Visual Six Sigma

Making Data Analysis Lean

IAN COX
MARIE A. GAUDARD
PHILIP J. RAMSEY
MIA L. STEPHENS
LEO T. WRIGHT

WILEY

John Wiley & Sons, Inc.

Published by John Wiley & Sons, Inc., Hoboken, New Jersey.
Published simultaneously in Canada.

For general information on our other products and services or for technical support, please contact our Customer Care Department within the United States at (800) 762-2974, outside the United States at (317) 572-3993 or fax (317) 572-4002.

Wiley also publishes its books in a variety of electronic formats. Some content that appears in print may not be available in electronic books. For more information about Wiley products, visit our web site at www.wiley.com.

Library of Congress Cataloging-in-Publication Data:

Cox, Ian, 1956–
    Visual six sigma : making data analysis lean / Ian Cox . . . [et al.].
        p.   cm. – (Wiley & SAS business series)
    Includes bibliographical references and index.
        ISBN 978-0-470-50691-2 (cloth)
    1. Six sigma (Quality control standard)   2. Decision support systems.   3. Decision making–Statistical methods.   4. Organizational effectiveness.   I. Title.
    HD30.213.C69 2010
    658.4'013–dc22

                                                                    2009025216

ISBN-13 978-0-470-50691-2

Printed in the United States of America.

10 9 8 7 6 5 4 3 2 1

Wiley & SAS Business Series

The Wiley & SAS Business Series presents books that help senior-level managers with their critical management decisions.

Titles in the Wiley and SAS Business Series include:

Business Intelligence Competency Centers: A Team Approach to Maximizing Competitive Advantage by Gloria J. Miller, Dagmar Brautigam, and Stefanie V. Gerlach

Case Studies in Performance Management: A Guide from the Experts by Tony C. Adkins

CIO Best Practices: Enabling Strategic Value with Information Technology by Joe Stenzel

Credit Risk Scorecards: Developing and Implementing Intelligent Credit Scoring by Naeem Siddiqi

Customer Data Integration: Reaching a Single Version of the Truth by Jill Dyché and Evan Levy

Enterprise Risk Management: A Methodology for Achieving Strategic Objectives by Gregory Monahan

Fair Lending Compliance: Intelligence and Implications for Credit Risk Management by Clark R. Abrahams and Mingyuan Zhang

Information Revolution: Using the Information Evolution Model to Grow Your Business by Jim Davis, Gloria J. Miller, and Allan Russell

Marketing Automation: Practical Steps to More Effective Direct Marketing by Jeff LeSueur

Performance Management: Finding the Missing Pieces (to Close the Intelligence Gap) by Gary Cokins

Performance Management: Integrating Strategy Execution, Methodologies, Risk, and Analytics by Gary Cokins

Credit Risk Assessment: The New Lending System for Borrowers, Lenders, and Investors by Clark R. Abrahams and Mingyuan Zhang

Business Intelligence Success Factors: Tools for Aligning Your Business in the Global Economy by Olivia Parr Rud

The Data Asset: How Smart Companies Govern Their Data for Business Success by Tony Fisher

Demand-Driven Forecasting: A Structured Approach to Forecasting by Charles Chase

The New Know: Innovation Powered by Analytics by Thornton May

For more information on any of the above titles, please visit www.wiley.com.

Contents

CHAPTER 4   Reducing Hospital Late Charge Incidents   57

               Framing the Problem   58
               Collecting Data   59
               Uncovering Relationships   62
               Uncovering the Hot Xs   90
               Identifying Projects   103
               Conclusion   103

CHAPTER 5   Transforming Pricing Management in a Chemical Supplier   105

               Setting the Scene   106
               Framing the Problem: Understanding the Current
                   State Pricing Process   107
               Collecting Baseline Data   112
               Uncovering Relationships   121
               Modeling Relationships   147
               Revising Knowledge   152
               Utilizing Knowledge: Sustaining the Benefits   159
               Conclusion   162

CHAPTER 6   Improving the Quality of Anodized Parts   165

               Setting the Scene   166
               Framing the Problem   167
               Collecting Data   169
               Uncovering Relationships   183
               Locating the Team on the VSS Roadmap   196
               Modeling Relationships   197
               Revising Knowledge   210
               Utilizing Knowledge   229
               Conclusion   231
               Note   232

CHAPTER 7   Informing Pharmaceutical Sales and Marketing   233

               Setting the Scene   235
               Collecting the Data   235
               Validating and Scoping the Data   237
               Investigating Promotional Activity   263
               A Deeper Understanding of Regional Differences   282
               Summary   291
               Conclusion   292

Preface

The purpose of this book is to show how, using the principles of Visual Six Sigma, you can exploit data to make better decisions more quickly and easily than you would otherwise. We emphasize that your company does not need to have a Six Sigma initiative for this book to be useful. Clearly there are many data-driven decisions that, by necessity or by design, fall outside the scope of a Six Sigma effort, and in such cases we believe that Visual Six Sigma is ideal. We seek to show that Visual Six Sigma can be used by a lone associate, as well as a team, to address data-driven questions, with or without the support of a formal initiative like Six Sigma.

To this end, we present six case studies that show Visual Six Sigma in action. These case studies address complex problems and opportunities faced by individuals and teams in a variety of application areas. Each case study was addressed using the Visual Six Sigma Roadmap, described in Chapters 2 and 3. As these case studies illustrate, Visual Six Sigma is about exploration and discovery, which means that it is not, and never could be, an entirely prescriptive framework.

As well as using the case studies to convey the Visual Six Sigma Roadmap, we also want to use them to illustrate Visual Six Sigma techniques that you can reuse in your own setting. To meet this goal, sometimes we have deliberately compromised the lean nature of the Visual Six Sigma Roadmap in order to take the opportunity to show you extra techniques that may not be strictly necessary to reach the conclusion or business decision. Striking the balance this way means that you will see a wider repertoire of techniques from which to synthesize an approach to Visual Six Sigma that works for you.

Because of its visual emphasis, Visual Six Sigma opens the doors for non-statisticians to take active roles in data-driven decision making, empowering them to leverage their contextual knowledge to pose relevant questions, get good answers, and make sound decisions. You may find yourself working on a Six Sigma improvement project, a design project, a data mining inquiry, or a scientific study— all of which require decision making based on data. After working through this book, we hope that you will be able to make data-driven decisions in your specific situation quickly, easily, and with great assurance.

How This Book Is Organized

This book is organized in two parts. Part I contains an introductory chapter that presents the three Visual Six Sigma strategies, a chapter on Visual Six Sigma, and a chapter introducing JMP statistical software (from SAS® Institute), which will be used throughout the case studies.

Case studies are presented in Part II. These case studies follow challenging real-world projects from start to finish. Through these case studies, you will gain insight into how the three Visual Six Sigma strategies combine to expedite project execution in the real world. Each case study is given its own chapter, which can be read independently from the rest. A concise summary of the storyline opens each case study. Although these case studies are real, we use fictitious names for the companies and individuals to preserve confidentiality.

Within each case study, visualization methods and other statistical techniques are applied at various stages in the data analysis process in order to better understand what the data are telling us. For those not familiar with JMP, each case study also contains the relevant how-to steps so that you may follow along and see Visual Six Sigma in action.

The data sets used in the case studies are available at http://support.sas.com/visualsixsigma. Here you can also find the exhibits shown in the case studies, allowing you to see screen captures in color. Additional Visual Six Sigma resource materials will be made available on the Web site, as appropriate.

We have used different fonts to help identify the names of data tables, of columns in data tables, and commands. Data table names are shown in **bold Times New Roman**, while the names of columns (which are variable names) are shown in Helvetica. The names of commands are shown in **bold Helvetica**.

A Word about the Software

The ideas behind Visual Six Sigma are quite general, but active learning—in our view the only kind of learning that works—requires that you step through the case studies and examples in this book to try things out for yourself. For more information about JMP and to download a trial version of the software, visit www.jmp.com/demo.

JMP is available on Windows, Mac, and Linux platforms. The step-by-step instructions in this book assume that you are working in Windows. Mac and Linux users should refer to the JMP documentation for details on differences. This book is based on JMP version 8.0.1.

Acknowledgments

Central to this book are the case studies that allow us to show Visual Six Sigma in some specific, real-world settings. We would like to thank all those who had a hand in shaping the case studies, giving specific mention to Joe Ficalora (Global Services for Sigma Breakthrough Technologies Inc., SBTI), who contributed the "Reducing Hospital Late Charge Incidents" case study in Chapter 4, Andrew Ruddick (Catalyst Consulting) for the "Transforming Pricing Management in a Chemical Supplier" case study in Chapter 5, and Andy Liddle (Catalyst Consulting) for the "Improving a Polymer Manufacturing Process" case study in Chapter 8. Their contributions were valuable in making the book more relevant and useful to prospective readers and are indicative of a consulting approach that is both pragmatic and enlightened.

The book was substantially improved by suggestions from the following individuals: Mark Bailey, Monica Beals, Duane Hayes, Bradley Jones, Ann Lehman, Paul Marovich, Tonya Mauldin, Malcolm Moore, Heath Rushing, Laura Ryan, and Scott Wise. We greatly appreciate their time, interest, valuable feedback, and insights.

This project was greatly facilitated by Stacey Hamilton and Stephenie Joyner, of SAS Publishing. Their support, encouragement, and attention to detail at every step of this adventure were invaluable.

Finally, we would like to thank John Leary, Dave Richardson, and Jon Weisz for their support and encouragement in the writing of this book. A special thank-you goes to John Sall and the JMP Development Team for their work on a visionary product that makes Visual Six Sigma possible.

PART I

Background

CHAPTER 1

Introduction

What Is Visual Six Sigma?

Visual Six Sigma leverages interactive and dynamic graphical displays to help transform data into sound decisions. It is not an algorithm. It is a creative process that employs visual techniques in the discovery of new and useful knowledge, leading to quicker and better decisions than do the methods in general use today. It signals a new generation of Six Sigma techniques.

At the heart of Six Sigma is the concept of data-driven decision making, that is, of exploiting the data from measurements or simulations on your product or service at various points in its lifecycle. Visual Six Sigma aims to produce better alignment between Six Sigma practice and the key idea of discovery, producing benefits for all those who have a stake in solving problems and in making improvements through data. Visual Six Sigma consists of three main strategies:

1. Using dynamic visualization to literally *see* the sources of variation in your data.
2. Using exploratory data analysis techniques to *identify key drivers and models*, especially for situations with many variables.
3. Using confirmatory statistical methods only when the conclusions are not obvious.

Six Sigma programs often use the so-called DMAIC approach for team-based process improvement or problem-solving efforts. The acronym DMAIC stands for the major phases in a team's project: *Define, Measure, Analyze, Improve*, and *Control*. DMAIC provides a structure for a team's efforts, just as an overall Six Sigma program provides a structure for a company's efforts. Each phase of DMAIC comes with a list of techniques that are considered appropriate in that phase; the team moves from one phase to another, using this sequence of techniques as a general guide. In a similar way, Six Sigma projects aimed at design follow various structures, such as *Define, Measure, Analyze, Design*, and *Validate* (DMADV) and *Identify, Design, Optimize*, and *Validate* (IDOV).

Visual Six Sigma is not a replacement for the DMAIC, DMADV, or IDOV frameworks. Rather, Visual Six Sigma supports these frameworks by simplifying and enhancing methods for data exploration and discovery whenever they are needed. In addition, when circumstances make a full-blown project-based or team-based approach undesirable or unworkable, Visual Six Sigma can still be used by individual contributors such as you. In a nutshell, Visual Six Sigma helps to make the DMAIC and design structures—and data analysis in general—lean.

Moving beyond Traditional Six Sigma

It is our belief that the tools, techniques, and workflows in common use with Six Sigma efforts are typically not aligned with the key idea of discovery. In the early days of Six Sigma, relevant data rarely existed, and a team was often challenged to collect data on its own. As part of the Measure phase, a team usually conducted a brainstorming session to identify which features of a process should be measured. In some sense, this brainstorming session was the team's only involvement in hypothesis generation. The data collected were precious, and hypothesis testing methods were critical in separating signals from noise.

Project teams struggling with a lack of useful data generally rely on an abundance of subjective input, and often require hypothesis testing to minimize the risk of bad decisions. This emphasis on hypothesis testing is reasonable in an environment where data are sparse. In contrast, today's Six Sigma teams often find warehouses of data that are relevant to their efforts. Their challenge is to wade through the data to discover prominent features, to separate the remarkable from the unremarkable.

These data-rich environments call for a shift in emphasis from confirmatory methods, such as hypothesis testing, to exploratory methods with a major emphasis on the display of data to reveal prominent features that are hidden in the data. Since the human interpretation of the data context is a vital part of the discovery process, these exploratory techniques cannot be fully automated. Also, with large quantities of data, hypothesis testing itself becomes less useful—statistical significance comes easily, and may have little to do with practical importance.

Of course, the simple abundance of data in a warehouse does not guarantee its relevance for improvement or problem solving. In fact, it is our experience that teams working in what they believe to be data-rich environments sometimes find that the available data are of poor quality, or are largely irrelevant to their efforts. Visualization methods can be instrumental in helping teams quickly reach this conclusion. In these cases, teams need to revert to techniques such as brainstorming, cause-and-effect diagrams, and process maps, which drive efforts to collect the proper data. But, as we shall see, even in situations where only few relevant data are available, visualization techniques, supported as appropriate by confirmatory methods, prove invaluable in identifying telling features of the data.

Making Data Analysis Lean

Discovery is largely supported by the generation of hypotheses—conjectures about relationships and causality. Today's Six Sigma teams, and data analysts in the business world in general, are often trained with a heavy emphasis on hypothesis testing, with comparatively little emphasis given to hypothesis generation and discovery. They are often hampered in their problem solving and improvement efforts by the inability to exploit exploratory methods, which could enable them to make more rapid progress, often with less effort.

In recent times, we have seen incredible advances in visualization methods, supported by phenomenal increases in computing power. We strongly believe that the approaches now allowed by these methods are underutilized in current Six Sigma practice. It is this conviction that motivated us to write this book. We hope you find it useful as you shape and build your own real-world Six Sigma experience.

Requirements of the Reader

This leads to another important point, namely, that you are "part of the system." Discovery, whether practiced as an individual or as a team sport, involves both divergent and convergent thinking; both creativity and discipline are required at different times. You should bear this in mind when forming a team or when consulting with individuals, since each person will bring his or her own skill set, perspective, and strength to the discovery process. Given the need to be data driven, we also need to recognize one of the basic rules of using data, which is that any kind of analysis (no matter how simple or complex) that treats data simply as a list of numbers is doomed to failure. To say it differently: All data are contextual, and it is this context and the objectives set out for the project that must shape the analysis and produce useful recommendations for action. As a practitioner, your main responsibility should always be to understand what the numbers in the data actually mean in the real world. In fact, this is the only requirement for putting the ideas in this book into practice in your workplace.

CHAPTER 2

Six Sigma and Visual Six Sigma

This chapter introduces the key ideas behind Six Sigma and Visual Six Sigma, where our focus is on the latter. Six Sigma is a huge topic, so we only have space to mention some of its essential ideas. There are already numerous well-written books and articles dealing with the many and diverse aspects of Six Sigma as commonly practiced.[1] We also note that, today, digital tools (software, databases, visual media, etc.) are leveraged extensively in Six Sigma initiatives.[2]

Our goal in this chapter is to provide an overview of Six Sigma so that you start to see how Visual Six Sigma fits into this picture. However, it is worth pointing out in advance that you can gain an appreciation of the power of visualization techniques only by working with data that relate to real problems in the real world.

Background: Models, Data, and Variation

There is no doubt that science and technology have transformed the lives of many and will continue to do so. Like many fields of human endeavor, science proceeds by building pictures, or *models*, of what we think is happening. These models can provide a framework in which we attempt to influence or control inputs so as to provide better outputs. Unlike the models used in some other areas, the models used in science are usually constructed using data that arise from measurements made in the real world.

At the heart of the scientific approach is the explicit recognition that we may be *wrong* in our current world view. Saying this differently, we recognize that our models will always be imperfect, but by confronting them with data, we can strive to make them better and more useful. Echoing the words of George Box, one of the pioneers of industrial statistics, we can say, "Essentially, all models are wrong, but some are useful."[3]

Models

The models of interest in this book can be conceptualized as shown in Exhibit 2.1. This picture demands a few words of explanation:

- In this book, and generally in Six Sigma, the outcomes of interest to us are denoted by Ys. For example, Y1 in Exhibit 2.1 could represent the event that someone will apply for a new credit card after receiving an offer from a credit card company.

- Causes that may influence a Y will be shown as Xs. To continue the example, X1 may denote the age of the person receiving the credit card offer.
- Rather than using a lengthy expression such as "we expect the age of the recipient to influence the chance that he or she will apply for a credit card after receiving an offer," we can just write Y = f(X). Here, f is called a *function*, and Y = f(X) describes *how* Y changes as X changes. If we think that Y depends on more than one X, we simply write an expression like Y = f(X1, X2). Since the function f describes how the inputs X1 and X2 affect Y, the function f is called a *signal function*.
- Note that we have two different kinds of causes: (X1, X2, X3), shown in the diagram with solid arrows, and (X4, X5, X6), shown with dotted arrows. The causes with dotted arrows are the causes that we do not know about or care about, or causes that we can't control. Often, these are called *noise* variables. In a sense, noise variables are not part of the model. For example, X4 could be the number of credit cards that the recipient of the offer already has, or the time since the recipient received a similar offer. The function that represents the combined effect of the noise variables on Y is called a *noise function*, and is sometimes referred to simply as *error*.
- Just because we do not know about the noise variables does not mean that they do not influence Y. If X4, X5, or X6 change, as they typically will, then they will necessarily lead to some apparently inexplicable *variation* in the outcome Y, even when we do our best to keep X1, X2, and X3 fixed. For example, whether an offer recipient applies for a new credit card may well be influenced by the number of credit cards that the recipient already has.

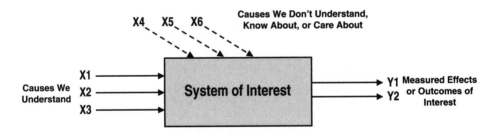

Y1 = Signal Function1(X1, X2, X3) + Noise Function1(X4, X5, X6)

Y2 = Signal Function2(X1, X2, X3) + Noise Function2(X4, X5, X6)

EXHIBIT 2.1   Modeling of Causes before Improvement

As you can see in the exhibit, a key aspect of such a model is that it focuses on some specific aspects (i.e., X1, X2, and X3) in order to better understand them. By intention or lack of knowledge, the model necessarily omits some aspects that may actually be important (X4, X5, and X6).

Depending on whether you are being optimistic or pessimistic, Six Sigma can be associated with improvement or problem solving. Very often, an explicit model relating the Ys to Xs may not exist; to effect an improvement or to solve a problem, you need to develop such a model. The process of developing this model first requires arriving at a starting model, and then confronting that model with data to try to improve it. Later in this chapter, in the section "Visual Six Sigma: Strategies, Process, Roadmap, and Guidelines," we discuss a process for improving the model.

If you succeed in improving it, then the new model might be represented as shown in Exhibit 2.2. Now X4 has a solid arrow rather than a dotted arrow. When we gain an understanding of noise variables, we usually gain leverage in explaining the outcome (Y) and, hence, in making the outcome more favorable to us. In other words, we are able to make an improvement.

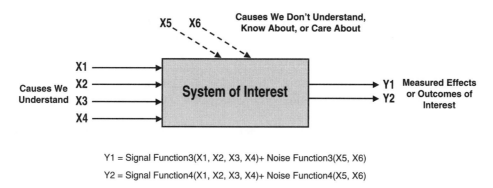

$$Y1 = \text{Signal Function3}(X1, X2, X3, X4) + \text{Noise Function3}(X5, X6)$$

$$Y2 = \text{Signal Function4}(X1, X2, X3, X4) + \text{Noise Function4}(X5, X6)$$

EXHIBIT 2.2 Modeling of Causes after Improvement

Measurements

The use of data-driven models to encapsulate and predict how important aspects of a business operate is still a new frontier. Moreover, there is a sense in which a scientific approach to business is more challenging than the pursuit of science itself. In science, the prevailing notion is that knowledge is valuable for its own sake. But for any business striving to deliver value to its customers and stakeholders—usually in competition with other businesses doing the same thing—knowledge does *not necessarily* have an intrinsic value. This is particularly so since the means to generate, store, and use data and knowledge are in themselves value-consuming, including database and infrastructure costs, training costs, cycle time lost to making measurements, and so on.

Therefore, for a business, the only legitimate driving force behind a scientific, data-driven approach that includes modeling is *a failure to produce or deliver what is required*. This presupposes that the business can assess and monitor what is needed, which is a non-trivial problem for at least two reasons:

1. A business is often a cacophony of voices, expressing different views as to the purpose of the business and needs of the customer.
2. A measurement process implies that a value is placed on what is being measured, and it can be very difficult to determine what should be valued.

It follows that developing a useful measurement scheme can be a difficult, but vital, exercise. Moreover, the analysis of the data that arise when measurements are actually made gives us new insights that often suggest the need for making new measurements. We will see some of this thinking in the case studies that follow.

Observational versus Experimental Data

Before continuing, it is important to note that the data we will use come in two types, depending on how the measurements of Xs and Ys are made: observational data and experimental data. Exhibit 2.1 allows us to explain the crucial difference between these two types of data.

1. *Observational data* arise when, as we record values of the Ys, the values of the Xs are allowed to change at will. This occurs when a process runs naturally and without interference.
2. *Experimental data* arise when we deliberately *manipulate* the Xs and then record the corresponding Ys.

Observational data tend to be collected with relatively little control over associated Xs. Often we simply assume that the Xs are essentially constant over the observational period, but sometimes the values of a set of Xs are recorded along with the corresponding Y values.

In contrast, the collection of experimental data requires us to force variation in the Xs. This involves designing a plan that tells us exactly how to change the Xs in the best way, leading to the topic of experimental design, or *design of experiments* (DOE). DOE is a powerful and far-reaching approach that has been used extensively in manufacturing and design environments.[4] Today, DOE is finding increasing application in non-manufacturing environments as well.[5] The book *Introduction to Design of Experiments with JMP Examples* guides readers in designing and analyzing experiments using JMP.[6]

In both the manufacturing and non-manufacturing settings, DOE is starting to find application in the Six Sigma world through discrete choice experiments.[7] In such experiments, users or potential users of a product or service are given the chance to express their preferences, allowing you to take a more informed approach to tailoring and trading off the attributes of a design. Because one attribute can be price, such methods allow you to address an important question—What will users pay money for? We note that JMP has extensive, easy-to-use facilities for both the design and analysis of choice models.

Even in situations where DOE is relevant, preliminary analysis of observational data is advised to set the stage for designing the most appropriate and powerful experiment. The case studies in this book deal predominantly with the treatment of observational data, but Chapters 6 and 8 feature aspects of DOE as well.

Six Sigma

Some common perceptions and definitions of Six Sigma include:

- A management philosophy.
- Marketing hype.
- A way to transform a company.
- A way to create processes with no more than 3.4 defects per million opportunities.

- Solving problems using data.
- A way to use training credits.
- Something a company has to do before Lean.
- Making improvements using data.
- A way to make money from consulting, training, and certification.
- A pseudo-religion.
- A way to get your next job.
- Something a company does after Lean.

In spite of this diversity, there seems to be broad agreement that a Six Sigma initiative involves a variety of stakeholders and is a project-based method utilizing cross-functional teams. A performance gap is the only legitimate reason for spending the time and resources needed to execute a Six Sigma project. From this point of view, questions such as the following are vital to a Six Sigma deployment:

- How big should the performance gap be to make a project worth doing?
- How can you verify that a project did indeed have the expected impact?

However, for reasons of space, our brief discussion will address only the steps that are followed in a typical Six Sigma project once it has gained approval, and what resources are needed to execute it.

Using the background presented in the beginning of this chapter, we offer our own succinct definition of Six Sigma:

Six Sigma *is the management of sources of variation in relation to performance requirements.*

Here, *management* refers to some appropriate modeling activity fed by data. Depending on both the business objectives and the current level of understanding, management of sources of variation can mean:

- Identifying and quantifying sources of variation.
- Controlling sources of variation.
- Reducing sources of variation.
- Anticipating sources of variation.

A Six Sigma deployment effort typically starts with the following infrastructure:

- A *senior executive*, often a president or chief executive officer, provides the necessary impetus and alignment by assuming a leadership role.
- An *executive committee*, working operationally at a level similar to that of the senior executive, oversees the Six Sigma deployment.
- A *champion* sponsors and orchestrates an individual project. This individual is usually a member of the executive committee and has enough influence to remove obstacles or allocate resources without having to appeal to a more senior individual.

- A *process owner* has the authority and responsibility to make improvements to operations.
- A *black belt* supports project teams, taking a leadership role in this effort. This individual is a full-time change agent who is allocated to several projects. A black belt is usually a quality professional, but is often not an expert on the operational processes within the scope of the project.
- A *green belt* works part-time on a project or perhaps leads a smaller-scope project.
- A *master black belt* mentors the Six Sigma community (black belts and green belts), often provides training, and advises the executive committee. A master black belt must have a proven track record of effecting change and be a known and trusted figure. This track record is established by having successfully completed and led numerous Six Sigma projects, ideally within the same organization.

To guide Six Sigma projects that seek to deliver bottom-line results in the short or medium term, black belts typically use the *Define, Measure, Analyze, Improve,* and *Control* (DMAIC) structure, where DMAIC is an acronym for the five phases involved:

1. *Define.* Define the problem or opportunity that the project seeks to address, along with the costs, benefits, and the customer impact. Define the team, the specific project goals, the project timeline, and the process to be improved.
2. *Measure.* Construct or verify the operational definitions of the Ys, also called *critical to quality* (CTQ) metrics and measures. Plot a baseline showing the level and current variation of the Ys. Quantify how much variation there is in the measurement process itself, in order to adjust the observed variation in the Ys and to improve the measurement process, if needed. Brainstorm or otherwise identify as many Xs as possible, in order to include the Xs that represent root causes.
3. *Analyze.* Use process knowledge and data to determine which Xs represent root causes of variation in the Ys.
4. *Improve.* Find the settings for Xs that deliver the best possible values for the Ys, develop a plan to implement process changes, pilot the process changes to verify improvement in the Ys, and institutionalize the changes.
5. *Control.* Lock in the performance gains from the Improve phase.

Depending on the state of the process, product, or service addressed by the project, a different set of steps is sometimes used. For instance, for products or processes that are being designed or redesigned, the *Define, Measure, Analyze, Design, Verify* (DMADV) or the *Identify, Design, Optimize, Validate* (IDOV) framework is often used. These structures form the basis of Design for Six Sigma (DFSS).[8] Briefly, the phases of the DMADV approach consist of the following:

- *Define.* Similar to the Define phase of DMAIC.
- *Measure.* Determine internal and external customer requirements, measure baseline performance against these requirements, and benchmark against competitors and industry standards.

- *Analyze.* Explore product and process design options for satisfying customer requirements, evaluate these options, and select the best design(s).
- *Design.* Create detailed designs of the product and process, pilot these, and evaluate the ability to meet customer requirements.
- *Verify.* Verify that the performance of the product and process meets customer requirements.

This brings us back full circle to our own definition: Six Sigma is the management of sources of variation in relation to performance requirements. With a little thought, perhaps you can see how large parts of DMAIC, DMADV, or IDOV involve different ways to manage variation. For example, a DFSS project would involve techniques and tools to "anticipate sources of variation" in the product, process, or service.

Variation and Statistics

In the previous section, we mentioned the following aspects of managing variation:

- Identifying and quantifying sources of variation.
- Controlling sources of variation.
- Reducing sources of variation.
- Anticipating sources of variation.

The first point, "Identifying and quantifying sources of variation," is a vital step and typically precedes the others. In fact, Six Sigma efforts aside, many businesses can derive useful new insights and better knowledge of their processes and products simply by understanding what their data represent and by interacting with their data to literally *see* what has not been seen before. Identification of sources of variation is a necessary step before starting any modeling associated with other Six Sigma steps. Even in those rare situations where there is already a high level of understanding about the data and the model, it would be very unwise to begin modeling without first investigating the data. Every set of data is unique, and in the real world, change is ubiquitous, including changes in the patterns of variation.

Given that the study of variation plays a central role in Six Sigma, it would be useful if there were already a body of knowledge that we could apply to help us make progress. Luckily, there is: *statistics*! One of the more enlightened definitions of statistics is *learning in the face of uncertainty*; since variation is a form of uncertainty, then the relevance of statistics becomes immediately clear.

Yet, statistics tends to be underutilized in understanding uncertainty. We believe that one of the reasons is that the fundamental difference between an *exploratory* study and a *confirmatory* study is not sufficiently emphasized or understood. This difference can be loosely expressed as the difference between *statistics as detective* and *statistics as judge*. Part of the difficulty with fully appreciating the relevance of *statistics as detective* is that the process of discovery it addresses cannot fully be captured within an algorithmic or theoretical framework. Rather, producing new and valuable insights from data relies on heuristics, rules of thumb, serendipity, and contextual knowledge. In contrast, *statistics as judge* relies on deductions that follow from a structured body of knowledge, formulas, statistical tests, and p-value guideposts.

The lack of appreciation of *statistics as detective* is part of our motivation in writing this book. A lot of traditional Six Sigma training overly emphasizes *statistics as judge*. This generally gives an unbalanced view of what Six Sigma should be, as well as making unrealistic and overly time-consuming demands on practitioners and organizations.

Six Sigma is one of many applications where learning in the face of uncertainty is required. In any situation where statistics is applied, the analyst will follow a process, more or less formal, to reach findings, recommendations, and actions based on the data.[9] There are two phases in this process:

1. Exploratory Data Analysis.
2. Confirmatory Data Analysis.

Exploratory Data Analysis (EDA) is nothing other than a fancy name for *statistics as detective*, whereas *Confirmatory Data Analysis* (CDA) is simply *statistics as judge*. In technical jargon, the emphasis in EDA is on hypothesis *generation*. In EDA efforts, the analyst searches for clues in the data that help identify theories about underlying behavior. In contrast, the focus of CDA is hypothesis *testing and inference*. CDA consists of confirming these theories and behaviors. CDA follows EDA, and together they make up *statistical modeling*. A recent paper by Jeroen de Mast and Albert Trip provides a detailed discussion of the crucial role of EDA in Six Sigma.[10]

Making Detective Work Easier through Dynamic Visualization

To solve a mystery, a detective has to spot clues and patterns of behavior and then generate working hypotheses that are consistent with the evidence. This is usually done in an iterative way, by gathering more evidence and by enlarging or shifting the scope of the investigation as knowledge is developed. So it is with generating hypotheses through EDA.

We have seen that the first and sometimes only step in managing uncertainty is to identify and quantify sources of variation. Building on the old adage that "a picture is worth a thousand words," it is clear that graphical displays should play a key role here. This is especially desirable when the software allows you to interact freely with these graphical views. Thanks to the advance of technology, most Six Sigma practitioners now have capabilities on their desktops that were only the province of researchers 10 years ago, and were not even foreseen 30 years ago. Although not entirely coincidental, we are fortunate that the wide availability of this capability comes at a time when data volumes continue to escalate.

Incidentally, many of the statistical methods that fall under CDA and that today are in routine use by the Six Sigma community, were originally developed for *squeezing the most* out of a small volume of data, often with the use of nothing more than a calculator or a pen and paper. Increasingly, the Six Sigma practitioner is faced with a quite different challenge, whereby the sheer volume of data (rows and columns) can make the application of statistical testing, should it be needed, difficult and questionable.

At this point, let us consider the appropriate role of visualization and, tangentially, data mining within Six Sigma. Visualization, which has a long and interesting history of its own, is conventionally considered valuable in three ways:[11]

1. Checking raw data for anomalies (EDA).
2. Exploring data to discover plausible models (EDA).
3. Checking model assumptions (CDA).

Given the crucial role of communication in Six Sigma, we can add two additional ways in which visualization has value:

4. Investigation of model outcomes (EDA and CDA).
5. Communication of results to others (EDA and CDA).

There is a wide variety of ways to display data visually. Many of these, such as histograms, scatterplots, Pareto plots, and box plots, are already in widespread use. However, the simple idea of providing multiple, linked views of data with which you can interact via software takes current Six Sigma analysis to another level of efficiency and effectiveness. For example, imagine clicking on a bar in a Pareto chart and seeing the corresponding points in a scatterplot become highlighted. Imagine what can be learned! But, unfortunately, a lot of software is relatively static, offering little more than a computerized version of what is possible on the printed page. In contrast, we see the dynamic aspect of good visualization software as critical to the detective work of EDA, which relies on an unfolding, rather than pre-planned, set of steps.

Visualization remains an active area of research, particularly when data volumes are high.[12] But there are already many new, useful graphical displays. For example, the parallel coordinates plots used for visualizing data with many columns are well known within the visualization community, but have not yet spread widely into the Six Sigma world.[13]

Additionally, although there are established principles about the correct ways to represent data graphically, the fact that two individuals will perceive patterns differently means that good software should present a wide repertoire of representations, ideally all dynamically linked with one another.[14] We hope to demonstrate through the case studies that this comprehensive dynamic linking is a powerful capability for hypothesis generation. To emphasize this desirable aspect, from now on, we will refer to *dynamic visualization*, rather than simply visualization.

Not only does dynamic visualization support EDA when data volumes are large, but it is also our experience that dynamic visualization is very powerful when data volumes are modest. For instance, if the distributions of two or more variables are linked together, you can quickly and easily see the *balance* of the data, that is, which values or levels of one variable occur with those of another. If the data are perfectly balanced, then tabulation may also provide the same insight, but if the data are only nearly balanced or if they are unbalanced, as is more often the case, the linked distributions will usually be much more easily interpreted. With dynamic visualization, we can assess many views of the data quickly and efficiently.

The mention of large data volumes inevitably raises the topic of *data mining*. This is a rapidly moving field, so that a precise definition is difficult. Essentially, data mining is the process of sorting through large amounts of data and picking out relevant information using techniques from machine learning and statistics.[15] In many cases, the data are split into at least two sets, and a model is built using one set, then tested or validated on the second set. Once the model is built, it is used to *score* new data as they arrive, thereby making (hopefully) useful predictions.

As with traditional statistical analysis, there are several processes that you can use in data mining.[16] In most data-mining applications, the software used automates each step in the process, usually involving some prescribed stopping rule to determine when there is no further structure in the data to model. As such, many data-mining efforts have a strong flavor of CDA. However, EDA can bring high value to data-mining applications, especially in Six Sigma settings. In our case studies, we will see two such applications.

Visual Six Sigma: Strategies, Process, Roadmap, and Guidelines

In this section, we will explore the three strategies that underlie Visual Six Sigma. We then present the Visual Six Sigma Data Analysis Process that supports these strategies through six steps, and define the Visual Six Sigma Roadmap that expands on three of the key steps. This section closes with guidelines that help you assess your performance as a Visual Six Sigma practitioner.

Visual Six Sigma Strategies

As mentioned earlier, Visual Six Sigma exploits the following three key strategies to support the goal of managing variation in relation to performance requirements:

1. Using dynamic visualization to literally *see* the sources of variation in your data.
2. Using exploratory data analysis techniques to *identify key drivers and models*, especially for situations with many variables.
3. Using confirmatory statistical methods only when the conclusions are not obvious.

Note that with reference to the section titled "Variation and Statistics," Strategy 1 falls within what was called EDA, or *statistics as detective*. Strategy 3 falls within what we defined as CDA, or *statistics as judge*. Strategy 2 has aspects of both EDA and CDA.

Earlier, we stressed that by working in the EDA mode of *statistics as detective* we have to give up the possibility of a neat conceptual and analytical framework. Rather, *the proper analysis of our data has to be driven by a set of informal rules or heuristics that allow us to make new, useful discoveries*. However, there are still some useful principles that can guide us. Jeroen de Mast and Albert Trip offer an excellent articulation and positioning of these principles in the Six Sigma context.[17] Unsurprisingly, these principles are applicable within Visual Six Sigma, and appear in a modified form in the Visual Six Sigma Roadmap presented later (Exhibit 2.4).

As you recall from Chapter 1, one of the goals of Visual Six Sigma is to equip users who know their business with some simple ideas and tools to get from data to decisions easily and quickly. Indeed, we would argue that the only prerequisite for a useful analysis, other than having high-quality data, is knowledge of what the different variables that are being analyzed actually represent. We cannot emphasize strongly enough this need for contextual knowledge to guide interpretation; it is not surprising that this is one of the key principles listed by de Mast and Trip.

As mentioned earlier, a motivating factor for this book is our conviction that the balance in emphasis between EDA and CDA in Six Sigma is not always correct. Yet another motivation for this book is to address the perception that a team must adhere strictly to the phases of DMAIC, even when the data or problem context does not warrant doing so. The use of the three key Visual Six Sigma strategies provides the opportunity to reengineer the process of going from data to decisions. In part, this is accomplished by freeing you, the practitioner, from the need to conduct unnecessary analyses.

Visual Six Sigma Process

We have found the simple process shown in Exhibit 2.3 to be effective in many real-world situations. We refer to this in the remainder of the book as the *Visual Six Sigma (VSS) Data Analysis Process*.

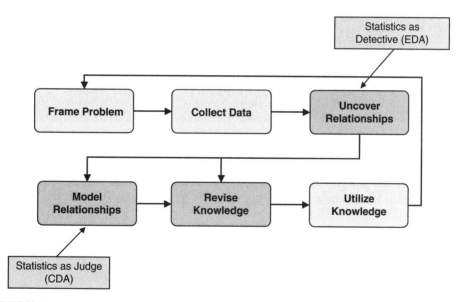

EXHIBIT 2.3   Visual Six Sigma Data Analysis Process

This gives rise to the subtitle of this book, *Making Data Analysis Lean*. As the exhibit shows, it may not always be necessary to engage in the "Model Relationships" activity. This is reflective of the third Visual Six Sigma strategy. An acid test for a Six Sigma practitioner is to ask, "If I *did* have a useful model of Ys against Xs from CDA, how would it change my recommended actions for the business?"

The steps in the Visual Six Sigma Data Analysis Process may be briefly described as follows:

- *Frame Problem.* Identify the specific failure to produce what is required (see prior section titled "Measurements"). Identify your general strategy for improvement, estimate the time and resources needed, and calculate the likely benefit if you succeed. Identify the Y or Ys of interest.

- *Collect Data.* Identify potential Xs using techniques such as brainstorming, process maps, data mining, *failure modes and effects analysis* (FMEA), and subject matter knowledge. Passively or actively collect data that relate these to the Ys of interest.
- *Uncover Relationships.* Validate the data to understand their strengths, weaknesses, and relevance to your problem. Using exploratory tools and your understanding of the data context, generate hypotheses and explore whether and how the Xs relate to the Ys.
- *Model Relationships.* Build statistical models relating the Xs to the Ys. Determine statistically which Xs explain variation in the Ys and may represent causal factors.
- *Revise Knowledge.* Optimize settings of the Xs to give the best values for the Ys. Explore the distribution of Ys as the Xs are allowed to shift a little from their optimal settings. Collect new data to verify that the improvement is real.
- *Utilize Knowledge.* Implement the improvement and monitor or review the Ys with an appropriate frequency to see that the improvement is maintained.

Visual Six Sigma Roadmap: Uncover Relationships, Model Relationships, and Revise Knowledge

In this section, we expand on the three steps in the Visual Six Sigma Data Analysis Process that benefit the most from the power of visual methods: Uncover Relationships, Model Relationships, and Revise Knowledge. These activities are reflective of where we see the biggest opportunities for removing waste from the process of going from data to decisions.

The Visual Six Sigma Roadmap in Exhibit 2.4 guides you through these three important steps. Given that the displays used for visualization and discovery depend on your own perceptive and cognitive style, the Visual Six Sigma Roadmap focuses

EXHIBIT 2.4   The Visual Six Sigma Roadmap: What We Do

Visual Six Sigma Roadmap - What We Do
Uncover Relationships
Dynamically visualize the variables one at a time
Dynamically visualize the variables two at a time
Dynamically visualize the variables more than two at a time
Visually determine the Hot Xs that affect variation in the Ys

Model Relationships
For each Y, identify the Hot Xs to include in the signal function
Model Y as a function of the Hot Xs; check the noise function
If needed, revise the model
If required, return to the Collect Data step and use DOE

Revise Knowledge
Identify the best Hot X settings
Visualize the effect on the Ys should these Hot X settings vary
Verify improvement using a pilot study or confirmation trials

on the goal, or the *what*, of each step. However, in Chapter 3, we will make specific suggestions about *how* each step can be accomplished using JMP.

The Roadmap uses the Six Sigma convention that a variable is usually assigned to a Y role (an outcome or effect of interest) or to an X role (a possible cause that may influence a Y). The phrase *Hot X* in Exhibit 2.4 relates to the fact that according to the available data this variable really does appear to have an impact on the Y of interest. Of course, in order to make such a determination, this X variable must have been included in your initial picture of how the process operates. Those X variables that are not Hot Xs, in spite of prior expectations, can be thought of as being moved into the noise function for that Y. Other terms for Hot X are *Red X* and *Vital X*. Whatever terminology is used, it is important to understand that for any given Y there may be *more than one* X that has an impact, and, in such cases, it is important to understand the *joint* impact of these Xs.

Note that, although the designations of Y or X for a particular variable are useful, whether a variable is a Y or an X depends on how the problem is framed and on the stage of the analysis. Processes are often modeled as both *serial* (a set of connected steps) and *hierarchical* (an ordered grouping of levels of steps, where one step at a higher level comprises a series of steps at a lower level). Indeed, one of the tough choices to be made in the Frame Problem step (Exhibit 2.3) is to decide on an appropriate level of detail and granularity for usefully modeling the process. Even when a manufacturing process is only moderately complex, it is often necessary to use a divide-and-conquer approach in process and product improvement and design efforts. Improvement and design projects are often divided into small pieces that reflect how the final product is made and operates. Thankfully, in transactional situations modeling the process is usually more straightforward.

Earlier, we used the phrase "data of high quality." Although data cleansing is often presented as an initial step prior to any data analysis, we feel that it is better to include this vital activity as part of the Uncover and Model Relationships steps (Exhibit 2.3), particularly when there are large numbers of variables. For example, it is perfectly possible to have a multivariate outlier that is not an outlier in any single variable. Thus the assessment of data quality and any required remedial action is understood to be woven into the Visual Six Sigma Roadmap.

We should also comment on the need to understand the measurement process that is behind each variable in your data. Variously known as a *Gauge Repeatability and Reproducibility* (Gauge R&R) study or a *Measurement System Analysis* (MSA) study, this is critically important. It is only when you understand the pattern of variation resulting from repeatedly measuring the *same* item that you can correctly interpret the pattern of variation when you measure *different* items of that type.[18]

In many ways, an MSA is best seen as an application of DOE to a measurement process, and properly the subject of a Visual Six Sigma effort of its own. To generalize, we would say that:

- In a transactional environment, the conventional MSA is often too sophisticated.
- In a manufacturing environment, the conventional MSA is often not sophisticated enough.

As an example of the second point: If the process to measure a small feature is automated, involving robot handling and vision systems, then the two Rs in Gauge R&R (corresponding to repeatability and reproducibility variation) may not be of interest. Instead we may be concerned with the variation when the robot loads and orients the part, when the camera tracks to supposedly fixed locations, and when the laser scans in a given pattern to examine the feature.

The Revise Knowledge activity is where we try to integrate what we have learned in the Uncover Relationships and possibly the Model Relationships steps with what we already know. There are many aspects to this, and most of them are particular to the specific context.

Regardless, one of the vital tasks associated with the Revise Knowledge step is to consider how, or if, our new findings will generalize. Note that Step 4 in Model Relationships already alerts us to this kind of problem, but this represents an extreme case.

Perhaps unsurprisingly, the best way to tackle this issue is to collect additional, new data via *confirmatory runs* to check how these fit with what we now expect. This is particularly important when we have changed the settings of the Hot Xs to achieve what appear to be better outcomes. As we acquire and investigate more and more data under the new settings, we have more and more assurance that we did indeed make a real improvement. Many businesses develop elaborate protocols to manage the risk of making such changes. Although there are some statistical aspects, there are at least as many contextual ones, so it is difficult to give general guidance.

In any case, confirmatory runs, no matter how they are chosen, are an expression of the fact that learning should be cumulative. Assuming that the performance gap continues to justify it, the continued application of the Visual Six Sigma Data Analysis Process (Exhibit 2.3) gives us the possibility of a virtuous circle.

Guidelines

Finally, the following are some guidelines that may help you as a practitioner of Visual Six Sigma:

- Customer requirements of your process or product should establish the context and objectives for all the analyses you conduct.
- These objectives can always be rephrased in terms of the identification, control, reduction, and/or anticipation of sources of variation.
- If you do not measure it, then you are guessing.
- If you do not know the operational definition of your measurement or the capability of your measurement process, then you are still guessing.
- If you spend more time accessing and integrating data than with Visual Six Sigma, then your information system needs to be carefully examined.
- The choice of which variables and observational units to include in constructing a set of data should be driven by your current process or product understanding and the objectives that have been set.
- Given that you have made such a choice, you need to be concerned about how your findings are likely to generalize to other similar situations.
- Any analysis that ignores business and contextual information and tries to just manipulate numbers will always fail.
- Any dataset has information that can be revealed by dynamic visualization.
- Models are used to make predictions, but a useful prediction need not involve a formal model.

- All models are wrong, but some are useful.
- The more sophisticated the model you build, the more opportunity for error in constructing it.
- If you cannot communicate your findings readily to business stakeholders, then you have failed.
- If the course of action is not influenced by your findings, then the analysis was pointless.

Conclusion

In this chapter, we have given an overview of Six Sigma and Visual Six Sigma. The "Six Sigma" section presented our definition of Six Sigma as the management of variation in relation to performance requirements, and briefly described some wider aspects of Six Sigma. The section "Variation and Statistics" emphasized the key role of *statistics as detective*, namely, EDA. The next section dealt briefly with dynamic visualization as a prerequisite for successful detective work, while the section "Visual Six Sigma: Strategies, Process, Roadmap, and Guidelines" aimed to summarize the three key strategies and the process that will allow you to solve data mysteries easily, more quickly, and with less effort. Through the Visual Six Sigma Data Analysis Process and the Visual Six Sigma Roadmap, the application of these strategies will be illustrated in the case studies.

Chapter 3 aims to familiarize you a little with JMP, the enabling technology we use for Visual Six Sigma. Its purpose is to equip you to follow the JMP usage in the Visual Six Sigma case studies that form the heart of this book. With the background in Chapter 3 and the step-by-step details given in the case studies, you will be able to work along with the investigators in the case study chapters, reproducing their graphs and reports. Maybe you will even venture beyond their analyses to discover new knowledge on your own! In any case, you will learn to use a large repertoire of techniques that you can then apply to your own decision-making capabilities.

Notes

1. Mikel Harry and Richard Schroeder, *Six Sigma: The Breakthrough Management Strategy Revolutionizing the World's Top Corporations* (New York, NY: Random House, 2006); Thomas Pyzdek, *The Six Sigma Handbook: A Complete Guide for Greenbelts, Blackbelts and Managers at All Levels* (New York, NY: McGraw-Hill, 2003); and George Eckes, *The Six Sigma Revolution: How General Electric and Others Turned Process into Profits* (New York, NY: John Wiley & Sons, Inc., 2003).
2. See references to Digital Six Sigma at http://www.motorola.com/content.jsp?globalObject Id=1958-4152 (accessed 5 July 2009).
3. George E. P. Box and Norman R. Draper, *Empirical Model-Building and Response Surfaces* (New York, NY: John Wiley & Sons, Inc., 1987), 424.
4. George E. P. Box, William G. Hunter, and Stuart J. Hunter, *Statistics for Experimenters: Design, Innovation, and Discovery* (Hoboken, NJ: John Wiley & Sons, Inc., 2005); Marvin Lentner and Thomas Bishop, *Experimental Design and Analysis, 2nd Edition* (Blacksburg, VA: Valley Book Co., 1986); Ronald Moen, Thomas W. Nolan, and Lloyd P. Provost, *Improving Quality through Planned Experimentation* (New York, NY: McGraw-Hill,

1991); and Douglas C. Montgomery, *Design and Analysis of Experiments, 6th Edition* (Hoboken, NJ: John Wiley & Sons, Inc., 2005).

5. Charles W. Holland and David W. Cravens, "Fractional Factorial Experimental Designs in Marketing Research," *Journal of Marketing Research* 10, no. 3 (1973): 270–276; and Forrest W. Breyfogle, *Implementing Six Sigma: Smarter Solutions Using Statistical Methods, 2nd Edition* (Hoboken, NJ: John Wiley & Sons, Inc., 2003).

6. Jacques Goupy and Lee Creighton, *Introduction to Design of Experiments with JMP Examples, Third Edition* (Cary, NC: SAS Press, 2007).

7. Bryan K. Orme, *Getting Started with Conjoint Analysis: Strategies for Product Design and Pricing Research* (Research Publishers LLC, 2004).

8. Clyde M. Creveling, Jeff Slutsky, and Dave Antis, *Design for Six Sigma in Technology and Product Development* (New York, NY: Pearson Education, 2003); and Basem El-Haik and David M. Roy, *Service Design for Six Sigma: A Roadmap for Excellence* (Hoboken, NJ: John Wiley & Sons, Inc., 2005).

9. There are many variations of this process, but one example, not too far removed from Six Sigma, can be found in Chris Chatfield, *Problem Solving: A Statistician's Guide, 2nd Edition* (New York, NY: Chapman & Hall, 1995).

10. Jeroen de Mast and Albert Trip, "Exploratory Data Analysis in Quality Improvement Projects," *Journal of Quality Technology* 4, no. 39 (2007): 301–311.

11. See article at the York University Consulting Service Web site http://www.math.yorku.ca/SCS/Gallery/historical.html (accessed 5 July 2009); Leland Wilkinson and Anand Anushka, "High-Dimensional Visual Analytics: Interactive Exploration Guided by Pairwise Views of Point Distributions," *IEEE Transactions on Visualization and Computer Graphics* 12, no. 6 (2006): 1363–1372.

12. For an example, see Antony Unwin, Martin Theus, and Heike Hofmann, *Graphics of Large Datasets: Visualizing a Million* (New York: Springer, 2006).

13. Alfred Inselberg, *Parallel Coordinates: Visual Multidimensional Geometry and Its Applications* (New York, NY: Springer, 2008).

14. Edward R. Tufte, *The Visual Display of Quantitative Information, 2nd Edition* (Cheshire, CT: Graphics Press, 2001).

15. See, for example, Trevor Hastie, R. Tibshirani, and J. H. Freidman, *The Elements of Statistical Learning: Data Mining, Inference and Prediction* (New York, NY: Springer, 2001).

16. For example, see the article on "SEMMA" at http://www.sas.com/offices/europe/uk/technologies/analytics/datamining/miner/semma.html (accessed 23 July 2007).

17. Jeroen de Mast and Albert Trip, "Exploratory Data Analysis in Quality Improvement Projects," *Journal of Quality Technology* 4, no. 39 (2007): 301–311.

18. Larry B. Barrentine, *Concepts for R&R Studies, 2nd Edition* (Milwaukee, WI: ASQ Quality Press, 2002); and Richard K. Burdick, Connie M. Borror, and Douglas C. Montgomery, *Design and Analysis of Gauge R&R Studies: Making Decisions with Confidence Intervals in Random and Mixed ANOVA Models* (Philadelphia, PA: Society for Industrial and Applied Mathematics, 2005).

CHAPTER 3

A First Look at JMP®

This chapter provides you some initial familiarity with JMP, the enabling software that we use for Visual Six Sigma. Here the intention is simply to provide sufficient background to allow you to follow the use of JMP in the six case studies that appear in Part Two of the book. In Chapter 2, we explained the roles of *statistics as detective*, also known as *exploratory data analysis* (EDA), and *statistics as judge*, also known as *confirmatory data analysis* (CDA), within Visual Six Sigma. Although we emphasize the usefulness of EDA in this book, it is important to mention that JMP also has very comprehensive CDA capabilities, some of which are illustrated in our case studies.

JMP is a statistical package that was developed by the SAS Institute Inc. First appearing in October 1989, it originally was designed to take full advantage of a graphical user interface that at the time was only available through the Apple Macintosh. JMP has enjoyed continual development ever since those early days. Today JMP is available on the Windows, Macintosh, and Linux operating systems, having a similar look and feel on each. The specifics presented in this chapter relate to the Windows version of JMP. If you are using the Mac or Linux operating systems, please refer to the appropriate manual.[1]

From the beginning, JMP was conceived as statistical software for EDA. It has a visual emphasis, and is nimble and quick owing to the fact that data tables are completely placed into local memory. This eliminates accessing and reading from the hard drive, resulting in high-speed performance, since access delays only happen when a table is initially read or finally written. It is worth noting that, although other software packages target Six Sigma analysis running in a Windows environment, many have a DOS heritage that makes it difficult or impossible to fully support dynamic visualization and the unfolding analysis style required for EDA.[2]

Of course, what makes JMP visual and nimble is best illustrated with examples. We start to give examples in the next section and invite you to follow along. We remind you that the data tables used in this book are available on the book's Web site (http://support.sas.com/visualsixsigma).

The Anatomy of JMP

This section gives you some basic background on how JMP works. We talk about the structure of data tables, modeling types, obtaining reports, visual displays and dynamic linking of displays, and window management.

Opening JMP

When you first open JMP, two windows will appear. The one in the foreground is the **Tip of the Day** window, which provides helpful tips and features about JMP (Exhibit 3.1 shows **Tip 2**). We recommend that you use these tips until you become familiar with JMP. Unchecking **Show tips at startup** at the bottom left of the window will disable the display of the **Tip of the Day** window.

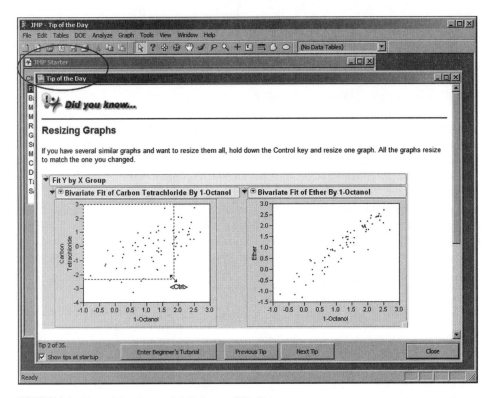

EXHIBIT 3.1   Tip of the Day and JMP Starter Windows

Behind the **Tip of the Day** window, you will find the **JMP Starter** window. This window shows an alternative way to access commands that can also be found in the main menu and toolbars. The commands are organized in groupings that may seem more intuitive to some users. You may prefer using the **JMP Starter** to using the menus. However, to standardize our presentation, we will illustrate features using the main menu bar. At this point, please close both of these windows.

To set a preference not to see the **JMP Starter** window on start-up, select **File > Preferences,** uncheck **Initial JMP Starter Window** under **General**, and click **OK** to save your preferences.

Data Tables

Data structures in JMP are called *data tables*. Exhibit 3.2 shows a portion of a data table that is used in the case study in Chapter 7 and which can be found in the data folder for Chapter 7. This data table, **PharmaSales.jmp**, contains monthly records on the performance of pharmaceutical sales representatives. The observations are keyed to 11,983 physicians of interest. Each month, information is recorded concerning the sales representative assigned to each physician and the sales activity associated with each physician. The data table covers an eight-month period. (A thorough description of the data is given in Chapter 7.)

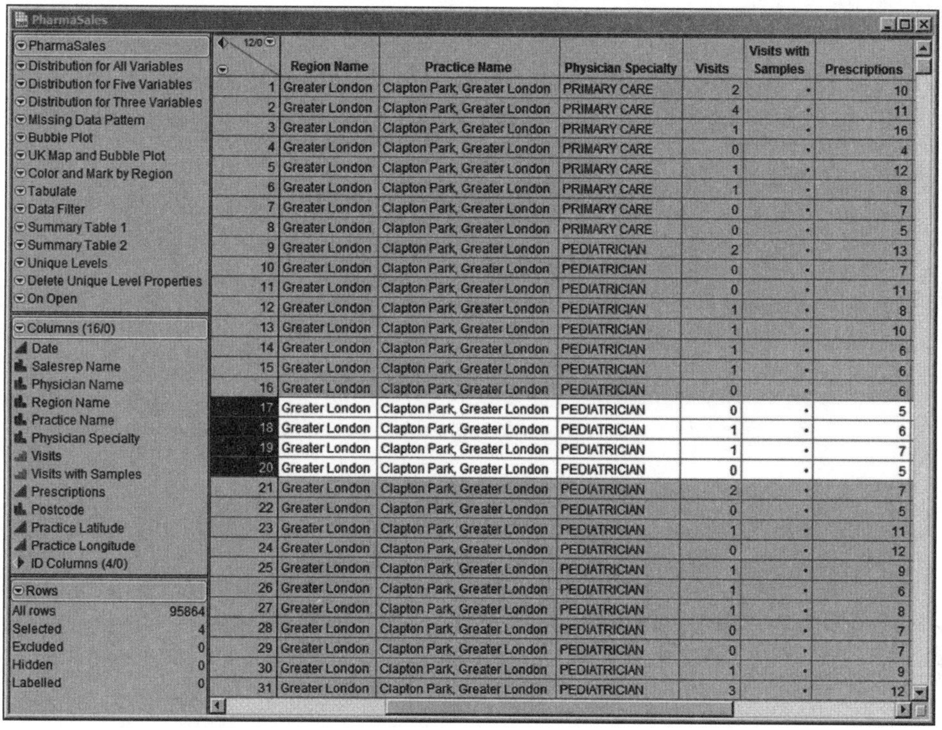

	Region Name	Practice Name	Physician Specialty	Visits	Visits with Samples	Prescriptions
1	Greater London	Clapton Park, Greater London	PRIMARY CARE	2	•	10
2	Greater London	Clapton Park, Greater London	PRIMARY CARE	4	•	11
3	Greater London	Clapton Park, Greater London	PRIMARY CARE	1	•	16
4	Greater London	Clapton Park, Greater London	PRIMARY CARE	0	•	4
5	Greater London	Clapton Park, Greater London	PRIMARY CARE	1	•	12
6	Greater London	Clapton Park, Greater London	PRIMARY CARE	1	•	8
7	Greater London	Clapton Park, Greater London	PRIMARY CARE	0	•	7
8	Greater London	Clapton Park, Greater London	PRIMARY CARE	0	•	5
9	Greater London	Clapton Park, Greater London	PEDIATRICIAN	2	•	13
10	Greater London	Clapton Park, Greater London	PEDIATRICIAN	0	•	7
11	Greater London	Clapton Park, Greater London	PEDIATRICIAN	0	•	11
12	Greater London	Clapton Park, Greater London	PEDIATRICIAN	1	•	8
13	Greater London	Clapton Park, Greater London	PEDIATRICIAN	1	•	10
14	Greater London	Clapton Park, Greater London	PEDIATRICIAN	1	•	6
15	Greater London	Clapton Park, Greater London	PEDIATRICIAN	1	•	6
16	Greater London	Clapton Park, Greater London	PEDIATRICIAN	0	•	6
17	Greater London	Clapton Park, Greater London	PEDIATRICIAN	0	•	5
18	Greater London	Clapton Park, Greater London	PEDIATRICIAN	1	•	6
19	Greater London	Clapton Park, Greater London	PEDIATRICIAN	1	•	7
20	Greater London	Clapton Park, Greater London	PEDIATRICIAN	0	•	5
21	Greater London	Clapton Park, Greater London	PEDIATRICIAN	2	•	7
22	Greater London	Clapton Park, Greater London	PEDIATRICIAN	0	•	5
23	Greater London	Clapton Park, Greater London	PEDIATRICIAN	1	•	11
24	Greater London	Clapton Park, Greater London	PEDIATRICIAN	0	•	12
25	Greater London	Clapton Park, Greater London	PEDIATRICIAN	1	•	9
26	Greater London	Clapton Park, Greater London	PEDIATRICIAN	1	•	6
27	Greater London	Clapton Park, Greater London	PEDIATRICIAN	1	•	8
28	Greater London	Clapton Park, Greater London	PEDIATRICIAN	0	•	7
29	Greater London	Clapton Park, Greater London	PEDIATRICIAN	0	•	7
30	Greater London	Clapton Park, Greater London	PEDIATRICIAN	1	•	9
31	Greater London	Clapton Park, Greater London	PEDIATRICIAN	3	•	12

EXHIBIT 3.2 Partial View of PharmaSales.jmp Data Table

A data table consists of a data grid and *data table panels*. The data grid consists of row numbers and data columns. Each row number corresponds to an observation, and the columns correspond to the variables. For observation 17, for example, the **Region Name** is Greater London, **Visits** has a value of 0, and **Prescriptions** has a value of 5. Note that for row 17 the entry in **Visits with Samples** is a dot. This is an indicator that the value for **Visits with Samples** is missing for row 17. Since **Visits with Samples** is a numeric variable, a dot is used to indicate that the value is missing. For a character variable, a blank is used to represent a missing value.

There are three panels, shown to the left of the data grid. The *table panel* is at the top left. In our example, it is labeled **PharmaSales**. Below this panel, we see the *columns panel* and the *rows panel*.

The table panel shows a listing of scripts. These are pieces of JMP code that produce analyses. A script can be run by clicking on the red triangle to the left of the script name and choosing **Run Script** from the drop-down menu. As you will see, you will often want to save scripts to the data table in order to reproduce analyses. This is very easy to do.

The last script in the list of scripts is an **On Open** script. When a script is given the name **On Open**, it is run whenever the data table is opened. In the data tables associated with the case studies that follow, you will often see **On Open** scripts. We use these to reinitialize the data table, to prevent you from inadvertently saving changes. If you wish to save work that you have added to a data table that contains an **On Open** script, we suggest that you delete that script (click on the red triangle next to it and choose **Delete**) and then save the table under a different name.

The columns panel, located below the table panel, lists the names of the columns, or variables, that are represented in the data grid. In Exhibit 3.2, we have 16 columns. The columns list contains a grouping of variables, called ID Columns, which groups four variables. Clicking on the blue disclosure icon next to ID Columns reveals the four columns that are grouped.

In the columns panel, note the small icons to the left of the column names. These represent the modeling type of the data in each column. JMP indicates the modeling type for each variable as shown in Exhibit 3.3.

◢ Continuous for numeric measurements
◢ Ordinal for measurements representing ordered categories
◢ Nominal for measurements representing unordered categories

EXHIBIT 3.3   Icons Representing Modeling Types

Specification of these modeling types tells JMP which analyses are appropriate for these variables. For example, JMP will construct a histogram for a variable with a continuous modeling type, but it will construct a bar graph and frequency table for a variable with a nominal modeling type. Note that our **PharmaSales.jmp** data table contains variables representing all three modeling types.

The rows panel appears beneath the columns panel. Here we learn that the data table consists of 95,864 observations. The numbers of rows that are **Selected**, **Excluded**, **Hidden**, and **Labelled** are also given in this panel. These four properties, called *row states*, reflect attributes that are assigned to certain rows, and that define how JMP utilizes those rows. For example, **Selected** rows are highlighted in the data table and plots, and can easily be turned into subsets. (In Exhibit 3.2, four rows (17–20) are selected.) **Excluded** rows are not included in calculations. **Hidden** rows are not shown in plots. **Labelled** rows are assigned labels that can be viewed in most plots.

Visual Displays and Text Reports

Commands can be chosen using the menu bar, the icons on the toolbar, or, as mentioned earlier, the **JMP Starter** window. We will use the menu bar in our discussion. Exhibit 3.4 shows the menu bar and default toolbars in JMP 8. Note that the name of the current data table is shown as part of the window's title. Also shown are the **File_Edit**, **Tools**, and **Data_Table_List** toolbars. This last toolbar shows a drop-down list of all open data tables; the selected data table is the current data table. Toolbars can be customized by selecting **Edit > Customize > Menus and Toolbars**.

EXHIBIT 3.4   Menu Bar and Default Toolbar in JMP 8

Reports can be obtained using the **Analyze** and **Graph** menus. JMP reports obtained from options under the **Analyze** menu provide visual displays (graphs) along with numerical results (text reports). Options under the **Graph** menu primarily provide visual displays, some of which are supported by analytical information.

The **Analyze** and **Graph** menus are shown in Exhibits 3.5 and 3.6. These high-level menus lead to submenus containing a wide array of visual and analytical tools, some of which are displayed in Exhibits 3.5 and 3.6. Other tools appear later in this chapter and in the case studies.

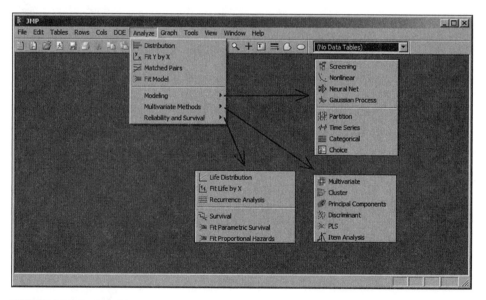

EXHIBIT 3.5   Analyze Menu

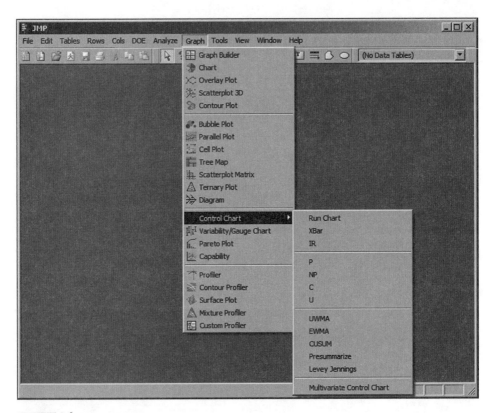

EXHIBIT 3.6   Graph Menu

We say that the menu choices under **Analyze** and **Graph** *launch* platforms. A platform is launched using a dialog that allows you to make choices about variable roles, plots, and analyses. A platform generates a *report* consisting of a set of related plots and tables with which you can interact so that the relevant features of the chosen variables reveal themselves clearly. We will illustrate this idea with the JMP **Distribution** platform.

Whenever you are given a data table, you should always start by under-standing what is *in* each variable. This can be done by using the **Distribution** platform. At this point, please open the data table **PharmaSales.jmp**. Clicking on **Analyze > Distribution**, with this data table active, opens the dialog window shown in Exhibit 3.7.

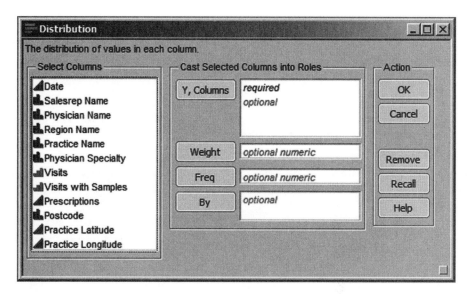

EXHIBIT 3.7   Distribution Dialog for PharmaSales.jmp

Suppose that we want to see distribution reports for **Region Name, Visits,** and **Prescriptions.** To obtain these, first select all three variable names in the **Select Columns** list by holding down the control key while selecting them. Enter them in the box called **Y, Columns**; you can do this either by dragging and dropping the column names from the **Select Columns** box to the **Y, Columns** box, or by clicking **Y, Columns.** You can also simply double-click each variable name individually. In Exhibit 3.8, these variables have been selected and given the **Y, Columns** role.

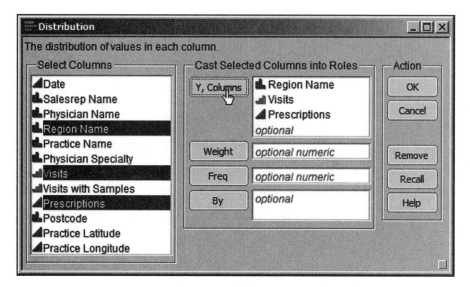

EXHIBIT 3.8   Distribution Dialog with Three Variables Chosen as Ys

Note that the modeling types of the three variables are shown in the **Y, Columns** box. Clicking **OK** gives the output shown in Exhibit 3.9. The graphs are given in a vertical layout to facilitate dynamic visualization of numerous plots at one time. This is the JMP default. However, under **File > Preferences > Platforms > Distribution**, you can set a preference for a stacked horizontal view by checking the **Stack** option. You can also make this choice directly in the report by choosing the appropriate option from the drop-down list of options obtained by clicking the red triangle next to **Distributions**, as we will illustrate later.

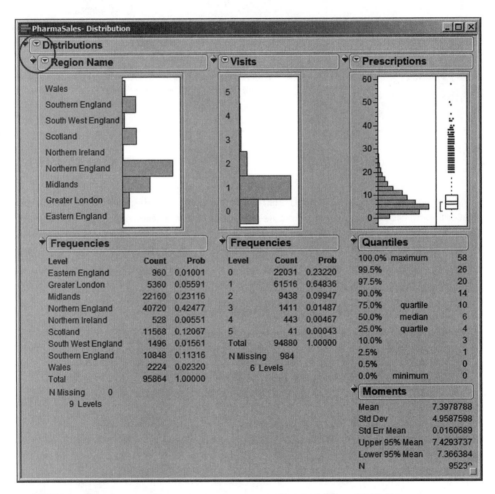

EXHIBIT 3.9   Distribution Reports for Region Name, Visits, and Prescriptions

The report provides a visual display, as well as supporting analytic information, for the chosen variables. Note that the different modeling types result in different output. For **Region Name**, a nominal variable representing unordered categories, JMP provides a bar graph as well as frequency counts and proportions (using the default alphanumeric ordering). **Visits**, an ordinal variable, is displayed using an ordered bar graph, accompanied by a frequency tabulation of the ordered values. Finally, the graph for **Prescriptions**, which has a continuous modeling type, is a histogram accompanied by a box plot. The analytic output consists of sample statistics, such as quantiles, sample mean, standard deviation, and so on.

Looking at the report for **Region Name**, we see that some regions have relatively few observations. Northern England is the region associated with roughly 42.5 percent of the rows. For **Visits**, we see that the most frequent value is one, and that at most five visits occur in any given month. Finally, we see that **Prescriptions**, the number of prescriptions written by a physician in a given month, has a highly right-skewed distribution, which is to be expected.

Additional analysis and graphical options are available in the menus obtained by clicking on the *red triangle icons*. If we click on the red triangle next to **Distributions** in the report shown in Exhibit 3.9, a list of options appears from which we can choose **Stack** (see Exhibit 3.10). This gives us the report in a stacked horizontal layout as shown in Exhibit 3.11. (Although the red triangle icons will not appear red in this text, we will continue to refer to them in this fashion, as it helps identify them when you are working directly in JMP.)

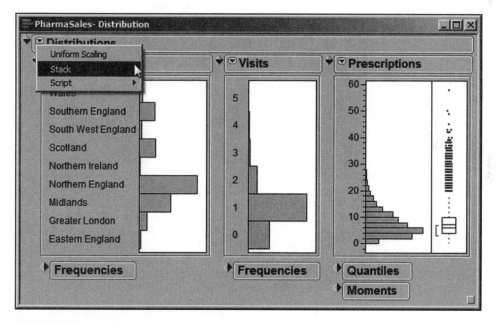

EXHIBIT 3.10   Distribution Whole Platform Options

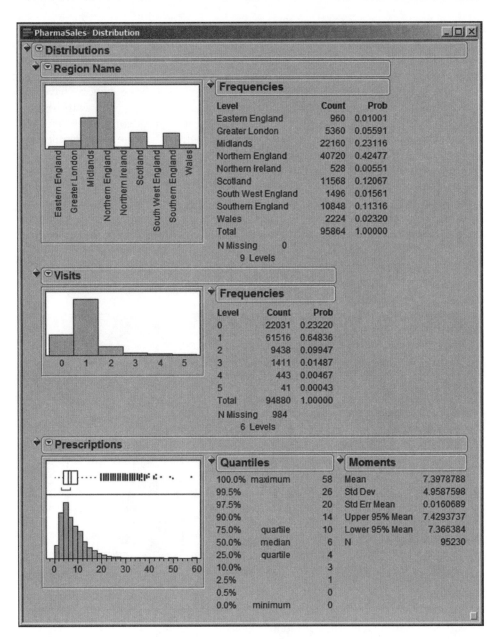

EXHIBIT 3.11   Stacked Layout for Three Distribution Reports

Further options, specific to the modeling type of each variable being studied, are given in the menu obtained by clicking the red triangle next to the variable name. Exhibit 3.12 shows the options that are revealed by clicking on the red triangle next to **Prescriptions**. These options are specific to a variable with a continuous modeling type.

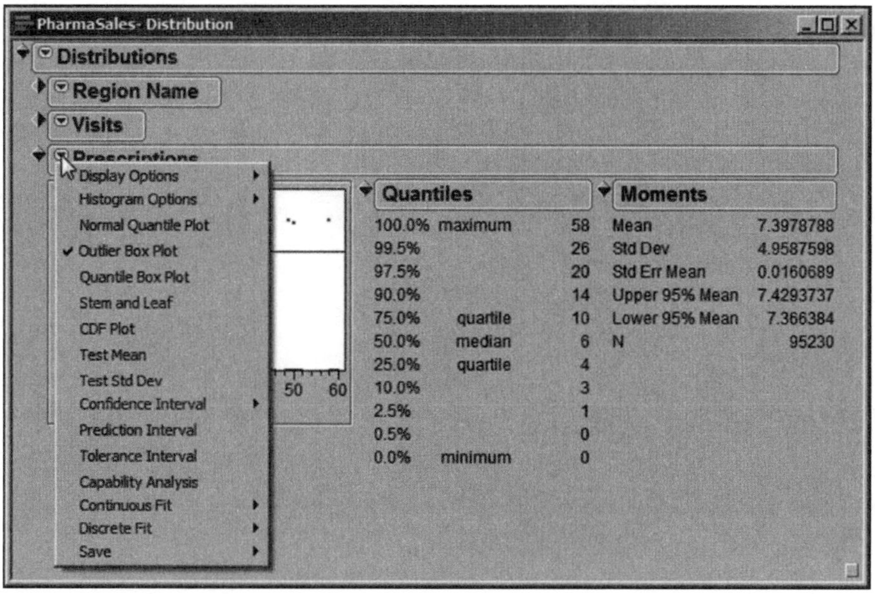

EXHIBIT 3.12 Variable-Specific Distribution Platform Options

The red triangles support the unfolding style of analysis required for EDA. They put *context sensitive* options right where you need them, allowing you to look at your data in a graphical format *before* deciding which analysis might best be used to describe, further investigate, or model this data.

You will also see blue and gray diamonds, called *disclosure icons*, in the report. These serve to conceal or reveal certain portions of the output in order to make viewing more manageable. In Exhibit 3.12, to better focus on **Prescriptions**, the disclosure icons for **Region Name** and **Visits** are closed to conceal their report contents. Note that the orientation of the disclosure icon changes, depending on whether it is revealing or concealing contents.

When you launch a platform, the initial state of the report can be controlled with the **Platforms** option under **File > Preferences**. Here, you can specify which plots and tables you want to see, and control the form of these plots and tables. *For the analyses in this book, we use the default settings unless we explicitly mention otherwise.* (If you have already set platform preferences, you may need to make appropriate changes to your preferences to exactly reproduce the reports shown above and in the remainder of the book.)

Dynamic Linking to Data Table

JMP dynamically links all plots that are based on the same data table. This is arguably its most valuable capability for EDA. To see what this means, consider the **PharmaSales.jmp** data table (Exhibit 3.2). Using **Analyze > Distribution**, we select Salesrep Name and Region Name as **Y, Columns**, and click **OK**. In the resulting report, click the red triangle icon next to **Distribution** to select **Stack.** Also, close the disclosure icon for **Frequencies** next to Salesrep Name. This gives the plots shown in Exhibit 3.13.

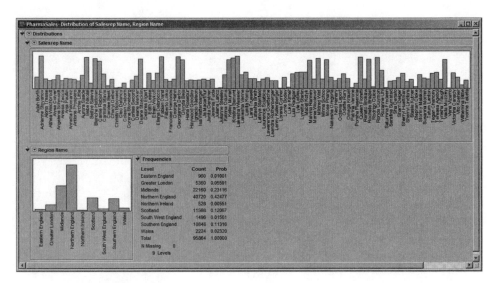

EXHIBIT 3.13   Distribution Reports for Region Name and Salesrep Name

Now, in the report for **Region Name**, we click in the bar representing Scotland. This selects the bar corresponding to Scotland, as shown in Exhibit 3.14. Simultaneously, areas in the **Salesrep Name** bar graph corresponding to rows with the **Region Name** of Scotland are also highlighted. In other words, we have identified the sales representatives who work in Scotland. Moreover, in the **Salesrep Name** graph, no bars are partially highlighted, indicating that all of the activity for each of the sales representatives identified is in Scotland. The proportion of a bar that is highlighted corresponds to the proportion of rows where the selected variable value (in this case, Scotland) is represented.

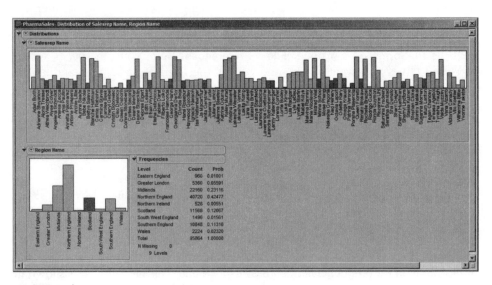

EXHIBIT 3.14   Bar for Region Name Scotland Selected

Now, what has happened behind the scenes is that the rows in the data table corresponding to observations having Scotland as the value for **Region Name** have been *selected* in the data grid. Exhibit 3.15 shows part of the data table. Note that the Scotland rows are highlighted. Also, note that the rows panel indicates that 11,568 rows have been selected.

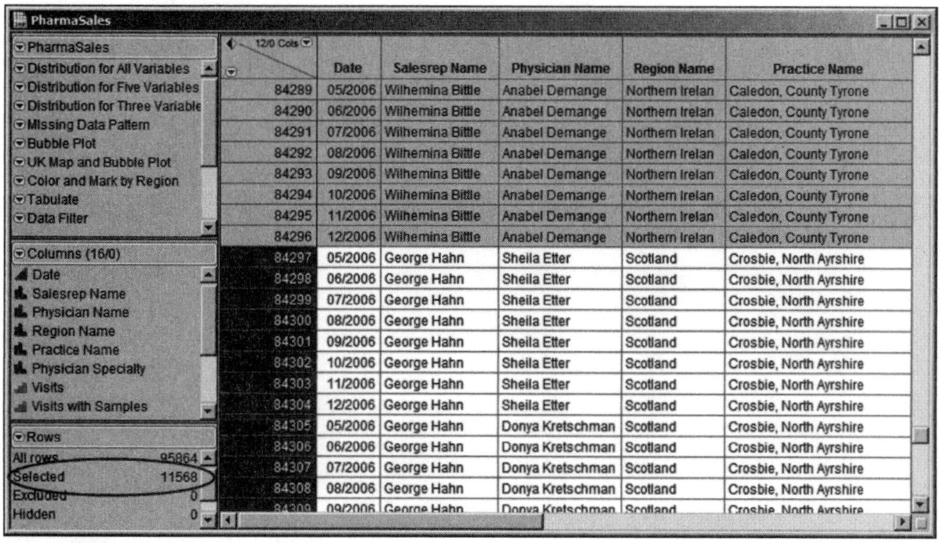

EXHIBIT 3.15   Partial View of Data Table Showing Selection of Rows with Region Name Scotland

Since these rows are selected in the data table, points and areas on plots corresponding to these rows will be highlighted, as appropriate. This is why the bars of the graph for **Salesrep Name** that correspond to representatives working in Scotland are highlighted. The sales representatives whose bars are highlighted have worked in Scotland, and because no bar is partially highlighted, we can also conclude that they have not worked in any other region.

Suppose that we are interested in identifying the region where a specific sales representative works. Let us look at the second sales representative in the **Salesrep Name** graph, Adrienne Stoyanov, who has a large number of rows. We can simply click on the bar corresponding to Adrienne in the **Salesrep Name** bar graph to highlight it, as shown in Exhibit 3.16.

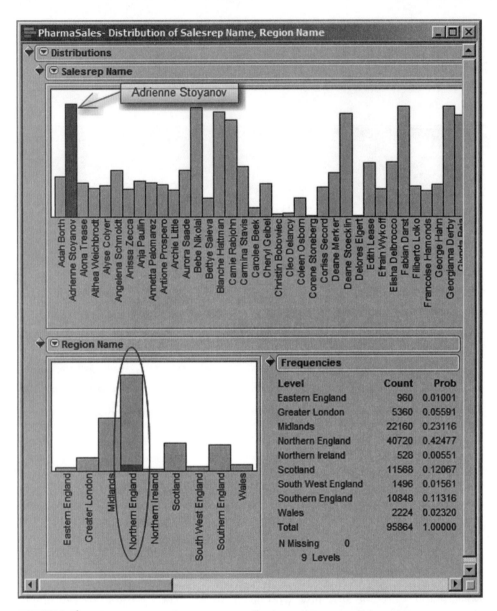

EXHIBIT 3.16 Distribution of Salerep Name with Adrienne Stoyanov Selected

This has the effect of selecting the 2,440 records corresponding to Adrienne in the data table (check the rows panel). We see that the bar corresponding to Northern England in the **Region Name** plot is partially highlighted. This indicates that Adrienne works in Northern England, but that she is only a small part of the Northern England sales force.

To view a data table consisting only of Adrienne's 2,440 rows, simply double-click on her bar in the **Salesrep Name** bar graph. A table (Exhibit 3.17) appears that contains only these 2,440 rows—note that all of these rows are selected, since the rows correspond to the selected bar of the histogram. This table is also assigned a

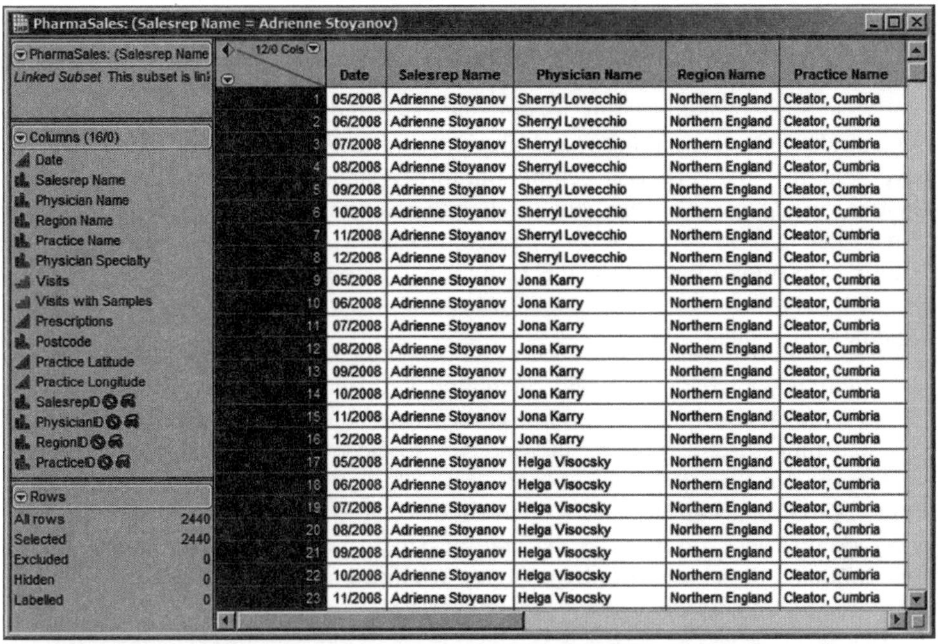

EXHIBIT 3.17 Data Table Consisting of 2,440 Rows with Salesrep Name Adrienne Stoyanov

descriptive name. If you have previously selected columns in the main data table, only those columns will appear in the new data table. Otherwise all columns will display in the new table, as shown in Exhibit 3.17. (We will explain how to deselect rows and columns next.)

To deselect the rows in this data table, left-click in the blank space in the lower triangular region located in the upper left of the data grid (Exhibit 3.18). Clicking in the upper right triangular region will deselect columns. Pressing the escape key while the data table is the active window will remove all row and column selections.

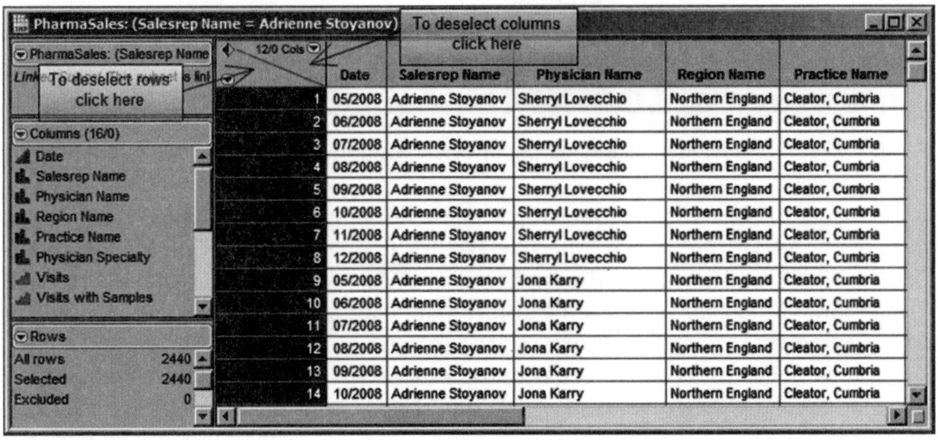

EXHIBIT 3.18 Deselecting Rows or Columns

Note that JMP also tries to link *between* data tables when it is useful. For example, when using the **Tables > Summary** menu option (described later), reports generated from summary data can be linked to reports based on the underlying data.

By way of review, in this section we have illustrated the ability of JMP to dynamically link data among visual displays and to the underlying data table. We have done this in a very basic setting, but this capability carries over to many other exciting visual tools. The flexibility to identify and work with observations based on visual identification is central to the software's ability to support Visual Six Sigma. The six case studies that follow this chapter will elaborate on this theme.

Window Management

In exploring your data, you will often find yourself with many data tables and reports simultaneously open. Of course, these can be closed individually. However, it is sometimes useful to close all windows, to close only data tables, or to close only report windows. JMP allows you to do this from the **Window** menu. Exhibit 3.19 shows our current JMP display. We have four open windows—two data tables and two reports. These are listed in the bottom panel of the **Window** drop-down. (We have arranged these windows by selecting **Window > Arrange > Cascade**.)

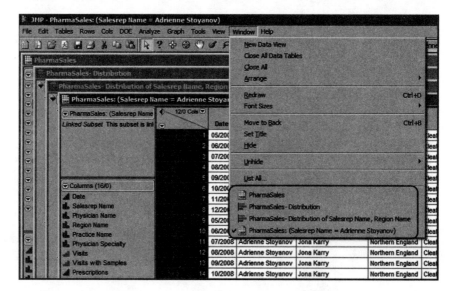

EXHIBIT 3.19   Window Menu Showing List of Open Windows

Note that **PharmaSales: (Salesrep Name = Adrienne Stoyanov)** has a checkmark next to it and, in the display, the title bar for that data table is highlighted. This indicates that this data table is the *current* data table. When running analyses on data, it is important to make sure that the appropriate data table is the current one—when a launch dialog is executed, commands are run on the current data table.

At this point, we could select **Window > Close All** or **Close All Data Tables**. Had a report been the active window, we would have been given the choice to **Close All Reports**. However, we want to continue our work with **PharmaSales.jmp**. So, for now, let us close the other three windows individually by clicking on the close button (**X**) in the top right corner of each window.

Visual Displays and Analyses Featured in the Case Studies

The visual displays and analyses that are featured in the case studies represent many different menu items in JMP. In this section, we will give a quick overview of the more basic items and where they can be found.

Graph

Techniques that have visual displays as their primary goal are available from the **Graph** menu shown earlier in Exhibit 3.6. Many of these displays allow you to view patterns in the data in three or more dimensions. The **Bubble Plot** is animated, giving one way for you to see behavior over time. In the case studies, we will see examples of the following:

- **Graph Builder** allows highly interactive simultaneous visualization of multiple variables using a wide variety of graphical elements.
- **Scatterplot 3D** gives a three-dimensional data view.
- **Bubble Plot** is a dynamic extension of a scatterplot that is capable of showing up to five dimensions (using x position, y position, size, color, and time).
- **Tree Map** is a two-dimensional version of a bar graph that allows visualization of variables with many levels.
- **Scatterplot Matrix** gives a matrix of scatterplots.
- **Diagram** is used to create cause-and-effect diagrams.
- **Control Chart** constructs a variety of control charts that, in particular, allow for phases.
- **Variability/Gauge Chart** is useful for measurement system analysis and for displaying data across the levels of multiple categorical variables, especially when the focus is on displaying the variation within and between groups.
- **Pareto Plot** gives a bar chart ordered by decreasing frequency of occurrence.
- **Capability** provides a goal plot as well as box plots to assess the performance of numerous responses.
- **Profiler** provides an interactive display that is used in optimization and simulation.
- **Surface Plot** creates three-dimensional, rotatable displays.

Analyze

Techniques that combine analytic results with supporting visual displays are found in the **Analyze** menu, as shown earlier in Exhibit 3.5. **Analyze** commands often produce displays similar to those found under the **Graph** menu. For example, a **Fit Model** analysis allows access to the profiler, which can also be accessed under **Graph**. As another example, under **Multivariate Methods > Multivariate**, a scatterplot matrix is presented. The selection **Graph > Scatterplot Matrix** also produces a scatterplot matrix. However, **Multivariate Methods > Multivariate** allows you to choose analyses not directly accessible from **Graph > Scatterplot Matrix**, such as pairwise correlations.

Each platform under **Analyze** performs analyses that are consistent with the modeling types of the variables involved. Consider the **Fit Y by X** platform, which addresses the relationship between two variables. If both are continuous, then **Fit Y by X** presents a scatterplot, allows you to fit a line or curve, and provides regression results. If Y is continuous and X is nominal, then the platform produces a plot of the data with comparison box plots, and allows you to choose an analysis of variance (ANOVA) report. If both X and Y are nominal, then a mosaic plot and contingency table are presented. If X is continuous and Y is nominal, a logistic regression plot and the corresponding analytic results are given. If one or both variables are ordinal, then, again, an appropriate report is presented.

This philosophy carries over to other platforms. The **Fit Model** platform is used to model the relationship between one or more responses and one or more predictors. In particular, this platform performs multiple linear regression analysis. The **Modeling** menu includes various modeling techniques, including neural nets and partitioning, which are usually associated with data mining.

Our case studies will take us to the following parts of the **Analyze** menu:

- **Distribution** provides histograms and bar graphs, distributional fits, and capability analysis.
- **Fit Y by X** gives scatterplots, linear fits, comparison box plots, mosaic plots, and contingency tables.
- **Fit Model** fits a large variety of models and gives access to a prediction profiler that is linked to the fitted model.
- **Modeling > Screening** fits models with numerous effects.
- **Modeling > Neural Net** fits flexible nonlinear models using hidden layers.
- **Modeling > Partition** provides recursive partitioning fits, similar to classification and regression trees.
- **Multivariate Methods > Multivariate** gives scatterplot matrices and various correlations.

Tables

Another menu that will be used extensively in our case studies is the **Tables** menu (Exhibit 3.20). This menu contains options that deal with data tables. The **Summary** platform is used to obtain summary information, such as means and standard

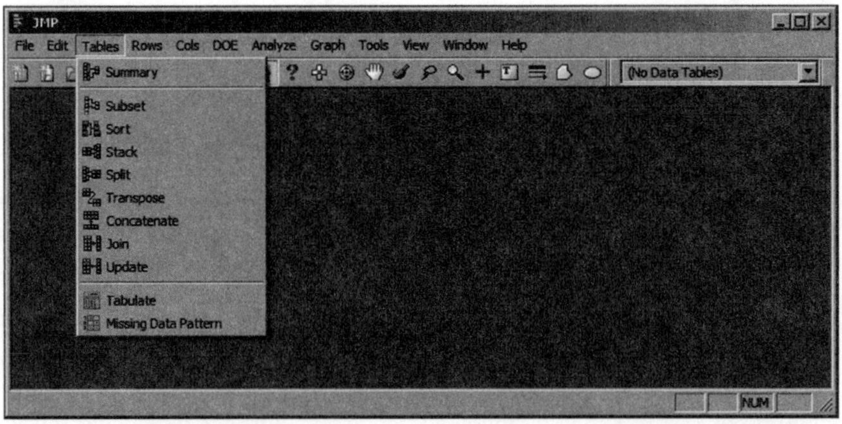

EXHIBIT 3.20   Tables Menu

deviations, for variables in a data table. **Subset** creates a new data table from selections of rows and columns in the current data table. **Sort** sorts the rows according to the values of a column or columns. **Stack**, **Split**, and **Transpose** create new data tables from the data in the current data table. **Join** and **Update** operate on two data tables, while **Concatenate** operates on two or more data tables.

Tabulate is an interactive way to build tables of descriptive statistics. **Missing Data Pattern** produces tables that help you determine if there are patterns or relationships in the structure of missing data in the current data table. Recall that for a numeric variable JMP uses "." to denote a missing value, while JMP uses an empty string for character data, which appears as a blank cell in a data table.

Our case studies will take us to the following platforms:

- **Summary** summarizes columns from the current data table in various ways.
- **Sort** sorts a data table by the values of designated columns.
- **Concatenate** combines rows from two or more data tables.
- **Tabulate** constructs tables of descriptive statistics in an interactive and flexible way.
- **Missing Data Pattern** creates a table describing where data are missing across a set of columns.

Rows

We will also use features that are found under the **Rows** menu. The **Rows** menu is shown in Exhibit 3.21, with the options under **Row Selection** expanded. The **Rows** menu allows you to exclude, hide, and label observations. You can assign colors

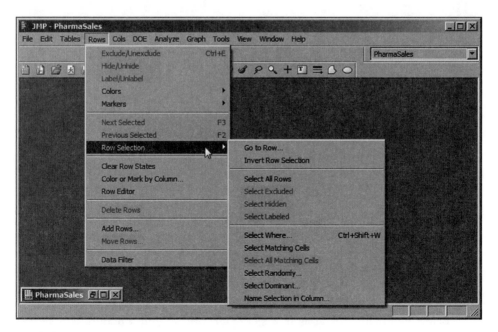

EXHIBIT 3.21   Rows Menu with Options for Row Selection Shown

and markers to the points representing observations. **Row Selection** allows you to specify various criteria for selecting rows, as shown.

A *row state* is a property that is assigned to a row. A row state consists of information on whether a specific row is selected, excluded from analysis, hidden so that it does not appear in plots, labeled, colored, or has a marker assigned to it. You often need to assign row states to rows interactively based on visual displays. The **Clear Row States** command removes any row states that you have assigned.

Data Filter will be used extensively in our case studies. This command provides a very flexible way for you to query the data interactively to identify meaningful, and possibly complex, subsets. It also provides a way of animating many of the visual displays in JMP. Depending on the analysis goal, subsets that you define using **Data Filter** can be easily selected and placed into their own data tables for subsequent analysis or excluded from the current analysis.

Columns

The **Cols** menu, shown in Exhibit 3.22, provides options dealing with column properties and roles, information stored along with columns, formulas that define column values, recoding of values, and more.

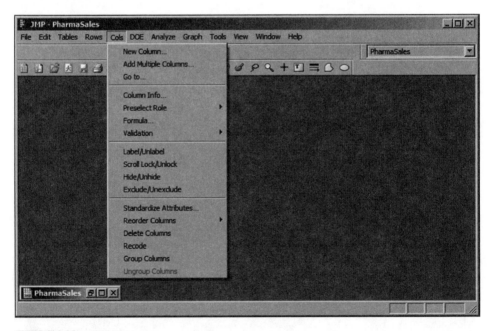

EXHIBIT 3.22   Cols Menu

The **Column Info** command opens a dialog that allows you to define properties that are saved as part of the column information. To access **Column Info** for a column, right-click in the column header area and choose **Column Info**. Exhibit 3.23 shows the **Column Info** dialog for Visits. For example, you can add a note describing the column (this has already been done), save specification limits, control limits, and so forth. When defining a new column, you can select **Formula** to define that column using a formula.

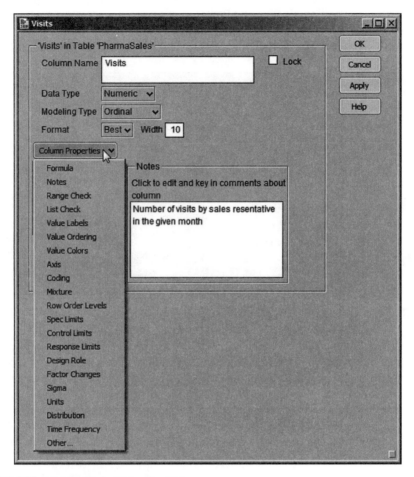

EXHIBIT 3.23   Column Info Dialog for Visits

In **Column Info** note that you can specify the data type and modeling type for your data. You can specify a format here as well.

DOE

In Chapter 2, we introduced the idea of experimental data, which arise when we deliberately manipulate the Xs. An *experimental design* is a list of trials or runs defined by specific settings for the Xs, with an order in which these runs should be performed. This design is used by an experimenter in order to obtain experimental data. JMP provides comprehensive support for generating experimental designs and modeling the results.

The **DOE** menu, shown in Exhibit 3.24, generates settings for a designed experiment, based on your choices of experimental design type, responses, and factors. There are nine major design groupings (**Custom Design** to **Taguchi Arrays** in the menu listing). The **Augment Design** platform provides options for adding runs to an existing design. The **Sample Size and Power** platform computes power, sample size, or effect size for a variety of situations, based on values that you set.

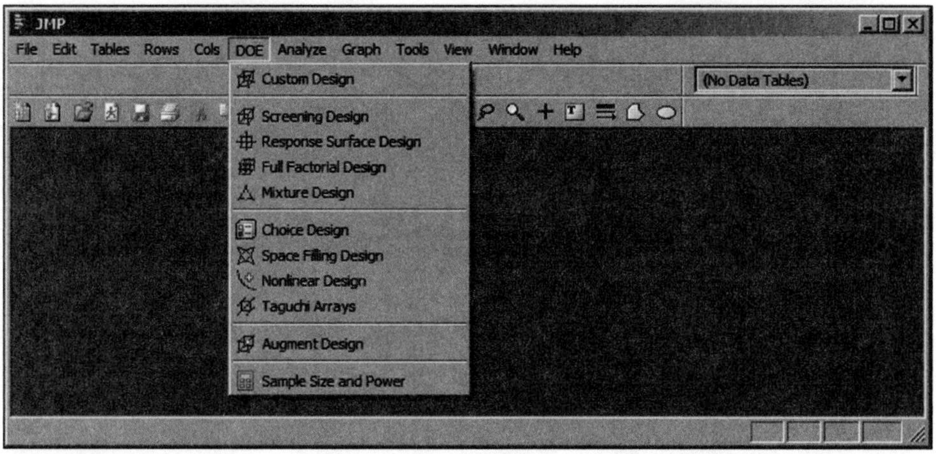

EXHIBIT 3.24   DOE Menu

The **Custom Design** platform allows great flexibility in design choices. In particular, **Custom Design** accommodates both continuous and categorical factors, provides designs that estimate user-specified interactions and polynomial terms, allows for situations with hard-to-change and easy-to-change factors (split-plot designs), and permits you to specify inequality constraints on the factors. The **Custom Design** platform is featured in one of our case studies (Chapter 6), while the **Full Factorial Design** platform is used in another (Chapter 8).

Scripts

As we have seen, the menus in JMP can be used to produce an incredible variety of visual displays and analyses. When you are starting out with JMP, you rarely need to look beyond these menus. However, more advanced users sometimes find the need to simplify repetitive tasks, or want to see custom analyses. These tasks can be programmed within JMP by using its scripting language, *JMP Scripting Language* (JSL).

A JMP script can be saved as a separate file, with a **.jsl** extension, or it can be saved as part of a data table. Our data table **PharmaSales.jmp** contains several JMP scripts that are saved as part of the data table in the table panel area. Consider the script **Distribution for Three Variables**. You can run this script by clicking on the red triangle to the left of the script and choosing **Run Script**, as shown in Exhibit 3.25.

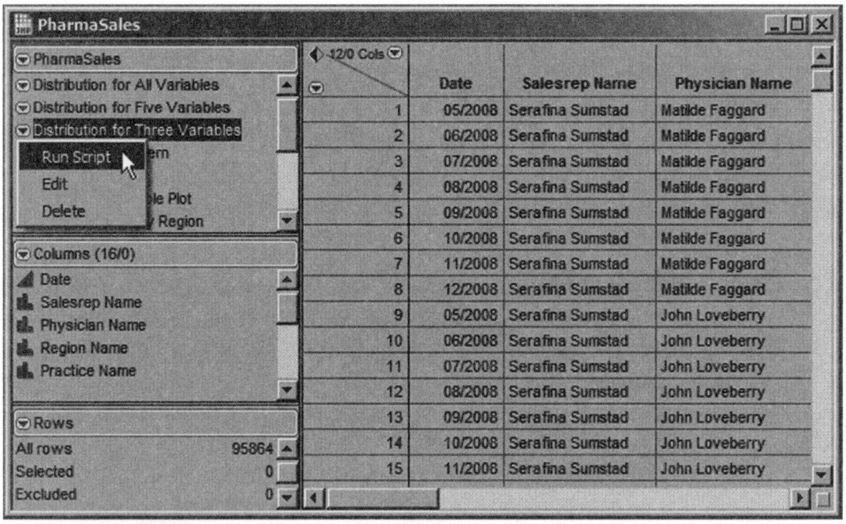

EXHIBIT 3.25 Running the Script Distribution for Three Variables

When you run this script, you obtain the report shown in Exhibit 3.26. This is the stacked layout that we obtained earlier in Exhibit 3.11. Scripts provide an easy way to document your work. When you have obtained a report that you want to reproduce, instead of saving the report, or parts of it, in a presentation file or document, you can simply save the script that produces the report to your data

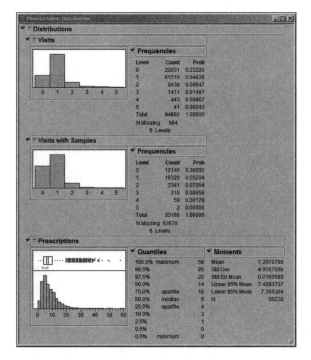

EXHIBIT 3.26 Distribution Report Obtained by Running Distribution for Three Variables

table. So long as the required columns are still in the table, the script will continue to work even if the data (rows) are refreshed or changed.

To save a script to produce this report, you would do the following. First, obtain the report by filling out the launch dialog as previously shown in Exhibit 3.8 and clicking **OK**. Then, from the red triangle menu options, select **Stack**. Now, click on the red triangle next to **Distributions** and choose **Script > Save Script to Data Table**, as shown in Exhibit 3.27. A new script, called **Distribution**, appears in the table panel.

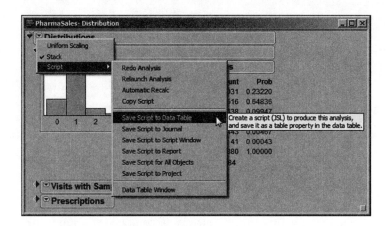

EXHIBIT 3.27   Saving a Script to the Data Table

You can rename or edit this script by clicking on its red triangle and choosing **Edit**. When you do this, you obtain the script window shown in Exhibit 3.28. This is the code that reproduces the report. In platforms other than **Distribution**, scripts can be saved in a similar way.

```
Table Property/Script for PharmaSales

Name: Distribution

Script  Distribution(
             Stack( 1 ),
             Nominal Distribution( Column( :Visits ), Horizontal Layout( 1
             Nominal Distribution(
                 Column( :Visits with Samples ),
                 Horizontal Layout( 1 ),
                 Vertical( 0 )
             ),
             Continuous Distribution(
                 Column( :Prescriptions ),
                 Horizontal Layout( 1 ),
                 Vertical( 0 )
             ),
             SendToReport(
                 Dispatch( {}, "Visits with Samples", OutlineBox, Close( 1
                 Dispatch( {}, "Prescriptions", OutlineBox, Close( 1 ) ),
                 Dispatch(
                     {"Prescriptions"},
                     "Distrib Outlier Box",
                     FrameBox

                                          OK    Cancel    Help
```

EXHIBIT 3.28   Distribution Script

Of course, scripts can be constructed from scratch, or pieced together from scripts that JMP automatically produces, such as the script in Exhibit 3.28. Some of the scripts in the data table **PharmaSales.jmp** are of this type.

In the case studies, you will see that the analysts frequently save scripts to their data tables. There are two reasons for this. First, we want you to have the scripts available in case you want to rerun their analyses quickly, so as to get to a point in the case study where you might have been interrupted. Second, we want to illustrate saving scripts because they provide an excellent way of documenting your analysis, allowing you to follow and recreate it in the future.

In Chapter 1 we mentioned that, on occasion, we have deliberately compromised the lean nature of the Visual Six Sigma Roadmap to show some JMP functionality that will be useful to you in the future. The saving of scripts is an example, because at one level scripts are not necessary and are therefore not lean. However, at another level, when you have obtained the critical reports that form the basis for your conclusions, scripts take on a lean aspect, because they help document results and mistake-proof further work.

Personalizing JMP

JMP provides many ways to personalize the user experience. These options range from specification of what the user wants to see by default in existing reports to creating customized reports for specific analysis or reporting tasks. Many features can be customized in the **Preferences** menu, located under **File**. More advanced customization may require the user to write or adapt scripts. We also mention the ability to **Journal**, located under **Edit**. This facility allows a user to document an analysis session.

Customization options include:

- Configuring the initial state of the report that a platform produces using **Preferences**.
- Deleting from or adding to a report.
- Combining several reports from different platforms.
- Defining custom analyses and reports.
- Adding to, deleting from, or rearranging menu items.
- Using **Journal** files to lay out a series of steps for users to take.

By allowing such a high degree of user customization, JMP enables users to best leverage their skills and capabilities. With relatively little effort, the software becomes a correct fit for an individual, or group of similar individuals.

Visual Six Sigma Data Analysis Process and Roadmap

As this quick tour of functionality may suggest, JMP has a very diverse set of features for both EDA and CDA. The earlier section "Visual Displays and Analyses Featured in the Case Studies" gave a preview of those parts of JMP that you will see again in later chapters. But, there is a danger that the section's techniques may have appeared as a laundry list, perhaps at odds with our contention in Chapter 2 that Visual Six Sigma is a way of *combining* such techniques to get value from data. Let's attempt to put the list of techniques into some context.

In Chapter 2, we discussed the outcome of interest to us, represented by Y, and the causes, or inputs that affect Y, represented by Xs. As we saw, Six Sigma practitioners often refer to the critical inputs, resources, or controls that determine Y as *Hot X*s. Although many Xs have the potential to affect an outcome, Y, the data may show that only certain of these Xs actually have an impact on the variation in Y. In our credit card example from Chapter 2, whether a person is an only child or not may have practically no impact on whether that person responds to a credit card offer. In other words, the number of siblings is not a Hot X. However, an individual's income level may well be a Hot X.

Consider the Visual Six Sigma Data Analysis Process, illustrated in Exhibit 3.29, which was first presented in Chapter 2. In your Six Sigma projects, first you determine the Y or Ys of interest during the Frame Problem step. Usually, these are explicit in the project charter or they follow as process outputs from the process map. In *Design for Six Sigma* (DFSS) projects, the Ys are usually the *Critical to Quality Characteristics* (CTQs).

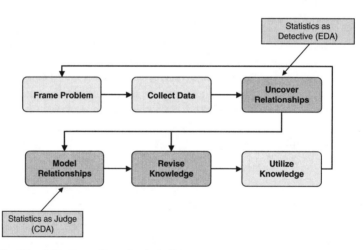

EXHIBIT 3.29   Visual Six Sigma Data Analysis Process

The Xs of potential interest are identified in the Collect Data step. To identify Xs that are potential drivers of the Ys, a team uses process maps, contextual knowledge, brainstorming sessions, cause-and-effect diagrams, cause-and-effect matrices, and other techniques. Once the Xs have been listed, you seek data that relate these Xs to the Ys. Sometimes these observational data exist in databases. Sometimes you have to begin data collection efforts to obtain the required information.

Once the data have been obtained, you face the issue of identifying the Hot Xs. This is part of the Uncover Relationships step. Once you have identified the Hot Xs, you may or may not need to develop an empirical model of how they affect the Ys. Developing this more detailed understanding is part of the Model Relationships step, which brings us back to the signal function, described in Chapter 2. You may need to develop a model that expresses the signal function for each Y in terms of the Hot Xs. Here we illustrate with *r* Hot Xs:

$$Y = f(X_1, X_2, \ldots, X_r)$$

Only by understanding this relationship at an appropriate level can you set the Xs correctly to best manage the variation in Y.

Identifying the Hot Xs and modeling their relationship to Y (for each Y) is to a large extent the crux of the Analyze phase of a DMAIC project, and a large part of the Analyze and Design phases of a DMADV project.

Exhibit 3.30 shows an expansion of the Visual Six Sigma Roadmap that was presented in Chapter 2. Recall that this Roadmap focuses on the three Visual Six Sigma Data Analysis Process steps that most benefit from dynamic visualization: Uncover Relationships, Model Relationships, and Revise Knowledge. In this expanded version, we show how a subset of the techniques listed earlier in this chapter can be used in a coordinated way to accomplish the goals of Visual Six Sigma. In our experience, this represents an excellent how-to guide for green belts who are starting the Analyze phase of a traditional Six Sigma project, or anyone who is simply faced with the need to understand the relationship between some set of inputs and some outcome measure outside a DMAIC or DMADV framework.

EXHIBIT 3.30   Visual Six Sigma Roadmap

Visual Six Sigma Roadmap

What We Do	How We Do It
Uncover Relationships*	
Dynamically visualize the variables one at a time	Distribution, Capability, Data Filter
Dynamically visualize the variables two at a time	Fit Y by X (Comparison Box Plots, Scatterplots, Mosaic Plots), Data Filter, Control Chart, Time Series
Dynamically visualize the variables more than two at a time	Variability Chart, Scatterplot Matrix, Graph Builder, Tree Map, Bubble Plot, Scatterplot 3D, Parallel Plots, Cell Plots
Visually determine the Hot Xs that affect variation in the Ys	Fit Y by X, Fit Model, Partition
* Use Data Filter, Colors, Markers, Brushing, Lassoing, and Selection of points throughout	
Model Relationships	
For each Y, identify the Hot Xs to include in the signal function	Fit Model, Screening, Profiler
Model Y as a function of the Hot Xs; check the noise function	Fit Model, Profiler, Simulation
If needed, revise the model	Fit Model
If required, return to the Collect Data step and use DOE	Custom Design, Sample Size and Power
Revise Knowledge	
Identify the best Hot X settings	Profilers
Visualize the effect on the Ys should these Hot X settings vary	Profilers, Simulation, Distribution, Capability, Goal Plot
Verify improvement using a pilot study or confirmation trials	Distribution, Control Charts, Capability, Goal Plot

However, remember that the EDA approach to uncovering relationships requires an unfolding style of analysis where your next step is determined by your interpretation of the previous result. So, although it is a great starting point to guide your usage of JMP in many situations, Exhibit 3.30 should never be followed slavishly or without thought. As you gain more familiarity with your data and with JMP, you may well develop your own Visual Six Sigma style that works better for you and your business.

Techniques Illustrated in the Case Studies

The remainder of the book contains six case studies drawn from real situations. Each illustrates a selection of techniques that support the Visual Six Sigma Roadmap. All of the case studies strongly emphasize uncovering relationships and therefore rely heavily on visualization techniques directed at discovery. The table in Exhibit 3.31 indicates which platforms and options, presented as JMP menu items, are illustrated in each case study.

We invite you to work through the case studies using the data tables provided. As mentioned earlier, the case studies assume that you are using the default settings in JMP (which you can reset under **File > Preferences** by clicking the **Reset to Defaults** button).

Conclusion

In this chapter, we have given an initial overview of JMP as the enabling technology for Visual Six Sigma. Our goal has been to familiarize you with JMP so that you are now able to follow the JMP usage in the case studies that show Visual Six Sigma in action.

The case studies are presented in the next six chapters. We remind you that there is a tension between illustrating Visual Six Sigma as a lean process and helping you see a variety of techniques and approaches that you can use in your future work. As we have stressed, Visual Six Sigma is not, and never can be, prescriptive. One of the keys to success is familiarity with JMP, and that is why we have sometimes deliberately compromised the purity of our Visual Six Sigma vision to show you patterns of use that will be useful as you embark on your own Visual Six Sigma journey.

Now let's start our detective work!

Notes

1. *JMP 8 User Guide*, Release 8 (Cary, NC: SAS Institute, 2008).
2. For more information about JMP, see www.jmp.com.

EXHIBIT 3.31 Platforms and Options Illustrated in the Case Studies

Menus	Platforms and Options	Chapter 4: Late Charge Incidents	Chapter 5: Pricing Management	Chapter 6: Anodized Parts	Chapter 7: Pharmaceutical Sales	Chapter 8: Polymer Manufacturing	Chapter 9: Cell Classification
Tables	Summary	X			X		
	Sort	X					
	Concatenate					X	
	Tabulate				X		
	Missing Data Pattern				X		
Rows	Exclude/Unexclude	X	X			X	X
	Hide/Unhide	X				X	X
	Colors/Markers					X	
	Row Selection	X				X	
	Clear Row States		X			X	
	Color or Mark by Column	X			X	X	X
	Data Filter	X			X	X	X
Cols	Column Info	X	X	X	X	X	X
	Column Properties	X	X	X	X	X	X
	Formula	X		X	X	X	X
	Hide/Unhide				X		X
	Exclude/Unexclude				X		X
	Group Columns				X		X
DOE	Custom Design			X			
	Save Factors and Responses			X			
	Full Factorial Design					X	

(Continued)

EXHIBIT 3.31 *(Continued)*

Menus	Platforms and Options	Chapter 4: Late Charge Incidents	Chapter 5: Pricing Management	Chapter 6: Anodized Parts	Chapter 7: Pharmaceutical Sales	Chapter 8: Polymer Manufacturing	Chapter 9: Cell Classification
Analyze	Distribution	X	X	X	X	X	X
	Histogram	X	X	X	X	X	X
	Capability			X		X	
	Continuous Fit					X	
	Frequency Distribution	X	X	X	X	X	X
	Fit Y by X	X	X		X	X	X
	Bivariate Fit	X			X	X	X
	Fit Line				X		
	Fit Special	X					
	Fit Polynomial				X		
	Contingency	X	X				X
	Oneway	X	X		X		
	Means Diamonds		X				
	Compare Means		X		X		
	Fit Model		X	X	X	X	X
	Standard Least Squares		X	X	X	X	
	Stepwise			X			X
	Random Effects (REML)				X		
	Nominal Logistic						X
	Modeling						
	Screening					X	X
	Neural Net					X	
	Partition		X				X
	Multivariate Methods—Multivariate						X
	Correlations						X
	Scatterplot Matrix						X

Graph							
	Graph Builder	X			X		X
	Scatterplot 3D	X			X		X
	Bubble Plot			X			
	Tree Map			X			X
	Scatterplot Matrix		X	X	X		
	Diagram (Ishikawa C&E)					X	
	Control Chart		X	X	X	X	X
	IR		X	X	X	X	X
	Xbar		X		X		
	Variability/Gauge Chart		X		X		
	Gauge RR		X		X		
	Attribute MSA				X		
	Pareto Plot				X		
	Capability (Goal Plot)		X		X		
	Profiler		X		X		
	Maximize Desirability		X		X		
	Sensitivity Indicators		X		X		
	Simulator		X		X		
	Contour Profiler				X		
	Surface Plot		X		X		X
Tools	Crosshairs	X	X		X		X
	Lasso						X

53

PART II

Case Studies

CHAPTER 4

Reducing Hospital Late Charge Incidents

This case study is set early in the deployment of a Lean Six Sigma initiative at a community hospital. A master black belt by the name of Alex Griffin was hired to help support the Lean Six Sigma effort. Management identified the billing department, and in particular late charges, as an area that tied up millions of dollars per year, and hence an area badly in need of improvement. This case study describes how Alex and Alice Griffith, an associate in the billing department, analyze billing data in order to define project opportunities for green belt teams.

The case study is almost entirely embedded in the Uncover Relationships stage of the Visual Six Sigma Data Analysis Process introduced in Chapter 2 (Exhibit 2.3). Alex and Alice are detectives, searching for clues that might explain the large number of late charges. Their work encompasses a number of the How-We-Do-It techniques described under Uncovering Relationships in Exhibit 3.30. Their findings will initiate the work of project teams; these teams will work through all six of the stages of the Visual Six Sigma Data Analysis Process.

In this case study, Alex and Alice analyze the late charge data for January 2008. The data set consists of 2,032 records with late charges. The columns include both nominal and continuous variables, as well as dates. Alex and Alice visualize their data using histograms, bar graphs, Pareto plots, control charts, scatterplots, mosaic plots, and tree maps, learning about potential outliers and conducting a missing data analysis along the way.

Exhibit 4.1 lists the JMP platforms and options that Alex and Alice will use in their discovery process. The data sets are available at http://support.sas.com/visualsixsigma. Based on what they learn, they will make several important recommendations to management. Read on to join Alex and Alice on their journey.

EXHIBIT 4.1   Platforms and Options Illustrated in This Case Study

Menus	Platforms and Options
Tables	Summary
	Sort
	Missing Data Pattern
Rows	Exclude/Unexclude
	Hide/Unhide
	Row Selection
	Data Filter
Cols	Column Info
	Column Properties
	Formula
Analyze	Distribution
	Histogram
	Frequency Distribution
	Fit Y by X
	Bivariate Fit
	Fit Special
	Contingency
	Oneway
Graph	Tree Map
	Control Chart
	IR
	Pareto Plot
Tools	Lasso
Other Options	Data View
	Select Points in a Plot
	Sort from Column Header
	Y Axis Specification, Reference Line

Framing the Problem

Alice Griffith has worked for a community hospital in the billing department for several years now. The hospital has recently initiated a Lean Six Sigma program to improve the efficiency and quality of its service, to increase patient satisfaction, and to enhance the hospital's already solid reputation within the community.

The hospital has hired a master black belt by the name of Alex Griffin to provide much needed support and momentum for the Lean Six Sigma initiative. Alex will be responsible for identifying and mentoring projects, providing training, and supporting and facilitating Lean Six Sigma efforts. Upper management has identified the billing department as particularly prone to problems and inefficiencies, and directs Alex to identify and prioritize realistic green belt projects within that area. Specifically, upper management mentions late charges as an area that ties up several million dollars per year.

It is in this context that Alex Griffin meets Alice Griffith. Alice is a devoted employee and a quick learner and has an enthusiastic personality. So, when management pairs her with Alex for the task of identifying projects, she is thrilled.

In accordance with their mandate, Alex and Alice proceed to address late charges, which have been a huge source of customer complaints, rework, and lost revenue. Alice describes late charges to Alex as follows:

> *Late charges can apply to both inpatients and outpatients. In both cases, tests or procedures are performed on a patient. The charge for each test or procedure is ideally captured at the time that the procedure is performed. However, a charge cannot be captured until the doctor's notes are completed, because the charge must be allocated to the relevant note. Sometimes notes aren't dictated and transcribed for as much as a week after the procedure date.*
>
> *Once the charge is captured, it waits for the billing activity to come around. The billing activity occurs a few days after the procedure date, allowing a short time so that all the charges related to that patient are accumulated. However, it is never really obvious what might still be outstanding or when all of these charges have rolled in. At this point, the hospital* drops the bill; *this is when the insurance companies or, more generally, the responsible parties, are billed for the charges as they appear at that point.*
>
> *Now, once the bill is dropped, no additional charges can be billed for that work. If charges happen to roll in after this point, then a credit has to be applied for the entire billed amount and the whole bill has to be recreated and submitted. Charges that roll in after the hospital drops the bill are called* late charges. *For example, an invoice of $200,000 might have to be redone for a $20 late charge, or the charge might simply be written off.*
>
> *If a patient is an inpatient, namely a patient who stays at least one night in the hospital, charges are captured during the patient's stay. No bill can be issued until the patient is discharged. A few days after discharge, the bill is dropped.*

By the way, the date is February 11, 2008, and Alice suggests to Alex that they begin their effort to identify green belt projects by examining some recent late charge data. She suggests looking at the January 2008 listing of late charges.

Collecting Data

Alice obtains the late charge report for January 2008, along with all other available information. She imports this data to a JMP file, which she calls **LateCharges.jmp** (see Exhibit 4.2 for a partial view of the data table). There are 2,032 records of late charges in January.

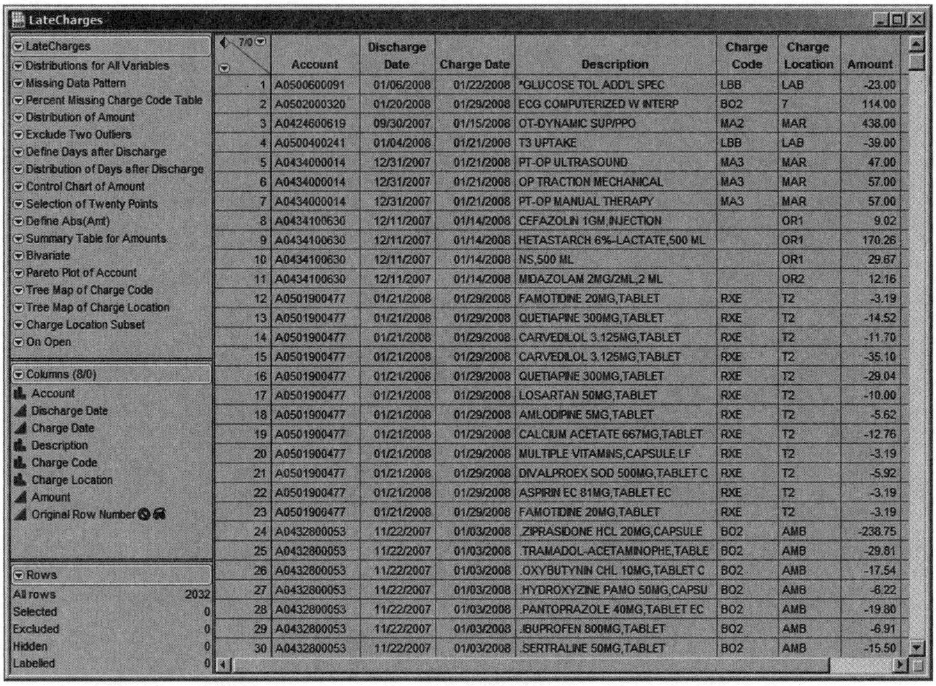

	Account	Discharge Date	Charge Date	Description	Charge Code	Charge Location	Amount
1	A0500600091	01/06/2008	01/22/2008	*GLUCOSE TOL ADD'L SPEC	LBB	LAB	-23.00
2	A0502000320	01/20/2008	01/29/2008	ECG COMPUTERIZED W INTERP	BO2	7	114.00
3	A0424600619	09/30/2007	01/15/2008	OT-DYNAMIC SUP/PPO	MA2	MAR	438.00
4	A0500400241	01/04/2008	01/21/2008	T3 UPTAKE	LBB	LAB	-39.00
5	A0434000014	12/31/2007	01/21/2008	PT-OP ULTRASOUND	MA3	MAR	47.00
6	A0434000014	12/31/2007	01/21/2008	OP TRACTION MECHANICAL	MA3	MAR	57.00
7	A0434000014	12/31/2007	01/21/2008	PT-OP MANUAL THERAPY	MA3	MAR	57.00
8	A0434100630	12/11/2007	01/14/2008	CEFAZOLIN 1GM,INJECTION		OR1	9.02
9	A0434100630	12/11/2007	01/14/2008	HETASTARCH 6%-LACTATE,500 ML		OR1	170.26
10	A0434100630	12/11/2007	01/14/2008	NS,500 ML		OR1	29.67
11	A0434100630	12/11/2007	01/14/2008	MIDAZOLAM 2MG/2ML,2 ML		OR2	12.16
12	A0501900477	01/21/2008	01/29/2008	FAMOTIDINE 20MG,TABLET	RXE	T2	-3.19
13	A0501900477	01/21/2008	01/29/2008	QUETIAPINE 300MG,TABLET	RXE	T2	-14.52
14	A0501900477	01/21/2008	01/29/2008	CARVEDILOL 3.125MG,TABLET	RXE	T2	-11.70
15	A0501900477	01/21/2008	01/29/2008	CARVEDILOL 3.125MG,TABLET	RXE	T2	-35.10
16	A0501900477	01/21/2008	01/29/2008	QUETIAPINE 300MG,TABLET	RXE	T2	-29.04
17	A0501900477	01/21/2008	01/29/2008	LOSARTAN 50MG,TABLET	RXE	T2	-10.00
18	A0501900477	01/21/2008	01/29/2008	AMLODIPINE 5MG,TABLET	RXE	T2	-5.62
19	A0501900477	01/21/2008	01/29/2008	CALCIUM ACETATE 667MG,TABLET	RXE	T2	-12.76
20	A0501900477	01/21/2008	01/29/2008	MULTIPLE VITAMINS,CAPSULE LF	RXE	T2	-3.19
21	A0501900477	01/21/2008	01/29/2008	DIVALPROEX SOD 500MG,TABLET C	RXE	T2	-5.92
22	A0501900477	01/21/2008	01/29/2008	ASPIRIN EC 81MG,TABLET EC	RXE	T2	-3.19
23	A0501900477	01/21/2008	01/29/2008	FAMOTIDINE 20MG,TABLET	RXE	T2	-3.19
24	A0432800053	11/22/2007	01/03/2008	.ZIPRASIDONE HCL 20MG,CAPSULE	BO2	AMB	-238.75
25	A0432800053	11/22/2007	01/03/2008	.TRAMADOL-ACETAMINOPHE,TABLE	BO2	AMB	-29.81
26	A0432800053	11/22/2007	01/03/2008	.OXYBUTYNIN CHL 10MG,TABLET C	BO2	AMB	-17.54
27	A0432800053	11/22/2007	01/03/2008	.HYDROXYZINE PAMO 50MG,CAPSU	BO2	AMB	-6.22
28	A0432800053	11/22/2007	01/03/2008	.PANTOPRAZOLE 40MG,TABLET EC	BO2	AMB	-19.80
29	A0432800053	11/22/2007	01/03/2008	.IBUPROFEN 800MG,TABLET	BO2	AMB	-6.91
30	A0432800053	11/22/2007	01/03/2008	.SERTRALINE 50MG,TABLET	BO2	AMB	-15.50

EXHIBIT 4.2 **Partial View of LateCharges.jmp Data Table**

There are seven columns of interest (the eighth column, which is hidden and excluded, gives the row number). The seven columns are described below:

1. *Account*. The account identifier. A patient can have several account numbers associated with a single stay. An account number is generated for each group of procedures or tests.
2. *Discharge Date*. The date when the patient was discharged from the hospital.
3. *Charge Date*. The date when the charge was captured internally. In other words, this is the date when the charge officially makes it into the hospital's billing system.
4. *Description*. The procedure description as it appears on the charge invoice.
5. *Charge Code*. The originating finance group charge area. For example, RXE refers to medication ordered in an emergency.
6. *Charge Location*. The physical area within the hospital where the charge originated.
7. *Amount*. The dollar amount of the late charge. Credits have a negative value.

Alex is a frequent JMP user and feels comfortable with the software, while Alice is a relative newcomer to JMP. But Alice is a quick learner and she likes to document her work. She asks Alex if there is a way to save these descriptions to the data table. Alex shows her how to do this for the Account column.

Alex right-clicks in the column header area for Account. As shown in Exhibit 4.3, this opens a context-sensitive menu. From this menu, Alex chooses **Column Info**.

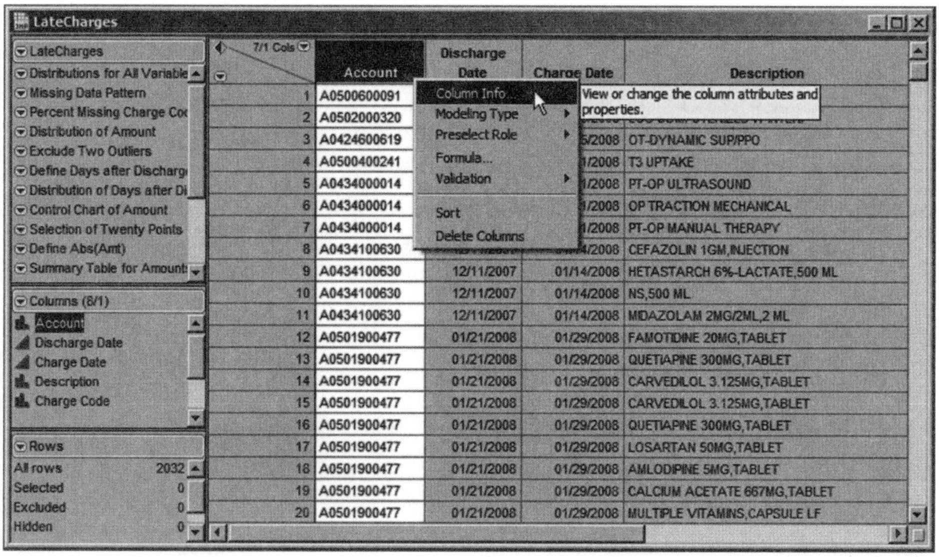

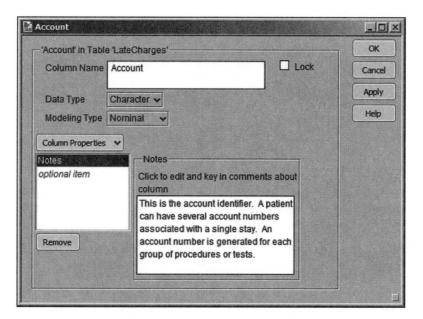

EXHIBIT 4.3   Column Info Selection from Context-Sensitive Menu

This opens the column information window. From the list that appears when Alex clicks the down arrow to the right of **Column Properties**, he chooses **Notes**. Then he types the column description into the text box (Exhibit 4.4). Having seen how this is done, Alice repeats the process for the other six columns. These **Notes** are already included in the data table **LateCharges.jmp** (Exhibit 4.2).

EXHIBIT 4.4   Column Info Window with Note Describing the Account Column

Uncovering Relationships

Given their goal to identify projects, Alex and Alice will not need to work through all six steps in the Visual Six Sigma Data Analysis Process. They nonetheless follow the guidance that the Visual Six Sigma Roadmap provides for the Uncover Relationships step. They will use dynamic linking to explore their variables one at a time and several at a time. Given the nature of their data, they will often need to connect anomalous behavior that they identify using plots to the records in their data table. This connection is made easy by dynamic linking. Their exploration will also include an analysis of missing records.

Visualizing the Variables One at a Time

Alex and Alice begin to explore their data. Their first step consists of obtaining **Distribution** reports for the seven variables. To do this, following Alex's direction, Alice selects **Analyze > Distribution**. She populates the launch dialog as shown in Exhibit 4.5.

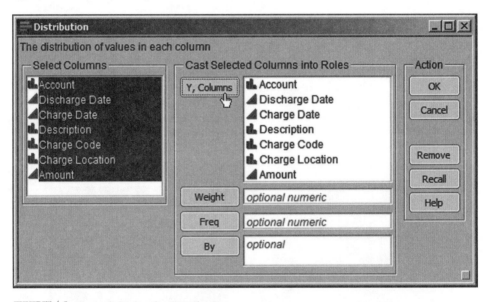

EXHIBIT 4.5   Launch Dialog for Distribution

When Alice clicks **OK**, the report that is partially shown in Exhibit 4.6 appears. Alice notes that Account and Description are nominal variables with many levels. The bar graphs are not necessarily helpful in understanding such variables.

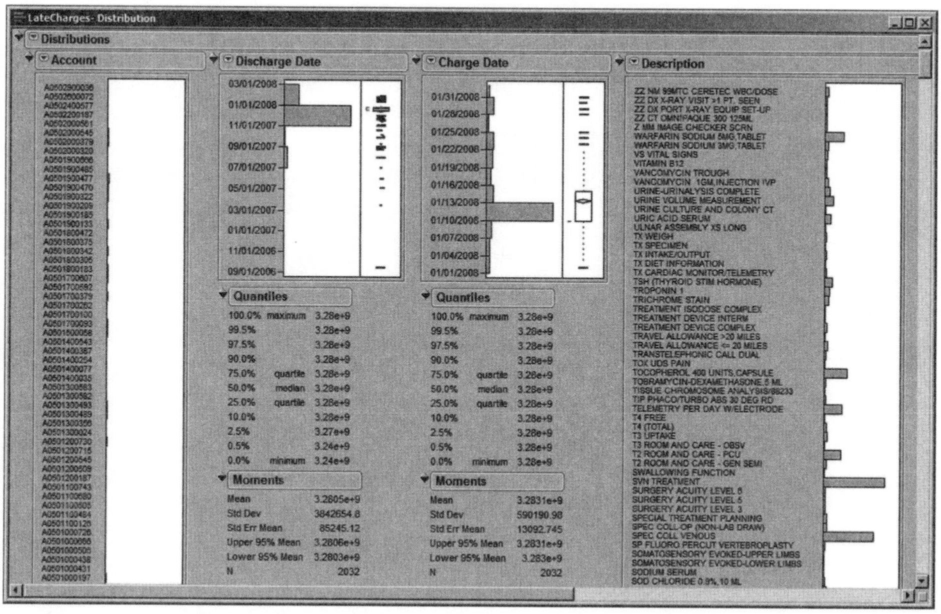

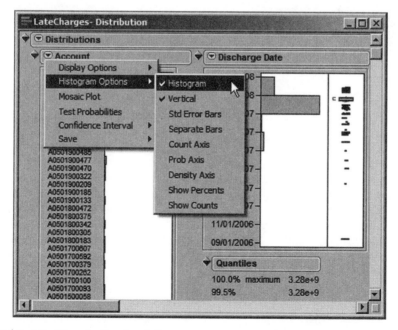

EXHIBIT 4.6 Partial View of Distribution Report

So, for each of these, Alice clicks on the red triangle associated with the variable in question, chooses **Histogram Options**, and unchecks **Histogram** (see Exhibit 4.7). This leaves only the **Frequencies** for these two variables in the report.

EXHIBIT 4.7 Disabling the Bar Graph Presentation

Alice is confused by the results under **Discharge Date** and **Charge Date** shown in Exhibit 4.8. The data for these two variables consist of dates in a month/day/year format. However, the values that appear under **Quantiles** and **Moments** are numeric.

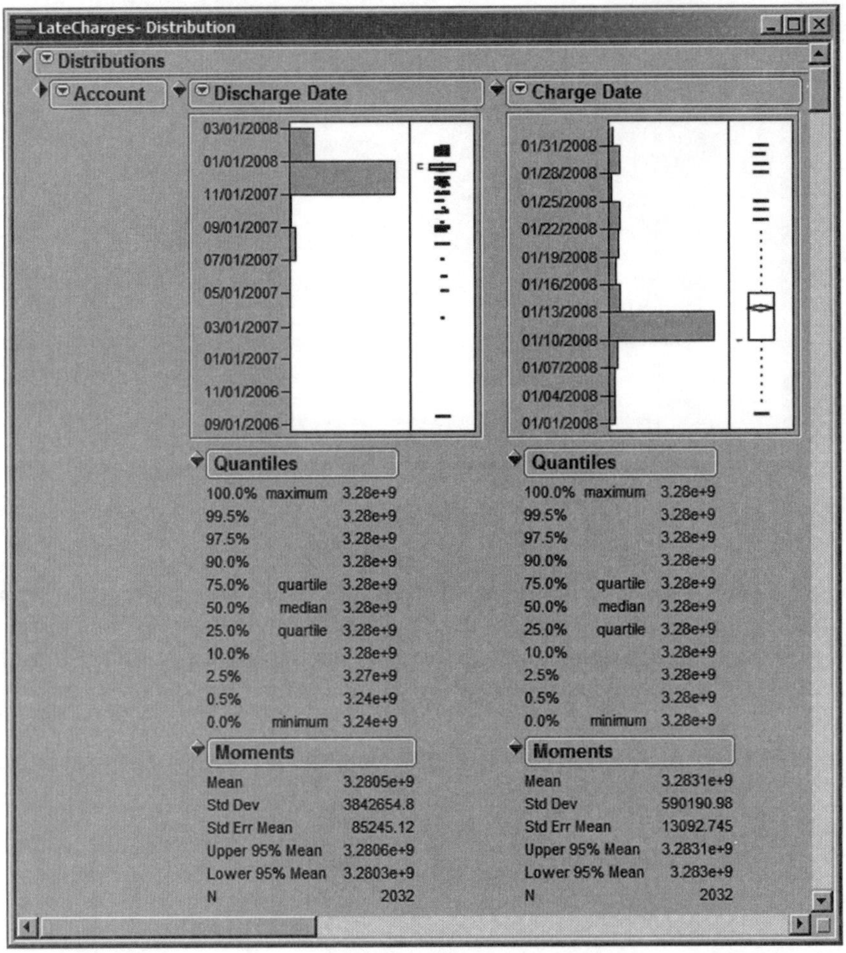

EXHIBIT 4.8   Reports for Discharge Date and Charge Date

Alex explains to Alice that in JMP dates are stored as the number of seconds since January 1, 1904. When **Distribution** is run on a column that has a date format, the number-of-seconds values appear in the **Quantiles** and **Moments** panels. These number-of-seconds values can be converted to a typical date using a JMP date format. To illustrate, Alex right-clicks on the **Discharge Date** column header and selects **Column Info**. In that dialog, he shows Alice that JMP is using **m/d/y** as the **Format** to display the dates.

Alex explains that to change the **Quantiles** to a date format, Alice should double-click on the number-of-seconds values in the **Quantiles** panel. This opens a pop-up menu. From the **Format** options, Alice chooses **Date > m/d/y**. Alice does this for both **Quantiles** panels. Then she clicks on the disclosure icons for the **Moments** panels to close them, since the **Moments** report for the dates is not of use to her. The new view, shown in Exhibit 4.9, makes her much happier.

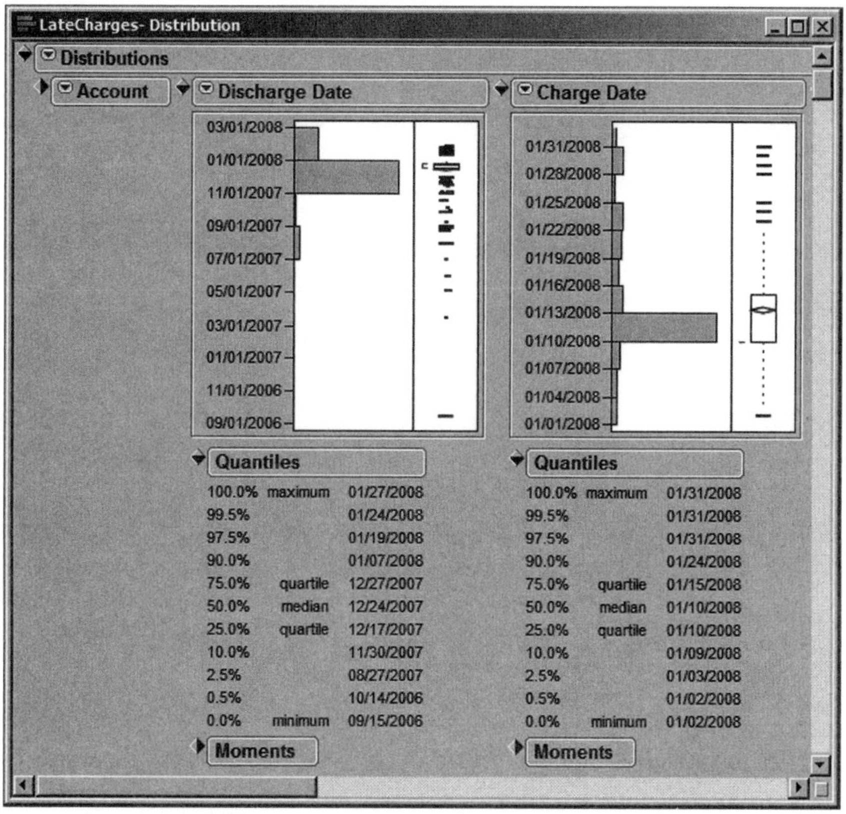

EXHIBIT 4.9   Discharge Date and Charge Date with Date Format for Quantiles

Alex and Alice are both amazed that JMP can create histograms for date fields. Seeing the distribution of discharge dates involved in the January 2008 late charge data is very useful. They like the report as it now appears, and so they save the script to the data table as **Distributions for All Variables.** (See the "Scripts" section in Chapter 3 for details on how to save a script.)

By studying the output for all seven columns in the report, Alex and Alice learn that:

- Account: There are 390 account numbers involved, none of which are missing.
- Discharge Date: The discharge dates range from 9/15/2006 to 1/27/2008, with 50 percent of the discharge dates ranging from 12/17/2007 to 12/27/2007 (see Exhibit 4.9). None of these are missing.
- Charge Date: As expected, the charge dates all fall within January 2008 (see Exhibit 4.9). None of these are missing.
- Description: There are 414 descriptions involved, none of which are missing.

- **Charge Code**: There are 46 distinct charge codes, but 467 records are missing charge codes.
- **Charge Location**: There are 39 distinct charge locations, with 81 records missing charge location.
- **Amount**: The amounts of the late charges range from −$6,859 to $28,280. There appears to be a single, unusually large value of $28,280 and a single outlying credit of $6,859. About 50 percent of the **amounts** are negative, and so constitute credits. (See Exhibit 4.10, where Alice has chosen **Display Options > Horizontal Layout** from the menu obtained by clicking the red triangle next to **Amount**.) None of these are missing.

Amount		
Quantiles		
100.0% maximum	28279.8	
99.5%	1114.26	
97.5%	561.4	
90.0%	114	
75.0% quartile	34	
50.0% median	0	
25.0% quartile	-25.86	
10.0%	-94	
2.5%	-338.18	
0.5%	-1019	
0.0% minimum	-6859.3	

Moments	
Mean	24.046914
Std Dev	687.48122
Std Err Mean	15.251023
Upper 95% Mean	53.956195
Lower 95% Mean	-5.862366
N	2032

EXHIBIT 4.10   Distribution Report for Amount

Understanding the Missing Data

The missing values in the **Charge Code** and **Charge Location** columns are somewhat troublesome, as they represent a fairly large proportion of the late charge records. Alex reminds Alice that JMP has a way to look at the missing value pattern across a collection of variables. He suggests that she select **Tables > Missing Data Pattern**. Here, he tells her to enter all seven of her columns in the **Add Columns** column box. She does this, clicks **OK**, and obtains the new data table shown in Exhibit 4.11. (The script **Missing Data Pattern** in the data table **LateCharges.jmp** creates the **Missing Data Pattern** table.)

	Count	Number of columns missing	Patterns	Account	Discharge Date	Charge Date	Description	Charge Code	Charge Location	Amount
1	1491	0	0000000	0	0	0	0	0	0	0
2	74	1	0000010	0	0	0	0	0	1	0
3	460	1	0000100	0	0	0	0	1	0	0
4	7	2	0000110	0	0	0	0	1	1	0

EXHIBIT 4.11   Missing Data Pattern Report

A value of one in a column indicates that there are missing values, while the number of missing values for that pattern is shown in the **Count** column. Alice sees that:

- There are 1,491 records with no missing values.
- There are 74 records with missing values only in the **Charge Location** column.
- There are 460 records with missing values only in the **Charge Code** column.
- There are 7 records with missing values in both the **Charge Code** and **Charge Location** columns.

So, 534 records contain only one of **Charge Location** or **Charge Code**. Are these areas where the other piece of information is considered redundant? Or would the missing information actually be needed? These 534 records represent over 25 percent of the late charge records for January 2008. Alex and Alice agree that improving or refining the process of providing this information is worthy of a project. If the information is redundant, or can be entered automatically, then this could simplify the information flow process. If the information is not input because it is difficult to do so, the project might focus on finding ways to facilitate and mistake-proof the information flow.

Just to get a little more background on the missing data, Alex suggests checking to see which locations have the largest numbers of missing charge codes. While holding down the control key, Alice selects rows 3 and 4 of the **Missing Data Pattern** table, thereby selecting the 467 rows in **LateCharges.jmp** where Charge Code is missing. In the **LateCharges.jmp** data table, Alice right-clicks on **Selected** in the rows panel and selects **Data View** (see Exhibit 4.12).

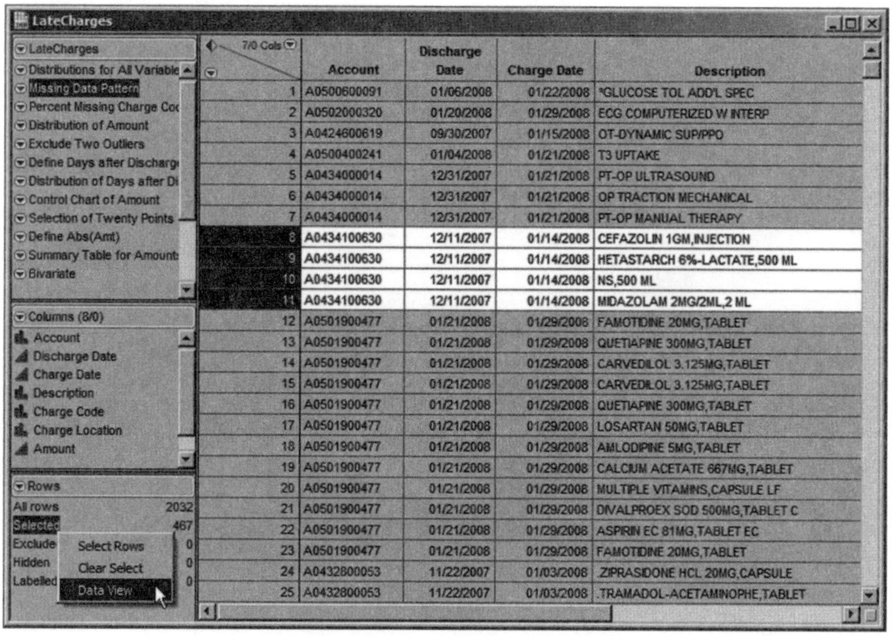

EXHIBIT 4.12   Selection of Data View from Rows Panel

This produces a new data table consisting of only the 467 rows where **Charge Code** is missing. Alice sees that all rows in this new data table are selected since they are linked to the main data table. So she deselects the rows in her **Data View** table by clicking in the bottom triangle in the upper left corner of the data grid (see Exhibit 3.18).

With this 467-row table as the current data table, Alice constructs a Pareto chart by selecting **Graph > Pareto Plot** and entering **Charge Location** as **Y, Cause** (Exhibit 4.13).

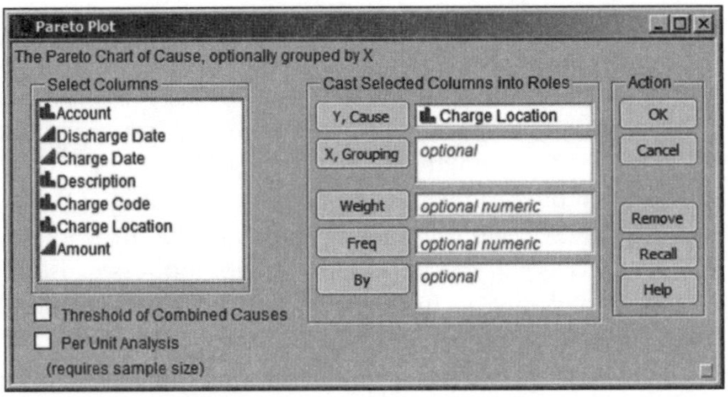

EXHIBIT 4.13   Launch Dialog for Pareto Plot of 467-Row Data Table

When she clicks **OK**, Alice sees the **Pareto Plot** in Exhibit 4.14. The plot shows that **Charge Locations** LB1 and T2 have the highest occurrence of missing data for **Charge Code**. *Hmmm!* Now Alex is wondering about the percentage of **Charge Code** entries that are missing for these areas. Is the percentage much higher than for other areas?

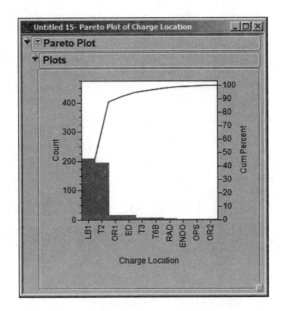

EXHIBIT 4.14   Pareto Plot of Charge Location

To address Alex's question, Alice would like to construct a table containing a row for each of the 39 different values of Charge Location; each row should show the Charge Location and the percentage of rows that are missing Charge Code for that location. Alice thinks she can do this using **Tables > Summary**.

First, she closes the **Data View** table and makes sure that **LateCharges.jmp** is the active window. She selects **Tables > Summary** and enters Charge Location into the **Group** panel. For each Charge Location, she wants JMP to compute the percent missing for Charge Code. To that end, she selects Charge Code in the **Select Columns** list. Then she clicks the **Statistics** button and selects **N Missing** from the drop-down menu (see Exhibit 4.15). She clicks **OK**.

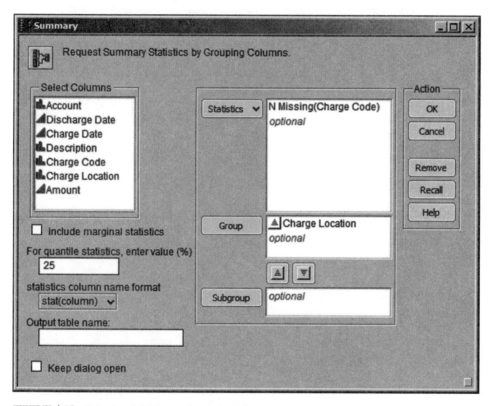

EXHIBIT 4.15   Populated Summary Launch Dialog

The resulting data table, which JMP automatically names **LateCharges By (Charge Location)**, is shown in Exhibit 4.16. Each of the 39 Charge Location values has a row. Row 1 corresponds to the value that indicates that Charge Location is missing. The N Rows column indicates how many rows in the data table **LateCharges.jmp** assume the given value of Charge Location. The third column gives the number of rows for which Charge Code is missing.

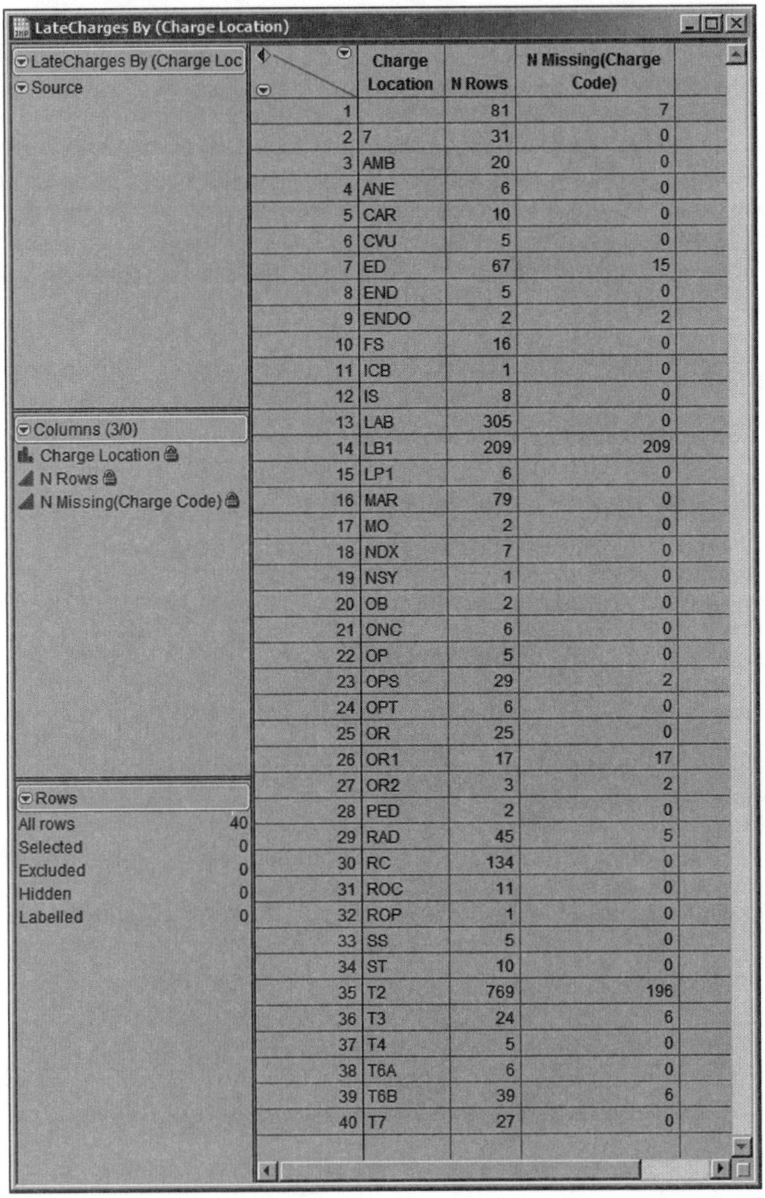

LateCharges By (Charge Location)

LateCharges By (Charge Loc
Source

Columns (3/0)
Charge Location
N Rows
N Missing(Charge Code)

Rows
All rows 40
Selected 0
Excluded 0
Hidden 0
Labelled 0

	Charge Location	N Rows	N Missing(Charge Code)
1		81	7
2	7	31	0
3	AMB	20	0
4	ANE	6	0
5	CAR	10	0
6	CVU	5	0
7	ED	67	15
8	END	5	0
9	ENDO	2	2
10	FS	16	0
11	ICB	1	0
12	IS	8	0
13	LAB	305	0
14	LB1	209	209
15	LP1	6	0
16	MAR	79	0
17	MO	2	0
18	NDX	7	0
19	NSY	1	0
20	OB	2	0
21	ONC	6	0
22	OP	5	0
23	OPS	29	2
24	OPT	6	0
25	OR	25	0
26	OR1	17	17
27	OR2	3	2
28	PED	2	0
29	RAD	45	5
30	RC	134	0
31	ROC	11	0
32	ROP	1	0
33	SS	5	0
34	ST	10	0
35	T2	769	196
36	T3	24	6
37	T4	5	0
38	T6A	6	0
39	T6B	39	6
40	T7	27	0

EXHIBIT 4.16   Summary Data Table

To obtain the percentage of rows with missing values of Charge Code, Alice needs to construct a formula, which she does with Alex's help. She creates a new column in the data table **LateCharges By (Charge Location)** by double-clicking in the column header area to the right of the third column, N Missing(Charge Code). She names the new column Percent Missing Charge Code. Alice clicks off the column header and then right-clicks back on it. This opens a context-sensitive menu, from which she selects **Formula** (Exhibit 4.17).

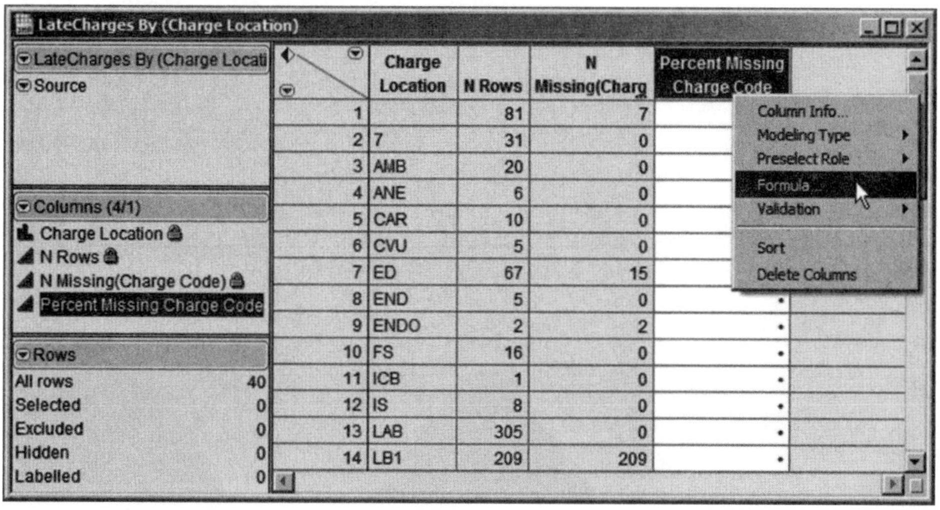

EXHIBIT 4.17   Menu with Formula Selection

This has the effect of opening the formula editor (Exhibit 4.18).

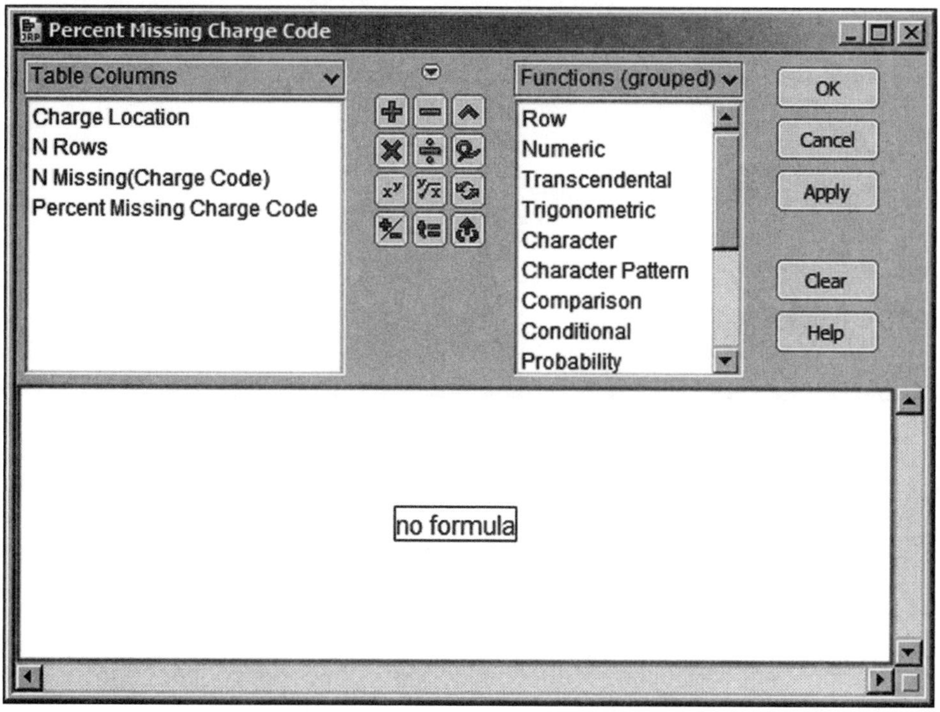

EXHIBIT 4.18   Formula Editor

To write her formula, Alice clicks on **N Missing(Charge Code)** in the **Table Columns** list at the top left of the formula editor. This enters that column into the editor window. Then Alice clicks the division symbol on the keypad. This creates a fraction and opens a highlighted box for the denominator contents. Now Alice selects **N Rows** from the **Table Columns** list. Since the denominator box was highlighted, the column **N Rows** is placed in that box. To turn this ratio into a percentage, she clicks the outer rectangle to highlight the entire fraction, selects the multiplication symbol from the keypad, and enters the number 100 into the highlighted box that appears. The formula appears as shown in Exhibit 4.19.

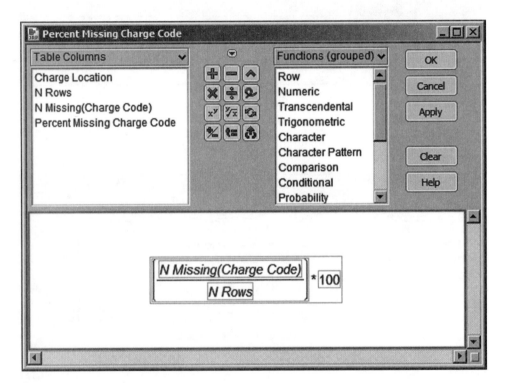

EXHIBIT 4.19   Formula for Percent Missing Charge Code

Clicking **OK** closes the formula editor and populates the new column with these calculated values (Exhibit 4.20).

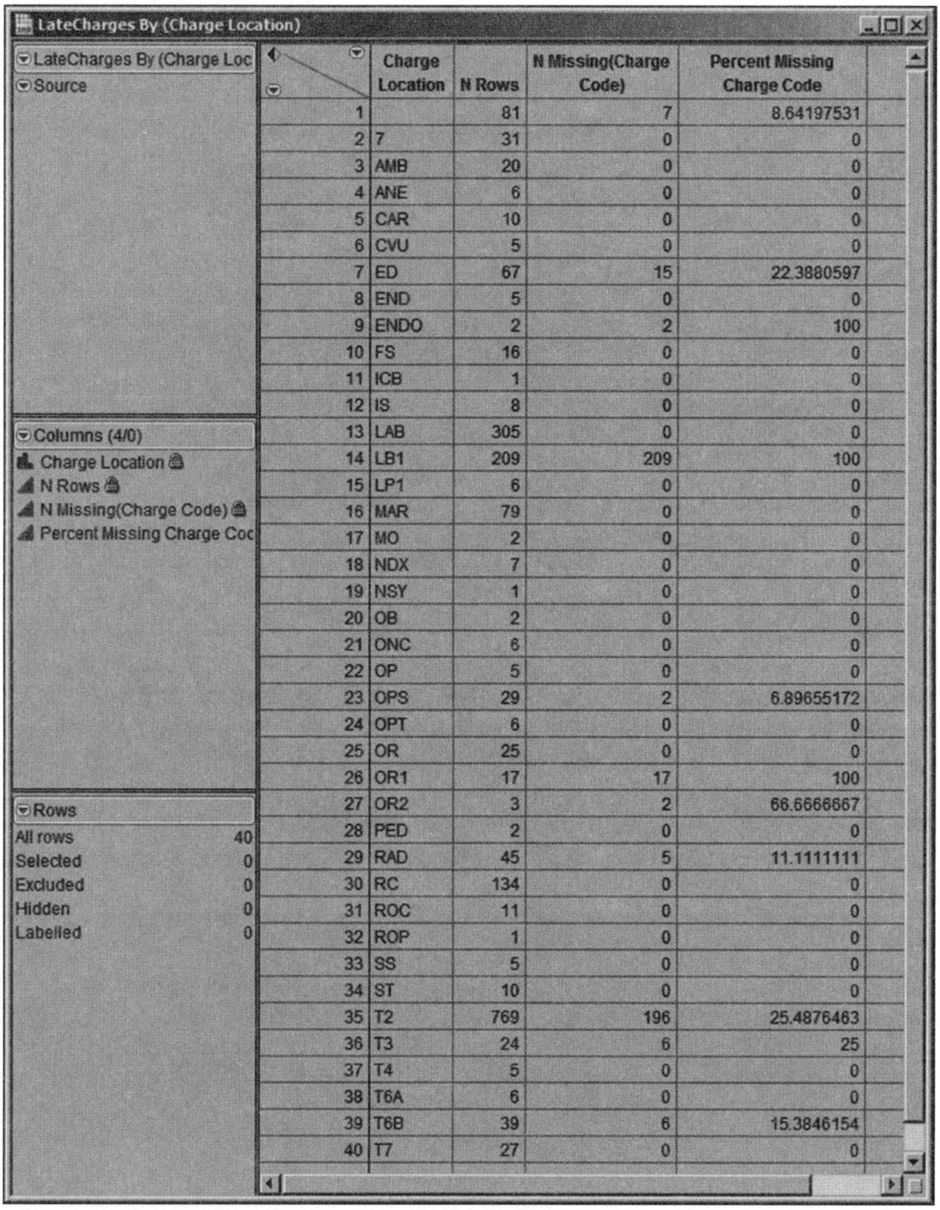

	Charge Location	N Rows	N Missing(Charge Code)	Percent Missing Charge Code
1		81	7	8.64197531
2	7	31	0	0
3	AMB	20	0	0
4	ANE	6	0	0
5	CAR	10	0	0
6	CVU	5	0	0
7	ED	67	15	22.3880597
8	END	5	0	0
9	ENDO	2	2	100
10	FS	16	0	0
11	ICB	1	0	0
12	IS	8	0	0
13	LAB	305	0	0
14	LB1	209	209	100
15	LP1	6	0	0
16	MAR	79	0	0
17	MO	2	0	0
18	NDX	7	0	0
19	NSY	1	0	0
20	OB	2	0	0
21	ONC	8	0	0
22	OP	5	0	0
23	OPS	29	2	6.89655172
24	OPT	6	0	0
25	OR	25	0	0
26	OR1	17	17	100
27	OR2	3	2	66.6666667
28	PED	2	0	0
29	RAD	45	5	11.1111111
30	RC	134	0	0
31	ROC	11	0	0
32	ROP	1	0	0
33	SS	5	0	0
34	ST	10	0	0
35	T2	769	196	25.4876463
36	T3	24	6	25
37	T4	5	0	0
38	T6A	6	0	0
39	T6B	39	6	15.3846154
40	T7	27	0	0

Side panels:

LateCharges By (Charge Loc)
Source

Columns (4/0)
- Charge Location
- N Rows
- N Missing(Charge Code)
- Percent Missing Charge Coc

Rows
All rows 40
Selected 0
Excluded 0
Hidden 0
Labelled 0

EXHIBIT 4.20 Table with Percent Missing Charge Code Column

Alice notices that some percents are given to a large number of decimal places, while others have no decimal places. In order to obtain a uniform format, she right-clicks on the column header again. This time, Alice chooses **Column Info**. This opens the column information window. Under **Format**, Alice chooses **Fixed Dec** and indicates that she would like one decimal place (Exhibit 4.21). (Another approach to constructing this column would have been for Alice to have entered the fraction only, without multiplying by 100. Then, under **Column Info**, she could have chosen **Percent** from the **Format** list.)

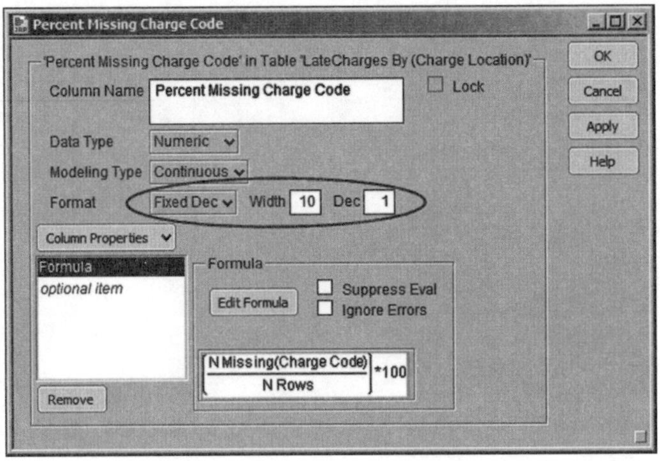

EXHIBIT 4.21 Column Info Dialog Showing Alice's Selected Format

This looks much better. Now Alice would like to see these percentages sorted in decreasing order. Again she right-clicks in the column header area where she selects **Sort**. This sorts the Percent Missing Charge Code column in ascending order. However, Alice repeats this and sees that the second **Sort** sorts in decreasing order. She obtains the data table partially shown in Exhibit 4.22.

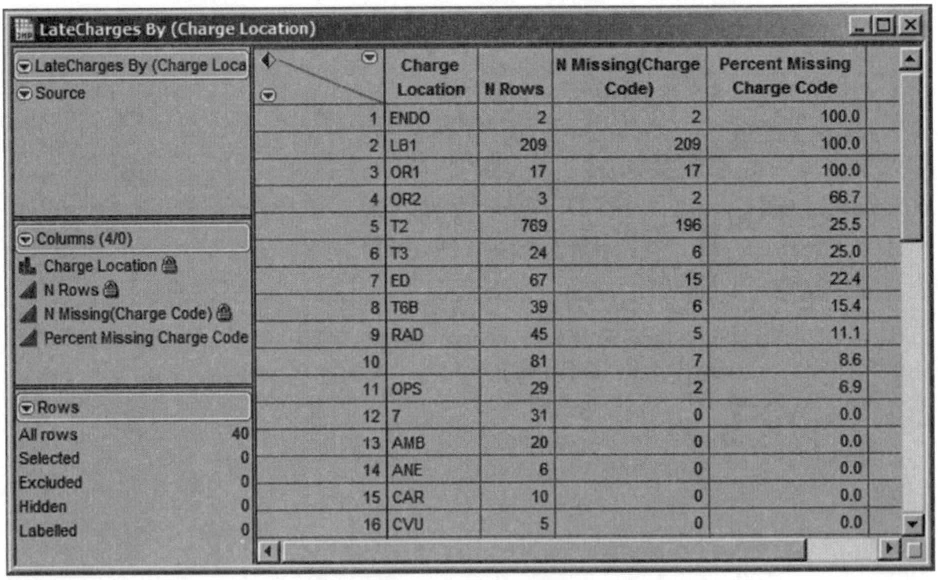

	Charge Location	N Rows	N Missing(Charge Code)	Percent Missing Charge Code
1	ENDO	2	2	100.0
2	LB1	209	209	100.0
3	OR1	17	17	100.0
4	OR2	3	2	66.7
5	T2	769	196	25.5
6	T3	24	6	25.0
7	ED	67	15	22.4
8	T6B	39	6	15.4
9	RAD	45	5	11.1
10		81	7	8.6
11	OPS	29	2	6.9
12	7	31	0	0.0
13	AMB	20	0	0.0
14	ANE	6	0	0.0
15	CAR	10	0	0.0
16	CVU	5	0	0.0

EXHIBIT 4.22 Partial View of Sorted Summary Data Table with New Column

This data table indicates that for the January 2008 data LB1 and OR1 are always missing **Charge Code** for late charges, while T2 has missing **Charge Code** values about 25 percent of the time. This is useful information, and Alex and Alice decide that this will provide a good starting point for a team whose goal is to address the missing data issue.

With Alex's help, Alice figures out how to capture the script that JMP has written to recreate this sorted table. She saves this script to the data table **LateCharges.jmp** with the name **Percent Missing Charge Code Table**. This will make it easy for her to recreate her work at a later date. She closes all open data tables other than **LateCharges.jmp**.

Analyzing Amount

Alex would like to look more carefully at the two outliers in the histogram for **Amount**. With **LateCharges.jmp** as the active window, Alice runs **Analyze > Distribution** with Amount as **Y, Columns**. She clicks **OK**. From the menu obtained by clicking the red triangle next to **Distribution**, she chooses **Stack** to obtain the report in Exhibit 4.23. Alice saves this script as **Distribution of Amount**.

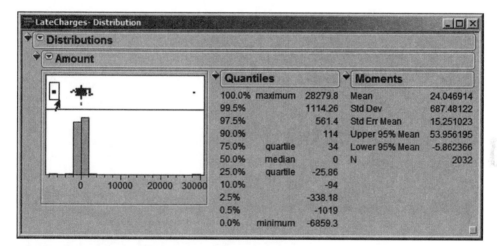

EXHIBIT 4.23   **Distribution Report for Amount Showing One Outlier Selected**

She selects the outlier to the left by clicking, holding the click, and drawing a rectangle around the point (shown in Exhibit 4.23). Then Alice holds down the shift key to add the outlier to the right to her selection, drawing a rectangle around it as well. In the rows panel in the data table, she looks at the number **Selected** to verify that both points are selected.

Alice would like to see the data records corresponding to these two points in a separate data table. To do this, she right-clicks in the rows panel on **Selected**. From the context-sensitive menu, she selects **Data View**. This creates the data table shown in Exhibit 4.24.

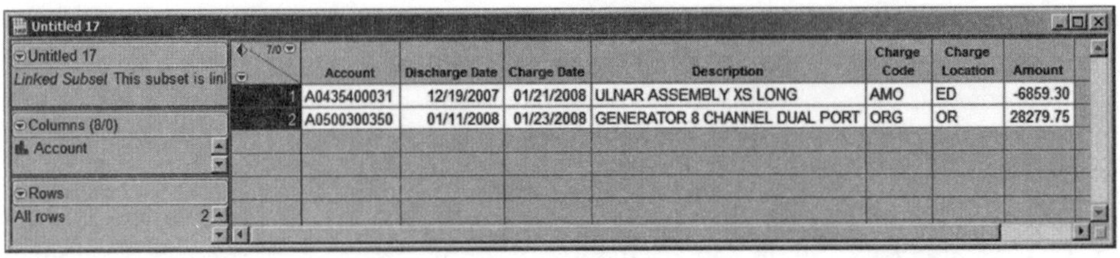

EXHIBIT 4.24 Data View of the Two Outliers on Amount

Alice looks more closely at the two outlying amounts. The first record is a credit (having a negative value). She examines the late charge data for several prior months and eventually finds that this appears to be a credit against an earlier late charge for an amount of $6859.30. The second record corresponds to a capital equipment item, and so Alice makes a note to discuss this with the group that has inadvertently charged it here, where it does not belong.

For now, Alex and Alice decide to exclude these two points from further analysis. So, Alice closes the data table created by **Data View** and makes the data table **LateCharges.jmp** active. Then she selects **Rows > Exclude** and **Rows > Hide**; this has the effect of both excluding the two selected rows from further calculations and hiding them in all graphs. Alice checks the rows panel to verify that the two points are **Excluded** and **Hidden**. Alex saves a script to the data table to recreate the outlier exclusion. He calls the script **Exclude Two Outliers**.

Alice reruns the **Distribution** report by running the script **Distribution of Amount**. This gives her the report shown in Exhibit 4.25. Note that **N** is now 2,030, reflecting the fact that the two rows containing the outlying values are excluded.

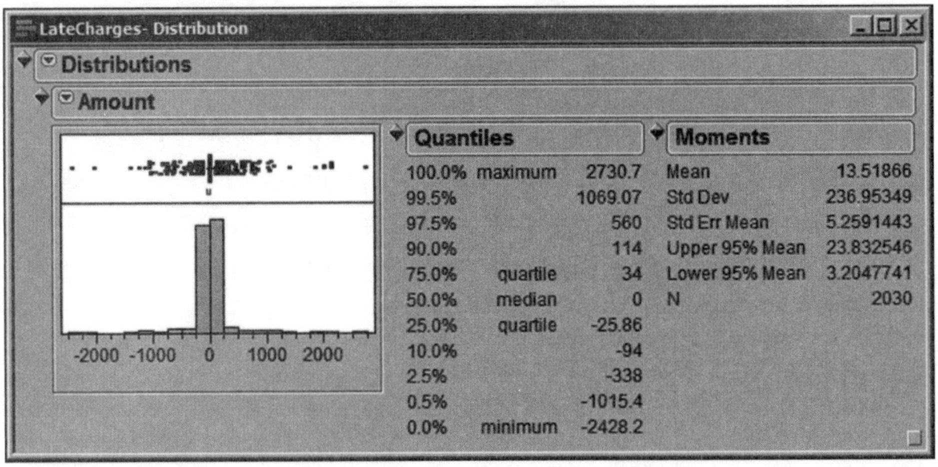

EXHIBIT 4.25 Distribution Report for Amount with Two Outliers Removed

The symmetry of the histogram for **Amount** about zero is striking. Alice notes that the percentiles shown in the **Quantiles** report are nearly balanced about zero, so many late charges are in fact credits. Are these credits for charges that were billed in a timely fashion? The fact that the distribution is balanced about zero raises the possibility that this is not so, and that they are actually credits for charges that were also late. Alex and Alice agree that this phenomenon warrants further investigation.

Visualizing the Variables Two at a Time: Days after Discharge

Alice is rather surprised that late charges are being accumulated in January 2008 for patients with discharge dates in 2006. In fact, 25 percent of the late charges are for patients with discharge dates preceding 12/17/2007, making them very late indeed.

To get a better idea of how delinquent these are, Alice defines a new column called **Days after Discharge**. She defines this column by a formula that takes the difference, in days, between **Charge Date** and **Discharge Date**. She chooses **Formula** from **Column Info** and asks Alex how she should write the required formula.

Alex reminds Alice that JMP saves dates as numeric data, defined as the number of seconds since January 1, 1904. The date formats convert such a value in seconds to a readable date. For example, the value 86400, which is the number of seconds in one day, will convert to 01/02/1904 using the JMP **m/d/y** format. With his coaching, Alice enters the formula shown in Exhibit 4.26.

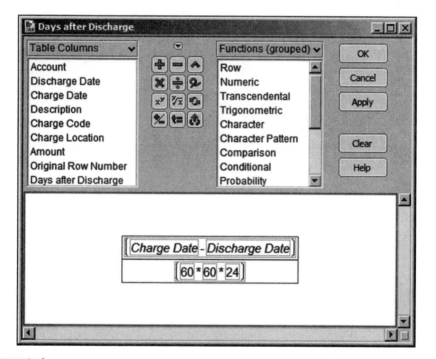

EXHIBIT 4.26   Formula for Days after Discharge

Alice reasons that **Charge Date** – **Discharge Date** gives the number of seconds between these two dates. This means that to get a result in days she needs to divide by the number of seconds in a day, namely, 60*60*24. Alice clicks **OK** and the difference in days appears in the new column. (This column can also be obtained by running the script **Define Days after Discharge**.)

Now, both Alice and Alex are aware that this difference is only an indicator of lateness and not a solid measure of days late. For example, a patient might be in the hospital for two weeks, and the late charge might be the cost of a procedure done on admittance or early in that patient's stay. For various reasons, including the fact that charges cannot be billed until the patient leaves the hospital, the procedure date is not tracked by the hospital billing system. Thus, Discharge Date is simply a rough surrogate for the date of the procedure, and Days after Discharge undercounts the number of days that the charge is truly late.

Alice obtains a distribution report of Days after Discharge using the **Distribution** platform, choosing **Stack** from the **Distributions** red triangle menu. This report is shown in Exhibit 4.27. (The script is saved as **Distribution of Days after Discharge.**)

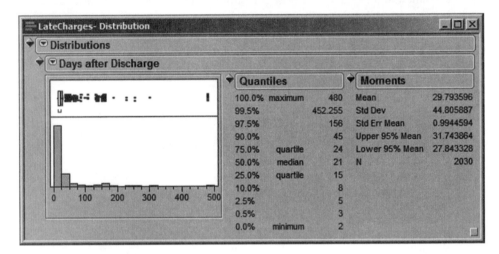

EXHIBIT 4.27   Distribution Report for Days after Discharge

Alex and Alice see that there were some charges that were at least 480 days late. By selecting the points corresponding to the 480 days in the box plot above the histogram, Alice and Alex proceed to view the ten relevant records using **Data View** (see Exhibit 4.28).

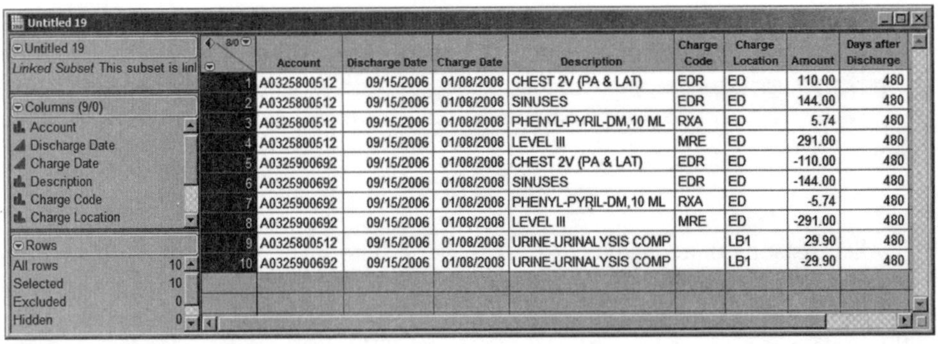

EXHIBIT 4.28   Data View of Rows with 480 Days after Discharge

They notice that only two **Account** numbers are involved, and they suspect, given that there is only one value of **Discharge Date**, that these might have been for the same patient. Alice deselects the rows. To arrange the charges by account number, Alice sorts on **Account** by right-clicking on its column header and choosing **Sort** (Exhibit 4.29).

		Account	Discharge Date	Charge Date	Description	Charge Code	Charge Location	Amount	Days after Discharge
	1	A0325800512	09/15/2006	01/08/2008	CHEST 2V (PA & LAT)	EDR	ED	110.00	480
	2	A0325800512	09/15/2006	01/08/2008	SINUSES	EDR	ED	144.00	480
	3	A0325800512	09/15/2006	01/08/2008	PHENYL-PYRIL-DM, 10 ML	RXA	ED	5.74	480
	4	A0325800512	09/15/2006	01/08/2008	LEVEL III	MRE	ED	291.00	480
	5	A0325800512	09/15/2006	01/08/2008	URINE-URINALYSIS COMP		LB1	29.90	480
	6	A0325900692	09/15/2006	01/08/2008	CHEST 2V (PA & LAT)	EDR	ED	-110.00	480
	7	A0325900692	09/15/2006	01/08/2008	SINUSES	EDR	ED	-144.00	480
	8	A0325900692	09/15/2006	01/08/2008	PHENYL-PYRIL-DM, 10 ML	RXA	ED	-5.74	480
	9	A0325900692	09/15/2006	01/08/2008	LEVEL III	MRE	ED	-291.00	480
	10	A0325900692	09/15/2006	01/08/2008	URINE-URINALYSIS COMP		LB1	-29.90	480

EXHIBIT 4.29   Data View of Rows with 480 Days after Discharge Grouped by Account

They notice something striking: Every single charge to the first **Account** (rows 1 to 5) is credited to the second **Account** (rows 6 to 10)! This is very interesting. Alice and Alex realize that they need to learn more about how charges make it into the late charges database. Might it be that a lot of these records involve charge and credit pairs, that is, charges along with corresponding credits?

Visualizing the Variables Two at a Time: A View by Entry Order

At this point, Alice and Alex close this **Data View** table. They are curious as to whether there is any pattern to how the data are entered in the data table. They notice that the entries are not in time order—neither **Discharge Date** nor **Charge Date** is in order. They consider constructing control charts based on these two time variables, but neither of these would be particularly informative about the process by which late charges appear.

To simply check if there is any pattern in how the entries are posted, Alex decides that they should construct an **Individual Measurement** chart, plotting the **Amount** values as they appear in row order. Alice selects **Graph > Control Chart > IR** and populates the launch dialog as shown in Exhibit 4.30. Note that Alice unchecks the box for **Moving Range**; they simply want to see a plot of the data by row number.

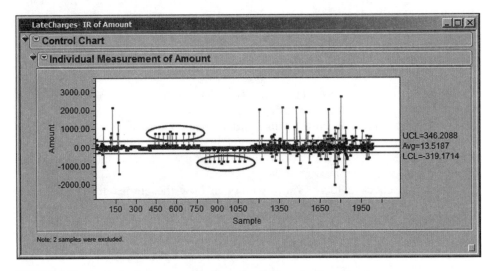

EXHIBIT 4.30   Launch Dialog for Individual Measurement Control Chart

The control chart for **Amount** is shown in Exhibit 4.31. (The script is called **Control Chart of Amount**.)

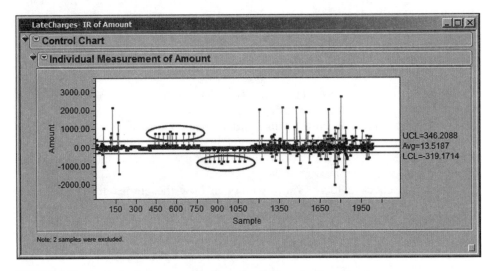

EXHIBIT 4.31   Individual Measurement Chart for Amount by Row Number

There is something going on that is very interesting. There are many positive charges that seem to be offset by negative charges (credits) later in the data table. For example, Alice notes that, as shown by the ellipses in Exhibit 4.31, there are several large charges that are credited in subsequent rows of the data table.

Alice selects the points in the ellipse with positive charges using the arrow tool, drawing a rectangle around these points. This selects ten points. Then, while holding down the shift key, she selects the points in the ellipse with negative charges. Alternatively, you can select **Tools > Lasso** or go to the tool bar to get the **Lasso** tool, which allows you to select points by enclosing them with a freehand curve. Holding the shift key while you select a second group of points retains the previous selection. (The script **Selection of Twenty Points** selects these points.)

In all, Alice has selected 20 points, as she can see in the rows panel of **Late-Charges.jmp**. Alice right-clicks on **Selected** in the rows panel and selects **Data View**. She obtains the table in Exhibit 4.32. The table shows that the first ten amounts were charged to a patient who was discharged on 12/17/2007 and credited to a patient who was discharged on 12/26/2007.

	Account	Discharge Date	Charge Date	Description	Charge Code	Charge Location	Amount	Days after Discharge
1	A0434300267	12/17/2007	01/10/2008	T2 ROOM AND CARE - PCU		T2	750.00	24
2	A0434300267	12/17/2007	01/10/2008	T2 ROOM AND CARE - PCU		T2	750.00	24
3	A0434300267	12/17/2007	01/10/2008	T2 ROOM AND CARE - PCU		T2	750.00	24
4	A0434300267	12/17/2007	01/10/2008	T2 ROOM AND CARE - PCU		T2	750.00	24
5	A0434300267	12/17/2007	01/10/2008	CT THORAX W/O CONTRAST	2T8	T2	869.00	24
6	A0434300267	12/17/2007	01/10/2008	T2 ROOM AND CARE - PCU		T2	750.00	24
7	A0434300267	12/17/2007	01/10/2008	T2 ROOM AND CARE - PCU		T2	750.00	24
8	A0434300267	12/17/2007	01/10/2008	T2 ROOM AND CARE - PCU		T2	750.00	24
9	A0434300267	12/17/2007	01/10/2008	T2 ROOM AND CARE - PCU		T2	750.00	24
10	A0434300267	12/17/2007	01/10/2008	T2 ROOM AND CARE - PCU		T2	750.00	24
11	A0435200437	12/26/2007	01/10/2008	T2 ROOM AND CARE - PCU		T2	-750.00	15
12	A0435200437	12/26/2007	01/10/2008	T2 ROOM AND CARE - PCU		T2	-750.00	15
13	A0435200437	12/26/2007	01/10/2008	T2 ROOM AND CARE - PCU		T2	-750.00	15
14	A0435200437	12/26/2007	01/10/2008	T2 ROOM AND CARE - PCU		T2	-750.00	15
15	A0435200437	12/26/2007	01/10/2008	CT THORAX W/O CONTRAST	2T8	T2	-869.00	15
16	A0435200437	12/26/2007	01/10/2008	T2 ROOM AND CARE - PCU		T2	-750.00	15
17	A0435200437	12/26/2007	01/10/2008	T2 ROOM AND CARE - PCU		T2	-750.00	15
18	A0435200437	12/26/2007	01/10/2008	T2 ROOM AND CARE - PCU		T2	-750.00	15
19	A0435200437	12/26/2007	01/10/2008	T2 ROOM AND CARE - PCU		T2	-750.00	15
20	A0435200437	12/26/2007	01/10/2008	T2 ROOM AND CARE - PCU		T2	-750.00	15

EXHIBIT 4.32 Data View of Ten Positive Amounts That Are Later Credited

Is this just an isolated example of a billing error? Or is there more of this kind of activity? This finding propels Alex and Alice to take a deeper look at credits versus charges.

Visualizing the Variables Two at a Time: Amount and Abs(Amt)

To investigate these apparent charge-and-credit occurrences more fully, Alex suggests constructing a new variable representing the absolute **Amount** of the late charge. This new variable will help them investigate the amount of money tied up in late charges. It will also allow them to group the credits and charges.

At this point, Alex and Alice close all open data tables except for **Late-Charges.jmp**. Alice creates a new column to the right of Days after Discharge, calling it **Abs(Amt)**. As before, she right-clicks in the header area and selects **Formula** to open the formula editor. She selects **Amount** from the list of **Table Columns**. With Amount in the editor window, she chooses **Numeric** under **Functions (grouped)** and selects **Abs** (Exhibit 4.33). This applies the absolute value function to Amount. She clicks **OK** to close the formula editor and to evaluate the formula. (This column can also be obtained by running the script **Define Abs(Amt)**.)

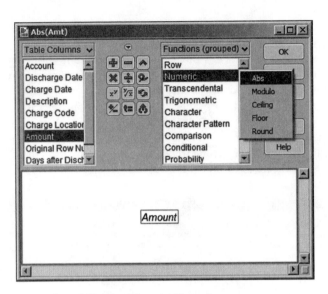

EXHIBIT 4.33 Construction of Absolute Amount Formula

To calculate the amount of money tied up in the late charge problem, Alex suggests that Alice use **Tables > Summary**. Alice fills in the launch dialog as shown in Exhibit 4.34, first selecting **Amount** and **Abs(Amt)** as shown and then choosing **Sum** from the drop-down list obtained by clicking the **Statistics** button.

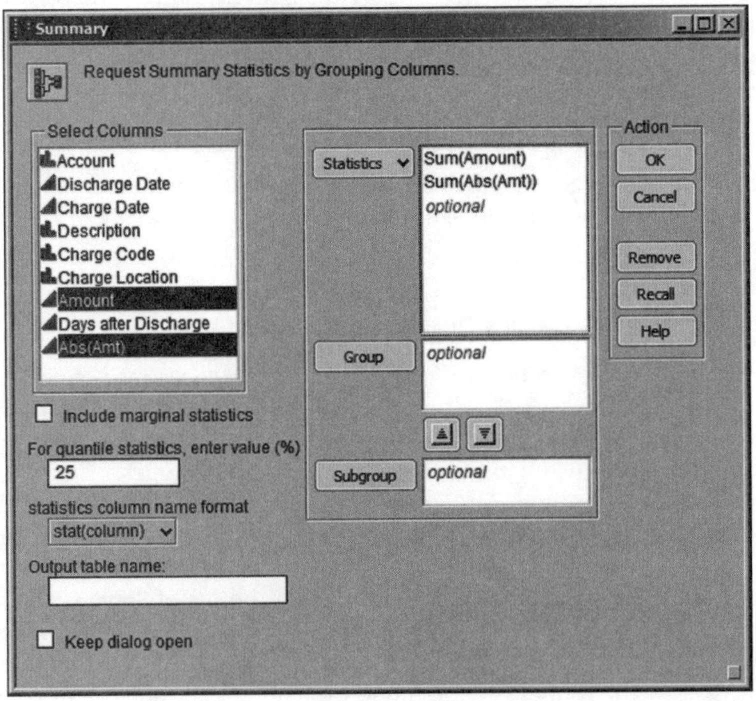

EXHIBIT 4.34 Summary Dialog for Calculation of Total Dollars in Amount and Abs(Amt)

When she clicks **OK**, she obtains the data table shown in Exhibit 4.35, which shows that the total for **Abs(Amt)** is $186,533, while the sum of actual dollars involved, **Sum(Amount)**, is $27,443. The only thing that Alex and Alice can conclude is that a high dollar amount is being tied up in credits. (The script for this summary table is called **Summary Table for Amounts**.)

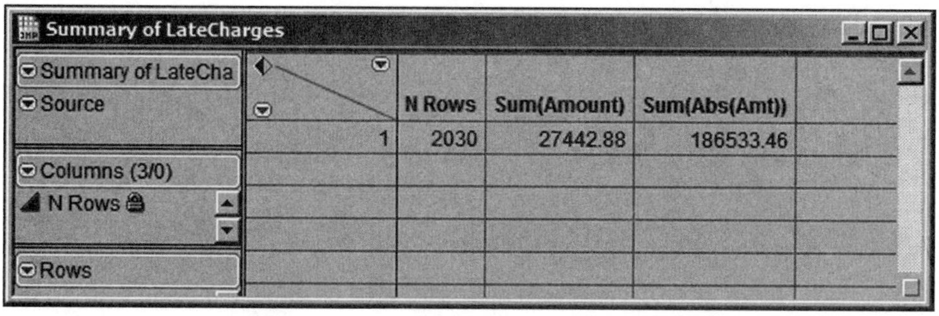

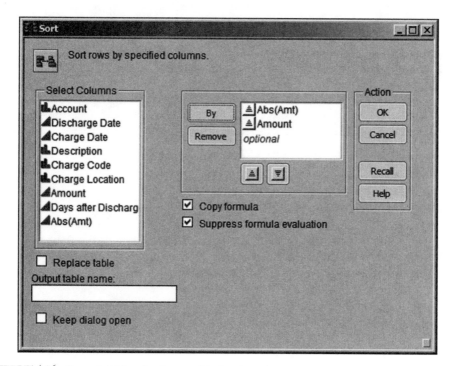

EXHIBIT 4.35 Summary Table Showing Sum of Amount and Abs(Amt)

To better understand the credit and charge situation, Alice closes the **Summary** data table, goes back to her **LateCharges.jmp** table, and constructs a new data table using **Tables > Sort**. She sorts on **Abs(Amt)**, with a secondary sort on **Amount** (see Exhibit 4.36).

EXHIBIT 4.36 Launch Dialog for Sort on Abs(Amt) and Amount

Once you have constructed this sorted data table, we suggest that you close it and work with the table **LateCharges_Sorted.jmp** instead. In that data table, the **Days after Discharge** column has been moved in order to juxtapose **Amount** and **Abs(Amt)** for easier viewing.

The new table reveals that 82 records have $0 listed as the late charge amount. Alice and Alex make note that someone needs to look into these records to figure out why they are appearing as late charges. Are they write-offs? Or are the zeros errors?

Moving beyond the zeros, Alice and Alex start seeing interesting charge-and-credit patterns. For an example, see Exhibit 4.37. There are 21 records with **Abs(Amt)** equal to $4.31. Seven of these have **Amount** equal to $4.31, while the remaining 14 records have **Amount** equal to −$4.31. Alex and Alice notice similar patterns repeatedly in this table—one account is credited, another is charged.

	Account	Discharge Date	Charge Date	Description	Charge Code	Charge Location	Days After Disharge	Amount	Abs(Amt)
441	A0500300262	01/11/2008	01/24/2008	MAGNESIUM CITRAT	RXE	T6B	14	-4.05	4.05
442	A0500700471	01/10/2008	01/18/2008	MAGNESIUM CITRAT	RXE	T6B	9	-4.05	4.05
443	A0424100080	12/26/2007	01/10/2008	HEPARIN FLUSH 100		T6B	158	-4.31	4.31
444	A0424200099	12/26/2007	01/10/2008	HEPARIN FLUSH 100		T6B	155	-4.31	4.31
445	A0435200437	01/05/2008	01/18/2008	NS,20 ML		ED	16	-4.31	4.31
446	A0435200437	12/19/2007	01/14/2008	NS,2 ML		T2	16	-4.31	4.31
447	A0435200437	12/30/2007	01/10/2008	NS,2 ML		T2	16	-4.31	4.31
448	A0435800035	11/29/2007	01/11/2008	HEPARIN FLUSH 100	RXE	T7	14	-4.31	4.31
449	A0433603153	12/31/2007	01/10/2008	EPINEPHRINE 1-1000,		OR1	27	-4.31	4.31
450	A0433603153	08/31/2007	01/31/2008	LIDOCAINE 2% (MDV		OR1	27	-4.31	4.31
451	A0435400111	08/31/2007	01/31/2008	HEPARIN FLUSH 100	BO2	T6B	25	-4.31	4.31
452	A0436300404	12/17/2007	01/10/2008	NS,2 ML	RXE	T6A	12	-4.31	4.31
453	A0431600679	12/17/2007	01/10/2008	LIDOCAINE 2% (MDV	RXE		44	-4.31	4.31
454	A0431600679	12/17/2007	01/10/2008	EPINEPHRINE 1-1000,	RXE		44	-4.31	4.31
455	A0434100162	12/08/2007	01/10/2008	NS,20 ML	3T7	T3	36	-4.31	4.31
456	A0436600069	12/06/2007	01/10/2008	NS,2 ML	RXE	OB	11	-4.31	4.31
457	A0423800130	08/28/2007	01/31/2008	HEPARIN FLUSH 100		T6B	153	4.31	4.31
458	A0423800130	08/29/2007	01/31/2008	HEPARIN FLUSH 100		T6B	153	4.31	4.31
459	A0434300267	12/26/2007	01/10/2008	NS,20 ML		ED	25	4.31	4.31
460	A0434300267	12/15/2007	01/10/2008	NS,2 ML		T2	25	4.31	4.31
461	A0434300267	12/15/2007	01/10/2008	NS,2 ML		T2	25	4.31	4.31
462	A0433603134	11/29/2007	01/11/2008	EPINEPHRINE 1-1000,		OR1	34	4.31	4.31
463	A0433603134	12/08/2007	01/14/2008	LIDOCAINE 2% (MDV		OR1	34	4.31	4.31
464	A0432800053	11/22/2007	01/03/2008	DICYCLOMINE HCL	BO2	AMB	43	-5.56	5.56
465	A0501900477	01/21/2008	01/29/2008	AMLODIPINE 5MG,TA	RXE	T2	7	-5.62	5.62

Left panel:
LateCharges_Sorted
- LateCharges_Sorted
- Source
- Summary Table
- On Open

Columns (9/2)
- Account
- Discharge Date
- Charge Date
- Description
- Charge Code
- Charge Location
- Days After Discharge
- Amount
- Abs(Amt)

Rows
All rows	2032
Selected	21
Excluded	2
Hidden	2
Labelled	0

EXHIBIT 4.37   Partial Data Table Showing Charges Offset by Credits

To get a better handle on the extent of the charge-and-credit issue, Alice decides that she wants to compare actual charges to what the revenue would be if there were no credits. The table **LateCharges_Sorted.jmp** is still her current table. She constructs a table using **Tables > Summary**, where she requests the sum of the **Amount** values for each value of **Abs(Amt)** by selecting **Abs(Amt)** as a group variable (see Exhibit 4.38). She clicks **OK**.

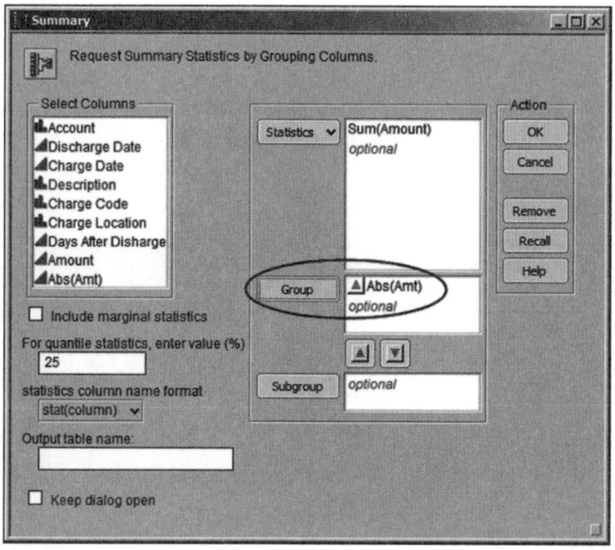

EXHIBIT 4.38 Summary Dialog for Comparison of Net Charges to Revenue If No Credits

In the summary data table that is created, Alice defines a new column called Sum If No Credits, using the formula Abs(Amt) × N Rows. This new variable gives the total amount of the billed charges, were there no credits. She saves a script to recreate this data table, called **Summary Table**, to **LateCharges_Sorted.jmp**. A portion of the table is shown in Exhibit 4.39. For example, note the net credit of $30.17 shown for the 21 charges with Abs(Amt) of $4.31 in row 10 of this summary table; one can only conclude that a collection of such transactions belies a lot of non-value-added time and customer frustration.

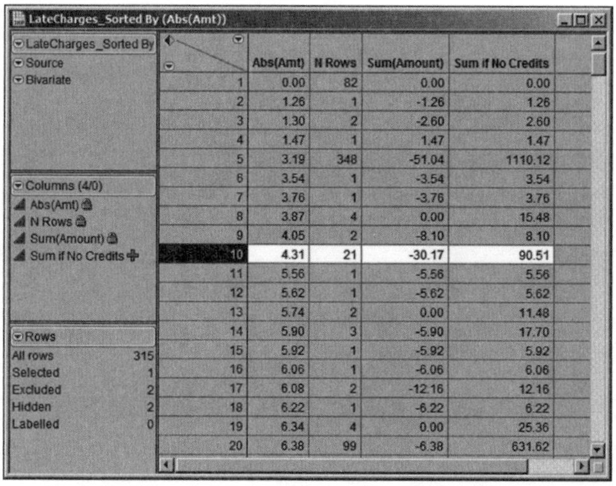

	Abs(Amt)	N Rows	Sum(Amount)	Sum if No Credits
1	0.00	82	0.00	0.00
2	1.26	1	-1.26	1.26
3	1.30	2	-2.60	2.60
4	1.47	1	1.47	1.47
5	3.19	348	-51.04	1110.12
6	3.54	1	-3.54	3.54
7	3.76	1	-3.76	3.76
8	3.87	4	0.00	15.48
9	4.05	2	-8.10	8.10
10	4.31	21	-30.17	90.51
11	5.56	1	-5.56	5.56
12	5.62	1	-5.62	5.62
13	5.74	2	0.00	11.48
14	5.90	3	-5.90	17.70
15	5.92	1	-5.92	5.92
16	6.06	1	-6.06	6.06
17	6.08	2	-12.16	12.16
18	6.22	1	-6.22	6.22
19	6.34	4	0.00	25.36
20	6.38	99	-6.38	631.62

EXHIBIT 4.39 Summary Table Comparing Net Charges to Revenue If No Credits

This table by itself is interesting. But Alice wants to go one step further. She wants a plot that shows how the actual charges compare to the charges if there were no credits. Alex suggests a scatterplot. So Alice selects **Analyze > Fit Y by X** to construct a scatterplot of Sum(Amount) by Sum if No Credits. She enters Sum(Amount) as **Y, Response** and Sum if No Credits as **X, Factor**. When she clicks **OK**, she obtains the report in Exhibit 4.40.

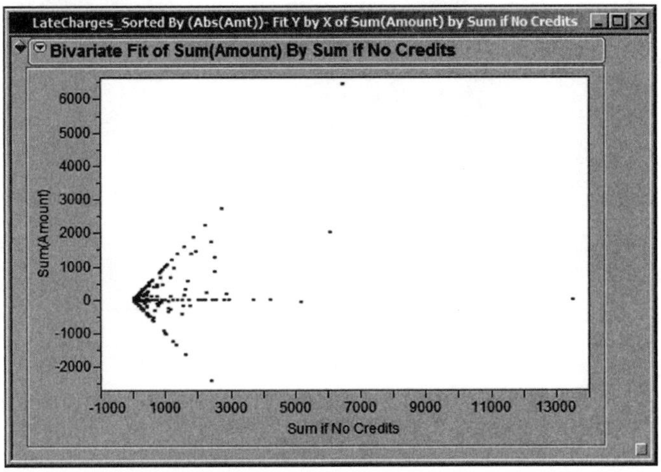

EXHIBIT 4.40   Bivariate Fit of Sum(Amount) by Sum if No Credits

The scatterplot shows some linear patterns, which Alice surmises represent the situations either where there are no credits at all or where all instances of a given Abs(Amt) are credited. To see better what is happening, she fits three lines to the data on the plot. She does this by clicking on the red triangle at the top of the report and choosing **Fit Special** (see Exhibit 4.41).

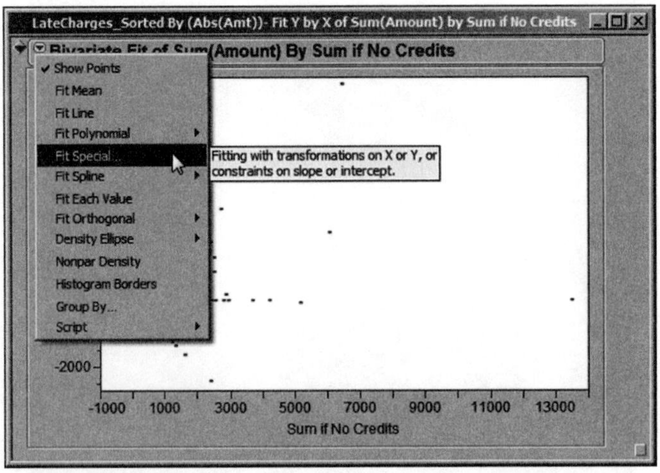

EXHIBIT 4.41   Fit Special Selection

This opens a dialog that allows Alice to choose among various special fits. What Alice wants to do is to fit three specific lines, all with intercept 0:

- The line with slope 1 covers points where the underlying **Amount** values are all positive.
- The line with slope 0 covers points where the charges are exactly offset with credits.
- The line with slope −1 covers points where all of the underlying late charge **Amount** values are negative (credits).

To fit the first line, Alice checks the two boxes at the bottom of the dialog to constrain the intercept and the slope, and enters the values 0 and 1, respectively, as shown in Exhibit 4.42. The other lines are fit in a similar fashion.

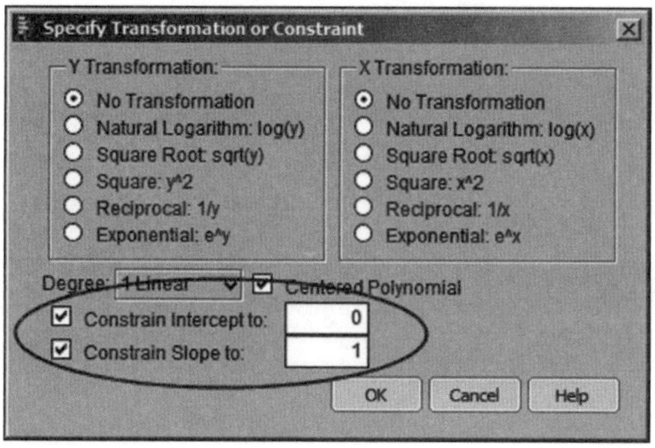

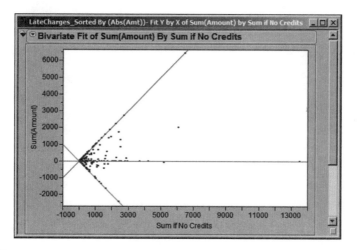

EXHIBIT 4.42   Dialog Choices for Line with Slope 1

Alice's final plot is shown in Exhibit 4.43. She saves the script as **Bivariate**.

EXHIBIT 4.43   Scatterplot of Sum(Amount) by Sum If No Credits

The graph paints a striking picture of how few values of **Abs(Amt)** are unaffected by credits. Only those points along the line with slope 1 are not affected by credits. The points on or near the line with slope 0 result from a balance between charges and credits, while the points on or near the line with slope −1 reflect almost all credits. The graph shows many charges being offset with credits. From inspection of the data, Alex and Alice realize that these often reflect credits to one account and charges to another. This is definitely an area where a green belt project would be of value.

Visualizing the Variables Two at a Time: Revisiting Days after Discharge

Alex raises the issue of whether there is a pattern in charges, relating to how long it has been since the patient's discharge. For example, do credits tend to appear early after discharge, while overlooked charges show up later? To address this question, Alice closes all of her open reports and data tables, leaving only **LateCharges.jmp** open. She selects **Analyze > Fit Y by X**, entering Amount as **Y, Response** and Days after Discharge as **X, Factor**. Alice clicks **OK**.

In the resulting plot, she adds a horizontal reference line at the $0 **Amount**. To do this, she moves her cursor to the vertical axis until it becomes a hand, as shown in Exhibit 4.44.

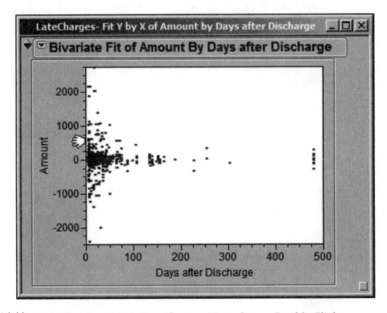

EXHIBIT 4.44 Accessing the Y Axis Specification Menu from a Double-Click

Then, she double-clicks to open the **Y Axis Specification** menu shown in Exhibit 4.45. In the dialog box, Alice simply clicks **Add** to add a reference line at 0.

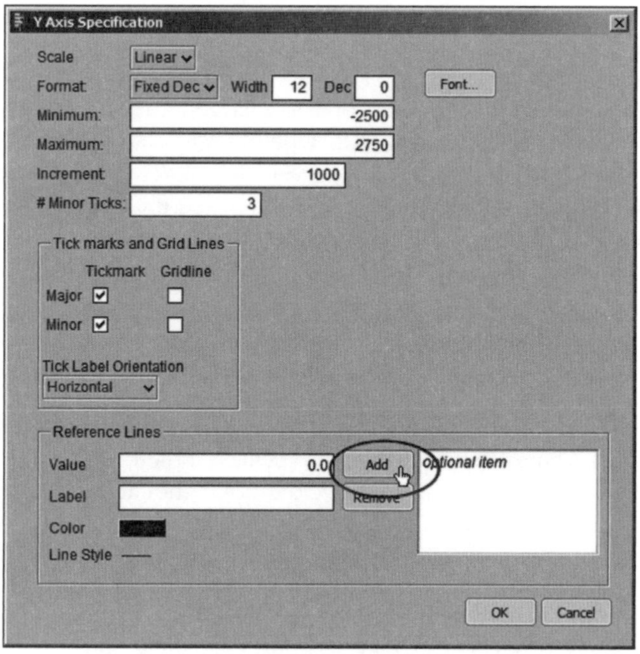

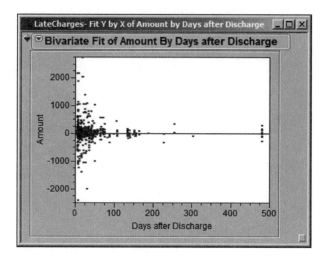

EXHIBIT 4.45   Adding a Reference Line to the Scatterplot

The resulting plot is shown in Exhibit 4.46. Alice saves the script that produced this plot to **LateCharges.jmp** as **Bivariate**. The resulting scatterplot shows no systematic relationship between the Amount of the late charge and Days after Discharge. However, the plot does show a pattern consistent with charges and corresponding credits. It also suggests that large dollar charges and credits are dealt with sooner after discharge, rather than later.

EXHIBIT 4.46   Scatterplot of Amount versus Days after Discharge

Uncovering the Hot Xs

At this point, Alex and Alice have learned a great deal about their data. They are ready to begin exploring the drivers of late charges, to the extent possible with their limited data. They are interested in whether late charges are associated with particular accounts, charge codes, or charge locations. They suspect that there are too many distinct descriptions to address without expert knowledge and that the Description data should be reflected in the Charge Code entries.

In their pursuit of the Hot Xs, Alex and Alice will use Pareto plots, tree maps, and the data filter, together with dynamic linking.

Exploring Two Unusual Accounts

At this point, it seems reasonable for Alice to construct Pareto plots for each of these variables: Account, Charge Code, and Charge Location. But, to gauge the effect of each variable on late charges, she and Alex decide to weight each variable by Abs(Amt), as this gives a measure of the magnitude of impact on late charges.

Alice closes all data tables and reports other than **LateCharges.jmp**. Recall that there were 389 different accounts represented in the data. To construct a Pareto plot, Alice selects **Graph > Pareto Plot**. She inserts Account as **Y, Cause** and Abs(Amt) as **Weight**. When she clicks **OK**, she sees a Pareto chart with 389 bars, some so small that they are barely visible (see Exhibit 4.47).

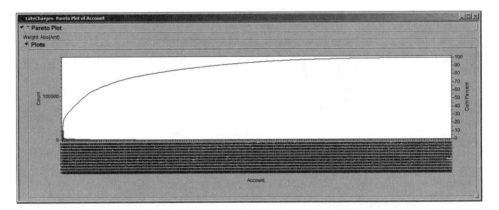

EXHIBIT 4.47   Pareto Plot for Account

She realizes that these barely visible bars correspond to Accounts with very small frequencies and/or Abs(Amts). To combine these into a single bar, Alice clicks on the report's red triangle and selects **Causes > Combine Causes** (Exhibit 4.48).

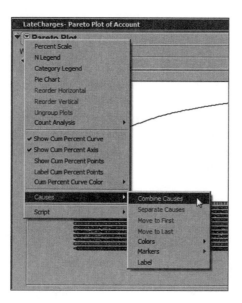

EXHIBIT 4.48   Selection of Combine Causes

This opens a dialog window in which Alice clicks the radio button next to **Last causes** and asks JMP to combine the last 370 causes. Alice saves the script for this plot to the data table as **Pareto Plot of Account.** The resulting chart is shown in Exhibit 4.49.

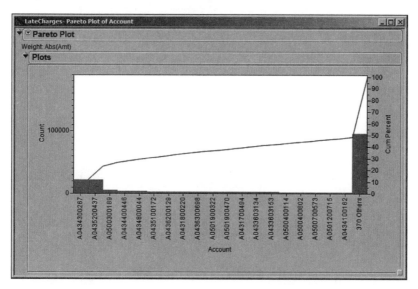

EXHIBIT 4.49   Pareto Plot of Account with Last 370 Causes Combined

The plot shows that two patient accounts represent the largest proportion of absolute dollars. In fact, they each account for $21,997 in absolute dollars out of the total of $186,533. Alice sees this by clicking each bar.

Alice is interested in the raw values of **Amount** that are involved for these two accounts. She selects the records corresponding to both accounts by holding down the control key while clicking on their bars in the **Pareto** plot. This selects 948 records. She goes back to the **LateCharges.jmp** data table and, using **Data View**, creates a table containing only these 948 records. (Alternatively, Alice could have created this table by double-clicking on either bar in the Pareto chart while holding the control key.) All rows are selected in her new data table; to clear the selection, Alice chooses **Rows > Clear Row States**.

For these two accounts, Alice wants to see if the Amount values have similar distributions. So, with this new data table active, she selects **Analyze > Fit Y by X**. She enters Amount as **Y, Response** and Account as **X, Factor**. When she clicks **OK**, Alice obtains the plot shown in Exhibit 4.50.

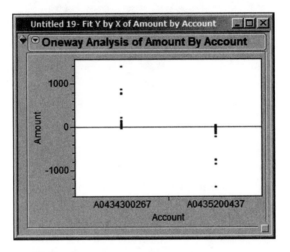

EXHIBIT 4.50   Oneway Plot for Two Accounts

Alice thinks that some of the points are overwriting each other, and so she checks to see if there is a way to better display these points. She clicks on the red triangle and selects **Display Options > Points Jittered**. This gives the plot in Exhibit 4.51.

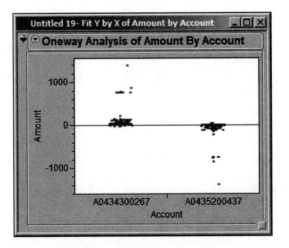

EXHIBIT 4.51   Oneway Plot for Two Accounts with Points Jittered

The plot in Exhibit 4.51 strongly suggests that amounts from the second account are being credited and charged to the first account. Sorting twice by **Abs(Amt)** in the data table consisting of the 948 records for these two accounts to obtain a descending sort, Alice sees the pattern of charges and credits clearly (Exhibit 4.52). Also, to better distinguish the rows corresponding to the two accounts, Alice selects a single cell containing account number A0434300267, and then uses **Rows > Row Selection > Select Matching Cells** to select all rows corresponding to that account number.

	Account	Discharge Date	Charge Date	Description	Charge Code	Charge Location	Amount	Days after Discharge	Abs(Amt)
1	A0434300267	12/17/2007	01/10/2008	ENDOSCOPY LEVEL 2	ORC	END	1394.00	24	1394.00
2	A0435200437	12/26/2007	01/10/2008	ENDOSCOPY LEVEL 2	ORC	END	-1394.0	15	1394.00
3	A0434300267	12/17/2007	01/10/2008	CT THORAX W/O CONTRAS	2T8	T2	869.00	24	869.00
4	A0435200437	12/26/2007	01/10/2008	CT THORAX W/O CONTRAS	2T8	T2	-869.00	15	869.00
5	A0434300267	12/17/2007	01/10/2008	LEVEL VI	EDM	ED	767.00	24	767.00
6	A0435200437	12/26/2007	01/10/2008	LEVEL VI	EDM	ED	-767.00	15	767.00
7	A0434300267	12/17/2007	01/10/2008	T2 ROOM AND CARE - PCU		T2	750.00	24	750.00
8	A0434300267	12/17/2007	01/10/2008	T2 ROOM AND CARE - PCU		T2	750.00	24	750.00
9	A0434300267	12/17/2007	01/10/2008	T2 ROOM AND CARE - PCU		T2	750.00	24	750.00
10	A0434300267	12/17/2007	01/10/2008	T2 ROOM AND CARE - PCU		T2	750.00	24	750.00
11	A0434300267	12/17/2007	01/10/2008	T2 ROOM AND CARE - PCU		T2	750.00	24	750.00
12	A0434300267	12/17/2007	01/10/2008	T2 ROOM AND CARE - PCU		T2	750.00	24	750.00
13	A0434300267	12/17/2007	01/10/2008	T2 ROOM AND CARE - PCU		T2	750.00	24	750.00
14	A0434300267	12/17/2007	01/10/2008	T2 ROOM AND CARE - PCU		T2	750.00	24	750.00
15	A0434300267	12/17/2007	01/10/2008	T2 ROOM AND CARE - PCU		T2	750.00	24	750.00
16	A0435200437	12/26/2007	01/10/2008	T2 ROOM AND CARE - PCU		T2	-750.00	15	750.00
17	A0435200437	12/26/2007	01/10/2008	T2 ROOM AND CARE - PCU		T2	-750.00	15	750.00
18	A0435200437	12/26/2007	01/10/2008	T2 ROOM AND CARE - PCU		T2	-750.00	15	750.00
19	A0435200437	12/26/2007	01/10/2008	T2 ROOM AND CARE - PCU		T2	-750.00	15	750.00
20	A0435200437	12/26/2007	01/10/2008	T2 ROOM AND CARE - PCU		T2	-750.00	15	750.00
21	A0435200437	12/26/2007	01/10/2008	T2 ROOM AND CARE - PCU		T2	-750.00	15	750.00
22	A0435200437	12/26/2007	01/10/2008	T2 ROOM AND CARE - PCU		T2	-750.00	15	750.00
23	A0435200437	12/26/2007	01/10/2008	T2 ROOM AND CARE - PCU		T2	-750.00	15	750.00
24	A0435200437	12/26/2007	01/10/2008	T2 ROOM AND CARE - PCU		T2	-750.00	15	750.00
25	A0434300267	12/17/2007	01/10/2008	ESOPHAGRAM	2T8	T2	219.00	24	219.00
26	A0435200437	12/26/2007	01/10/2008	ESOPHAGRAM	2T8	T2	-219.00	15	219.00

Columns (10/3): Account, Discharge Date, Charge Date, Description, Charge Code, Charge Location, Amount, Original Row Number, Days after Discharge, Abs(Amt)

Rows: All rows 948, Selected 474, Excluded 0, Hidden 0, Labelled 0

EXHIBIT 4.52 Partial Data Table Showing Amounts for Top Two Accounts

Alternatively, Alice could have selected one such cell and right-clicked in the highlighted row area to the left of the account number. This opens a context-sensitive menu from which she can choose **Select Matching Cells** (Exhibit 4.53).

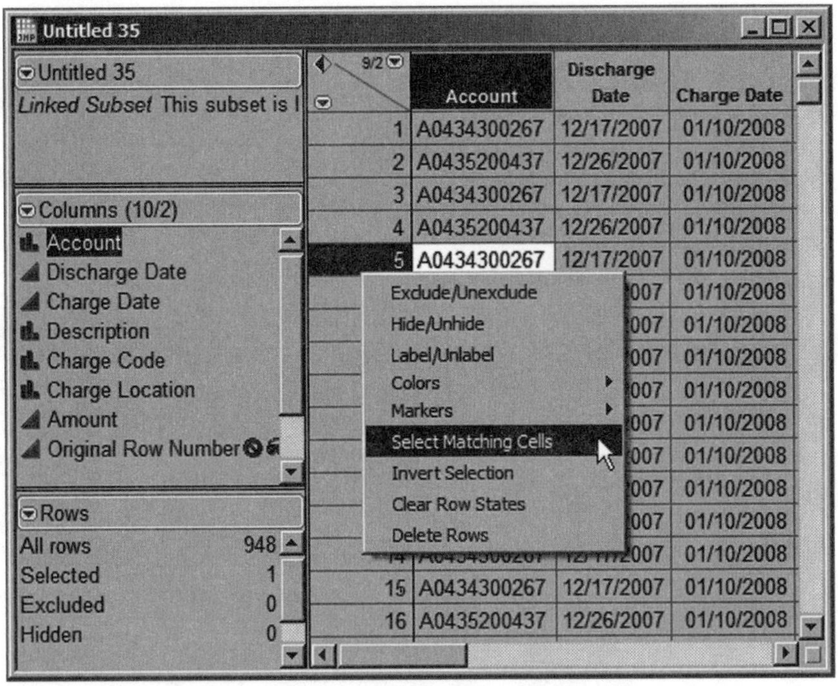

EXHIBIT 4.53   Context-Sensitive Menu for Selecting Matching Cells

This analysis confirms the need to charter a team to work on applying charges to the correct account. Alex and Alice document what they have learned and then close this 948-row table.

Exploring Charge Code and Charge Location

Alex and Alice now turn their attention to **Charge Code** and **Charge Location**, making sure that **LateCharges.jmp** is active. They keep in mind that about 25 percent of records are missing values of at least one of these variables. They consider constructing Pareto charts, but again, because of the large number of levels, they would have to combine causes. Alice wants to try a *tree map*; this is a plot that uses rectangles to represent categories.

Alice selects **Graph > Tree Map**. She enters Charge Code as **Categories**. Then, at Alex's direction, she enters Abs(Amt) as **Sizes**. Alex explains that the sizing results in rectangles with areas that are approximately proportional to the *sum* of the values in the size column. In other words, a size variable is analogous to a weighting variable. Alex asks her to enter **Abs(Amt)** as **Coloring**. This will assign an intensity scale to the rectangles based on the mean of the specified value within each category. Alex also indicates that Abs(Amt) should be entered as **Ordering**. This asks JMP to try to put rectangles that are of similar sizes relative to Abs(Amt) close to each other. The completed launch dialog is shown in Exhibit 4.54.

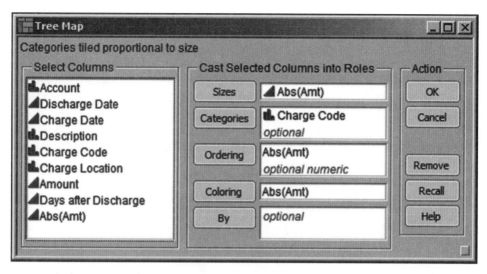

EXHIBIT 4.54   Launch Dialog for Tree Map of Charge Code

When Alice clicks **OK**, the plot in Exhibit 4.55 appears. On the screen, this exhibit displays the default blue-to-red intensity scale. For this book, we present it with a white-to-black scale, with black representing the grouping with the highest mean **Abs(Amt)**. Alice saves the script as **Tree Map of Charge Code**.

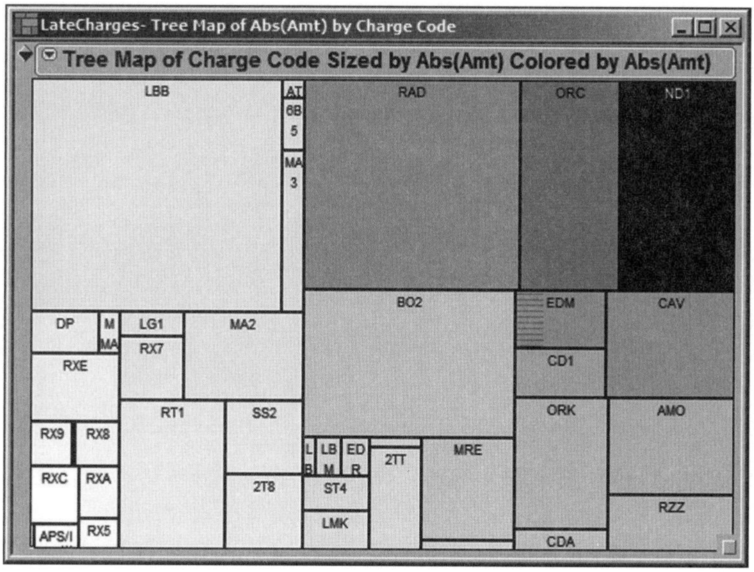

EXHIBIT 4.55   Tree Map of Charge Code: Sized, Colored, and Ordered by Abs(Amt)

Studying the tree map, Alice and Alex note that there are five charge codes—LBB, RAD, BO2, ND1, and ORC—that have large areas. This means that these charge codes account for the largest percentages of absolute dollars (one can show that, in total, they account for 85,839 out of a total of 186,533 absolute dollars). One of these charge codes, ND1, is colored black. This means that although the total absolute dollars accounted for by ND1 is less than, say, for LBB, the mean of the absolute dollars is higher.

Alex clicks in the ND1 area in the tree map; this has the effect of selecting the rows with an ND1 **Charge Code** in the data table. Then he obtains a **Data View** (Exhibit 4.56). There are only seven records involved, but they are all for relatively large charges. He notes that these charges appear from 7 to 18 days after discharge. Also, none of these are credits. Alice and Alex conclude that addressing late charges in the ND1 **Charge Code** is important.

		Account	Discharge Date	Charge Date	Description	Charge Code	Charge Location	Amount	Days after Discharge	Abs(Amt)
	1	A0500700573	01/07/2008	01/14/2008	OVERNIGHT POLYSOMOGRAM	ND1	NDX	2150.00	7	2150.00
	2	A0435400116	12/19/2007	01/05/2008	OPSG WITH CPAP OR BILEVEL	ND1	NDX	2023.00	17	2023.00
	3	A0501200715	01/12/2008	01/21/2008	OVERNIGHT POLYSOMOGRAM	ND1	NDX	2150.00	9	2150.00
	4	A0500400802	01/04/2008	01/14/2008	OVERNIGHT POLYSOMOGRAM	ND1	NDX	2150.00	10	2150.00
	5	A0435300201	12/18/2007	01/05/2008	OPSG WITH CPAP OR BILEVEL	ND1	NDX	2023.00	18	2023.00
	6	A0500600098	01/06/2008	01/14/2008	SOMATOSENSORY EVOKED-L	ND1	NDX	488.00	8	488.00
	7	A0500600098	01/06/2008	01/14/2008	SOMATOSENSORY EVOKED-U	ND1	NDX	488.00	8	488.00

EXHIBIT 4.56 Data View of the Seven Charge Code ND1 Rows

Alice applies this same procedure to select the ORC records, which are shown in Exhibit 4.57. Here, there are 14 records and a number of these are credits. Some are charge and credit pairs. The absolute amounts are relatively large.

		Account	Discharge Date	Charge Date	Description	Charge Code	Charge Location	Amount	Days after Discharge	Abs(Amt)
	1	A0434300267	12/17/2007	01/10/2008	ENDOSCOPY LEVEL 2	ORC	END	1394.00	24	1394.00
	2	A0435200437	12/26/2007	01/10/2008	ENDOSCOPY LEVEL 2	ORC	END	-1394.00	15	1394.00
	3	A0501700607	01/24/2008	01/31/2008	GENERAL ANESTHESIA PER	ORC	ANE	-137.20	7	137.20
	4	A0501700607	01/24/2008	01/31/2008	GENERAL ANESTHESIA PER	ORC	ANE	137.20	7	137.20
	5	A0501700607	01/24/2008	01/31/2008	SURGERY ACUITY LEVEL 3	ORC	OR	-616.20	7	616.20
	6	A0501700607	01/24/2008	01/31/2008	SURGERY ACUITY LEVEL 3	ORC	OR	249.60	7	249.60
	7	A0500300189	01/04/2008	01/10/2008	GENERAL ANESTHESIA PER	ORC	ANE	-1019.20	6	1019.20
	8	A0500300189	01/04/2008	01/10/2008	GENERAL ANESTHESIA PER	ORC	ANE	431.20	6	431.20
	9	A0500300189	01/04/2008	01/10/2008	SURGERY ACUITY LEVEL 6	ORC	OR	-2428.20	6	2428.20
	10	A0500300189	01/04/2008	01/10/2008	ADDITIONAL NURSE/MINUTE	ORC	OR	-408.00	6	408.00
	11	A0500300189	01/04/2008	01/10/2008	SURGERY ACUITY LEVEL 6	ORC	OR	1060.20	6	1060.20
	12	A0500300189	01/04/2008	01/10/2008	ADDITIONAL NURSE/MINUTE	ORC	OR	192.00	6	192.00
	13	A0432700209	11/24/2007	01/10/2008	GUIDEWIRE 1.6MM	ORC	OR	70.50	47	70.50
	14	A0432700209	11/24/2007	01/10/2008	SCREW CANNULATED 4.5MM	ORC	OR	349.28	47	349.28

EXHIBIT 4.57 Data View of the 14 Charge Code ORC Rows

She also looks at each of the remaining top five **Charge Codes** in turn. For example, the LBB **Charge Code** consists of 321 records and represents a mean absolute dollar amount of $87 and a total absolute dollar amount of $28,004. There appear to be many credits, and many charge and credit pairs. From this analysis, Alex and Alice agree that **Charge Code** is a good way to stratify the late charge problem.

But how about **Charge Location**? They both realize that **Charge Location** defines the area in the hospital where the charge originates, and consequently identifies the staff groupings who must properly manage the information flow. Alice selects **Graph > Tree Map** once again. She clicks on the **Recall** button, which reinserts the settings used in her previous analysis (Exhibit 4.54). However, she now wants to replace Charge Code with Charge Location. This is easily done. She selects Charge Code in the **Categories** text box, clicks on the **Remove** button, and inserts Charge Location into the **Categories** box. Alice obtains the plot shown in Exhibit 4.58. She saves the script as **Tree Map of Charge Location**.

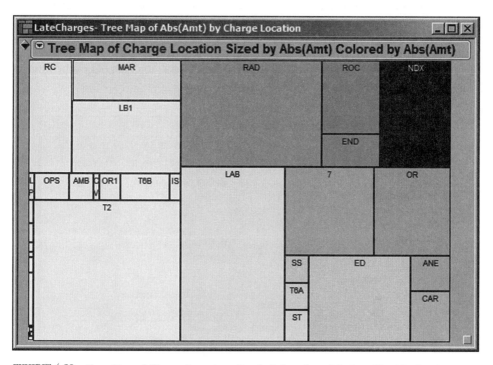

EXHIBIT 4.58   Tree Map of Charge Location: Sized, Colored, and Ordered by Abs(Amt)

The eight largest rectangles in this graph are: T2, LAB, RAD, ED, 7, LB1, NDX, and OR. These eight Charge Locations consist of 1,458 of the total 2,030 records, and represent 140,115 of the total of 186,533 absolute dollars. Alice and Alex both wonder about location 7, and make a note to find out why this location uses an apparently odd code.

Next, Alice and Alex examine each of these groupings individually using the process of selecting the rectangle and creating a table using **Data View**. One interesting finding is that Charge Location NDX consists of exactly the seven Charge Code ND1 records depicted in Exhibit 4.56. So it may be that the NDX location only deals with the ND1 code, suggesting that the late charge problem in this area might be easier to solve than in other areas.

But this raises an interesting question for Alex. He is wondering how many late charge Charge Code values are associated with each Charge Location. Alex thinks that the larger the number of charge codes involved, the higher the complexity of information flow, and the higher the likelihood of errors, particularly of the charge-and-credit variety.

To address this question in a manageable way, Alice suggests that they select all records corresponding to the eight largest **Charge Location** rectangles and use **Fit Y by X** to create a mosaic plot. In the tree map, Alice selects the eight charge locations T2, LAB, RAD, ED, 7, LB1, NDX, and OR, holding down the shift key to add values to the selection. She notes that in the rows panel of the data table 1,458 rows appear as selected. She right-clicks on **Selected** in the rows panel and selects **Data View**. This produces a table containing only those 1,458 rows; as usual in such a table, all the rows are selected, so Alice deselects them. (A script that produces this data table is saved to **LateCharges.jmp** as **Charge Location Subset**. The data table is labeled as **Charge Location Subset** in the exhibits that follow.)

Using this data table, Alice selects **Analyze > Fit Y by X**, and populates the launch dialog as shown in Exhibit 4.59.

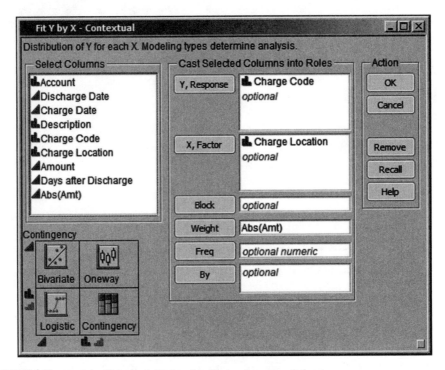

EXHIBIT 4.59   Fit Y by X Launch Dialog for Charge Location Subset

Note that for consistency Alice weights this plot by **Abs(Amt)**. She clicks **OK** to obtain the report in Exhibit 4.60. (In the data table produced by the script **Charge Location Subset**, this mosaic plot is obtained by running the script called **Contingency**.)

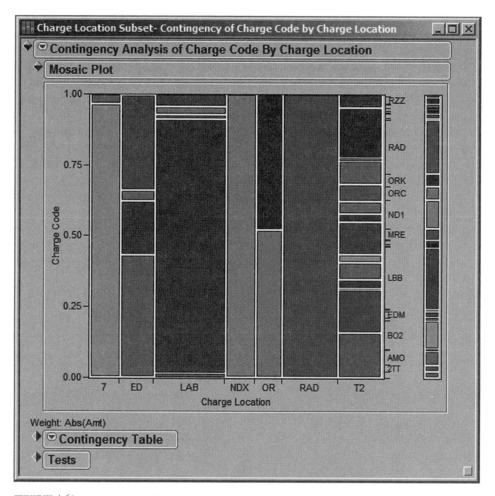

EXHIBIT 4.60   Mosaic Plot of Charge Code by Charge Location, Weighted by Abs(Amt)

Alice and Alex find it noteworthy that **Charge Location** T2 deals with a relatively large number of **Charge Code** values. This is precisely the location that had 25 percent of its **Charge Code** values missing, so the sheer volume of codes associated with T2 could be a factor. The remaining areas tend to deal with small numbers of **Charge Code** values. In particular, NDX and RAD each only have one **Charge Code** represented in the late charge data. NDX and RAD may deal with other codes, but the January 2008 late charges for each of these two areas are only associated with a single code.

Alex and Alice note that except perhaps for T2 these charge locations tend to have charge codes that seem to be unique to the locations. In the colored version of the mosaic plot viewed on a computer screen, one can easily see that there is very little redundancy, if any, in the colors within the vertical bars for the various charge locations.

"Wait a minute," says Alice. "Where is LB1?" The LB1 **Charge Location** does not appear in the mosaic plot—only seven locations are shown. Alex reminds

Alice that **Charge Code** is entirely missing for the LB1 **Charge Location**, as they learned in their earlier analysis of the relationship between **Charge Code** and **Charge Location**.

With that mystery solved, Alex and Alice turn their attention back to the mosaic plot in Exhibit 4.60. Both Alex and Alice, who are approaching the bifocal years, want to double-check their vision. They decide to use distribution plots to better see how **Charge Code** varies by **Charge Location**.

Alice makes the subset data table containing the 1,458 rows the current data table. She selects **Analyze > Distribution** and enters **Charge Code** as **Y** and **Charge Location** as the **By** variable. When she clicks **OK**, she obtains an alert message indicating: "Column Charge Code from table Charge Location=LB1 has only missing values." She realizes that this is because **Charge Location** LB1 has missing data for all rows. She clicks **OK** to move beyond the error alert.

When the distribution report opens, Alice clicks on the red triangle next to the first **Distribution** report and chooses **Stack** (see Exhibit 4.61). This converts the report to a horizontal layout with the histograms stacked, as shown in Exhibit 4.62.

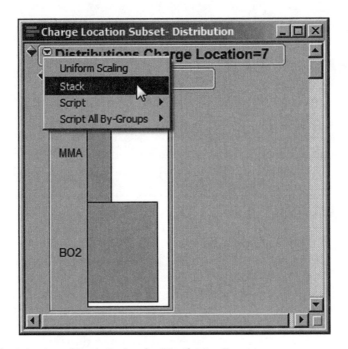

EXHIBIT 4.61   Selection of Stack Option for Distribution Report

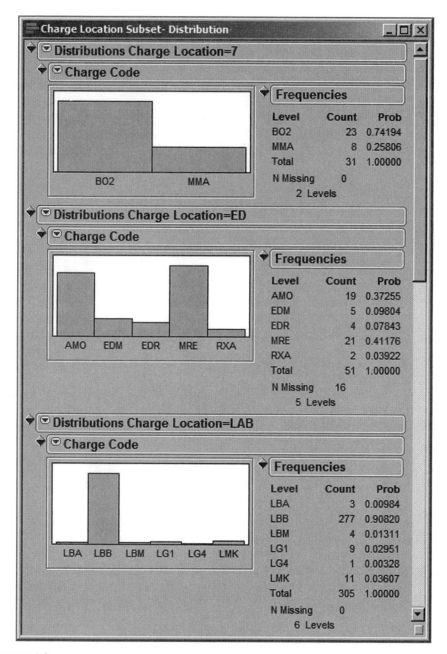

EXHIBIT 4.62   Partial View of Stacked Distributions for Charge Locations

Now Alice selects **Rows > Data Filter**, chooses Charge Code as the variable of interest, and clicks **Add**. (The script **Distributions and Data Filter** in the subset table produces both reports.) Alice clicks on each of the Charge Code values in turn in the data filter menu and scrolls to see which bar graphs in the **Distribution** report reflect records with that Charge Code. They find that almost all of the Charge Code values only appear in one of the locations. RXA is one exception, appearing both for ED and T2 (see Exhibit 4.63).

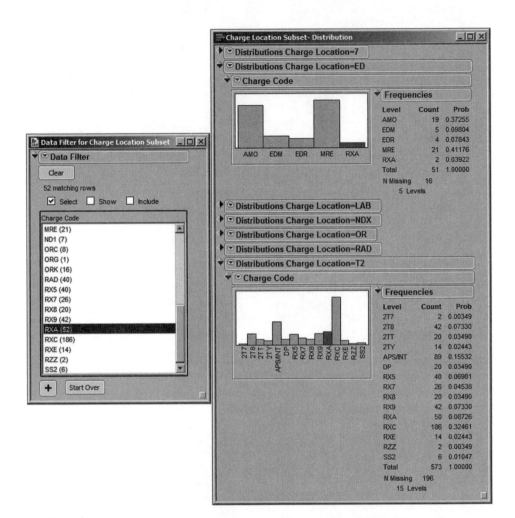

EXHIBIT 4.63   Data Filter and Distribution Display Showing Charge Code RXA

Alex and Alice also conduct a small study of the **Description** information, using tree maps and other methods. They conclude that the **Description** information could be useful to a team addressing late charges, given appropriate contextual knowledge. But they believe that **Charge Location** might provide a better starting point for defining a team's charter.

Given all they have learned to this point, Alex and Alice decide that a team should be assembled to address late charges, with a focus on the eight **Charge Location** areas. For some of these areas, late charges seem to be associated with **Charge Codes** that are identified as prevalent by the tree map in Exhibit 4.55, and that would give the team a starting point in focusing their efforts.

Identifying Projects

Alex and Alice are ready to make recommendations to management relative to areas that should be addressed by green belt project teams. Recall that the January data showed that the late charge problem involves 186,533 absolute dollars. Here are the rationale and recommendations that Alex and Alice make to management:

- First and foremost, a team should be assembled and chartered with developing a value stream map of the billing process. This will provide future teams with a basis for understanding and simplifying the process. The non-value-added time, or wait times, will indicate where cycle-time improvement efforts should be focused. Meanwhile, teams can be chartered to address the problems below. These teams and the value-stream mapping team need to stay in close contact.
- There is a pervasive pattern of charges being offset by credits. A team should be organized to determine what drives this phenomenon and to find a way to eliminate this rework.
- There are 85,839 absolute dollars tied up in six charge codes, and 140,115 absolute dollars tied up in eight charge locations. Since the codes used in the locations seem proprietary to the locations, the recommendation is that a green belt project team should be given the task of reducing the level of late charges, and that the initial focus be these eight areas. Take note that one of these areas, T2, deals with many charge codes, which may entail using a different approach in that area.
- Two complex accounts were found that contributed greatly to the late charges in January. In fact, 984 of the 2,030 records of late charges in January involved transactions for these two accounts. The absolute dollars involved were $43,995. A green belt team should investigate whether this was the result of a special cause or whether such occurrences are seen regularly. In either case, the team should suggest appropriate ways to keep the problem from recurring.
- There is also a tendency to not report the charge code. For example, one of the locations, LB1, is always missing the charge code entry. A team should be formed to address this issue. Is the information redundant and hence unnecessary? Is the information not useful? Is it just too difficult to input this information? The team should address this information flow, and make appropriate recommendations.

Conclusion

As mentioned at the start of this chapter, this case study is almost entirely embedded in the Uncover Relationships stage of the Visual Six Sigma Data Analysis Process (Exhibit 3.29). Alex and Alice take on the role of detectives, searching for clues. They use a number of the How-We-Do-It techniques described under Uncovering Relationships in Exhibit 3.30. Their exploration has been quite unstructured and oriented toward their personal learning and thinking styles, yet they have learned a great deal very quickly.

Using the dynamic visualization and dynamic linking capabilities available in JMP, Alex and Alice have discovered interesting relationships that have business value. JMP has facilitated data screening, exploration, and analysis. In a very short time, these two associates performed analyses that allowed them to define four major problem focus areas. Also, their visual displays made sense to management, lending credibility and strength to their recommendations.

CHAPTER 5

Transforming Pricing Management in a Chemical Supplier

S ix Sigma is often assumed to be the prerogative of black belts, quality engineers, or continuous improvement professionals working in manufacturing environments where the culture and approach are amenable to the rigor and discipline of statistically based data analysis. This case study illustrates how Visual Six Sigma may be successfully applied in the world of sales and marketing, a world conventionally seen as being driven more by art and intuition than by data analysis and science. Specifically, we will see how Visual Six Sigma is used to drive a new way of conceptualizing and managing the pricing process of a multinational chemicals supplier.

Polymat Ltd., a manufacturer of polymeric materials that are sold into a range of commodity and specialty applications, faces growing competition from new manufacturing facilities, primarily in China and India. Market prices have declined steadily over a period of several years. Against this backdrop, Jane, a skilled black belt, is enlisted to help arrest the steady price decline.

Jane assembles a small team, and together they construct what they hope will prove to be a useful set of data. These data capture information from two sales campaigns that attempted to renegotiate prices so as to meet at least a 5 percent price increase. The campaigns cover two very different periods, one where Polymat's product was in undersupply and one where it was in oversupply. In addition to the actual percentage price increase that the sales representative was able to negotiate for each sale, the data set also includes ratings of the experience levels of the sales representative and buyer, and a classification of the value of each sale as seen from the buyer's point of view.

The two experience levels, together with the perceived value of the sale and a few other variables, constitute Jane's Xs. Her Ys are percentage price increase and a nominal variable that reflects whether the target 5 percent increase was met. Failure to meet the 5 percent target defines a *defect* in the negotiating process.

Jane and her team explore this data, first assessing the capability of the pricing process and then uncovering relationships between the Xs and Ys. Given that one Y is continuous and the other is nominal, she uses traditional modeling techniques as well as partitioning to explore relationships with the Xs.

Guided by her data exploration, Jane identifies several key areas for improvement: training of sales representatives, negotiating sales based on the knowledge of the product's value to the buyer, providing appropriate guidelines for sales managers, and accounting for the prevailing supply/demand balance when setting pricing targets. Addressing these areas leads to improvements in the pricing process, which Jane continues to monitor over a period of time.

Jane and her team work through all of the steps of the Visual Six Sigma Data Analysis Process. Exhibit 5.1 lists the JMP platforms and options that Jane uses in her analysis. The data sets are available at http://support.sas.com/visualsixsigma. We invite you to join Jane and her team by working through this case study to see how Visual Six Sigma can lead to substantial improvements in sales and marketing.

EXHIBIT 5.1   Platforms and Options Illustrated in This Case Study

Menus	Platforms and Options
Rows	Exclude/Unexclude
	Clear Row States
Cols	Column Info
	Column Properties
Analyze	Distribution
	Histogram
	Frequency Distribution
	Fit Y by X
	Contingency
	Oneway
	Means Diamonds
	Compare Means
	Fit Model
	Standard Least Squares
	Modeling
	Partition
Graph	Diagram (Ishikawa C&E)
	Control Chart
	IR
Other Options	Automatic Recalc
	Broadcast Command
	Control Charts—Phases
	Value Colors

Setting the Scene

Polymat Ltd., headquartered in England, is a manufacturer of polymeric materials that are sold into a range of commodity and specialty applications. A leader in a steadily growing market, Polymat faces increased competition owing to large-scale competitive investments in new manufacturing facilities, primarily in China and India. As a consequence of the growing availability of product from these far-eastern factories, market prices have shown a steady decline over a period of several years.

Bill Roberts is the recently appointed commercial director for Polymat. He has an excellent track record of business turnaround and has been appointed specifically to reverse Polymat's steady decline in profitability. During his first three months, Bill carries out a major review of each part of the Polymat business. He finds many things that concern him, but is particularly worried about the possibility of further price decline, because he knows that further significant cost cutting is not possible. In reviewing this with his colleagues, Bill realizes that despite several recent attempts to impose price increases, margin and profitability have continued to be eroded.

Bill is aware that the market ultimately defines the price. However, having visited a number of customers, Bill has a hunch that his sales representatives are leaving money on the table in their price negotiations. Motivated by his recent attendance at an exciting conference on process management, Bill is determined to apply *process thinking* to this difficult challenge. He knows that new perspectives in sales and marketing are required to help Polymat halt or reverse the price decline. So he decides to go out and hire the best Six Sigma black belt he can find.

One month later, Jane Hamilton, a highly experienced black belt trained in Visual Six Sigma, is on the job. During her first meeting with Bill, she is given very clear directions: "Go out and fix my pricing process—it's broken!" he tells her. She immediately gets to work.

Framing the Problem: Understanding the Current State Pricing Process

Jane has a few key ideas in mind that help her focus her initial efforts. She realizes that she needs to form a team in order to have the relevant expertise available. She also needs data in order to identify the root causes that will direct her to solutions. Jane's initial thinking is to design a data set using historical data.

In a previous project, Jane employed an approach based on a Product Categorization Matrix. This tool is based on the idea that the seller should view the product from the perspective of the buyer. Jane feels strongly that such a tool could put sales representatives in a stronger negotiating position for certain products. Consequently, Jane intends to integrate product categorization data into the team's investigation.

Defining the Process

Quickly, Jane pulls together a small team consisting of two sales representatives, a sales clerk, and a Polymat financial analyst familiar with the IT system who knows how to access invoice and sales data. The team members agree that they should focus on improving the *pricing management* process, that is, the process that consists of setting price targets, negotiating prices with customers, and invoicing and tracking orders after a successful sale. To define the scope and focus of the initial work, the team starts by drawing a high-level map of this process (see Exhibit 5.2).

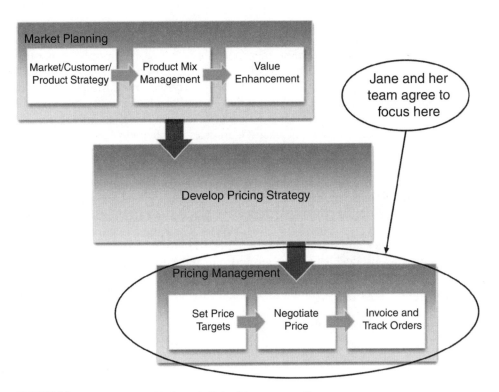

EXHIBIT 5.2   Process Map of Polymat's Price Management Process

Jane checks this scope with Bill, who confirms that this is the right place to start; his management team is already undertaking a strategic review of the market planning process and is looking to simplify Polymat's product range. Bill makes it clear that he expects Jane to help drive improvement in the operational implementation of the stipulated market plans and pricing strategies. This is where he believes a Six Sigma approach will be most beneficial.

Based on discussions with Bill and other members of the management team, Jane also realizes that recent attempts to renegotiate prices with customers have by and large been unsuccessful. Working with the financial analyst on her team, she uncovers data connected to four separate attempts to increase prices over the last two years. Each of these was directed at achieving a 5 percent price increase across Polymath's customer base. None of the four attempts were successful in meeting this target.

Constructing an Analysis Data Set

In thinking about her analysis data set, Jane decides that her main Y will be a measure of the price increase. For each sale, she defines this as the difference between the price charged for the product after the negotiated increase and the price that would have been charged before the increase, divided by the price before the increase. This measure eliminates any currency exchange rate fluctuations that might otherwise complicate the analysis.

Jane also realizes that prevailing market conditions have a pronounced effect on price. The market for Polymat products is highly volatile and can change from demand exceeding supply (a shortage) to supply exceeding demand (an oversupply) in just 6 to 12 months, depending on a number of factors:

- Cyclical characteristics of end user markets (e.g., packaging, electronics).
- Fluctuating oil prices (a key raw material).
- New polymer supply factories coming online (mainly in China and the Far East).

Based simply on market forces, Jane expects that when demand exceeds supply a higher price should be viable (and vice versa). However, she needs to verify that this expectation is supported by the data. So, to better understand the situation, Jane decides to baseline the capability of the current pricing management process using a detailed assessment of two of the recent attempts to impose a unilateral price increase.

After intensive planning and some brainstorming with the team to identify useful data for this investigation, it becomes clear to Jane that information on the experience of the sales representative and on the sophistication of the buyer involved in each sale will be vital. With this in mind, Jane realizes that it does not make sense simply to use a large set of unstructured and possibly uninformative sales data. Instead, she decides to retroactively design and assemble a data set for her baseline assessment. This will both ensure that she has data on the relevant background variables and minimize the time she spends researching and constructing the values of related variables.

Jane constructs the data set for her baseline assessment as follows:

- **Products.** Working with a member of the Polymat marketing department, she selects 20 products as the basis for the study. These products represent a range of both commodity and specialty product types as defined in the Polymat marketing plan. The products are sold in volume and have a respectable (> 30 percent) combined market share.
- **Customers.** Polymat is the market leader in four territories: the United Kingdom, France, Germany, and Italy. Jane wants to ensure that the study includes a range of customers from each of these territories. To that end, for each of the 20 products, 3 customers representing a range of different sizes are chosen from each of the 4 regions. Here, customer *size* is defined as the annual volume in sales made by Polymat to that customer. This results in a total of 240 customers being represented: 3 customers for each of 20 products for each of 4 regions.
- **Supply/Demand Balance.** To include the effect of market conditions in the analysis, Jane indentifies two price increase campaigns that were run under different conditions. In the first case, the market was tight, that is, demand was close to exceeding supply and there was a relative shortage of polymer product. In the second case, 12 months later, the market had shifted to a point where, owing to new factories coming online, there was oversupply.

Based on this retroactive design, Jane constructs a data table whose rows are defined by all possible combinations of the 20 products, the 12 customers (3 in each of the 4 regions), and the 2 supply/demand balance periods. This leads to

$20 \times 12 \times 2 = 480$ records. For each of the combinations of product, customer, and supply/demand balance period, Jane obtains the following information for a sale:

- **Sales Representative Experience.** Jane and her team believe that the experience of the sales representative is a factor of interest, because at Polymat there is no fixed price for each product. Sales representatives have the responsibility of negotiating the best price based on general guidelines and pricing targets set by their sales manager. Consequently, the price that a customer pays for a product depends on the outcome of the negotiation with the buyer. Jane works with the sales manager to sort the sales representatives into three categories of experience: high, medium, and low. Their categorization is based on each representative's number of years of general sales experience and industry-specific knowledge. For example, a sales representative designated with high experience has over ten years of sales experience and in excess of five years selling at Polymat or a similar business.
- **Buyer Sophistication.** Because negotiation is a two-way undertaking, Jane wants to explore the relationship between the experience of the sales representative and the experience of the buyer. She expects that price negotiations will differ based on whether an inexperienced sales representative is selling to an experienced and skilled buyer, or vice versa. Jane sits down with the sales manager to categorize the buyer sophistication for each customer that bought one of the 20 products under consideration. High buyer sophistication is allocated to customers whose buyers are highly professional and highly trained, whereas low buyer sophistication is assigned to customers whose buyers are less highly trained or skilled.
- **Product Category.** This is a categorization of a product and customer into one of four classes, based on how the buying organization views and uses the product. The Product Categorization Matrix section that follows describes this categorization and Jane's use of it.
- **Annual Volume Purchased.** This is the total amount spent by each customer for this product over the year in which the supply/demand balance period falls.
- **% Price Increase (Y).** This is computed by taking the difference between the price charged for the product after the negotiated increase and the price that would have been charged before the increase, and dividing this difference by the price before the increase.

Product Categorization Matrix

Jane is concerned about the simple specialty–commodity split that marketing uses to describe Polymat's products. Luckily, in a previous role, she was responsible for a project in which purchasing operations were redesigned. As part of that project, Jane developed a simple tool to encourage buyers to think differently about what they did, where they spent their time, and where they should focus to reduce the costs of the products they bought.

Jane decides to turn this thinking on its head and apply the same idea to Polymat's pricing process. "After all," she reflects, "if you are selling a product and want to get the best price, it's certainly a good idea to think of the product and its value in the same way that a customer would."

Jane pulls the team members together over lunch for a discussion of her proposed approach. She explains that the Product Categorization Matrix will help them to see the product from the *buyer's* viewpoint, and so should be more informative than the specialty–commodity split that just sees things from the *seller's* point of view. Jane goes on to say that each sale of a product to a customer can be placed into a two-by-two grid based on the requirements of the buying organization (Exhibit 5.3).

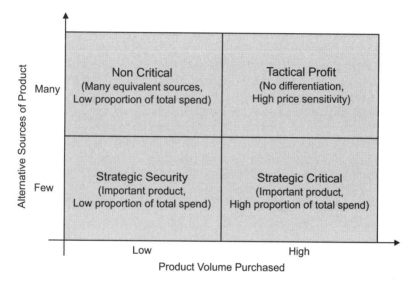

EXHIBIT 5.3   The Product Categorization Matrix

The vertical axis, *Alternative Sources of Product*, represents the buyer's supply vulnerability relative to the product in question. The axis is scaled from Few to Many, referring to the number of potential suppliers. It represents the buyer's risk, posing the question, "What happens if the current seller cannot provide the product?" For example, if the buyer cannot obtain an equivalent product elsewhere or if the product is specific to the buyer's process, then that sale's value on Alternative Sources of Product is Few.

The horizontal axis, *Product Volume Purchased*, represents the product's relative cost to the buyer. This axis is scaled from Low to High. If a product represents a high proportion of the buyer's spend, the Product Volume Purchased rating of the sale is High.

The four quadrants of the matrix are:

1. **Strategic Security.** This quadrant contains products for which the buyer has few alternatives. These products may be unique or specific to the customer's process but represent a low proportion of the buyer's spending. These products should be able to command a high price and the buyer should be relatively insensitive to price increases. The key task of the buyer is to ensure the security of his

business by guaranteeing a supply of these strategic products almost at any cost.

2. **Strategic Critical.** This quadrant contains products for which the buyer's spending is very high. Small changes in price will have a high impact on the buyer's overall spending. Therefore, the buyer will typically be more sensitive to price. The critical task of the buyer is to purchase these strategic products at minimal cost.

3. **Tactical Profit.** For products in this quadrant, the buyer has several options, as there are competitive products with similar characteristics available from alternative vendors. The product in this category represents a high proportion of the buyer's spending, so the buyer will make tactical purchasing decisions based on maximizing his profit. In marketing terms, products in this category are typical commodity products. There is little differentiation and high price sensitivity—hence, it will be very difficult to increase the price for these products. Any attempt to do so will encourage the buyer to purchase from a competitor and the business will be lost.

4. **Non Critical.** Products in this quadrant are commodity products that represent small-volume purchases for the buyer. There are many equivalent products available, and the products represent a small overall cost. Decisions regarding the purchase of these products will be based on criteria other than price, such as ease of doing business, lead time, and similar factors.

The buyer will typically expend effort in two areas of the matrix: the Strategic Security products and the Strategic Critical products. The buyer will be sensitive to price in two areas: Strategic Critical and Tactical Profit. The buyer's ultimate strategy is to move all of his products to the Tactical Profit quadrant, where he can play one supplier against another, or at least to make his suppliers *believe* that their products are in this quadrant!

As Jane emphasizes, this product categorization is based on the *use* of the product. A particular product may be Strategic Security for customer A because alternative products do not give the same consistency of performance in customer A's manufacturing process, whereas for customer B, that same product may be Non Critical, being one of several alternatives that can deliver the consistency that customer B requires.

As the team quickly realizes, this approach to thinking about price sensitivity is situational—it is quite different from simply setting a list price for each product, and will give Polymat's sales representatives greater insight into the price increase a specific transaction may bear. With the team's support, Jane holds a series of meetings with the appropriate sales and marketing personnel to apply their account knowledge in categorizing the transactions included in the baseline data set. When this work is completed, she is happy to see that all four types of sale are broadly represented in the baseline data.

Collecting Baseline Data

Now Jane and her team embark on the process of obtaining the historical data and verifying its integrity. Once this is done, they will compute some baseline measures.

Obtaining the Data

Recall that Jane has decided to study two periods during which 5 percent price increases were targeted. She has identified 20 products and, for each product, 12 customers representing various sizes and regional locations (3 customers per region). Each of these product and customer combinations had sales in each of two periods: oversupply and shortage. This results in 480 different product-by-customer-by-period combinations.

Having identified the data required, the corresponding invoice figures are directly downloaded from Polymat's data warehouse into a standard database. After entering the Product Categorization Matrix categories determined earlier, along with the sales representative experience and buyer sophistication rankings, Jane loads the data from the two ill-fated pricing interventions into JMP for further investigation. The raw data are given in the first ten columns in the 480-row data table **BaselinePricing.jmp** (Exhibit 5.4).

BaselinePricing

Left panel:
- BaselinePricing
- Distributions for All Variables
- Baseline Contingency
- Contingency for Defect (<=5%
- Oneway of % Price Increase
- Oneway with Comparison Circ
- Partition - No Splits
- Value Colors
- Partition - Eight Splits
- Model - % Price Increase
- Cause And Effect Diagram
- On Open

Columns (11/0):
- Product Code
- Region
- Customer ID
- Supply Demand Balance
- Sales Rep
- Sales Rep Experience
- Buyer Sophistication
- Product Category
- Annual Volume Purchased
- % Price Increase
- Defect (<=5%)+

Rows:
- All rows 480
- Selected 0
- Excluded 0
- Hidden 0
- Labelled 0

	Product Code	Region	Customer ID	Supply Demand Balance	Sales Rep	Sales Rep Experience	Buyer Sophistication
1	1	France	181	Oversupply	Didier	Medium	Medium
2	1	France	181	Shortage	Didier	Medium	Medium
3	1	France	201	Oversupply	Danielle	Medium	High
4	1	France	201	Shortage	Danielle	Medium	High
5	1	France	221	Oversupply	Marie	High	Medium
6	1	France	221	Shortage	Marie	High	Medium
7	1	Germany	121	Oversupply	Hans	Low	High
8	1	Germany	121	Shortage	Hans	Low	High
9	1	Germany	141	Oversupply	Michael	Low	Medium
10	1	Germany	141	Shortage	Michael	Low	Medium
11	1	Germany	161	Oversupply	Ernst	High	High
12	1	Germany	161	Shortage	Ernst	High	High
13	1	Italy	61	Oversupply	Marco	High	Low
14	1	Italy	61	Shortage	Marco	High	Low
15	1	Italy	81	Oversupply	Marina	Medium	Low
16	1	Italy	81	Shortage	Marina	Medium	Low
17	1	Italy	101	Oversupply	Angelo	Medium	Medium
18	1	Italy	101	Shortage	Angelo	Medium	Medium
19	1	UK	1	Oversupply	Martin	High	High
20	1	UK	1	Shortage	Martin	High	High
21	1	UK	21	Oversupply	Elizabeth	High	Low
22	1	UK	21	Shortage	Elizabeth	High	Low
23	1	UK	41	Oversupply	Lee	Low	High
24	1	UK	41	Shortage	Lee	Low	High
25	2	France	182	Oversupply	Didier	Medium	Medium
26	2	France	182	Shortage	Didier	Medium	Medium
27	2	France	202	Oversupply	Danielle	Medium	Medium
28	2	France	202	Shortage	Danielle	Medium	Medium

EXHIBIT 5.4   Partial View of Baseline Pricing Data Table

Jane is thinking more and more about the failure of a sale to achieve a 5 percent price increase as a defect; she has even heard some members of the management team refer to this failure as a *pricing defect*. She adds an eleventh column to the data that indicates whether the given sale has this defect. She calls this column **Defect (<=5%)**, and defines it using a formula, as indicated by the + sign next to the column name in the columns panel to the left of the data grid. Jane foresees using this column as an easy categorization of whether the price obtained for the given sale met the mandated increase. For her current purposes, Jane will consider any sale that exhibits a pricing defect to be defective.

The columns in the data table are described in Exhibit 5.5. Note that only the last two variables are Ys. The rest are Xs that Jane believes may be useful in her understanding of the resulting price increases. Jane assigns appropriate data modeling types to her variables: Most are nominal, but **Sales Rep Experience** and **Buyer Sophistication** are ordinal, while **Annual Volume Purchased** and **% Price Increase** are continuous.

EXHIBIT 5.5 Description of Columns in the Baseline Pricing Data Table

Column	Description
Product Code	Product identifier
Region	Region of facility making the purchase
Customer ID	Customer identifier
Supply Demand Balance	Prevailing market conditions when a price increase was made (Shortage or Oversupply)
Sales Rep	Name of sales representative
Sales Rep Experience	Sales representative's experience level
Buyer Sophistication	Customer's level of buying sophistication
Product Category	Category of product when sold to a particular customer
Annual Volume Purchased	Total amount spent by the customer for this product over the year in which the supply/demand balance period falls
% Price Increase	Percentage price increase defined as $100 \times$ (Price After – Price Before)/Price Before, where Price After = invoiced price after the price increase was implemented, and Price Before = invoiced price before the price increase was implemented
Defect (<=5%)	Categorization as a defect based on whether the % Price Increase is less than or equal to 5%

Verification of Data Integrity

Jane wants to perform a quick check to make sure that the data she has imported into JMP are what she expects. She also wants to check that the incidence of the categories in her nominal variables is large enough to allow useful analysis. For example, if only 2 percent of records were not defective, then the data would be of questionable value in helping to determine which Xs affect the response **Defect (<=5%)**. There would simply not be very many records with a nondefective outcome.

To take a quick look at her data, Jane obtains **Distribution** analyses for *all* of her columns. She selects **Analyze > Distribution** and enters all 11 of her variables as **Y, Columns** (see Exhibit 5.6).

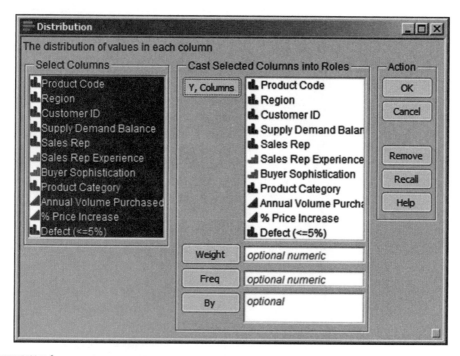

EXHIBIT 5.6   Distribution Dialog with All Variables Entered

When she clicks **OK**, Jane sees the reports partially shown in Exhibit 5.7. From the first four reports, she verifies that her 20 product codes, 4 regions, 240 customers, and 2 periods of supply/demand balance are represented in equal proportions. She looks at the remaining reports to learn that:

- **Sales Rep**: A reasonable number of sales representatives are represented.
- **Sales Rep Experience**: The experience levels of these sales representatives span the three categories, with reasonable representation in each.
- **Buyer Sophistication**: Buyers of various sophistication levels are represented in almost equal proportions.
- **Product Category**: Each of the four product categories is well-represented, with the smallest having a 17.5 percent representation.
- **Annual Volume Purchased**: The distribution of volume purchased for these products is consistent with what Jane expected.
- **% Price Increase**: This shows a slightly right-skewed distribution, which is to be expected—Jane will analyze this Y further once she finishes her verification.
- **Defect (<=5%)**: This shows that about 72 percent of all records are defects according to the 5 percent cut-off and that 28 percent are not. The representation in the two groupings is adequate to allow further analysis.

Just in passing, Jane notices that JMP does something very nice in terms of ordering the categories for nominal variables. The default is for JMP to list these in alphabetical order in plots; for example, the **Sales Rep** names are listed in reverse alphabetical order in the plot and in direct order in the frequency table in Exhibit 5.7.

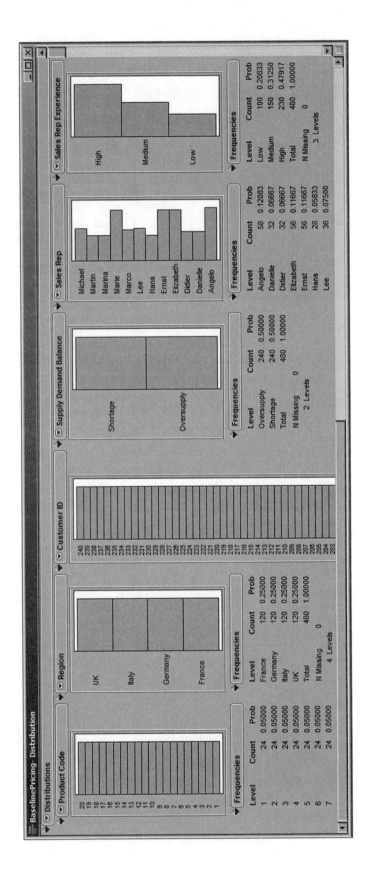

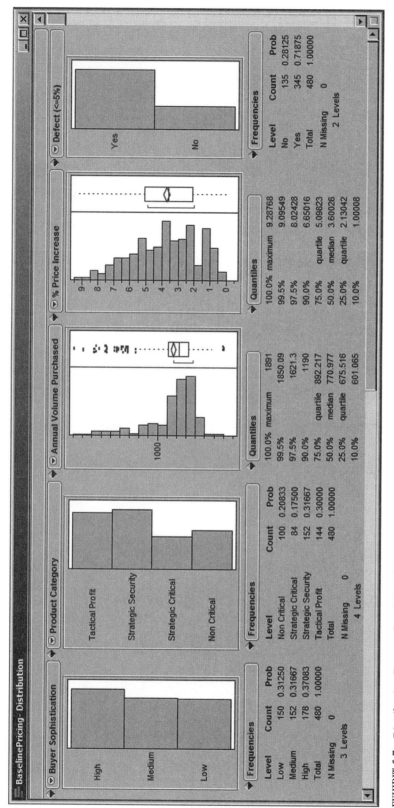

EXHIBIT 5.7 Distribution Reports for all Variables

117

But, JMP uses some intelligence in ordering the categories of **Sales Rep Experience** and **Buyer Sophistication**. Both have Low, Medium, and High categories, which JMP places in their context-based order, rather than alphabetical order.

Because Jane wants to document her work and be able to reproduce it easily later on, she saves the script that created this report to her data table as **Distributions for All Variables**. She will save scripts for most of her analyses because this allows her to recreate her analyses easily. However, we emphasize that when you are working on your own projects you need not save scripts unless you want to document or easily reproduce your work.

Satisfied that her data are consistent with her intended design and that the distributions of the nondesigned variables make sense and provide reasonable representation in the categories of interest, Jane initiates her baseline analysis.

Baseline Analysis

The purpose of Jane's baseline analysis is to understand the capability of the current pricing management process under the two different market conditions of Oversupply and Shortage. She has already seen (Exhibit 5.7) that the overall defect rate is about 0.72. An easy way to break this down by the two **Supply Demand Balance** conditions is to construct a mosaic plot and contingency table.

Jane selects **Analyze > Fit Y by X**, and populates the dialog as shown in Exhibit 5.8. She thinks of **Defect (<=5%)** as the response (Y) and **Supply Demand Balance** as

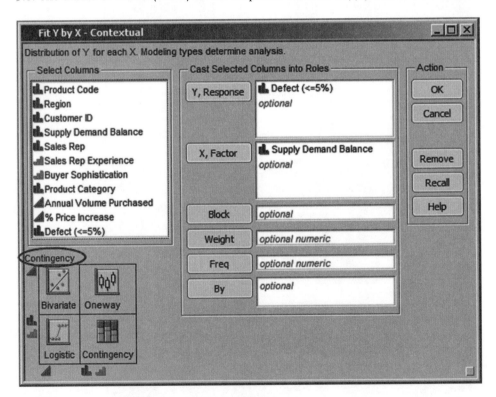

EXHIBIT 5.8   Fit Y by X Dialog for Defect (<=5%)

an X that might explain some of the variation in Y. The schematic in the lower left area of the dialog indicates that because both X and Y are nominal, the resulting report will be a **Contingency** analysis.

When she clicks **OK**, Jane sees the report shown in Exhibit 5.9 (note that she has closed the disclosure icon for **Tests**). She sees immediately that the percentage of defective sales is much larger in periods of Oversupply than in periods of Shortage, as represented by the areas in the **Mosaic Plot** (these appear blue on a computer screen).

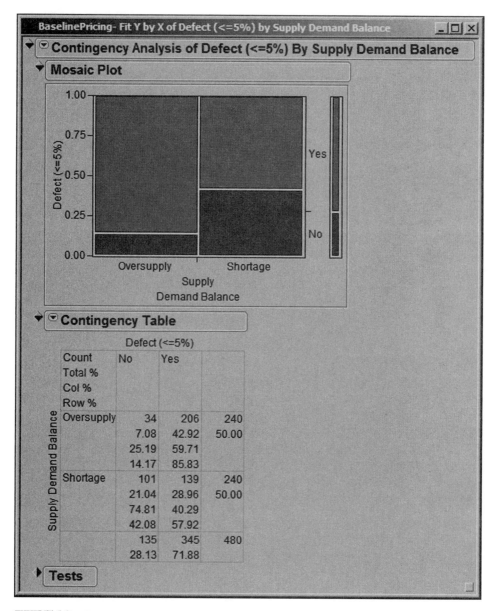

EXHIBIT 5.9   Contingency Report for Defect (<=5%)

The **Contingency Table** below the plot gives the **Count** of records in each of the classifications as well as the **Row %**. Jane sees that in periods of Oversupply about 86 percent (specifically, 85.83 percent) of the sales in her data table are defective, while in periods of Shortage, about 58 percent (specifically, 57.92 percent) are defective. Jane saves this script as **Baseline Contingency**.

This finding makes sense. However, if Jane relates what she sees to the expectation of Polymat's leadership team she starts to understand some of Bill Roberts's frustrations. Even in times of Shortage, when the account managers are in a strong negotiating position, Polymat suffers a high pricing defect rate—an estimated 58 percent of the sales are defective due to being negotiated so as to have an increase below the 5 percent target.

To assess baseline behavior in terms of the continuous Y, % Price Increase, Jane first refers back to the **Distribution** report that she constructed earlier. She clicks the red triangle next to % Price Increase, and from the menu that appears chooses **Display Options > Horizontal Layout**. This gives the layout shown in Exhibit 5.10. Jane sees that the mean % Price Increase is about 3.7 percent and that the percentage increases vary quite a bit, from 0 percent to about 9.3 percent.

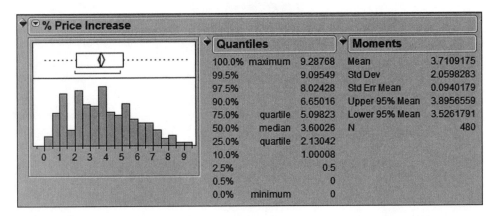

EXHIBIT 5.10   Distribution Report for % Price Increase

What about the breakdown by Supply Demand Balance? Jane selects **Distribution** from the **Analyze** menu. In the dialog box, she enters % Price Increase as **Y, Response** and enters Supply Demand Balance as a **By** variable. She clicks **OK**. In the resulting report, she selects **Stack** from the menu obtained by clicking the red triangle next to **Distributions Supply Demand Balance = Oversupply**. She obtains the report shown in Exhibit 5.11.

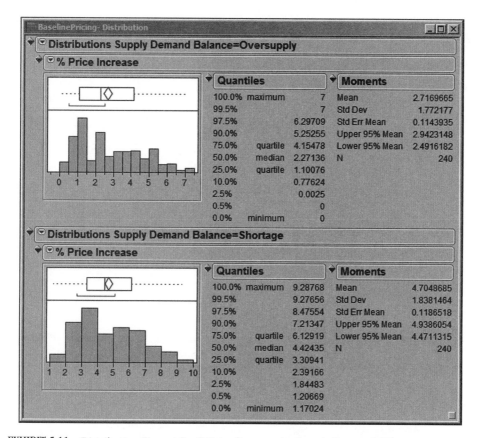

EXHIBIT 5.11   Distribution Report for % Price Increase by Supply Demand Balance

In periods of Oversupply, the report shows that the mean **% Price Increase** is about 2.7 percent, while in periods of Shortage it is 4.7 percent. Both means are below the desired 5 percent increase, with a much lower mean during periods of Oversupply, as one might expect.

Yet, for Jane this is an exciting initial finding! There is a high potential for improvement if the business can increase prices when market conditions are advantageous. Jane immediately uses her baseline analysis to entice Polymat's senior staff to increase their commitment to the project. Recognizing the power of appropriate language to change behavior, Jane also starts to reinforce the concept of a *pricing defect* within the leadership team. She is pleasantly surprised by how quickly Bill starts to use this language to drive a new way of thinking.

Uncovering Relationships

Jane is excited about moving on to the task of identifying Hot Xs. But first, she takes a little time to think through how she will structure the analysis of her data. She thinks back to the Visual Six Sigma Data Analysis Process (Exhibit 3.29) and observes that she is now at the Uncover Relationships step, which, if necessary, is followed by the Model Relationships step. Referring to the Visual Six Sigma Roadmap (Exhibit 3.30), she decides that she will:

- Use **Distribution** and dynamic visualization to better understand potential relationships among her variables.
- Plot her variables two at a time to determine if any of the Xs might have an effect on the Ys.
- Use multivariate visualization techniques to explore higher-dimensional relationships among the variables.

If Jane finds evidence of relationships using these exploratory techniques, and if she can corroborate this evidence with contextual knowledge, she could stop her analysis here. She would then proceed directly to proposing and verifying improvement actions as part of the Revise Knowledge step. This presumes that she can substantiate that her findings are indicative of real phenomena. However, since her data set is not very large, Jane decides that for good measure she will follow up with the Model Relationships step to try to confirm the hypotheses that she obtains from data exploration.

Dynamic Visualization of Variables Using Distribution

She begins to explore which Xs might be influencing the Ys by obtaining **Distribution** reports for all of her variables, as she did when she was verifying her data. Since she saved her script at that time, calling it **Distributions for All Variables**, she simply locates it in the table panel, clicks on the red triangle next to it, and selects **Run Script** from the list of options (Exhibit 5.12).

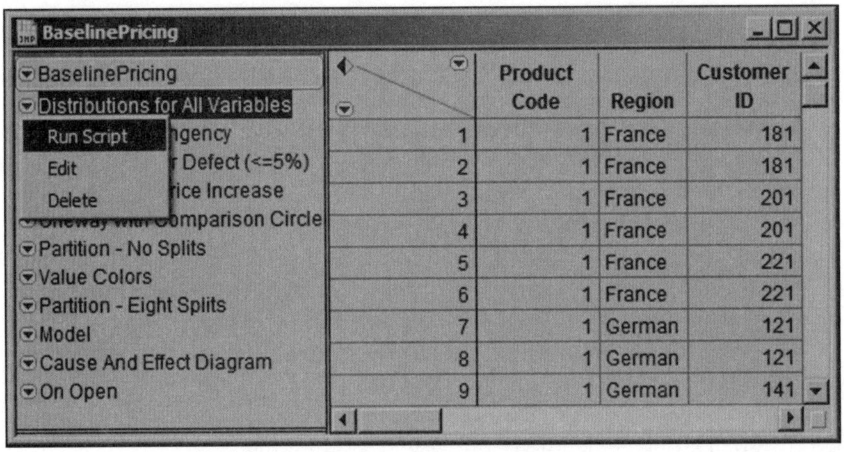

EXHIBIT 5.12   Running the Script Distributions for All Variables

Jane now starts to use dynamic linking in the **Distribution** platform to identify the Xs that influence the success or the lack of success of the two historical price increases under investigation. In the **Distribution** plot for Defect (<=5%), she clicks in the No bar (see Exhibit 5.13). This has the effect of selecting all those rows in the data table where Defect (<=5%) has the value No. In turn, this highlights the areas that represent these rows in all of the other **Distribution** plots. (Note that the plot for Customer ID is only partially shown in Exhibit 5.13, as it involves 240 bars.)

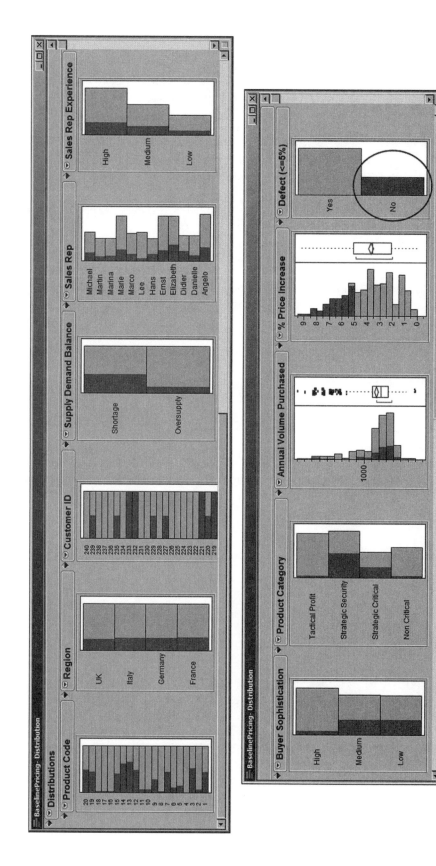

EXHIBIT 5.13   Highlighted Portions of Distributions Linked to Defect ($<=$5%) = No

123

Toggling between the Yes and No bars for **Defect (<=5%)** quickly shows Jane that **Supply Demand Balance**, **Buyer Sophistication**, and **Product Category** have different distributions, based on whether **Defect (<=5%)** is Yes or No. It also appears that **Defect (<=5%)** may be related to **Product Code** and **Customer ID**. This raises the question of how, in terms of root causes, these last two variables might affect pricing defects. Jane believes that the causal link is probably captured by how the customer views the product, namely, by the **Product Category** as assigned using the Product Categorization Matrix.

Interacting with the **Defect (<=5%)** bar chart in this way also shows Jane that price increase has little or no association with:

- **Region.** Whether a price increase is a defect does not appear to depend on region.
- **Sales Rep.** There is some variation in how sales representatives perform, but there is no indication that some are strikingly better than others at achieving the target price increases.
- **Sales Rep Experience.** Interestingly, the highly experienced account managers appear to be no more effective in increasing the price than those who are less experienced. (This is much to everyone's surprise.)
- **Annual Volume Purchased.** Sales representatives appear to be no better at raising prices with small customers than with large customers.

Jane wants to see the impact of **Product Category** on pricing defects. She first clears the selected bar in the bar graph for **Defect (<=5%)** by holding the control key while she clicks in the bar. Then she highlights *Strategic Security* and *Strategic Critical* in the **Distribution** report by clicking on these two bars in the **Product Category** plot while holding down the shift key. The impact on **Defect (<=5%)** is shown in Exhibit 5.14.

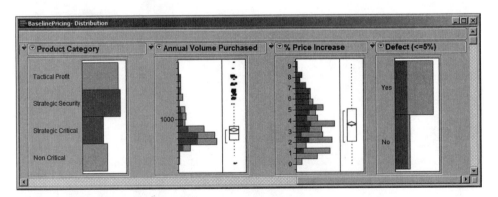

EXHIBIT 5.14   Impact of Strategic Product Categories on Defect (<=5%)

Note that almost all of the sales that met the price increase target, namely, where **Defect (<=5%)** has the value No, come from these two categories. Alternatively, clicking on the No bar in the **Defect (<=5%)** graph shows that almost all of these sales are either Strategic Security or Strategic Critical. This supports Jane's belief that **Product Category** captures the effect of **Product Code** and **Customer ID**.

However, the most interesting X appears to be **Buyer Sophistication**. Jane selects High values of this variable by clicking on the appropriate **Distribution** plot bar; after examining the remaining plots, she clicks on the Medium and Low values. With highly sophisticated buyers, the proportion of pricing defects is much higher than for buyers who have Medium or Low sophistication. Jane concludes that these buyers use highly effective price negotiations to keep prices low (Exhibit 5.15).

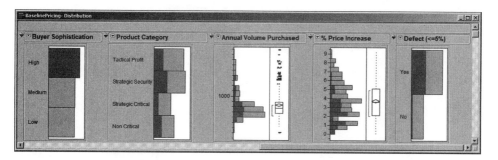

EXHIBIT 5.15   Impact of High Buyer Sophistication on Defect (<=5%)

To date, her exploratory analysis leaves Jane suspecting that the main Xs of interest are **Supply Demand Balance**, **Buyer Sophistication**, and **Product Category**. Although Jane has simply run **Distribution** analyses for her variables, she has used dynamic linking to study her variables two at a time by viewing the highlighted or conditional distributions. In the next section, Jane uses **Fit Y by X** to view her data two variables at a time.

Dynamic Visualization of Variables Two at a Time

The **Fit Y by X** platform, found under **Analyze**, provides reports that help identify relationships between pairs of variables. To get a better look at how Supply Demand Balance, Buyer Sophistication, and Product Category are related to Defect (<=5%), Jane selects **Analyze > Fit Y by X**. In the launch dialog, she enters Defect (<=5%) as **Y, Response** and Supply Demand Balance, Buyer Sophistication, and Product Category as **X, Factor** (Exhibit 5.16). Since two of her Xs are nominal and one is ordinal, while her Y is nominal, she sees from the small schematic in the bottom left of the launch dialog that JMP will provide a **Contingency** analysis for each pair of variables.

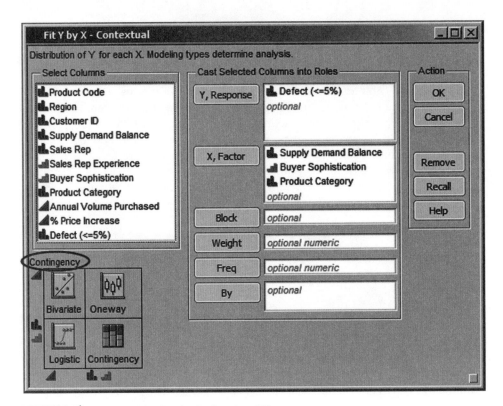

EXHIBIT 5.16   Fit Y by X Dialog for Defect (<=5%)

When she clicks **OK**, mosaic plots and contingency tables appear. The contingency tables that are shown by default include **Total %** and **Col %**, but Jane is only interested in **Count** and **Row %**. Jane would like to remove **Total %** and **Col %** from all three analyses. She also would prefer not to have to go through the keystrokes to do this individually for all three reports. Rather, she would like to run through the keystrokes once and have the commands *broadcast* to all three analyses. She knows that JMP makes this easy: One simply holds down the control key while selecting the desired menu options; this sends those choices to all other similar objects in the report.

So, holding down the control key to broadcast her changes to the other two contingency tables, Jane clicks on the red triangle next to the **Contingency Table** heading in one of the reports. Then, she unchecks **Total %**. She repeats this, unchecking **Col %**. Her output now appears as shown in Exhibit 5.17. (The script is called **Contingency for Defect (<=5%)**.)

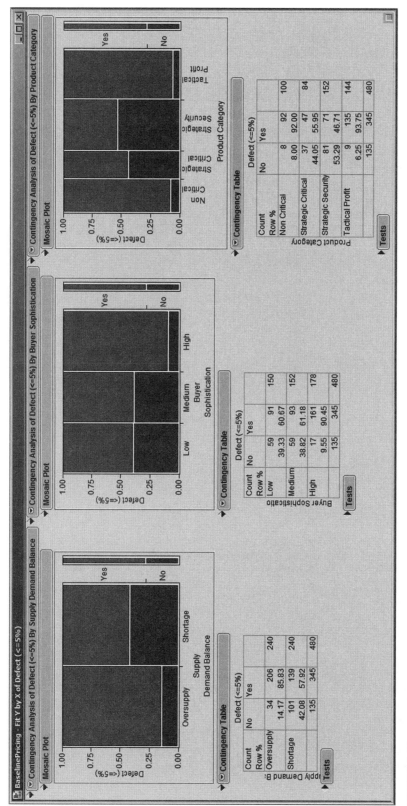

EXHIBIT 5.17   Three Contingency Reports for Defect (<=5%)

The plots and contingency tables show:

- **Supply Demand Balance.** Not surprisingly, there are fewer defective sales in periods of Shortage than in periods of Oversupply (58 percent versus 86 percent, respectively).
- **Buyer Sophistication.** There are more defective sales when dealing with highly sophisticated buyers (90 percent) than when dealing with medium or low sophistication buyers (about 61 percent for each group). In fact, there appears to be little difference between low and medium sophistication buyers relative to defective sales, although other variables might differentiate these categories.
- **Product Category.** This has a striking impact on defective sales. The defect rates for Strategic Critical and Strategic Security are 56 percent and 47 percent, respectively, compared to Non Critical and Tactical Profit, with defect rates of 92 percent and 94 percent, respectively.

This analysis is conducted with the nominal response, **Defect (<=5%)**. Will these results carry through for the continuous response, **% Price Increase**?

Jane proceeds to see how **Supply Demand Balance**, **Buyer Sophistication**, and **Product Category** are related to **% Price Increase**. She realizes that the variable **Defect (<=5%)** is simply a coarsened version of this continuous variable. As she did with **Defect (<=5%)**, Jane uses the **Fit Y By X** platform to look at **% Price Increase** as a function of each of these three potential Hot Xs.

She selects **Analyze > Fit Y by X** and, in the resulting dialog, assigns column roles as shown in Exhibit 5.18. Now the schematic at the bottom left of the launch window indicates that the analysis will be **Oneway**.

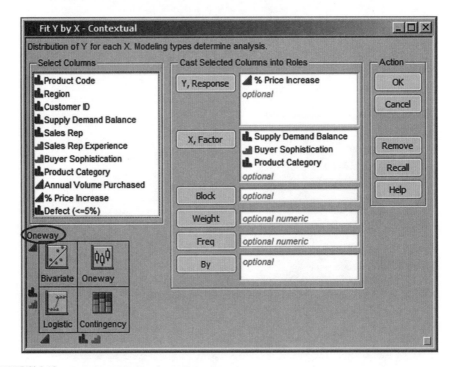

EXHIBIT 5.18   Fit Y by X Dialog for % Price Increase

The resulting report, shown in Exhibit 5.19, consists of three **Oneway** displays. Each of these displays has a red triangle drop-down menu, allowing the user to choose different options for each.

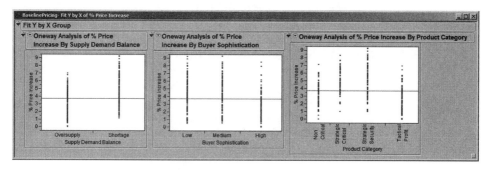

EXHIBIT 5.19 Three Oneway Reports for % Price Increase

The points in the plots seem to overwrite each other and Jane would like the plots to show the points individually without overlap. To do this, Jane holds down the control key (to broadcast her next command), clicks on one of the red triangles, and chooses **Display Options > Points Jittered**. This jitters the points nicely (Exhibit 5.20). Jane saves this script as **Oneway of % Price Increase**.

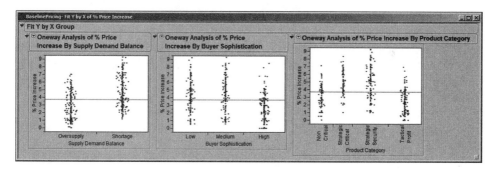

EXHIBIT 5.20 Three Oneway Reports for % Price Increase with Points Jittered

This is nice, and gives Jane a better idea of the distributions across the levels of each variable. But Jane would like a statistical guide to determine which levels differ. She knows that **Compare Means**, obtained from the red triangle menu, provides a visual representation of a statistical test for significant differences among the levels of the Xs.

When you choose **Compare Means** you will notice four options. Those most often used are **Each Pair, Student's t** and **All Pairs, Tukey HSD**. The difference between these two procedures is that the **Each Pair** option controls the risk of incorrectly concluding that two specific groups differ, while the **All Pairs** option controls this risk for all possible comparisons of two groups. The default level for both risks is 5 percent. The **All Pairs, Tukey HSD** option is the more conservative, and for this reason, Jane chooses to use this option. (We would encourage you to use the **All Pairs, Tukey HSD** option in general, unless you have good reason not to.)

Yet again, Jane would prefer not to make her next selections individually for each of the three predictors, so, as before, she broadcasts her commands. She holds down the control key, clicks on any one of the red triangles, and chooses **Compare Means > All Pairs, Tukey HSD**. To see the means on the plots, Jane also makes another choice: Again holding the control key while clicking a red triangle, she selects **Display Options > Means Diamonds**. She would also like calculated values for the means. Holding the control key, she clicks a red triangle and selects **Means and Std Dev**. (The script is saved as **Oneway with Comparison Circles**.)

The resulting report (Exhibit 5.21) shows the plots with *means diamonds* overlaid on the jittered points. The central horizontal line in each of these diamonds is plotted at the level of the sample mean for **% Price Increase** for that category. The top and bottom of each diamond defines a 95 percent confidence interval for the true category mean. Looking at these, Jane realizes that there are probably a number of statistically significant differences. For each variable, a table of means and standard deviations for each grouping is given below the plot.

The plot in Exhibit 5.21 also shows a new area to the right of the points containing *comparison circles*. These circles are a graphical way to test for differences in the means of the levels of each predictor. For example, take **Product Category**, which has four levels. There is one circle corresponding to each level. The top two circles in the plot in Exhibit 5.21 correspond to the levels Strategic Critical and Strategic Security.

Jane clicks on the circle corresponding to Strategic Critical. This causes the labels below the jittered points to change appearance. Now the label for Strategic Critical is in boldface type and, on her computer screen, it is red, while the circle for Strategic Security appears red on her screen, but is not bolded. Since both circles are red, this means that the mean **% Price Increase** does not differ significantly for these two levels. However, the circles for Non Critical and Tactical Profit are gray. This means that the mean **% Price Increase** for each of these two categories differs significantly from the mean **% Price Increase** for Strategic Critical, the bolded category.

In the grayscale plot shown in Exhibit 5.21, you will notice that the label for Strategic Critical is in boldface text, while the label for Strategic Security is not bolded. This indicates that these two groups do not differ statistically. The other two labels, Non Critical and Tactical Profit, are in non-boldface, italicized text, indicating that these two do differ statistically from Strategic Critical.

Jane remembers a very important point from her training. Some students incorrectly assumed that groups were statistically significantly different if and only if their circles did not overlap. It is true that groups with nonoverlapping circles differ statistically. However, she learned that, in fact, groups with overlapping circles can also differ significantly (on screen, when one is selected, they will have different colors).

To illustrate, in the **Product Category** plot, Jane clicks on the lowest circle, which corresponds to Tactical Profit. The Tactical Profit circle does overlap with the Non Critical circle. Yet, on the screen, the Tactical Profit circle is bold red and the Non Critical circle is gray, indicating that the categories differ statistically.

Exhibit 5.21 also shows Oversupply selected for **Supply Demand Balance**. The circles do not overlap, indicating that the two groupings, Oversupply and Shortage,

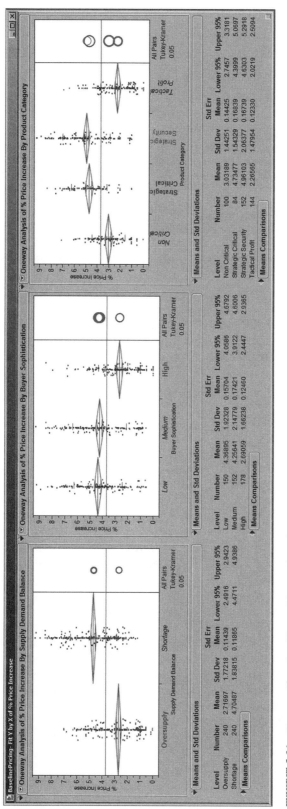

EXHIBIT 5.21 Reports Showing Means Diamonds and Comparison Circles

131

differ statistically in their effect on **% Price Increase**. For **Buyer Sophistication**, High sophistication buyers are selected. They differ statistically in their effect on **% Price Increase** from Medium and Low sophistication buyers. By clicking on the circle for Medium sophistication buyers, Jane sees that the Medium and Low sophistication groups do not differ statistically.

Continuing her analysis, Jane clicks on circles corresponding to other levels of variables in Exhibit 5.21 one by one to see which differ relative to **% Price Increase**. Recalling that two categories differ with statistical significance only if, when she clicks on one of the circles, the other changes to gray, she concludes that:

- The mean **% Price Increase** differs significantly based on the **Supply Demand Balance**, with higher increases in periods of Shortage.
- The mean **% Price Increase** for High **Buyer Sophistication** is significantly lower than for Medium or Low sophistication levels, while these last two do not differ significantly.
- The means of **% Price Increase** for the Strategic Critical and Strategic Security **Product Category** levels are each significantly higher than for the Non Critical and Tactical Profit levels, although the means for Strategic Critical and Strategic Security do not differ significantly.
- The mean **% Price Increase** for Non Critical products is significantly higher than for Tactical Profit products.

The **Means Comparisons** reports, whose blue disclosure icons are closed in Exhibit 5.21, are analytic reports containing the results that give rise to the comparison circles. For exploratory purposes, Jane knows that it suffices to examine the comparison circles.

Jane realizes that she has identified which levels differ with *statistical* significance. *Practical* importance is quite another matter. In the report (Exhibit 5.21), she studies the actual means and their confidence intervals. For example, relative to **Buyer Sophistication**, she notes that High sophistication buyers had mean **% Price Increase** values of about 2.7 percent, with a confidence interval for the true mean ranging from about 2.4 to 2.9 percent (**Lower 95%** and **Upper 95%** refer to the confidence interval limits). For less sophisticated buyers, these increases are much higher—about 4.3 percent for Medium and 4.4 percent for Low sophistication levels.

In a similar fashion, Jane studies the other Xs. Then, in her usual tidy way, she saves this script to the data table, calling it **Oneway with Comparison Circles**.

This exploratory **Fit Y by X** analysis has provided Jane with evidence that there are differences in **% Price Increase** based on a number of levels of these three Xs. Given this evidence, Jane is comfortable thinking of **Supply Demand Balance**, **Buyer Sophistication**, and **Product Category** as Hot Xs for the continuous Y, **% Price Increase**. Of course, she will need to verify that these are indeed Hot Xs. She realizes that there may well be interactions among the potential Xs and that these will not be evident without a multivariate analysis. To that end, she now proceeds to an exploration of multivariate relationships among these variables.

Dynamic Visualization of Several Variables at a Time

THE INITIAL PARTITION REPORT   As mentioned, Jane realizes that the **Fit Y by X** analysis she has just undertaken only looks at one X at a time in relation to her Ys. This means that her conclusions to date may overlook multidimensional relationships among the Xs and Ys. She has both a nominal Y, **Defect (<=5%)**, and a continuous Y, **% Price Increase**. She could explore **Defect (<=5%)** using logistic regression or a partition analysis. Because of its ease of interpretation and the fact that she has several nominal Xs, some of which have many levels, she decides to use the **Partition** platform.

Jane understands that she will use partition as an exploratory method. There are no hypothesis tests that allow statistical validation of results. For confirmation of conclusions from a partition analysis, she will have to rely on contextual knowledge of the process and validation based on future data. (Note that later on, to study **% Price Increase**, Jane will use a multiple linear regression model, using **Fit Model**. This will provide a confirmatory analysis and bring new results to light.)

To obtain a partition analysis of **Defect (<=5%)**, Jane selects **Analyze > Modeling > Partition**. She enters **Defect (<=5%)** as **Y, Response**. Thinking about her Xs, she decides to enter all nine of them. This is her chance to find multivariate relationships, and there is no reason to miss any of these. So, she assigns the column roles shown in Exhibit 5.22.

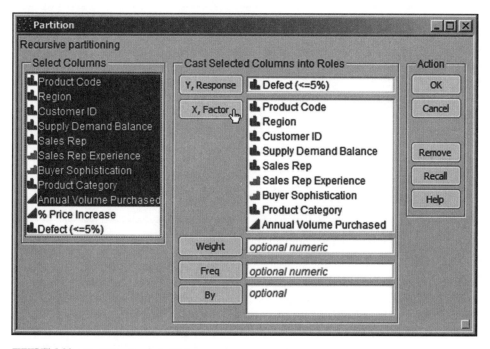

EXHIBIT 5.22   Partition Launch Dialog

Clicking **OK** provides an initial partition report. In order to display the proportion of defective sales versus nondefective sales shown in the single node in the report in Exhibit 5.23, Jane has chosen **Display Options > Show Split Prob** from the drop-down menu obtained by clicking the red triangle at the top of the report. This allows Jane to see the levels of Defect (<=5%) as well as the **Prob**, or proportion, of sales falling in each group (shown in Exhibit 5.23).

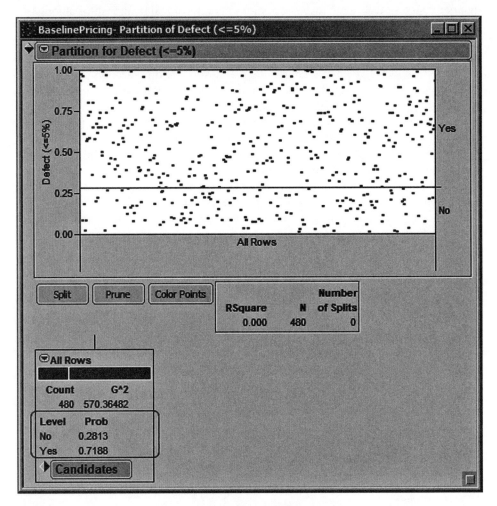

EXHIBIT 5.23   Initial Partition Report with Split Probabilities

APPLYING COLORS   Knowing that color always makes displays easier to understand, Jane clicks on **Color Points**, located under the plot and to the right of the **Split** and **Prune** buttons. This has the effect of assigning the color blue to all points associated with a pricing defect (Yes) and the color red to points where there is no pricing defect (No). Jane also sees that by choosing this coloring option the colors are displayed next to each row number in the data table (Exhibit 5.24). (You may want to work through this specific analysis on your computer in order to see the colors.)

Product Code	Region	Customer ID	Supply Demand Balance	Sales Rep	Sales Rep Experience
1	1 France	181	Oversupply	Didier	Medium
2	1 France	181	Shortage	Didier	Medium
3	1 France	201	Oversupply	Danielle	Medium
4	1 France	201	Shortage	Danielle	Medium
5	1 France	221	Oversupply	Marie	High
6	1 France	221	Shortage	Marie	High
7	1 German	121	Oversupply	Hans	Low
8	1 German	121	Shortage	Hans	Low
9	1 German	141	Oversupply	Michael	Low
10	1 German	141	Shortage	Michael	Low
11	1 German	161	Oversupply	Ernst	High
12	1 German	161	Shortage	Ernst	High
13	1 Italy	61	Oversupply	Marco	High
14	1 Italy	61	Shortage	Marco	High
15	1 Italy	81	Oversupply	Marina	Medium
16	1 Italy	81	Shortage	Marina	Medium
17	1 Italy	101	Oversupply	Angelo	Medium
18	1 Italy	101	Shortage	Angelo	Medium
19	1 UK	1	Oversupply	Martin	High
20	1 UK	1	Shortage	Martin	High

EXHIBIT 5.24   Partial View of Data Table with Color Markers

"But wait a minute," Jane thinks. "This coloring sends the wrong message: Points where there are *no* defects are colored red (a color associated with danger), while the points where there *are* defects are colored blue." Jane thinks it might be good, for the purpose of presenting her results, if the points corresponding to no defects were colored green and those corresponding to defects were colored red.

To make this happen, Jane needs to define a *column property*, namely a property associated with a column or variable. She saves the script for her initial partition report to the data table, calling it **Partition – No Splits**, since she knows that she will want to rerun this report with the new colors. She closes her partition analysis. In the **Rows** menu, she selects **Clear Row States** to remove the blue and red color assignment.

Now she proceeds to assign a *value colors* property to the column Defect (<=5%). She right-clicks on Defect (<=5%) in the columns panel of **BaselinePricing.jmp**. (Alternatively, she could right-click in the column header.) She selects **Column Info**, and under **Column Properties** chooses **Value Colors** (see Exhibit 5.25). The colors that appear for the two values, No and Yes, are the colors that were assigned in the partition analysis (red and blue, respectively).

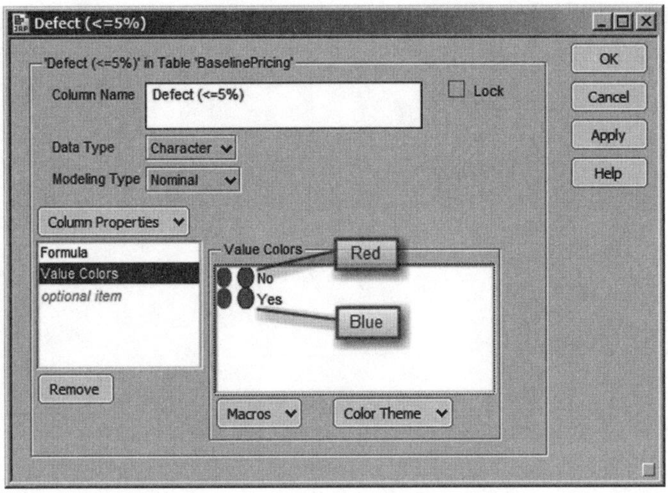

EXHIBIT 5.25 Value Colors for Defect (<=5%)

To change the color for No, Jane clicks on the red-filled ellipse next to No and chooses a bright green color from the palette that appears (see Exhibit 5.26). She repeats this process for Yes, choosing a bright red color for sales that are defective. Then she closes the dialog window by clicking **OK**. (The script **Value Colors** will create this column property.)

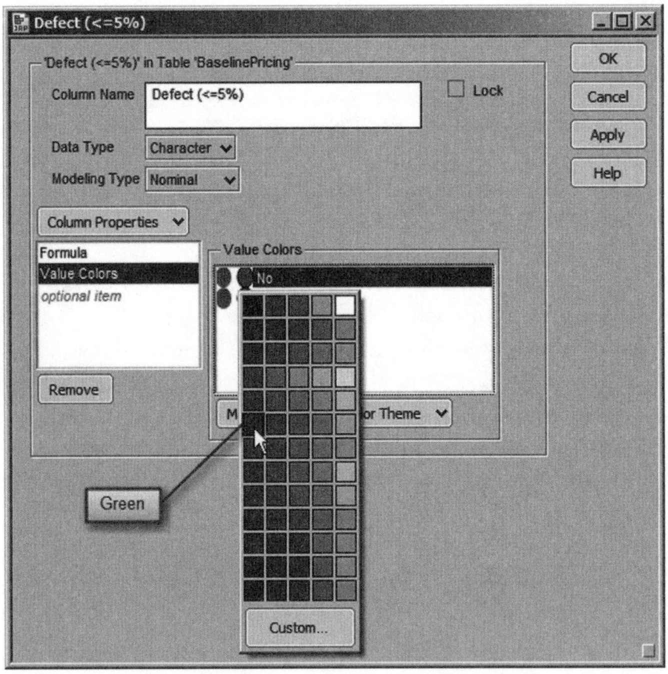

EXHIBIT 5.26 Changing the Color Assigned to No from Red to Green

Now, Jane runs the script **Partition – No Splits**. Although the bars in the node are now an informative green and red, the points in the plot are black, so she clicks on **Color Points** to apply the new coloring. She checks that points are colored as she wanted, red for defective sales (Yes) and green for nondefective sales (No). She also sees that the coloring for the points has been applied in the data table.

SPLITTING   At this point, Jane is ready to start *splitting* her data into groups or *nodes* that differentiate between defective and nondefective sales. At each split step, the partition algorithm finds the variable that best explains the difference between the two levels of **Defect (<=5%)**. The two groupings of values that best explain this difference are added as nodes to the diagram, so that repeated splits of the data produce a tree-like structure.

Jane realizes that she can split as many times as she likes, with the only built-in constraint being the *minimum size split*. This is the size of the smallest split grouping that is allowed. To see where this is set by default, Jane clicks on the red triangle at the top of the report and selects **Minimum Size Split**. The dialog window that appears indicates that the minimum size is set at 5. With 480 records, Jane thinks this might be small. It could allow for modeling noise, rather than structure. Jane thinks about this for a while and decides to specify a minimum size of 25 for her splits in order to help ensure that her analysis reveals true structure, rather than just the vagaries of this specific data set. So, she enters 25 as the **Minimum Size Split**, as shown in Exhibit 5.27, and clicks **OK**.

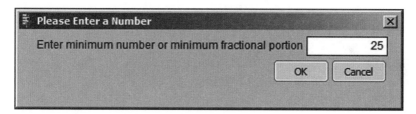

EXHIBIT 5.27   Setting the Minimum Size Split

Finally, she is ready to begin splitting. She clicks once on the **Split** button, obtaining the report in Exhibit 5.28. To her dismay, the first split is on the variable **Customer ID**. She sees that for a large group of customers all sales are defective, while for the other group of customers only about 33 percent of sales are defective. But this does not help her understand the root causes of why defects occur. She regrets having included **Customer ID** as a predictor.

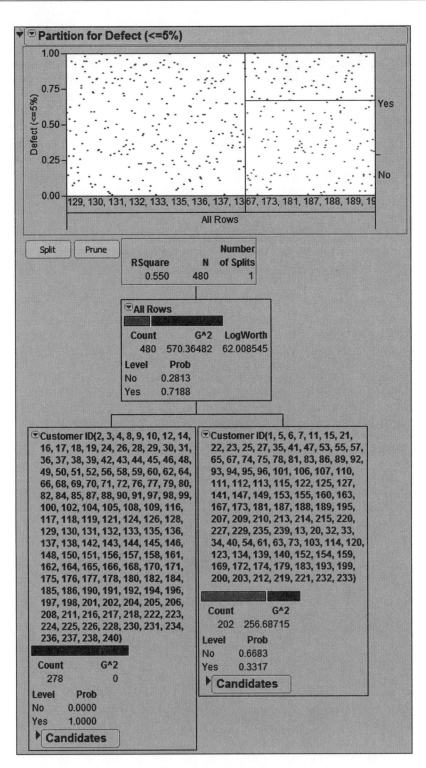

EXHIBIT 5.28   Partition with One Split on Customer ID

Ah, but she does not need to start her analysis over, although it would be very easy for her to do so. Instead, Jane clicks on the top red triangle and selects **Lock Columns** (Exhibit 5.29). As the menu tip points out, this will allow Jane to lock the Customer ID column out of her analysis.

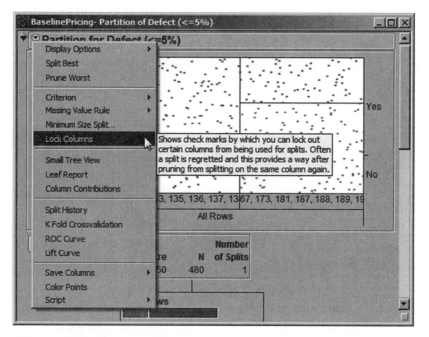

EXHIBIT 5.29   Selecting Lock Columns

Selecting **Lock Columns** inserts a list of the Xs to the right of the plot. In this list, Jane checks Customer ID. She then clicks on the **Prune** button to remove the split on Customer ID from the report (Exhibit 5.30).

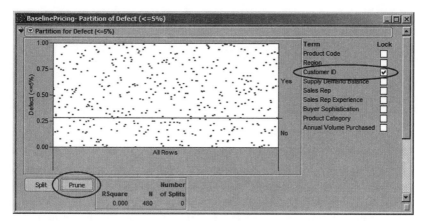

EXHIBIT 5.30   Locking Out Customer ID

She is ready to split once more. Clicking **Split** once provides a split on **Product Category** (Exhibit 5.31). Jane sees that the two categories Tactical Profit and Non Critical result in a 93 percent defective rate (node on the left). The Strategic Critical and Strategic Security categories have a 50 percent defective rate (node on the right). These proportions are reflected in the plot above the tree. Jane hopes that further splits will help explain more of the variation left unexplained, especially by the node on the right.

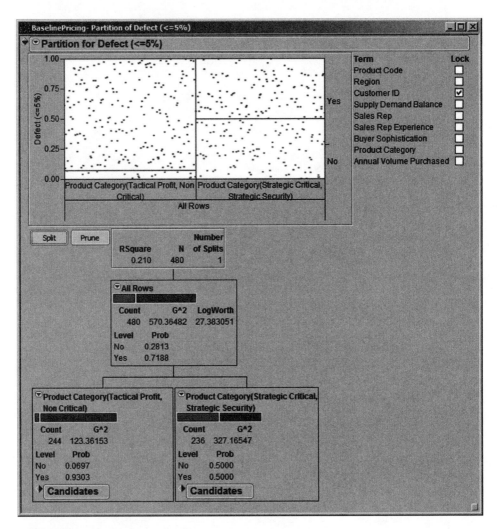

EXHIBIT 5.31   **Partition with First Split on Product Category**

A second split brings **Buyer Sophistication** into play (Exhibit 5.32). Jane sees that for the Strategic Critical and Strategic Security product categories, High sophistication buyers are associated with an 82 percent rate of defective sales, while Medium and Low sophistication buyers are associated with a 30 percent rate. This is fantastic information, reinforcing the notion that for high-profile product categories Polymat's sales representatives need to be better equipped to deal with highly sophisticated buyers.

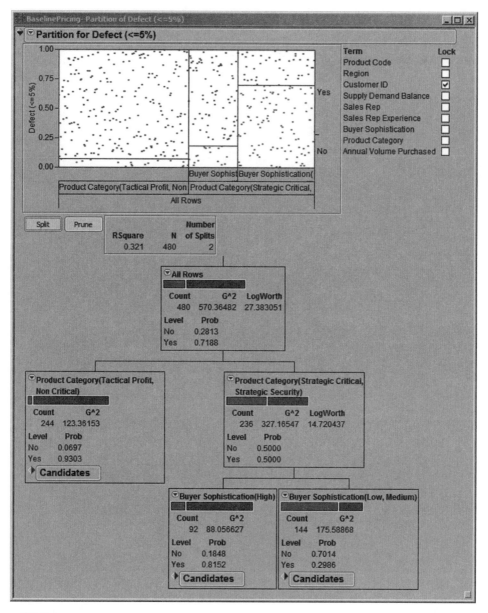

EXHIBIT 5.32   Partition with Two Splits

At this point, Jane decides to split until the stopping rule, a minimum size node of 25, ends the splitting process. She clicks on **Split** and keeps an eye on the **Number of Splits** in the information panel to the right of the **Split** and **Prune** buttons. As a result of the specified minimum size split, splitting stops after nine splits.

At this point, the tree is so big that it no longer fits on Jane's screen. She has to navigate to various parts of it to see what is going on. After a while, she checks the top red triangle menu and selects **Small Tree View**. A small tree (Exhibit 5.33) appears to the right of the plot and lock columns list. This small tree allows Jane to see the columns where splits have occurred, but it does not give the node detail. However, with the exception of Region at the bottom right, the splits are on the three variables that Jane has been thinking of as her Hot Xs.

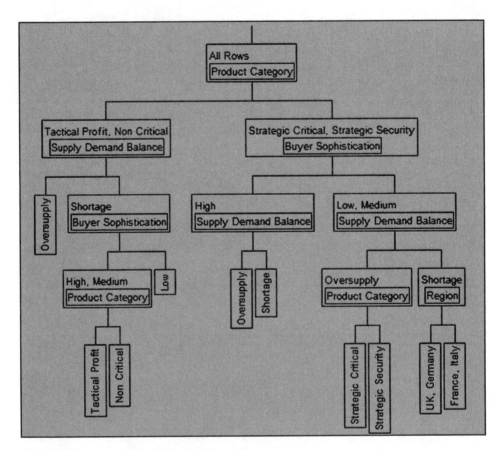

EXHIBIT 5.33   Small Tree View after Nine Splits

To better understand the split on **Region**, Jane navigates to that split in her large tree. It is at the bottom, all the way to the right (see Exhibit 5.34). The split on Region is a split of the 72 records that fall into the **Supply Demand Balance(Shortage)** node at this point in the tree (note that there are three splits on Supply Demand Balance). The **Supply Demand Balance(Shortage)** node contains relatively few records (2.78 percent) reflecting defective sales. The further split into the two groupings of regions attempts to explain the Yes values, using the fact that there are no defective sales in France or Italy at that point in the tree. But the proportions of Yes values in the two nodes are not very different (0.06 and 0.00).

Supply Demand Balance(Shortage)

Count	G^2	LogWorth
72	18.277999	0.4861888

Level	Prob
No	0.9722
Yes	0.0278

Region(UK, Germany)

Count	G^2
35	15.332277

Level	Prob
No	0.9429
Yes	0.0571

▸ **Candidates**

Region(France, Italy)

Count	G^2
37	0

Level	Prob
No	1.0000
Yes	0.0000

▸ **Candidates**

EXHIBIT 5.34   Nodes Relating to Split on Region

Jane does not see this as useful information. She suspects this was one of the last splits, so she clicks the **Prune** button once. Looking at the **Small Tree View**, she sees that this split has been removed and so concludes that it was the ninth split. She is content to proceed with her analysis based on the tree with eight splits. She saves the script for this analysis as **Partition—Eight Splits**.

PARTITION CONCLUSIONS   Jane continues to study her large tree. She sees evidence of several local interactions. For example, for Tactical Profit and Non Critical products, **Buyer Sophistication** explains variation in times of Shortage (Exhibit 5.35) but not necessarily in times of Oversupply, with the Low sophistication buyers resulting in substantially fewer defects (66.67 percent) than High and Medium sophistication buyers (96.25). Again the message surfaces that sales representatives need to know how to negotiate with sophisticated buyers.

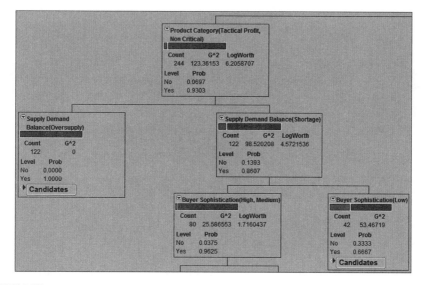

EXHIBIT 5.35   Example of a Local Interaction

Jane notices that she can obtain a summary of all the terminal nodes by selecting **Leaf Report** from the red triangle menu at the top of the report. The resulting **Leaf Report**, shown in Exhibit 5.36, describes all nine terminal nodes and gives their response probabilities (proportions) and counts.

Leaf Report

Response Prob

Leaf Label	No		Yes	
Product Category(Tactical Profit, Non Critical)&Supply Demand Balance(Oversupply)	0.0000		1.0000	
^&Supply Demand Balance(Shortage)&Buyer Sophistication(High, Medium)&Product Category(Tactical Profit)	0.0000		1.0000	
^&Supply Demand Balance(Shortage)&Buyer Sophistication(High, Medium)&Product Category(Non Critical)	0.0909		0.9091	
Product Category(Tactical Profit, Non Critical)&Supply Demand Balance(Shortage)&Buyer Sophistication(Low)	0.3333		0.6667	
Product Category(Strategic Critical, Strategic Security)&Buyer Sophistication(High)&Supply Demand Balance(Oversupply)	0.0652		0.9348	
Product Category(Strategic Critical, Strategic Security)&Buyer Sophistication(High)&Supply Demand Balance(Shortage)	0.3043		0.6957	
^&Buyer Sophistication(Low, Medium)&Supply Demand Balance(Oversupply)&Product Category(Strategic Critical)	0.1000		0.9000	
^&Buyer Sophistication(Low, Medium)&Supply Demand Balance(Oversupply)&Product Category(Strategic Security)	0.6667		0.3333	
Product Category(Strategic Critical, Strategic Security)&Buyer Sophistication(Low, Medium)&Supply Demand Balance(Shortage)	0.9722		0.0278	

Response Counts

Leaf Label	No		Yes	
Product Category(Tactical Profit, Non Critical)&Supply Demand Balance(Oversupply)	0		122	
^&Supply Demand Balance(Shortage)&Buyer Sophistication(High, Medium)&Product Category(Tactical Profit)	0		47	
^&Supply Demand Balance(Shortage)&Buyer Sophistication(High, Medium)&Product Category(Non Critical)	3		30	
Product Category(Tactical Profit, Non Critical)&Supply Demand Balance(Shortage)&Buyer Sophistication(Low)	14		28	
Product Category(Strategic Critical, Strategic Security)&Buyer Sophistication(High)&Supply Demand Balance(Oversupply)	3		43	
Product Category(Strategic Critical, Strategic Security)&Buyer Sophistication(High)&Supply Demand Balance(Shortage)	14		32	
^&Buyer Sophistication(Low, Medium)&Supply Demand Balance(Oversupply)&Product Category(Strategic Critical)	3		27	
^&Buyer Sophistication(Low, Medium)&Supply Demand Balance(Oversupply)&Product Category(Strategic Security)	28		14	
Product Category(Strategic Critical, Strategic Security)&Buyer Sophistication(Low, Medium)&Supply Demand Balance(Shortage)	70		2	

EXHIBIT 5.36   Leaf Report

Jane would like to see a listing of the node descriptions in decreasing order of proportion defective, in other words, with the proportions under the **Yes** heading under **Response Prob** listed in descending order. To obtain this, she right-clicks in the body of the **Leaf Report**, as shown in Exhibit 5.37, and selects **Sort by Column** from the list of options that appears. In the resulting dialog box, she chooses **Yes** and clicks **OK**. The sorted leaf report is shown in Exhibit 5.38.

Leaf Report

Response Prob

Leaf Label	No		Yes	
Product Category(Tactical Profit, Non Critical)&Supply Demand Balance(Oversupply)	0.0000		1.0000	
^&Supply Demand Balance(Shortage)&Buyer Sophistication(High, Medium)&Product Ca	0.0000		1.0000	
^&Supply Demand Balance(Shortage)&Buyer Sophistication(High, Medium)&Product Ca	0.0909		0.9091	
Product Category(Tactical Profit, Non Critical)&Supply Demand Balance(Shortage)&Buy	0.3333		0.6667	
Product Category(Strategic Critical, Strategic Security)&Buyer Sophistication(High)&Sup	0.0652		0.9348	
Product Category(Strategic Critical, Strategic Security)&Buyer Sophistication(High)&Sup	0.3043		0.6957	
^&Buyer Sophistication(Low, Medium)&Supply Demand Balance(Oversupply)&Product C	0.1000		0.9000	
^&Buyer Sophistication(Low, Medium)&Supply Demand Balance(Oversupply)&Product Category(Strategic Security)	0.6667		0.3333	
Product Category(Strategic Critical, Strategic Security)&Buyer Sophistication(Low, Medium)&Supply Demand Balance(Shortage)	0.9722		0.0278	

Menu options overlaying table:
Table Style ▶
Columns ▶
Sort by Column...
Make into Data Table
Make Combined Data Table
Make Into Matrix

EXHIBIT 5.37   Selection of Sort by Column in the Leaf Report

Leaf Report

Response Prob

Leaf Label	No	Yes
Product Category(Tactical Profit, Non Critical)&Supply Demand Balance(Oversupply)	0.0000	1.0000
^&Supply Demand Balance(Shortage)&Buyer Sophistication(High, Medium)&Product Category(Tactical Profit)	0.0000	1.0000
Product Category(Strategic Critical, Strategic Security)&Buyer Sophistication(High)&Supply Demand Balance(Oversupply)	0.0652	0.9348
^&Supply Demand Balance(Shortage)&Buyer Sophistication(High, Medium)&Product Category(Non Critical)	0.0909	0.9091
^&Buyer Sophistication(Low, Medium)&Supply Demand Balance(Oversupply)&Product Category(Strategic Critical)	0.1000	0.9000
Product Category(Strategic Critical, Strategic Security)&Buyer Sophistication(High)&Supply Demand Balance(Shortage)	0.3043	0.6957
Product Category(Tactical Profit, Non Critical)&Supply Demand Balance(Shortage)&Buyer Sophistication(Low)	0.3333	0.6667
^&Buyer Sophistication(Low, Medium)&Supply Demand Balance(Oversupply)&Product Category(Strategic Security)	0.6667	0.3333
Product Category(Strategic Critical, Strategic Security)&Buyer Sophistication(Low, Medium)&Supply Demand Balance(Shortage)	0.9722	0.0278

Response Counts

Leaf Label	No	Yes
Product Category(Tactical Profit, Non Critical)&Supply Demand Balance(Oversupply)	0	122
^&Supply Demand Balance(Shortage)&Buyer Sophistication(High, Medium)&Product Category(Tactical Profit)	0	47
^&Supply Demand Balance(Shortage)&Buyer Sophistication(High, Medium)&Product Category(Non Critical)	3	30
Product Category(Tactical Profit, Non Critical)&Supply Demand Balance(Shortage)&Buyer Sophistication(Low)	14	28
Product Category(Strategic Critical, Strategic Security)&Buyer Sophistication(High)&Supply Demand Balance(Oversupply)	3	43
Product Category(Strategic Critical, Strategic Security)&Buyer Sophistication(High)&Supply Demand Balance(Shortage)	14	32
^&Buyer Sophistication(Low, Medium)&Supply Demand Balance(Oversupply)&Product Category(Strategic Critical)	3	27
^&Buyer Sophistication(Low, Medium)&Supply Demand Balance(Oversupply)&Product Category(Strategic Security)	28	14
Product Category(Strategic Critical, Strategic Security)&Buyer Sophistication(Low, Medium)&Supply Demand Balance(Shortage)	70	2

EXHIBIT 5.38 Leaf Report Sorted by Proportion Defective Sales

Jane studies both the leaf report and her tree carefully to arrive at these conclusions:

- **Product Category** is the key determining factor for pricing defects. Pricing defects are generally less likely with Strategic Critical or Strategic Security products. However, with High sophistication buyers, a high defective rate can result even for these products, both in Oversupply (93.48 percent) and Shortage (69.57 percent) situations.
- **Buyer Sophistication** interacts in essential ways with **Product Category** and **Supply Demand Balance**. The general message is that for Strategic Critical and Strategic Security sales, pricing defects are much more likely with buyers of High sophistication (81.52 percent) than for those with Low and Medium sophistication (29.86 percent). In periods of Shortage, sales of these products to Low and Medium sophistication buyers result in very few defects (2.78 percent), but sales to High sophistication buyers have a high defective rate (69.57 percent).
- **Supply Demand Balance** also interacts in a complex way with **Product Category** and **Buyer Sophistication**. The general message is that for Strategic Critical and Strategic Security sales involving Low and Medium sophistication buyers, pricing defects are less likely when there is a Shortage rather than an Oversupply.

Jane reviews this analysis with the team. The team members concur that these conclusions make sense to them. Their lively discussion supports the suggestion that sales representatives are not equipped with tools to deal effectively with sophisticated buyers. Team members believe that sophisticated buyers exploit their power in the negotiation much more effectively than do the sellers. In fact, regardless of buyer sophistication, sales representatives may not know how to exploit their negotiating strength to its fullest potential in times of oversupply.

Also, the experiences of the team members are consistent with the partition analysis' conclusion that the only occasions when sales representatives are almost guaranteed to achieve at least a 5 percent price increase is when they are dealing with less sophisticated buyers in times of product shortage and selling products for which buyers have few other options for purchase. However, the team members do express some surprise that **Sales Rep Experience** did not surface as a factor of interest.

At this point, Jane takes stock of where she is relative to the Visual Six Sigma Data Analysis Process (Exhibit 5.39). She has successfully completed the Uncover Relationships step, having performed some fine detective work in uncovering actionable relationships among her Xs and Ys. Although all of her work to this point has been exploratory (EDA), given the amount of corroboration of her exploratory results by team members who know the sales area intimately, Jane feels that she could skip the Model Relationships step and move directly to the Revise Knowledge step. This would have the advantage of keeping her analysis lean. But she reflects that her data set is not large and that a quick modeling step using traditional confirmatory analysis might be good insurance. So, she proceeds to undertake this analysis.

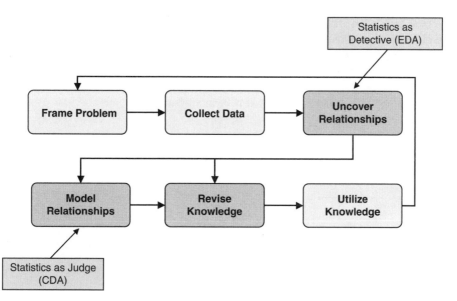

EXHIBIT 5.39   Visual Six Sigma Data Analysis Process

Modeling Relationships

For a traditional confirmatory analysis, Jane needs to use an analysis method that permits hypothesis testing. She could use logistic regression, with **Defect** (<=5%) as her nominal response. However, Jane feels that the partition analysis provided a good examination of this response and, besides, the continuous variable **% Price Increase** should be more informative. For this reason, she decides to model **% Price Increase** as a function of the Xs using **Fit Model**.

But which Xs should she include? And what about interactions, which the partition analysis clearly indicated were of importance? **Fit Model** fits a multiple linear regression. Jane realizes that for a regression model, nominal variables with too many values can cause issues relative to estimating model coefficients. So she needs to be selective relative to which nominal variables to include. In particular, she sees no reason to include **Customer ID** or **Sales Rep**, as these variables would not easily help her address root causes even if they were significant.

Now **Region**, thinks Jane, is an interesting variable. There could well be interactions between **Region** and the other Xs, but she does not see how these would be helpful in addressing root causes. The sales representatives need to be able to sell in all regions. She decides to include **Region** in the model to verify whether there is a **Region** effect (her exploratory work has suggested that there is not), but not to include any interactions with **Region**.

Jane builds her model as follows. She selects **Fit Model** from the **Analyze** menu. She enters **% Price Increase** as **Y**, and then, in the **Select Columns** list, selects the five variables highlighted in Exhibit 5.40. Then, to include two-way interactions involving these five variables, she clicks on the arrow next to **Macro** and selects **Factorial to Degree** from the drop-down menu. By default, this enters the effects for a model that contains main effects and all two-way interactions.

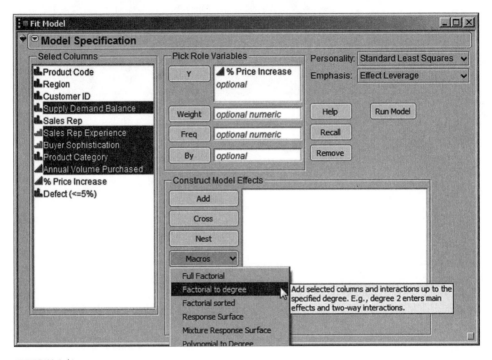

EXHIBIT 5.40   Fit Model Dialog

Now, she selects Region from the **Select Columns** list and clicks **Add** to add it to the **Constructed Model Effects** lists. The final **Fit Model** dialog is shown in Exhibit 5.41. From the menu obtained by clicking the red triangle next to **Model Specification**, Jane chooses **Save to Data Table**, which saves the script with the name **Model.** She renames it **Model—% Price Increase**.

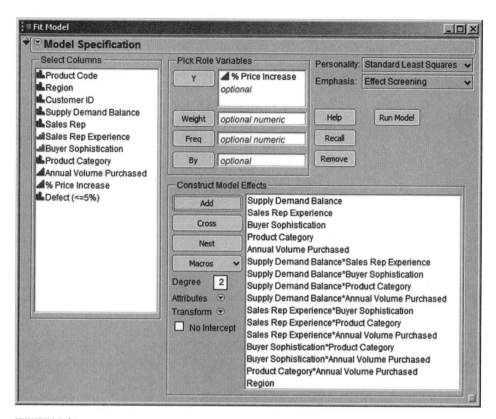

EXHIBIT 5.41   Populated Fit Model Dialog

Jane clicks **Run Model**, and the report in Exhibit 5.42 appears. Jane examines the **Actual by Predicted** plot, noticing that the data seem randomly spread about the solid line that describes the model. There are no apparent patterns or outliers. (We will not delve into the details of residual analysis or, more generally, multiple regression at this time; there are many good texts that cover this topic.) So Jane concludes that the model appears to provide a reasonable fit to the data.

The **Analysis of Variance** table shows a **Prob > F** value that is less than .0001. This indicates that the model successfully explains variability in the response.

When the report window first opens, the **Parameter Estimates** panel is open. Jane realizes that this table gives estimates of the model parameters and provides a significance test for each. However, four of her predictors are nominal. Two of these have three levels and one has four, so the model parameterization involves indicator variables associated with these levels and their associated two-way interactions. She clicks the disclosure icon to close this panel.

To determine which effects are significant, Jane proceeds to examine the **Effect Tests**. She uses the usual 0.05 cut-off value to determine which effects are significant. She looks through the list of **Prob > F** values, identifying those effects where **Prob > F**

| BaselinePricing- Fit Least Squares | | | | | | _ □ ✕ |

Response % Price Increase

Actual by Predicted Plot

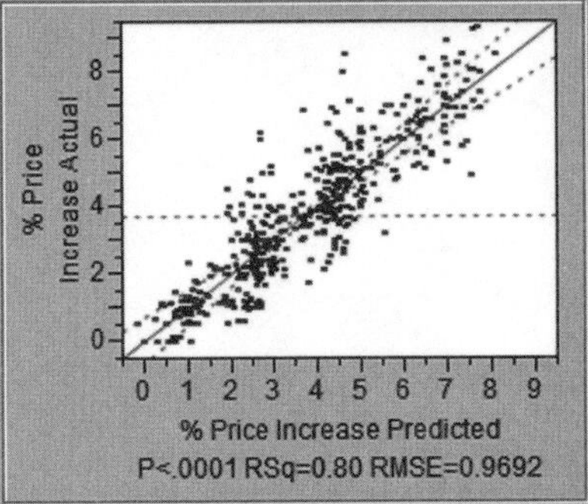

% Price Increase Actual (y-axis, 0 to 8)
% Price Increase Predicted (x-axis, 0 to 9)
P<.0001 RSq=0.80 RMSE=0.9692

Summary of Fit

Analysis of Variance

Source	DF	Sum of Squares	Mean Square	F Ratio
Model	43	1622.7680	37.7388	40.1734
Error	436	409.5776	0.9394	Prob > F
C. Total	479	2032.3455		<.0001*

Parameter Estimates

Effect Tests

Source	Nparm	DF	Sum of Squares	F Ratio	Prob > F
Supply Demand Balance	1	1	56.977520	60.6532	<.0001*
Sales Rep Experience	2	2	3.203608	1.7051	0.1830
Buyer Sophistication	2	2	69.722340	37.1101	<.0001*
Product Category	3	3	91.115833	32.3313	<.0001*
Annual Volume Purchased	1	1	0.064894	0.0691	0.7928
Supply Demand Balance*Sales Rep Experience	2	2	0.281898	0.1500	0.8607
Supply Demand Balance*Buyer Sophistication	2	2	0.021605	0.0115	0.9886
Supply Demand Balance*Product Category	3	3	0.385906	0.1369	0.9379
Supply Demand Balance*Annual Volume Purchased	1	1	0.226059	0.2406	0.6240
Sales Rep Experience*Buyer Sophistication	4	4	6.267709	1.6680	0.1564
Sales Rep Experience*Product Category	6	6	12.136324	2.1532	0.0465*
Sales Rep Experience*Annual Volume Purchased	2	2	3.322404	1.7684	0.1718
Buyer Sophistication*Product Category	6	6	79.382998	14.0840	<.0001*
Buyer Sophistication*Annual Volume Purchased	2	2	5.238695	2.7883	0.0626
Product Category*Annual Volume Purchased	3	3	3.370690	1.1960	0.3108
Region	3	3	1.215956	0.4315	0.7306

Effect Details

Scaled Estimates

Prediction Profiler

EXHIBIT 5.42   Fit Least Squares Report

is less than 0.05. She notes that JMP conveniently places asterisks next to these **Prob > F** values. The significant effects are:

- Supply Demand Balance
- Buyer Sophistication
- Product Category
- Sales Rep Experience*Product Category
- Buyer Sophistication*Product Category

What is very interesting is that **Sales Rep Experience** has appeared in the list. On its own, it is not significant, but it is influential through its interaction with **Product Category**. This is an insight that did not appear in the exploratory analyses that Jane had conducted. In fact, Jane's exploratory results led her to believe that **Sales Rep Experience** did not have an impact on defective sales negotiations. But you need to keep in mind that Jane's multivariate exploratory technique, the partition analysis, used a nominal version of the response. Nominal variables tend to carry less information than do their continuous counterparts. Also, partition and multiple linear regression are very different modeling techniques. Perhaps these two observations offer a partial explanation for why this interaction was not seen earlier.

To get a visual picture of the **Sales Rep Experience*Product Category** and the **Buyer Sophistication*Product Category** interactions, Jane locates the **Effect Details** panel in the report and clicks its disclosure icon. She first finds the subpanel corresponding to **Sales Rep Experience*Product Category**. She clicks the red triangle and selects **LSMeans Plot**. She then does the same for **Buyer Sophistication*Product Category**. These two plots show the means predicted by the model (Exhibit 5.43).

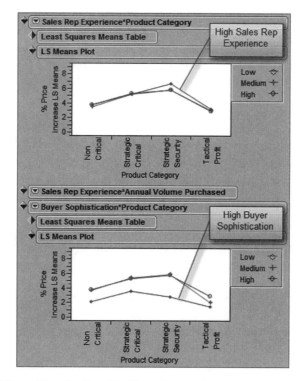

EXHIBIT 5.43   LSMeans Plots for Two Significant Interactions

From the first plot, Jane concludes that there is some evidence that High experience sales representatives tend to get slightly higher price increases than do Medium and Low experience sales representatives for Strategic Security products. (She opens the **Least Squares Means Table** to see that they average about 0.8 percent more.) *Hmmm*, she wonders. Do they know something that could be shared?

In the second plot, Jane sees the effect of High sophistication buyers—they negotiate lower price increases across all categories, but especially for Strategic Security products (about 3 percent lower than do Low or Medium sophistication buyers for those products). For Tactical Profit products, Medium sophistication buyers get lower price increases than do Low sophistication buyers. For other product categories, there is little difference between Medium and Low sophistication buyers. Clearly, there would be much to gain by addressing High sophistication buyers, especially when dealing with Strategic Security products.

Jane notes that these findings are consistent with and augment the conclusions that she has drawn earlier from her many exploratory analyses. She is ready to move on to addressing the problem of too many pricing defects.

Revising Knowledge

At this point, Jane is confident that she has identified a number of Hot Xs. She is ready to move on to the Revise Knowledge step of the Visual Six Sigma Data Analysis Process.

To find conditions that will optimize the pricing process, as well as to ensure that no significant Xs have been overlooked, Jane decides that she will involve her team members and a larger group of sales representatives in discussing her observations and conclusions and in suggesting ways to improve the pricing process. After all, the sales representatives are the ones working with the pricing management process on a daily basis, and Jane knows that their knowledge and support will be critical when she moves into the imminent improvement phase of this project.

Once this is accomplished, Jane will meet with Bill to formulate an improvement plan. She intends to monitor pricing over a short pilot period in a limited market segment to verify that the improvement plan will lead to sustainable benefits before changes are institutionalized.

Identifying Optimal Strategies

Jane sets up a number of workshops where she presents the findings of her data analysis. She is delighted and even surprised by the enthusiastic feedback that she receives. Typical comments are:

- "I really like what you showed me. . . . It's simple to understand and tells a really clear story."
- "I've been frustrated for a while. Now at last I can see what is going on."
- "At last—someone prepared to listen to us—we've been saying for some time that we need sales managers to understand some of our problems."

- "It really looks like we are being out-negotiated. If we focus on our strengths and exploit the great products we have, then I'm sure we can win."
- "We've allowed our competition to drive prices down for too long. We need to do something quickly, and this gives us some really good ideas."

Specifically the sales representatives highlight:

- The need for more training in negotiation skills.
- The need for more realistic sales management guidelines and price targets through a tailored price management process. A target 5 percent price increase across the board is seen by them as a very blunt instrument. They want a more finely tuned approach that aims for higher increases where Polymat has strong competitive advantage (as in the Strategic Security and Strategic Critical product categories), but lower target increases in commodity areas (as in the Tactical Profit product category). They strongly feel that this would allow them to focus their time and negotiating energy where the return on their investment is the highest.

Jane captures all the Xs that might lead to effective price increases, from both her analyses and ideas generated by the sales representatives, in a cause-and-effect diagram (Exhibit 5.44). She constructs this in JMP, using **Graph > Diagram**. Using boldfaced, italicized text, she highlights potential causes that are identified as important based on her data analysis and the sales representatives' discussions. She saves a script that reproduces her work to the data table, calling it **Cause and Effect Diagram**. (The reader is encouraged to consult the **Help** files to see how this diagram is constructed; search for *Ishikawa*. The data are in the table **CauseAndEffectTable.jmp**.)

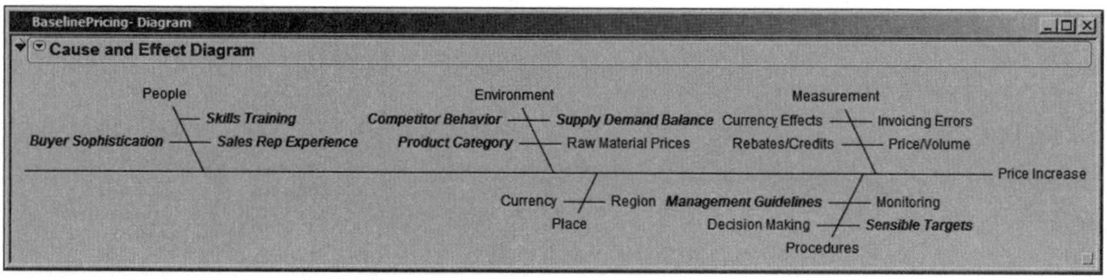

EXHIBIT 5.44 Cause-and-Effect Diagram for Price Increase

Jane now consolidates her findings for a summary meeting with Bill. She summarizes the Xs identified from a combination of the data analysis and the sales representatives' input in an Impact and Control Matrix, shown in Exhibit 5.45. From her experience, Jane finds this to be a powerful tool for crystallizing findings and directing an improvement strategy.

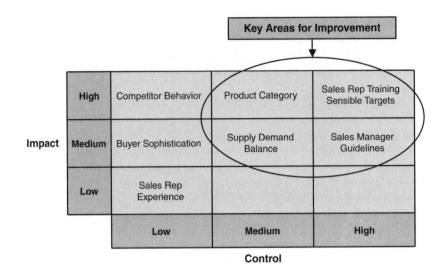

EXHIBIT 5.45   Impact and Control Matrix

The *Impact* axis is the relative size of the impact that an X has on overall process performance. For those Xs for which she has quantitative information, Jane uses this information to help make decisions on their degree of impact. However, for Xs where she has only qualitative information from the sales representatives, this assignment is necessarily more subjective.

The *Control* axis relates to the degree of control or influence that can be exercised on this X through process redesign. Environmental factors, such as **Buyer Sophistication**, are not things that can be influenced (absent unethical business practices)—sales representatives have to deal with the buyers who are facing them in the negotiation. However, the training of sales representatives, such as the type of training, frequency of training, and appropriateness of training, is within the control of Polymat.

Interestingly, Jane places **Supply Demand Balance** in the Medium Control category despite its appearance as an environmental factor outside Polymat's control. The reasoning behind this is that although **Supply Demand Balance** itself cannot be directly controlled, Polymat's leadership team *can* control the *timing* of any price increase in response to market conditions. She feels that this timing could be better managed to ensure that price increases are attempted only when the overall supply/demand balance is favorable, such as in periods of relative shortage.

The Xs toward the top right of the Impact and Control Matrix are clearly the ones on which Jane and the team should focus in the Improve phase of DMAIC. These Xs have a big impact and can be strongly influenced or controlled by better process design.

Improvement Plan

After his sponsor review meeting with Jane and the team, Bill is delighted. "I told you that I thought we were leaving money on the table in our pricing negotiations. Now, thanks to your fine work, I have the analysis that really convinces me!"

Moreover, Bill is extremely enthusiastic about the visual capabilities of JMP. He admits privately to Jane that he was concerned that he might not be able to convince his colleagues of the need to adopt a Six Sigma approach. His colleagues are not very process-oriented and have little time for what they view as the "statistical complexity of the Six Sigma approach." Bill can see that by using Visual Six Sigma he and Jane are better able to tell a simple but compelling story that shows a clear direction for Polymat's pricing efforts.

Together with Jane, Bill pulls together an improvement plan focusing on four key areas:

1. *Product Category.* The analysis has illustrated the power of Jane's product categorization method for Polymat. Because this work used only sample products and customers, Bill agrees to convene workshops to classify all of the significant products in Polymat's portfolio in this way. Bill and Jane also develop a review process to keep this classification current.
2. *Sales Representative Training.* The analysis highlighted the relative weakness of sales representatives in the price negotiation process. Sophisticated buyers are much more successful in keeping prices low than are sales representatives in negotiating prices up. This was reinforced by the sales representatives themselves, who requested more training in this area.

   Consequently, Bill agrees to focused training sessions to improve negotiation skills. These are to be directly linked to the new product categorization matrix to ensure that sales representatives fully exploit the negotiating strength provided by Polymat's Strategic Critical and Strategic Security products.
3. *New Rules for Supply/Demand Balance Decisions.* Recognizing the need to understand the prevailing supply/demand balance before adjusting pricing targets, Bill allocates one of his senior market managers to join Jane's team. His role is to develop a monitoring process using trade association data to track market dynamics by quarter. This process will be designed to take account of fluctuations in demand and also to track imports, exports, and the start-up of new suppliers. Business rules will flag when price increases are likely to be successful, and Polymat's leadership team will trigger the price management process to make an appropriate response.
4. *Price Management Process Redesign.* Bill agrees that a total re-engineering of the price management process is needed. Jane and Bill set up a workshop to begin the process redesign, and, during an intensive two-day offsite meeting, the workshop team develops a redesign with the following features:
   Step 1. Based on a target-setting worksheet, Polymat sales managers will review each key customer and product combination and agree to the percent price increase target *for that particular product at that customer.* This replaces the blanket 5 percent increase that has been used up to now. Typically, the targeted increase will be in the range 0–10 percent.
   Step 2. Using the worksheet, price negotiations will be tracked at weekly account reviews. The current status will be flagged using red-yellow-green traffic signals, so that sales managers can support the sales representatives' negotiations as needed.
   Step 3. At the agreed date of the price increases, the newly mandated price targets will be input into the order entry system for subsequent transactions.

Step 4. Following the price increases, the actual invoiced prices will be downloaded from the order entry system and checked against the new target. Any remaining pricing defects can then be remediated as necessary. A dashboard of summary reports will allow the Polymat business leadership team to track planned versus actual performance.

The leadership team agrees to take a phased approach to implementing the new process design, starting with a six-month pilot in one market segment. Unfortunately, the market seems to be switching from Oversupply to Shortage just as the pilot starts.

Verifying Improvement

About six months later, Jane sits down with Bill and some new data in JMP. Jane's new data table is called **PilotPricing.jmp**. It consists of data on all of the product and company combinations used in the previous study that had activity during the pilot period. Over the period of the pilot study, only three companies did not purchase the product that they had purchased during the baseline study. Consequently, the data table consists of 237 rows.

Jane immediately selects **Analyze > Distribution** and assigns % Price Increase to the **Y, Columns** role. She clicks **OK**. From the top red triangle, she selects **Stack**. The resulting report, shown in Exhibit 5.46, indicates that the new pricing management process has delivered a mean price increase of about 5.8 percent. Jane saves this script as **Distribution for % Price Increase**.

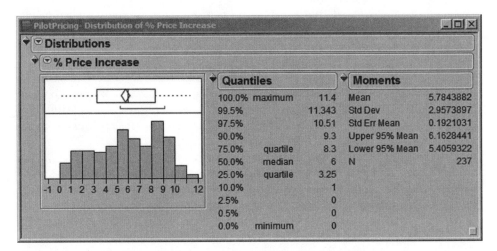

EXHIBIT 5.46   Distribution Report for % Price Increase during Pilot Study

Jane reminds Bill that the 5.8 percent figure should be compared with the baseline data when there was a supply shortage, which showed a mean increase of 4.7 percent. Although an approximate 1 percent gain in % Price Increase does not appear dramatic, Jane works this through to the bottom line and calculates that for the complete Polymat portfolio this is worth in excess of 2 million British pounds per year.

Jane then delves a little more deeply into the data to see the nature of underlying changes. She selects **Analyze > Distribution**, assigns the column roles as shown in Exhibit 5.47, and clicks **OK**. She saves the script as **Distribution for Five Variables**.

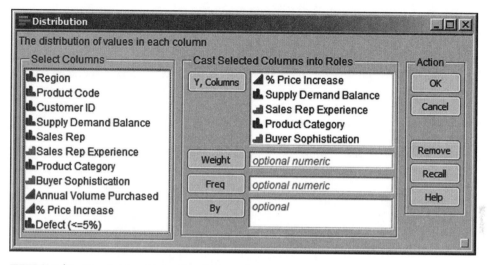

EXHIBIT 5.47   Distribution Dialog for Five Variables

She explores the data by clicking on bars in the graphs, just as she did when exploring the baseline data. She is intrigued by the following: When she shift-clicks on the Strategic Security and Strategic Critical bars in the **Product Category** bar chart, she sees that there has been a noticeable impact on **% Price Increase** (Exhibit 5.48).

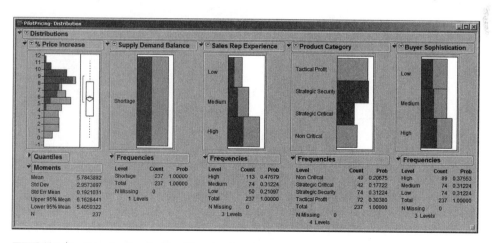

EXHIBIT 5.48   Distribution Report Showing Product Category Impact

In fact, the mean **% Price Increase** for these two categories is 8.12 percent! Jane sees this as follows. She selects the two bars of **Product Category** representing Tactical Profit and Non Critical. Next, she right-clicks in the bar graph and selects

Row Exclude. This excludes rows in the data table corresponding to Tactical Profit and Non Critical sales. Finally, Jane clicks on the red triangle next to **Distributions** and selects **Script > Automatic Recalc**.

The **Distribution** analysis automatically updates to show the report for only the unexcluded rows, namely, the Strategic Security and Strategic Critical sales. The **Distribution** report for % Price Increase shows that the mean for these sales is 8.12 percent. Going back to her baseline data, Jane verifies that the % Price Increase for these two categories during the Shortage period had been only 5.88 percent.

Jane reminds Bill that for these product categories sales representatives have a relatively strong negotiating position due to the small number of alternative options available to the buyer. After the improvements were put in place, the price increase for these products is strongly skewed to markedly higher levels, suggesting much more effective and targeted negotiations during the pilot.

Jane closes her **Distribution** report and selects **Rows > Clear Row States** to clear the exclusions from her previous analysis. Now she wants to see the impact of Product Category and Buyer Sophistication on % Price Increase. She selects **Analyze > Fit Y By X** with % Price Increase as **Y, Response** and Product Category and Buyer Sophistication as **X, Factor**. Using the same options that she used earlier, she obtains the report shown in Exhibit 5.49. (The script is **Oneway with Comparison Circles**.)

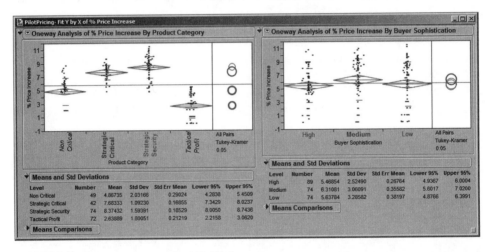

EXHIBIT 5.49   Oneway Reports for % Price Increase

The comparison circles (and associated tests) show no evidence of a Buyer Sophistication effect on % Price Increase. As expected, though, the Product Category effect is still present. The means for all four categories are given in this report: Strategic Critical and Strategic Security sales average an increase of 7.68 percent and 8.37 percent, respectively, while the other two categories average increases of 4.87 percent and 2.64 percent.

Jane takes the data, these reports, and a summary of her key findings from the pilot to a review meeting with Bill and the Polymat leadership team. Convinced by this study, the leadership team immediately gives the go-ahead to implement the new pricing management process as rapidly as possible across all operations.

Utilizing Knowledge: Sustaining the Benefits

Jane's project was initiated by Bill in response to frustration over a consistent Polymat price decline during an extended period due to:

- Increasing commoditization of products.
- Increasing competition from low-cost, far-eastern suppliers.

Bill had a hunch that sales representatives were weak in pricing negotiations, and Jane was able to clearly show that this was the case. She was also able to target specific areas where those negotiation skills could be improved. Exploiting the insights from a Visual Six Sigma analysis of failed attempts to increase price unilaterally, Jane adapted and promoted a practical and simple tool that was better able to capture the value proposition of products to customers. Using this tool allowed sales representatives to become better prepared for specific price negotiations and to receive support if necessary. The pricing management process was redesigned as an ongoing, data-driven business process to be triggered periodically when market or business conditions were deemed conducive to price changes. The results from the pilot indicate yearly revenue increases on the order of 2 million British pounds for Polymat's current operations.

In line with the price management process redesign, Bill now wants a monitoring mechanism that allows the Polymat leadership team to easily track what is happening to their prices over time, picking up early shifts and patterns that might give another means to trigger their pricing review activity. So, as the final step in the project, Jane is asked to provide Bill with a simple way to visually track shifts and trends in Polymat's prices, ideally using leading rather than lagging indicators, so that Polymat can react appropriately.

To do this, Jane draws inspiration from the idea of the Retail Price Index and creates a Polymat Price Index based on a collection of Polymat products. This index, which is based on the price of a fixed volume of these selected products and corrected for currency exchange fluctuations and inflation, will be monitored quarterly by the leadership team. The leadership team hopes to see the Polymat Price Index rise over time.

Jane writes a script to calculate this Price Index by quarter, then calculates the index for the year preceding the pilot and for the pilot period itself. The data are given in **PriceIndex1.jmp** (Exhibit 5.50).

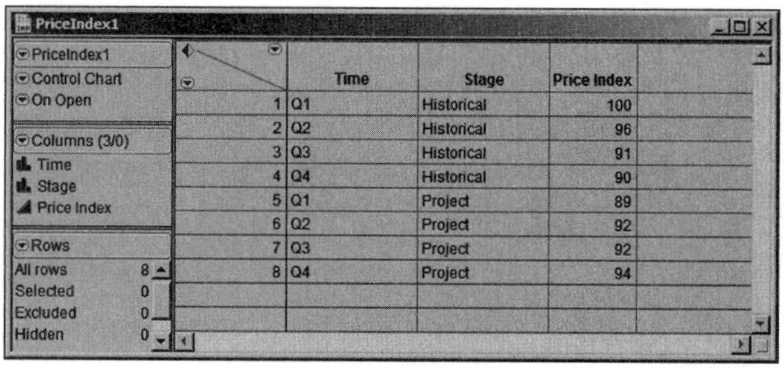

	Time	Stage	Price Index
1	Q1	Historical	100
2	Q2	Historical	96
3	Q3	Historical	91
4	Q4	Historical	90
5	Q1	Project	89
6	Q2	Project	92
7	Q3	Project	92
8	Q4	Project	94

EXHIBIT 5.50 Price Index Data Table for Historical and Pilot Periods

Jane's plan is to monitor this **Price Index** using an individual measurement chart (**Graph > Control Chart > IR**). She constructs this chart, using Price Index as **Process**, Time as **Sample Label**, and Stage as **Phase**. The dialog box is shown in Exhibit 5.51. The resulting chart is shown in Exhibit 5.52. She saves the script as **Control Chart**.

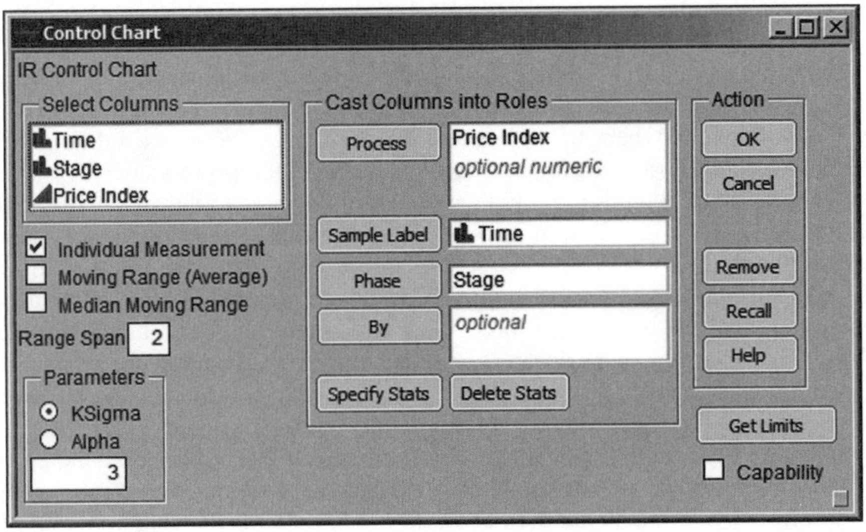

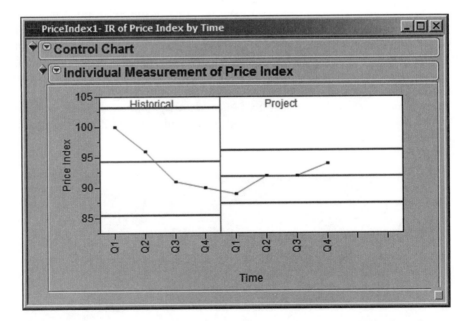

EXHIBIT 5.51   Control Chart Dialog for Polymat Price Index

EXHIBIT 5.52   Control Chart for Polymat Price Index over Historical and Pilot Periods

The upper and lower horizontal lines shown here for each level of **Stage** are *control limits* (they appear red on a computer screen). Jane is a bit disappointed because, although there *may* be a trend forming over the project period, there is no statistical evidence that that trend is anything more than random variation. No points in the Project period fall above the control limits, but there are only four points. Jane realizes that it may take time for the improvements to reveal themselves on a chart of this type. Jane continues to update her chart with quarterly data over the next three years.

Now, three years after project completion, Polymat is well-immersed in the use of Visual Six Sigma. Jane is able to calculate the Polymat Price Index over three **Stage** periods, the year prior to the initiation of the project (Historical), the year during which the project was conducted and tested (Project), and the three subsequent years (Post Project). The data table, **PriceIndex2.jmp**, is shown in Exhibit 5.53.

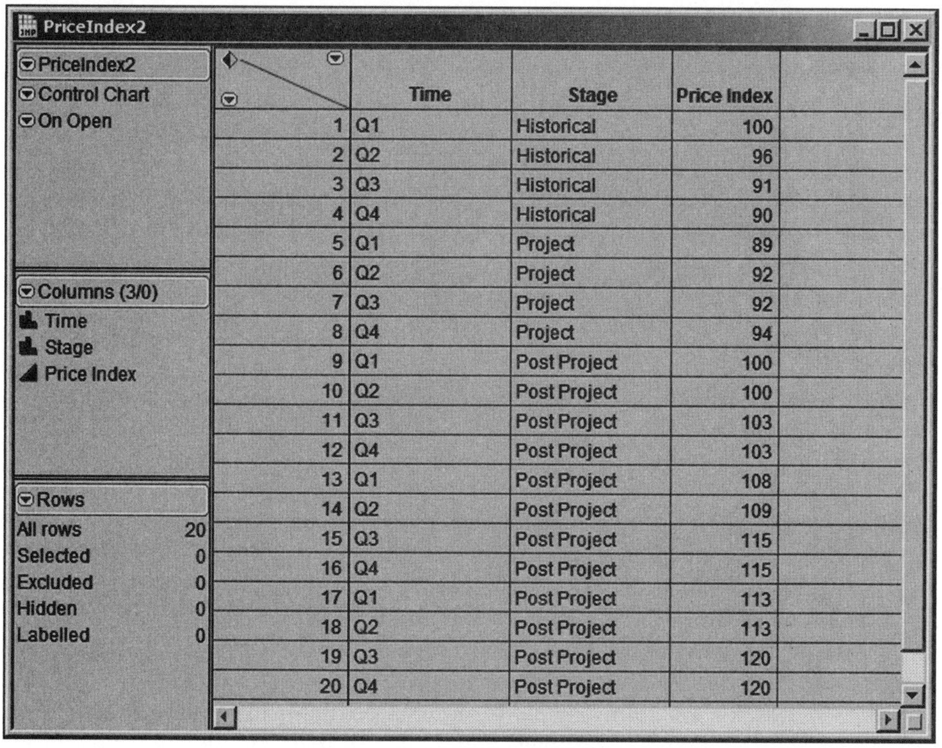

PriceIndex2

PriceIndex2
Control Chart
On Open

Columns (3/0)
Time
Stage
Price Index

Rows
All rows 20
Selected 0
Excluded 0
Hidden 0
Labelled 0

	Time	Stage	Price Index
1	Q1	Historical	100
2	Q2	Historical	96
3	Q3	Historical	91
4	Q4	Historical	90
5	Q1	Project	89
6	Q2	Project	92
7	Q3	Project	92
8	Q4	Project	94
9	Q1	Post Project	100
10	Q2	Post Project	100
11	Q3	Post Project	103
12	Q4	Post Project	103
13	Q1	Post Project	108
14	Q2	Post Project	109
15	Q3	Post Project	115
16	Q4	Post Project	115
17	Q1	Post Project	113
18	Q2	Post Project	113
19	Q3	Post Project	120
20	Q4	Post Project	120

EXHIBIT 5.53 Polymat Price Index Data Table

Jane wants to view the performance of the price management process over time. So, again, she selects **Graph > Control Chart > IR**, and assigns the column roles and options as shown in Exhibit 5.51. She clicks **OK** to obtain the plot in Exhibit 5.54, and then saves the report to the data table as **Control Chart**.

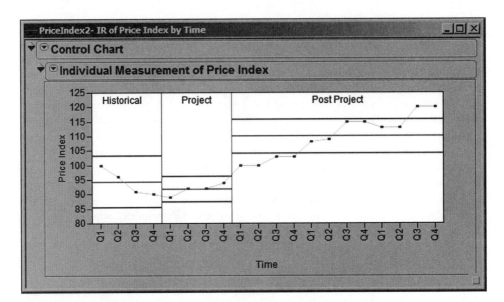

EXHIBIT 5.54   Control Chart for Polymat Price Index over Five Years

Bill, Jane, and, most important, the Polymat management team realize that control charts such as Exhibit 5.54 are powerful tools for tracking long-term trends in Polymat pricing. Clearly the improvement work is having an impact in halting and reversing the historical downward trend. Once the process stabilizes, control limits based on that stable period can be used as objective decision limits to flag changes in pricing.

Conclusion

This case study illustrates how Visual Six Sigma can be exploited beyond the traditional data-driven manufacturing and engineering areas. Almost any business involved in selling products or services generates data in its transactional activities, but such data are often used exclusively for accounting, rather than for improvement. In process terms, pricing and price management generally remain something of an art.

Pricing data is a very rich source of information about dynamics of the market and the relationship between suppliers and their customers. In our case study, using Visual Six Sigma reveals some dramatic insights. In response to these findings, a simple and pragmatic value analysis tool is developed to help sales representatives focus their price negotiations more effectively. In addition, new measurement tools are developed that enable the supplier to better align its price adjustments with shifts in market conditions.

Using Visual Six Sigma, the messages that were contained in Polymat's historical price change data revealed themselves as clear and unambiguous. These findings could be presented in ways that were not clouded in statistical language and that told a compelling story leading quickly to improvement opportunities. Although access to subject matter expertise was vital, Visual Six Sigma allowed Jane to make rapid progress with only the need for periodic consultations with other Polymat personnel.

These findings led to the development of simple but powerful approaches founded on measurements that were easily implemented. The sales representatives, sales managers, and Polymat's leadership team readily adopted these approaches because they were practical, gave new insights, and delivered visible and measurable benefits.

CHAPTER 6

Improving the Quality of Anodized Parts

E ven though defect reduction is often viewed as the overarching goal of a Six Sigma project, optimization is just as important. In this case study, we follow the efforts of a Six Sigma team working to both optimize an existing manufacturing process and reduce the number of defects it produces. The company is Components Inc., a manufacturer of aluminum components used in high-end audio equipment. The surfaces of these components are anodized and then dyed to produce a visually smooth, rich, black surface.

Unfortunately, Components Inc. currently has a significant problem with discoloration of their black components. Lot yields in manufacturing are extremely low, causing rework and compromising on-time delivery. Failure to fix this problem could cost Components Inc. its major customer and result in the loss of more than a million dollars.

Management assembles a Six Sigma project team, under the leadership of Sean Cargill, a black belt, whose charge it is to improve the yield of the anodizing process. This case study follows Sean and his team as they work through all of the steps of the Visual Six Sigma Data Analysis Process.

The team members make extensive use of dynamic visualization in achieving their goal. They identify four Ys and five Hot Xs that relate to yield. *Measurement System Analysis* (MSA) studies are conducted and the results are explored using variability charts. Specification limits for the four Ys are determined using EDA and visualization tools that include Distribution with dynamic linking, Graph Builder, Scatterplot Matrix, and Scatterplot 3D displays.

To understand how the yield can be increased, the team members design an experiment that has to satisfy various constraints. They fit models to the four Ys, simultaneously optimize the Xs using the prediction profiler, and then conduct simulations to estimate capability at the new optimal settings. This predicted capability is explored using a goal plot.

The new settings for the Xs are implemented in production and the project moves into its Control phase. A control chart of post-implementation data shows that the process is stable and highly capable, delivering predictable performance and high yields. The project is deemed a resounding success. The increased predictability of supply means that Components Inc. is able to retain its key customer, and the increased yield reduces annual scrap and rework costs by more than a million dollars.

The platforms and options used by Sean and his team are listed in Exhibit 6.1. Their data sets are available at http://support.sas.com/visualsixsigma. To share the excitement of this project team's journey, join Sean and his teammates as they tackle this ambitious project.

EXHIBIT 6.1   Platforms and Options Illustrated in This Case Study

Menus	Platforms and Options
Cols	Column Info
	Column Properties
	Formula
DOE	Custom Design
	Save Factors and Responses
Analyze	Distribution
	Histogram
	Capability
	Frequency Distribution
	Fit Model
	Standard Least Squares
	Stepwise
Graph	Graph Builder
	Scatterplot 3D
	Scatterplot Matrix
	Control Chart
	IR
	Variability/Gauge Chart
	Gauge RR
	Attribute MSA
	Capability (Goal Plot)
	Profiler
	Maximize Desirability
	Sensitivity Indicators
	Simulator
	Contour Profiler
Other Options	Broadcast Command
	Control Charts—Phases
	Copy Axis Settings
	Dynamic Linking of Profilers
	Row Legend
	Save Prediction Formula

Setting the Scene

Components Inc. is a manufacturer of aluminum components for high-end audio equipment. Components are anodized to protect against corrosion and wear, and the anodized parts are dyed to produce a smooth, rich, black surface that helps to make the final product visually pleasing. Components Inc. has one major customer, and, given the premium price of the equipment it assembles and sells, buyers are very sensitive to its workmanship and aesthetics, not just its audio performance.

In the spring of 2008, Components Inc. begins to experience what becomes a significant problem with chronic discoloration of the components it is making. Lot yields, determined by an outgoing visual inspection, range from 0 to 40 percent, so there is substantial rework and scrap. The low yields mean that on-time delivery of components in sufficient quantity is very poor. In addition, the quality of even the shipped components is often considered marginal when assessed by Components Inc.'s customers, so some lots that are shipped are returned. Unless Components Inc. can successfully improve yield and optimize the quality of its components, it stands to lose millions of dollars, as well as the business of its major customer.

Anodizing is an electrolytic process, used to increase the thickness and density of the natural oxide layer on the surface of metal parts. The anodized surfaces are porous, and the pores may be filled with a dye or a corrosion sealer to improve corrosion resistance. In the case of Components Inc., the pores are filled with a dye to obtain the required black color. The anodizing process used by Components Inc. is referred to as a Type II anodize, where the anodizing is done in a sulfuric acid bath. The parts are suspended in the acid bath and a direct current is applied in such a way that the parts become the anodes of an electrolytic cell (hence the term *anodize*). Oxygen is generated on the surfaces of the aluminum parts, causing a buildup of aluminum oxide. The parameters used in the anodizing process not only have a significant impact on the coated thickness, but also affect the shape and size of the pores that form in the coating. This, in turn, affects the ability of the anodized surface to retain dye or other coatings.

For Components Inc., a defect occurs and yield is reduced when the surface of an anodized part has either a purple or a smutty black appearance. The purple color varies from a very light to a deep purple, while the smutty black appearance gives the impression that the finish is smudged and not blemish-free. An acceptable surface has a rich, black, clear, and blemish-free appearance.

Framing the Problem

In June 2008, a Six Sigma project team is assembled and charged with improving the yield of the anodizing process. Sean Cargill, a black belt for Components Inc., is assigned the task of leading the Six Sigma project.

Sean brings the team together and initiates the Define phase of the project. In conjunction with the project sponsor and the assembled team, Sean develops the initial project charter, shown in Exhibit 6.2. Note that the team identifies process yield as the *Key Performance Indicator* (KPI). The team realizes that if this process measure improves, so will delivery performance.

EXHIBIT 6.2   Project Charter

Project Title	Improve Black Anodize Quality and Yield
Business Case	Specialty anodizing is considered an area for substantial profitable growth for Components Inc. The ability to manufacture high-quality specialty anodized items will increase Earnings Before Interest and Taxes (EBIT) and open new potential markets for Components Inc.'s products.
Problem/Opportunity Statement	Currently, the black anodizing process has very low daily yields, usually below 40%, and averaging 19%. This results in high scrap and rework costs. Also, Components Inc.'s largest customer is threatening to find another supplier if quality and on time delivery are not substantially improved. In the past six months, scrap and rework costs have totaled approximately $450,000 with on-time delivery below 60%.
Project Goal Statement and KPI (Key Performance Indicator)	Improve the black anodize process yield from 19% to a minimum of 90% by December 2008 (a six-month timeframe). The KPI is the lot by lot yield plotted on an individual measurement control chart.
Project Scope	The project will address only the black anodizing process. All other manufacturing steps are out of scope for this project.
Project Team	Sponsor: John Good Black belt: Sean Cargill Team Members: Mike Knott, David Barry, Nancy Wiles, Bob Barr, Mary Kendall

Sean and the team begin working on the project by constructing a process map for the anodizing process. To do this, they enlist the help of manufacturing personnel, which the team agrees is critical to success. Their map, shown in Exhibit 6.3, contains the basic process steps as well as key inputs (the boxes below each step) and outputs (the boxes above each arrow connecting the steps) at each step.

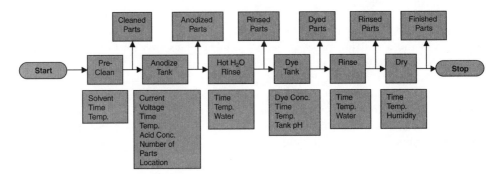

EXHIBIT 6.3   Process Map of the Anodizing Process

Sean then works with the team to define *critical to quality* (CTQ) output variables. The key measures of quality are the thickness of the anodize coating and the color of the parts. The anodize thickness is measured in thousandths of an inch using a backscatter radiation gauge. The color is qualitatively assessed by inspectors and measured quantitatively with a spectrophotometer. The spectrophotometer provides a color assessment based on the three-axis coordinate color scheme also known as the CIELAB (Commission Internationale de l'Eclairage) color space. Every color can be uniquely defined in a three-dimensional space using the attributes L*, a*, and b*. L* is a measure of lightness of the color (the range is 0–100 with lower values indicating darker color), a* is a measure of red/green (positive values indicate redness and negative values indicate greenness), and b* is a measure of yellow/blue (positive values indicate yellowness and negative values indicate blueness). Measurements are given in CIELAB units.

Thus, there are four continuous CTQs for the anodizing process: anodize coating thickness and the three color coordinates. Although the project charter identifies yield as the KPI, Sean and the team believe that these four continuous Y measurements determine yield. They realize that these measures will prove much more informative in the team's work than would the attribute-based percent yield measurement.

Collecting Data

Data collection is the usual focus of the Measure Phase of a Six Sigma project. Here, a team typically assesses the measurement systems for all key input and output variables, formulating operational definitions if required and studying variation in the measurement process. Once this is done, a team constructs a baseline for current process performance.

Relative to measurement processes, Sean is particularly concerned with the visual inspection that classifies parts as good or bad. However, prudence requires that measurement of the four Ys identified should also be examined. Sean asks the team to conduct MSAs on the three measurement systems: the backscatter gauge, the spectrophotometer, and the visual color inspection rating that classifies parts as good or bad.

Backscatter Gauge MSA

Since the capability of the backscatter gauge used to measure thickness has not been assessed recently, the team decides to perform its first MSA on this measurement system. The team learns that only one gauge is typically used, but that as many as 12 operators may use it to measure the anodize thickness of the parts.

Sean realizes that it is not practical to use all 12 operators in the MSA. Instead, he suggests that the team design the MSA using three randomly selected operators and five randomly selected production parts. He also suggests that each operator measure each part twice, so that an estimate of repeatability can be calculated. The resulting MSA design is a typical gauge R&R (repeatability and reproducibility) study, with two replications, five parts, and three operators. (Such a design can easily be constructed using **DOE > Full Factorial Design**.) Note that since the operators are randomly chosen from a larger group of operators, the variation due to operator will be of great interest.

To prevent any systematic effects from affecting the study (equipment warm-up, operator fatigue, etc.), Sean insists that the study be run in completely random order. The data table **ThicknessMSA_1.jmp** contains the run order and results (see Exhibit 6.4). **Thickness** is measured in thousandths of an inch.

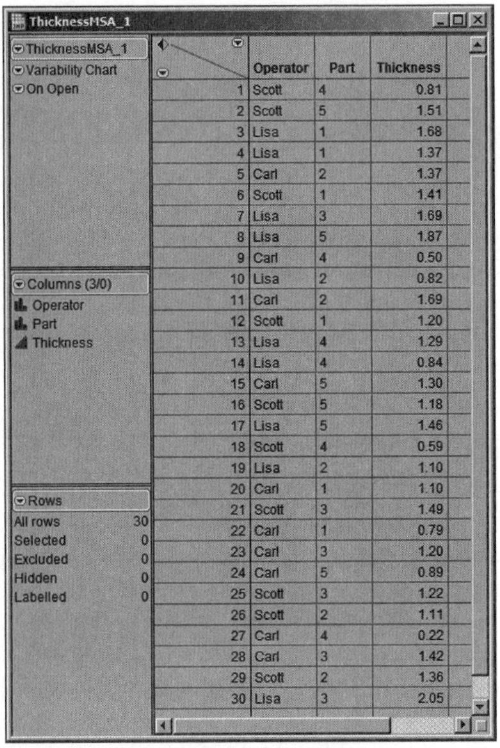

	Operator	Part	Thickness
1	Scott	4	0.81
2	Scott	5	1.51
3	Lisa	1	1.68
4	Lisa	1	1.37
5	Carl	2	1.37
6	Scott	1	1.41
7	Lisa	3	1.69
8	Lisa	5	1.87
9	Carl	4	0.50
10	Lisa	2	0.82
11	Carl	2	1.69
12	Scott	1	1.20
13	Lisa	4	1.29
14	Lisa	4	0.84
15	Carl	5	1.30
16	Scott	5	1.18
17	Lisa	5	1.46
18	Scott	4	0.59
19	Lisa	2	1.10
20	Carl	1	1.10
21	Scott	3	1.49
22	Carl	1	0.79
23	Carl	3	1.20
24	Carl	5	0.89
25	Scott	3	1.22
26	Scott	2	1.11
27	Carl	4	0.22
28	Carl	3	1.42
29	Scott	2	1.36
30	Lisa	3	2.05

EXHIBIT 6.4 Data Table for Backscatter Gauge MSA

The variability in measurements between operators (reproducibility) and within operators (repeatability) is of primary interest. Sean shows the team how to use the **Variability/Gauge Chart** platform, found in the **Graph** menu, to visualize this variation, filling in the launch dialog as shown in Exhibit 6.5.

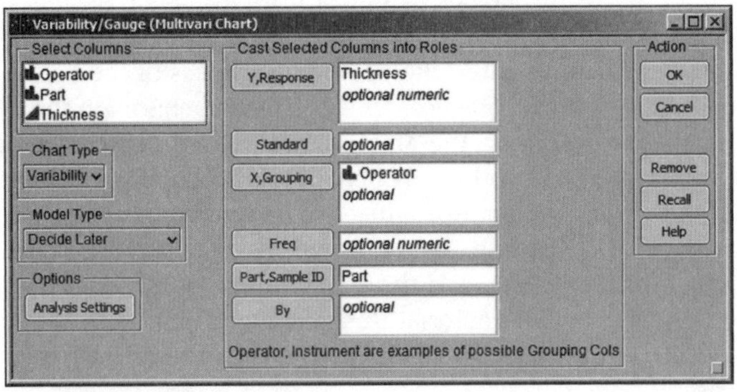

EXHIBIT 6.5 Launch Dialog for Variability Chart

Clicking **OK** yields the variability chart shown in Exhibit 6.6. Sean remembers that this chart is sometimes called a *Multi-Vari* chart.[1] The chart for Thickness shows, for each Operator and Part, the two measurements obtained by that Operator. These two points are connected by a **Range Bar**, and a small horizontal dash is placed at the mean of the two measurements. Beneath the chart for Thickness, Sean sees a **Std Dev** chart. This plots the standard deviation of the two measurements for each Operator and Part combination.

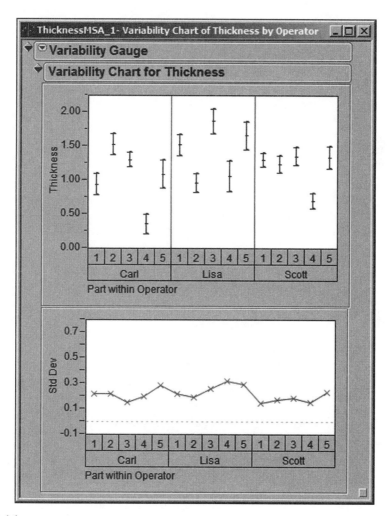

EXHIBIT 6.6   Variability Chart for Thickness MSA

Since there are only two values for each Operator and Part combination, and since this range is already illustrated in the Thickness chart, Sean removes the **Std Dev** plot from the display by clicking on the red triangle at the top of the report and unchecking **Std Dev Chart** in the resulting menu. In that menu, he also clicks **Connect Cell Means**, **Show Group Means**, and **Show Grand Mean** (Exhibit 6.7). These choices help group the data, thereby facilitating visual analysis. Sean saves this script to the data table as **Variability Chart**.

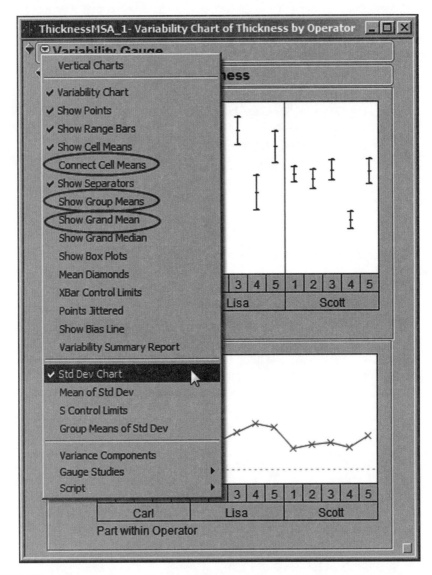

EXHIBIT 6.7   Selections Made under Variability Gauge Report Drop-Down Menu

Sean remembers, a little too late, that there is a JMP shortcut that allows the user to choose a number of options simultaneously from red triangle drop-down menus. If you hold the Alt key while clicking on the red triangle, a dialog containing all the menu commands and options appears, allowing you to check all that are of interest to you. This eliminates the need for repeated visits to the red triangle. (See Exhibit 6.8, where Sean's choices are shown.)

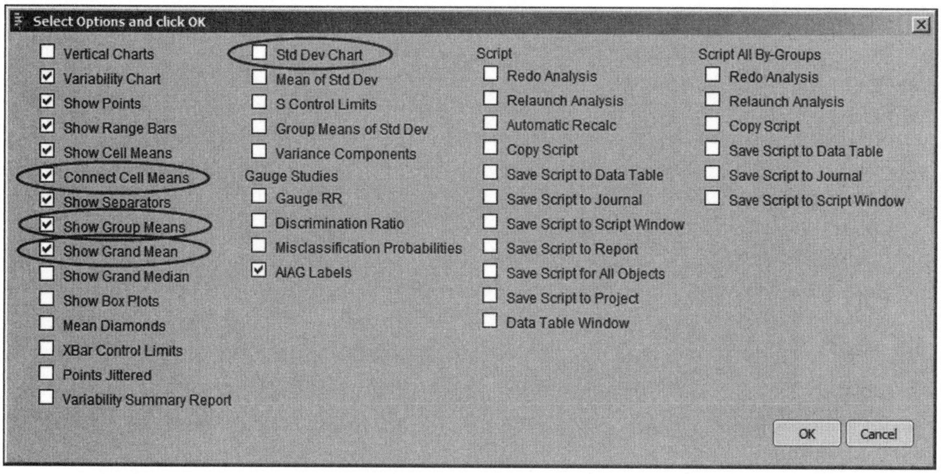

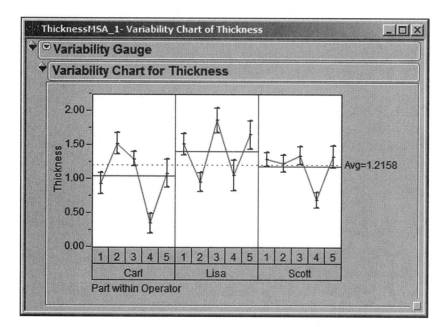

EXHIBIT 6.8 Select Options Dialog Obtained by Holding Alt Key

Sean's variability chart is shown in Exhibit 6.9. The chart shows that for the five parts, measured **Thickness** values range from about 0.25 (Carl's lowest reading for Part 4) to about 2.00 (Lisa's highest reading for Part 3). However, this variation includes **Part** variation, which is not of direct interest to the team at this point. In an MSA, interest focuses on the variation inherent in the *measurement* process itself.

EXHIBIT 6.9 Variability Chart for Backscatter Gauge MSA—Initial Study

Accordingly, the team members turn their focus to the measurement process. They realize that **Thickness** measurements should be accurate to at least 0.1 thousandths of an inch, since measurements usually range from 0.0 to 1.5 thousandths of an inch. The **Thickness** plot in Exhibit 6.9 immediately signals that there are issues.

- Measurements on the same **Part** made by the same **Operator** can differ by a value of from 0.20 to 0.45 thousandths. To see this, look at the vertical line (*range bar*) connecting the two measurements for any one **Part** within an **Operator**, and note the magnitude of the difference in the values of **Thickness** for the two measurements.
- Different operators differ in their overall measurements of the parts. For example, for the five parts, Carl gets an average value of slightly over 1.0 (see the solid line across the panel for Carl), while Lisa gets an average of about 1.4, and Scott averages about 1.2. For Part 1, for example, Carl's average reading is about 0.9 thousandths (see the small horizontal tick between the two measured values), while Lisa's is about 1.5, and Scott's is about 1.3.
- There are differential effects in how some operators measure some parts. In other words, there is an **Operator** by **Part** interaction. For example, relative to their measurements of the other four parts, Part 2 is measured high by Carl, low by Lisa, and at about the same level by Scott.

Even without a formal analysis, the team knows that the measurement process for **Thickness** must be improved. To gain an understanding of the situation, three of the team members volunteer to observe the measurement process, attempting to make measurements of their own and conferring with the operators who routinely make **Thickness** measurements.

These three team members observe and experience that operators have difficulty repeating the exact positioning of parts being measured using the backscatter gauge. Moreover, the gauge proves to be very sensitive to the positioning of the part being measured. They also learn that the amount of pressure applied to the gauge head on the part affects the **Thickness** measurement. In addition, the team members notice that operators do not calibrate the gauge in the same manner, which leads to reproducibility variation. They report these findings to Sean and the rest of the team.

Armed with this knowledge, the team and a few of the operators work with the metrology department to design a fixture that automatically locates the gauge on the part and adjusts the pressure of the gauge head on the part. At the same time, the team works with the operators to define and implement a standard calibration practice.

Once these changes are implemented, the team conducts another MSA to see if they can confirm improvement. Three different operators are chosen for this study. The file **ThicknessMSA_2.jmp** contains the results. Sean constructs a variability chart for these data (see Exhibit 6.10) following the procedure he used for the initial study. For his future reference, he saves the script to the data table as **Variability Chart**.

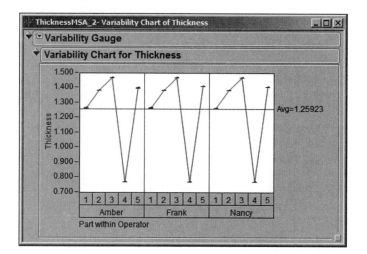

EXHIBIT 6.10   Variability Chart for Backscatter Gauge MSA—Confirmation Study

Now, Sean would like to see this new variability chart with the same scaling as he obtained in the chart shown in Exhibit 6.9. To accomplish this, in the variability chart for the initial MSA, he moves his cursor to hover over the vertical axis until it becomes a hand. At this point, Sean right-clicks to show a context-sensitive menu. Here, he chooses **Edit > Copy Axis Settings**, as shown in Exhibit 6.11. This copies the axis settings to the clipboard.

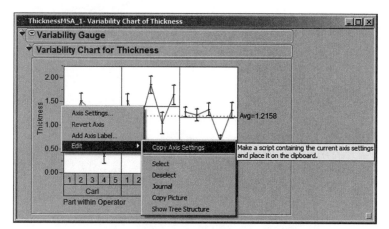

EXHIBIT 6.11   Copying Axis Settings from Initial Study Variability Chart

Now, with the variability chart for the data in **ThicknessMSA_2.jmp** active, he again hovers over the vertical axis until he sees a hand and then right-clicks. In the context-sensitive menu, he selects **Edit > Paste Axis Settings**.

The resulting chart is shown in Exhibit 6.12. Sean checks that it has the same vertical scale as was used in the plot for the initial study in Exhibit 6.9. The plot confirms dramatic improvement in both repeatability and reproducibility. In fact, the repeatability and reproducibility variation is virtually not visible, given the scaling of the chart. Sean saves the script as **Variability Chart Original Scaling**.

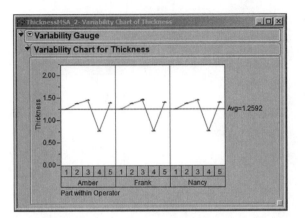

EXHIBIT 6.12   Rescaled Variability Chart for Backscatter Gauge MSA—Confirmation Study

The team follows this visual analysis with a formal gauge R&R analysis. Recall that the gauge should be able to detect differences of 0.1 thousandths of an inch. Sean clicks the red triangle next to **Variability Gauge** at the top of the report and chooses **Gauge Studies > Gauge RR** (Exhibit 6.13).

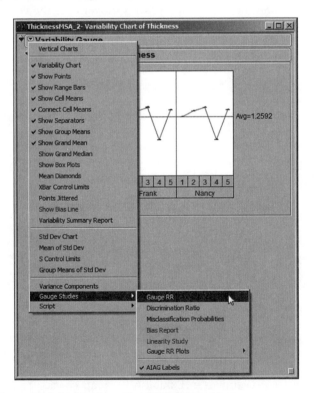

EXHIBIT 6.13   Gauge RR Selection from Variability Gauge Menu

This opens a dialog window asking Sean to select the **Variability Model**. Sean's effects are crossed, namely, each **Operator** measured each **Part**. So, he accepts the default selection of **Crossed** and clicks **OK**.

The next window that appears asks Sean to enter gauge R&R specifications (Exhibit 6.14). Since there are no formal specifications for **Thickness**, he does not enter a **Tolerance Interval** or **Spec Limits**. He simply clicks **OK**.

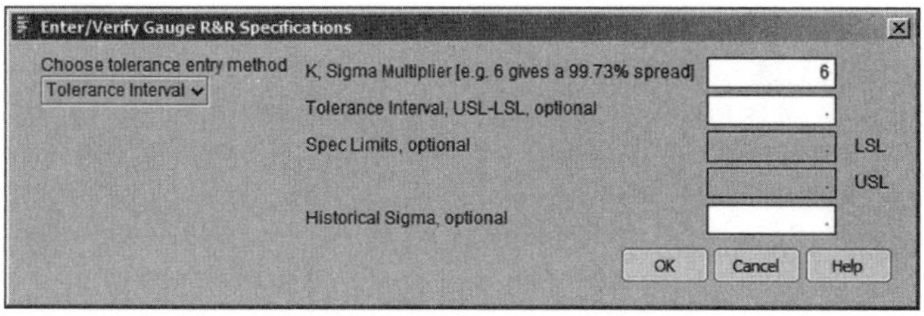

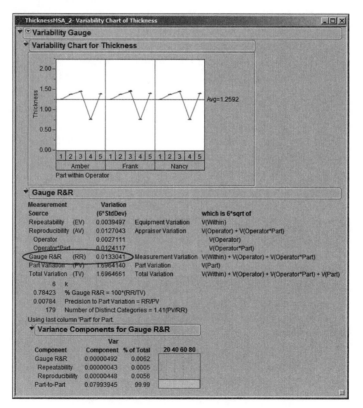

EXHIBIT 6.14   Gauge R&R Specifications Dialog

The resulting analysis is shown in Exhibit 6.15. It indicates a **Gauge R&R** value of 0.0133. This means that the measurement system variation, comprised of both repeatability and reproducibility variation, will span a range on the order of only 0.0133 thousandths of an inch.

EXHIBIT 6.15   Gauge R&R Report for Backscatter Gauge Confirmation Study

This indicates that the measurement system will easily distinguish parts that differ by 0.1 thousandths of an inch. Thanks to the new fixture and new procedures, the **Thickness** measurement process is now extremely capable. Sean saves this script to the data table as **Gauge R&R**.

Having completed the study of the backscatter gauge, Sean guides the team in conducting an MSA on the spectrophotometer used to measure color. Using an analysis similar to the one above, the team finds the spectrophotometer to be extremely capable.

Visual Color Rating MSA

At this point, Sean and his team address the visual inspection process that results in the lot yield figures. Parts are classified into one of three **Color Rating** categories: Normal Black, Purple/Black, and Smutty Black. Normal Black characterizes an acceptable part. Purple/Black and Smutty Black signal defective parts, and these may result from different sets of root causes. So, not only is it important to differentiate good parts from bad parts, it is also important to differentiate between these two kinds of bad parts.

Sean helps the team design an attribute MSA for the visual inspection process. Eight different inspectors are involved in inspecting color. Sean suggests using three randomly chosen inspectors as raters for the study. He also suggests choosing 50 parts from production, asking the team to structure the sample so that each of the three categories is represented at least 25 percent of the time. That is, Sean would like the sample of 50 parts to contain at least 12 each of the Normal Black, Purple/Black, and Smutty Black parts. This is so that accuracy and agreement relative to all three categories can be estimated with somewhat similar precision.

In order to choose such a sample and study the accuracy of the visual inspection process, the team identifies an in-house expert rater. Given that customers subsequently return some parts deemed acceptable by Components Inc., the expert rater suggests that he work with an expert rater from their major customer to rate the parts to be used in the MSA. For purposes of the MSA, the consensus classification of the parts by the two experts will be considered correct and will be used to evaluate the accuracy of the inspectors.

The experts rate the 50 parts that the team has chosen for the study. The data are given in the table **AttributeMSA_PartsOnly.jmp**. To see the distribution of the color ratings, Sean obtains a **Distribution** report for the column **Expert Rating** (Exhibit 6.16). He checks that all three categories are well represented and deems the 50-part sample appropriate for the study. (The script is called **Distribution**.)

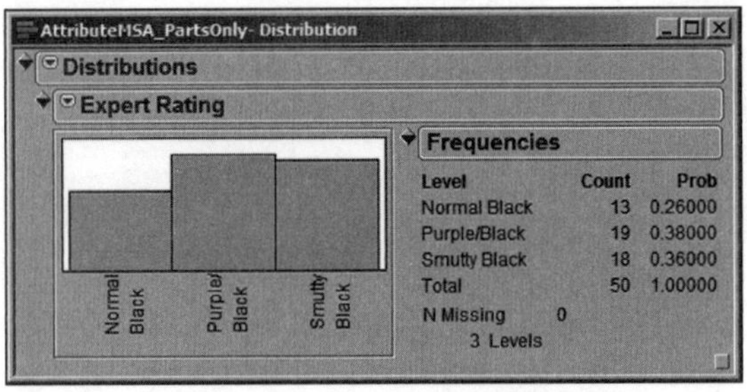

EXHIBIT 6.16   Expert Color Rating of Parts for Color Rating MSA

The team randomly selects three raters, Hal, Carly, and Jake, to participate in the MSA. Each rater will inspect each part twice. The team decides that, to minimize recall issues, the parts will be presented in random order to each rater on each of two consecutive days. The random presentation order is shown in the table **AttributeMSA.jmp**. The Part column shows the order of presentation of the parts on each of the two days. Note that the order for each of the two days differs. However, to keep the study manageable, the same order was used for all three raters on a given day. (Ideally, the study would have been conducted in a completely random order.) Note that the **Expert Rating** is also given in this table.

The team conducts the MSA and records the rating for each rater in the table **AttributeMSA.jmp**. Sean selects **Graph > Variability/Gauge Chart**, making sure to choose **Attribute** under **Chart Type**. He populates the launch dialog as shown in Exhibit 6.17 and clicks **OK**.

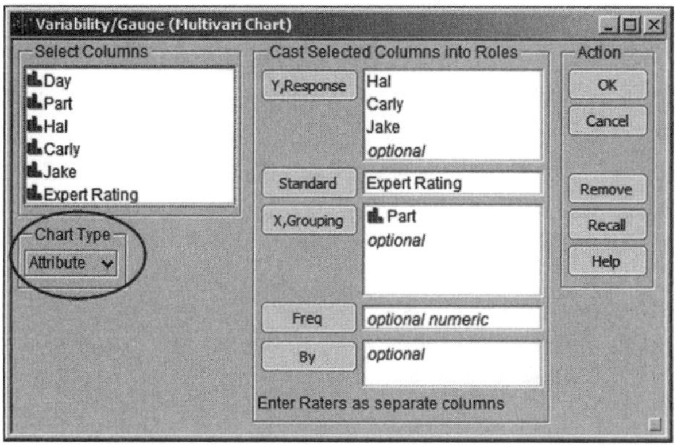

EXHIBIT 6.17   Launch Dialog for Attribute MSA

He obtains the report shown in Exhibit 6.18, where Sean has closed a few disclosure icons. As usual, in order to keep a record, Sean saves the analysis script, called **Attribute Chart**, to the data table.

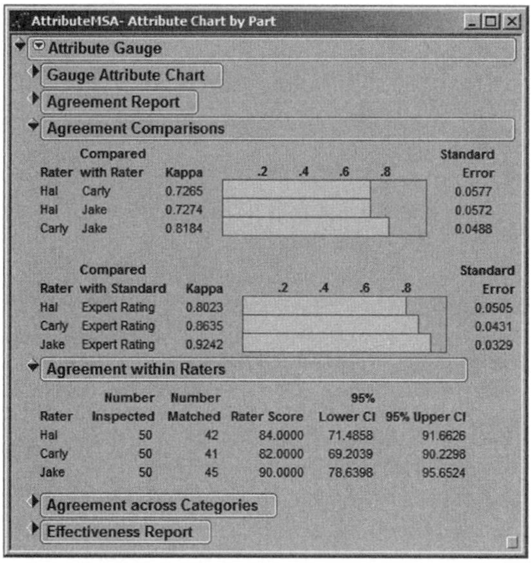

EXHIBIT 6.18   Agreement Reports for Color Rating MSA

Sean first focuses on the kappa values in the **Agreement Comparisons** panel, which assess interrater agreement, as well as agreement with the expert. Sean knows that kappa provides a measure of beyond-chance agreement. It is generally accepted that a kappa value between 0.60 and 0.80 indicates substantial agreement, while a kappa value greater than 0.80 reflects almost perfect agreement. In the **Agreement Comparisons** panel shown in Exhibit 6.18, Sean sees that all kappa values exceed 0.60. For comparisons of raters to other raters, kappa is always greater than 0.72. The kappa values that measure rater agreement with the expert all exceed 0.80.

Next, Sean observes that the **Agreement within Raters** panel indicates that raters are fairly repeatable. Each rater rated at least 80 percent of parts the same way on both days.

The effectiveness of the measurement system is a measure of accuracy, that is, of the degree to which the raters agree with the expert. Loosely speaking, the effectiveness of a rater is the proportion of correct decisions made by that rater. An effectiveness of 90 percent or higher is generally considered acceptable. Sean opens the disclosure icon for the **Effectiveness Report** in order to study the effectiveness of the measurement system (Exhibit 6.19).

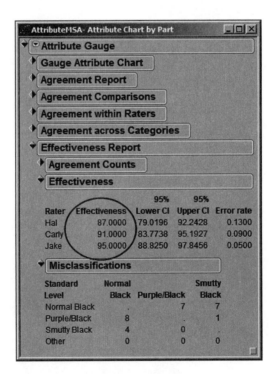

EXHIBIT 6.19   Effectiveness Report for Color Rating MSA

He notes that there is room for improvement, as one rater has an effectiveness score below 90 percent and another is at 91 percent. Also, since these three raters are a random selection from a larger group of raters, it may well be that other raters not used in the study will have effectiveness scores below 90 percent as well. The **Misclassifications** table gives some insight on the nature of the misclassifications.

Based on the effectiveness scores, Sean and the team take note that a study addressing improvements in accuracy is warranted. They include this as a recommendation for a separate project. However, for the current project, the team agrees to treat the visual **Color Rating** measurement system as capable at this point.

To summarize, the team has validated that the measurement systems for the four CTQ Ys and for yield are now capable. The team can now safely proceed to collect and analyze data from the anodize process.

Baseline

The anodize process is usually run in lots of 100 parts, where typically only one lot is run per day. However, occasionally, for various reasons, a complete lot of 100 parts is not available. Only those parts classified by the inspectors as Normal Black are considered acceptable. The project KPI, process yield, is defined as the number of Normal Black parts divided by the lot size, that is, the proportion of parts that are rated Normal Black.

The baseline data consist of two months' worth of lot yields, which are given in the file **BaselineYield.jmp**. Note that Sean has computed **Yield** in this file using a formula. If he clicks on the plus sign next to **Yield** in the columns panel, the formula editor appears, showing the formula (Exhibit 6.20).

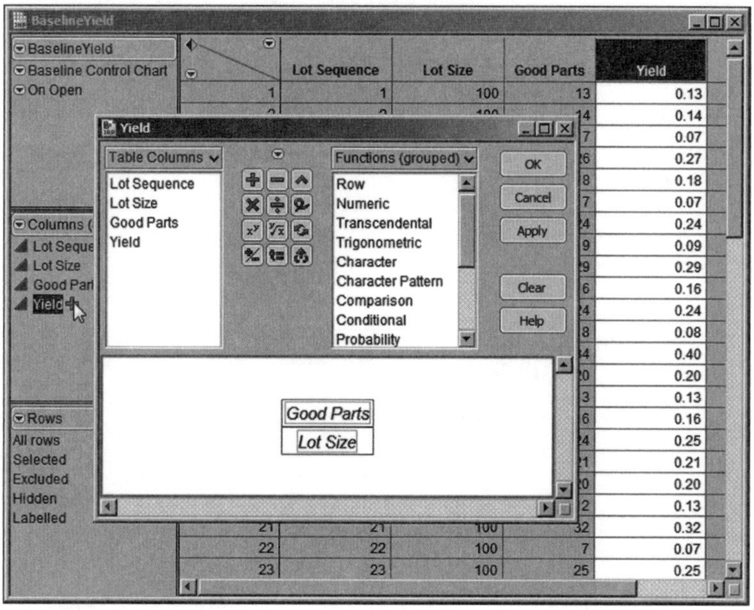

EXHIBIT 6.20   Formula for Yield

It might appear that **Yield** should be monitored by a p chart. However, Sean realizes that taken as a whole the process is not likely to be purely binomial (with a single, fixed probability for generating a defect). More likely, it will be a mixture of binomials because there are many extraneous sources of variation. For example, materials for the parts are purchased from different suppliers, the processing chemicals come from various sources and have varying shelf lives, and different operators run the parts. All of these contribute to the likelihood that the underlying proportion defective is not constant from lot to lot.

For this reason, Sean encourages the team to use an individual measurement chart to display the baseline data. To chart the baseline data, Sean selects **Graph > Control Chart > IR**. Here, *IR* represents Individual and Range, as control charts for both can be obtained. He populates the launch dialog as shown in Exhibit 6.21. Note that Sean has unchecked the box for **Moving Range (Average)**; he views this as redundant, given that he will see the ranges in the chart for Yield.

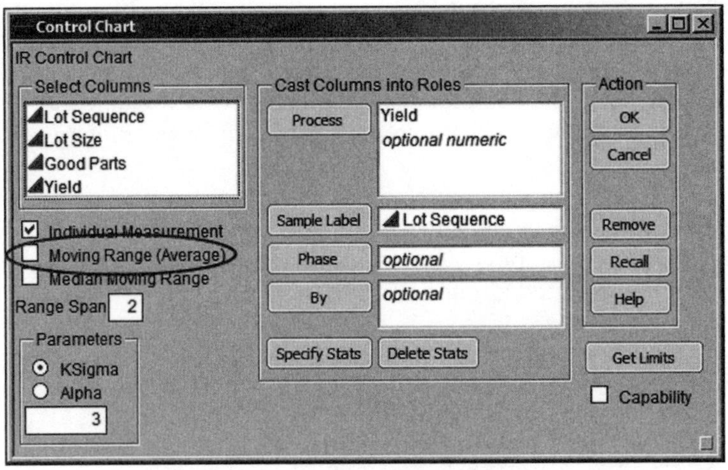

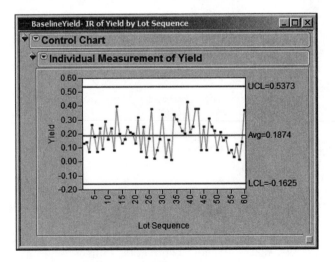

EXHIBIT 6.21   Launch Dialog for IR Chart of Yield

Sean clicks **OK** and saves the script for the resulting report to the data table as **Baseline Control Chart**. The chart appears in Exhibit 6.22.

EXHIBIT 6.22   Control Chart of Baseline Yield Data

The team is astounded to see that the average process yield is so low: 18.74 percent. The process is apparently stable, except perhaps for an indication of a shift starting at lot 34. In other words, the process is producing this unacceptably low yield primarily because of common causes of variation, namely, variation that is inherent to the process. Therefore, the team realizes that improvement efforts will have to focus on common causes. In a way, this is good news for the team. It should be easy to improve from such a low level. However, the team's goal of a yield of 90 percent or better is a big stretch!

Data Collection Plan

At this point, Sean and the team engage in serious thinking and animated discussion about the direction of the project. Color Rating is a visual measure of acceptability given in terms of a nominal (attribute) measurement. Sean and his team realize that a nominal measure does not provide a sensitive indicator of process behavior. This is why they focused, right from the start, on Thickness and the three color measures, L*, a*, and b*, as continuous surrogates for Color Rating.

Sean sees the team's long-range strategy as follows. The team will design an experiment to model how each of the four continuous Ys varies as a function of various process factors. Assuming that there are significant relationships, Sean will find optimal settings for the process factors. But what does "optimal" mean? It presumes that Sean and the team know where the four responses need to be in order to provide a Color Rating of Normal Black.

No specification limits for Thickness, L*, a*, and b* have ever been defined. So, Sean and his team members conclude that they need to collect data on how Color Rating and the four continuous Ys are related. In particular, they want to determine if there are ranges of values for Thickness, L*, a*, and b* that essentially guarantee that the Color Rating will be acceptable. These ranges would provide specification limits for the four responses, allowing the team and, in the long term, production engineers to assess process capability with respect to these responses.

They decide to proceed as follows. Team members will obtain quality inspection records for lots of parts produced over the past six weeks. For five randomly selected parts from each lot produced, they will research and record the values of Color Rating, Thickness, L*, a*, and b*.

It happens that 48 lots were produced during that six-week period. The team collects the measurements and summarizes them in the data table **Anodize_ColorData.jmp**.

Uncovering Relationships

Sean's thinking is that a visual analysis of the data in **Anodize_ColorData.jmp** will give the team some insight on whether certain ranges of Thickness, L*, a*, and b* are associated with the acceptable Normal Black value of Color Rating, while other ranges are associated with the defective values Purple/Black and Smutty Black. In other words, he wants to see if good parts can be separated from bad parts based on the values of the four continuous Ys. If so, then those values would suggest specification limits that should result in good parts.

Sean realizes that this is a multivariate question. Even so, it makes sense to him to follow the Visual Six Sigma Roadmap (Exhibit 3.30), uncovering relationships by viewing the data one variable at a time, then two variables at a time, and then more than two at a time.

Using Distribution

To begin the process of uncovering relationships, the team obtains distribution plots for **Color Rating** and for each of **Thickness, L*, a*,** and **b***. To construct these plots, Sean selects **Analyze > Distribution** and enters all five variables as **Y, Columns** (Exhibit 6.23).

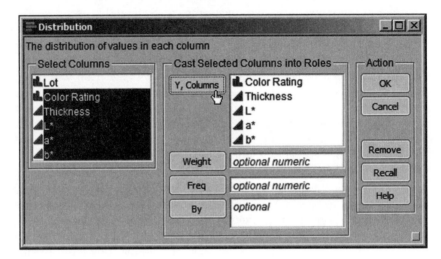

EXHIBIT 6.23   Distribution Launch Dialog

When he clicks **OK**, the team sees the plots in Exhibit 6.24. Sean saves this script to the data table as **Distribution for Five Reponses**.

The distribution of **Color Rating** shows a proportion of good parts (Normal Black) of 22.5 percent. This is not unexpected, given the results of the baseline analysis. However, the team members are mildly surprised to see that the proportion of Smutty Black parts is about twice the proportion of Purple/Black parts. They also notice that the distributions for **Thickness, L*, a*,** and **b*** show clumpings of points, rather than the expected mound-shaped pattern.

Anodize_ColorData- Distribution

Distributions

Color Rating

Thickness

L*

a*

b*

Frequencies

Level	Count	Prob
Normal Black	54	0.22500
Purple/Black	60	0.25000
Smutty Black	126	0.52500
Total	240	1.00000
N Missing	0	
3 Levels		

Quantiles (Thickness)

100.0%	maximum	1.36
99.5%		1.35385
97.5%		1.31
90.0%		1.24
75.0%	quartile	1.15
50.0%	median	0.95
25.0%	quartile	0.73
10.0%		0.641
2.5%		0.60025
0.5%		0.57
0.0%	minimum	0.57

Quantiles (L*)

100.0%	maximum	14.86
99.5%		14.7411
97.5%		12.8933
90.0%		11.499
75.0%	quartile	10.9175
50.0%	median	9.42
25.0%	quartile	7.8825
10.0%		7.37
2.5%		7.1205
0.5%		7.01615
0.0%	minimum	7.01

Quantiles (a*)

100.0%	maximum	10.61
99.5%		10.5608
97.5%		8.43875
90.0%		7.859
75.0%	quartile	4.6825
50.0%	median	1.525
25.0%	quartile	0.865
10.0%		0.633
2.5%		0.43
0.5%		0.3641
0.0%	minimum	0.36

Quantiles (b*)

100.0%	maximum	1.43
99.5%		1.4259
97.5%		1.1885
90.0%		0.679
75.0%	quartile	0.3525
50.0%	median	-0.67
25.0%	quartile	-4.345
10.0%		-5.639
2.5%		-8.0533
0.5%		-9.0949
0.0%	minimum	-9.14

Moments (Thickness)

Mean	0.95125
Std Dev	0.2199888
Std Err Mean	0.0142002
Upper 95% Mean	0.9792236
Lower 95% Mean	0.9232764
N	240

Moments (L*)

Mean	9.5235833
Std Dev	1.6797658
Std Err Mean	0.1084284
Upper 95% Mean	9.7371807
Lower 95% Mean	9.3099859
N	240

Moments (a*)

Mean	2.8066667
Std Dev	2.8004923
Std Err Mean	0.180771
Upper 95% Mean	3.1627746
Lower 95% Mean	2.4505588
N	240

Moments (b*)

Mean	-1.668042
Std Dev	2.5830654
Std Err Mean	0.1667362
Upper 95% Mean	-1.339582
Lower 95% Mean	-1.996502
N	240

EXHIBIT 6.24   Distribution Reports for Five Response Variables

What Sean would really like to see are the values of **Thickness, L*, a*,** and **b***
stratified by the three categories of **Color Rating.** Realizing that there are many ways
to do this in JMP, Sean begins with the simple approach of clicking on the bars in
the bar graph for **Color Rating.** When Sean clicks on the bar for Smutty Black, the 126
rows corresponding to Smutty Black parts are selected in the data table, and JMP
shades all plots to represent these 126 points. The four histograms for **Thickness, L*,**
a*, and **b*** now appear as in Exhibit 6.25.

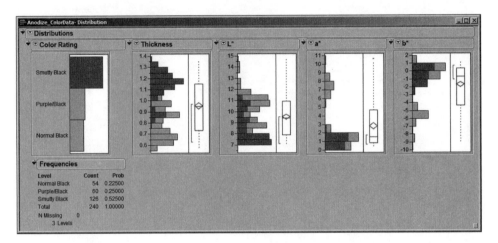

EXHIBIT 6.25   Histograms for Thickness, L*, a*, and b*, Shaded by Smutty Black

Note that Sean has removed the selection of **Quantiles** and **Moments** from the
reports for the continuous variables. He did this by holding down the control key
while clicking on a red triangle next to any one of the continuous variables, releasing
it, selecting **Display Options > Moments** to uncheck **Moments,** and then repeating
this for **Quantiles.** Holding the control key in this fashion *broadcasts* commands
from one report to all similar reports in a window. Sean saves the script that gives
this view as **Distribution 2.**

Studying the plots in Exhibit 6.25, Sean and his team members begin to see that
only certain ranges of values correspond to Smutty Black parts. Next, Sean clicks
on the Purple/Black bar, and the shaded areas change substantially (Exhibit 6.26).
Again, he and the team see that very specific regions of **Thickness, L*, a*,** and **b***
values correspond to Purple/Black parts.

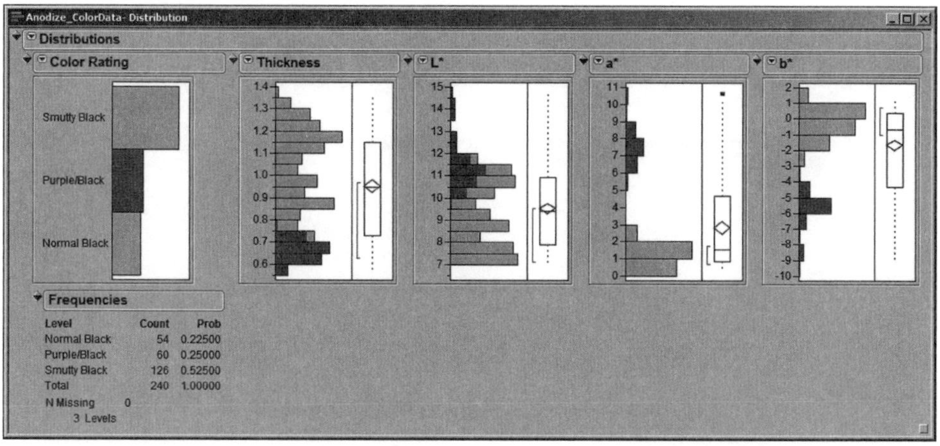

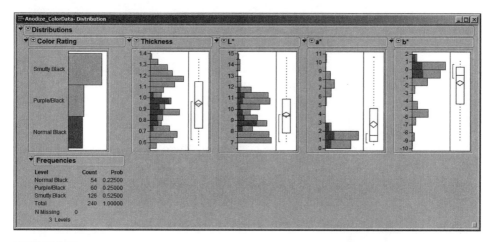

EXHIBIT 6.26   Histograms for Thickness, L*, a*, and b*, Shaded by Purple/Black

However, of primary interest is which values of **Thickness**, **L***, **a***, and **b*** cor-respond to Normal Black parts. Sean clicks on the Normal Black bar in the **Color Rating** distribution plot. The shaded areas now appear as in Exhibit 6.27.

EXHIBIT 6.27   Histograms for Thickness, L*, a*, and b*, Shaded by Normal Black

Sean notes that there is a specific range of values for each of the four responses where the parts are largely of acceptable quality. In general, Normal Black parts have **Thickness** values in the range of 0.7 to 1.05 thousandths of an inch. In terms of color, for Normal Black parts, Sean notes that **L*** values range from roughly 8.0 to 12.0, **a*** values from 0.0 to 3.0, and **b*** values from −1.0 to 2.0.

Using Graph Builder

Actually, Sean thinks it would be neat to see these distributions in a single, matrix-like display. He recalls that JMP 8 has a new feature called **Graph Builder**. This is an interactive platform for exploring many variables in a graphical way.

Sean clears previously selected rows by selecting **Rows > Clear Row States**. Then he selects **Graph > Graph Builder**. The initial template is shown in Exhibit 6.28. Sean observes that this template is split into zones for dragging and dropping variables.

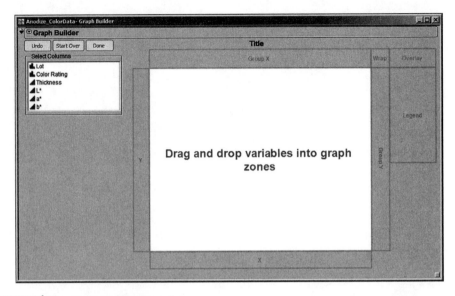

EXHIBIT 6.28   Graph Builder Template

Sean begins by dragging Thickness to the **Y** zone at the left of the display area. This results in a display of jittered points, showing the distribution of Thickness. Next, Sean drags the variable Color Rating to the **Group X** zone at the top of the display area. As shown in Exhibit 6.29, this groups the points for Thickness according to the three levels of Color Rating: Normal Black, Purple/Black, and Smutty Black. It is easy to see how the values of Thickness differ across the three categories of Color Rating.

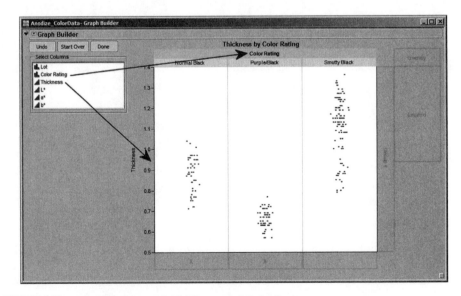

EXHIBIT 6.29   Graph Builder with Thickness and Color Rating

Sean would like to see this kind of picture for all four responses. He adds **L***
to the vertical axis by dragging it to the **Y** zone below **Thickness**. When a bottom-
justified blue polygon appears, as shown in Exhibit 6.30, Sean drops **L***.

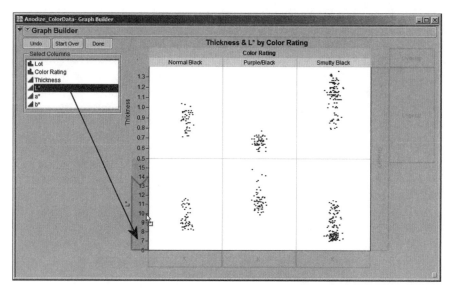

EXHIBIT 6.30   Adding Additional Variables to the Y Zone

He repeats this process with **a*** and **b***, always dragging these new variables until
a bottom-justified blue polygon appears before dropping them in the **Y** zone. He
makes a few mistakes in doing this, which he easily corrects by clicking the **Undo** button at the top left of the report window. This results in the plot shown in Exhibit 6.31.

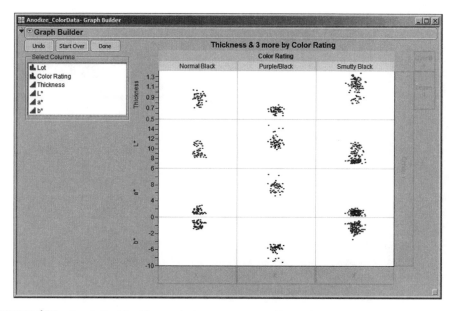

EXHIBIT 6.31   Graph Builder Plot with Four Ys, Grouped by Color Rating

Sean and his team study this plot and conclude that Normal Black parts and Purple/Black parts generally appear to have distinct ranges of response values, although there is some overlap in L* values. Normal Black parts and Smutty Black parts seem to share common response values, although there are some systematic tendencies. For example, Normal Black parts tend to have lower Thickness values than do Smutty Black parts.

Although the points help show the differences in the distributions across the categories of Color Rating, Sean would like to see histograms. To switch to histograms, Sean again uses the idea of broadcasting a command. He holds down the control key as he right-clicks in the plot. Then he releases the control key, and in the context-sensitive menu that appears, he selects **Points > Change to > Histogram**, as shown in Exhibit 6.32.

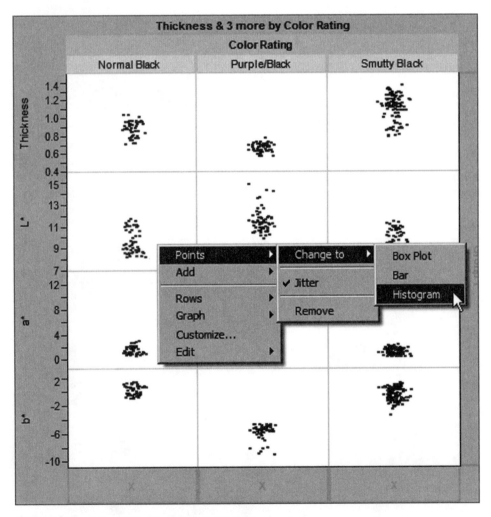

EXHIBIT 6.32 Context-Sensitive Menu with Options

This replaces the points in each of the 12 panels with histograms, as shown in Exhibit 6.33. Here, Sean has rescaled the axes a bit to separate the histograms for the four variables.

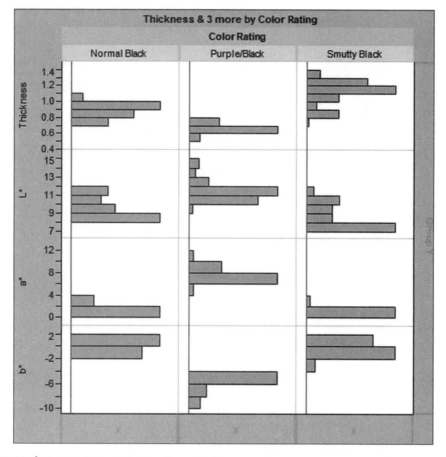

EXHIBIT 6.33   Final Graph Builder Plot with Histograms

This is a compact way to view and present the information that Sean and his team visualized earlier by clicking on the bars of the bar graph for **Color Rating**. It shows the differences in the values of the four response variables across the categories of **Color Rating**, all in a single plot. Sean saves the script for this plot as **Graph Builder**.

Using Scatterplot Matrix

Next, Sean uses a scatterplot matrix to help the team members in their efforts to define specification ranges for the four Ys. He finds the **Scatterplot Matrix** platform under the **Graph** menu, enters the four responses (**Thickness, L*, a*,** and **b***) as **Y, Columns**, and clicks **OK**. This gives the plot shown in Exhibit 6.34.

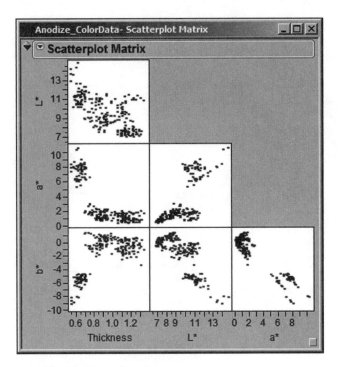

EXHIBIT 6.34 Scatterplot Matrix for Four Responses

Sean wants to distinguish the Color Rating groupings in this plot. To obtain different markers (and colors) for the points, Sean right-clicks in one of the scatterplot panels. This opens a context-sensitive menu, where Sean selects **Row Legend**. In the resulting **Mark by Column** dialog, he chooses Color Rating, sets **Markers** to **Standard**, and checks **Make Window with Legend** (see Exhibit 6.35). He clicks **OK**. (The script **Color and Mark by Color Rating** produces these colors and markers, but not the legend window.)

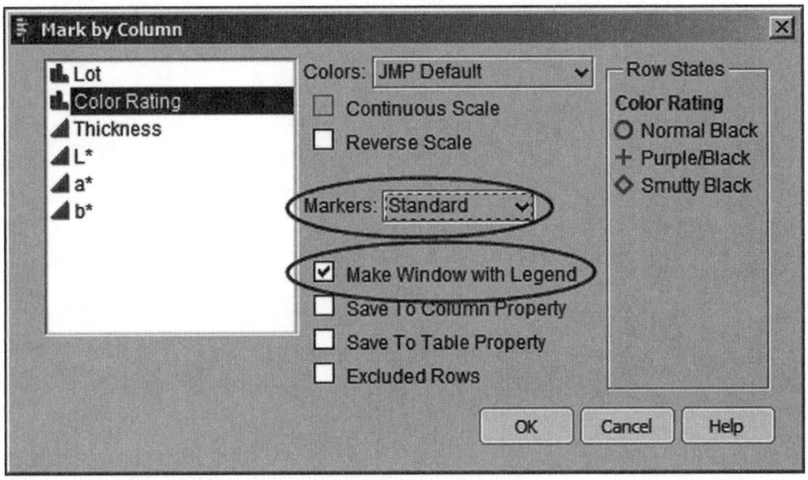

EXHIBIT 6.35 Mark by Column Menu Selections

When Sean clicks **OK**, the markers and colors are applied to the points in the scatterplot matrix. A legend appears in the matrix panel, and although Sean does not need it at this point, a small legend window is created (Exhibit 6.36). For later reference, Sean saves the script for the scatterplot to the data table as **Scatterplot Matrix**.

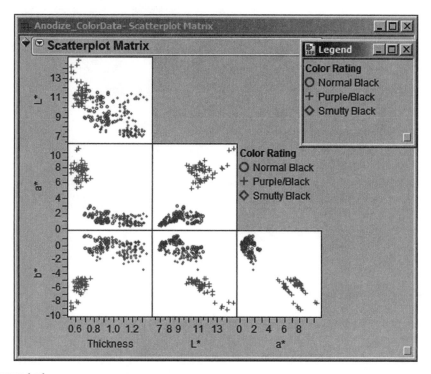

EXHIBIT 6.36   Scatterplot Matrix with Legend and Legend Window

Sean begins to explore the scatterplot matrix. He notices that when he clicks on the text **Normal Black** in the legend (Exhibit 6.37), the points that correspond to Normal Black in all the scatterplots (the circles) are highlighted. (These circles are bright red on a computer screen.) Using the legend, Sean can click on each **Color Rating** in turn. This highlights the corresponding points in the plots, bringing them to the forefront.

The regions in the scatterplot matrix associated with each **Color Rating** are more distinct than the regions shown in the histograms. The Purple/Black parts occur in very different regions than do Normal Black and Smutty Black. More interestingly, whereas the Normal Black and Smutty Black parts were difficult to distinguish using single responses, in the scatterplot matrix Sean sees that they seem to fall into fairly distinct regions of the b* and L* space. In other words, joint values of b* and L* might well distinguish these two groupings.

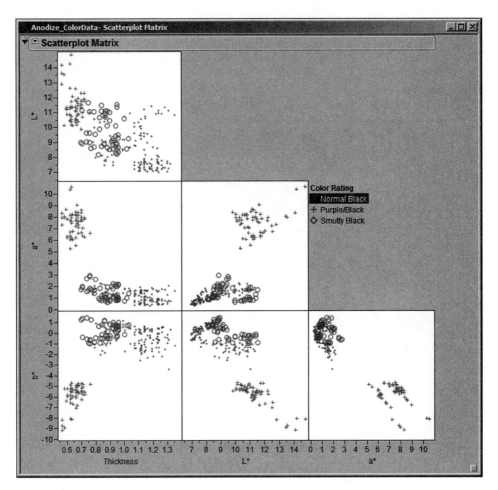

EXHIBIT 6.37   Scatterplot Matrix with Normal Black Parts Highlighted

Using Scatterplot 3D

The regions that differentiate Color Rating values are even more striking when viewed in three dimensions. Sean selects **Graph > Scatterplot 3D** to see yet another view of the data, entering his responses in the order Thickness, L*, a*, and b*, and clicking **OK**. Here, Sean's legend window comes in handy. He places it next to the scatterplot 3D window and clicks on each Color Rating in turn.

Exhibit 6.38 shows the plot with Thickness, L*, and a* on the axes, and with points corresponding to Normal Black (again shown by circles here, but with a red color on screen) highlighted using the legend for Color Rating. Using either the drop-down lists at the bottom of Exhibit 6.38 or the arrow to their right, Sean is able to view three-dimensional plots of all possible combinations of the four response measures.

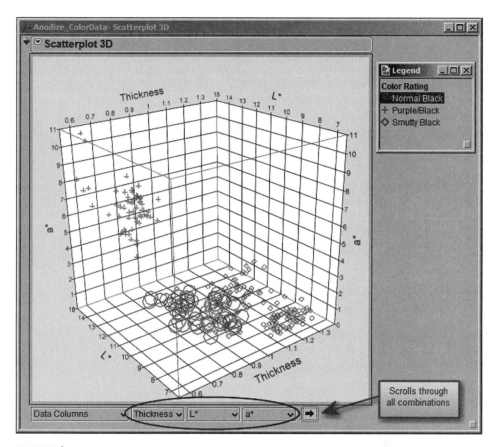

EXHIBIT 6.38   Scatterplot 3D with Normal Black Parts Highlighted

In each plot, Sean places his cursor in the plot, then clicks and drags to rotate the plot so that he can see patterns more clearly. It seems clear that Color Rating values are associated with certain ranges of Thickness, L*, a*, and b*, as well as with multivariate functions of these values. At this point, Sean saves the script as **Scatterplot 3D** and clears any row selections.

Proposing Specifications

Using the information from the histograms and the two- and three-dimensional scatterplots, the team feels comfortable in proposing specifications for the four Ys that should generally result in acceptable parts. Although the multidimensional views suggested that combinations of the response values could successfully distinguish the three Color Rating groupings, the team members decide that for the sake of practicality and simplicity they will propose specification limits for each Y individually.

Exhibit 6.39 summarizes the proposed targets and specification ranges for the four Ys. The team members believe that these will suffice in distinguishing Normal Black parts from the other two groupings and, in particular, from the Smutty Black parts. (You might want to check these limits against the appropriate 3D scatterplots.)

EXHIBIT 6.39   Specifications for the Four CTQ Variables

Variable	Target	Specification Range
Thickness	0.9	± 0.2
L*	10.0	± 2.0
a*	2.0	± 2.0
b*	0.0	± 2.0

At this point, we note that the team could have used more sophisticated analytical techniques such as discriminant analysis and logistic regression to further their knowledge about the relationship between **Color Rating** and the four CTQ variables. However, the simple graphical analyses provided the team with sufficient knowledge to move to the next step.

Locating the Team on the VSS Roadmap

This project was cast as a formal Six Sigma project, following the DMAIC structure. Let's take a step back to see how the team's application of the DMAIC cycle fits with the Visual Six Sigma Data Analysis Process and with the Visual Six Sigma Roadmap (Exhibits 3.29 and 3.30).

- *Frame the Problem* corresponds to the Define phase.
- *Collect Data* corresponds to the Measure phase. Here, the team collected data for its MSA studies and for the baseline control chart. The team also collected a set of historical data that relates **Color Rating**, the team's primary, but nominal, Y, to four continuous Ys, namely **Thickness**, **L***, **a***, and **b***, that provide more detailed information than **Color Rating**.
- *Uncover Relationships* occurs in the Analyze phase. The team members first visualized the five variables using the Distribution platform. In this report, they dynamically explored relationships between **Color Rating** and **Thickness**, **L***, **a***, and **b***. They constructed a plot using Graph Builder that summarized this information. Next, they dynamically visualized the variables two at a time with a scatterplot matrix and then three at a time using Scatterplot 3D.
- *Model Relationships*, which will occur in the next section, bridges the Analyze and Improve phases. Here the team members identify and determine the impact of potential Hot Xs by modeling the relationships between the Xs and the Ys and optimizing settings of the Xs.
- *Revise Knowledge*, where a team addresses the question of how new knowledge will generalize, is part of the Improve phase. Often, in revising knowledge, a team runs confirmation trials to assess whether its expectations will be met.
- *Utilize Knowledge* includes part of the Improve phase as well as all of the Control phase. Here, the solution identified by the team is implemented together with a way to check that the improvement is real and to assure that it is maintained over time.

Modeling Relationships

In initial brainstorming sessions to identify causes of bad parts, the team identified five possible Hot Xs:

- Coating variables: Anodize Temperature, Anodize Time, and Acid Concentration.
- Dye variables: Dye Concentration and Dye pH.

It is time to determine whether these are truly Hot Xs, and to model the relationships that link **Thickness, L*, a***, and **b*** and these Xs. So, Sean will guide the team in conducting a designed experiment. These five process factors may or may not exert a causal influence. The designed experiment will indicate whether they do and, if so, will allow the team to model the Ys as functions of the Xs. The team will use these models to optimize the settings of the input variables in order to maximize yield.

Although **Color Rating** is the variable that ultimately defines yield, Sean knows that using a nominal response in a designed experiment is problematic—a large number of trials would be required in order to establish statistical significance. Fortunately, the team has learned that there are strong relationships between **Thickness, L*, a***, and **b**, and the levels of **Color Rating**. Accordingly, Sean and his team decide that the four responses will be **L*, a*, b***, and **Thickness**. There will be five factors: **Anodize Temp, Anodize Time, Acid Conc, Dye Conc,** and **Dye pH.**

With the data from this experiment in hand, Sean plans to move to the Model Relationships phase of the Visual Six Sigma Data Analysis Process (Exhibit 3.29). He will use the guidance given under Model Relationships in the Visual Six Sigma Roadmap (Exhibit 3.30) to direct his analysis.

Developing the Design

The team now faces a dilemma in terms of designing the experiment, which must be performed on production equipment. Due to the poor yields of the current process, the equipment is in continual use by manufacturing. Negotiating with the production superintendent, Sean secures the equipment for two consecutive production shifts, during which the team will be allowed to perform the experiment. Since the in-process parts, even prior to anodizing, have high value, and all the more so given the poor yields, the team needs to use as few parts as possible in the experiment. Given these practical considerations, the team determines that at most 12 experimental trials can be performed and decides to run a single part at each of these experimental settings.

Sean points out to the team members that if they employ a two-level factorial treatment structure for the five factors (a 2^5 design), 32 runs will be required. Obviously, the size of the experiment needs to be reduced. Sean asks for a little time during which he will consider various options.

Sean's first thought is to perform a 2^{5-2} fractional factorial experiment, which is a quarter fraction of the full factorial experiment. With the addition of two center runs, this experiment would have a total of ten runs. However, Sean realizes, with the help of the JMP Screening Design platform (**DOE > Screening Design**), that the 2^{5-2} fractional factorial is a resolution III design, which means that some main effects are aliased with two-way interactions. In fact, for this particular design, each main effect is aliased with a two-way interaction.

Sean discusses this idea with the team members, but they decide that it is quite possible that there are two-way interactions among the five factors. They determine that a resolution III fractional factorial design is not the best choice here. As Sean also points out, for five experimental factors there are ten two-way interaction terms. Along with the five main effects, the team would need at least 16 trials to estimate all possible two-way interactions, the main effects, and the intercept of the statistical model. However, due to the operational constraints this is not possible, so the team decides to continue the discussion with two experts, who join the team temporarily.

Recall that the anodize process occurs in two steps:

Step 1   The anodize coating is applied.
Step 2   The coated parts are dyed in a separate tank.

The two experts maintain that interactions cannot occur between the two dye tank factors and the three anodize tank factors, although two-way interactions can certainly occur among the factors within each of the two steps. If the team does not estimate interactions between the factors in each of the two anodize process steps, only four two-way interactions need to be estimated:

- Anodize Temperature*Anodize Time
- Anodize Temperature*Acid Concentration
- Anodize Time*Acid Concentration
- Dye Concentration*Dye pH

So with only ten trials, it will be possible to estimate the five main effects, the four two-way interactions of importance, and the intercept. This design is now feasible. Sean and his teammates are reasonably comfortable proceeding under the experts' assumption, realizing that any proposed solution will be verified using confirmation trials before it is adopted.

Another critical piece of knowledge relative to designing the experiment involves the actual factors settings to be used. With the help of the two experts that the team has commandeered, low and high levels for the five factors are specified. The team members are careful to ensure that these levels are aggressive relative to the production settings. Their thinking is that if a factor or interaction has an effect, they want to maximize the chance that they will detect it.

Sean now proceeds to design the experiment. He realizes that the design requirements cannot be met using a classical design. Fortunately, he knows about the **Custom Design** platform in JMP (**DOE > Custom Design**). The **Custom Design** platform allows the user to specify a constraint on the total possible number of trials and to specify the effects to be estimated. The platform then searches for optimal designs (using either the D- or I-optimality criterion) that satisfy the user's requirements.

Sean selects **DOE > Custom Design** and adds the responses and factors as shown in Exhibit 6.40. Note that the four Ys are entered in the **Responses** panel, along with their *response limits* (**Lower Limit**, **Upper Limit**), which Sean sets to the specification limits. For each response, the goal is to match the target value, so Sean leaves **Goal** set at **March Target**. (JMP defines the target value to be the midpoint of the response limits.) Sean retains the default **Importance** value of 1, because he currently has no reason to think that any one response is of greater importance than another in obtaining good color quality. Sean also specifies the five factors and their low and high levels in the **Factors** panel.

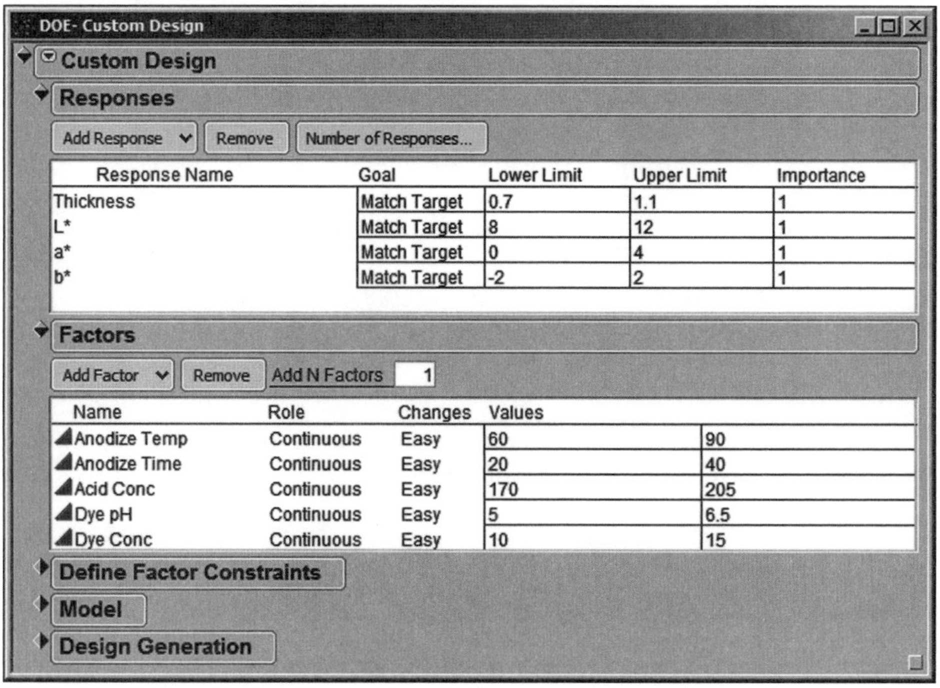

DOE- Custom Design

Custom Design

Responses

Add Response | Remove | Number of Responses...

Response Name	Goal	Lower Limit	Upper Limit	Importance
Thickness	Match Target	0.7	1.1	1
L*	Match Target	8	12	1
a*	Match Target	0	4	1
b*	Match Target	-2	2	1

Factors

Add Factor | Remove | Add N Factors | 1

Name	Role	Changes	Values	
Anodize Temp	Continuous	Easy	60	90
Anodize Time	Continuous	Easy	20	40
Acid Conc	Continuous	Easy	170	205
Dye pH	Continuous	Easy	5	6.5
Dye Conc	Continuous	Easy	10	15

Define Factor Constraints

Model

Design Generation

EXHIBIT 6.40   Custom Design Dialog Showing Responses and Factors

In the menu obtained by clicking on the red triangle, Sean finds the option to **Save Responses** and **Save Factors**, and he does so for future reference. JMP saves these simply as data tables. (If you don't want to enter this information manually, click on the red triangle to **Load Responses** and **Load Factors**. The files are **Anodize_CustomDesign_Responses.jmp** and **Anodize_CustomDesign_Factors.jmp**.)

Initially, the **Model** panel shows the list of main effects. To add the desired two-way interactions, while holding the shift key, Sean selects the three anodize factors, Anodize Temp, Anodize Time, and Acid Conc, in the list of **Factors**. Then, he clicks on **Interactions** in the **Model** panel, selecting **2nd**. This is illustrated in Exhibit 6.41. This adds the three interactions to the **Model** panel. Sean adds the single Dye pH*Dye Conc interaction in a similar fashion.

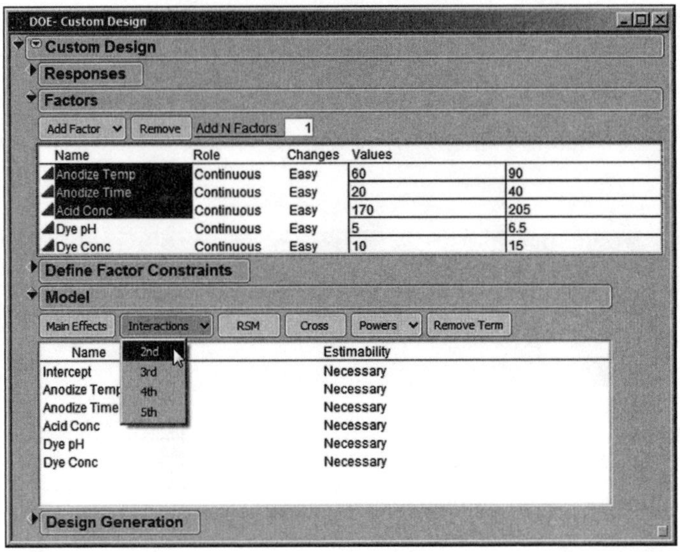

EXHIBIT 6.41   Adding the Anodize Interactions to the Model List

In the **Design Generation** panel, Sean specifies 10 runs (next to **User Specified**). He wants to reserve 2 of his 12 runs for center points. The completed dialog is shown in Exhibit 6.42.

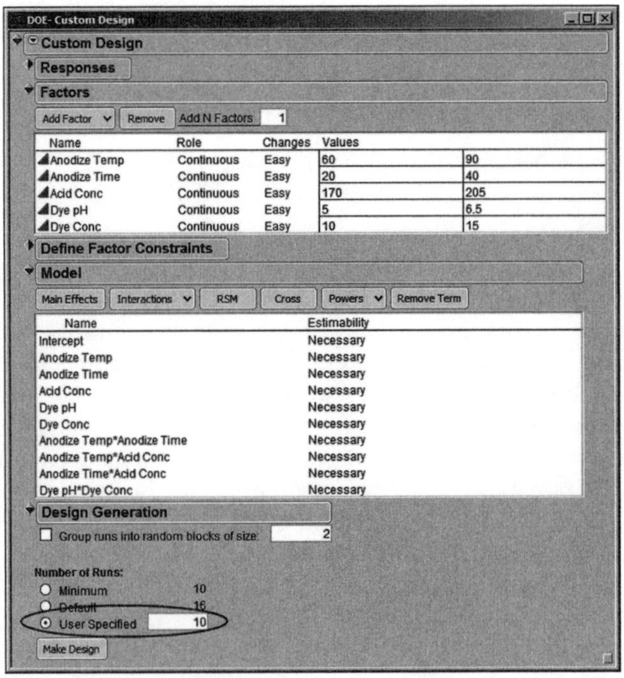

EXHIBIT 6.42   Completed Dialog Showing Custom Design Settings

When Sean clicks **Make Design**, JMP constructs the requested design, showing it in the **Custom Design** dialog. Sean's design is shown in Exhibit 6.43. The design that you obtain will very likely differ from this one. This is because the algorithm used to construct custom designs involves a random starting point. The random seed changes each time you run the algorithm. To obtain the same design every time, you can set the random seed, selecting **Set Random Seed** from the red triangle menu. (For Sean's design, the random seed is 31675436.)

Sean inspects his design (Exhibit 6.43) and finds that it makes sense. He examines the **Output Options** panel and agrees with the default that the **Run Order** be randomized. He specifies 2 as the **Number of Center Points**, including these to estimate pure error and to check for lack of fit of the statistical models. Then he clicks **Make Table**.

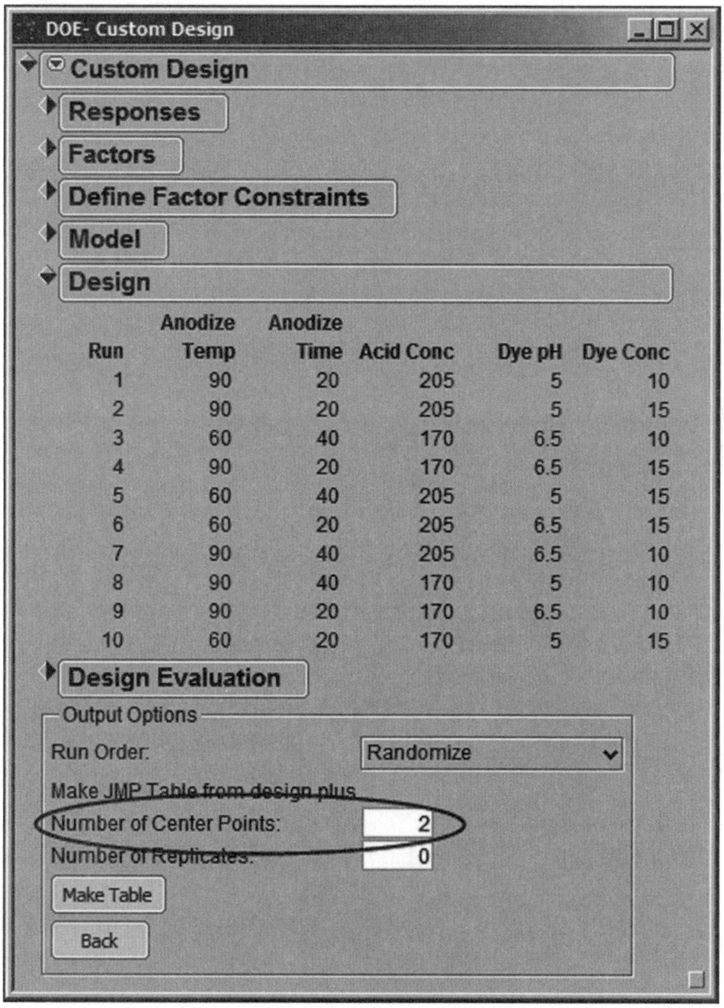

EXHIBIT 6.43   Custom Design Runs and Output Options

The data table generated by JMP for Sean's design is called **Anodize_CustomDesign_Table.jmp** and is shown in Exhibit 6.44. Note that two center points have been specified; these appear in the randomization as trials 3 and 8. Sean and the team are delighted to see that JMP has saved the script for the model that the team will eventually fit to the data. It is called **Model** and is located in the table panel in the upper left corner of the data table. This script defines the model that Sean specified when he built the design, namely, a model with five main effects and four two-way interactions. (To see this, run the script.)

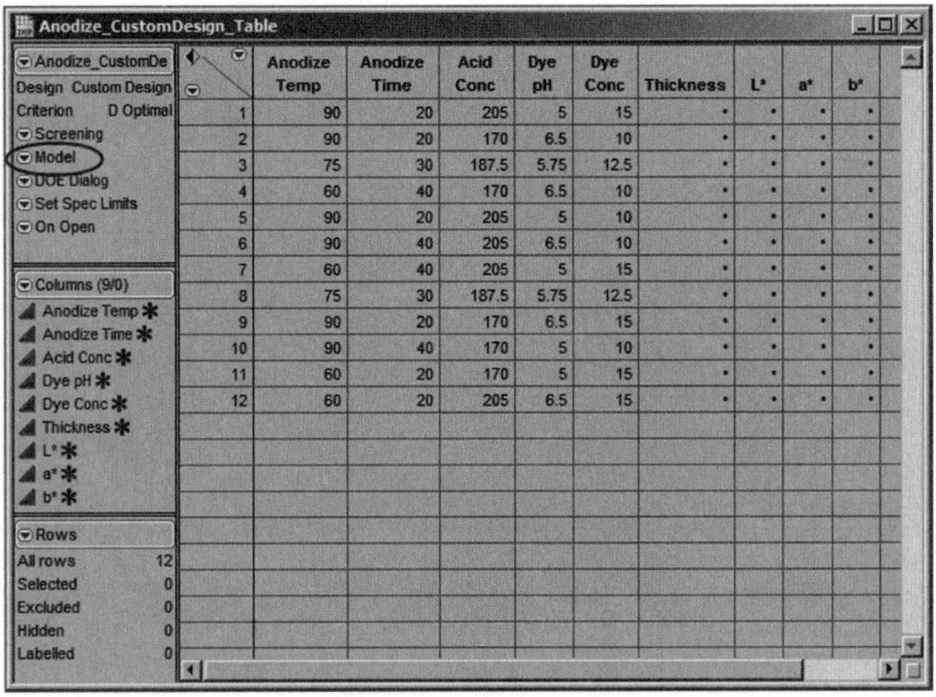

		Anodize Temp	Anodize Time	Acid Conc	Dye pH	Dye Conc	Thickness	L*	a*	b*
	1	90	20	205	5	15	•	•	•	•
	2	90	20	170	6.5	10	•	•	•	•
	3	75	30	187.5	5.75	12.5	•	•	•	•
	4	60	40	170	6.5	10	•	•	•	•
	5	90	20	205	5	10	•	•	•	•
	6	90	40	205	6.5	10	•	•	•	•
	7	60	40	205	5	15	•	•	•	•
	8	75	30	187.5	5.75	12.5	•	•	•	•
	9	90	20	170	6.5	15	•	•	•	•
	10	90	40	170	5	10	•	•	•	•
	11	60	20	170	5	15	•	•	•	•
	12	60	20	205	6.5	15	•	•	•	•

EXHIBIT 6.44 Design Table Generated by Custom Design

Sean notices that JMP has saved two other scripts to this data table. One of these scripts, **Screening**, runs a screening analysis. In this analysis, a saturated model is fit. Sean will not be interested in this analysis, since he has some prior knowledge of the appropriate model. The other script, **DOE Dialog**, reproduces the **DOE > Custom Design** dialog used to obtain this design.

Sean also notices the asterisks next to the variable names in the columns panel (Exhibit 6.45). He clicks on these to learn that JMP has saved a number of **Column Properties** for each of the factors: **Coding**, **Design Role**, and **Factor Changes**. Clicking on any one of these takes Sean directly to that property in **Column Info**. Similarly, for each response, **Response Limits** has been saved as a **Column Property**.

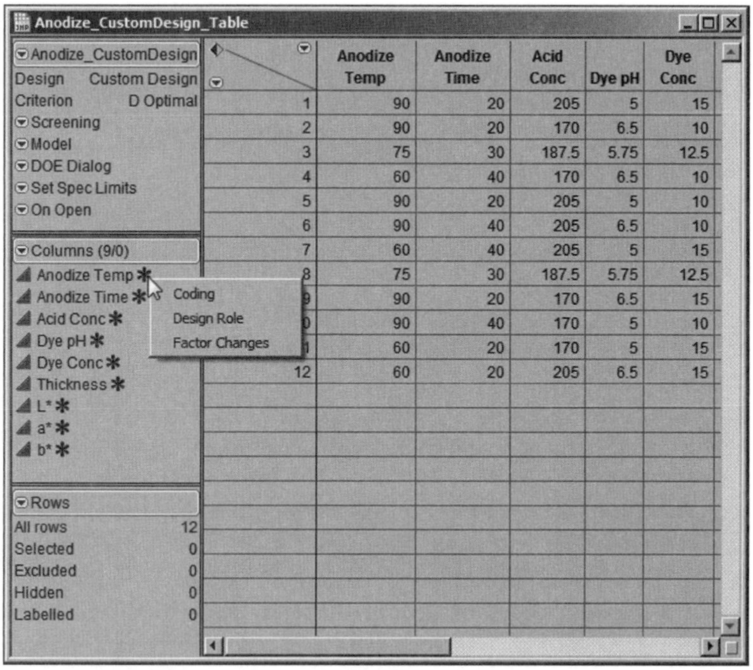

EXHIBIT 6.45   Column Properties for Anodize Temp

Sean decides to add each response's specification limits as a column property. He believes this information will be useful later, when determining optimal settings for the factors. To set specification limits for **Thickness**, Sean right-clicks in the header for the **Thickness** column. From the menu that appears, he chooses **Column Info**. In the **Column Info** window, from the **Column Properties** list, Sean selects **Spec Limits**. He populates the **Spec Limits** box as shown in Exhibit 6.46.

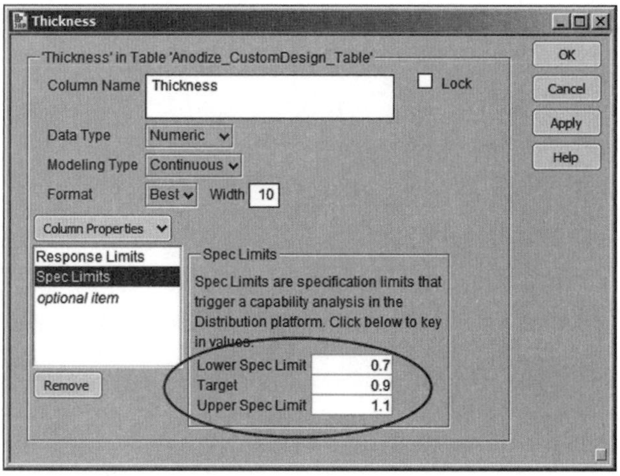

EXHIBIT 6.46   Dialog for Thickness Spec Limits

In a similar fashion, Sean saves **Spec Limits** as a column property for each of L*, a*, and b*. These will be useful later on. (The script **Set Spec Limits** will set the specification limits for all four responses at once.)

Conducting the Experiment

The team is now ready to perform the experiment. Sean explains the importance of following the randomization order and of resetting all experimental conditions between runs. The team appreciates the importance of these procedures and plans the details of how the experiment will be conducted. The team also decides to number the parts in order to mistake-proof the process of taking measurements.

The team members proceed to conduct the experiment. The design and measured responses are given in the data table **Anodize_CustomDesign_Results.jmp** (Exhibit 6.47).

	Anodize Temp	Anodize Time	Acid Conc	Dye pH	Dye Conc	Thickness	L*	a*	b*
1	90	20	205	5	15	0.71	9.26	1.42	-2.13
2	90	20	170	6.5	10	0.99	3.61	3.16	-1.74
3	75	30	187.5	5.75	12.5	0.74	10.55	3.86	-2.78
4	60	40	170	6.5	10	0.41	17.13	6.23	-3.95
5	90	20	205	5	10	0.72	3.99	-0.42	1.15
6	90	40	205	6.5	10	1.06	3.02	-0.52	2.24
7	60	40	205	5	15	0.79	14.37	3.92	-3.38
8	75	30	187.5	5.75	12.5	0.77	11.27	3.49	-2.79
9	90	20	170	6.5	15	1.02	8.11	4.23	-4.89
10	90	40	170	5	10	1.09	2.39	-1.64	0.11
11	60	20	170	5	15	0.39	17.34	7.22	-7.93
12	60	20	205	6.5	15	0.47	19.05	7.75	-5.56

EXHIBIT 6.47   Results of Designed Experiment

Uncovering the Hot Xs

It is time to analyze the data, and Sean and the team are very excited! Sean will attempt to identify significant factors by modeling each response separately, using the **Fit Model** platform. For each of the four responses, Sean follows this strategy:

- Examine the data for outliers and possible lack of fit, using the **Actual by Predicted** plot as a visual guide. Check the **Lack Of Fit Test**, which can be conducted thanks to the two center points, in order to confirm his visual assessment of the **Actual by Predicted** plot.
- Find a best model by eliminating effects that appear insignificant.
- Save the prediction formula for the best model as a column in the data table.
- Save the script for the best model to the data table for future reference.

Sean's plan, once this work is completed, is to use the **Profiler** to find factor level settings that will simultaneously optimize all four responses.

Sean runs the **Model** script saved in the table information panel. This will fit models to all four responses. But Sean wants to examine these one by one, starting with the model for Thickness. So he removes the other three responses from the **Fit Model** dialog by selecting them in the **Y** text box and clicking the **Remove** button.

Then Sean clicks **Run Model** to run the full model for Thickness. In the report, from the red triangle drop-down menu, he chooses **Row Diagnostics > Plot Actual by Predicted**. The report for the model fit to Thickness, shown in Exhibit 6.48, shows no significant lack of fit—both the **Actual by Predicted** plot and the formal **Lack Of Fit** test support this conclusion (the p-value for the **Lack of Fit** test is **Prob > F =** 0.6238). Note that this is a nice example of Exploratory Data Analysis (the **Actual by Predicted** plot) being reinforced by Confirmatory Data Analysis (the **Lack Of Fit** test).

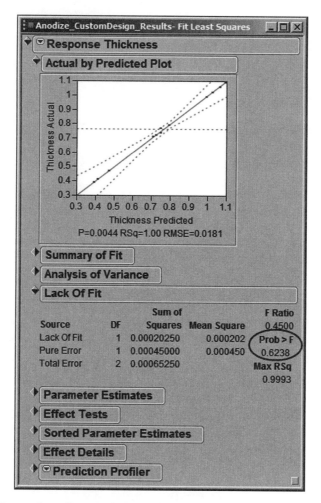

EXHIBIT 6.48   Report for Full Model for Thickness

Since the model appears to fit, Sean checks the **Analysis of Variance** panel and sees that the overall model is significant (Exhibit 6.49). He knows that he could examine the **Effect Tests** table to see which effects are significant. However, he finds it easier to interpret the **Sorted Parameter Estimates** table (Exhibit 6.49), which gives a graph where the size of a bar is proportional to the size of the corresponding effect. He examines the Prob > |t| values, and sees that two of the two-way interactions, Anodize Temp*Anodize Time and Dye pH*Dye Conc, do not appear to be significant (Sean decides that a significant p-value is one that is less than 0.05).

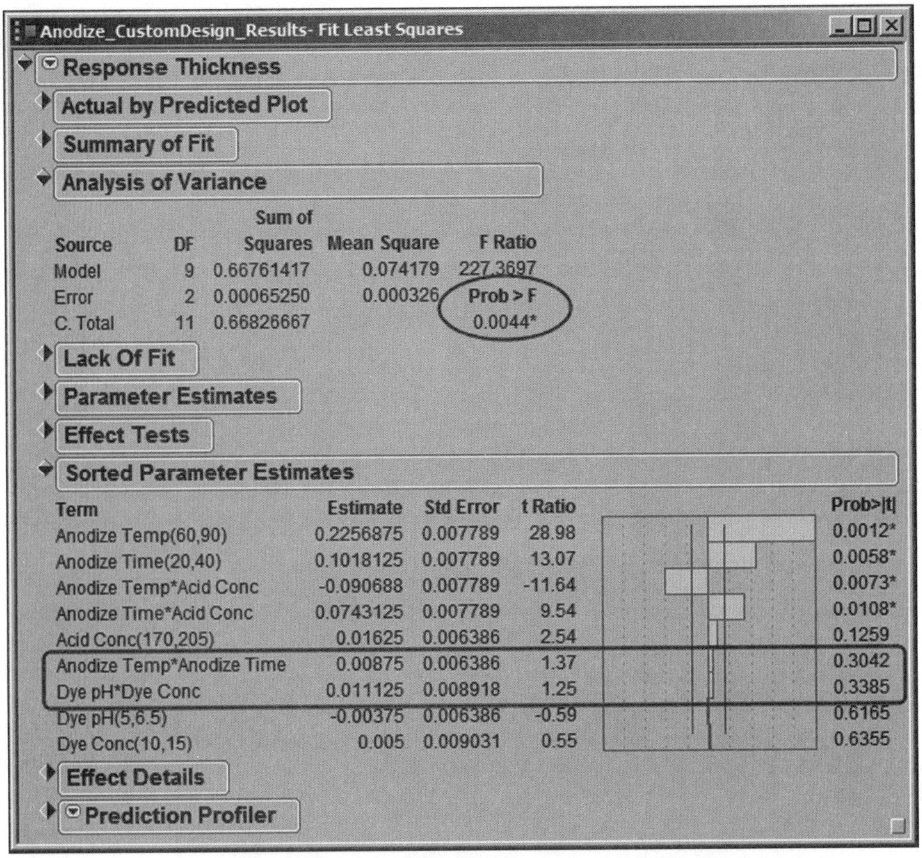

Anodize_CustomDesign_Results- Fit Least Squares

Response Thickness

Actual by Predicted Plot

Summary of Fit

Analysis of Variance

Source	DF	Sum of Squares	Mean Square	F Ratio
Model	9	0.66761417	0.074179	227.3697
Error	2	0.00065250	0.000326	Prob > F
C. Total	11	0.66826667		0.0044*

Lack Of Fit

Parameter Estimates

Effect Tests

Sorted Parameter Estimates

Term	Estimate	Std Error	t Ratio		Prob>|t|
Anodize Temp(60,90)	0.2256875	0.007789	28.98		0.0012*
Anodize Time(20,40)	0.1018125	0.007789	13.07		0.0058*
Anodize Temp*Acid Conc	-0.090688	0.007789	-11.64		0.0073*
Anodize Time*Acid Conc	0.0743125	0.007789	9.54		0.0108*
Acid Conc(170,205)	0.01625	0.006386	2.54		0.1259
Anodize Temp*Anodize Time	0.00875	0.006386	1.37		0.3042
Dye pH*Dye Conc	0.011125	0.008918	1.25		0.3385
Dye pH(5,6.5)	-0.00375	0.006386	-0.59		0.6165
Dye Conc(10,15)	0.005	0.009031	0.55		0.6355

Effect Details

Prediction Profiler

EXHIBIT 6.49   ANOVA and Sorted Parameter Estimates for Full Model for Thickness

At this point, Sean can opt for one of two approaches. He can reduce the model manually or he can use a stepwise procedure. In the past, he has done model reduction manually, but he has learned that JMP has a **Stepwise** platform that allows him to remove effects from a model for a designed experiment in a way that is consistent with the hierarchy of terms. So he tries both approaches.

In the manual approach, Sean removes the least significant of the two interaction terms from the model, namely, Dye pH*Dye Conc. The **Fit Model** dialog remains open, and so it is easy to remove this term from the **Model Effects** box. He refits the model without this term, notes that **Dye Conc** is the next least significant term, removes it, and refits the model. Next, each in turn, **Dye pH** and **Anodize Temp*Anodize Time** are removed from the model. At this point, all remaining terms are significant at the 0.05 level (Exhibit 6.50).

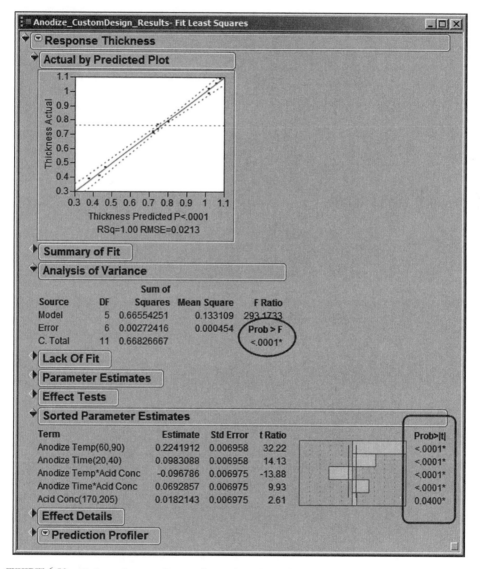

EXHIBIT 6.50   Fit Least Squares Report for Reduced Thickness Model

In the stepwise approach, Sean asks JMP to reduce the model exactly as he has just reduced it. He needs to rerun the full model for **Thickness**, since he was modifying the **Fit Model** dialog just now. He reruns the script **Model** and removes the other three responses, since model reduction is only done for one response at a time. Under **Personality**, he chooses **Stepwise**, as shown in Exhibit 6.51.

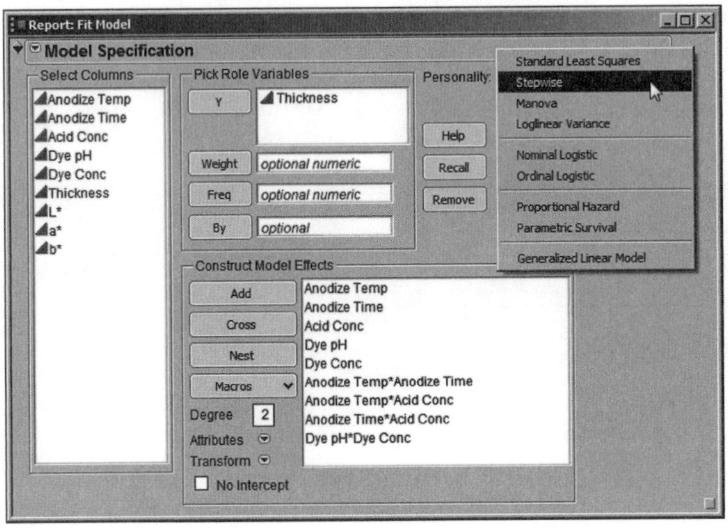

EXHIBIT 6.51   Selection of Stepwise Regression from Fit Model Dialog

When Sean clicks **Run Model**, the **Fit Stepwise** dialog box opens. He clicks on **Enter All** to enter all effects into the model. Then he sets up the dialog options as shown in Exhibit 6.52: He sets **Prob to Leave** to 0.05, so that effects will be removed if their p-values exceed 0.05; he sets the **Direction** to **Backward**, so that effects are removed in turn (and effects are not entered); and he chooses **Restrict** under **Rules**. This last choice removes effects in a fashion consistent with the hierarchy of terms. For example, a main effect is not removed so long as an interaction involving the main effect is significant.

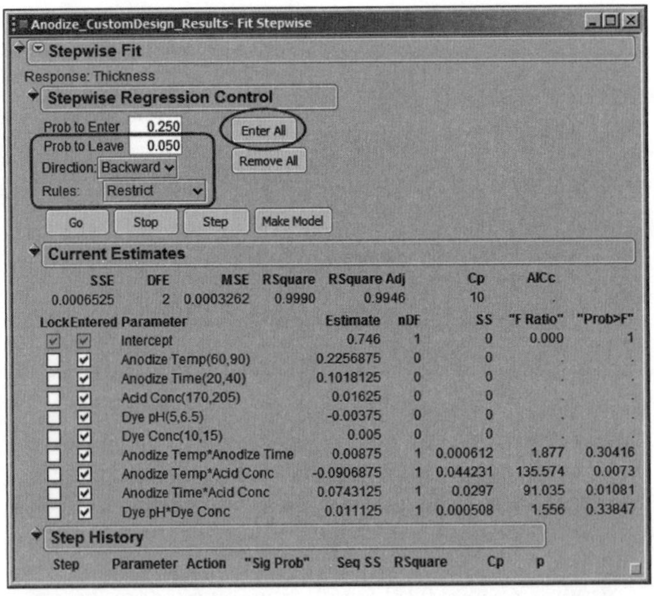

EXHIBIT 6.52   Fit Stepwise Dialog Settings for Thickness Model Reduction

At this point, Sean can click **Step** to view the removal of terms one by one, or he can click **Go** to have the reduction done all at once. Either way, the procedure ends with four effects removed, as shown in Exhibit 6.53.

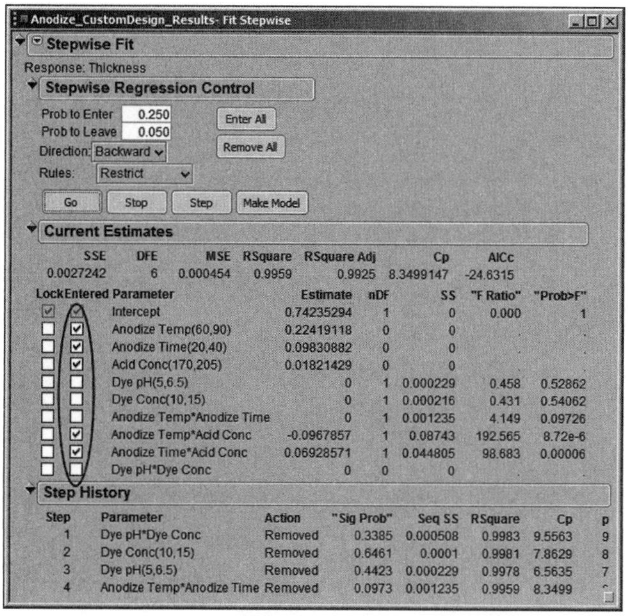

EXHIBIT 6.53   Results of Stepwise Reduction for Thickness

Now, in the **Fit Stepwise** dialog, Sean clicks **Make Model**. This creates a **Stepped Model** dialog to fit the reduced model (Exhibit 6.54). He notes that this is the same model that he obtained using the manual approach.

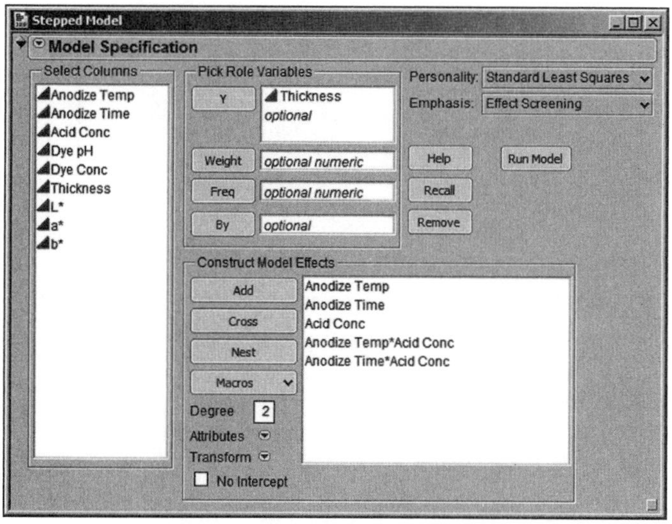

EXHIBIT 6.54   Stepped Model Dialog for Reduced Model for Thickness

Sean observes that these are precisely the significant effects left in the model that he reduced manually, whose analysis is shown in Exhibit 6.50. He adopts this as his reduced and final model for Thickness.

Sean notices that the final Thickness model contains two significant interactions. He also notes that only factors in the anodizing step of the process are significant for Thickness. Thus, the team finds that the model is in good agreement with engineering knowledge, which indicates that factors in the dye step should not have an impact on anodize thickness. Sean saves a script that creates the fit model dialog for his final Thickness model to the data table as **Thickness Model**.

Sean uses the stepwise approach in a similar fashion to determine final models for each of the other three responses. These models are also saved to the table information panel in the data table **Anodize_CustomDesign_Results.jmp** (see Exhibit 6.55). Each of the models for L*, a*, and b* includes factors from both the anodizing and dyeing processes.

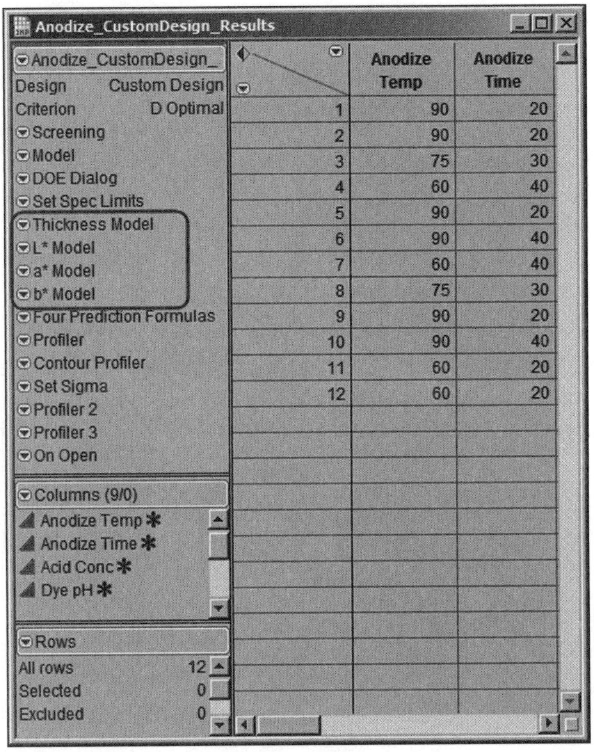

EXHIBIT 6.55   Final Model Scripts for Four Responses

Revising Knowledge

In the Visual Six Sigma Data Analysis Process, the Model Relationships step is followed by Revise Knowledge (see Exhibit 3.29). This is where we identify the best settings for the Hot Xs, visualize the effect of variation in the settings of the Hot Xs, and grapple with the extent to which our conclusions generalize. Having developed models for the four responses and, in the process, identified the Hot Xs, Sean and his team now proceed to the Revise Knowledge step.

Determining Optimal Factor Level Settings

Sean and his teammates are pleased with their four different models for the responses. At this point, their intent is to identify settings of the five Xs that optimize these four Ys. Sean knows that factor settings that optimize one response may, in fact, degrade performance with respect to another response. For this reason, it is important that *simultaneous* optimization be conducted relative to a sound measure of desirable performance.

In the Analyze Phase, the team defined target values and specification limits for the four Ys, hoping to guarantee acceptable color quality for the anodized parts. Using these targets and specifications as a basis for optimization, Sean guides the team in performing multiple optimization in JMP.

JMP bases multiple optimization on a *desirability function*. Recall that when Sean entered his responses in the custom design dialog he noted that the goal for each response was to **Match Target**, and he entered the specification limits as response limits—see the **Lower Limit** and **Upper Limit** entries under **Responses** in Exhibit 6.40. Note also that Sean assigned equal **Importance** values of 1 to each response (also Exhibit 6.40). (What is important is the ratio of these values; for example, they could equally well have all been assigned as 0.25.)

The desirability function constructs a single criterion from the response limits and importance values. This function weights the responses according to importance and, in a **Match Target** situation, places the highest desirability on values in the middle of the response range (the user can manually set the target elsewhere, if desired). The desirability function is a function of the set of factors that is involved in the union of the four models. In Sean's case, since each factor appears in at least one of the models, the desirability function is a function of all five process factors.

In JMP, desirability functions are accessed from the **Profiler**, which is often called the *Prediction Profiler* to distinguish it from the several other profilers that JMP provides. Sean knows that the **Profiler** for a single response can be found in the **Fit Model** report for that response. He also knows that when different models are fit to multiple responses the **Profiler** should be accessed from the **Graph** menu. So, he selects **Graph > Profiler**, realizing almost immediately that he has acted prematurely. He must first save prediction formulas for each of the responses; otherwise, JMP will not have the underlying models available to optimize.

So, he returns to the table **Anodize_CustomDesign_Results.jmp**. He needs to save the four prediction formulas to the data table. He does this as follows:

- He runs the script that he has saved for the given response (**Thickness Model, L* Model, a* Model, or b* Model**).
- In the **Fit Model** dialog, he clicks **Run Model**.
- In the report, he clicks the red triangle at the top and chooses **Save Columns > Prediction Formula**.

This inserts a *Pred Formula* column in the data table for each response—these will appear as the final four columns in the data table (Exhibit 6.56). (Alternatively, you can run the script **Four Prediction Formulas**.)

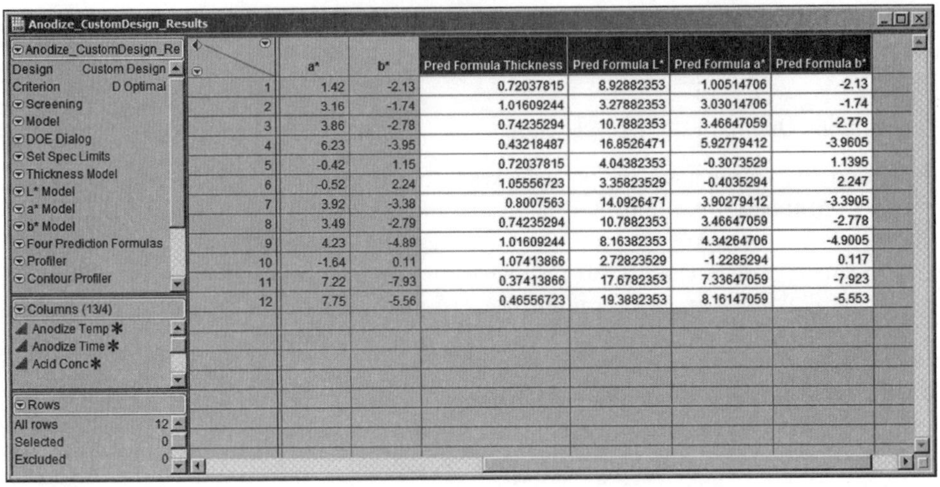

	a*	b*	Pred Formula Thickness	Pred Formula L*	Pred Formula a*	Pred Formula b*
1	1.42	-2.13	0.72037815	8.92882353	1.00514706	-2.13
2	3.16	-1.74	1.01609244	3.27882353	3.03014706	-1.74
3	3.86	-2.78	0.74235294	10.7882353	3.46647059	-2.778
4	6.23	-3.95	0.43218487	16.8526471	5.92779412	-3.9605
5	-0.42	1.15	0.72037815	4.04382353	-0.3073529	1.1395
6	-0.52	2.24	1.05556723	3.35823529	-0.4035294	2.247
7	3.92	-3.38	0.8007563	14.0926471	3.90279412	-3.3905
8	3.49	-2.79	0.74235294	10.7882353	3.46647059	-2.778
9	4.23	-4.89	1.01609244	8.16382353	4.34264706	-4.9005
10	-1.64	0.11	1.07413866	2.72823529	-1.2285294	0.117
11	7.22	-7.93	0.37413866	17.6782353	7.33647059	-7.923
12	7.75	-5.56	0.46556723	19.3882353	8.16147059	-5.553

EXHIBIT 6.56 Columns Containing Prediction Formulas for Final Models

Each of these columns is defined by the formula for the model for the specified response. For example, the prediction formula for **a*** is given in Exhibit 6.57.

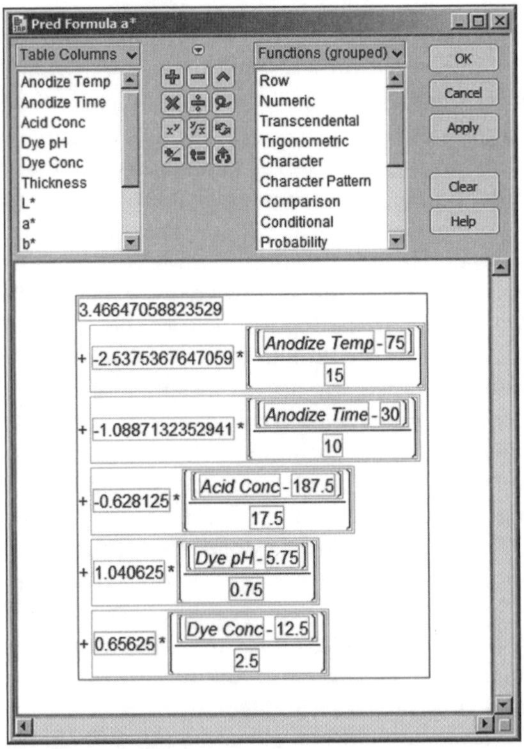

$$3.46647058823529$$

$$+ -2.5375367647059 * \frac{[\text{Anodize Temp} - 75]}{15}$$

$$+ -1.0887132352941 * \frac{[\text{Anodize Time} - 30]}{10}$$

$$+ -0.628125 * \frac{[\text{Acid Conc} - 187.5]}{17.5}$$

$$+ 1.040625 * \frac{[\text{Dye pH} - 5.75]}{0.75}$$

$$+ 0.65625 * \frac{[\text{Dye Conc} - 12.5]}{2.5}$$

EXHIBIT 6.57 Prediction Formula for a*

Now, confident that he has laid the infrastructure, Sean returns to **Graph > Profiler** and enters the four prediction formulas as **Y, Prediction Formula**. Exhibit 6.58 shows the configuration of the launch dialog.

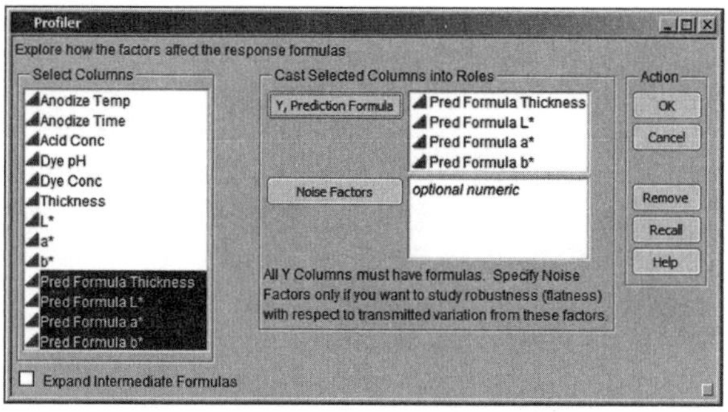

EXHIBIT 6.58   Launch Dialog for Graph > Profiler

When Sean clicks **OK**, the **Profiler** appears with desirability functions displayed in the rightmost column (Exhibit 6.59). This column is associated with each response's individual desirability function. For each response, the maximum desirability value is 1.0, and this occurs at the midpoint of the response limits. The least desirable value is 0.0, and this occurs near the lower and upper response limits. (Since Sean's specifications are symmetric, having the highest desirability at the midpoint makes sense. We reiterate that the user can change this.) The cells in the bottom row in Exhibit 6.59 show traces, or cross-sections, for the desirability function associated with the simultaneous optimization of all four responses.

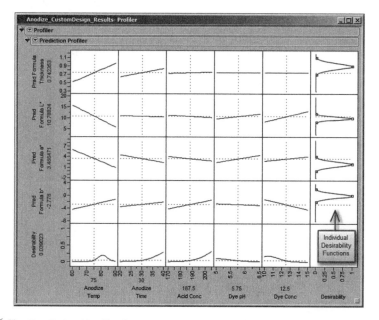

EXHIBIT 6.59   Prediction Profiler for Four Responses

Recall that the response limits for **b*** were −2.0 and +2.0. To better understand the desirability function, Sean double-clicks in the desirability panel for **b***, given in the rightmost column. He sees the dialog displayed in Exhibit 6.60. He notes that −2.0 and +2.0 are given desirability close to 0, namely, 0.0183, and that the midpoint between the response limits, 0, is given desirability 1. If he wanted to change any of these settings, Sean could do so in this dialog. Satisfied, Sean clicks **Cancel** to close the **Response Goal** dialog.

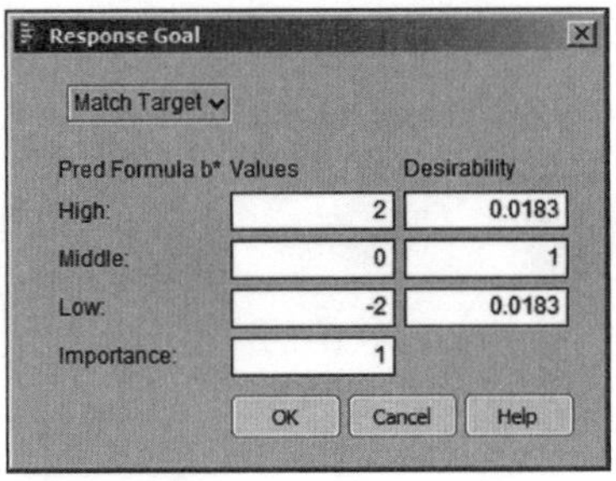

EXHIBIT 6.60   Response Goal Dialog for b*

The profiler is dynamically linked to the models for the responses. When the profiler first appears, the dotted (red) vertical lines in the panels are set to the midpoint of the predictor values. Sean shows the team that by moving the dotted (red) vertical line for a given process factor one can see the effect of changes on the four responses. This powerful dynamic visualization technique enables what-if inquiries such as "What happens if we increase **Anodize Time**?" The team explores various scenarios using this feature, before returning to the goal of optimization.

To perform the optimization, Sean selects the **Maximize Desirability** option from the red triangle in the **Prediction Profiler** panel. Sean's results for the multiple response optimization of the four responses are shown in Exhibit 6.61. However, since there are many solutions to such an optimization problem, the results you obtain may differ from Sean's. (Sean's specific results can be obtained by running the script **Profiler** in **Anodize_CustomDesign_Results.jmp**.)

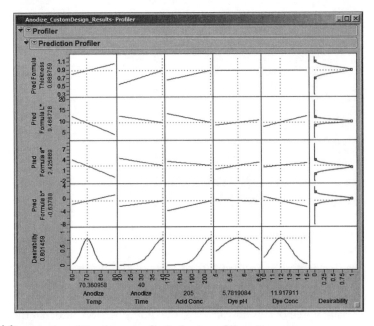

EXHIBIT 6.61   Results of Simultaneous Optimization of Four Responses

The wealth of information concerning the responses and the process variable settings provided in this visual display amazes Sean and his team. At the bottom of the display (in gray in Exhibit 6.61, in red on a screen), he sees optimal settings for each of the five process variables. To the left of the display (again, gray in Exhibit 6.61 and red on a screen), he sees the predicted mean response values associated with these optimal settings.

Sean notes that the predicted mean levels of all four responses are reasonably close to their specified targets, and are well within the specification limits. It does appear that further optimization could be achieved by considering higher values of **Anodize Time** and **Acid Conc**, since the optimal settings of these variables are at the extremes of their design ranges. Sean makes a note to consider expanding these ranges in a future experiment.

Linking with Contour Profiler

One of the team members asks Sean if there is a way to see other settings that might optimize the overall desirability. Even though the optimal factor settings obtained are feasible in this case, it is always informative to investigate other possible optimal or near-optimal settings.

Sean reflects a bit and then concludes that the **Contour Profiler** would be useful in this context. He realizes that he can access the **Contour Profiler** from the red triangle menu next to **Profiler**. But he would prefer to see it in a separate window, which is possible if he accesses it from the **Graph** menu. So, he selects **Graph > Contour Profiler**, enters all four prediction formulas as **Y, Prediction Formula** in the dialog, and clicks **OK**. The report shown in Exhibit 6.62 appears. (Sean saves the script as **Contour Profiler**.)

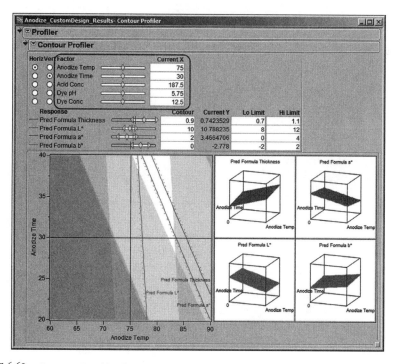

EXHIBIT 6.62   Contour Profiler for Four Prediction Formulas

The report shows contours of the four prediction formulas, as well as small surface plots for these formulas. Additional contour lines can be added by selecting **Contour Grid** from the red triangle next to **Contour Profiler**. Sean does not do that yet.

Sean observes that in the top part of the **Contour Profiler** report the **Current X** values are the midpoints of the design intervals. Recall that these were the initial settings for the factors in the **Prediction Profiler** as well. Sean would like to set these factor levels at the optimal settings as determined earlier using the **Prediction Profiler**.

To do this, he places the two profilers side-by-side. First, Sean links the two profilers. He does this by clicking on the red arrow next to **Prediction Profiler** and choosing **Factor Settings > Link Profilers**, as shown in Exhibit 6.63. This causes the **Contour Profiler** to update to the settings in the **Prediction Profiler**.

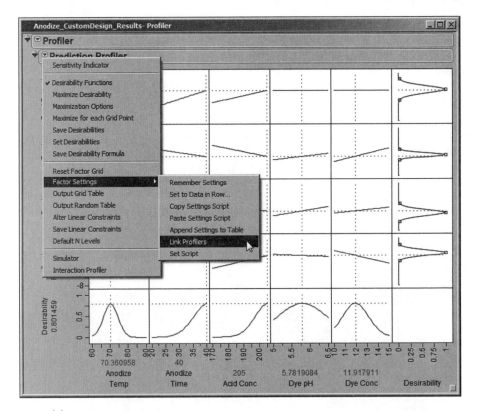

EXHIBIT 6.63   Linking the Profilers

By now, Sean has lost his optimal settings in the **Prediction Profiler**. So, once he has linked the two profilers, in the **Prediction Profiler**, he reruns **Maximize Desirability**. The settings for **Current X** in the **Contour Profiler** update to match the optimal settings found in the **Prediction Profiler** (Exhibit 6.64). (If the optimal settings are still showing in your **Prediction Profiler** when you link the profilers, you do not need to rerun **Maximize Desirability**.)

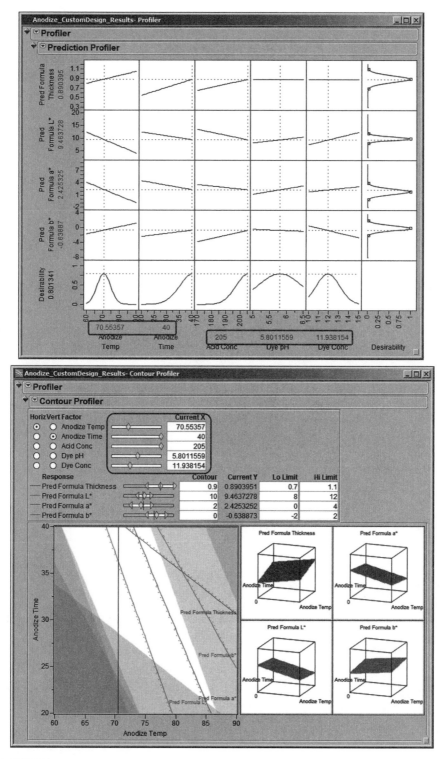

EXHIBIT 6.64   Linked Profilers

Now Sean illustrates how, by making choices of **Horiz** and **Vert Factor** in the **Contour Profiler** and by moving the sliders next to these or by moving the crosshairs in the contour plot, one can see the effect of changing factor settings on the predicted responses. One can see the effect on overall desirability by checking the **Prediction Profiler**, which updates as the factor settings are changed in the **Contour Profiler**. Sean chooses settings for the **Contour Grid**, obtained from the **Contour Profiler** red triangle menu, as appropriate to better view responses.

Sean and his team agree that the **Contour Profiler** and its ability to link to the **Prediction Profiler** is an extremely powerful tool in terms of exploring alternative factor level settings. In some cases it might be more economical, or necessary for other reasons, to run at settings different from those found to be optimal using the **Prediction Profiler**. This tool allows users to find alternative settings and to gauge their effect on desirability as well as on the individual response variables. At this point, Sean closes the **Contour Profiler**. Since they have been exploring various settings of the predictors, Sean runs the script **Profiler** to retrieve his optimal settings.

Sensitivity

The **Prediction Profiler** report provides two ways to assess the sensitivity of the responses to the settings of the process variables: desirability traces and a sensitivity indicator.

Notice that the last row of the **Prediction Profiler** display, repeated in Exhibit 6.65, contains desirability traces for each of the process variables. These traces represent the overall sensitivity of the combined desirability functions to variation in the settings of the process factors. For example, Sean observes that the desirability trace for **Anodize Temp** is peaked, with sharply descending curves on either side of the peak. Thus, the desirability function is more sensitive to variation in the setting of **Anodize Temp** than, say, to **Dye pH**, which is much less peaked by comparison. Variation in the setting of **Anodize Temp** will cause significant variation in the desirability of the responses.

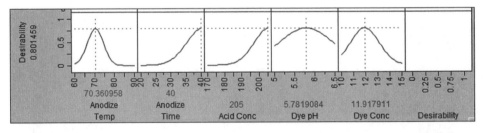

EXHIBIT 6.65   Desirability Traces in Last Row of Prediction Profiler

Sean clicks the red triangle in the **Prediction Profiler** report panel and selects **Sensitivity Indicator**. These indicators appear in Exhibit 6.66 as small triangles in each of the response profiles. (Note that Sean has used the grabber tool to rescale some of the axes so that the triangles are visible; place your cursor over an axis and the grabber tool will appear.) The height of each triangle indicates the relative sensitivity of that response at the corresponding process variable's setting. The triangle points up or down to indicate whether the predicted response increases or decreases, respectively, as the process variable increases.

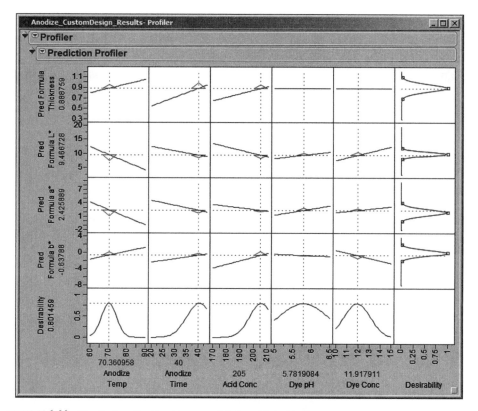

EXHIBIT 6.66 Prediction Profiler Report with Sensitivity Indicators

For Anodize Temp, Sean notices that Pred Formula L* and Pred Formula a* both have relatively tall downward-pointing triangles, indicating that according to his models both L* and a* will decrease fairly sharply with an increase in Anodize Temp. Similarly, Sean sees that Pred Formula Thickness and Pred Formula b* have upward-pointing triangles, indicating that those responses will increase with an increase in Anodize Temp.

Sean is puzzled by the horizontal traces and lack of sensitivity indicators for Dye pH and Dye Conc in the row for Pred Formula Thickness. In fact, he is about to write to JMP Technical Support, when he remembers that not all factors appear in all prediction formulas. In fact, he remembers now that the dye variables did not appear in the model for Thickness. So, it makes sense that horizontal lines appear, and that no sensitivity indicators are given, since Dye pH and Dye Conc do not have an effect on Thickness.

From the sensitivity analysis, Sean concludes that the joint desirability of the responses will be quite sensitive to variation in the process variables in the region of the optimal settings. The team reminds him that some process experts did not believe, prior to the team's experiment, that the anodize process, and especially color, was sensitive to Anodize Temp. It is because of this unfounded belief that temperature is not controlled well in the current process. The team views this lack of control over temperature as a potentially large contributor to the low yields and substantial run-to-run variation seen in the current process.

Confirmation Runs

The team now thinks it has a potential solution to the color problem. Namely, the process should be run at the optimized settings for the Ys, while controlling the Xs as tightly as possible. The Revise Knowledge step in the Visual Six Sigma Roadmap (see Exhibit 3.30) addresses the extent to which our conclusions generalize. Gathering new data through confirmation trials at the optimal settings will either provide support for the model or indicate that the model falls short of describing reality.

To see if the optimal settings actually do result in good product, Sean suggests that the team conduct some confirmation runs. Such confirmation is essential before implementing a systemic change to how a process operates. In addition to being good common sense, this strategy will address the skepticism of some of the subject matter experts who are not involved with the team.

With support from the production manager, the team performs two confirmatory production runs at the optimized settings for the process variables. The results of these confirmation runs are very favorable—not only do both lots have 100 percent yields, but the outgoing inspectors declare these parts uniformly to have the best visual appearance they have ever seen. The team also ships some of these parts to Components Inc.'s main customer, who reports that these are the best they have received from any supplier.

Projected Capability

At this point, the team is ready to develop an implementation plan to run the process at the new optimized settings. However, Sean restrains the team from doing this until the capability of the new process is estimated. Sean points out that this is very important, since some of the responses are quite sensitive to variation in the process variables.

In Design for Six Sigma (DFSS) applications, estimation of response distribution properties is sometimes referred to as *response distribution analysis*. Predictive models, or more generally *transfer functions*, are used to estimate or simulate the amount of variation that will be observed in the responses as a function of variation in the model inputs.

Sean and his team set out to obtain estimates of the variation in the process variables for the current production process. They learn that they can control **Anodize Time** with essentially no error. Standard deviation estimates for the remaining variables are shown in Exhibit 6.67.

EXHIBIT 6.67   Estimated Standard Deviations for
Process Factors

Process Factor	Estimated Standard Deviation
Anodize Temp	1.542
Acid Conc	1.625
Dye pH	0.100
Dye Conc	0.323

In the data table **Anodize_CustomDesign_Results.jmp**, for each of these four Xs, Sean enters these values as the **Column Property** called **Sigma** in **Column Info**. He does not specify a **Sigma** property for Anodize Time, which the team will treat as fixed. (**Set Sigma** is a script that enters these values as **Sigma** column properties.)

As Sean knows from his participation in DFSS projects, the **Prediction Profiler** in JMP includes an excellent simulation environment. He accesses it by selecting **Simulator** from the menu obtained by clicking the red triangle next to **Prediction Profiler**. Sean saves this script as **Profiler 2**.

Exhibit 6.68 displays the simulation report. Keep in mind that your settings will likely differ from those shown in the exhibit. However, the script **Profiler 2** reproduces the settings shown in the exhibit.

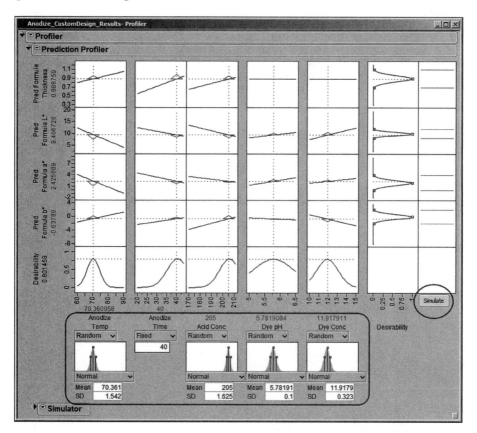

EXHIBIT 6.68 Simulation at Optimal Settings with Specified Process Factor Distributions

JMP automatically defaults to **Normal** distributions and inserts the optimal settings as **Mean** and the standard deviations specified as **Sigma** in the column properties as **SD**. These settings appear, with histograms showing the specified process variable distributions, at the bottom of the output. Sean uses the normal distributions that are given by default, but he realizes that several distributions are available for use.

Sean clicks on the **Simulate** button, located to the far right. This causes JMP to simulate 5,000 rows of factor values for which simulated response values are calculated. Histograms for these simulated response values appear above the **Simulate** button, as shown in Exhibit 6.69.

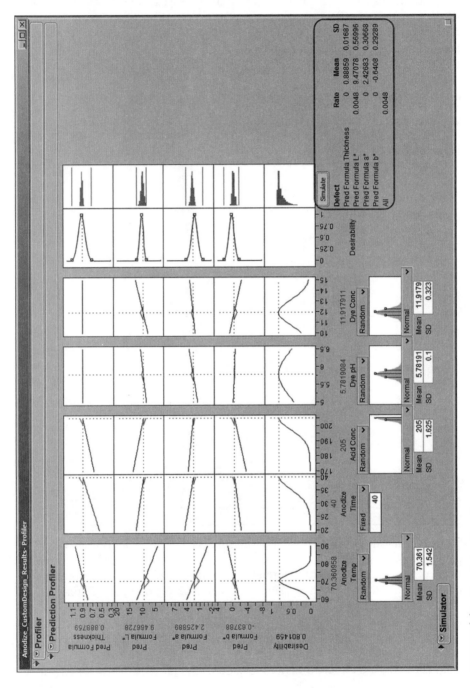

EXHIBIT 6.69   Simulation Results

Based on the simulation results, the **Prediction Profiler** also calculates estimated defective rates for each of the four responses. The team notices that the estimated defective rate for L* is 0.48 percent, which is higher than they would like. For the other three responses, at least to four decimal places, the estimated defective rate is 0. Sean remembers that one can obtain an estimate of *defective parts per million* (PPM) by right-clicking in the **Simulate** area and selecting **Columns > PPM**, as shown in Exhibit 6.70.

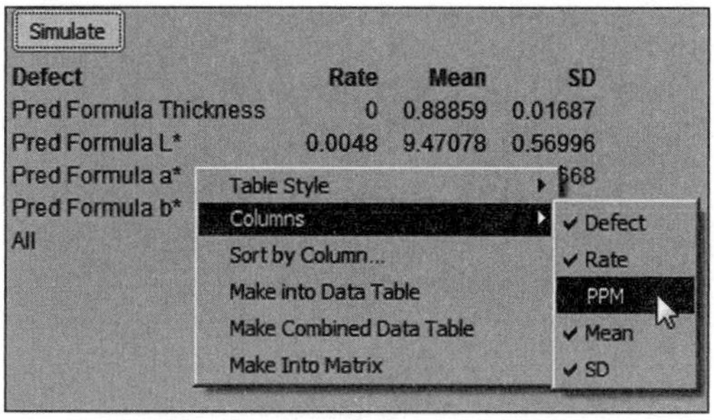

EXHIBIT 6.70   Obtaining a PPM Estimate in the Defect Report

Rerunning the simulation a few times indicates that an overall defect rate of 0.48 percent, corresponding to a PPM level of 4,800, is in the ballpark. The team takes note of this as a possible direction for further study or for a new project.

To obtain an estimate of the capability of the process when run at the new settings, Sean saves 5,000 simulated response values to a data table. Such a table is easily created within the **Prediction Profiler** using the **Simulator** panel (see Exhibit 6.71). After clicking on the disclosure icon for **Simulate to Table**, Sean clicks on **Make Table** to run the simulation. Once the table appears, Sean saves this simulated data table for future reference as **Anodize_CustomDesign_Simulation.jmp**.

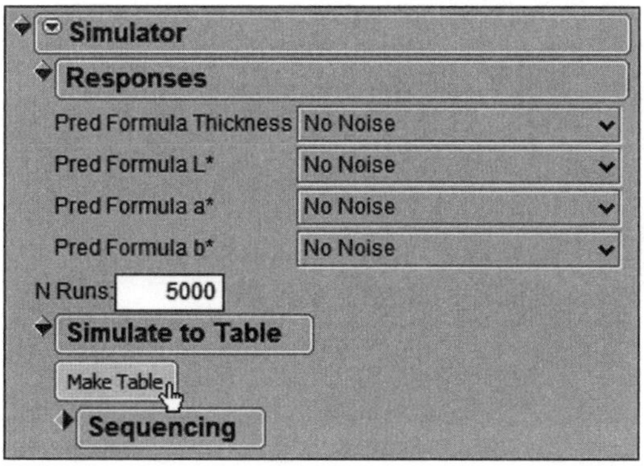

EXHIBIT 6.71   Simulating a Data Table with 5,000 Values

The data table consisting of the simulated data contains a script called **Distribution**. Sean runs this script, which provides histograms and capability analyses for all four predicted responses. The capability analyses are provided because specification limits were saved to the column information for the original responses, and JMP carried those to the prediction formulas.

The report for **Pred Formula Thickness**, based on the simulated results, is shown in Exhibit 6.72. For **Pred Formula Thickness**, the capability, as measured by Cpk, is 3.691. Also, note that the process is slightly off center. (The reader needs to keep in mind that since the capability analyses are based on simulated data, these values will change whenever the simulation is run.)

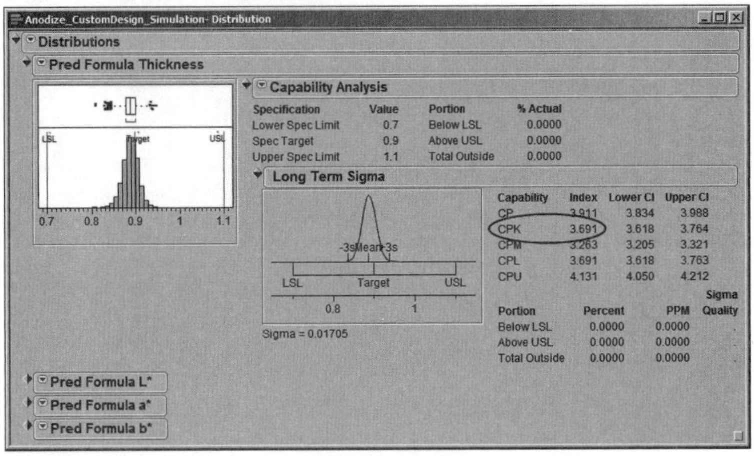

EXHIBIT 6.72   Capability Report for Predicted Thickness

Sean suddenly remembers that JMP has a platform designed to support the visualization of capability-related data when numerous responses are of interest. He has four responses, admittedly not a large number, but he is still interested in exploring his simulated capability data using this platform. While he still has the simulated data table as the current data table, Sean selects **Graph > Capability**. In the capability launch dialog, he enters all four prediction formulas (Exhibit 6.73).

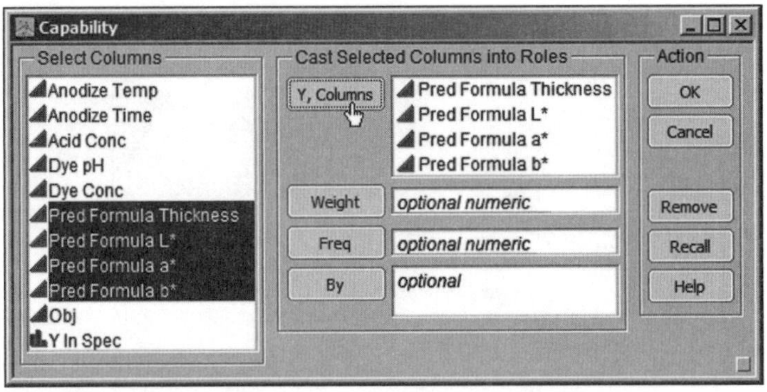

EXHIBIT 6.73   Launch Dialog for Capability

When Sean clicks **OK**, he obtains the report shown in Exhibit 6.74. The **Goal Plot** displays a point for each predicted response. The horizontal value for a response is its mean shift from the target divided by its specification range. The vertical value is its standard deviation divided by its specification range. The ideal location for a response is near (0,0); it should be on target and its standard deviation should be small relative to its specification range.

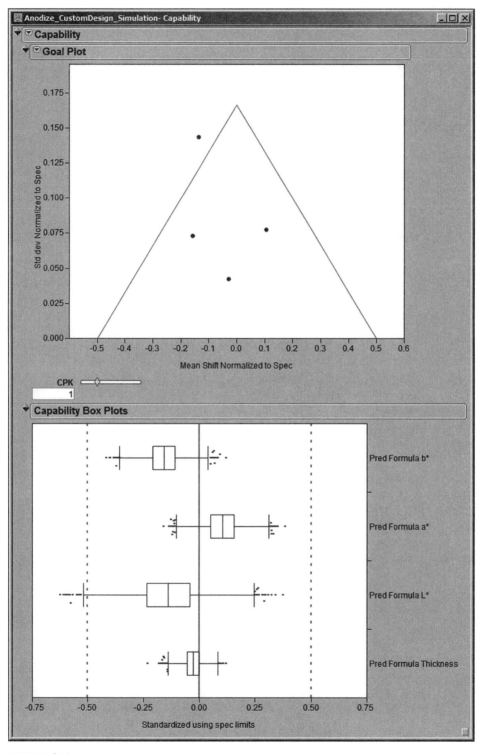

EXHIBIT 6.74 Capability Report for Four Simulated Responses

There is a slider at the bottom of the **Goal Plot** that is set, by default, to a **CPK** of 1. The slider setting defines a triangular, or *goal*, area in the plot, within which responses have Cpks that exceed 1.

The slider can be moved to change the **CPK** value and the corresponding goal area. Recall that a centered process with a Cpk of 1 has a 0.27 percent defective rate; such a process is generally considered unacceptable. Assuming that a process is stable and centered, a Cpk of 1.5 corresponds to a rate of 6.8 defective items per million.

Sean enters the value 1.5 into the **CPK** text box. The triangular region changes, but three of the four responses continue to fall in the Cpk-defined goal area. Sean looks at the red triangle options next to **Goal Plot** and notices that he can request **Goal Plot Labels**. He does so, and the plot that results is shown in Exhibit 6.75.

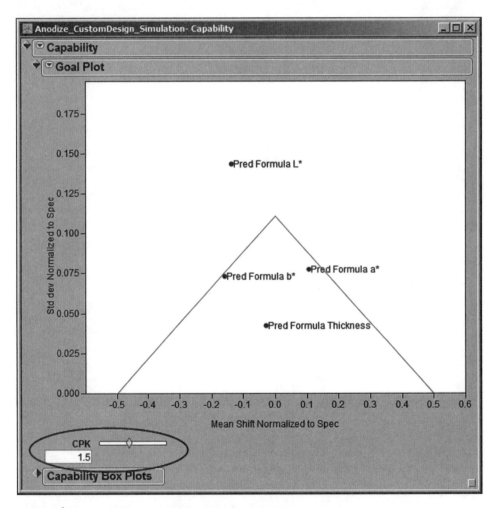

EXHIBIT 6.75   Goal Plot with Labels and Cpk Region at 1.5

Sean notes that Pred Formula L* falls outside the 1.5 Cpk region, while the three other predicted responses fall within that region. From the red triangle menu at the top level of the report, next to **Capability**, Sean selects **Capability Indices Report**. This report shows summary information for all four predicted responses, as well as their Cpk values (Exhibit 6.76). (Note that Sean has double-clicked on the **PPM** column to choose a decimal format.) It is clear that L* would benefit from further study and work.

Columns	LSL	Target	USL	Mean	Standard Deviation	CP	CPK	PPM
Pred Formula Thickness	0.7	0.9	1.1	0.888737	0.017046	3.910927	3.6907	0.00
Pred Formula L*	8	10	12	9.456406	0.574349	1.160734	0.8452	5615.11
Pred Formula a*	0	2	4	2.420672	0.311403	2.140849	1.6906	0.20
Pred Formula b*	-2	0	2	-0.63326	0.293705	2.269848	1.5511	1.63

EXHIBIT 6.76 Estimated Capability Values from Simulation

The second plot in Exhibit 6.74 gives **Capability Box Plots**. These are box plots constructed from the centered and scaled data. To be precise, the box plot is constructed from values obtained as follows: The response target is subtracted from each measurement, then this difference is divided by the specification range. Sean and his teammates see, at a glance, that except for Pred Formula Thickness the simulated responses fall off target, and, in the case of L*, some simulated values fall below the lower spec limit.

At this point, Sean saves his script as **Capability** and closes both his **Capability** report and the simulation table **Anodize_CustomDesign_Simulation.jmp**. As he reexamines results from the sensitivity analysis, he recalls that L* and a* are particularly sensitive to variation in Anodize Temp (Exhibit 6.66), which is not well controlled in the current process. The team suspects that if the variation in Anodize Temp can be reduced, then conformance to specifications will improve, particularly for L*.

The team members engage in an effort to find an affordable temperature control system for the anodize bath. They find a system that will virtually eliminate variation in the bath temperature during production runs. Before initiating the purchasing process, the team asks Sean to estimate the expected process capability if they were to control temperature with this new system.

Conservative estimates indicate that the new control system will reduce the standard deviation of Anodize Temp by 50 percent, from 1.5 to 0.75. To explore the effect of this change, Sean returns to **Anodize_CustomDesign_Results.jmp** and reruns the script **Profiler 2**. He changes the standard deviation for Anodize Temp at the bottom of the **Prediction Profiler** panel to 0.75. Since he hopes to be dealing in small defective rates based on this change, Sean changes the specification of **Normal** distributions for his process factors to **Normal Weighted** distributions. The **Normal Weighted** distribution implements a weighted sampling procedure designed for more precise estimation of small defective rates. These changes in the **Profiler** are shown in Exhibit 6.77. Sean saves the script for this analysis as **Profiler 3**.

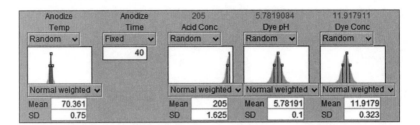

EXHIBIT 6.77 **Profiler Settings for Second Simulation**

Sean constructs a new 5,000-value simulated data table (**Anodize_CustomDesign_Simulation2.jmp**). He runs the **Distribution** script that is automatically saved in this table to obtain capability analyses, which he then studies. The **Capability Indices Report** that he obtains using **Graph > Capability** is shown in Exhibit 6.78. (Again, since these values are based on a simulation, the values you obtain may differ slightly.)

Anodize_CustomDesign_Simulation2- Capability

Capability

Goal Plot

Capability Indices

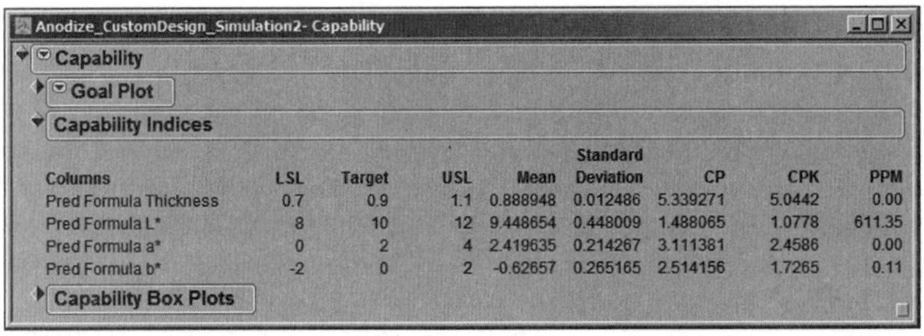

Columns	LSL	Target	USL	Mean	Standard Deviation	CP	CPK	PPM
Pred Formula Thickness	0.7	0.9	1.1	0.888948	0.012486	5.339271	5.0442	0.00
Pred Formula L*	8	10	12	9.448654	0.448009	1.488065	1.0778	611.35
Pred Formula a*	0	2	4	2.419635	0.214267	3.111381	2.4586	0.00
Pred Formula b*	-2	0	2	-0.62657	0.265165	2.514156	1.7265	0.11

Capability Box Plots

EXHIBIT 6.78 **Estimated Capability Values Based on Reduction of Anodize Temp Standard Deviation**

Sean and the team are very pleased. The new capability analyses indicate that Thickness, a*, and b* have extremely high capability values and very low PPM defective rates. Most important, the PPM rate for L* has dropped dramatically, and it now has a Cpk value of about 1.1.

Sean asks the team to run some additional confirmation trials at the optimal settings, exerting tight control of Anodize Temp. Everyone is thrilled when all trials result in 100 percent yield. Sean wonders if perhaps the specification limits for L* could be widened, without negatively affecting the yield. He makes a note to launch a follow-up project to investigate this further.

At this point, the team is ready to recommend purchase of the new temperature control system and to begin operating at the settings identified in the optimization. Sean guides the team in preparing an implementation plan. The team, with Sean's support, reports its findings to the management team. With the capability calculations as leverage, the team recommends the purchase of the anodize bath temperature control equipment. Management agrees with the implementation plan and the recommendations, and instructs the team members to implement their solution. With this, the project enters the Control Phase.

Utilizing Knowledge

In a formal DMAIC project, the utilization of knowledge begins in the Improve Phase and continues into the Control phase. As part of its Control Phase activities, the team prepares a comprehensive control plan for the anodize process. The plan includes specification of the optimum settings for the five Xs, as well as the new protocol for controlling the variation of these variables. The control plan also specifies the use of statistical process control to monitor the Xs, the four Ys, and the project KPI, process yield. Recall that the project goal was to improve the anodize process yield from 19 percent to a minimum of 90 percent, and to sustain that improvement.

About four months after the new process settings and controls are implemented, Sean and his team collect the associated data, including the final yield numbers. They add the yield values to a data table that contains yields for the initial 60-lot baseline period (**BaselineYieldAll.jmp**).

The team decides to continue to use an individual measurement chart to monitor process yield. Recall that although the yield measure is truly a proportion defective, Sean had reason to choose an individual measurement chart, rather than a p chart, to monitor this proportion. Sean makes **BaselineYieldAll.jmp** the active window. He selects **Graph > Control Chart > IR** and populates the launch dialog as shown in Exhibit 6.79. The column **Phase** is used to generate control limits for each portion of the data (Before and After). (The script is **Control Phase Control Chart**.)

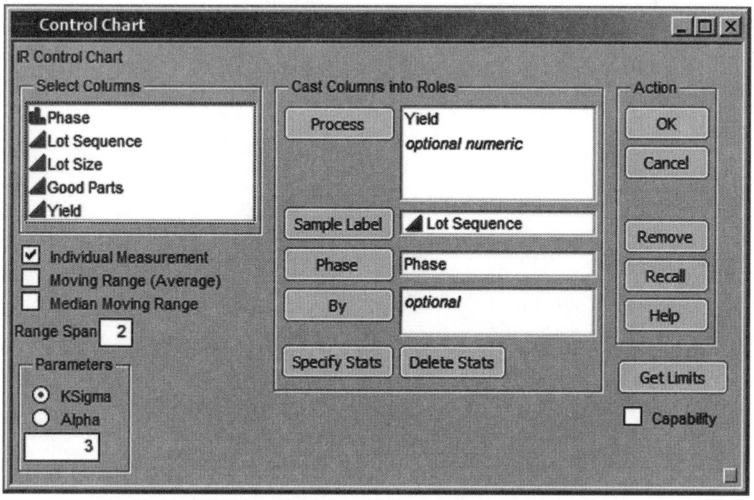

EXHIBIT 6.79   Launch Dialog for Individual Measurement Chart for Yield

The chart is shown in Exhibit 6.80. The team is delighted! The chart shows that the process is yielding, on average, close to 99 percent. This greatly exceeds the team's goal of improving daily yield to at least 90 percent.

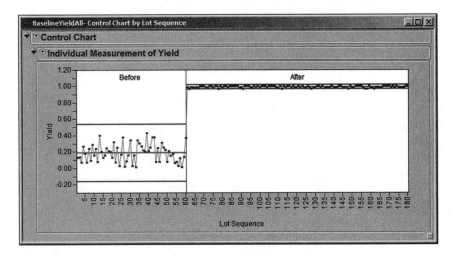

EXHIBIT 6.80   Before and After Control Charts for Yield

To better see the Control phase detail, Sean reruns the control chart, entering
Phase as a **By** variable rather than as a **Phase**. Exhibit 6.81 shows the resulting
control charts (the script is **Control Charts by Phase**). The process is consistently
yielding at least 96 percent.

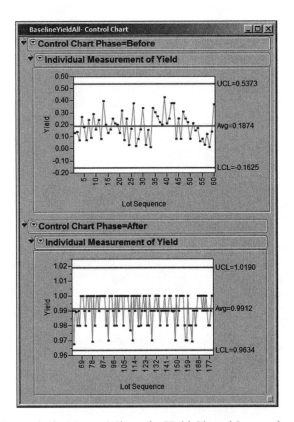

EXHIBIT 6.81   Before and After Control Charts for Yield, Plotted Separately

At this point, the project is deemed a success. Prior to celebrating and disbanding, the team members transition the process monitoring responsibility to the production manager, who will ensure that the process continues to perform at a high level. Sean and the team also document what they have learned and make recommendations for future improvement projects relating to this process.

Conclusion

Using this case study, let us review how the Visual Six Sigma Data Analysis Process aligns with the DMAIC framework, and how the Visual Six Sigma Roadmap was used to make progress quickly:

- Frame the Problem occurred in the Define phase.
- Collect Data began in the Measure phase, where the team collected data for its MSA studies and for the baseline control chart. Also, the team collected a set of historical data relating **Color Rating**, the team's primary, but nominal, Y, to four continuous Ys, namely **Thickness, L*, a*,** and **b***, that were thought to provide more detailed information than **Color Rating** itself.
- Uncover Relationships was the goal of the Analyze phase. The team members first visualized the five Ys one at a time using **Distribution**, also using dynamic linking to start to explore conditional distributions. Then, they dynamically visualized the variables two at a time with a **Scatterplot Matrix**. Finally, they dynamically visualized the variables more than two at a time using **Scatterplot 3D**. From the relationships that they uncovered, they were able to define specification limits for **Thickness, L*, a*,** and **b*** that corresponded to nondefective Normal Black parts.
- Model Relationships occurred in the Analyze and Improve phases. Here, the team studied five potential Hot Xs for the four continuous Ys. A customized experiment that allowed the team to identify which Hot Xs to include in each of the four signal functions was designed and conducted. The resulting models were visualized using the **Prediction Profiler**.
- Revise Knowledge also occurred as part of the Improve phase. New settings for the Hot Xs were identified that would simultaneously optimize all four Ys. Confirmation runs were obtained to provide some assurance that operating at the new optimal settings was likely to deliver the expected results. Finally, the JMP simulator was used to visualize the impact that variation about these optimal settings would have on the Ys.
- Utilize Knowledge was the goal of both the Improve and Control phases. Here, the knowledge developed by the team was institutionalized as the new way of running the process.

This case study shows how a Six Sigma team used visualization and confirmatory methods to solve a challenging industrial problem. The team's efforts resulted in a multimillion-dollar cost reduction for Components Inc. In addition, the elimination of rework resulted in significantly increased capacity in the anodize process. Components Inc. was able to use this newfound capacity to accommodate the increased demand for the parts that resulted from the dramatic improvements in quality and on-time delivery.

Our case study demonstrates how the dynamic visualization, analytic, and simulation capabilities of JMP played a prominent role in uncovering information and in modeling relationships that led to the resolution of a tough problem. Without these capabilities, and the Visual Six Sigma Roadmap to guide them, the team would have faced a much longer and more difficult path trying to find a workable solution.

Note

1. Robert D. Zaciewski and Lou Németh, "The Multi-Vari Chart: An Underutilized Quality Tool," *Quality Progress* 28, no. 10 (October 1995), 81–83.

CHAPTER 7

Informing Pharmaceutical Sales and Marketing

S ix Sigma is often positioned as a project-based approach. Certainly using identifiable and well-defined projects aligns well with approaches to managing change, and change management can be an important aspect in spreading the use of data within a company. But insofar as Visual Six Sigma makes data analysis lean, it has an important role to play within companies whose operations and organizations do not or cannot support the traditional project infrastructure, as well as for projects that by their nature do not require a formal structure. This scenario looks at one such project set in one such company.

Pharma Inc. is a pharmaceutical firm that markets drugs addressing several therapeutic areas. Rick Fincham is a recently hired sales manager who is responsible for U.K. operations. Although Rick is very experienced in sales, he is still learning about how Pharma Inc.'s sales operations run and perform.

Executive management perceives that Pharma Inc. has lost ground recently. Consequently, Rick has been asked to look into the recent performance of his sales force. Specifically, Rick has been asked to:

- Verify the claims of the marketing group that a limited promotion for Pharma Inc.'s major product, run from May through December 2008, was very successful.
- Determine whether there are regional differences in performance relative to sales of Pharma Inc.'s major product.

However, Rick also sees this as an opportunity to learn more about what happens in the field.

To answer the questions posed above, Rick downloads company data on the monthly performance of the sales representatives for May through December 2008. The data table is large, containing 95,864 rows and 16 columns. The data consist of a number of nominal demographic variables, as well as a few continuous and ordinal variables. The number of prescriptions for Pharma Inc.'s product written by physicians is the major Y of interest.

Rick's data are typical of large observational data sets. As such, Rick first spends some time assessing and dealing with the quality of the data. He moves on to obtain a better understanding of the deployment of his sales force using a bubble plot to display the location of the practices visited and their associated sales representatives. In answering the questions posed to him, Rick uses summary tables, oneway analyses with comparison circles, regression plots, and even an animated bubble plot.

Rick finds that the promotion was indeed successful. He identifies regional differences. He also uncovers what seems to be an uncanny and suspicious adherence to an unstated operational rule that each physician should be visited once per month.

The upshot of his single-handed analysis is that he can easily answer the questions posed by the executive management, using results and arguments supported by data and informed by visual displays that make it easy for him to get his points across. In addition, Rick uncovers a number of interesting facts that will help him to manage and deploy his sales force more effectively in the future.

Had Rick simply used a spreadsheet, by far the most common tool used for such analyses, he would not have arrived at his conclusions so quickly, if at all. He certainly would have struggled to construct informative graphical displays and to apply appropriate statistical techniques, and it is very likely that he would not have noticed the one-visit-per-month behavior. In short, it is probable that the useful new insights that Rick obtained from his quick visual analysis would not have been gained.

The platforms and options that Rick employs are listed in Exhibit 7.1. The data sets that he uses are available at http://support.sas.com/visualsixsigma. Rick would

EXHIBIT 7.1   Platforms and Options Illustrated in This Case Study

Menus	Platforms and Options
Tables	Summary
	Tabulate
	Missing Data Pattern
Rows	Color or Mark by Column
	Data Filter
Cols	Column Info
	Column Properties
	Formula
	Hide/Unhide
	Exclude/Unexclude
	Group Columns
Analyze	Distribution
	Histogram
	Frequency Distribution
	Fit Y by X
	Bivariate Fit
	Fit Line
	Fit Polynomial
	Oneway
	Compare Means
	Fit Model
	Standard Least Squares
	Random Effects (REML)
Graph	Bubble Plot
	Tree Map
Other Options	Broadcast Command
	Create a Script (from Existing Script)
	Edit Script
	Group By (In Bivariate Fit)
	Make into Data Table
	Run Script
	Save Script to Data Table

really enjoy your company as he explores his sales data set. You might be able to uncover some information that he overlooked. Give it a try!

Setting the Scene

Pharma Inc. markets drugs addressing several therapeutic areas, competing for market share and revenue with other companies doing the same thing. Rick Fincham, a recently hired sales manager for Pharma Inc., is responsible for U.K. operations. He has been in his position only three months, having previously been a senior account executive with a larger company. Although as an industry veteran Rick is very familiar with the general landscape, he has yet to come to terms with the nuances of exactly how Pharma Inc.'s operations run and perform.

Even though the markets view Pharma Inc. as generally doing well, executive management thinks that the company has lost ground recently. So, early in 2009, Rick is chartered to look into the recent performance of his sales force to shed light on some issues related to the perceived decline. He himself sees this as a chance to get better acquainted with exactly what happens in the field and why.

More specifically, Rick's manager, the vice president of sales and marketing, has asked him to:

- Verify the claims of the marketing group that a limited promotion they ran for Pharma Inc.'s major product from May through December 2008 was very successful.
- Determine if there are regional differences in performance relative to sales of Pharma Inc.'s major product.

Outside of work, Rick is a keen golfer and plays regularly with his partner, Arthur Ford, who is an engineering manager at a high-tech manufacturing company. While Rick was in his previous position, Arthur had convinced him to use JMP for data analysis. Knowing how visually oriented JMP is, Rick sees that it would be very useful in exploring the data that he intends to collect for the task at hand. He also knows that if he needs help he can count on his golfing buddy to give him guidance!

Collecting the Data

Each sales representative works his or her own territory, which is a geographic region of the United Kingdom defined by a collection of postal codes. A given territory contains physicians arranged in practices, where each physician has a particular medical specialty. The physicians write prescriptions for patients who visit their practices, aiming to provide them with the best possible care within the prevailing constraints. A sales representative will periodically make calls on a prescribing physician to promote the use of Pharma Inc.'s products, while representatives from competing companies do the same thing. During a visit, if a promotion is running, the sales representative may leave behind a promotional sample kit. Sales representatives control their own time and, before Rick joined, typically met with their sales manager about once a year.

Rick downloads company data on the performance of the sales representatives for May through December 2008 into a Microsoft® Excel spreadsheet. He intends to use this data to address both of the questions posed by his manager. He realizes that there has been some turnover in the sales force in 2008, but this has been minor. For his purposes, Rick decides that he will only include data for sales representatives who dealt with the same physicians for the entire eight-month period. He eliminates those few sales representatives who were active for only a portion of the eight months.

At this point, Rick easily imports his Excel data into a single JMP table called **PharmaSales_RawData.jmp**. The data table contains 95,864 rows and 16 columns. A partial view of the data table is given in Exhibit 7.2.

■ PharmaSales_RawData							
			Date	SalesrepID	Salesrep Name	PhysicianID	Physician Name
▼ PharmaSales_RawData		1	05/2008	107	Serafina Sumstad	168786	Matilde Faggard
▼ On Open		2	06/2008	107	Serafina Sumstad	168786	Matilde Faggard
		3	07/2008	107	Serafina Sumstad	168786	Matilde Faggard
▼ Columns (16/0)		4	08/2008	107	Serafina Sumstad	168786	Matilde Faggard
▲ Date		5	09/2008	107	Serafina Sumstad	168786	Matilde Faggard
▮ SalesrepID		6	10/2008	107	Serafina Sumstad	168786	Matilde Faggard
▮ Salesrep Name		7	11/2008	107	Serafina Sumstad	168786	Matilde Faggard
▮ PhysicianID		8	12/2008	107	Serafina Sumstad	168786	Matilde Faggard
▮ Physician Name		9	05/2008	107	Serafina Sumstad	175675	John Loveberry
▮ RegionID		10	06/2008	107	Serafina Sumstad	175675	John Loveberry
▮ Region Name		11	07/2008	107	Serafina Sumstad	175675	John Loveberry
▮ PracticeID		12	08/2008	107	Serafina Sumstad	175675	John Loveberry
▮ Practice Name		13	09/2008	107	Serafina Sumstad	175675	John Loveberry
▮ Physician Specialty		14	10/2008	107	Serafina Sumstad	175675	John Loveberry
▲ Visits		15	11/2008	107	Serafina Sumstad	175675	John Loveberry
▲ Visits with Samples		16	12/2008	107	Serafina Sumstad	175675	John Loveberry
▲ Prescriptions		17	05/2008	107	Serafina Sumstad	434070	Maryanne Schnicke
▮ Postcode		18	06/2008	107	Serafina Sumstad	434070	Maryanne Schnicke
▲ Practice Latitude		19	07/2008	107	Serafina Sumstad	434070	Maryanne Schnicke
▲ Practice Longitude		20	08/2008	107	Serafina Sumstad	434070	Maryanne Schnicke
		21	09/2008	107	Serafina Sumstad	434070	Maryanne Schnicke
▼ Rows		22	10/2008	107	Serafina Sumstad	434070	Maryanne Schnicke
All rows	95864	23	11/2008	107	Serafina Sumstad	434070	Maryanne Schnicke
Selected	0	24	12/2008	107	Serafina Sumstad	434070	Maryanne Schnicke
Excluded	0						
Hidden	0						
Labelled	0						

EXHIBIT 7.2   Partial View of PharmaSales_RawData.jmp

The columns are listed and described in Exhibit 7.3. Each row in the data table is uniquely defined by **Date, Salesrep Name,** and **Physician Name.** The variables **Visits, Visits with Samples,** and **Prescriptions** give the number of occurrences in the month defined by **Date.** Note that the four ID columns are simply codings of the corresponding Name columns, so that one of each pair is redundant.

EXHIBIT 7.3   Variable Descriptions for PharmaSales_RawData.jmp

Column Name	Description
Date	Month and year of current record
SalesrepID	Sales representative identifier
Salesrep Name	Name of the sales representative
PhysicianID	Physician identifier
Physician Name	Name of the prescribing physician
RegionID	Region identifier
Region Name	Name of the region
PracticeID	Practice identifier
Practice Name	Name of the practice
Physician Specialty	Specialty of the physician
Visits	Number of visits made by the sales representative to this physician this month
Visits with Samples	Number of visits during which a promotional sample kit is left by the sales representative with this physician this month
Prescriptions	Number of prescriptions for Pharma Inc.'s product written by this physician this month
Postcode	Location (postal code) of the practice
Practice Latitude	Latitude of the practice
Practice Longitude	Longitude of the practice

Recall that we use Ys to represent responses and Xs to represent variables that might affect the Ys. **Prescriptions** is the main Y variable of interest. **Visits** and **Visits with Samples** may be considered as input or X variables, because they are under the control of the sales representatives and are expected to have an impact on **Prescriptions**, or as Y variables, since they are the outcomes of past choices made by the sales representatives. Aside from **Practice Latitude** and **Practice Longitude**, which are used for mapping purposes, the other variables are either ancillary variables or stratifying variables that describe how Rick's sales system is currently configured and operated, and the environment in which it has to function.

Validating and Scoping the Data

Before starting to understand how the data can help answer the questions raised by the marketing vice president, Rick's first goal is to get a feel for what is actually *in* his data. Questions such as the following come to mind:

- How many sales representatives are there and where do they operate?
- How many practices are there?
- How many physicians are in each practice?

In his initial review of the data, Rick also wants to look at the general quality of the data, since he has seen problems with this in the past. He is reminded of the old saying, "Garbage in, garbage out."

Preparing the Data Table

Rick decides to do some preliminary preparation of his data table. He will enter descriptions of the variables in each column and then group, exclude, and hide the ID columns. He will save his documented and reorganized data table in a new file called **PharmaSales.jmp**.

The steps quickly described in this section illustrate some useful features of JMP that can be used for documenting and simplifying your work environment. Although these steps may initially seem like unnecessary overhead, our view is that mistake proofing and a right-first-time approach is useful in any context. Often, the lean nature of these steps is not revealed until later. In this case, imagine a similar request to Rick the following year. But, for a quick analysis, these steps are unnecessary.

With that in mind, if you prefer to skip this section, feel free to proceed directly to the next section, "Dynamic Visualization of Variables One and Two at a Time." If, however, you want to follow along with Rick, please open the file **PharmaSales_RawData.jmp**.

INSERTING NOTES In order to document the data, Rick inserts a **Notes** property in each column describing the contents of that column. We will see how he does this for the column Visits with Samples.

Rick selects the column Visits with Samples by clicking in the column header. Next he selects **Cols > Column Info**. Alternatively, he can right-click on the header of the Visits with Samples column and choose **Column Info** (Exhibit 7.4). In the **Column Info** dialog, Rick chooses **Notes** from the **Column Properties** menu (Exhibit 7.5). This opens a **Notes** text box, where Rick types "Number of visits when the sales representative left a sample kit in the given month" (Exhibit 7.6). He clicks **OK** to close the **Column Info** dialog.

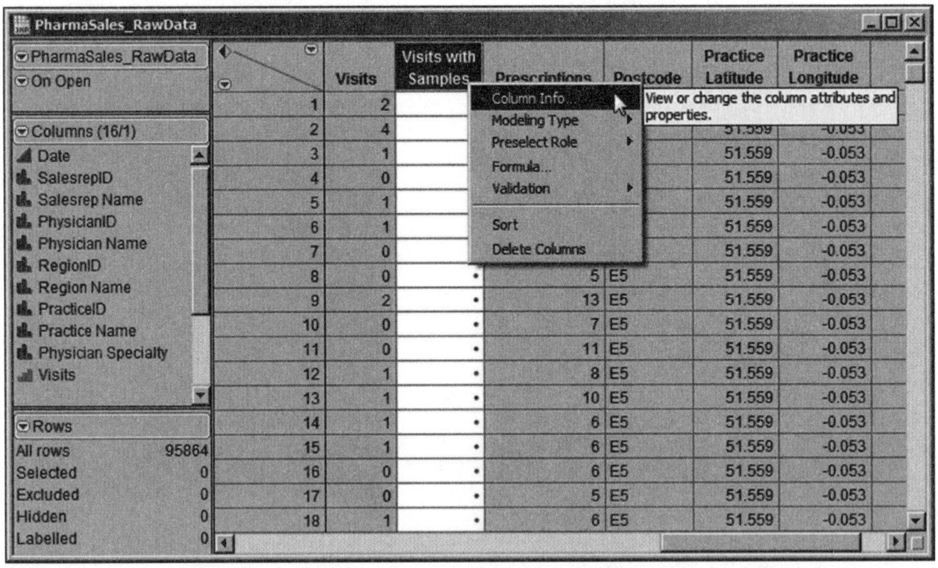

EXHIBIT 7.4 Column Info Obtained from Right-Click on Column Header

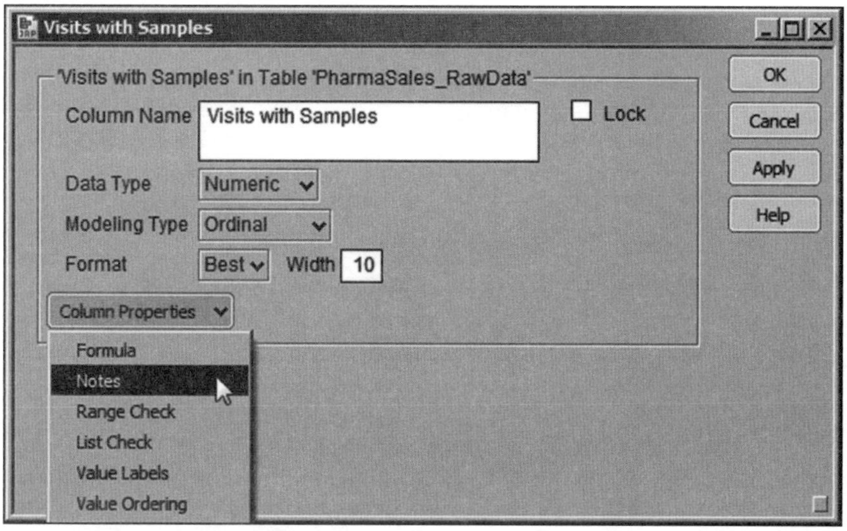

EXHIBIT 7.5   Column Properties Menu

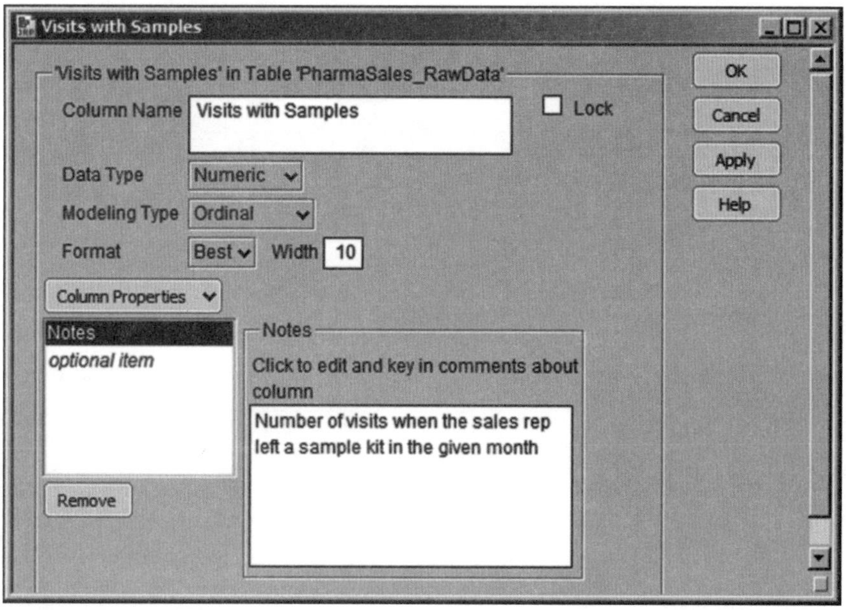

EXHIBIT 7.6   Column Info Dialog with Note for Visits with Samples

Following this procedure, Rick inserts notes for all columns.

GROUPING COLUMNS   Rick observes that the four ID columns are redundant. He does not want to delete them but would like to hide them so that they do not appear in the data table and to exclude them from variable selection lists for analyses. He does this as follows.

- He selects the four ID columns in the columns panel, holding the control key for multiple selections.
- He right-clicks in the highlighted area. This opens a context-sensitive menu.
- From this menu, he chooses **Group Columns** (Exhibit 7.7). This groups the four columns as shown in Exhibit 7.8.

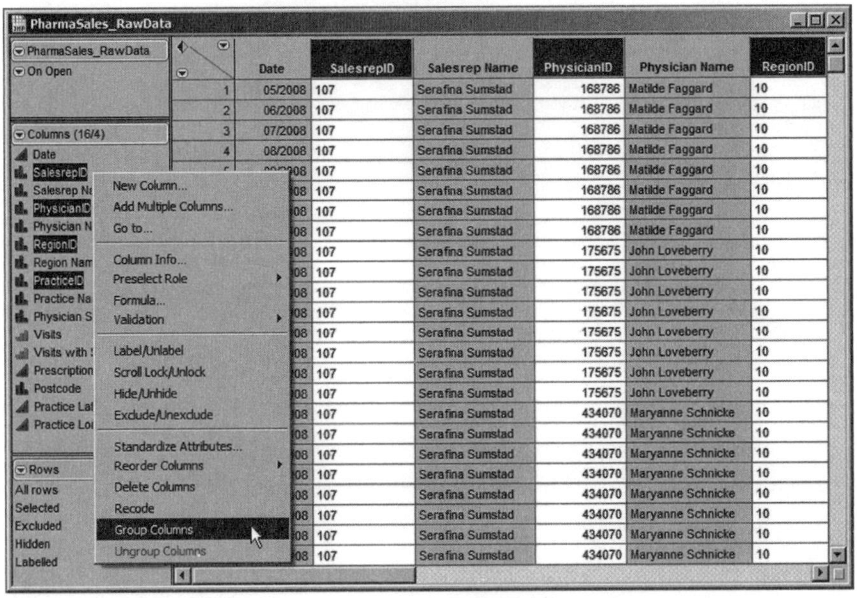

EXHIBIT 7.7   Context-Sensitive Columns Panel Menu Showing Group Columns Selection

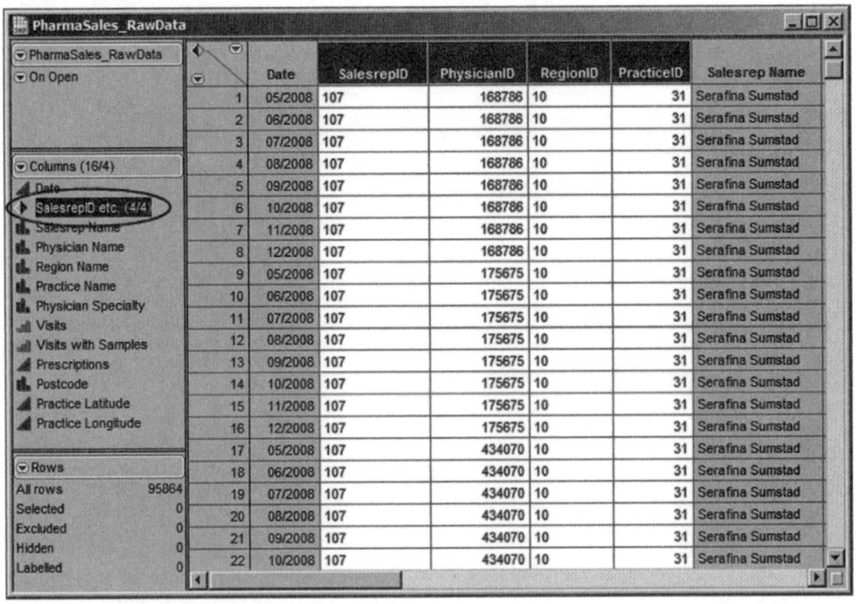

EXHIBIT 7.8   Columns Panel Showing Grouped Columns

By double-clicking on the name of the grouping, Rick renames the grouping to
ID Columns. Rick then clicks on the disclosure icon next to the ID Columns grouping
to reveal the four ID columns. He clicks on ID Columns, selecting the entire grouping.
With the ID Columns grouping selected, Rick right-clicks on the selection to open
the context-sensitive menu shown in Exhibit 7.7. This time, he chooses **Exclude/
Unexclude**. This places an exclusion icon next to each column in the grouping. He
opens the context-sensitive menu once again and chooses **Hide/Unhide**. This places
a mask-like icon next to each column indicating that it is hidden. The ID grouping
in the column panel now appears as shown in Exhibit 7.9.

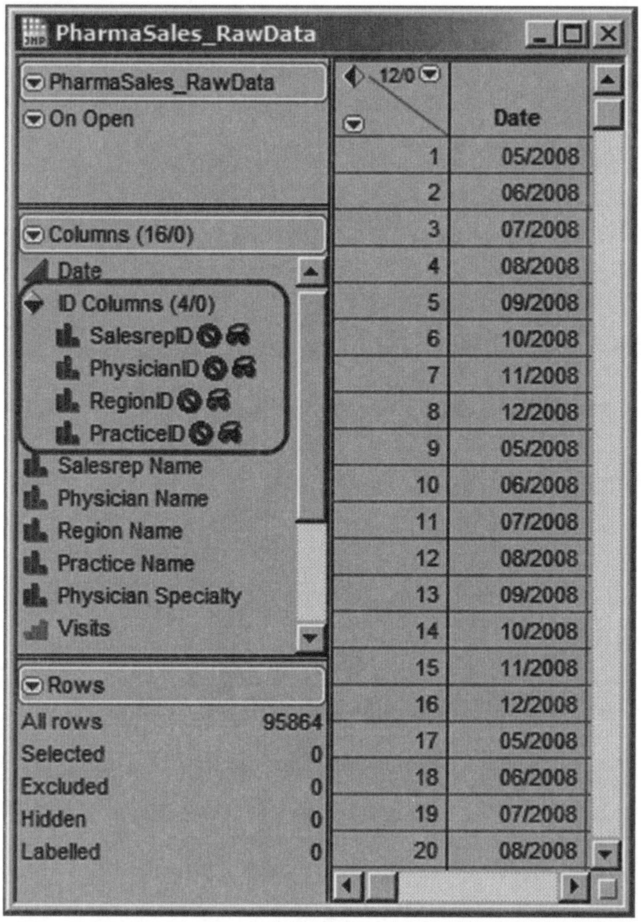

EXHIBIT 7.9   Columns Panel with ID Columns Grouped, Excluded, and Hidden

Finally, Rick closes the disclosure icon next to ID Columns. Then, he clicks on
ID Columns and, while holding the click, drags that grouping down to the bottom of
the columns list, as shown in Exhibit 7.10. Now Rick is happy with the configuration
of the data table, and he saves it as **PharmaSales.jmp**. (If you wish to save the file
you have created, *please* use a different name.)

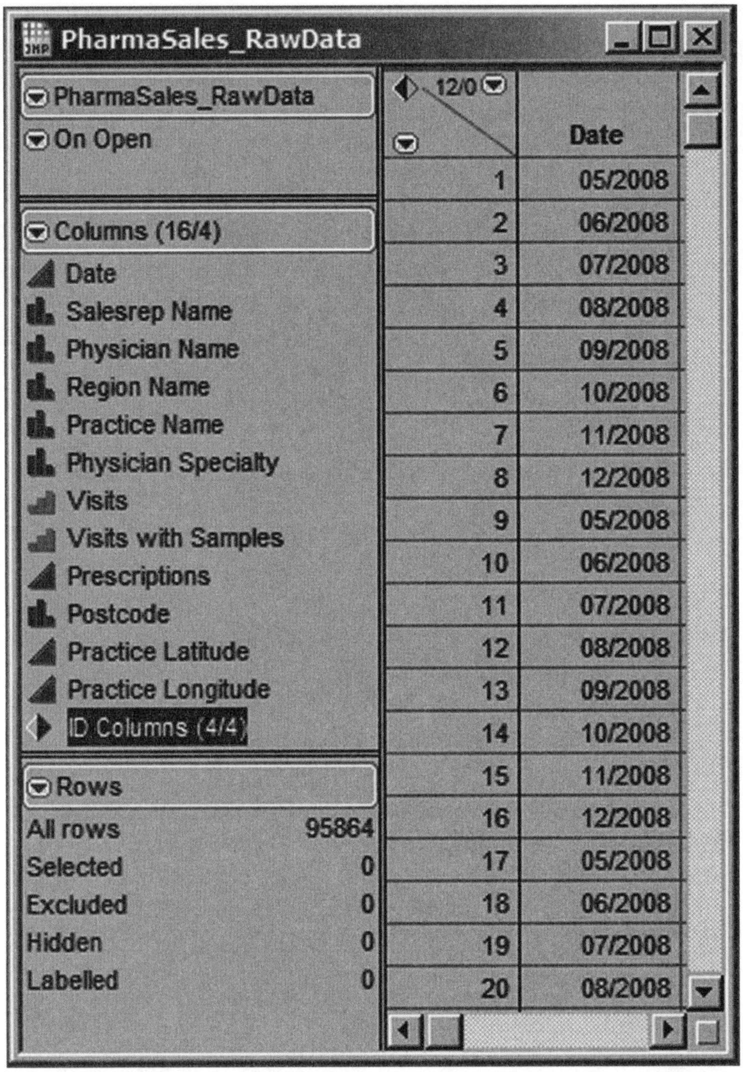

EXHIBIT 7.10   Final Configuration of Columns Panel with ID Columns at Bottom of List

Dynamic Visualization of Variables One and Two at a Time

At this point, you may open **PharmaSales.jmp**, which is precisely the data table that Rick has prepared for his analysis. You will notice that the table **PharmaSales.jmp** contains scripts. These will be created or inserted later on in the case study. If you prefer to replicate this work entirely on your own, then continue using the data table that you created based on **PharmaSales_RawData.jmp** after following the steps in the section "Preparing the Data Table."

The first thing that Rick does is to run **Distribution** on all of the variables. He selects **Analyze > Distribution** and enters all the variables as **Y, Columns** (see Exhibit 7.11).

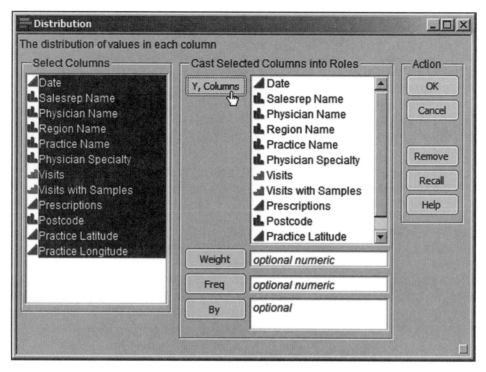

EXHIBIT 7.11   Distribution Dialog with All Variables Entered

When he clicks **OK**, he sees the report that is partially shown in Exhibit 7.12. Since some of Rick's nominal variables have many levels, their bar graphs are huge and not very informative, and they cause the default report to be extremely long. Rick notices this for **Physician Name,** in particular.

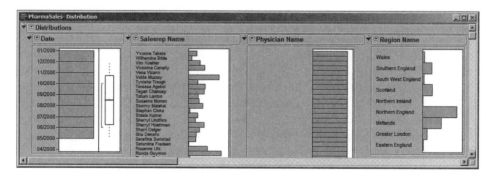

EXHIBIT 7.12   Partial View of Distribution Report for All Variables

For now, although some of the smaller bar graphs are useful, Rick decides to remove all of the bar graphs. He does this as follows:

- He holds down the control key.
- While doing so, he clicks on the red triangle next to one of the nominal variable names (he picks **Salesrep Name**).
- He releases the control key at this point.
- From the drop-down menu, he selects **Histogram Options > Histograms**.

This last selection deselects the **Histogram** option, removing it for **Salesrep Name**. But, since Rick held the control key while clicking on the red triangle, this command was *broadcast* to all other nominal and ordinal variables in the report. So, all of the bar graphs have been removed. Rick saves the script for this report to the data table, naming it **Distribution for All Variables**.

Rick peruses the report. He observes the following:

- **Date.** Rick recalls that JMP stores dates internally as the number of seconds since January 1, 1904. The numbers that he sees under **Quantiles** and **Moments** are this internal representation for dates. But the histogram indicates all that Rick needs to know, namely, that eight months of data are represented and there are equal numbers of rows corresponding to each month.
- **Salesrep Name.** Scrolling down to the bottom of the frequency table, Rick sees that there are 103 sales representatives.
- **Physician Name.** Scrolling down to the bottom of the frequency table, Rick sees that there are 11,983 physicians represented and that each has eight records, presumably one for each of the eight months.
- **Region Name.** There are nine regions. Northern England and Midlands have the most records.
- **Practice Name.** There are 1,164 practices.
- **Physician Specialty.** There are 15 specialties represented. There are 376 rows for which this information is missing.
- **Visits.** There can be anywhere from 0 to 5 visits made to a physician in a given month. Typically, a physician receives one or no visits. There are 984 rows for which this information is missing.
- **Visits with Samples.** There can be anywhere from 0 to 5 visits with samples made to a physician in a given month. Typically, a physician receives one or no such visits. There are 62,678 rows for which this information is missing.
- **Prescriptions.** The distribution for the number of prescriptions for Pharma Inc.'s product written by a physician in a given month is right-skewed. The average number of prescriptions written is 7.40, and the number can range from 0 to 58.
- **Postcode, Practice Latitude, Practice Longitude.** There is no missing data (note that, under **Moments, N** = 95864), and the values seem to make sense.

Now that he has taken a preliminary look at all of his data, Rick is ready to study some of his key descriptive variables more carefully. These key variables include **Date, Salesrep Name, Region Name, Practice Name,** and **Physician Specialty**. Given the large number of physicians, he decides not to include **Physician Name** in this list.

Rick thinks of these variables in two ways. He uses **Region Name** as an example. First, **Region Name** will allow him to *stratify* his data, namely to view it by its layers or values. In other words, he will learn if some regions differ from others; this information will help him develop his understanding of root causes.

However, Rick also thinks of variables such as these as *chunk variables*.[1] Rick likes to use this term because it emphasizes the fact that his descriptive variables are large, indiscriminate, omnibus groupings of very specific root causes. Each of these variables will require further investigation if it turns out to be of interest. For example, a regional difference could be caused by any, or some combination, of the following more specific causes within a region: the educational, financial, or social level of patients; the knowledge level or specialties of physicians; the causes of underlying medical conditions; the hiring practices and management of sales representatives, or their training or attitude; and so on.

To view distributions for his five key chunk variables, Rick uses **Analyze > Distribution**. The launch dialog is shown in Exhibit 7.13.

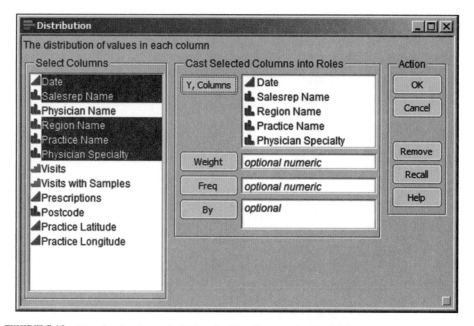

EXHIBIT 7.13   Distribution Launch Dialog for Five Descriptive Variables

In the resulting report, Rick closes the disclosure icons for **Quantiles** and **Moments** under the **Date** report, since these are given in seconds since January 1, 1904, and since the histogram gives him all the information he needs. By inspecting the **Distribution** report and by clicking judiciously on the histogram bars, Rick can immediately see some interesting things. For example, by clicking on the bar for Northern England under **Region Name** (Exhibit 7.14) he observes:

- The names of the sales representatives who work in that region.
- The names of the practices located in that region.
- The physician specialties represented in that region.

PharmaSales - Distribution

▷ Distributions

▷ Date
01/2009
12/2008
11/2008
10/2008
09/2008
08/2008
07/2008
06/2008
05/2008
04/2008

▷ Quantiles
▷ Moments

▷ Salesrep Name

Yvonne Takata
Wilhelmina Battle
Vito Koehler
Victorina Cassidy
Vera Vizarro
Valda Mauzey
Tynisha Travagli
Teressa Agatol
Tatum Lanton
Susanna Morren
Stormy Malakai
Stephan Cloke
Stasia Autrey
Sherry Lindfors
Sherryl Huettman
Shan Daley
Sha DeLeo
Serafina Sumstad
Saturnina Frydeen
Roxanne Uhl
Ronda Guymon
Rodrigo Guice
Rochelle Braziel
Renaldo Baker
Queen Foretti
Porsha Plasencia
Patrina Verone
Omega Oquist
Odette Rary
Octavia Leport
Ned Heeney
Nakisha Regusa
Moises Prang
Minna Schoo
Millard Wett
Mavis Hooker
Malvina Raenay
Mabel Kotyk
Lynette Starin
Lyla Letsos
Lisa Redigan
Luke Kilmer
Lorrie Rooksy
Leonny Kaltenberger
Leandra Rothenberger
Lawrence Goettsche
Lawrence Scialhca

▷ Region Name

South England
South West England
Scotland
Northern Ireland
Northern England
Midlands
Greater London
Eastern England

▷ Frequencies

Level	Count	Prob
Eastern England	960	0.01001
Greater London	5360	0.05591
Midlands	22160	0.23116
Northern England	40726	0.42477
Northern Ireland	528	0.00551
Scotland	11568	0.12067
South West England	1496	0.01561
Southern England	10848	0.11316
Wales	2224	0.02320
Total	95864	1.00000

N Missing 0
9 Levels

▷ Practice Name

Yoxall, Greater London
Wylde Green, West Midlands
Wylam, Northumberland
Wycombe Marsh, Buckinghamshire
Worcester, Hereford and Worcester
Woodbury, Berkshire
Woodford Bridge, Greater London
Wirral, Merseyside
Wirral, Hampshire
Whiteley, Hampshire
Whitefield, Greater Manchester
Weybridge, Surrey
Westhoughton, Greater Manchester
Westbourne, Bournemouth
West Worthing, West Sussex
West Derby, Merseyside
West Bromwich, West Midlands
Wellingborough, Northamptonshire
Watton, Hereford and Worcester
Walton, Merseyside
Wallasey, Merseyside
Upton, Merseyside
Tinsdon Colliery, County Durham
Trafford Park, Greater Manchester
Totland, Isle of Wight
Tonbridge, Kent
Tile Cross, West Midlands
Thornaby-on-Tees, Stockton-on-Tees
Talsarnau, Gwynedd
Swindon, Sutton
Stretford, Greater Manchester
Stony Stratford, Milton Keynes
Stoneferry, Kingston upon Hull
Stockton-on-Tees, Stockton-on-Tees
Stockport, Greater Manchester
Station Town, County Durham
Stansted Mountfitchet, Essex
Stanmore, Greater London
Stalybridge, Greater Manchester
St Bees, Cumbria
St Albans, Hertfordshire
Springwell, Tyne and Wear
Speke, Merseyside
Southchurch, Essex
Southbourne, Bournemouth
South Shields, Tyne and Wear

▷ Physician Specialty

RHEUMATOLOGY
PSYCHIATRIST
PRIMARY CARE
PEDIATRICS
PEDIATRICIAN
PED
OTHER
NEUROLOGIST
MP0INTERNAL MEDICINE PEDIATRI
INTERNAL MEDICINE
GENERAL PRACTICE
FAMILY PRACTICE
FAM
CHNCHILD NEUROLOGIST
ADOLESCENT MEDICINE

▷ Frequencies

Level	Count	Prob
ADOLESCENT MEDICINE	24	0.00025
CHNCHILD NEUROLOGIST	88	0.00092
FAM	8	0.00008
FAMILY PRACTICE	13888	0.14335
GENERAL PRACTICE	856	0.00896
INTERNAL MEDICINE	5240	0.05488
MP0INTERNAL MEDICINE PEDIATRI	48	0.00050
NEUROLOGIST	1632	0.01709
OTHER	200	0.00209
PED	8	0.00008
PEDIATRICIAN	21872	0.22905
PEDIATRICS	5856	0.06133
PRIMARY CARE	45568	0.47721
PSYCHIATRIST	256	0.00268

EXHIBIT 7.14 Partial View of Distribution Report for Five Descriptive Variables

He continues by selecting other bars for other variables. For example, Rick clicks on the Internal Medicine bar under **Physician Specialty** and notes that only roughly a third of practices cover that specialty. When he is finished exploring, he saves the script, naming it **Distribution for Five Variables**. He clears his row selections by selecting **Rows > Clear Row States** (or by pressing the escape key while the data table is the active window).

Having developed a feeling for some of the variables describing sales operations, Rick now turns his attention to the monthly outcomes data. He begins by obtaining a **Distribution** report for Visits, Visits with Samples, and Prescriptions. At the top of the report, to better see the layout of the data, he clicks on the red triangle next to **Distributions** and chooses **Stack** from the menu. This stacks the histograms and presents each horizontally (Exhibit 7.15). Rick saves the script as **Distribution for Three Variables.**

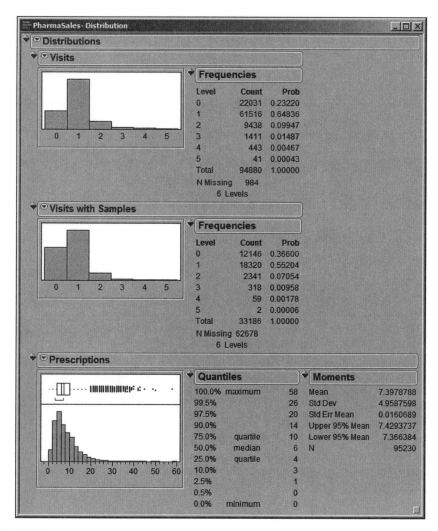

EXHIBIT 7.15   Distribution Report for Three Outcomes Variables

These distributions show Rick the following, some of which he observed earlier:

- The numbers of monthly **Visits** by sales representatives range from 0 to 5.
- About 23 percent of the time a physician is not visited in a given month. About 65 percent of the time a physician receives exactly one visit in a given month. However, about 12 percent of the time, a physician receives two or more visits in a given month.
- There are 984 records for which **Visits** is missing.
- There are 62,678 records missing an entry for **Visits with Samples**. Rick suspects that this could be for locations where the promotion was not run—he recalls being told that the promotion was limited in scope.
- For the rows where **Visits with Samples** was reported, about 37 percent of the time no sample kit was left.
- The monthly numbers of **Prescriptions** written by each physician vary from 0 to 58.
- Generally, physicians write relatively few prescriptions for Pharma Inc.'s main product each month. They write 6 or fewer prescriptions 50 percent of the time.
- However, when **Visits with Samples** is one or two, more **Prescriptions** are written than when it is zero. Rick sees this by clicking on the bars for **Visits with Samples**.
- The number of promotional visits appears to be much smaller than the total number of visits. Rick sees this by looking at the bar graph for **Visits** while clicking on the bars for **Visits with Samples**.

Now, Rick arranges the **Distribution** plots for his chunk variables and the **Distribution** plots for his outcome measures so that he can see both on his screen. He finds it convenient to deselect the **Stack** option for his outcome measures (see Exhibit 7.16). Now he clicks in the bars of his chunk variables to see if there are any systematic relationships with the outcome measures. For example, are certain regions associated with larger numbers of visits than others? Or do certain specialties write more prescriptions? Exhibit 7.16 illustrates the selection of Midlands from **Region Name**. Rick notes that Midlands is associated with a large proportion of the **Visits with Samples** data and that it has a bimodal distribution in terms of **Prescriptions**.

All told, though, Rick does not see any convincing relationships at this point. He realizes that he will need to aggregate the data over the eight-month period in order to better see relationships. Meanwhile, he wants to get a better sense of the quality of the data, and then move on to his private agenda, which is to better understand how his sales force is deployed.

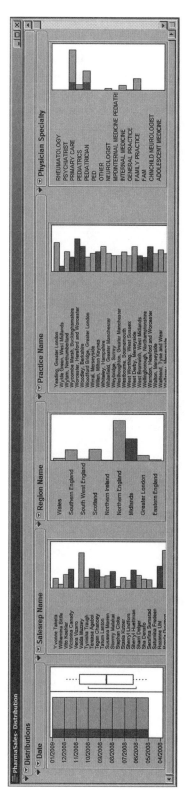

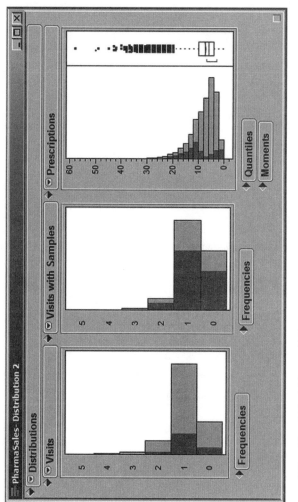

EXHIBIT 7.16   Arrangement of Five Chunk Variables and Three Outcome Measures

Missing Data Analysis

Having seen that some variables have a significant number of missing values, Rick would like to get a better understanding of this phenomenon. He notices, by browsing the JMP menu bar, that JMP has a platform for missing data analysis, located in the **Tables** menu. Selecting **Tables > Missing Data Pattern**, Rick chooses all 12 columns in the **Select Columns** list and adds them as shown in Exhibit 7.17.

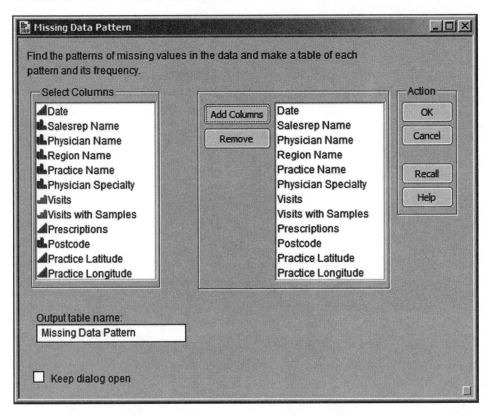

EXHIBIT 7.17   Missing Data Launch Dialog

Clicking **OK** gives him a summary table. This eight-row table is partially shown in Exhibit 7.18. Rick saves the script as **Missing Data Pattern**.

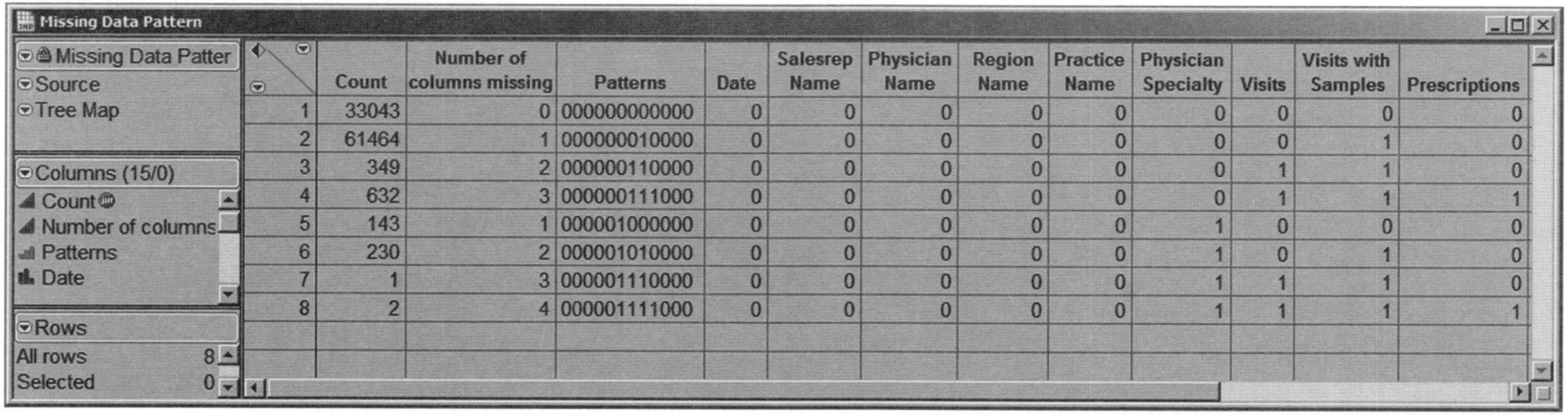

	Count	Number of columns missing	Patterns	Date	Salesrep Name	Physician Name	Region Name	Practice Name	Physician Specialty	Visits	Visits with Samples	Prescriptions
1	33043	0	000000000000	0	0	0	0	0	0	0	0	0
2	61464	1	000000010000	0	0	0	0	0	0	0	1	0
3	349	2	000000110000	0	0	0	0	0	0	1	1	0
4	632	3	000000111000	0	0	0	0	0	0	1	1	1
5	143	1	000001000000	0	0	0	0	0	1	0	0	0
6	230	2	000001010000	0	0	0	0	0	1	0	1	0
7	1	3	000001110000	0	0	0	0	0	1	1	1	0
8	2	4	000001111000	0	0	0	0	0	1	1	1	1

Missing Data Patter...
Source
Tree Map

Columns (15/0)
Count
Number of columns
Patterns
Date

Rows
All rows 8
Selected 0

EXHIBIT 7.18   Partial View of Missing Data Pattern Table

251

In the **Missing Data Pattern** table, Rick considers the columns from Date to Practice Longitude. Each of these columns contains the values 0 or 1, with a 0 indicating no missing data, while a 1 indicates missing data. He observes that the Patterns column is a 12-digit string of 0s and 1s formed by concatenating the entries of the columns Date to Practice Longitude. A 0 or 1 is used to indicate if there are missing data values in the column corresponding to that digit's place.

The table has eight rows, reflecting the fact that there are eight distinct missing data patterns. For example, row 1 of the Count column indicates that there are 33,043 rows that are not missing data on any of the 12 variables. Row 2 of the Count column indicates that there are 61,464 rows where *only* the eighth variable, Visits with Samples, is missing. Row 3 indicates that there are 349 records where only the two variables Visits and Visits with Samples are missing. Rick decides that he needs to follow up to find out if data on Visits with Samples was entered for only those locations where the promotion was run.

Rick thinks that a Pareto plot showing the eight missing data patterns and their frequencies might be useful as a visual display. But he notices that a **Tree Map** script is included in the **Missing Data Pattern** table and recalls that a tree map is analogous to a Pareto plot, but that it tiles the categories into a rectangle, permitting a more condensed display when one has many categories. Selecting **Run Script** from the red triangle next to **Tree Map**, Rick sees the display in Exhibit 7.19.

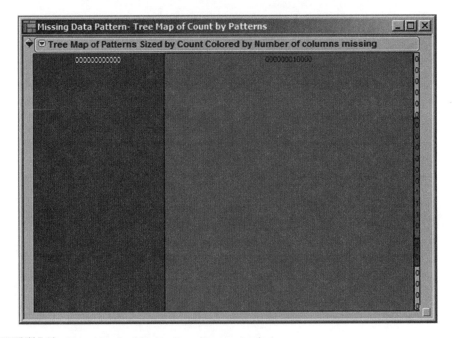

EXHIBIT 7.19   Tree Map for Missing Data Pattern Analysis

The areas of the rectangles and the legends within them show the pattern of the layout of the data relative to missing values. The large rectangle to the left represents the rows that have no missing data. The second rectangle from the left—the largest—represents the 61,464 records where Visits with Samples is the only variable that is missing data. The small area to the right consists of the six rectangles that correspond to rows 3 to 8 of the **Missing Data Pattern** table. Two of these are barely visible, corresponding to rows 7 and 8, which have one and two entries, respectively.

Rick views these smaller rectangles with no concern. They account for very little of the total available data. Note, however, that for some specific detailed analyses Rick might want assurance that there is no systematic pattern associated with missing data, even for small rectangles. For example, if he were interested in comparing sales representatives across practices and if the missing data for Prescriptions were associated with a few select practices, this would be cause for concern.

Consequently, Rick is primarily concerned with the missing data for Visits with Samples. Rick returns to his **PharmaSales.jmp** data table and runs the script **Distribution for Five Variables**. Then, back in the **Missing Data Pattern** table, he selects those rows, rows 1 and 5, for which Visits with Samples is not missing. This selects the corresponding rows in the main data table, and these rows are now highlighted in the **Distribution** graphs. Rick scans the distributions for patterns (see Exhibit 7.20). He notes that Region Name shows a pattern: Bars for exactly three regions are highlighted, and they are almost entirely highlighted.

Rick speculates that the promotion was run in only these three regions. He makes a few phone calls and finally connects with the IT associate who was responsible for coordinating and entering the data from the promotion. She confirms that the promotion was run in only three regions: Southern England, Northern Ireland, and Midlands. Further, she confirms that for those six regions where the promotion was not run the Visits with Samples field was left empty. She also confirms that in the three regions where the promotion was run, missing values appear when the sales representative did not report whether a sample kit was left on a given visit (this happened fairly rarely, as seen in Exhibit 7.20).

Rick feels much better upon hearing this news. He sees no other missing data issues that need to be addressed at this point. He selects **Window > Close All Reports** to close all the reports that he has opened. Then he closes the **Missing Data Pattern** table as well. He is left with **PharmaSales.jmp** as his only open window. Here, he deselects the selected rows by selecting **Rows > Clear Row States**; alternatively, he could have clicked in the lower triangle at the upper left of the data grid, or pressed the escape key.

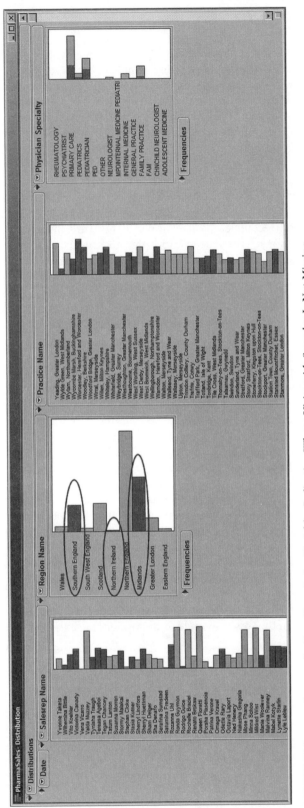

EXHIBIT 7.20 Distributions for Four Descriptive Variables Indicating Where Visits with Samples Is Not Missing

Dynamic Visualization of Sales Representatives and Practices Geographically

From the Distribution reports, Rick knows that most of the sales representative activity is in Northern England and the Midlands. He is anxious to see a geographical picture showing the practices assigned to his sales representatives and how these are grouped into regions. To get this geographical view, Rick selects **Graph > Bubble Plot** and assigns column roles as shown in Exhibit 7.21.

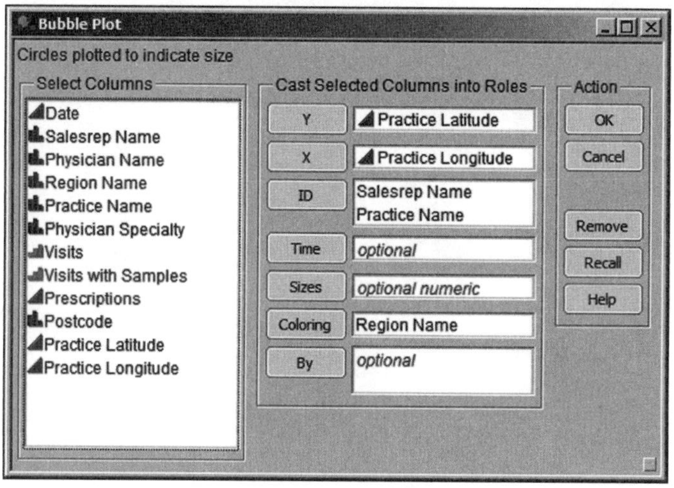

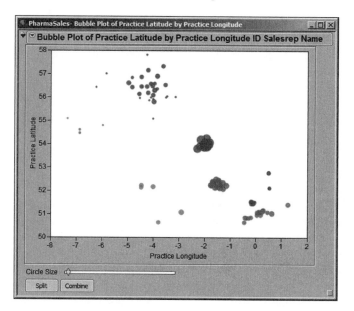

EXHIBIT 7.21   Launch Dialog for Bubble Plot

When he clicks **OK**, he obtains the plot in Exhibit 7.22. Although this is a pretty picture, it is not what Rick envisioned. The colors (on screen) help him see where the various practices are, but he would like to see these bubbles overlaid on a map of the United Kingdom. He saves this initial script as **Bubble Plot**.

EXHIBIT 7.22   Bubble Plot Showing Practice Locations Colored by Region Name

Then he calls his golfing buddy, who refers him to someone who has written a JMP graphics script that draws a U.K. map. Rick is able to obtain that script and adds it to the bubble plot script that he has saved. He saves this new script to **PharmaSales.jmp**, calling it **UK Map and Bubble Plot**. When he runs the adapted script, he obtains the plot in Exhibit 7.23.

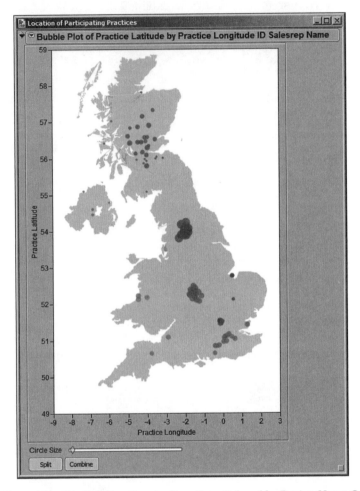

EXHIBIT 7.23 Bubble Plot Showing Practice Locations Colored by Region Name Overlaid on Map of the United Kingdom

To make the regions easier to identify, Rick constructs a legend window. To do this, he selects **Rows > Color or Mark by Column**. He chooses **Region Name** and checks the **Make Window with Legend** box, as shown in Exhibit 7.24. For later use, he also selects **Standard** from the **Markers** list. (The colors and markers, but not the legend window, can be obtained by running the script **Color and Mark by Region**.)

When he clicks **OK**, a small window showing the color legend appears on his screen. He places this window so that he can simultaneously view both it and his plot of the United Kingdom. When Rick clicks on a **Region Name** in the legend window

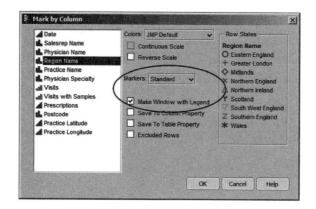

EXHIBIT 7.24   Dialog for Color or Mark by Column

(Northern Ireland is selected in Exhibit 7.25), the names of the sales representatives assigned to the corresponding practices appear in the plot of the United Kingdom. By doing this for each region, Rick identifies the sales representatives and locates the practices for each of the nine regions.

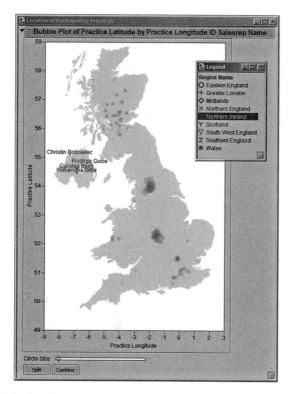

EXHIBIT 7.25   Bubble Plot Showing Practice Locations with Legend Window

By hovering with the arrow tool over the bubble indicated in the plot on the left in Exhibit 7.26, Rick sees that this apparently strange, wet territory belongs to

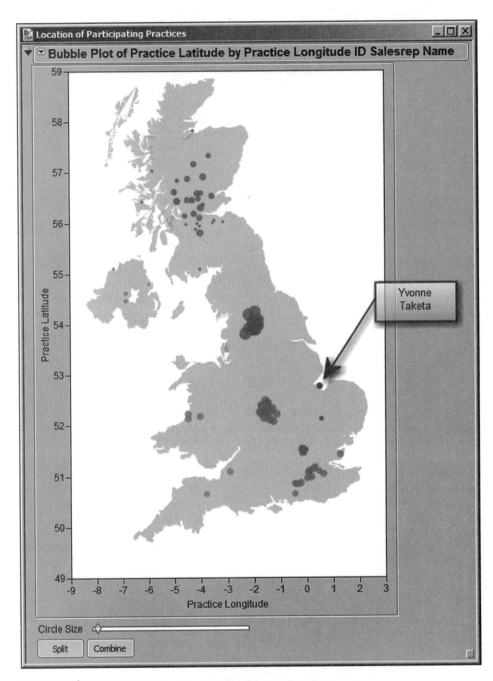

EXHIBIT 7.26   Bubble Plots Showing Yvonne Taketa's Practices

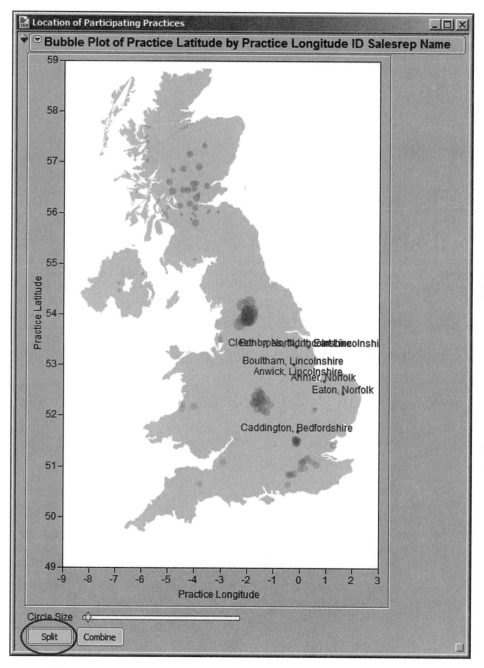

EXHIBIT 7.26 *(Continued)*

Yvonne Taketa. But by selecting that bubble and clicking the **Split** button at the bottom, Rick sees her assigned practices (see the plot to the right in Exhibit 7.26).

This makes it clear to Rick what is happening—Yvonne's practices just happen to have a mean location that falls in the North Sea. Selecting the **Combine** button makes the display on the right in Exhibit 7.26 revert to the display on the left. Using the display on the left, Rick can see the geographical center of each sales representative's activities.

To remove the selection of Yvonne Taketa, Rick clicks elsewhere in the plot. Next, he selects **Split All** from the red triangle at the top of the report. This shows the location of all the practices in the United Kingdom. Selecting **Combine All** causes the display to revert to the initial display. With this background, Rick feels that he has a good sense of where his sales force and their practices are located. He closes his open reports and the legend window.

Dynamic Visualization of Sales Representatives and Practices with a Tabular Display

At this point, Rick wants to see a list of each sales representative's practices and physicians. To do this, he selects **Tables > Tabulate,** choosing to **Build table using** a **Dialog** and entering first Practice Name and then Physician Name in the **Grouping** list, as shown in Exhibit 7.27.

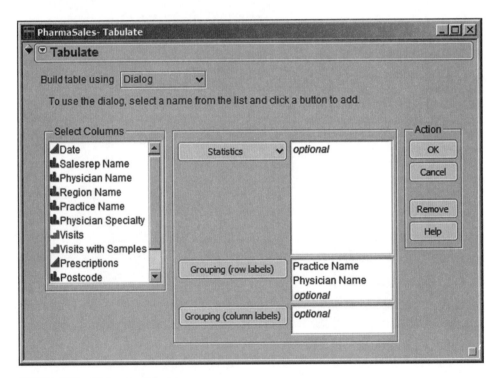

EXHIBIT 7.27   Dialog for Tabulate

The resulting table is partially shown in Exhibit 7.28. Rick saves this work in a script called **Tabulate**. Rick expects this tabulation to be quite large, and the vertical scroll bar in the report window confirms this. Incidentally, the fact that each row of the tabulation consists of 8 values (note the **N** = 8 column) confirms that Rick does have the eight-month prescribing record for each physician.

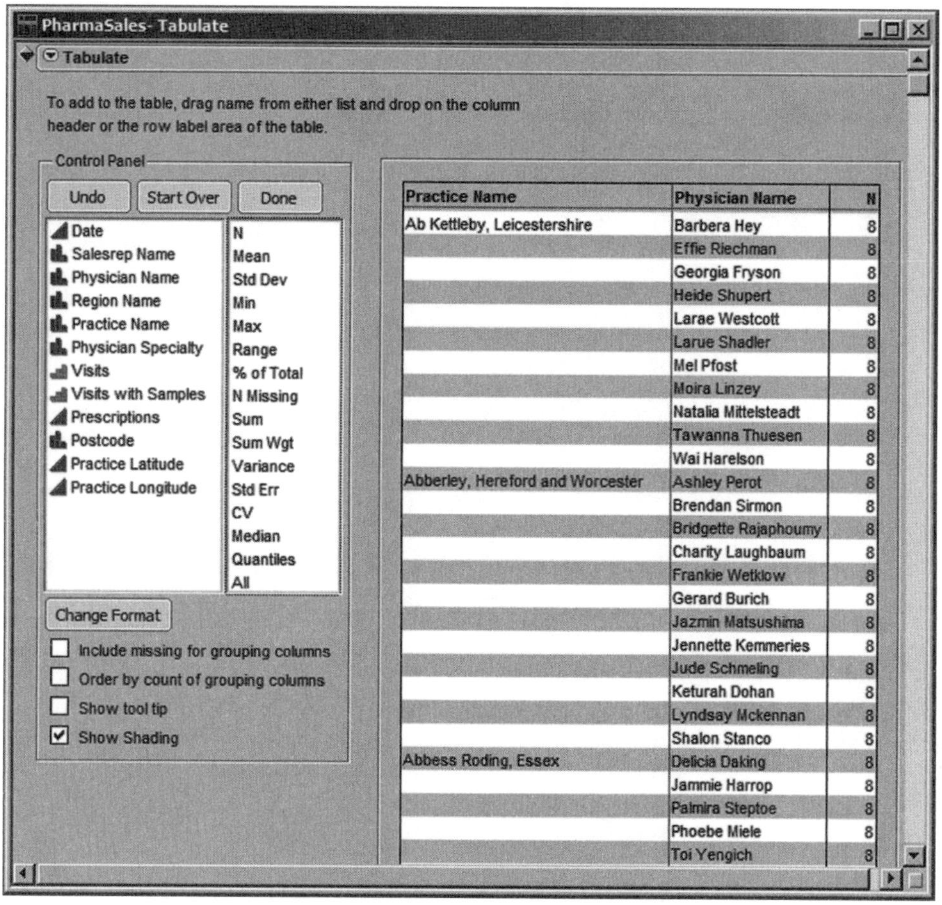

Practice Name	Physician Name	N
Ab Kettleby, Leicestershire	Barbera Hey	8
	Effie Riechman	8
	Georgia Fryson	8
	Heide Shupert	8
	Larae Westcott	8
	Larue Shadler	8
	Mel Pfost	8
	Moira Linzey	8
	Natalia Mittelsteadt	8
	Tawanna Thuesen	8
	Wai Harelson	8
Abberley, Hereford and Worcester	Ashley Perot	8
	Brendan Sirmon	8
	Bridgette Rajaphoumy	8
	Charity Laughbaum	8
	Frankie Wetklow	8
	Gerard Burich	8
	Jazmin Matsushima	8
	Jennette Kemmeries	8
	Jude Schmeling	8
	Keturah Dohan	8
	Lyndsay Mckennan	8
	Shalon Stanco	8
Abbess Roding, Essex	Delicia Daking	8
	Jammie Harrop	8
	Palmira Steptoe	8
	Phoebe Miele	8
	Toi Yengich	8

EXHIBIT 7.28 Table Showing All Practices and Physicians

To make the tabulation more manageable, Rick selects **Rows > Data Filter**. He then selects the Salesrep Name column under **Add Filter Columns** and clicks the **Add** button. He unchecks **Select** and checks **Show** and **Include**, in order to show the rows for a selected sales representative. Choosing **Show** hides all rows in the data table *not* selected by the **Data Filter** settings and choosing **Include** excludes these rows as well.

Rick arranges the **Data Filter** report and the **Tabulate** report side-by-side. Now, when he clicks on a Salesrep Name in the **Data Filter** window, the **Tabulate** report shows the Practice Names and associated information for only that Salesrep Name. This is illustrated for Alona Trease in Exhibit 7.29.

Practice Name	Physician Name	N
Adversane, West Sussex	Chanda Kaeser	8
	Christian Ludke	8
	Cristie Bergantzel	8
	Deb Edmerson	8
	Denise Lemert	8
	Laquanda Roegge	8
	Maddie Arent	8
	Nancee Perella	8
	Quintin Gneiser	8
	Rachal Breitenbucher	8
	Stephaine Lupi	8
	Tamesha Faraone	8
Alphamstone, Essex	Dori Szuba	8
	Gilbert Harcar	8
	Hortencia Gunyon	8
	Kanesha Jappa	8
	Rhoda Gooding	8
	Tiera Dorset	8
Alton, Hampshire	Cheyenne Brackman	8
	Chin Derosa	8
	Fidela Marander	8
	Livia Foshay	8
	Milda Schueren	8
	Niesha Redgate	8
	Tyrone Fratercangelo	8
	Venita Taurino	8
Balls Cross, West Sussex	Abby Placide	8
	Adeline Ohmie	8
	Andres Hasch	8
	Chelsie Grimmett	8
	Kori Savich	8
	Mana Bekker	8
	Numbers Michl	8
	Susie Whittmore	8
	Vickey Rademan	8
	Yong Lies	8

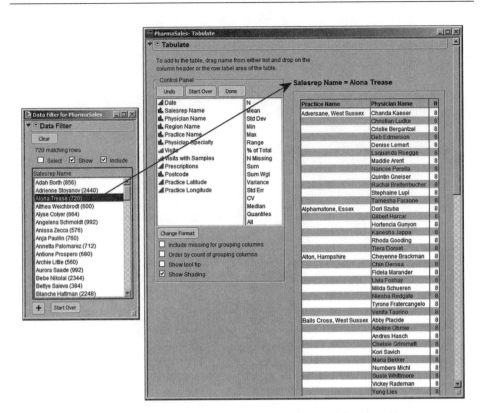

EXHIBIT 7.29 Linking of Data Filter to Tabulate Report, Illustrated for Alona Trease

But to see this information more easily, Rick selects the **Animation** command from the red triangle in the **Data Filter**, resulting in the view shown in Exhibit 7.30. He saves this work in a script called **Data Filter**.

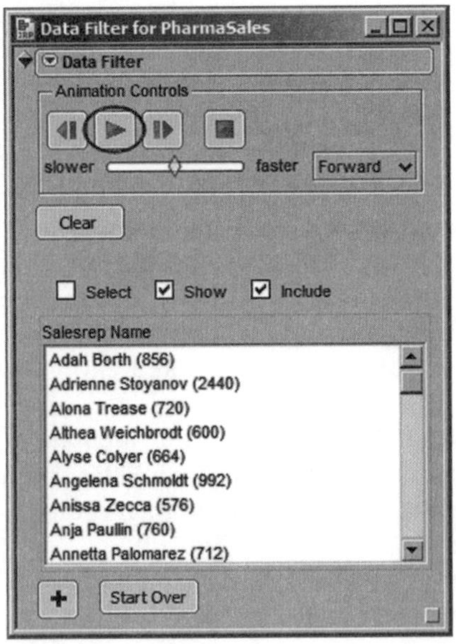

EXHIBIT 7.30 Settings for Data Filter for Animation of Tabulate Report

In the **Data Filter**, he clicks the blue arrow to begin the animation. This causes JMP to loop in turn over all the values of **Salesrep Name**, updating the tabulation report to reflect the current choice as it does so. As he watches the animation, Rick sees that there are some sales representatives calling on just a very few physicians, whereas some are calling on very many. He assumes this is due to some sales representatives working part time and makes a note to check this with the human resources department. See, for example, Exhibit 7.31, showing Cleo Delancy, who works with only one practice comprised of seven physicians.

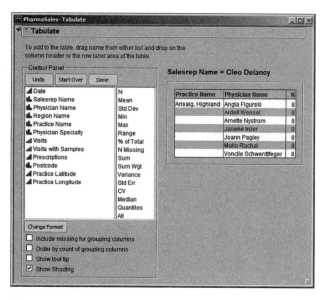

EXHIBIT 7.31 Tabulate Report for Cleo Delancy

Once he is finished, Rick presses the **Clear** button in the **Data Filter** window to remove the row states applied by the **Data Filter**. Then he closes the **Data Filter** along with the **Tabulate** report.

At this point, Rick concludes that he has a clean set of data and that he has a good grasp of its content. He also feels that he has fulfilled his private agenda, which was to learn about the distribution of his sales force. The visual and dynamic capabilities provided by JMP have been extremely helpful to him in this pursuit—he has very quickly learned things he could never have learned using a spreadsheet. Now, finally, he is ready to roll up his sleeves and address the business questions posed by his manager.

Investigating Promotional Activity

Rick's first task is to verify the claims of the marketing group that the test promotion they ran in 2008 was successful. The promotion was run from May through December 2008 in three regions: Midlands, Northern Ireland, and Southern England.

Rick's first thought is to look at total prescriptions written per physician across the eight months for which he has data, and to see if the three promotion regions stand out. To accomplish this, he must construct a summary table giving the sum for the relevant variables over the eight-month period. This will allow him to compare the 2008 physician totals across regions, taking into account physician variability. But Rick is also interested in how prescription totals vary by region when considering the number of visits. Do the promotional regions stand out from the rest in terms of prescriptions written if we account for the number of visits per physician?

Preparing a Summary Table

Rick begins by creating a data table that summarizes his data across physicians. First, he makes sure that colors and markers by **Region Name** are still applied to his data table. (If yours are not, then please run the script **Color and Mark by Region**.) To create a summary table, he selects **Tables > Summary**. Thinking carefully about what to summarize, Rick decides that he will want to sum Visits, Visits with Samples, and Prescriptions across Physician Name. To populate the dialog correctly, he first selects all three of the variables that he wants to sum and then goes to the **Statistics** drop-down list, where he selects **Sum** (Exhibit 7.32). When he clicks on **Sum**, the list box to the right of **Statistics** shows the three variables, Sum(Visits), Sum(Visits with Samples), and Sum(Prescriptions).

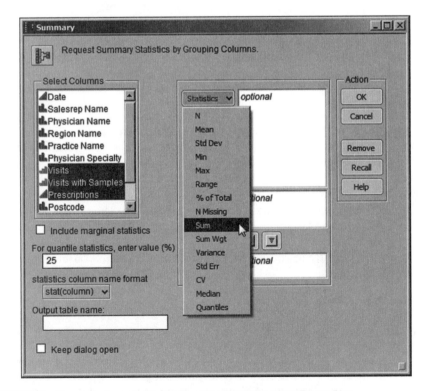

EXHIBIT 7.32   Summary Launch Dialog Showing Statistics Drop-Down List

Next, Rick devotes some thought to the other columns that should appear in his summary table. Surely, **Physician Name** is one of these, since that is the column on whose values he wants the summary to be based. In fact, he hopes to see 11,983 rows—one for each **Physician Name**. But he would also like to have **Region Name** included in the summary table, as well as **Salesrep Name**. These last two variables should not define additional grouping classes, since each **Physician Name** is associated with only one **Salesrep Name** and only one **Region Name** over the eight months. So Rick includes these in the **Group** list. When he has done this, the launch dialog appears as in Exhibit 7.33.

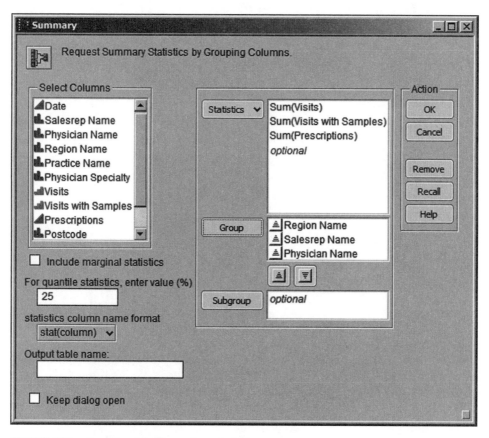

EXHIBIT 7.33   Completed Summary Launch Dialog

When Rick clicks **OK**, he obtains the data table that is partially shown in Exhibit 7.34. To his delight, Rick notes that this summary table has inherited the row markers that were present in **PharmaSales.jmp**, and that there are indeed 11,983 rows in the summary.

At this point, Rick (or you, if you were conducting a similar analysis) would normally save this summary table as a new table for reuse later. However, to make it easy for you to recreate the summary table, we have saved a script in **PharmaSales.jmp** that does this. The script is called **Summary Table 1**. If you are interested in how this is done, see the section "Additional Details" at the end of this chapter.

PharmaSales By (Region Name, Salesrep Name, Physician Name)

PharmaSales By (Region Nam

Source

Columns (7/0)
- Region Name
- Salesrep Name
- Physician Name
- N Rows
- Sum(Visits)
- Sum(Visits with Samples)
- Sum(Prescriptions)

Rows	
All rows	11983
Selected	0
Excluded	0
Hidden	0
Labelled	0

	Region Name	Salesrep Name	Physician Name	N Rows	Sum(Visits)	Sum(Visits with Samples)	Sum(Prescriptions)
1	Eastern England	Coleen Osborn	Alvin Halfacre	8	6	•	50
2	Eastern England	Coleen Osborn	Chantel Flythe	8	8	•	63
3	Eastern England	Coleen Osborn	Charmaine Stuczynski	8	7	•	53
4	Eastern England	Coleen Osborn	Cherly Hammerstad	8	9	•	61
5	Eastern England	Coleen Osborn	China Hentz	8	5	•	77
6	Eastern England	Coleen Osborn	Cinda Kruzan	8	5	•	55
7	Eastern England	Coleen Osborn	Clarissa Kostelecky	8	8	•	57
8	Eastern England	Coleen Osborn	Claudette Accetta	8	4	•	53
9	Eastern England	Coleen Osborn	Danuta Hantz	8	4	•	57
10	Eastern England	Coleen Osborn	Diann Brendeland	8	5	•	47
11	Eastern England	Coleen Osborn	Don Dimarzio	8	7	•	44
12	Eastern England	Coleen Osborn	Emil Englebert	8	8	•	69
13	Eastern England	Coleen Osborn	Ernestina Buboltz	8	6	•	61
14	Eastern England	Coleen Osborn	Franklin Katzberg	8	8	•	46
15	Eastern England	Coleen Osborn	Georgeanna Ramo	8	8	•	71
16	Eastern England	Coleen Osborn	Giovanna Vanderjagt	8	10	•	54
17	Eastern England	Coleen Osborn	Glen Capouch	8	9	•	60
18	Eastern England	Coleen Osborn	Grover Hasak	8	9	•	66
19	Eastern England	Coleen Osborn	Hilaria Borsh	8	4	•	57
20	Eastern England	Coleen Osborn	Iesha Feauto	8	5	•	57

EXHIBIT 7.34 Partial View of Summary Table

Uncovering Relationships: Prescriptions versus Region

EXPLORATORY APPROACH: COMPARISON CIRCLES Rick's first thought is to compare values of Sum(Prescriptions) across Region Name to see if the promotion regions had significantly more prescriptions written than did the nonpromotion regions. So, making sure that his summary table is active, Rick selects **Analyze > Fit Y by X**. He inserts Sum(Prescriptions) as **Y, Response** and Region Name as **X, Factor**. When he clicks **OK**, he obtains the plot shown in Exhibit 7.35.

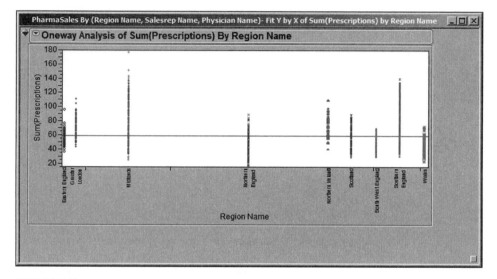

EXHIBIT 7.35   Oneway Plot of Sum(Prescriptions) by Region Name

Rick notes that the regions are not spread uniformly across the horizontal axis. He figures out that this is meant to illustrate the sizes of the groupings—regions with many observations get a bigger share of the axis than do regions with few observations. This is why Midlands and Northern England, the regions with the most data, have a comparatively large share of the axis. He also notes that the points are all lined up, and he suspects that with 11,983 records in his data table some of the data points overwrite each other.

To fix the overwriting, Rick clicks on the red triangle at the top of the report and chooses **Display Options > Points Jittered**. He also would prefer that the regions be spread evenly across the horizontal axis. To address this, in the red triangle menu, Rick chooses **Display Options** and unchecks **X Axis proportional**. The resulting display is shown in Exhibit 7.36.

As expected, Rick sees the huge density of points representing Northern England. But his real interest is in the promotion regions: Midlands, Northern Ireland, and Southern England. Indeed, there appear to be more prescriptions being written in these three regions. Rick thinks about how he can verify this more formally. Ah, he remembers: *comparison circles*! These provide a visual representation of statistical tests that compare pairs of categories, which here consist of regions.

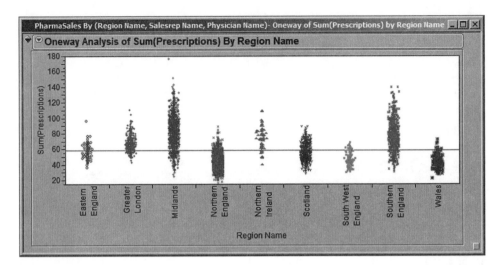

EXHIBIT 7.36   Oneway Plot with New Display Options

Rick clicks on the red triangle at the top of the report and selects **Compare Means > All Pairs, Tukey HSD** (see Exhibit 7.37). He chooses the **All Pairs, Tukey HSD** option (rather than **Each Pair, Student's t**) because he will be making pairwise comparisons of nine regions. There are $(9 \times 8) / 2 = 36$ possible pairs to compare. So, Rick wants to control the overall error rate for the collection of 36 tests at 0.05. (HSD stands for *honestly significant difference*.) If Rick had chosen the **Each Pair, Student's t** option,

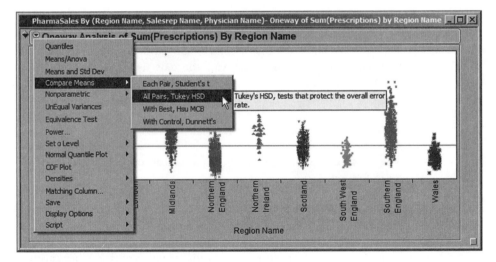

EXHIBIT 7.37   Compare Means Options

each individual comparison would have a 0.05 false alarm rate. Over 36 tests, this could result in a very large overall false alarm rate $(1 - (1 - 0.05)^{36} = 0.84$, or 84 percent). Note that JMP refers to the false alarm rate as the *error rate*.

When he clicks the **All Pairs, Tukey HSD** option, Rick obtains comparison circles, as he expects. These appear in a new area to the right of the dot plots, as shown in Exhibit 7.38. Some analytic output is also provided in the **Means Comparisons** panel, but Rick realizes that all the information he needs is in the circles. Rick saves his script to the summary data table as **Oneway**.

Rick reminds himself of how the comparison circles work. There is one circle for each value of the nominal variable. So here, there will be one circle for each value of **Region Name**. Each circle is centered vertically at the mean for the category to which it corresponds. When you click on one of the circles, it turns a bold red on the screen, as does its corresponding label on the X axis. Each other circle either turns gray or normal red (but not bold red). The circles that turn gray correspond to categories that significantly differ from the category chosen. The other circles that turn red correspond to categories that do *not* significantly differ from the chosen category.

With this in mind, Rick clicks on the tiny topmost circle. He sees from the bold red label on the plot that this circle corresponds to the Midlands. He infers that it is tiny because Midlands has so many observations. Once that circle is selected, he sees that all of the other circles and axis labels are gray. This means that Midlands differs significantly from all of the other regions. Technically stated, each of the eight pairwise tests comparing the mean of **Sum(Prescriptions)** for Midlands to the mean **Sum(Prescriptions)** for another region is significant using the Tukey procedure.

Next, Rick clicks on the big circle that is second from the top, shown in Exhibit 7.39. He is not surprised that this corresponds to Northern Ireland—the circle is large because there is comparatively little data for Northern Ireland. All the other circles turn gray except for the very small circle contained within and near the top of Northern Ireland's circle. By clicking on that circle, Rick sees that it corresponds to Southern England. He concludes that Northern Ireland differs significantly from all regions other than Southern England relative to prescriptions written.

Exploring comparison circles relies heavily on color and is therefore very easy to do on a computer screen. With grayscale printed output, such as that in Exhibit 7.39, one must look carefully at the labels on the horizontal axis. Note that the label for Northern Ireland is bold gray. Labels that correspond to regions that differ significantly from Northern Ireland are italicized. Those that do not differ significantly are not italicized. Note that the label for Southern England is the only label other than Northern Ireland's that is not italicized.

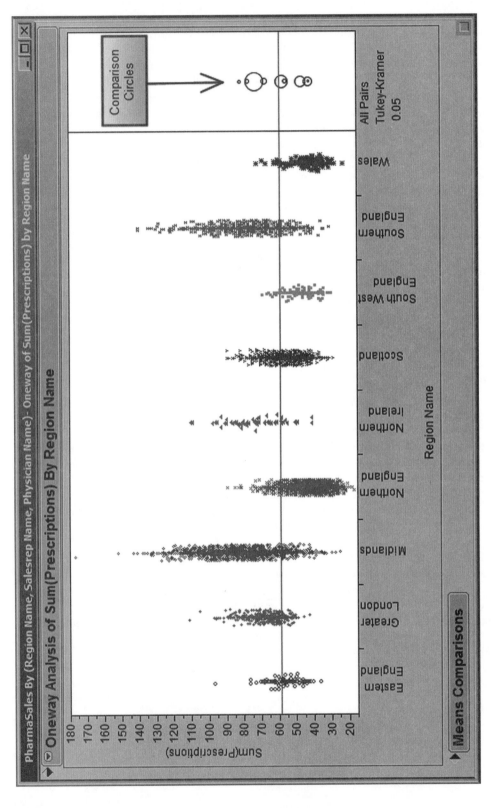

EXHIBIT 7.38   Comparison Circles

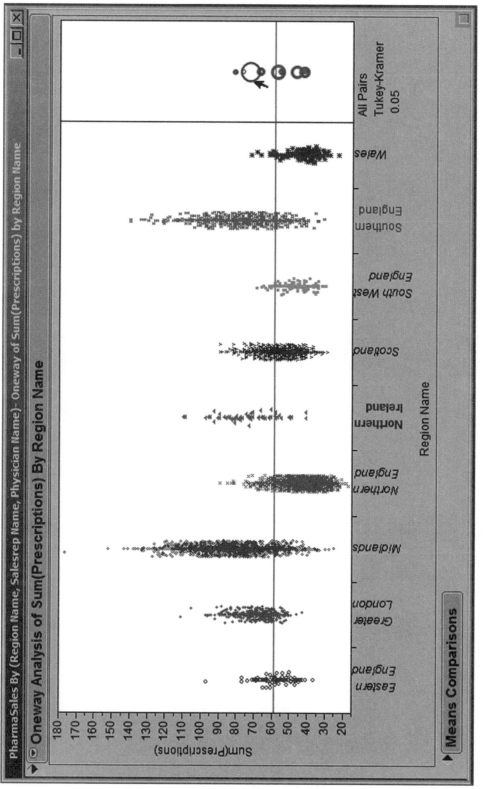

EXHIBIT 7.39 Comparison Circles with Northern Ireland Selected

Rick peruses the report in the **Means Comparisons** panel. He discovers a table that summarizes the significant differences among regions (see Exhibit 7.40, where this table is enclosed in a rectangle). Rick sees that this table divides his nine regions into six groups based on an associated letter, and that each of these groups differs significantly from the other groups. This table is sometimes called a *Connecting Letters* report.

Midlands (letter A) has significantly more sales than all of the other regions. Next come Southern England and Northern Ireland, both of which are associated with the letter B and can't be distinguished statistically, but both have significantly more sales than the regions associated with the letters C, D, E, and F. The smallest numbers of sales are associated with Wales and Northern England. The Connecting Letters report also provides the **Mean** number of prescriptions written by physicians in each of the regions. These vary from 42.5 in Wales and Northern England to 81.6 in Midlands.

Means Comparisons

Comparisons for all pairs using Tukey-Kramer HSD

q*	Alpha
3.10232	0.05

Abs(Dif)-LSD

	Midlands	Southern England	Northern Ireland	Greater London	Eastern England	Scotland	South West England	Wales	Northern England
Midlands	-1.06391	3.359905	3.780781	12.63307	20.4294	24.65416	32.04686	36.54036	38.20982
Southern England	3.359905	-1.52061	-0.95088	7.795781	15.67814	19.76978	27.27761	31.7524	33.26249
Northern Ireland	3.780781	-0.95088	-6.89246	0.51739	9.341374	12.24283	20.6573	24.8977	25.52727
Greater London	12.63307	7.795781	0.51739	-2.16326	5.858787	9.750601	17.42605	21.86893	23.17974
Eastern England	20.4294	15.67814	9.341374	5.858787	-5.11159	-1.944	6.285959	10.58533	11.36658
Scotland	24.65416	19.76978	12.24283	9.750601	-1.944	-1.47252	6.022741	10.4997	12.02605
South West England	32.04686	27.27761	20.6573	17.42605	6.285959	6.022741	-4.09473	0.24828	1.158146
Wales	36.54036	31.7524	24.8977	21.86893	10.58533	10.4997	0.24828	-3.35834	-2.32538
Northern England	38.20982	33.26249	25.52727	23.17974	11.36658	12.02605	1.158146	-2.32538	-0.78485

Positive values show pairs of means that are significantly different.

Level		Mean
Midlands	A	81.621300
Southern England	B	76.949115
Northern Ireland	B	72.909091
Greater London	C	67.283582
Eastern England	D	57.500000
Scotland	D	55.682573
South West England	E	46.582888
Wales	F	42.589928
Northern England	F	42.476621

Levels not connected by same letter are significantly different.

EXHIBIT 7.40 Connecting Letters Report

Rick really likes this table and wants to present it as part of a Microsoft® PowerPoint presentation. He would like to turn this into a nicely formatted table for the presentation and therefore wants to put the results into an Excel file where he can format the cell contents and add borders. He right-clicks in the interior portion of the table area. This opens a context-sensitive menu, shown in Exhibit 7.41, and Rick notices that he can choose to **Make into Data Table**. He chooses this option, and the output is converted to a JMP data table that Rick then copies and pastes into Excel. The JMP data table is shown in Exhibit 7.42. Here, Rick has right-clicked in the column header for Mean, selected **Column Info**, and changed the format to display only two decimal places.

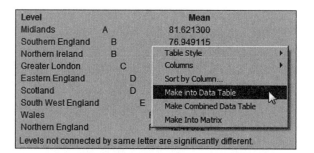

Level		Mean
Midlands	A	81.621300
Southern England	B	76.949115
Northern Ireland	B	
Greater London	C	
Eastern England	D	
Scotland	D	
South West England	E	
Wales	F	
Northern England	F	

Table Style ▶
Columns ▶
Sort by Column...
Make into Data Table
Make Combined Data Table
Make Into Matrix

Levels not connected by same letter are significantly different.

EXHIBIT 7.41   Context-Sensitive Menu in Means Comparisons Panel

	Level	Column 2	Column 3	Column 4	Column 5	Column 6	Column 7	Mean
1	Midlands	A						81.62
2	Southern England		B					76.95
3	Northern Ireland		B					72.91
4	Greater London			C				67.28
5	Eastern England				D			57.50
6	Scotland				D			55.68
7	South West England					E		46.58
8	Wales						F	42.59
9	Northern England						F	42.48

EXHIBIT 7.42   Data Table Showing Connecting Letters Report

Rick is excited about these results. He has learned that physicians in the three promotional regions wrote significantly more prescriptions over the eight-month promotional period than did those in the six nonpromotional regions. He has also learned that physicians in Midlands wrote significantly more prescriptions than those in Northern Ireland or Southern England. He is intrigued by why this would be the case and makes a note to follow up at his next meeting with the sales representatives.

Rick also notes that there are significant differences in the nonpromotional regions as well. Physicians in Northern England (the region with the largest number of physicians) and Wales wrote the smallest numbers of prescriptions. He wants to understand why this is the case. But, he firmly keeps in mind that many factors could be driving such differences. It is all too easy to think that the sales representatives in these two regions are not working hard enough. But, for example, there could be cultural differences among patients and physicians that make them less likely to request or prescribe medications. There could be age, experience, or specialty differences among the physicians. Rick realizes that many causal factors could be driving these regional differences.

MODEL TO ACCOUNT FOR SALES REPRESENTATIVE EFFECT   When Rick discusses his results with his golfing buddy, Arthur indicates that there might be a subtle problem with the way that Rick conducted his tests. Each value in **Sum(Prescriptions)** represents the total number of prescriptions written by a given physician over the eight-month period. But, the number of prescriptions written by a given physician could be driven by the sales representative, and each sales representative has a number of assigned physicians. This means that the values of **Sum(Prescriptions)** are not independent, as required by the **Compare Means** test that Rick used. Rather, they are correlated: **Sum(Prescriptions)** values for physicians serviced by a given sales representative are likely to be more similar than **Sum(Prescriptions)** values for physicians across the collection of sales representatives. If, in fact, the number of prescriptions written is highly dependent on the particular sales representative, then the tests that Rick used previously are not appropriate. Arthur points out that Rick's **Compare Means** analysis ignored the sales representative effect (**Salesrep Name**).

Arthur tells Rick that there are two options that would lead to more appropriate analyses: Aggregate the data to the sales representative level and then use **Compare Means**, or construct a model that accounts for the effect of **Salesrep Name**. Rick is intrigued by this second approach, and so Arthur shows him how to do this.

Using the summary data table as the current data table, he tells Rick to select **Analyze > Fit Model**. In the **Fit Model** launch dialog, he tells Rick to enter **Sum(Prescriptions)** as **Y** and to add both **Region Name** and **Salesrep Name** as model effects. Arthur explains that Rick is interested in the variability contributed by sales representatives within a region, rather than in comparing one sales representative to another. This means that Rick should treat **Salesrep Name** as a *random effect*. Arthur shows Rick how to indicate this: He must select **Salesrep Name** in the **Construct Model Effects** box and then click the red triangle next to **Attributes** at the bottom left of the **Construct Model Effects** box, selecting **Random Effect** (see Exhibit 7.43). This places the **& Random** designation next to **Salesrep Name** in the **Model Effects** box. Rick saves this launch dialog to his data table as a script called **Model with Random Effect**.

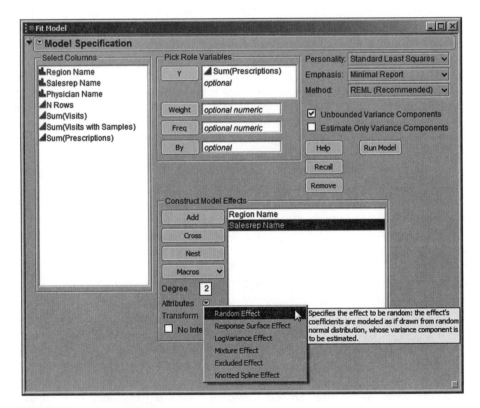

EXHIBIT 7.43   Fit Model Dialog

By treating **Salesrep Name** as a random effect, Rick will obtain an estimate of the variation due to sales representatives within a region. Arthur also points out that the sales representatives are *nested* within a region. In other words, a given sales representative works in only one region and his or her effect on another region cannot be assessed. The analysis that JMP provides takes this into account automatically.

When he clicks **Run Model**, Rick obtains the report shown in Exhibit 7.44. Rick immediately sees that **Region Name** is significant, even when properly accounting for the sales representative effect. Arthur explains that this test for **Region Name** is based on the variability due to sales representatives, not physicians, as opposed to the comparison circle tests that Rick used earlier.

Rick also sees that **Salesrep Name** accounts for only 0.042 percent of the total variation. The **Residual** variation, which accounts for most of the variation, is the variation due to physicians. It follows that within a region most of the variation is due to physician, not sales representative, differences. This indicates that the earlier conclusions that Rick drew from his analysis using comparison circles are actually not misleading.

PharmaSales By (Region Name, Salesrep Name, Physician Name)- Fit Least Squares

Response Sum(Prescriptions)

Summary of Fit

RSquare	0.637237
RSquare Adj	0.636995
Root Mean Square Error	12.7603
Mean of Response	58.79162
Observations (or Sum Wgts)	11983

Parameter Estimates

Random Effect Predictions

REML Variance Component Estimates

Random Effect	Var Ratio	Var Component	Std Error	95% Lower	95% Upper	Pct of Total
Salesrep Name	0.0004246	0.069132	0.2169141	-0.35602	0.494283	0.042
Residual		162.82515	2.1125522	158.76267	167.04632	99.958
Total		162.89428				100.000

-2 LogLikelihood = 95026.661056

Covariance Matrix of Variance Component Estimates

Iterations

Fixed Effect Tests

Source	Nparm	DF	DFDen	F Ratio	Prob > F
Region Name	8	8	132.3	2426.873	<.0001*

Effect Details

EXHIBIT 7.44   Fit Model Report

Arthur also points out that Rick can obtain an analog of comparison circles from this report. He tells Rick to open the **Effect Details** panel. The **Region Name** panel shows the **Least Squares Means Table** for Sum(Prescriptions). Clicking the red triangle next to **Region Name** opens a list of options from which Rick chooses **LSMeans Tukey HSD**. This presents pairwise comparisons based on the current model (Exhibit 7.45).

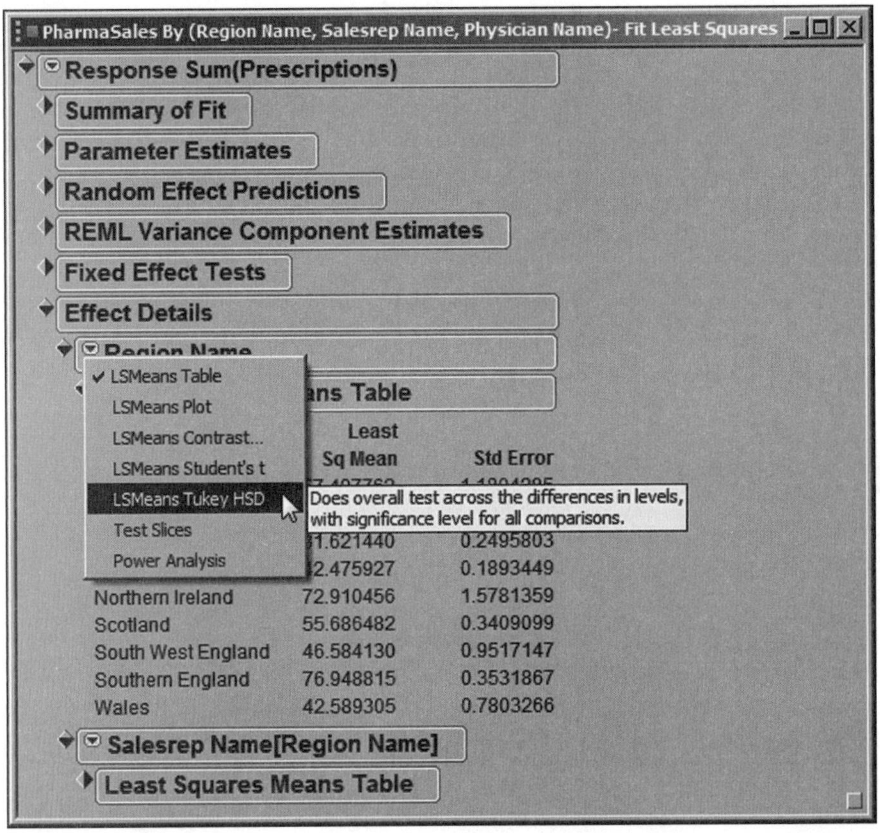

EXHIBIT 7.45   Effect Details Options for Region Name

The test results are represented in matrix form as shown in Exhibit 7.46. The first row in each cell of the matrix gives the mean difference between the two regions. Sean notes that some differences are large. Pairs of regions with results in gray (red on the screen) are significantly different (with an overall false alarm rate of 0.05). If the results are black, the difference is not statistically significant. The Connecting Letters report below the matrix summarizes the differences.

Note that these conclusions are exactly the same as those that Rick obtained using his simpler **Compare Means** approach. But, had the data contained substantial variability due to sales representatives, these conclusions might well have differed from those he obtained earlier.

PharmaSales By (Region Name, Salesrep Name, Physician Name)- Fit Least Squares

▼ Response Sum(Prescriptions)

▼ Effect Details

  ▼ Region Name

   ▼ LSMeans Differences Tukey HSD

α= 0.050

Mean[i]-Mean[j] Std Err Dif Lower CL Dif Upper CL Dif	Eastern England	Greater London	Midlands	Northern England	Northern Ireland	Scotland	South West England	Southern England	Wales
Eastern England	0	-9.7874	-24.124	15.0218	-15.413	1.81128	10.9136	-19.451	14.9085
	0	1.28231	1.20652	1.19552	1.97077	1.22867	1.5163	1.23213	1.41503
	0	-13.795	-27.896	11.2825	-21.541	-2.0279	6.16217	-23.302	10.478
	0	-5.7795	-20.352	18.7611	-9.2842	5.6505	15.6651	-15.6	19.3389
Greater London	9.78745	0	-14.336	24.8093	-5.6252	11.5987	20.7011	-9.6636	24.6959
	1.28231	0	0.55964	0.5355	1.65572	0.60591	1.07549	0.6129	0.92726
	5.77954	0	-16.097	23.1185	-10.768	9.69999	17.316	-11.587	21.7793
	13.7953	0	-12.576	26.5001	-0.4821	13.4975	24.0862	-7.7399	27.6125
Midlands	24.1237	14.3362	0	39.1455	8.71098	25.935	35.0373	4.67262	39.0321
	1.20652	0.55964	0	0.31328	1.59775	0.4225	0.9839	0.43247	0.81927
	20.3516	12.5759	0	38.1137	3.74889	24.6026	31.9336	3.3037	36.4476
	27.8957	16.0966	0	40.1773	13.6731	27.2673	38.141	6.04155	41.6167
Northern England	-15.022	-24.809	-39.146	0	-30.435	-13.211	-4.1082	-34.473	-0.1134
	1.19552	0.5355	0.31328	0	1.58945	0.38996	0.97037	0.40074	0.80297
	-18.761	-26.5	-40.177	0	-35.371	-14.451	-7.1732	-35.754	-2.6514
	-11.283	-23.118	-38.114	0	-25.498	-11.97	-1.0432	-33.192	2.42466
Northern Ireland	15.4127	5.62525	-8.711	30.4345	0	17.224	26.3263	-4.0384	30.3212
	1.97077	1.65572	1.59775	1.58945	0	1.61454	1.8429	1.61717	1.76052
	9.28423	0.4821	-13.673	25.4979	0	12.21	20.5919	-9.061	24.847
	21.5412	10.7684	-3.7489	35.3711	0	22.238	32.0608	0.98428	35.7953
Scotland	-1.8113	-11.599	-25.935	13.2106	-17.224	0	9.10235	-21.262	13.0972
	1.22867	0.60591	0.4225	0.38996	1.61454	0	1.01093	0.49088	0.85155
	-5.6505	-13.497	-27.267	11.9701	-22.238	0	5.91879	-22.804	10.4172
	2.02794	-9.7	-24.603	14.451	-12.21	0	12.2859	-19.721	15.7772
South West England	-10.914	-20.701	-35.037	4.1082	-26.326	-9.1024	0	-30.365	3.99483
	1.5163	1.07549	0.9839	0.97037	1.8429	1.01093	0	1.01514	1.23072
	-15.665	-24.086	-38.141	1.04317	-32.061	-12.286	0	-33.564	0.11673
	-6.1622	-17.316	-31.934	7.17324	-20.592	-5.9188	0	-27.166	7.87292
Southern England	19.4511	9.66361	-4.6726	34.4729	4.03836	21.2623	30.3647	0	34.3595
	1.23213	0.6129	0.43247	0.40074	1.61717	0.49088	1.01514	0	0.85653
	15.5997	7.73991	-6.0415	33.192	-0.9843	19.7209	27.1658	0	31.6614
	23.3024	11.5873	-3.3037	35.7538	9.06099	22.8038	33.5635	0	37.0576
Wales	-14.908	-24.696	-39.032	0.11338	-30.321	-13.097	-3.9948	-34.36	0
	1.41503	0.92726	0.81927	0.80297	1.76052	0.85155	1.23072	0.85653	0
	-19.339	-27.612	-41.617	-2.4247	-35.795	-15.777	-7.8729	-37.058	0
	-10.478	-21.779	-36.448	2.65142	-24.847	-10.417	-0.1167	-31.661	0

Level		Least Sq Mean
Midlands	A	81.621440
Southern England	B	76.948815
Northern Ireland	B	72.910456
Greater London	C	67.285208
Eastern England	D	57.497762
Scotland	D	55.686482
South West England	E	46.584130
Wales	F	42.589305
Northern England	F	42.475927

Levels not connected by same letter are significantly different.

▼ Salesrep Name[Region Name]

EXHIBIT 7.46   Tukey HSD Pairwise Comparisons

With this, Rick thanks Arthur for his help. He feels much more comfortable now that he has a rigorous way to analyze his data. However, he reflects that he learned a lot from the simple, slightly incorrect comparison circle analysis. He closes all report windows but keeps his summary table open.

Uncovering Relationships: Prescriptions versus Visits by Region

Reflecting on the regional differences, Rick starts to wonder if the number of visits has an effect on a physician's prescribing habits. Do more visits tend to lead to more prescriptions for Pharma Inc.'s main product? Or, do physicians tire of visits by sales representatives, leading perhaps to a negative effect? Do more sample kits lead to more prescriptions, as one might expect?

Rick proceeds to develop insight into these issues by running **Fit Y by X**, with Sum(Prescriptions) as **Y, Response** and Sum(Visits) as **X, Factor**. After he clicks **OK**, he selects **Fit Line** from the red triangle. He obtains the **Bivariate Fit** plot shown in Exhibit 7.47.

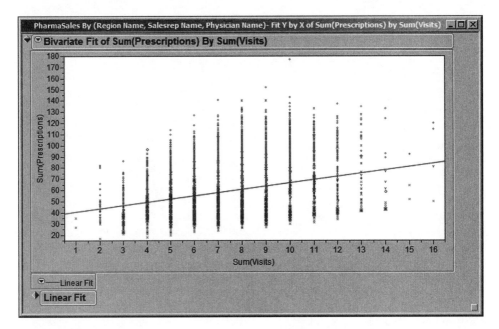

EXHIBIT 7.47   Bivariate Plot for Sum(Prescriptions) by Sum(Visits)

Rick reminds himself that the X axis represents the total number of visits paid to the given physician by the sales representative over the eight-month period. It does appear that at least to a point more visits result in more prescriptions being written. Given the pattern of points on the plot and the fact that at some point additional visits will have diminishing returns, Rick suspects that there may be a little curvature to the relationship. So, he starts thinking about a quadratic fit. But, he would like to see such a fit for each of the nine regions, that is, by the values of **Region Name**.

First, Rick removes the line he has fit to all of the data. To do this, he clicks on the red triangle next to **Linear Fit** at the bottom left of the plot and chooses **Remove Fit**. Now he clicks on the red triangle at the top of the report and chooses **Group By**. This opens the dialog window shown in Exhibit 7.48. Rick chooses **Region Name** and clicks **OK**. This directs JMP to group the rows by **Region Name** so that further fits are performed for the data corresponding to each value of **Region Name**, rather than for the data set as a whole.

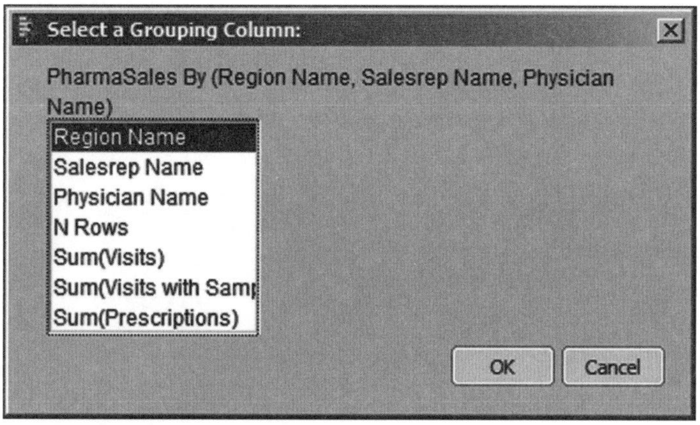

EXHIBIT 7.48   Group By Dialog

With this done, Rick returns to the red triangle at the top of the report and selects **Fit Polynomial > 2, quadratic**. He obtains the plot in Exhibit 7.49, which shows nine second-degree polynomial fits, one for each region. When he sees this, Rick is immediately struck by the three curves that start out fairly low in comparison to the others but that exceed the others as **Sum(Visits)** increases. Which regions are these?

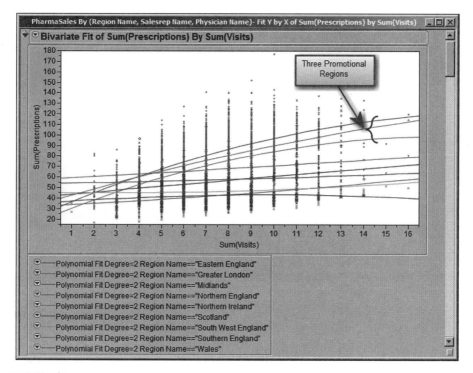

EXHIBIT 7.49   Quadratic Fits to Each of the Nine Regions

To better identify the regions, Rick right-clicks in the plot and chooses **Row Legend** from the context-sensitive menu that appears. A **Mark by Column** dialog window opens, where Rick selects Region Name from the list and specifies **Standard Markers**, as shown in Exhibit 7.50.

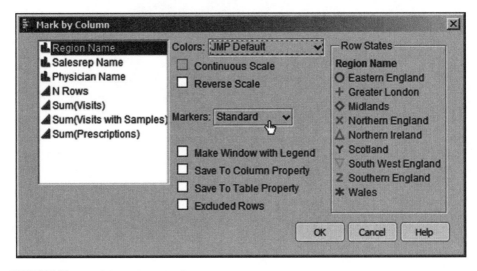

EXHIBIT 7.50   Mark by Column Dialog

When Rick clicks **OK**, a legend appears in his bivariate fit report. Rick finds that when he clicks on each region name in turn the points in the plot corresponding to that region are highlighted. This makes it easy for him to see how the different regions behave relative to Sum(Visits) and Sum(Prescriptions). Exhibit 7.51 shows the plot with Northern Ireland selected.

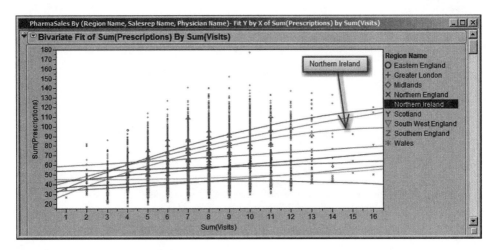

EXHIBIT 7.51   Bivariate Plot with Northern Ireland Selected

From the legend colors, Rick is able to tell that the three curves that start out low and proceed to exceed the others are for the three promotional regions. This suggests that leaving sample kits behind makes a big difference. Rick makes a mental note to run a similar analysis with Sum(Visits with Samples) as **X, Factor** in a few minutes.

The plot suggests that some of the other six regions may not see an increase in the number of prescriptions written with increased visits. Rick quickly peruses the **Prob > F** values for the model tests in the **Analysis of Variance** tables (realizing that these tests suffer from the same deficiency as his comparison circles did in his previous analysis and so are not technically correct). Models that are associated with **Prob > F** values less than 0.05 are marked by asterisks and can be considered significant. He sees that the **Prob > F** values for Eastern England, Southwest England, and Wales do not indicate that the quadratic fits are significant (nor are linear fits, which Rick also checks). This suggests that in these regions the sales representatives may need to do something other than increase visit frequency if they wish to increase sales. Rick saves this script to the data table as **Bivariate Fit 1**.

Yes, indeed, Rick is already planning a second bivariate fit! For this second fit, Rick selects **Analyze > Fit Y by X**, and enters Sum(Prescriptions) as **Y, Response** and Sum(Visits with Samples) as **X, Factor**. He repeats the steps that he took for the previous plot, grouping by Region Name, fitting second-degree polynomials to each region, and obtaining a row legend within the plot. He obtains the plot shown in Exhibit 7.52, where once again Northern Ireland is selected. He saves this second report as **Bivariate Fit 2**.

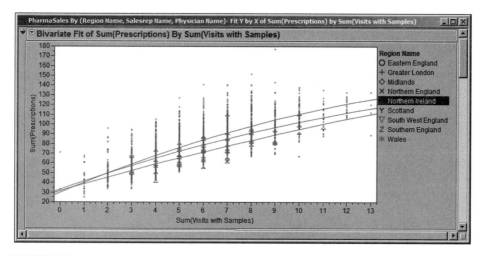

EXHIBIT 7.52   Bivariate Plot for Promotional Regions with Sum(Visits with Samples) on X Axis

Since only the three promotional regions had nonmissing data on Visits with Samples, these are the only three regions for which fits are possible. All three polynomial fits are significant. It seems clear that up to a point the more frequently the sales representative visited and left sample kits behind, the larger the number of prescriptions written. This analysis provides more evidence that the promotion was successful.

Of course, it raises the question about limits. When does one reach the point of diminishing returns relative to the number of visits with sample kits being left? This is an important marketing question. Rick wants to think about how to address this question before he raises it with his vice president. For now, though, Rick is confident that the promotion was successful, and he can use his plots to communicate the results to the vice president. Rick closes his summary table and all open reports and clears row states.

A Deeper Understanding of Regional Differences

Rick's next charge is to determine whether there are regional differences in performance relative to sales of Pharma Inc.'s major product. He realizes that he has already gone a long way toward answering this question. Yes, there are statistical differences between the regions, as indicated by the **Compare Means** analysis illustrated in Exhibit 7.39 and reinforced by the model that accounts for the sales representative effect (Exhibit 7.44). Rick can say that in terms of total prescriptions written over the eight-month period the regions fall into six groups, as shown in Exhibit 7.42. The important questions now revolve around the practical extent of such differences and which chunk factors are related to the differences.

So at this point, Rick wants to go beyond the counts of written prescriptions. Again, he has already done some of the work to understand the relationship between the number of prescriptions and the number of visits. Now he wants to see if he can gain additional insight by seeing this from the perspective of the sales representatives and by taking into account behavior over time. In fact, when Rick thinks about this, he realizes that he would like to see, on a year-to-date basis, how the total number of prescriptions written by each sales representative's physicians is related to the total number of visits. But he would also like to be able to visualize the effect of the total number of physicians assigned to a sales representative and to easily identify the sales representatives' regions. In short, Rick wants a more informative version of the scatterplots presented in the bivariate reports in the previous section.

Rick has seen demos using the JMP bubble plot animation to show changes in the scatter of points over time. He quickly realizes that he must do some data preparation before using this visualization tool—he needs to summarize his data across sales representatives and to define year-to-date summaries of **Prescriptions** and **Visits**.

Rick does this aggregation in JMP. If you have the need to perform a similar aggregation in a project, you could use a spreadsheet, but generally using JMP will be faster, easier, and more flexible. We give the details of the JMP aggregation in the final section, "Additional Details." But for now it suffices to say that Rick writes a script for his aggregation and saves it to **PharmaSales.jmp** as **Summary Table 2**. You should run this script at this point.

The script constructs Rick's aggregated data table (Exhibit 7.53). For each month, the columns **Visits YTD** and **Prescriptions YTD** contain the year-to-date sums of the corresponding variables *for each sales representative*. Rick recalls that there are 103 sales representatives. There should be eight YTD values for each sales representative, and so his new table should contain 824 rows, which it does.

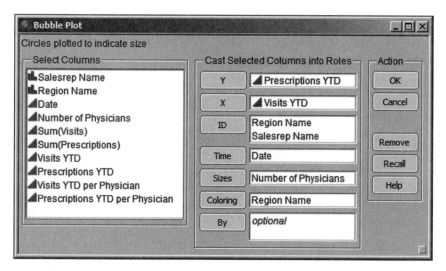

	Visits YTD	Prescriptions YTD	Visits YTD per Physician	Prescriptions YTD per Physician
1	87	1012	0.8	9.5
2	181	2089	1.7	19.5
3	283	3187	2.6	29.8
4	378	4231	3.5	39.5
5	478	5249	4.5	49.1
6	578	6281	5.4	58.7
7	673	7318	6.3	68.4
8	768	8339	7.2	77.9
9	293	1604	1.0	5.3
10	565	3208	1.9	10.5
11	826	4762	2.7	15.6
12	1132	6447	3.7	21.1
13	1404	8054	4.6	26.4
14	1688	9597	5.5	31.5
15	1956	11268	6.4	36.9
16	2237	12892	7.3	42.3
17	92	910	1.0	10.1
18	170	1809	1.9	20.1
19	264	2775	2.9	30.8
20	354	3722	3.9	41.4

EXHIBIT 7.53   Partial View of Summary Table Giving YTD Aggregation

At this point, Rick is ready to construct an animated bubble plot. He decides to look at the relationship between **Prescriptions YTD** and **Visits YTD**, with bubbles sized by **Number of Physicians** and colored by **Region Name** over the time period defined by **Date**. Bubbles will be identified by either the **Salesrep Name** or the **Region Name**. He selects **Graph > Bubble Plot**, and fills in the launch dialog as shown in Exhibit 7.54.

EXHIBIT 7.54   Bubble Plot Launch Dialog for Prescriptions YTD versus Visits YTD

When Rick clicks **OK**, he obtains the bubble plot shown in Exhibit 7.55, which shows the picture for May 2008. He saves this script as **Bubble Plot 1**. There is one bubble per **Region Name**, since this was the first **ID** variable. By clicking **Step** at the bottom left of the plot, Rick can follow the relationship through the eight-month period. Exhibit 7.56 shows the relationship in December 2008.

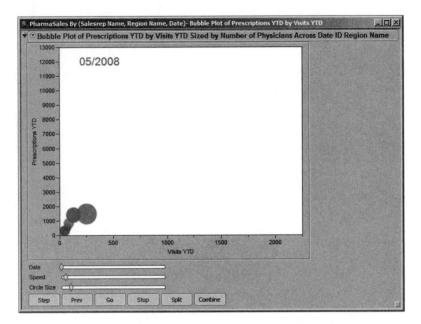

EXHIBIT 7.55   Bubble Plot for Prescriptions YTD versus Visits YTD, May 2008

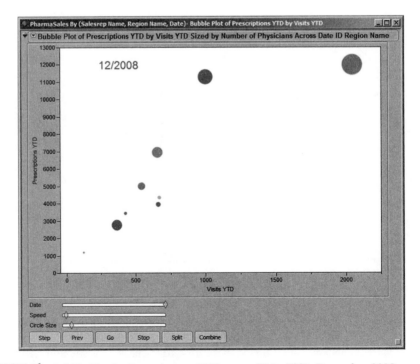

EXHIBIT 7.56   Bubble Plot for Prescriptions YTD versus Visits YTD, December 2008

Now, Rick needs to take a moment to figure out what is being plotted. The vertical center of each bubble is at the average of **Prescriptions YTD** for the given region. The horizontal center is at the average of **Visits YTD** for the given region. The sizes of the bubbles are proportional to the number of physicians in the regions.

Rick notices that he can animate the plot by clicking **Go**. He does this and finds it interesting that the two top regions, as shown in the December plot (Exhibit 7.56), achieve the same general average prescription totals, yet one requires many more visits on average than the other.

To find out which two regions these are, he selects **All Labels** from the red triangle. The labels appear on the plot (Exhibit 7.57), and Rick sees that the regions of interest are Midlands and Northern England. Ah, Midlands was part of the promotion while Northern England was not. He finds it striking that sales representatives in Midlands attained roughly the same mean number of prescriptions as did representatives in Northern England, but with far fewer visits.

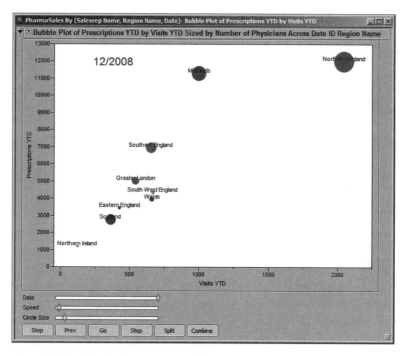

EXHIBIT 7.57 Bubble Plot for Prescriptions YTD versus Visits YTD, December 2008, with Labels

Rick clicks **Go** again and notices that Midlands and Northern England tend to have the same general mean level of **Prescriptions YTD** over time. However, Rick notes that Midlands, whose bubble is smaller than Northern England's, evidently has fewer, perhaps about half as many, physicians as does Northern England. Perhaps, thinks Rick, the sales representatives in Northern England have a larger physician workload than do the sales representatives in Midlands and so have to make more visits. Perhaps he should be looking at year-to-date prescriptions and year-to-date visits *per physician*?

But first, Rick wants to see this plot with the bubbles split by **Salesrep Name**. He clicks on the red triangle and unchecks **All Labels**, then returns to the red triangle and clicks **Split All**. Now, for each month, he sees a single bubble for each sales representative. He animates the plot and observes what is happening. (Exhibit 7.58 shows the plot for December 2008.)

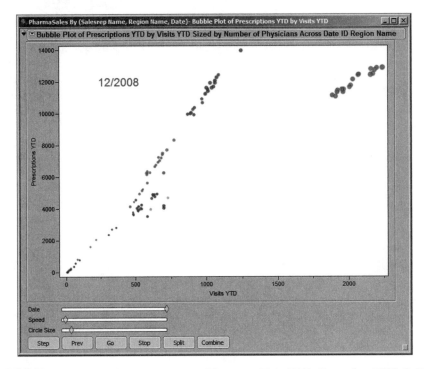

EXHIBIT 7.58   Bubble Plot for Prescriptions YTD versus Visits YTD, December 2008, Split by Salesrep Name

Viewing the plot over time, he finds it interesting that the sales representative bubbles within a region stay tightly clustered, indicating that the aggregated numbers of visits are fairly homogeneous within regions, as are the aggregated prescription totals. He also notices that the circle sizes differ greatly from region to region, but are fairly uniform within regions, meaning that the number of physicians assigned to sales representatives may differ dramatically for different regions, but that within regions the allocation is fairly consistent. It does appear that a typical sales representative in Northern England has more physicians than a typical sales representative in Midlands. This plot provides useful information and could help Rick in thinking about ways to realign the sales force to make it more effective.

Now Rick returns to his idea of normalizing by **Number of Physicians**. The two columns that Rick will need, **Visits YTD per Physician** and **Prescriptions YTD per Physician**, are already inserted in the summary table. He constructed these columns by creating new columns and using the formula editor. For example, the formula for the column **Visits YTD per Physician** is shown in Exhibit 7.59. To view it, in the data table, click on the plus sign to the right of **Visits YTD per Physician** in the columns panel.

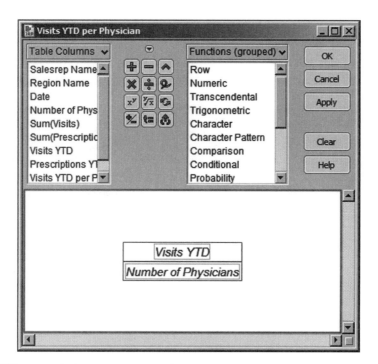

EXHIBIT 7.59   Formula for Visits YTD per Physician

Next, Rick selects **Graph > Bubble Plot** and fills in the launch dialog using the new variables, Prescriptions YTD per Physician versus Visits YTD per Physician, as the **Y** and **X** variables, respectively, and the other variable choices as shown in Exhibit 7.60. He clicks **OK** and saves the script as **Bubble Plot 2**.

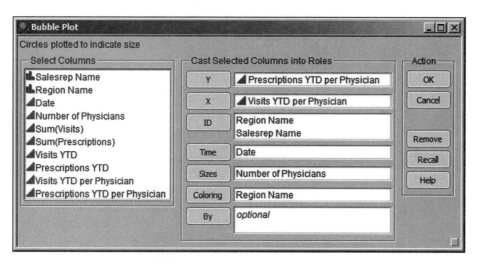

EXHIBIT 7.60   Bubble Plot Launch Dialog for Prescriptions YTD per Physician versus Visits YTD per Physician

As before, Rick selects **All Labels**. Rick also selects **Trail Bubbles** and **Trail Lines** from the red triangle options. Then, Rick animates the plot to see how the regions behave over the eight-month period. The plot for December 2008 is shown in Exhibit 7.61.

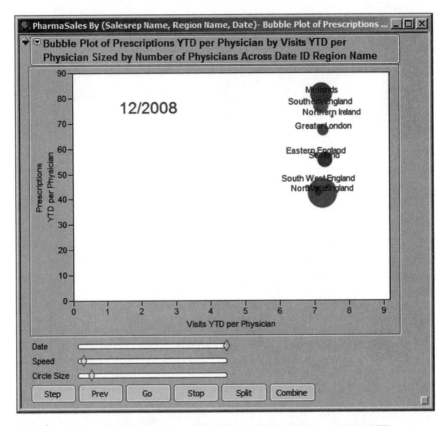

EXHIBIT 7.61   Bubble Plot for Prescriptions YTD per Physician versus Visits YTD per Physician, December 2008

Rick is struck by how similar the regions are in terms of Visits YTD per Physician. He realizes that the norm for visits to physicians is one visit per month. But the data show this happening with almost uncanny regularity.

He wonders if perhaps sales representatives make one visit per month to each practice, and then count this as a visit to all physicians at that practice even though they do not meet individually with all the physicians there. In other words, what does it mean to "make a visit to a physician?" Does it mean that the sales representative talks with the physician face to face? Or that the representative talks with a secretary or technician? Or that the representative simply drops in and leaves a card? And, is it possible that the data are not quite representative of reality? Rick notes that he needs to discuss this with the representatives when they next meet.

Rick considers the plot for 12/2008. By selecting various bubbles and holding down the shift key to select more than one region, Rick is able to select Midlands and Northern England (Exhibit 7.62). Since he has enabled **Trail Bubbles** and **Trail Lines**, the plot shows the bubbles for the preceding months. Rick sees that these two regions drift further apart over time, with Midlands greatly exceeding Northern England in mean number of Prescriptions YTD per Physician. So, even accounting for number of physicians, Midlands is ahead, providing more confirmation that the promotion enhanced sales.

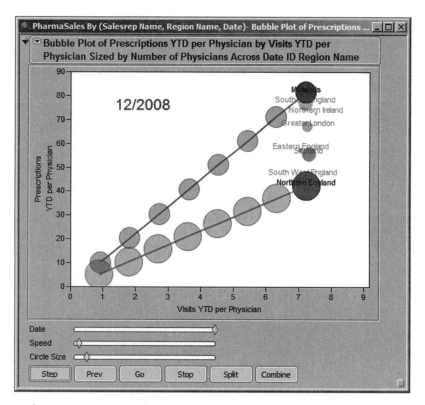

EXHIBIT 7.62   Bubble Plot for Prescriptions YTD per Physician versus Visits YTD per Physician, December 2008, Two Regions Selected

Without the need for animation, the trail bubbles highlight that almost suspicious regularity in Visits YTD per Physician. This is a mystery that Rick needs to unravel.

Rick deselects these two regions, and then deselects **All Labels** and selects the **Split All** option to see the individual sales representative behavior. Once again, he animates the plot. He notes that there is a little less regularity in the Visits YTD per Physician for individual sales representatives, with Scotland showing the most variability. He stops the plot at 12/2008 and selects various sales representatives in order to view their trails. He sees some small amount of variability, but not nearly as much as he might expect. Again, the question of what the sales representatives are recording comes to Rick's mind. And are the representatives in Scotland using different criteria? (See Exhibit 7.63, where the plot on the left shows trails for six Scotland sales representatives, while the plot on the right shows trails for six sales representatives from other regions.)

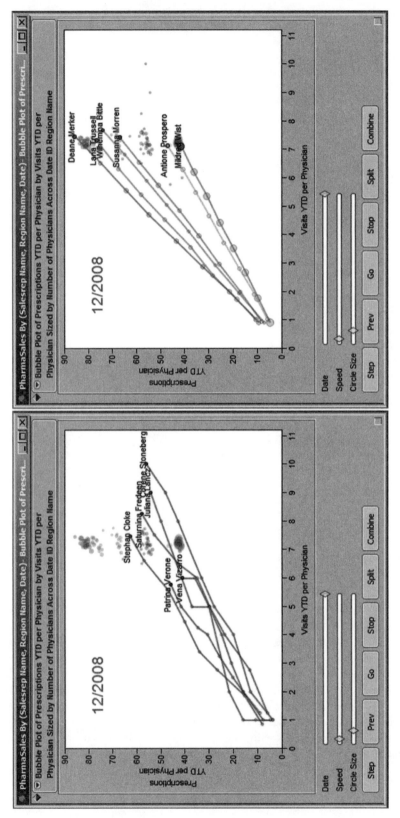

EXHIBIT 7.63   Bubble Plots Showing Trails for Selected Sales Representatives, from Scotland Only on Left, from Other Regions on Right

Summary

Rick now gathers his findings and recommendations from his investigations relative to the two tasks he was given by his sales and marketing vice president, which were to:

- Verify the claims of the marketing group that a limited promotion they ran for Pharma Inc.'s major product from May through December 2008 was very successful.
- Determine whether there are regional differences in performance relative to sales of Pharma Inc.'s major product.

As for the first task, given the available evidence, the 2008 promotional activity in Midlands, Southern England, and Northern Ireland did have a positive impact, just as the marketing group had claimed. Physicians in these regions averaged 81.6, 77.0, and 72.9 prescriptions, respectively, over the eight-month period (Exhibit 7.42). Meanwhile, physicians in the best nonpromotional region, Greater London, averaged 67.3 prescriptions. In the worst nonpromotional regions, Wales and Northern England, physicians averaged 42.5 prescriptions over that eight-month period. The oneway plot in Exhibit 7.39 shows the picture by region with the data summarized by physician, and the bubble plot in Exhibit 7.61 shows the picture summarized by sales representative and adjusted by the number of physicians per sales representative.

Rick also learns that more visits by sales representatives generally lead to more prescriptions being written for Pharma Inc.'s major product (Exhibit 7.51). This effect is especially true when representatives leave promotional sample kits.

Relating to the second task, Rick's initial analysis of the data shows that some sales representatives are in contact with many physicians, whereas others are in contact with far fewer physicians, and that this depends on the region. Even though he does not have to account for sales representatives' time, he would like to understand better why this difference occurs, because he may then be able to increase the yield of his sales force as a whole in the future. But, more to the point, Rick has learned that there are large differences in sales between the different regions. Rather than simply attributing this to a failure of his sales force in some regions, he is prepared to consider that this may also be due to regional differences in the physician and population demographics.

One issue that his data analysis has surfaced is the extreme regularity of monthly visits over almost all regions. When data are this regular, Rick knows that there is probably some underlying reason. He needs to convey to the sales representatives that there will not be negative consequences if they fail to adhere to a one-visit-per-month doctrine, so long as they show good performance overall.

As a first step, he will initiate interviews with some selected sales representatives so that he can learn something about this issue, as well as why there is so much variation in number of physicians assigned to sales representatives in the different regions. He expects to realign his sales force in 2009 and would like to do this in an effective, logical fashion. He also needs to enlist the sales representatives' help in creating operational definitions of concepts that are being measured, such as *a visit to a physician*. Clear definitions will provide meaningful data, which will support better knowledge, decisions, and operational effectiveness in the future.

Conclusion

Using visual techniques, Rick has been able to construct a good understanding of the operation of his sales force and to answer the two questions posed to him by his manager in a complete and compelling manner. Rick's work in the section "Validating and Scoping the Data" was largely directed toward his personal goal of obtaining better knowledge of his sales force. In the "Investigating Promotional Activity" and "A Deeper Understanding of Regional Differences" sections, he addressed the business questions posed by his manager. The analysis that led to the required answers in these two sections was clean, quick, and compelling, and much more efficient than anything Rick could have done without JMP.

This case study is a good example of where force-fitting important business questions either into a project framework or into the traditional Six Sigma DMAIC methodology would be ill-advised and counterproductive. Rick Fincham's analysis raises two major points:

1. Sales data are likely to be more, not less, complex than the data presented here, and there are likely to be more records. Questions relating to data quality, the distribution of missing values, and the balance of the data (namely, which levels of descriptive variables occur jointly) become crucial. As this case study seeks to show, understanding these issues is a necessary step in any kind of sensible analysis. Once these patterns of variation are understood, the analysis itself is often relatively straightforward given a typical set of business objectives.
2. A key requirement of software used in an analysis such as this one is that it should allow you to easily construct insights from real-world, unruly data. Answering one question typically leads to several other questions, and static reports with fixed hierarchies do not lend themselves to this pattern of use. The process of discovery is necessarily personal, so software should aspire to provide a wide repertoire of techniques that allow you to visualize patterns of variation in your data in an unfettered way. Rick's analysis took one direction, but there are many others that might have been taken.

Additional Details

In this section, we provide you with details relating to three items, two of which were mentioned in the case study. The first subsection gives a description of a script that provides the number of unique levels for each variable and saves these levels to **Column Info**. The second subsection explains how to save a script to create a summary table to the main data table, as is done in the data table **PharmaSales.jmp**. The third subsection sketches how to create a formula for a year-to-date summation.

Unique Levels Script

As we have seen, some of the nominal variables in the **PharmaSales.jmp** data table have a large number of levels, which makes studying their bar graphs difficult. The data table **PharmaSales.jmp** contains a script called **Unique Levels** that produces a table that gives the counts of the number of distinct levels of each variable, sorting the columns in order of decreasing frequency relative to the number of levels. For each variable, the script also places these levels into the **Column Info** dialog as a column property. When nominal variables have a large number of levels, this script can be useful as a preliminary data check.

When you run this script, the table in Exhibit 7.64 appears.

PharmaSales_UniqueLevels

	Column Name	Number of Unique Levels
1	Physician Name	11983
2	PhysicianID	11983
3	Practice Name	1164
4	Postcode	1164
5	PracticeID	1164
6	Practice Longitude	1043
7	Practice Latitude	1026
8	Salesrep Name	103
9	SalesrepID	103
10	Prescriptions	48
11	Physician Specialty	16
12	Region Name	9
13	RegionID	9
14	Date	8
15	Visits	7
16	Visits with Samples	7

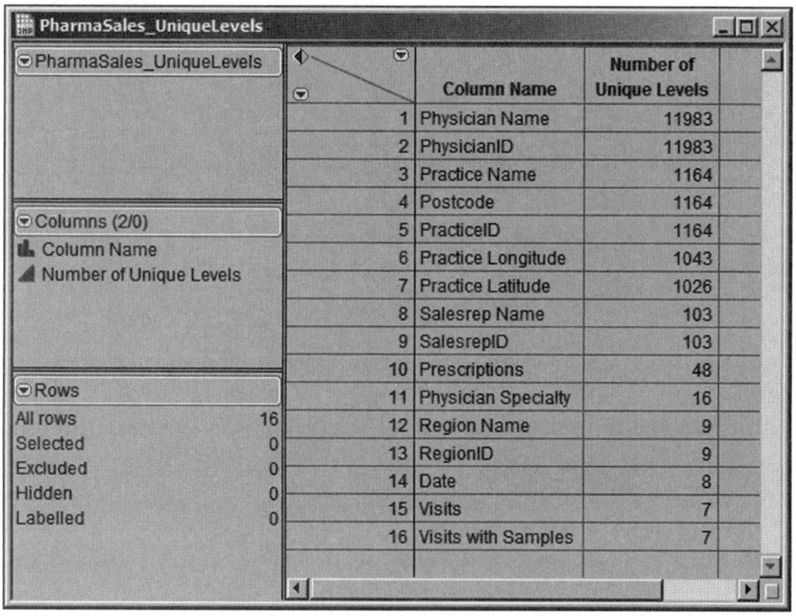

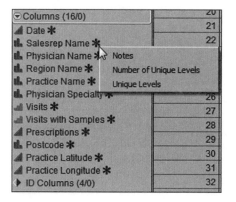

EXHIBIT 7.64 Table Giving Number of Distinct Levels for Each Variable in PharmaSales.jmp

Also, you will note that in **PharmaSales.jmp** asterisks appear next to each variable name in the columns panel. For example, if you click on the asterisk next to Salesrep Name, a list showing the column properties associated with that variable appears, as shown in Exhibit 7.65. The script has placed two new properties in **Column Info**: **Number of Unique Levels** and **Unique Levels**.

EXHIBIT 7.65 List of Column Properties for Salesrep Name

Click on **Unique Levels**. This opens the **Column Info** dialog, and the unique levels of Salesrep Name, namely the names of all the sales representatives, are shown in the text window (Exhibit 7.66).

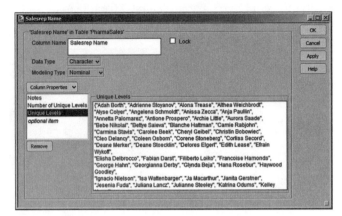

EXHIBIT 7.66   Unique Levels for Salesrep Name, Shown in Column Info Dialog

The script **Delete Unique Levels** removes the column properties inserted by the **Unique Levels** script. If you find these scripts useful, you can copy them to other JMP tables.

Saving a Script to Create a Summary Data Table

This section describes how you would save a script that creates a summary table to the parent data table. Recall that Rick created a summary data table from the data in **PharmaSales.jmp** (Exhibit 7.34) by selecting **Tables > Summary** and filling out the dialog as shown in Exhibit 7.67.

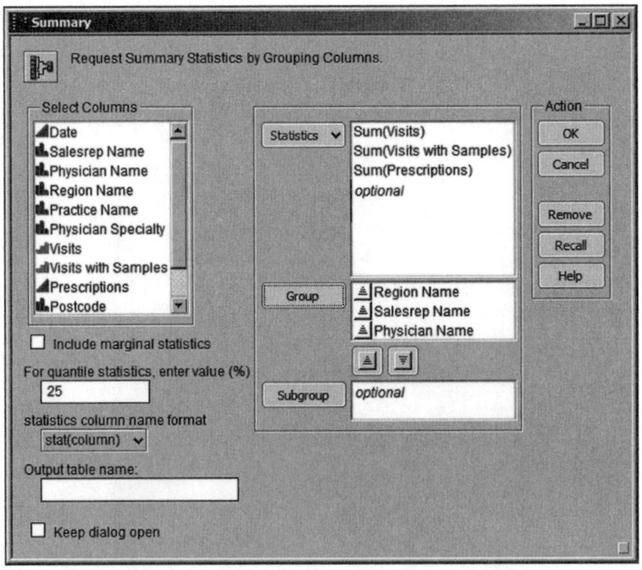

EXHIBIT 7.67   Dialog for Summary Table 1

When you run this summary dialog, in the resulting summary table you will see a script called **Source**. This is the script that creates the summary table. To run the summary from a script in the main data table, you need only copy the **Source** script to the parent data table, namely, to **PharmaSales.jmp**.

So, with **PharmaSales.jmp** active, run the dialog in Exhibit 7.67. In the summary table, click on the red triangle next to **Source**, choose **Edit**, and copy the script to the clipboard. Then, close the script window and make the data table **PharmaSales.jmp** active. In this data table, click on the red triangle next to **PharmaSales** in the data table panel (Exhibit 7.68) and choose **New Property/Script**.

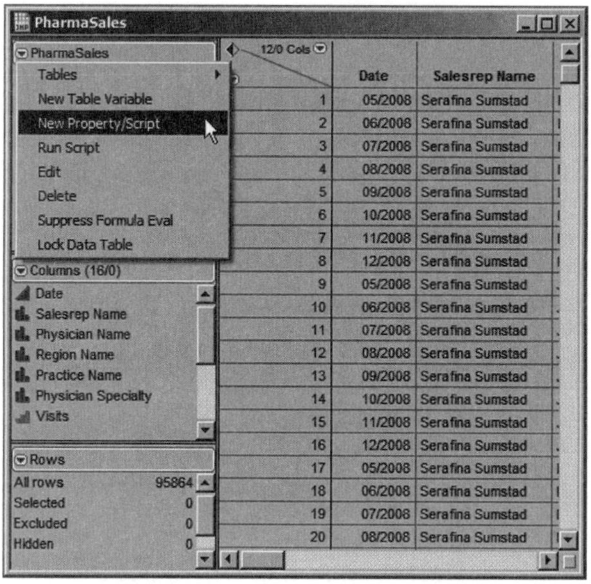

EXHIBIT 7.68   New Property/Script Option in Data Table Panel

This opens a text window where you can paste the **Source** script. Here, we have named the script **Summary Table 3** to distinguish it from the two summary scripts that are already saved. The text window is shown in Exhibit 7.69. Just to be sure that this works, click **OK** and run the script.

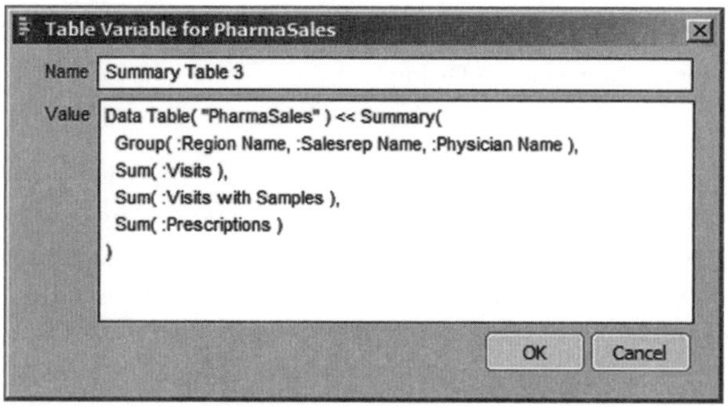

EXHIBIT 7.69   Summary Table Script Window

Constructing a Year-to-Date Summary Table

In this section, we give the details of how Rick accumulates his outcome variables on a year-to-date basis as required in the data table given by the script **Summary Table 2**. To begin, Rick makes his main table, **PharmaSales.jmp**, the active table. He first needs to aggregate Prescriptions and Visits for each sales representative each month. In other words, he wants to sum these two variables over the physicians serviced by each sales representative. To do this, Rick selects **Tables > Summary**, completes the launch dialog as shown in Exhibit 7.70, and then clicks **OK**.

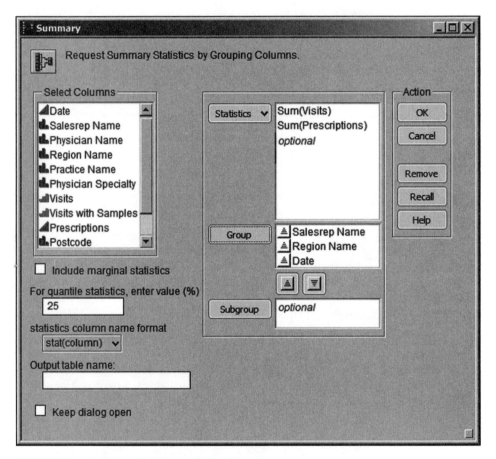

EXHIBIT 7.70   Summary Table Launch Dialog

In the resulting data table, Rick sees a column called N Rows. This is the total number of rows in **PharmaSales.jmp** for each sales representative in the given month. Rick realizes that this is just the number of physicians assigned to the given sales representative. For this reason, he renames the N Rows column to Number of Physicians (Exhibit 7.71).

		Salesrep Name	Region Name	Date	Number of Physicians	Sum(Visits)	Sum(Prescriptions)
▾ PharmaSales By (Salesrep N	1	Adah Borth	Southern England	05/2008	107	87	1012
▾ Source	2	Adah Borth	Southern England	06/2008	107	94	1077
▾ Bubble Plot 1	3	Adah Borth	Southern England	07/2008	107	102	1098
▾ Bubble Plot 2	4	Adah Borth	Southern England	08/2008	107	95	1044
▾ Columns (6/1)	5	Adah Borth	Southern England	09/2008	107	100	1018
↓ Salesrep Name	6	Adah Borth	Southern England	10/2008	107	100	1032
↓ Region Name	7	Adah Borth	Southern England	11/2008	107	95	1037
◢ Date	8	Adah Borth	Southern England	12/2008	107	95	1021
◢ Number of Physicians	9	Adrienne Stoyanov	Northern England	05/2008	305	293	1604
◢ Sum(Visits)	10	Adrienne Stoyanov	Northern England	06/2008	305	272	1604
◢ Sum(Prescriptions)	11	Adrienne Stoyanov	Northern England	07/2008	305	261	1554
▾ Rows	12	Adrienne Stoyanov	Northern England	08/2008	305	306	1685
All rows 824	13	Adrienne Stoyanov	Northern England	09/2008	305	272	1607
Selected 0	14	Adrienne Stoyanov	Northern England	10/2008	305	284	1543
Excluded 0	15	Adrienne Stoyanov	Northern England	11/2008	305	268	1671
Hidden 0							
Labelled 0							

EXHIBIT 7.71   Partial View of Summary Data Table

At this point, Rick wants to add year-to-date sums of **Visits** and **Prescriptions** to this data table. He will do this by creating two new columns, called **Visits YTD** and **Prescriptions YTD**, using formulas. His plan is to base year-to-date sums on the **Date** column, summing only one row for May, two rows (May and June) for June, and so on. We will not describe how these formulas are defined in detail, but we sketch Rick's approach in the context of the formula for **Visits YTD**.

First, by double-clicking in the empty column header area to the right of **Sum(Prescriptions)**, Rick opens a new column. He names this new column **Visits YTD**. Then he right-clicks in the header area to open the context-sensitive menu, where he chooses **Formula**. This opens the formula editor window. Under **Table Columns**, Rick selects **Date**. This enters **Date** into the formula editor.

Just a reminder about dates in JMP: Any date is stored as a continuous value representing the number of seconds since January 1, 1904. Available under **Column Info**, the date formats translate the number of seconds into recognizable date formats such as the m/y (month/year) format used for **Date** in **PharmaSales.jmp**.

Back to Rick, who has **Date** entered into the formula editor. Rick wants to define a partial sum for each value of **Date**. To do this, he will use the **Match** function, available under the **Conditional** grouping. But he would prefer not to have to type each of the dates into the **Match** function in order to define the partial sum that is appropriate for that value of **Date**. So, he uses a JMP shortcut. With **Date** in the formula editor and selected (there should be a red rectangle around it), Rick *holds down the shift key as he clicks on* **Conditional** *in the list of* **Functions (grouped)**. At that point, he releases the shift key and selects **Match** (Exhibit 7.72).

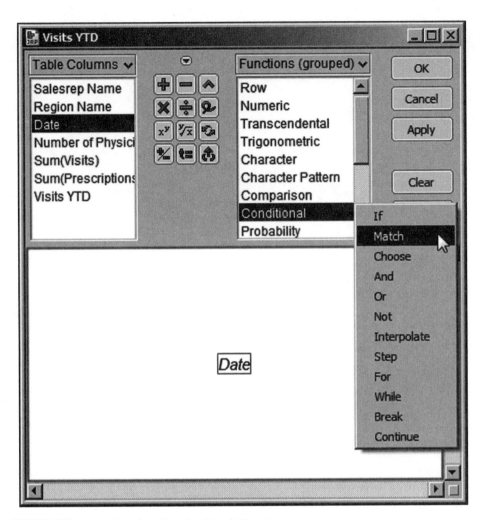

EXHIBIT 7.72 Formula Editor Showing Match Function

Holding down the shift key while choosing **Conditional** causes JMP to list each possible value of **Date** as a conditional argument to the **Match** function. The resulting function template appears as shown in Exhibit 7.73. Each date is shown using its internal representation as the number of seconds since January 1, 1904. However, since the dates are listed in increasing order, it is clear to Rick that the value 3292444800 represents May 2008, 3295123200 represents June 2008, and so on.

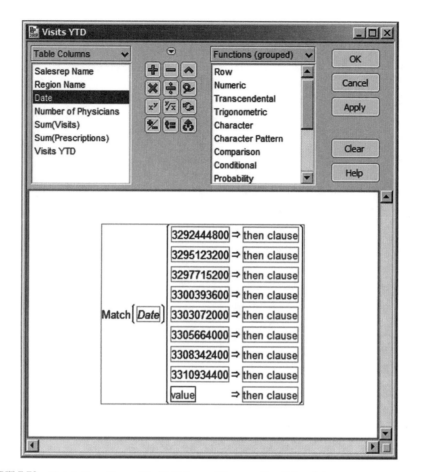

EXHIBIT 7.73   Match Function with All Values of Date as Conditional Arguments

Now Rick can enter the partial sum functions for each date. The finished formula is shown in Exhibit 7.74, where we have enlarged the first four sums for visibility. For May 2008, the partial sum is simply the value of Sum(Visits) for the current row. Rick enters this into the **then clause** rectangle by selecting the **then clause** text area, selecting Sum(Visits) under **Table Columns**, and, while it is selected (surrounded by the red rectangle) in the formula editor, clicking on **Row** under **Functions (grouped)** and choosing **Subscript**, then going to **Row** again and choosing **Row** (to fill the **Subscript** box). The formula tells JMP that if the month is May 2008, then Visits YTD should return the value of Sum(Visits) in the current row.

To construct the formula for June, Rick begins by copying his formula for May, which is Sum(Visits) subscripted by **Row( )**, into the formula rectangle for June 2008. Then he clicks a plus sign and defines the second summand shown in Exhibit 7.74. Here, for the subscript, he selects repeatedly under the **Row** formula grouping: first, **Subscript**, next **Lag**, then **Row**. He continues building his partial sums in this fashion, entering appropriate values for the lag argument. He uses a similar approach to construct Prescriptions YTD.

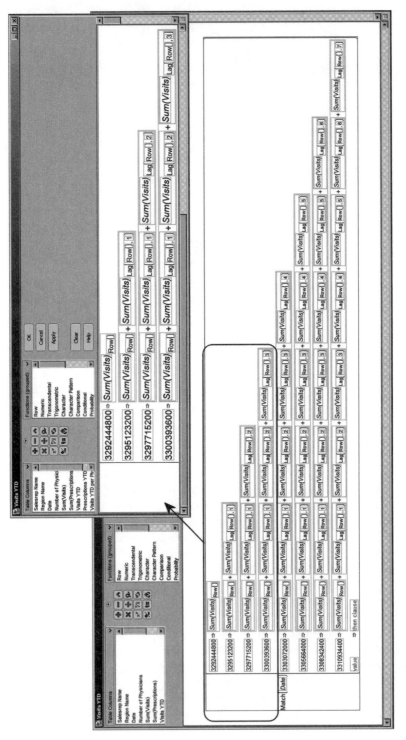

EXHIBIT 7.74   Formula for Visits YTD

To view these formulas on your screen, run the script **Summary Table 2** in **PharmaSales.jmp**. In the columns panel, click on the plus sign next to Visits YTD or Prescriptions YTD.

Note

1. Ellis R. Ott, *Process Quality Control* (New York, NY: McGraw-Hill, 1975), 87; and Ronald Moen, Thomas W. Nolan, and Lloyd P. Provost, *Quality Improvement through Planned Experimentation, Second Edition* (New York, NY: McGraw-Hill, 1999), 60.

CHAPTER 8

Improving a Polymer Manufacturing Process

The British company MoldMat Ltd. manufactures granulated white plastic at a plant in Britain and supplies it to a molding plant in Italy, where it is made into white garden chairs and tables. However, the molding process goes through intermittent phases when its product quality drops, leading to yield losses at both the polymer and the molding plants. When a crisis occurs, teams are formed to tackle the problem, but the problem usually disappears for no apparent reason.

After yet another mysterious crisis occurs and resolves itself, Carl Linton, a young engineer with black belt training in Six Sigma, is tasked to solve the problem once and for all. Together with a small project team, Carl identifies two characteristics (Ys) that are of paramount importance relative to quality and yield: the polymer's *melt flow index* (MFI) and its *color index* (CI).

Carl and his team reanalyze data collected by the most recent crisis team. Because suspected relationships between the two responses and eight process factors fail to reveal themselves in this analysis, Carl suspects that measurement variation may be clouding results. Consequently, Carl and his team conduct *Measurement System Analysis* (MSA) studies on the measured Ys and Xs. The problematic variables turn out to be MFI (one of the two Ys) and filler concentration (one of the Xs).

Once the repeatability and reproducibility issues for these two variables are addressed, Carl and his team gather new data. They initiate their analysis by visualizing the data one variable at a time and two variables at a time. Then, they proceed to modeling relationships using the screening platform. They develop useful models for MFI and CI that include terms that might otherwise have been overlooked had Carl not used the screening platform.

The profiler is used to optimize MFI and CI simultaneously. Using sound estimates of the expected variation in the Hot Xs, Carl simulates the expected distributions for MFI and CI at the optimal settings. This confirms that the parts per million (PPM) rate should be greatly reduced. After running some successful confirmation trials, the changes are implemented.

One and a half years later, not a single batch of white polymer has been rejected by the molding plant. The savings from rejected batches alone amount to about £750,000 per annum. Additionally, because there are now no processing restrictions on the molding plant, savings of £2,100,000 per annum are being realized by MoldMat's big customer. This, in turn, leads to increased sales for MoldMat. These savings came at very little cost, as project-related expenditures were minimal.

Carl's odyssey takes him and his team through all of the steps of the Visual Six Sigma Data Analysis Process. In particular, he engages in some interesting work involving MSAs and modeling using the screening platform. A list of platforms and options used by Carl is given in Exhibit 8.1. The data sets he uses can be found at http://support.sas.com/visualsixsigma. Please join Carl and his team as they solve a very tough but typical manufacturing problem.

EXHIBIT 8.1   Platforms and Options Illustrated in This Case Study

Menus	Platforms and Options
Tables	Concatenate
Rows	Exclude/Unexclude
	Hide/Unhide
	Colors/Markers
	Row Selection
	Clear Row States
	Data Filter
Cols	Column Info
	Column Properties
	Formula
DOE	Full Factorial Design
Analyze	Distribution
	Histogram
	Capability
	Continuous Fit
	Frequency Distribution
	Fit Y by X
	Bivariate Fit
	Fit Model
	Standard Least Squares
	Modeling
	Screening
Graph	Scatterplot Matrix
	Control Chart
	IR
	Xbar
	Variability/Gauge Chart
	Gauge RR
	Profiler
	Maximize Desirability
	Sensitivity Indicators
	Simulator
	Surface Plot
Tools	Crosshairs
Other Options	Column Label/Unlabel
	Control Charts—Phases
	Copy/Paste in a Data Table (Using Fill)
	Data View
	Non-normal Capability
	Save Prediction Formula
	Save Script to Data Table
	Select Points in a Plot

Setting the Scene

For the past 25 years, MoldMat Ltd. has supplied the plastic used by one of its major customers in Italy in making white garden furniture. Over the years, mysterious crises occur during which the flowability of the plastic leads to low yields for both MoldMat and its Italian customer. To date, all efforts to find the root causes of these crises have failed. After the most recent crisis, a new team is formed, led by an engineer named Carl Linton, a black belt with training in Visual Six Sigma.

Manufacturing Process

White garden chairs and furniture command a very good price, but they are difficult to make owing to the impact of whitening agents on plastic flowability. Getting the right balance of whiteness and flow is not easy. As the proportion of additives in the mix increases to make the plastic whiter, the flow of the plastic is impaired.

The process for making white plastic begins with the preparation of a filler mixture, or *slurry*. The white filler, which is an inert powder, is sourced from a number of quarries in Africa. It is mixed with unpurified river water in a stirred tank in the filler preparation section of the MoldMat polymer plant (Exhibit 8.2). The filler preparation tank is agitated and held at a target concentration. The tank is topped off each day with filler and water. Small amounts of a viscosity modifier are added to the slurry if the viscosity gets too high.

Clear plastic is made by heating and stirring a monomer in a batch reactor until it polymerizes. To make the white plastic, the filler slurry is added to the monomer in the polymerization reactor at the start of the polymerization process. When the polymerization reaction is complete, the molten polymer is granulated and packed. The MoldMat plant in England makes three batches of white plastic per day, running a 24-hour schedule every day of the week.

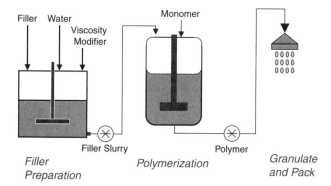

EXHIBIT 8.2   White Polymer Manufacturing Process

The polymer plant tests every batch of polymer. A sample from each completed batch is taken and tested for:

- Color (whiteness), measured on a colorimeter using a color index.

- Melt flow, measured as a melt flow index in an off-line laboratory test. This is an indicator of how well the polymer will process in the downstream molding plant.
- Filler content of the polymer.

Typical Crisis

Crises have occurred two or three times a year ever since a new product was introduced ten years ago. Here is a typical sequence of events.

The Italian molding plant will have several months of normal processing before starting to experience problems with flowability. When this happens, technicians in the molding plant check the processing parameters, and if these look reasonable they question the quality of the polymer. The MoldMat plant engineers check that the polymer is in specification and verify that there is nothing wrong with the test equipment. This leads the processing plant engineers to suspect that the molding processing parameters have changed.

After a few more days of bad processing, the molding plant engineers will ask for some different polymer to run as a trial. This requires a fresh start for molding production. The molding plant must empty the polymer silos to run the trial polymer. The purged material is sold as scrap, which is accounted for as a loss in the MoldMat plant yield.

By this time, the output of the molding plant is well behind schedule, and customers are running out of chairs. The business suffers substantial lost margin and opportunity.

Meanwhile, rapid action teams have been assembled from across Europe. A plethora of helpful theories and their associated solutions are developed, such as:

- The filler supplier is inconsistent and should be replaced.
- Last week's heavy rain has altered the pH of the water supply, which has affected the reaction chemistry.
- The MFI specification is too high, so batches of polymer at the bottom end of the specification range should be the only ones used.
- Abnormal ambient temperatures and humidity are to blame.
- The filler is not evenly distributed through the polymer, and agglomerates are blocking the flow channels in the molds.

Process changes are made, trials are run, and data are gathered. But none of the changes ever conclusively solve the problem.

Then, mysteriously, the problem goes away. The molding process gradually improves with everyone convinced that their pet theory or solution was the one that made the difference. All is well until the next time.

Forming a Team

After one particularly bad crisis, the manufacturing director, Edward Constant, has finally had enough. MoldMat has started to implement Visual Six Sigma, and the black belts from the first wave of training are anxious to start driving improvement. Edward is skeptical about Visual Six Sigma, but he is prepared to give it a go—after all, nothing else has worked.

Carl Linton, a bright young engineer who has only recently moved to the polymer plant, is one of the first trainees. Edward has met him a few times and is impressed by his openness to new ideas and his approach to problem solving. Given the numerous false starts, Edward figures that Carl's lack of detailed knowledge of MoldMat's operations could actually be an advantage, provided that he works with people who have the right mix of experience. Edward agrees to act as the project sponsor.

At their first meeting, Edward tells Carl that he will give him all the help he needs. "Everyone has an opinion on the best solution, but I have never been satisfied that anyone has properly done any rigorous analysis, let alone identified the root cause of the problem so that it can be conclusively fixed," he says. "This problem has been around for ten years, so a few more months are not going to make that much difference. The best advice I can give you is to take your time and to trust nothing and no one, unless you have personally verified the data and have worked through it in a methodical way. I don't want any more crises. If the process can work most of the time, then it should be able to work all of the time."

Edward knows that a change of polymer can immediately affect the processing performance of the molding plant, even if the polymer batches meet the polymer specifications. So he directs Carl to focus on the polymer plant first. He urges him to talk to a wide range of people in both the polymer and molding plants. But above all, he directs Carl to collect some data.

Carl and Edward decide to form a small project team comprised of Carl and the following associates:

- Henry, the polymer plant quality manager.
- Bill, a polymer chemist from a technical support group.
- Roberto, a process engineer from the Italian molding plant.

To ensure that the Visual Six Sigma methodology and tools are correctly applied, Tom, a well-seasoned and culturally savvy master black belt from MoldMat's training partner, supports Carl. Carl and Tom assemble the team and review its objectives. To ensure that all team members share a common language and approach, Tom and Carl schedule and conduct an impromptu training session in Visual Six Sigma and JMP.

Framing the Problem

To frame the problem, Carl and his team develop a formal project charter. Additionally, they obtain customer input that directs them to focus on two critical process characteristics, melt flow index and color index.

Developing a Project Charter

During their first team meeting, Carl and his team members draw a high-level process map (Exhibit 8.3). They also decide to review yield data from both the polymer and molding plants to confirm the size and frequency of the problem.

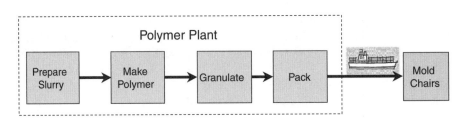

EXHIBIT 8.3 High-level Process Map of White Polymer Molding Process

There have been many arguments about white polymer quality. Although there is a polymer specification, the molding plant has long suspected that it does not fully reflect the true requirements of their process. After a long discussion, the team agrees on the following *Key Performance Indicator* (KPI) definition for the project:

Daily yield, *calculated as the weight of good polymer divided by the weight of total polymer produced.*

Good polymer *is polymer that can be successfully processed by the molding plant.*

Total polymer produced *will include product that fails to meet the polymer plant specifications, plus any polymer that, although meeting polymer plant specifications, is subsequently scrapped or rejected in the molding plant.*

Carl collects some historical data on daily yield and imports it into a data table that he names **BaselineYieldData.jmp**. Part of this data table is shown in Exhibit 8.4. The data table contains two columns, **Date** and **Yield**, and covers a period of a little over three years.

	Date	Yield
1	07/28/2004	100.00
2	07/29/2004	96.87
3	07/30/2004	89.42
4	07/31/2004	95.66
5	08/01/2004	99.03
6	08/02/2004	100.00
7	08/03/2004	93.05
8	08/04/2004	89.62
9	08/05/2004	93.25
10	08/06/2004	96.26
11	08/07/2004	95.71
12	08/08/2004	93.61
13	08/09/2004	92.17
14	08/10/2004	91.99
15	08/11/2004	90.07

BaselineYieldData — BaselineYieldData, Control Chart, Data Filter, On Open. Columns (2/0): Date, Yield. Rows: All rows 1125, Selected 0, Excluded 0, Hidden 0, Labelled 0.

EXHIBIT 8.4 Partial View of BaselineYieldData.jmp

Note that Carl has designated Yield as a **Label** variable, as evidenced by the yellow label icon next to Yield in the columns panel in Exhibit 8.4. He did this by right-clicking on Yield in the columns panel and selecting **Label/Unlabel**. With this property, when the arrow tool hovers over a point in a plot, that point's value of Yield will appear. Carl thinks this may be useful later on.

Carl decides to construct an *individual measurement* (IR) control chart to see how Yield varies over time. He realizes that the distribution of Yield measurements is likely to be skewed since there is an upper limit of 100 percent, so control limits calculated using an individual measurement control chart may not be appropriate. Nonetheless, he decides to use the individual measurement chart in an exploratory fashion.

To construct this chart, he selects **Graph > Control Chart > IR**. In the dialog he enters Yield as **Process** and Date as **Sample Label**. As shown in Exhibit 8.5, he also unchecks the **Moving Range (Average)** box, as this is not of interest to him at this point—he is only interested in the **IR** chart. Carl then clicks **OK**.

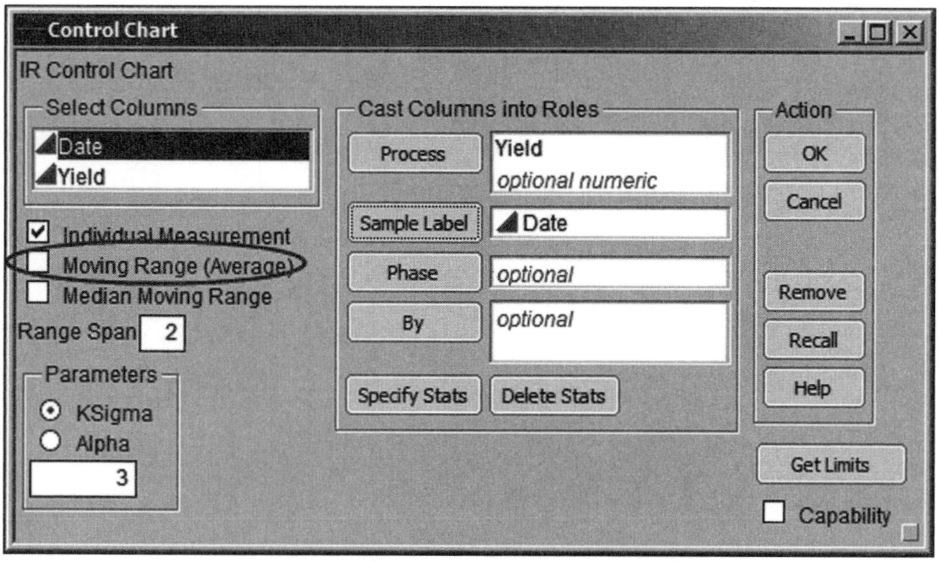

EXHIBIT 8.5   Launch Dialog for IR Chart of Baseline Yield Data

The resulting chart is shown in Exhibit 8.6. This chart clearly shows periods of high yields, each followed by a crisis, with a total of nine crises over the period (two of these crisis periods are marked in Exhibit 8.6). The average Yield over this time period is about 88 percent, and Carl notes that, as expected, the process is far from stable.

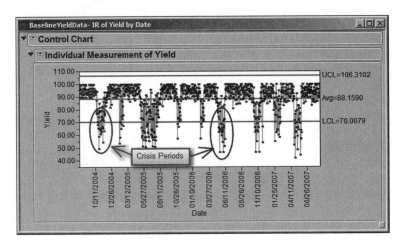

EXHIBIT 8.6   IR Chart of Baseline Yield Data

Following good documentation practice, Carl saves a script to the data table to reproduce this chart. He does this by clicking on the red triangle next to **Control Chart** in the report window and choosing **Script > Save Script to Data Table**. By default, the script is called **Control Chart**.

Recall that Carl has designated Yield as a **Label** variable. To get some idea of what the noncrisis Yield values might be, Carl lets his arrow tool hover over various points to see their yields, and decides that crisis periods can be loosely defined by collections of batches with Yield values below 85.

Carl is curious about the likely yield of the process had it not been affected by these crisis periods. Just to get a sense of the noncrisis yields, he decides to construct a control chart with crisis batches, defined as batches with yields below 85, excluded. The **Data Filter**, found under **Rows**, provides an easy way to *filter out* data values. Carl selects **Rows > Data Filter**. In the dialog window that appears, he selects Yield and clicks **Add**. The dialog window now appears as in Exhibit 8.7.

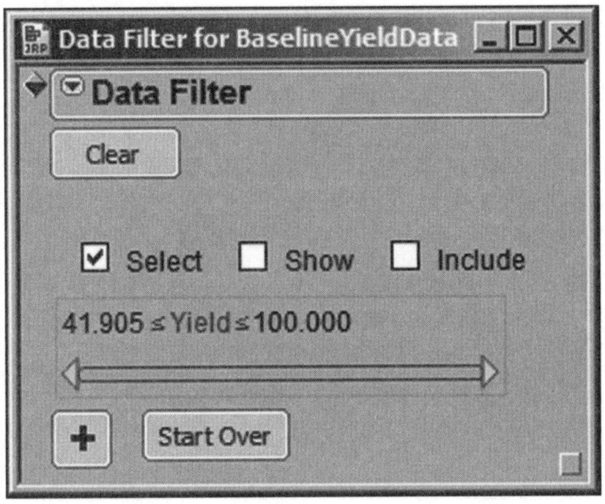

EXHIBIT 8.7   Data Filter Dialog with Yield Added

Carl would like to include only those rows with yields of at least 85. To do this, Carl clicks on the minimum value for **Yield** above the slider in the dialog box; this is shown as 41.905 in Exhibit 8.7. When he clicks on 41.905, a text box appears into which he types 85. Because **Select** is checked, the **Data Filter** selects all rows where **Yield** is at least 85. To include only these rows in calculations, Carl checks the **Include** box. But he also unchecks **Select**, because he does not need to have these rows selected.

Now Carl's dialog appears as shown in Exhibit 8.8. He checks his data table to see that 280 rows have been excluded and scrolls to verify that these are the crisis yield rows. He clicks on the red arrow in the report window next to **Data Filter** and selects **Script > Save Script to Data Table**. This saves the script for the data filter with the default name **Data Filter**.

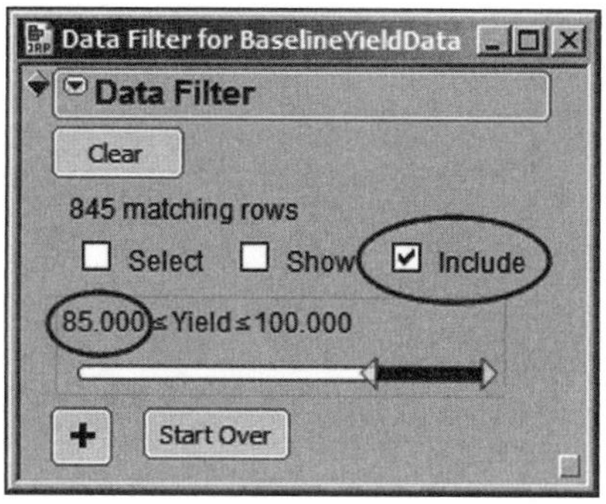

EXHIBIT 8.8   Data Filter Dialog Settings to Exclude Crisis Rows

Now that crisis rows have been excluded, Carl reruns his **Control Chart** script. His new control chart is shown in Exhibit 8.9. Although the crisis points were excluded from the control chart calculations, they were not hidden, so they appear gray on the plot. This is good—Carl did not want anyone to forget that these periods had occurred. He notes that the overall **Yield** for the noncrisis days is about 94 percent. This will help him and his teammates determine a goal for their project.

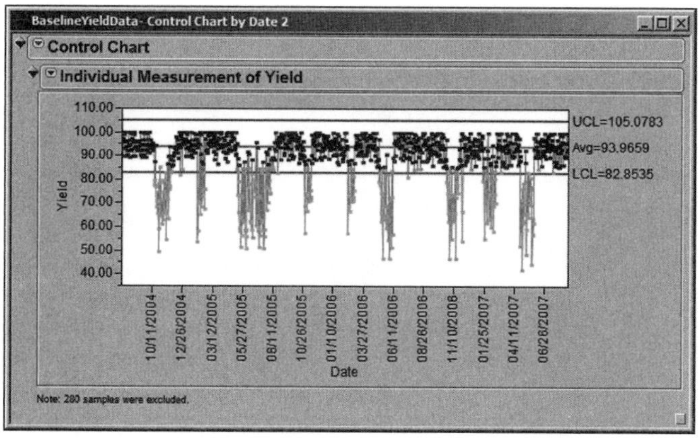

EXHIBIT 8.9   IR Chart with Crisis Periods Excluded

Carl closes his data table at this point. With this information as background, the team reconvenes to agree upon the problem statement and project goal, and to define the specific scope and focus of the project.

The team drafts a project charter, shown in Exhibit 8.10. As instructed, the team members decide to focus on the polymer plant. They set a goal of achieving an average yield of 95 percent by the end of the year. It is late August—this gives them four months. They know that if they can eliminate the crises, they can expect a 94 percent yield. But, knowing that they will be constructing detailed knowledge of the process, they feel that they can even do a little better.

EXHIBIT 8.10   Project Charter

Project Title	Improve White Polymer Process Yield
Business Case	The manufacture of white polymer results in periodic flowability crises at a large Italian customer's molding plant. The molding plant sells suspect polymer at scrap prices. These crises have been going on for years and, although the crises resolve temporarily, they continue to recur, causing significant disruption and great financial loss for both MoldMat and its customer.
	Demand for white furniture keeps increasing, and the molding plant in Italy can't afford to be down due to lack of acceptable white polymer. The molding plant has to turn orders away in crisis periods, causing a significant loss in revenue and great dissatisfaction.
Problem/Opportunity Statement	It is estimated that, due to the crisis periods, the polymer plant suffers a yield loss of about £700,000 per year in scrap material. There is the opportunity to recover at least £700,000 annually in what would otherwise be scrap.
	Also, a significant margin loss is generated by the molding plant, which has to turn orders away in crisis periods. If the problem could be fixed, the accounting department estimates that the company would realize an additional £2,000,000 of revenue annually.
Project Goal Statement and KPI (Key Performance Indicator)	Increase the average yield of white polymer from 88 percent to 95 percent or higher by December 31, 2007 (four months).
	Daily yield will be plotted using an individual measurement control chart.
Project Scope	The polymer plant's part of the process.
Project Team	Sponsor: Edward Constant
	Black belt and polymer process engineer: Carl Linton
	Team members:
	Henry Doyle, the polymer plant quality manager
	Bill Wright, a polymer chemist from a technical support group
	Roberto Valentino, a process engineer from the Italian molding plant

At this point, Carl checks in with Edward to ensure that he is comfortable with the project charter and the team's proposed direction. Edward is very impressed with the clarity of the team's work to date and likes the idea that the project goal was chosen based on sound data. He is quick to approve of the team's charter and direction.

Identifying Customer Requirements

Next, the team members need to explore the following questions:

- What are the true requirements of the molding plant?
- Why are these requirements met at some times but not at others?
- What is changing?

To this end, during their next meeting, they produce a SIPOC map to help them gain a better understanding of the process steps and to identify where they should focus within the polymer plant (Exhibit 8.11).

Suppliers	Inputs	Process	Outputs	Customers
Umboga A Kuanga A Kuanga B	Filler	Prepare Slurry	Filler Slurry	Polymerization
North West Water Authority	Water			
Slurry Preparation	Filler Slurry	Make Polymer	Polymer	Granulation
Monomers Inc.	Monomer			
Granulation	Polymer	Granulate	Granules	Packing
Packing	Granules	Pack	Bags	Molding Plant

EXHIBIT 8.11   SIPOC Map for White Polymer Process

The team also proceeds to collect *voice of the customer* (VOC) information from the immediate customers of the process, namely, the stakeholders at the molding plant. Through interviews, team members collect information from molding plant technicians and managers. There are many comments reflecting that plant's frustration, such as the following:

- "I don't want any crises caused by poor polymer."
- "Your polymer is not consistent."
- "I don't believe you when you say you are in spec."
- "I need to be able to make good white molding all the time."
- "You are killing my business."
- "We can't continue with these scrap levels."

But the team also collects specific information about the technical requirements of the molding process. They diagram their analysis in the form of a *Critical to Quality* tree, a portion of which is shown in Exhibit 8.12. Two primary characteristics quickly emerge:

- The molding plant has specified that in order for the polymer to process well on their equipment, the polymer's *melt flow index*, or MFI, must fall between lower and upper specification limits of 192 and 198 (with a target of 195).
- The polymer's *color index*, or CI, must meet the whiteness specification. The maximum possible CI value is 100, but the only requirement is that CI must exceed a lower specification limit of 80.

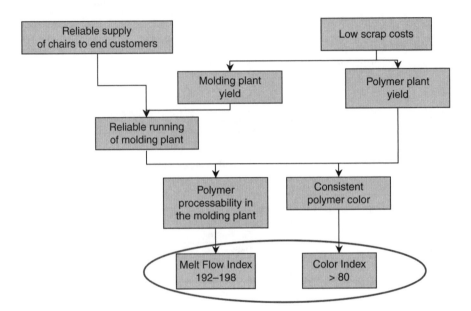

EXHIBIT 8.12   Partial Critical to Quality Tree for Molding Plant VOC

Reviewing Historical Data

Carl and his team are now ready to start thinking about data. They decide that a good starting point is to review the prior crisis team's data and analysis.

Data from Prior Crisis Team

To their surprise and delight, the team members find that the prior crisis team had used many Six Sigma tools in investigating possible causes of the problem. In particular, the team members had developed an *Input/Output* process map (Exhibit 8.13) to help identify the potential Xs that might be driving variation in MFI, CI, and, consequently, Yield. They used the Xs and Ys identified in their process map to determine the data they should collect.

Filler
Water
Quarry
X_7
pH
X_4
Monomer
Prepare Slurry
Make Polymer
Granulate
Pack
Mold Chairs
Y_1 MFI
Y_2 CI
Y_3 Yield
X_1 SA
X_2 M%
X_5 Viscosity
X_3 Xf
X_6 Ambient Temp
X_8 Shift

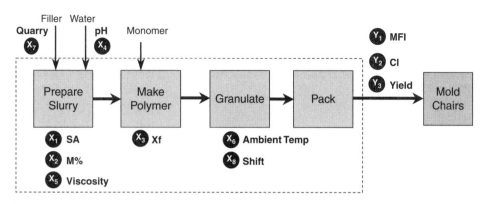

EXHIBIT 8.13 Input/Output Process Map of White Polymer Process

Carl obtains a spreadsheet of the data collected by the crisis team and imports this into a JMP table, which he calls **CrisisTeamData.jmp**. The data consist of measurements for the Xs and Ys identified in the process map for 127 batches over about a six-week period. A partial view of the data file is shown in Exhibit 8.14.

CrisisTeamData
CrisisTeamData
Distribution
Control Charts
On Open
Columns (12/0)
Batch Number
MFI
CI
Yield
SA
M%
Xf
pH
Viscosity
Ambient Temp
Quarry
Shift
Rows
All rows 127
Selected 0
Excluded 0
Hidden 0
Labelled 0

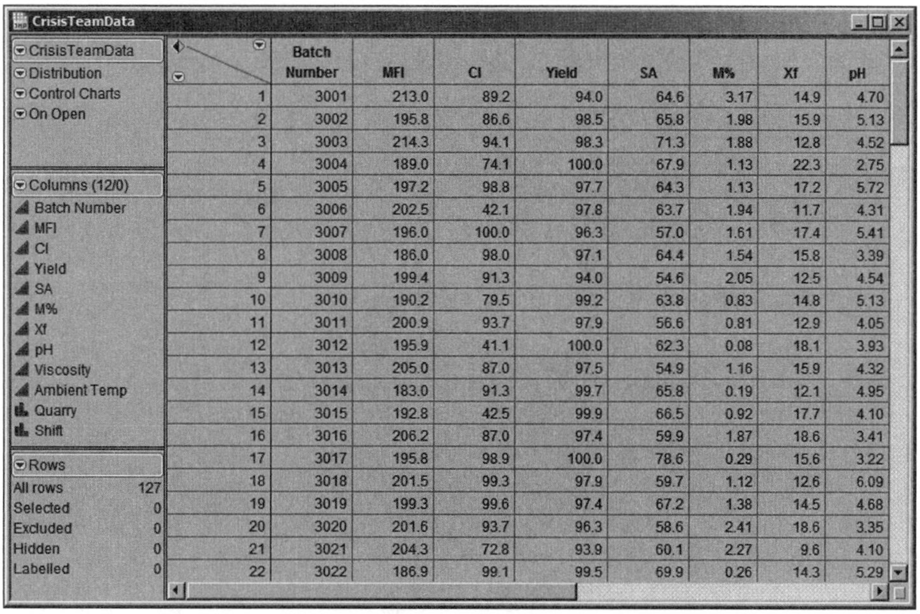

	Batch Number	MFI	CI	Yield	SA	M%	Xf	pH
1	3001	213.0	89.2	94.0	64.6	3.17	14.9	4.70
2	3002	195.8	86.6	98.5	65.8	1.98	15.9	5.13
3	3003	214.3	94.1	98.3	71.3	1.88	12.8	4.52
4	3004	189.0	74.1	100.0	67.9	1.13	22.3	2.75
5	3005	197.2	98.8	97.7	64.3	1.13	17.2	5.72
6	3006	202.5	42.1	97.8	63.7	1.94	11.7	4.31
7	3007	196.0	100.0	96.3	57.0	1.61	17.4	5.41
8	3008	186.0	98.0	97.1	64.4	1.54	15.8	3.39
9	3009	199.4	91.3	94.0	54.6	2.05	12.5	4.54
10	3010	190.2	79.5	99.2	63.8	0.83	14.8	5.13
11	3011	200.9	93.7	97.9	56.6	0.81	12.9	4.05
12	3012	195.9	41.1	100.0	62.3	0.08	18.1	3.93
13	3013	205.0	87.0	97.5	54.9	1.16	15.9	4.32
14	3014	183.0	91.3	99.7	65.8	0.19	12.1	4.95
15	3015	192.8	42.5	99.9	66.5	0.92	17.7	4.10
16	3016	206.2	87.0	97.4	59.9	1.87	18.6	3.41
17	3017	195.8	98.9	100.0	78.6	0.29	15.6	3.22
18	3018	201.5	99.3	97.9	59.7	1.12	12.6	6.09
19	3019	199.3	99.6	97.4	67.2	1.38	14.5	4.68
20	3020	201.6	93.7	96.3	58.6	2.41	18.6	3.35
21	3021	204.3	72.8	93.9	60.1	2.27	9.6	4.10
22	3022	186.9	99.1	99.5	69.9	0.26	14.3	5.29

EXHIBIT 8.14 Partial View of Table Containing Crisis Team Data

The columns in the data table are described in Exhibit 8.15. Note that there are three Ys and eight Xs of interest. Carl realizes that even though the table does not have an explicit date or time column, the sequential values of Batch Number define the processing order.

EXHIBIT 8.15   Description of Variables in CrisisTeamData.jmp

Variable Type	Name	Description
ID	Batch Number	Identifying number for slurry batch
Ys	MFI	Melt flow index of the polymer
	CI	Color index of the polymer
	Yield	Weight of good polymer as determined by the molding plant, divided by weight of total polymer produced
Xs	SA	Amps for slurry tank stirrer
	M%	Viscosity modifier percent measured in the filler slurry tank
	Xf	Percent of filler in the polymer
	pH	pH of the slurry
	Viscosity	Viscosity of the slurry
	Ambient Temp	Ambient temperature in the slurry tank area
	Quarry	Quarry of origin for filler
	Shift	Shift during which batch was processed

Reanalyzing the Historical Data

The first thing that the team wants to know is how the process behaved, in terms of Ys, over the six-week period reviewed by the previous crisis team. But, Carl insists that they first run **Distribution** for all of the variables (except **Batch Number**). In his training, Carl learned from Tom, his mentor for this project, that this is an important first step in any data analysis.

Carl selects **Analyze > Distribution**, adds all eleven Xs and Ys as **Y, Columns**, and clicks **OK**. He saves the script for this analysis with the default name, **Distribution**.

The team reviews the resulting plots. Of particular interest are the Yield values that fall below 85 percent. Carl selects these in the box plot to the right of the Yield histogram. He does this by using the arrow tool inside the box plot area, clicking and dragging a rectangle that includes these points as shown in Exhibit 8.16.

This action selects the corresponding rows in the data table—Carl checks to find that 14 rows have been selected. Consequently, the values corresponding to these 14 low-yielding batches are highlighted in the histograms for all of the variables. For example, the team sees that the 14 crisis **Yield** batches had very low **SA** values. To remove the selection of the 14 rows, Carl selects **Rows > Clear Row States**.

Looking at the histograms, one of the team members points out that the distribution of **CI** is not bell-shaped. Carl agrees and observes that this is not unusual, given that **CI** has a natural upper bound of 100 percent. But, the team is now aware that they must keep this in mind when using certain statistical techniques, such as individual measurement control charts and capability analysis, both of which assume that measured values are normally distributed.

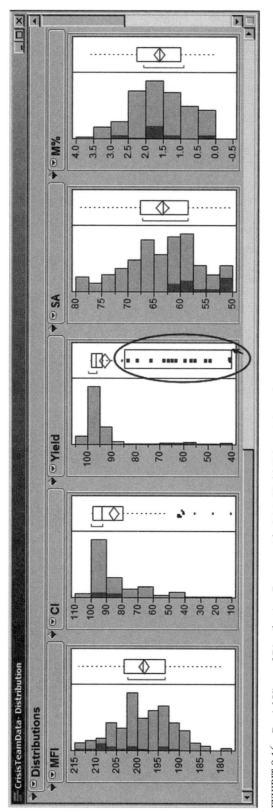

EXHIBIT 8.16 Partial View of Distribution Report with Crisis Yield Values Selected

At this point, the team is eager to see how the three Ys behave over time. Carl constructs individual measurement control charts for these three responses by selecting **Graph > Control Chart > IR**. He inserts MFI, CI and Yield in the **Process** list and Batch Number as the **Sample Label** and unchecks **Moving Range**. When he clicks **OK,** the charts as shown in Exhibit 8.17 appear. Once again, Carl saves the script to the data table, double-clicking on the name to change it to **Control Charts**.

For the most part, MFI seems to be stable. There are no points outside the control limits. When Carl clicks on the red triangle for MFI and chooses **Tests > All Tests**, some points signal unstable situations based on these additional tests. But what is more troubling is that MFI averages 198.4 over this time period. The team's VOC analysis indicated that 198 is the upper specification limit for MFI!

The control chart for CI immediately shows the problem with applying a normality-based control chart to highly skewed data. Nonetheless, there are indications of special causes. The plot also shows some very large and regular dips in CI. There are many excursions below the lower specification limit of 80. This leaves the team members puzzled, especially because the dips do not align with the one crisis period that is so evident in the Yield control chart.

The team considers the idea of running capability analyses for these three responses. However, the **IR** chart clearly shows that MFI is not capable, since the process average exceeds the upper specification limit. Each of CI and Yield is affected by special causes. The corresponding points could be removed prior to running capability analyses, but it is not all that easy to tell exactly which points result from special causes. Finally, Carl's team decides that there is not much to gain by running formal capability analyses on these data.

Carl turns his attention to the crisis team's modeling efforts. Reading through their documentation, Carl sees that team members had analyzed the data using multiple regression, hoping that this might help them determine whether any of the Xs had a significant effect on the three key responses. The team had identified **M%** and **Viscosity** as being significantly related to MFI, but had not found any of the Xs to be related to CI.

Carl finds this last result especially curious. There are several reasons that such an analysis might lead to no significant factors:

- One or more key Xs are missing.
- One or more higher-order terms involving the specified Xs are missing.
- Measurement variation in the Ys or Xs is too large and is masking the systematic patterns in the Ys caused by process variation in the Xs.

Carl meets with members of the crisis team to discuss the reasoning that led to their final choice of Xs and Ys; they convince him that they did not overlook any critical Xs. After this meeting, Carl reanalyzes their data, introducing higher-order terms. He finds some significant relationships, but these don't seem conclusive in terms of the process, especially as they relate to CI. This suggests to Carl that measurement variation may be clouding results.

Carl and his team meet to determine how to proceed. The team members agree that it is possible that measurement variation in the Ys or Xs could be large relative to the systematic variation caused by the Xs. They fully support Carl's proposal to assess the magnitude of the measurement variation.

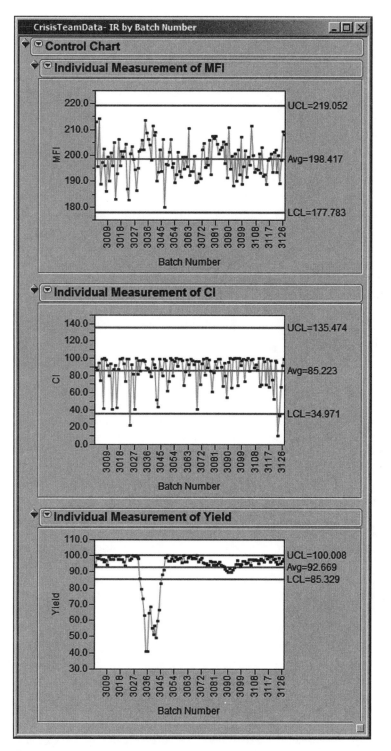

EXHIBIT 8.17   IR Charts for MFI, CI, and Yield, Crisis Team Data

Measurement System Analysis

As a general principle, measurement systems for key variables should always be evaluated before engaging in data collection efforts. Since measurement uncertainty or error is suspected as being part of the reason previous attempts to find root causes of the polymer problems failed, it is all the more important that Carl's team thoroughly study the measurement systems for all the variables identified by the process map.

Carl's team learns that recent routine MSAs indicate that Cl; polymer weight, which forms the basis for the Yield calculation; SA; M%; pH; Viscosity; and Ambient Temp are being measured with very capable instruments and methods. However, the measurement systems for MFI and Xf have not been evaluated in the recent past. Furthermore, given how these measurements are made, the team realizes that they may be prone to problems.

MSA for MFI

MFI is measured using a melt flow meter during an off-line laboratory test. Four instruments are available within the laboratory to perform the test, and there are three different laboratory technicians who do the testing. There is no formal calibration for the instruments. When Carl's team members interview the technicians who perform the test, they get the impression that the technicians do not necessarily use a standardized procedure.

Carl meets with the technicians and their manager to discuss the desired consistency of the measurement process and to enlist their support for an MSA. He reminds them that for characteristics with two-sided specification limits, a guideline that is often used is that the measurement system range, measured as six standard deviations, should take up at most 10 percent of the *tolerance range*, which is the difference between the upper and the lower specification limits. Since the upper and lower specification limits for MFI are 198 and 192, respectively, the guideline would thus require the measurement system range not to exceed 10% × (198 − 192) = 0.6 MFI units.

Carl also mentions that there are guidelines as to how precise the measurement system should be relative to part-to-part, or process, variation: The range of variability of a highly capable measurement system should not exceed 10 percent of the part-to-part (or, in this case, the batch-to-batch) variability.

Given these guidelines, Carl suggests that an MSA for MFI might be useful, and the technicians and their manager agree. He learns from the technicians that the test is destructive. MFI is reported in units of grams per ten minutes. The protocol calls for the test to run over a half-hour period, with three measurements taken on each sample at prescribed times, although due to other constraints in the laboratory the technicians may not always be available precisely at these set times. Each of these three measurements is normalized to a ten-minute interval, and the three normalized values are averaged. From preparation to finish, a test usually takes about 45 minutes to run.

Using this information, Carl designs the structure for the MSA. Since the test is destructive, true repeatability of a measurement is not possible. However, Carl reasons, and the technicians agree, that a well-mixed sample from a batch can be divided into smaller samples that can be considered identical. The three technicians who perform the test all want to be included in the study, and they also want to have all four instruments included. Carl suggests that the MSA should be conducted using samples from three randomly chosen batches of polymer and that each technician make two repeated measurements for each batch by instrument combination.

This leads to 72 tests: 3 batches × 3 technicians × 4 instruments × 2 measurements. Since each test is destructive, a sample from a given batch of polymer will have to be divided into 24 aliquots for testing. For planning purposes, it is assumed that the MSA design will permit three tests to be run per hour, on average, using three of the four instruments. This leads to a rough estimate of 24 hours for the total MSA. With other work intervening, the technicians conclude that they can finish the MSA comfortably in four or five workdays.

Next, Carl designs the experiment for the MSA. To do this, he selects **DOE > Full Factorial Design**. The resulting dialog window is shown in Exhibit 8.18.

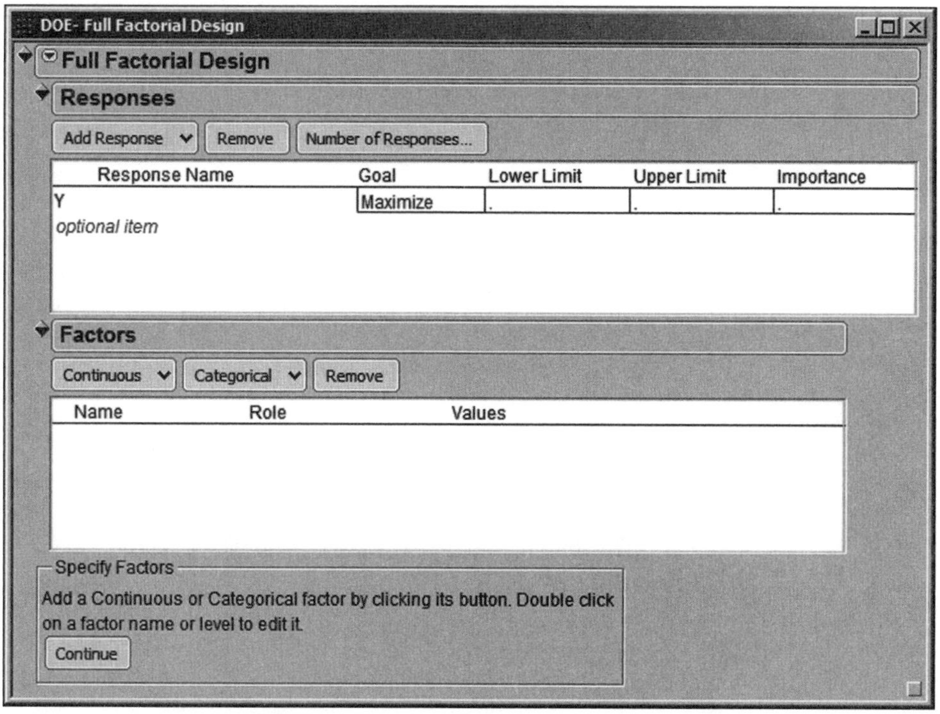

EXHIBIT 8.18   DOE Full Factorial Design Dialog

Carl double-clicks on the response, **Y**, and renames it MFI. He notes the default goal of **Maximize** that JMP specifies. Since this is an MSA, there is no optimization goal relative to the response. He decides to simply leave this as is, since it will not affect the design. Next, by clicking on the **Categorical** button under **Factors**, he adds two three-level categorical factors and one four-level categorical factor. He renames these factors and specifies their values as shown in Exhibit 8.19.

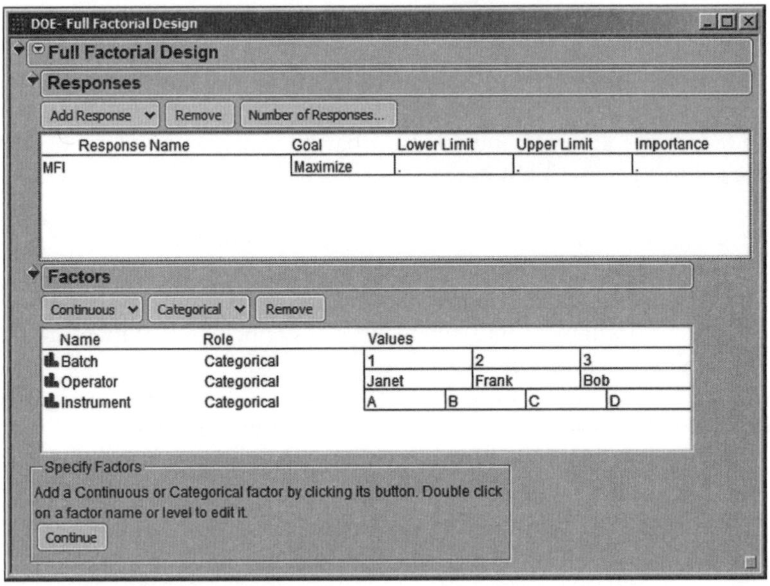

EXHIBIT 8.19   DOE Full Factorial Design Dialog with Response and Factors Specified

Carl then clicks **Continue**. He notes that the design, as specified so far, consists of 36 runs. Carl sees from the default specification that the **Run Order** will be randomized. Since two samples should be run at each of these 36 settings, he inserts a value of 1 in the box for **Number of Replicates**, as shown in Exhibit 8.20. Then he clicks **Make Table** and the design table, partially shown in Exhibit 8.21, appears. (Note that your table will likely appear different due to the fact that the run order is randomized.)

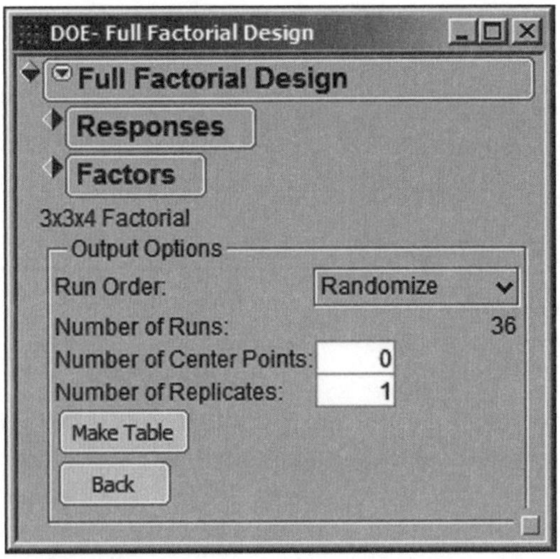

EXHIBIT 8.20   DOE Full Factorial Design Output Options

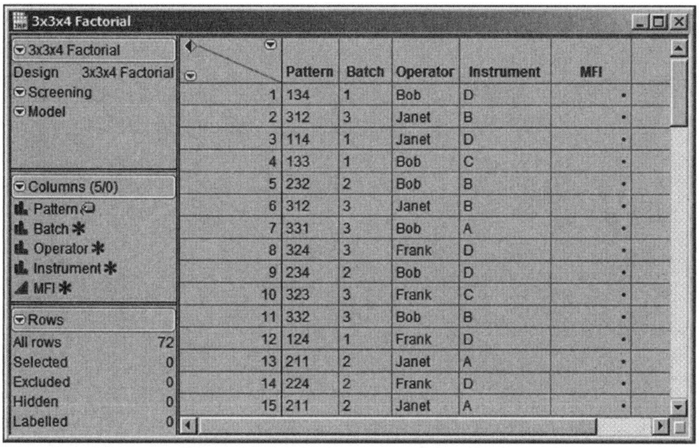

	Pattern	Batch	Operator	Instrument	MFI
1	134	1	Bob	D	•
2	312	3	Janet	B	•
3	114	1	Janet	D	•
4	133	1	Bob	C	•
5	232	2	Bob	B	•
6	312	3	Janet	B	•
7	331	3	Bob	A	•
8	324	3	Frank	D	•
9	234	2	Bob	D	•
10	323	3	Frank	C	•
11	332	3	Bob	B	•
12	124	1	Frank	D	•
13	211	2	Janet	A	•
14	224	2	Frank	D	•
15	211	2	Janet	A	•

EXHIBIT 8.21 MSA Design Table

Carl notices that the **DOE – Full Factorial Design** dialog remains open; this is useful in case changes need to be made to the design that has been generated. As mentioned earlier, the runs are randomized. To the extent possible, the experiment will be run in this order. When JMP creates this design, it assumes that the goal is to model or optimize a process, so it automatically saves two scripts, **Screening** and **Model**, to the data table. But, since the data are being gathered for a measurement system analysis, Carl realizes that these scripts are not appropriate, and so he deletes them.

The technicians conduct the experiment over the course of the next week and enter their results into the data table that Carl has prepared. This table, containing the design and results, is called **MSA_MFI_Initial.jmp** and is partially shown in Exhibit 8.22.

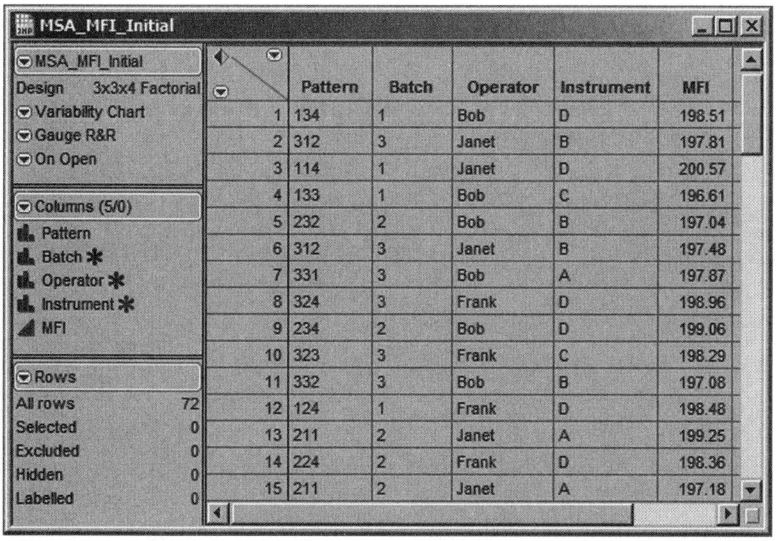

	Pattern	Batch	Operator	Instrument	MFI
1	134	1	Bob	D	198.51
2	312	3	Janet	B	197.81
3	114	1	Janet	D	200.57
4	133	1	Bob	C	196.61
5	232	2	Bob	B	197.04
6	312	3	Janet	B	197.48
7	331	3	Bob	A	197.87
8	324	3	Frank	D	198.96
9	234	2	Bob	D	199.06
10	323	3	Frank	C	198.29
11	332	3	Bob	B	197.08
12	124	1	Frank	D	198.48
13	211	2	Janet	A	199.25
14	224	2	Frank	D	198.36
15	211	2	Janet	A	197.18

EXHIBIT 8.22 Partial View of Data Table for Initial MFI MSA

Carl's team regroups to analyze the data. With this data table as the active window, Carl uses the JMP MSA platform, selecting **Graph > Variability/Gauge Chart**. He populates the dialog as shown in Exhibit 8.23 and clicks **OK**. Carl reflects for a moment on how easy it was to include **Instrument** as part of the analysis—traditional gauge R&R studies are usually limited to estimating variability due to operators and parts. The **Variability/Gauge Chart** platform makes including additional sources of variability trivial.

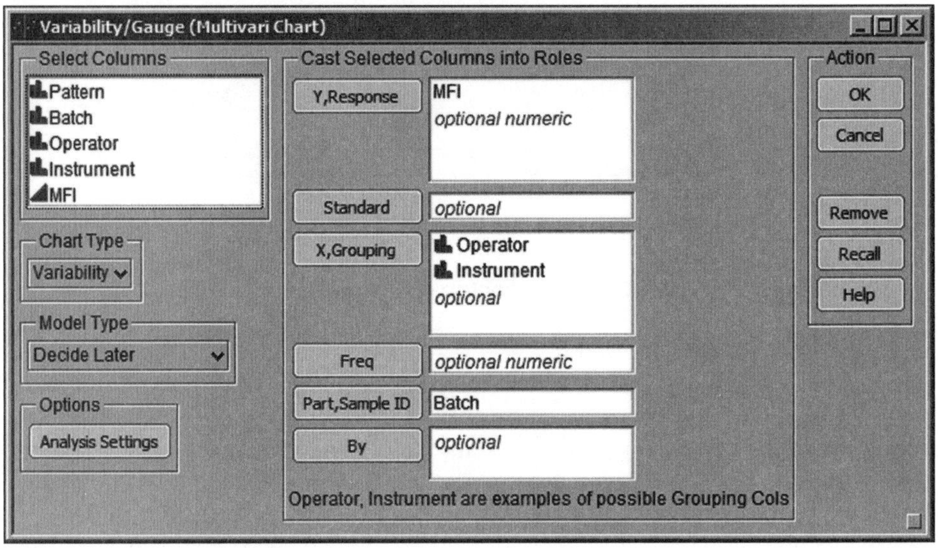

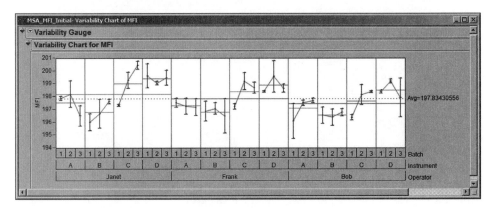

EXHIBIT 8.23   Launch Dialog for MFI MSA

In the menu obtained by clicking on the red triangle, he selects, one by one, **Connect Cell Means**, **Show Group Means**, and **Show Grand Mean**. This allows Carl and his teammates to get a sense of the variability between **Batches**, between **Instruments**, and between **Operators**. He deselects the **St Dev Chart** option, realizing that sufficient information on spread is given by the vertical distance between the two points in each cell. The resulting **Variability Chart** is shown in Exhibit 8.24. He saves the script with the name **Variability Chart**.

EXHIBIT 8.24   Variability Chart for Initial MFI MSA

It is immediately apparent from the variability chart that some sample measurements can vary by as much as three units when being measured by the same Operator with the same Instrument. For example, see Bob's measurement of Batch 3 with Instrument D. Carl clicks on these two points while holding down the shift key to select both. (Alternatively, he could draw a rectangle around them.) Then he goes to the data table, where he sees that the two rows have been selected. To create a table consisting of only these two rows, Carl right-clicks on **Selected** in the rows panel, as shown in Exhibit 8.25, and chooses **Data View**. This creates a data table containing only Bob's two measurements for Batch 3 with Instrument D.

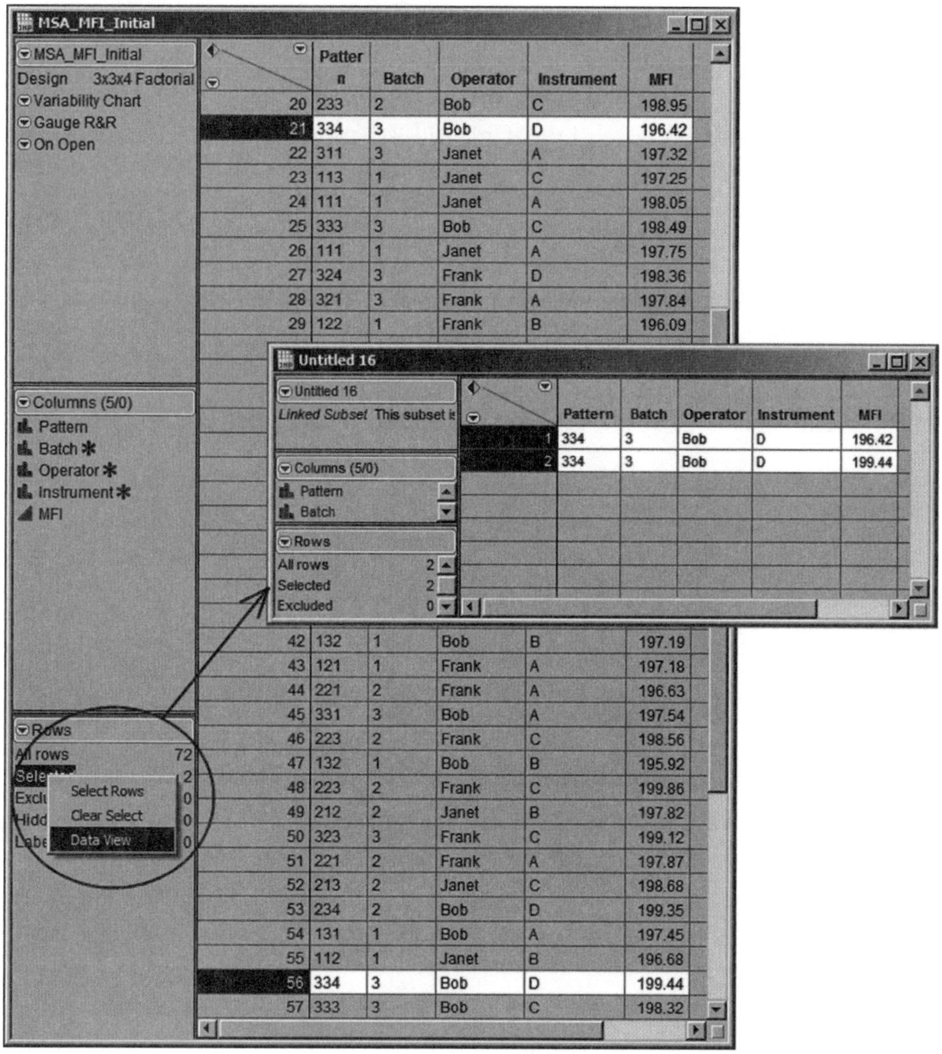

EXHIBIT 8.25   Data View Selection to Create a Subset Table of Selected Rows

The table shows that one measurement is 196.42 while the other is 199.44. Given the fact that the **MFI** measurement system variability should not exceed 0.6 units, this signals a big problem. A sample that falls within the specification limits can easily give a measured **MFI** value that falls outside the specification limits. For example, when Bob measured **Batch** 3, one of his measurements indicated that the batch fell within the specification limits (192 to 198), while another measurement indicated that it was not within the specification limits. The variability in measurements made on the same batch by the same operator with the same instrument is too large to permit accurate assessment of whether product is acceptable.

Carl wants to delve a bit deeper to determine where improvement efforts should focus. Is the larger problem *repeatability* (same batch, same operator, same instrument) or *reproducibility* (same batch, different operators, different instruments)? He performs a **Gauge R&R** analysis. To do this, he selects **Gauge Studies > Gauge RR** from the red triangle in the variability chart report. In the dialog box that appears, he sees that **Crossed** is chosen by default. He is happy with this choice, because his design is *crossed*: Every **Operator** uses every **Instrument** for every **Batch**. He clicks **OK**.

JMP performs some intensive calculations at this point, so Carl has a short wait before the dialog, shown in Exhibit 8.26, appears. There, Carl notices that the default number of standard deviations used to define the measurement system range is six. Assuming normality, this range will contain 99.73 percent of measurement values, and it also corresponds to the guidelines that he is using to assess the performance of the measurement system. The tolerance range for **MFI**, namely USL − LSL, is 198 − 192 = 6. Carl enters this as the **Tolerance Interval** and clicks **OK**.

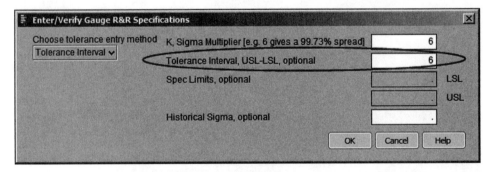

EXHIBIT 8.26   Enter/Verify Gauge R&R Specifications Dialog

The report shown in Exhibit 8.27 appears (the script is saved as **Gauge R&R)**. In the **Gauge R&R** panel, the entry for **Gauge R&R** under the column **Measurement Source** indicates that the MFI measurement system is taking up 7.32 units, which is 122 percent of the tolerance range. This is clearly indicative of a poor measurement system—its variability range exceeds the tolerance range!

Furthermore, both the repeatability and reproducibility variation are quite large and similar in magnitude, with repeatability variation using 5.13 units of the tolerance range and reproducibility variation using 5.23 units. The largest contributors to reproducibility variation are **Instrument** (3.99 units) and **Instrument** interacting with **Batch**, denoted **Instrument*Batch** (2.67 units). The analysis indicates that both the

```
MSA_MFI_Initial- Variability Chart of MFI                                    _□×

▼ ⊽ Variability Gauge
  ▶ Variability Chart for MFI
  ▼ Gauge R&R

                              Variation      % of
   Measurement Source        (6*StdDev)   Tolerance                    which is 6*sqrt of
   Repeatability        (EV)  5.1278252      85.46    Equipment Variation    V(Within)
   Reproducibility      (AV)  5.2258989      87.10    Appraiser Variation    V(Total)-V(Batch)-V(Within)
    Operator                  0.4521374       7.54                           V(Operator)
    Instrument                3.9851557      66.42                           V(Instrument)
    Operator*Instrument       1.2400928      20.67                           V(Operator*Instrument)
    Operator*Batch            1.1282729      18.80                           V(Operator*Batch)
    Instrument*Batch          2.6711571      44.52                           V(Instrument*Batch)
    Operator*Instrument*Batch 1.1305820      18.84                           V(Operator*Instrument*Batch)
   Gauge R&R            (RR)  7.3215170     122.03    Measurement Variation  V(Total)-V(Batch)
   Part Variation       (PV)  1.6009261      26.68    Part Variation         V(Batch)
   Total Variation      (TV)  7.4945030     124.91    Total Variation        V(Total)

        6    k
   97.6918   % Gauge R&R = 100*(RR/TV)
    4.5733   Precision to Part Variation = RR/PV
        0    Number of Distinct Categories = 1.41(PV/RR)
        6    Tolerance = USL-LSL
   1.22025   Precision/Tolerance Ratio = RR/(USL-LSL)
   Using last column 'Batch' for Part.

  ▼ Variance Components for Gauge R&R

                         Var
    Component        Component  % of Total    20 40 60 80
    Gauge R&R        1.4890170     95.44
     Repeatability   0.7304053     46.81
     Reproducibility 0.7586117     48.62
     Part-to-Part    0.0711935      4.56
```

EXHIBIT 8.27   Gauge R&R Report for Initial MFI MSA

repeatability and reproducibility variation must be addressed and that team members should concentrate on variation connected with Instrument when they address reproducibility.

A *variance component* is an estimate of a variance. The primary variance components of interest are given in the **Variance Components for Gauge R&R** panel, where Carl finds estimates of the variance in MFI values due to:

- **Repeatability:** Repeated measurements of the same part by the same operator with the same instrument.
- **Reproducibility:** Repeated measurements of the same part by different operators using different instruments.
- **Part-to-Part:** Differences in the parts used in the MSA; here parts are represented by batches.

Note that the variance components for **Repeatability** and **Reproducibility** sum to the variance component for **Gauge R&R**, which is an estimate of the measurement process variance. The total variance is the sum of the **Gauge R&R** variance component and the **Part-to-Part** variance component. In an MSA, we are typically not directly interested in part-to-part variation. In fact, we often intentionally choose parts that represent a range of variability.

The bar graph in the **Variance Components for Gauge R&R** panel shows that the **Gauge R&R** variance component is very large compared to the **Part-to-Part** variance component. This suggests that the measurement system has difficulty distinguishing batches. Also, the bar graph indicates that the repeatability and reproducibility variances, where **Instrument** variation is included in the latter, are essentially of equal magnitude, again pointing out that both must be addressed.

MSA for Xf

Next, the team enlists technicians in conducting an MSA for **Xf**. The test that measures **Xf**, called the *ash test*, measures the concentration of filler in the final polymer as a percent of total weight. The **Xf** value reported for a given batch is the mean of two or three ash measurements per batch. Adjustments are made to the next batch based on the results of a test on the previous batch. The ash measurement involves taking a sample of polymer, weighing it, heating it in an oven to remove all the organic material, then weighing the remaining inorganic content, which is virtually all filler. The ratio of the filler weight to the initial weight is the reported result and reflects the concentration of filler.

This is a relatively time-consuming test that takes about one hour per sample. So, it is imperative that this is taken into consideration when designing the study. Also, like the test for **MFI**, the ash test is a destructive test, meaning that repeated measurements will not be true replicates. However, as in the MSA for **MFI**, a sample will be collected from the batch and divided into aliquots; these aliquots will be considered similar enough to form a basis for repeatability estimates.

A single dedicated oven is used for the test. Three instruments are available within the laboratory to perform the weight measurements, and there are six different technicians who do the testing. The team decides that an MSA involving all six technicians would be too time-consuming, so three of the technicians are randomly chosen to participate. A study is designed using samples from 3 randomly chosen batches of polymer. These will be measured on each of the 3 instruments by each of the 3 technicians. Again, 2 repetitions of each measurement will be taken.

This results in a total of 54 tests, with each technician performing 18 tests. At an hour per test, this will take each technician about 18 hours in total; however, the technicians can complete other work while the samples are in the oven. The laboratory manager agrees that this is an acceptable amount of time. The constraint on the duration of the study is the oven, which can be used for only one sample at a time. So, a two-week period is designated for the study, with the intent that **Xf** samples will be worked in between other ash tests performed as part of the laboratory's regular work. The **Xf** study is completely randomized. As mentioned earlier, to come as close to true repeated measurements as possible, a single sample is taken from each of the three batches of polymer, and the resulting sample is divided into the 18 required aliquots.

The study is conducted, and the design and results are given in **MSA_Xf_ Initial.jmp**. The first thing that the team wants to see is a variability chart. As before, Carl selects **Graph > Variability/Gauge Chart**, and enters: Xf as **Y,Response**; Operator then Instrument as **X,Grouping**; and Batch as **Part,Sample ID**. He clicks **OK**. From the red triangle, he again chooses **Connect Cell Means**, **Show Group Means**, and **Show**

Grand Mean, and deselects **Std Dev Chart**. He obtains the graph shown in Exhibit 8.28 and saves the script as **Variability Chart**.

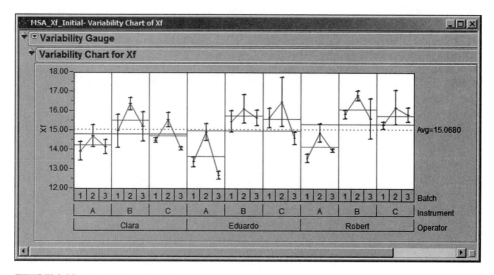

EXHIBIT 8.28   Variability Chart for Initial Xf MSA

The team members observe that given the variability in readings it is impossible to differentiate the batches. For example, a team member points out that measurements made by one of the technicians, Eduardo, using **Instrument** B do not distinguish the three batches. Repeatability variation seems large as well. Consider Eduardo's two measurements of Batch 2 using **Instrument** C—they appear to differ by about 2.5 units. Moreover, it appears that measurements made with **Instrument** A are systematically lower than those made with the other two instruments.

Carl proceeds to obtain a gauge R&R analysis. From the red triangle in the variability chart report, he chooses **Gauge Studies > Gauge RR**. He clicks **OK** to accept the **Crossed** default in the model type menu. Again, there is a short wait before the next dialog box appears. Since no tolerance interval has been specified for Xf, when the **Enter/Verify Gauge R&R Specifications** dialog opens, Carl simply clicks **OK**. The report in Exhibit 8.29 appears. He saves the script as **Gauge R&R**.

Since no tolerance range for Xf has ever been determined, the key to whether Xf is being measured with enough precision is determined by whether it can distinguish different batches, in this case the three batches that were used for the study. (Carl realizes that in the production setting two or three measurements are typically taken, which increases precision. But his intent in this MSA is to estimate the precision of a single measurement.)

Carl focuses on the **Variance Components for Gauge R&R** report. He notes that the **Gauge R&R** variance component is much larger than the **Part-to-Part** variance component. As was the case for MFI, this is indicative of a measurement system in trouble. Carl notes that the reproducibility and repeatability variance components are large and comparable in size.

Turning his attention to the **Gauge R&R** report, Carl studies the column **Variation (6*StdDev)**, which gives variation in units of percent ash. The ranges of percent

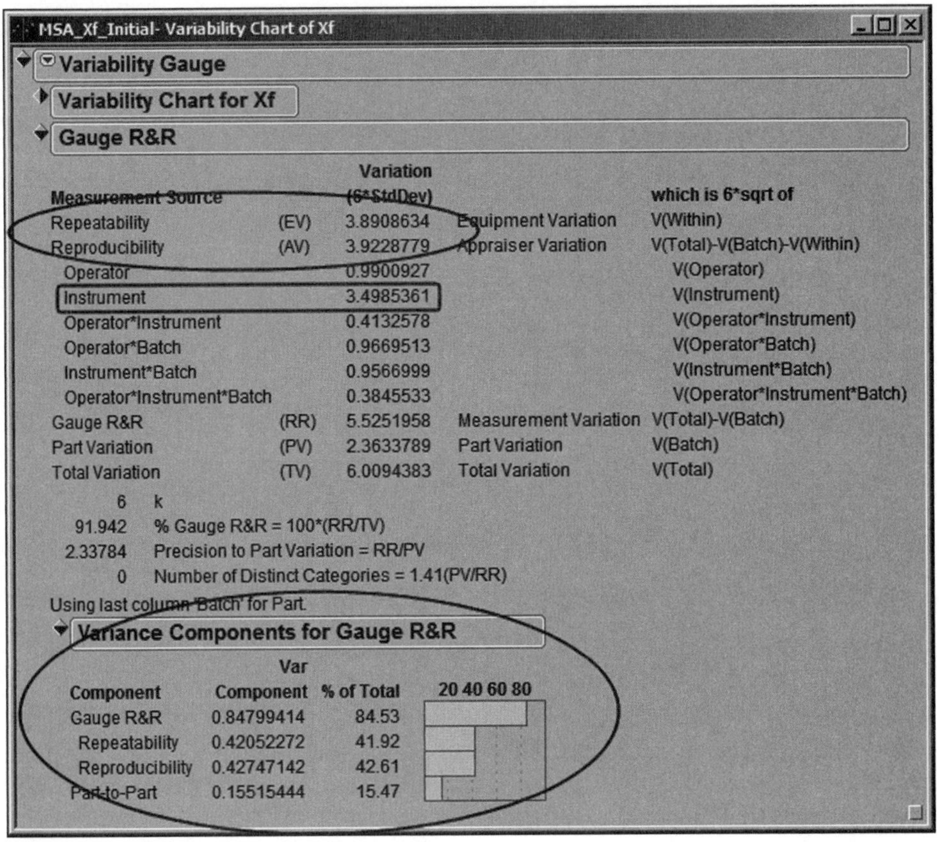

EXHIBIT 8.29   Gauge R&R Report for Initial Xf MSA

ash units taken up by repeatability and reproducibility variation are quite similar, 3.89 percent and 3.92 percent, respectively. However, what stands out immediately is that Instrument is by far the largest source of reproducibility variation, taking up 3.50 percent ash units. It is clear that the two main issues to be dealt with are the repeatability and the Instrument reproducibility, which in this case involves three scales.

Setting a New Timeline and Fixing the Measurement Systems

The findings from the MSAs for MFI and Xf deal a major blow to the project timetable. But Carl and his team realize that they cannot proceed until these measurement issues are resolved. Furthermore, based on the results of the MSAs, the team determines that the historical data obtained by the crisis team are largely useless. Carl's team will need to collect new data. The team estimates that in total this will cause at least a three-month delay to the project—six weeks to sort out the measurement issues and then another six weeks to obtain enough new data to analyze.

Carl explains the situation to his sponsor. After the initial shock, Edward is very supportive. "So, that means that we have been flying blind for the last ten years. But at least it explains why we have never been able to resolve this issue. Go get some good data and let's see what it tells us!"

With this guidance, Carl and his team enlist the help of the technicians and engineers who know the measurement processes for **MFI** and **Xf**. Together they begin work on improving the measurement systems.

Fixing the **MFI** measurement process requires the team to address the root causes of the high repeatability variation, reproducibility variation due to instrument, and variation due to the instrument and batch interaction. Observation of the process reveals that after being removed from the slurry tank, samples can sit for different lengths of time waiting to be analyzed. Also, processing steps can occur in various orders and experience time delays. It is suspected that this is a major cause of the repeatability variation. After careful study, a standard operating procedure is developed specifying the sequence of operations and timeline to be followed in processing the samples.

The other issue, reproducibility, revolves around the four melt flow meters. Here, a quick examination of the four meters in use shows that two of them are older units, and that the dies are quite worn. This could account for the differences in how the instruments measure overall as well as for batch-specific differences, which are quantified in the **Instrument*Batch** interaction. As part of the improvement strategy, these two units are replaced with new units, and the set of four is tested and calibrated to ensure consistent readings.

Analysis of the measurement process for **Xf** by the team and technicians also revealed two key issues whose root causes need to be addressed. The first of these is oven control. Sometimes technicians have other tasks that make it difficult to wait until the oven has reached its target temperature or to leave the sample in for the prescribed length of time. This explains the repeatability issues that surfaced in the MSA.

A two-part solution is proposed and approved. First, an oven probe, with a portable remote monitor capable of broadcasting alerts, is purchased. In addition, work assignments are reorganized so that a technician is always in the area of the oven when a test is being run.

The second issue relates to the instrument reproducibility problem. The team learns that the scales that are being used to weigh the filler are archaic analog scales. They are replaced by high-precision digital scales. Finally, to control other sources of variation, standardized operating procedures for testing **Xf** are developed and implemented with the help of the technicians.

Follow-up MSAs for MFI and Xf

After implementing these improvements to both measurement systems, Carl's team designs follow-up measurement system studies.

The follow-up MSA for **MFI** has the same structure as did the initial study. The results are given in the table **MSA_MFI_Final.jmp**. The variability chart is shown in Exhibit 8.30, and the **Gauge R&R** results are given in Exhibit 8.31. Carl saves the scripts and names them **Variability Chart** and **Gauge R&R**, respectively.

The team members and technicians look at the variability chart and are delighted! Compared to the variability among the three batches, there is very little repeatability or reproducibility variation evident.

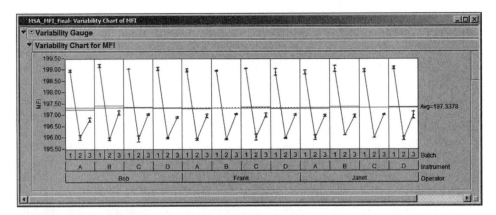

EXHIBIT 8.30   Variability Chart for Follow-Up MFI MSA

EXHIBIT 8.31   Gauge R&R Report for Follow-Up MFI MSA

Carl notes that the **Gauge R&R** value given in the **Gauge R&R** panel is 0.61. This means that the measurement system only takes up about 0.61 units, which is almost exactly 10 percent of the tolerance range (recall that the specification limits are 192 and 198). The measurement system is now sufficiently accurate in classifying batches as good or bad relative to the specification limits on MFI. Also, the measurement system is doing well relative to the variation in batches—Carl notes that the **Number of Distinct Categories** value is 14.

As for **Xf**, the follow-up MSA is conducted with the three technicians who were not part of the original study. The results are given in **MSA_Xf_Final.jmp**. The variability chart is shown in Exhibit 8.32, and the **Gauge R&R** results are shown in Exhibit 8.33. Again, Carl has saved the scripts as **Variability Chart** and **Gauge R&R**, respectively.

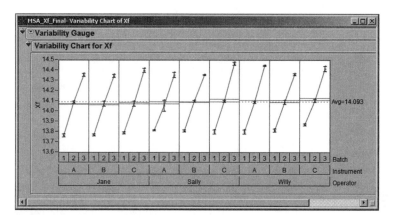

EXHIBIT 8.32 Variability Chart for Follow-Up Xf MSA

MSA_Xf_Final- Variability Chart of Xf

Variability Gauge

Variability Chart for Xf

Gauge R&R

Measurement Source		Variation (6*StdDev)		which is 6*sqrt of
Repeatability	(EV)	0.1623171	Equipment Variation	V(Within)
Reproducibility	(AV)	0.1148701	Appraiser Variation	V(Total)-V(Batch)-V(Within)
Operator		0.0641409		V(Operator)
Instrument		0.0392444		V(Instrument)
Operator*Instrument		0.0105340		V(Operator*Instrument)
Operator*Batch		0.0453434		V(Operator*Batch)
Instrument*Batch		0.0679982		V(Instrument*Batch)
Operator*Instrument*Batch		0.0273902		V(Operator*Instrument*Batch)
Gauge R&R	(RR)	0.1988517	Measurement Variation	V(Total)-V(Batch)
Part Variation	(PV)	1.1682859	Part Variation	V(Batch)
Total Variation	(TV)	1.1850882	Total Variation	V(Total)

6	k
16.7795	% Gauge R&R = 100*(RR/TV)
0.17021	Precision to Part Variation = RR/PV
8	Number of Distinct Categories = 1.41(PV/RR)

Using last column Batch for Part.

Variance Components for Gauge R&R

Component	Var Component	% of Total	20 40 60 80
Gauge R&R	0.00109839	2.82	
Repeatability	0.00073186	1.88	
Reproducibility	0.00036653	0.94	
Part-to-Part	0.03791367	97.18	

EXHIBIT 8.33 Gauge R&R Report for Follow-Up Xf MSA

Once again, the team members and technicians are pleased. Compared to the variability among the three batches, there is little repeatability or reproducibility variation.

The **Gauge R&R** value given in the **Gauge R&R** panel is 0.199 units, while the **Part Variation**, referring to batches in this case, is 1.168. Although these three batches were randomly selected, Carl acknowledges that they may not provide a good estimate of process variability. He notes that it would make sense to obtain a control-chart-based estimate of process variability for future comparisons.

All the same, Carl examines the **Precision to Part Variation**, which is 0.199/ 1.168 = 0.170, shown near the bottom of the **Gauge R&R** panel. This indicates that the measurement system is reasonably efficient at distinguishing batches based on **Xf** measurements. The team had hoped that this ratio would be 10 percent or less, but 17 percent is quite respectable. Also, the **Number of Distinct Categories** is 8, which is usually considered adequate. (In fact, based on this analysis, the decision was made to stop the practice of measuring two or more samples from each batch.)

To ensure that both the **MFI** and **Xf** measurement systems continue to operate at their current levels, measurement control systems are introduced in the form of periodic checks, monthly calibration, semiannual training, and annual MSAs.

Uncovering Relationships

With reliable measurement systems in place, the team now embarks on the task of collecting meaningful process data. The team members collect data on all batches produced during a five-week period. They measure the same variables as were measured by the crisis team, with the assurance that these new measurements have greater precision. The data are presented in the JMP data table **VSSTeamData.jmp**.

Carl's analysis plan is to do preliminary data exploration, to plot control charts for **MFI** and **CI**, to check the capability of these two responses, and then to attempt to uncover relationships between the Xs and these two Ys. He keeps his Visual Six Sigma Roadmap, repeated in Exhibit 8.34, clearly in view at all times.

EXHIBIT 8.34   The Visual Six Sigma Roadmap

Visual Six Sigma Roadmap

What We Do	How We Do It
Uncover Relationships	
Dynamically visualize the variables one at a time	Distribution, Capability, Data Filter
Dynamically visualize the variables two at a time	Fit Y by X (Comparison Box Plots, Scatterplots, Mosaic Plots), Data Filter, Control Chart, Time Series
Dynamically visualize the variables more than two at a time	Variability Chart, Scatterplot Matrix, Graph Builder, Tree Map, Bubble Plot, Scatterplot 3D, Parallel Plots, Cell Plots
Visually determine the Hot Xs that affect variation in the Ys	Fit Y by X, Fit Model, Partition
Use Data Filter, Colors, Markers, Brushing, Lassoing, and Selection of points throughout	
Model Relationships	
For each Y, identify the Hot Xs to include in the signal function	Fit Model, Screening, Profiler
Model Y as a function of the Hot Xs; check the noise function	Fit Model, Profiler, Simulation
If needed, revise the model	Fit Model
If required, return to the Collect Data step and use DOE	Custom Design, Sample Size and Power
Revise Knowledge	
Identify the best Hot X settings	Profilers
Visualize the effect on the Ys should these Hot X settings vary	Profilers, Simulation, Distribution, Capability, Goal Plot
Verify improvement using a pilot study or confirmation trials	Distribution, Control Charts, Capability, Goal Plot

Visualizing One Variable at a Time

To clear his workspace, Carl first closes all open windows in JMP, and then opens **VSSTeamData.jmp**. As he did for the crisis team's data, Carl's first step is to run **Distribution** for all of the variables except **Batch Number**. He selects **Analyze > Distribution** and adds all 11 Xs and Ys. Once he clicks **OK**, Carl saves the script for this report as **Distribution**.

The first five histograms are shown in Exhibit 8.35. Carl and his teammates note the following:

- MFI appears to have a mound-shaped distribution, except for some values of 206 and higher.
- CI is, as expected, left-skewed.
- Yield seems to exhibit some outliers in the form of extremely low values.

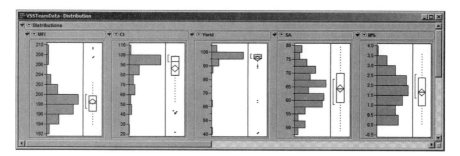

EXHIBIT 8.35   Five of the 11 Distribution Reports

As he did with the crisis team's data, Carl selects those points that reflect low Yield values, specifically, those four points that fall below 85 percent. He does this by clicking and drawing a rectangle that includes these points using the arrow tool inside the box plot area, as shown in Exhibit 8.36. The highlighting in the other histograms indicates that these four crisis Yield rows had very high MFI values and very low SA values. This is good news, since it is consistent with knowledge that the crisis team obtained. It also suggests that crisis yields are related to Ys, such as MFI, and perhaps influenced by Xs, such as SA. Interestingly, though, all four rows have CI values that exceed the lower specification limit.

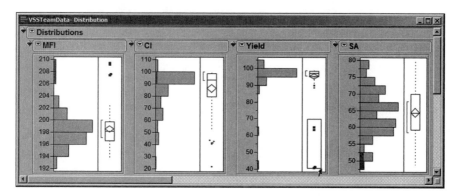

EXHIBIT 8.36   Distribution Reports with Four Crisis Yield Values Selected

A striking aspect of the histograms for **MFI** and **CI** is the relationship of measurements to the specification limits. Recall that **MFI** has lower and upper specification limits of 192 and 198, respectively, and that **CI** has a lower specification limit of 80. Carl closes his **Distribution** report for all his variables, and reruns **Distribution** for only **MFI** and **CI**. From the **Quantiles** panel for **MFI**, he sees that all 110 observations exceed the lower specification limit of 192 and that about 50 percent of these exceed the upper specification of 198. About 25 percent of **CI** values fall below the lower specification of 80. He saves the script as **Distribution – MFI and CI**.

Carl keeps this report open for now. To get a view of how often the specifications on these two variables are jointly met, Carl selects **Rows > Data Filter**. He selects **MFI**, clicks **Add**, then clicks on the maximum value of 209.350 above the slider and changes it to 198. This selects all rows where **MFI** meets the specification limits. Next, Carl clicks on the plus sign in the bottom left corner of the **Data Filter** dialog, selects **CI**, and clicks **Add**. In the range of **CI** values shown above the **CI** slider, he changes the minimum value of 21.90 to 80. When he clicks away from that text box, all records that meet both specification limits are selected. The completed **Data Filter** dialog is shown in Exhibit 8.37. He saves the script as **Data Filter**.

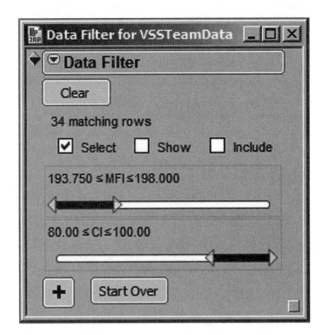

EXHIBIT 8.37   Data Filter Dialog to Select In-Specification Batches

The updated **Distribution** report is shown in Exhibit 8.38. The highlighted areas represent batches that meet the specifications on both **MFI** and **CI**. To obtain a count of these batches, Carl checks the **Selected** area of the rows panel in the data table: Only 34 out of 110 batches conform to the specifications for both responses. It is clear that the current process is not capable of meeting these specification limits.

Before he closes the **Data Filter** dialog, Carl clicks the **Clear** button at the top of the dialog to remove the **Selected** row states imposed by the **Data Filter**.

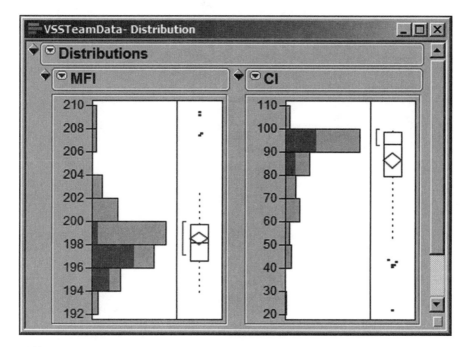

EXHIBIT 8.38   Distribution Reports with In-Specification Batches Highlighted

With this as background, Carl and his team proceed to see how the three Ys behave over time. As before, Carl constructs individual measurement charts for these three responses by selecting **Graph > Control Chart > IR**. He inserts MFI, CI, and Yield in the **Process** list, Batch Number as the **Sample Label**, unchecks **Moving Range**, and clicks **OK**. Carl saves this script to the data table and calls it **Control Charts**.

The resulting charts are shown in Exhibit 8.39. There is clear evidence of one crisis period relative to Yield. Carl selects the four low Yield values and sees that these correspond to the four MFI values that greatly exceed the upper control limit. As seen before, the control limits for CI are not very meaningful because of the extreme non-normality of its distribution.

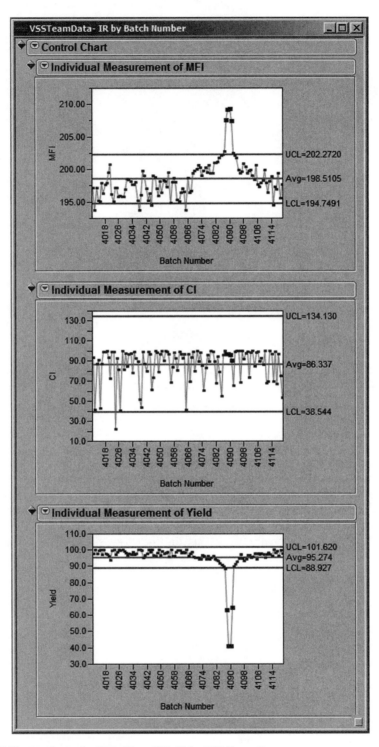

EXHIBIT 8.39   IR Charts for MFI, CI, and Yield for VSS Team Data

Carl thinks that it might be a good idea to track these four outlying rows in subsequent analyses. He has selected these four points in the **Yield** control chart, which means that their corresponding rows are selected in the data table. Carl selects **Rows > Markers** and chooses hollow square markers, as shown in Exhibit 8.40. Then he selects **Rows > Colors** and chooses a bright red color for the square markers.

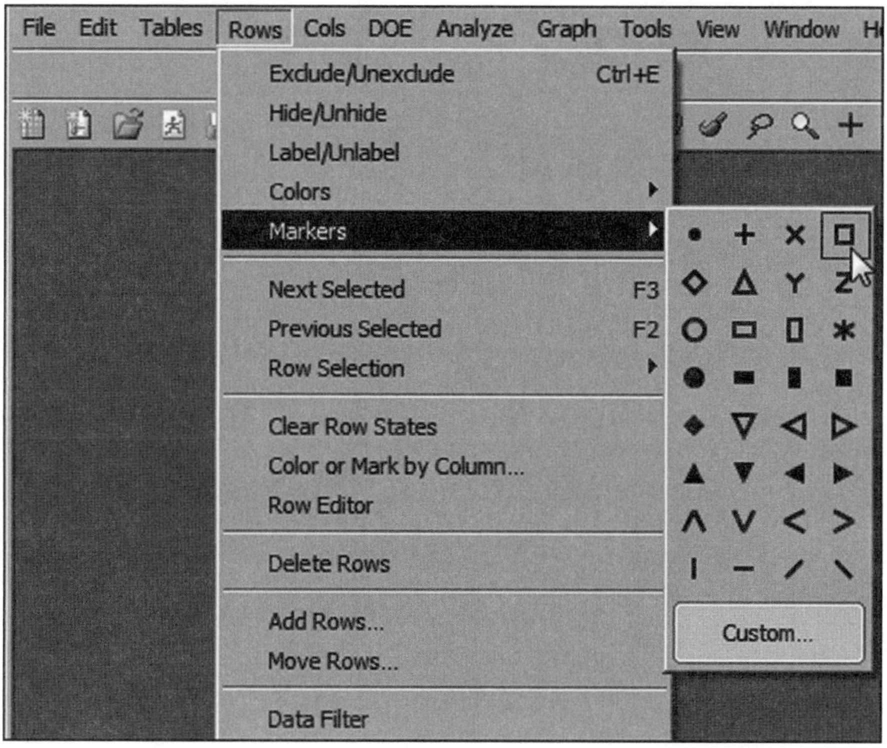

EXHIBIT 8.40   Selection of Markers for Four Rows

Now the points in the control chart appear as shown in Exhibit 8.41. Points associated with these four rows will appear marked in all subsequent plots, until the markers are removed. (If you prefer to simply set these markers using a script, run the script **Markers for Outliers**.)

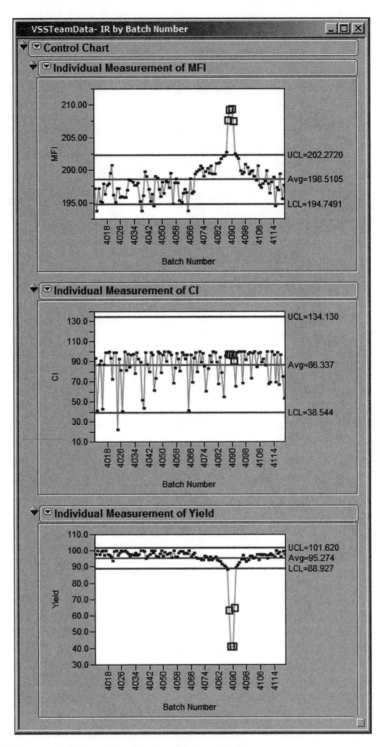

EXHIBIT 8.41   Control Charts Showing Four Rows with Markers

One of the team members observes that there was advance warning of the crisis on the MFI and Yield charts in the form of a trend that began perhaps around batch 4070. Had MFI been monitored by a control chart, this trend might have alerted engineers to an impending crisis. Carl agrees but observes that this assumes a strong relationship between MFI and Yield. And this is as good a time as any to see if this really is a strong relationship.

Visualizing Two Variables at a Time

So, Carl selects **Fit Y by X** and enters Yield as **Y, Response** and MFI as **X, Factor**. Clicking **OK** gives the plot shown in Exhibit 8.42. Yes, indeed, the relationship between these two Ys is a strong one. The four outliers clearly suggest that high MFI values are associated with crisis level yields. (Note that the points for the outliers appear smaller than they did in Exhibit 8.40 because Carl has deselected the rows.) He saves the script as **Bivariate – Yield by MFI**.

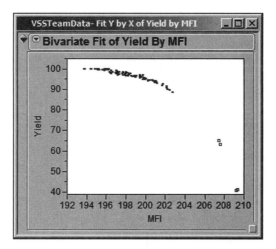

EXHIBIT 8.42   Bivariate Plot of Yield by MFI

To better see the effect of meeting the MFI specification limits on Yield, Carl clicks on the crosshairs tool in the toolbar (Exhibit 8.43). When he clicks in the plot with this tool, it turns into crosshairs. He holds the mouse button and drags to set the vertical line at the upper specification for MFI, namely, MFI = 198, and then moves the crosshairs up to the data values (Exhibit 8.44). He notes that for any MFI value of 198 or lower, Yield exceeds 95 percent. It does appear that meeting the MFI specifications would help eliminate crisis periods.

EXHIBIT 8.43   Crosshair Tool

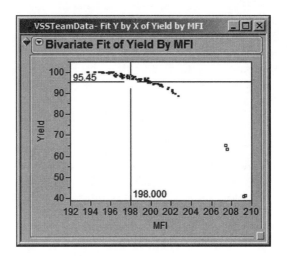

EXHIBIT 8.44   Bivariate Plot of Yield by MFI with Crosshairs

Carl decides it might be useful to view scatterplots for all the variables of interest. He selects **Graph > Scatterplot Matrix**. In the box for **Y, Columns**, he enters all of the variables from MFI to Shift, as shown in Exhibit 8.45.

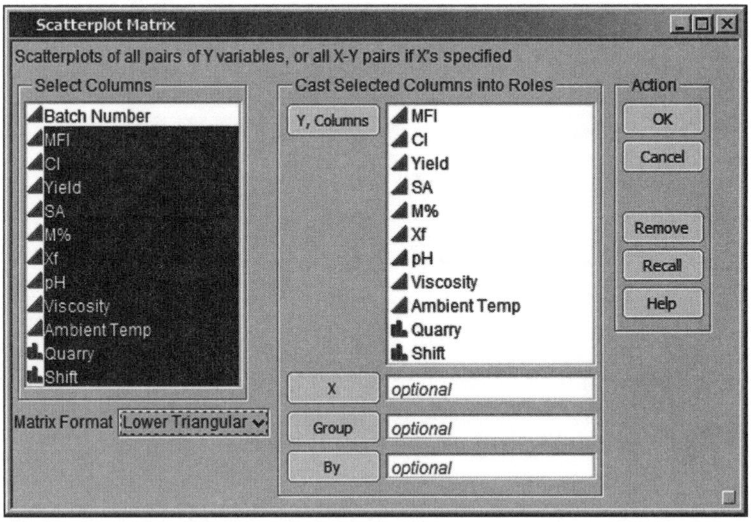

EXHIBIT 8.45   Launch Dialog for Scatterplot Matrix

Clicking **OK** gives the scatterplot matrix shown in Exhibit 8.46. Carl saves the script to the data table as **Scatterplot Matrix**. The matrix shows all possible scatterplots, including scatterplots that involve the two nominal variables, **Quarry** and **Shift**. For the nominal values involved in these scatterplots, the points are jittered randomly within the appropriate level. Carl and his teammates immediately notice the four crisis points appearing prominently in the Yield and MFI scatterplots.

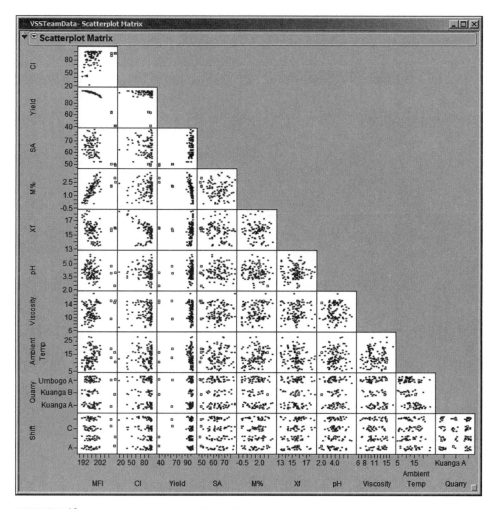

EXHIBIT 8.46   Scatterplot Matrix of All Variables

Since these four points affect the scaling of the plots, making it difficult to see other relationships, Carl selects them in one of the plots, then right-clicks and chooses **Row Exclude** from the menu that appears. Carl is happy to see that once these points are excluded the axes automatically rescale to remove useless whitespace.

In an empty part of the plot (so that the current row selection remains in force), he right-clicks again and chooses **Row Hide**. This hides the four points in all the plots. Carl checks the rows panel in the data table to be sure that they are excluded and hidden, and they are. The updated matrix is shown in Exhibit 8.47.

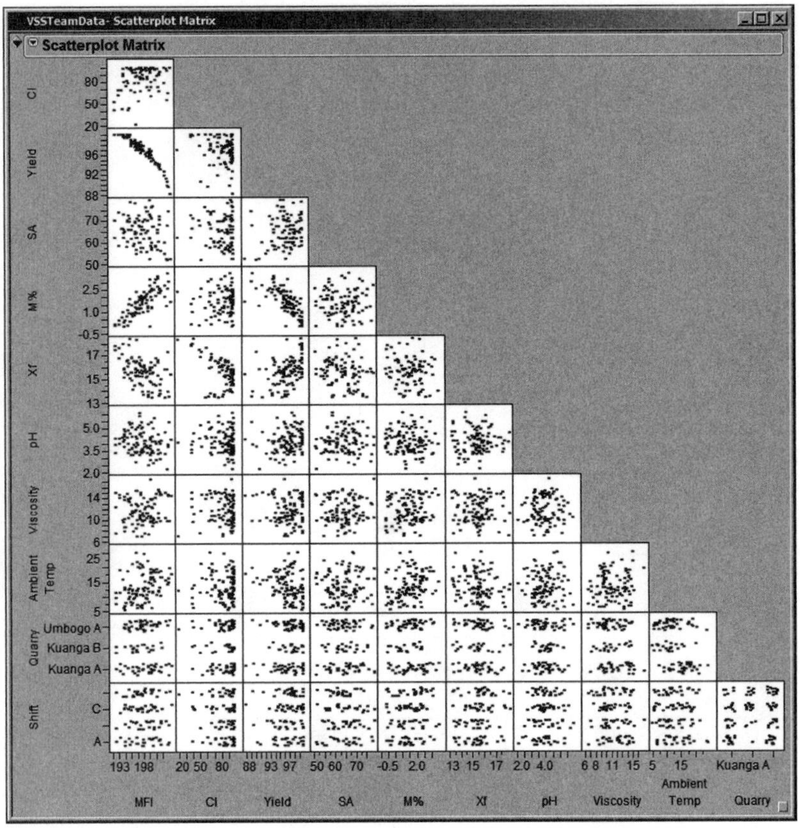

EXHIBIT 8.47   Scatterplot Matrix of All Variables with Four Outliers Excluded

Viewing down the columns from left to right, Carl sees evidence of bivariate relationships between:

- Yield and MFI
- M% and MFI
- Xf and MFI
- Xf and CI (this is a nonlinear relationship)
- M% and Yield
- Quarry and Ambient Temp

It could be that the relationship between Yield and M% reflects the more basic relationship between MFI and M%. In any case, there appear to be relationships between Xs and Ys and, in particular, between the two more fundamental Ys, MFI and CI, and the Xs. Interestingly, there is a relationship between two Xs, Ambient Temp and Quarry. A member of Carl's team investigates and learns that a container of material from a single quarry is used consistently over a period of days until it needs to be replaced, so the fact that there is an association between material and ambient temperature is expected.

One of the team members wants to see the apparent nonlinear relationship between Xf and CI more clearly. Carl agrees that this is a good idea. To include the four outlier rows for this next exploratory analysis, Carl chooses the commands **Rows > Exclude/Unexclude** and **Rows > Hide/Unhide** (these are toggles). The four rows remain selected.

Next, Carl selects **Analyze > Fit Y by X**, enters CI as **Y, Response** and Xf as **X, Factor**, and then clicks **OK**. The plot in Exhibit 8.48 appears. Carl saves the script as **Bivariate**. Everyone notes the highly nonlinear relationship: Both low and high values of Xf are associated with CI values that fail to meet the lower specification limit of 80. Also, the four rows that represent MFI outliers are not outliers relative to the relationship between Xf and CI. Carl saves the script as **Bivariate – CI by Xf**.

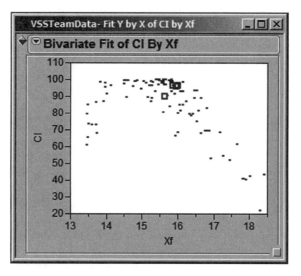

EXHIBIT 8.48   Bivariate Plot of CI by Xf

One team member starts speculating about setting a specification range on **Xf**, maybe requiring **Xf** to fall between 14.0 and 15.5. Carl responds that in fact the team must find operating ranges for all of the Xs. But he cautions that setting these operating ranges one variable at a time is not a good approach. Also, the operating ranges have to simultaneously satisfy specification limits on two Ys, both **MFI** and **CI**. Carl indicates that a statistical model relating the Xs to the Ys would reveal appropriate operating ranges and target settings for the Xs. This brings the team to the Model Relationships step of the Visual Six Sigma Data Analysis Process.

Modeling Relationships

The data exploration up to now has revealed several relationships between Xs, which may be Hot Xs, and the two Ys of interest, **MFI** and **CI**. At this point, Carl and the team embark on the task of modeling the relationships in a multivariate framework.

Carl formulates a plan and explains it to his teammates. First, they will develop two models, one that relates the Xs to **MFI** and one that relates the Xs to **CI**. By examining the results, they will determine Hot Xs for each response and reformulate the models in terms of these Hot Xs. Then, they will use the profiler to simultaneously optimize both models, finding the *best* settings for the entire collection of Hot Xs. Once this is accomplished, they will find optimal operating ranges for these Xs. They will then investigate how variation in the Hot Xs propagates to variation in the Ys.

Dealing with the Preliminaries

Carl struggles with the issue of what to do with the four **MFI** outliers. He realizes that he could include these four rows in the model development process and, once a model is selected, check to see if they are influential (using visual techniques and statistical measures such as Cook's D). Or, he could just develop models without them.

Looking back at the histograms and control charts for **MFI**, Carl sees that they are very much beyond the range of most of the **MFI** measurements. More to the point, they are far beyond the specification limits for **MFI**. The fact that they are associated with extremely low yields also points out that they are not in a desirable operating range.

Since Carl is interested in developing a model that will optimize the process, he needs a sound model over that desirable operating range. The outliers will not help in developing such a model, and, in fact, they might negatively affect this effort. With this as his rationale, Carl decides to exclude them from the model development process.

To exclude and hide the four outliers, Carl runs **Distribution** with Yield as **Y, Columns**. In the box plot part of the plot, he drags a rectangle to contain the four points. In the plot, he right-clicks and selects **Row Exclude** (see Exhibit 8.49). He right-clicks once more and selects **Row Hide**. He checks in the rows panel of the data table to make sure that four points are **Excluded** and **Hidden**. (If your four outlier rows are still selected, you can simply select **Row Exclude** and **Row Hide**; there is no need to select the points once more. Alternatively, whether they are selected or not, you can run the script **Exclude and Hide Outliers**.)

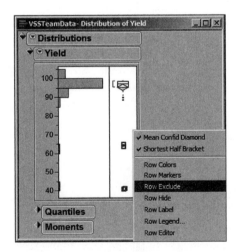

EXHIBIT 8.49   Excluding and Hiding the Four Outliers

In the interests of expediency for subsequent analyses, Carl decides to store the specification limits for MFI and CI in the data table. He right-clicks in the MFI column header and chooses **Column Info**. In the **Column Info** dialog, from the **Column Properties** list, he chooses **Spec Limits** (Exhibit 8.50).

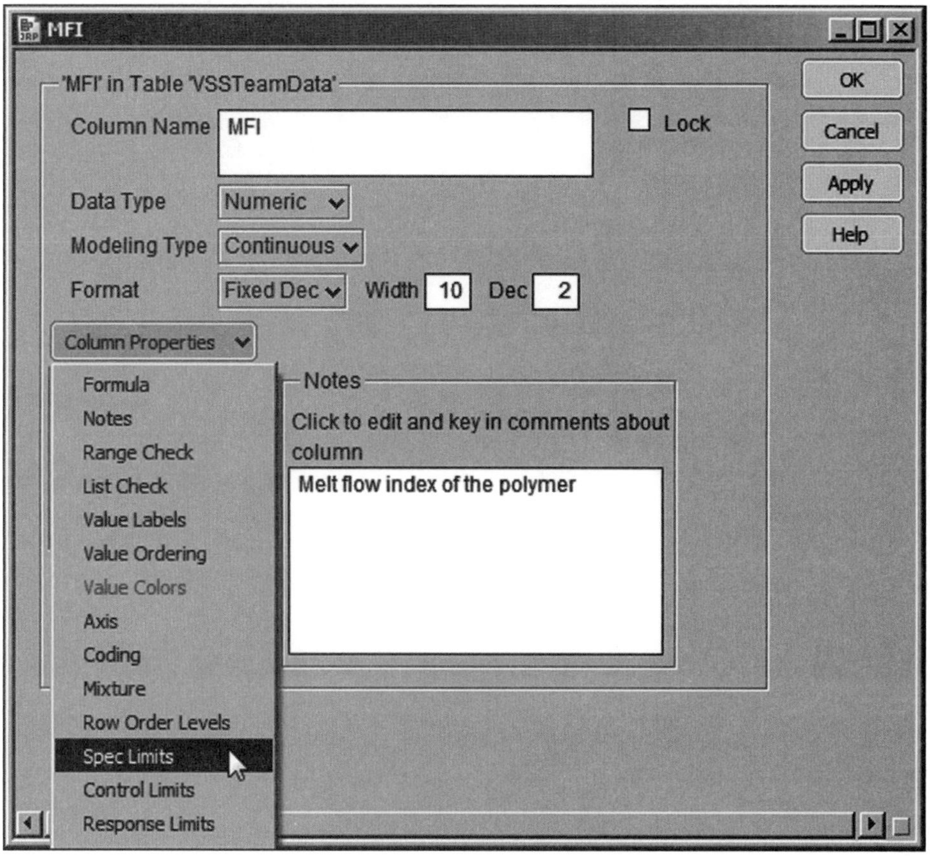

EXHIBIT 8.50   Column Properties with Spec Limits Chosen

He fills in the text boxes as shown in Exhibit 8.51, recording that the target is 195, with lower and upper specification limits of 192 and 198, respectively. He clicks **OK**. Carl proceeds in a similar fashion for CI, recording only a lower specification limit of 80. (If you wish to simply insert these by means of a script, run the script **Spec Limits**.)

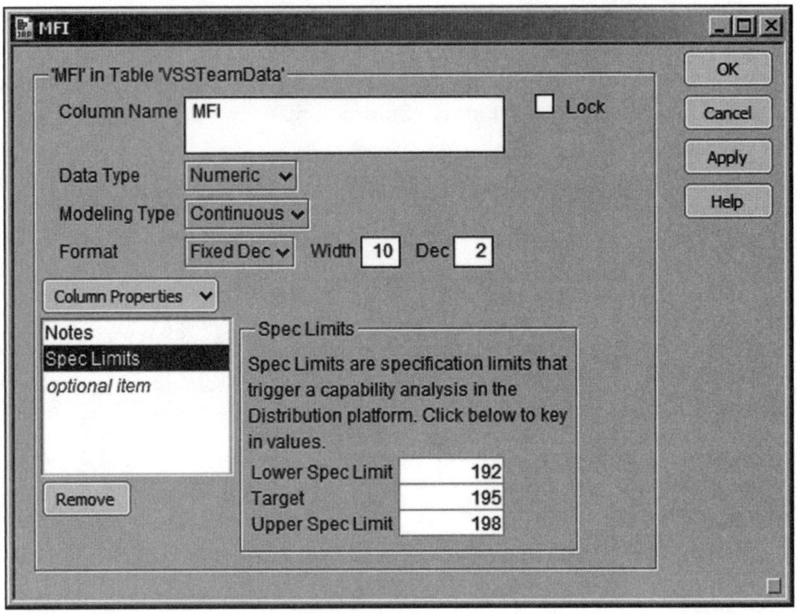

EXHIBIT 8.51   Spec Limits Property Menu for MFI

Plan for Modeling

Now Carl has another decision to make—how to build a model? There are a number of options: **Fit Model**, with manual elimination of inactive terms, **Fit Model** using the **Stepwise** personality for automated variable selection, or the **Screening** platform. Carl thinks: "Wow, something new—I have never tried screening!" The idea of using this platform intrigues him.

He decides to get some advice about the screening platform from his mentor, Tom. Over lunch together, Tom explains that the screening platform was developed to analyze the results of a two-level regular fractional factorial experiment and that it is in this situation where its performance is best. That being said, Tom tells Carl that the screening platform may also be useful when exploring observational data.

Tom also mentions that nominal variables should not be included when using the screening platform, since it will treat them as if they were measured on a continuous scale. He warns Carl to check the viability of the predictors he obtains through **Screening** by running **Fit Model** on the same selection. It is at this point that Carl might want to also include his nominal variables.

The conversation moves to a discussion of the nominal factors, Quarry and Shift. Keeping in mind that the purpose of this modeling effort is to find optimal settings for the process variables, Tom suggests that perhaps it does not make sense to include Shift in this modeling effort. None of the exploratory analysis to date has suggested that Shift affects the responses MFI and CI.

Just to ensure that multivariate relationships have not been overlooked, after lunch Carl pulls out his computer, and they conduct a quick partition analysis (**Analyze > Modeling > Partition**). They conclude that Shift and Quarry seem to have very little impact on MFI, where SA, M%, and Xf seem to be the drivers, and little impact on CI, where Xf and SA appear to be the drivers. (We encourage you to explore this on your own.)

Given that Shift cannot be controlled, and armed with the knowledge that it does not appear to affect either response in a serious way, Carl is content not including Shift in the modeling. But what about Quarry, which could be controlled if need be? Tom suggests that Carl add Quarry and its interactions with other linear terms once potential predictors have been identified using the screening platform.

Carl is comfortable with this plan. For each of MFI and CI, he will:

- Identify potentially active effects among the continuous Xs using **Screening**.
- Use these as effects in a **Fit Model** analysis.
- Add Quarry and its interactions with the linear terms identified by **Screening** to the effects list for the **Fit Model** analysis.
- Reduce the effect list to obtain a final model.

He will then use these final models to find settings of the Hot Xs that simultaneously optimize both MFI and CI. At that point, he also hopes to quantify the anticipated variability in both responses, based on the likely variation exhibited by the Hot Xs in practice.

Using Screening to Identify Potential Predictors

Carl and his teammates are ready for some exciting analysis. Carl selects **Analyze > Modeling > Screening**. He populates the launch dialog as shown in Exhibit 8.52.

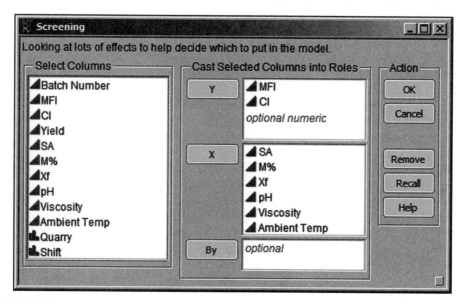

EXHIBIT 8.52   Launch Dialog for Screening Platform

Carl clicks **OK**. The report that appears is partially shown in Exhibit 8.53. Carl saves its script with the default name **Screening**. There are two analyses presented side-by-side, one for MFI and one for CI. Note that the disclosure icon for the CI report is closed in Exhibit 8.53. Carl intends to use these reports to develop separate models for these two responses. (If you are running this analysis on your own, please note that your p-values will not exactly match those shown in Exhibit 8.53. This is because the p-values are obtained using a simulation. However, the values should be very close, usually only differing in the third decimal place.)

Term	Contrast		Lenth t-Ratio	Individual p-Value	Simultaneous p-Value
M%	1.66323		29.60	<.0001*	<.0001*
Xf	-0.76681		-13.65	<.0001*	<.0001*
SA	-0.48106		-8.56	<.0001*	<.0001*
pH	-0.16781		-2.99	0.0042*	0.3198
Ambient Temp	0.16472		2.93	0.0046*	0.3566
Viscosity	0.04140		0.74	0.4606	1.0000
M%*M%	0.03425	*	0.61	0.5466	1.0000
M%*Xf	0.10389	*	1.85	0.0647	0.9912
Xf*Xf	0.03192	*	0.57	0.5751	1.0000
M%*SA	0.04252	*	0.76	0.4467	1.0000
Xf*SA	-0.19148	*	-3.41	0.0014*	0.1318
SA*SA	0.52375	*	9.32	<.0001*	<.0001*
M%*pH	0.03752	*	0.67	0.5037	1.0000
Xf*pH	-0.02356	*	-0.42	0.6825	1.0000
SA*pH	0.20801	*	3.70	0.0006*	0.0616
pH*pH	0.07120	*	1.27	0.2048	1.0000
M%*Ambient Temp	-0.09967	*	-1.77	0.0771	0.9966
Xf*Ambient Temp	-0.00205	*	-0.04	0.9718	1.0000
SA*Ambient Temp	-0.18758	*	-3.34	0.0019*	0.1525
pH*Ambient Temp	-0.01042	*	-0.19	0.8592	1.0000
Ambient Temp*Ambient Temp	-0.04483	*	-0.80	0.4230	1.0000
M%*Viscosity	0.09979	*	1.78	0.0768	0.9964
Xf*Viscosity	-0.00682	*	-0.12	0.9086	1.0000
SA*Viscosity	-0.02093	*	-0.37	0.7189	1.0000
pH*Viscosity	0.02717	*	0.48	0.6332	1.0000

EXHIBIT 8.53   Partial View of Screening Analysis Report for MFI

At this point, Carl reviews his notes on the screening platform and has another quick discussion with Tom. The screening platform fits as many terms as possible to a response to produce a *saturated* model. Because there are 106 rows (recall that four outliers were excluded), 105 separate terms or effects can be estimated.

Screening includes terms by first introducing linear terms, or *main effects* (the six factors), then all two-way interactions and squared terms in these six factors (there are 21 such terms), then three-way interactions and cubic terms, and so on, until no more effects can be fit. Second-order terms are introduced in an order determined by the significance of first-order terms, and this thinking continues with higher-order terms. In Carl's example, a large number of three-way interactions and cubic terms are included. This can be seen by examining the entries in the **Term** column.

The **Screening for MFI** report lists the 105 possible model terms. Carl recalls from his training that the analysis philosophy behind the **Screening** platform is that of *effect sparsity*, which is the idea that only a few of the potential or postulated model terms will actually be important in explaining variation in the response.[1] These important terms are often called *active* effects. The simulated p-values provide a means of classifying terms into signal or noise, and effect sparsity would lead us to always expect relatively few active terms.

The measure of the effect of a term is represented by its *contrast*. If the data were from a two-level orthogonal design, the contrast would be the effect of the factor—the difference between the mean at its high setting and the mean at its low setting. (See the JMP **Help** documentation for further details.)

The test statistic is *Lenth's t-Ratio*. Two types of p-values are provided. Now, as Carl was reminded in his recent talk with Tom, it is important to keep in mind that these p-values are obtained using simulation and that different, though very similar, p-values will be obtained when the analysis is rerun. For example, when you run the **Screening** script that Carl saved, you will see p-values that differ slightly from those shown in Exhibit 8.53.

But how do the two types of p-values, individual p-values and simultaneous p-values, differ? The *individual p-values* are analogous to p-values obtained for terms in a multiple linear regression. (Note that in the screening platform JMP highlights each term that has an individual p-value less than 0.10.) Now, with 105 terms, each being tested at a 5 percent significance level, a sizable number could easily appear to be significant just by chance alone. This is why the simultaneous p-values are important. The *simultaneous p-values* are adjusted for the fact that many tests are being conducted.

Carl remembers that in his training Tom discussed these two types of p-values in terms of Type I (false positive) and Type II (false negative) errors. A *false positive* amounts to declaring an effect significant when it is not. A *false negative* results in declaring an effect not to be significant when, in fact, it is. Neither of these errors is desirable, and there is always a trade-off between them: A false positive can result in costs incurred by controlling factors that don't have an effect; a false negative can overlook factors that are actually part of the causal system and that could be manipulated to produce more favorable outcomes. Tom believes that any inactive factors that are incorrectly included in a model have a way of exposing themselves in later analysis, so his recommendation here is to minimize false negatives at the expense of false positives.

Now, to relate these errors to the p-values, Carl realizes that using the **Individual p-values** might result in false positives, while using the **Simultaneous p-values** might result in false negatives. He resolves to strike a balance between these two possibilities.

With this in mind, Carl looks at the **Screening for MFI** report and wishes that the p-values could be sorted. Then he remembers that by right-clicking in a section of a report, JMP often provides options that users would like to have. When he right-clicks in the **Screening for MFI** report, to his delight, a menu appears with the option **Sort by Column** (Exhibit 8.54). Carl immediately clicks on that option, which opens a **Select Columns** menu (also shown in Exhibit 8.54), where he chooses to sort on the report column **Individual p-Value**.

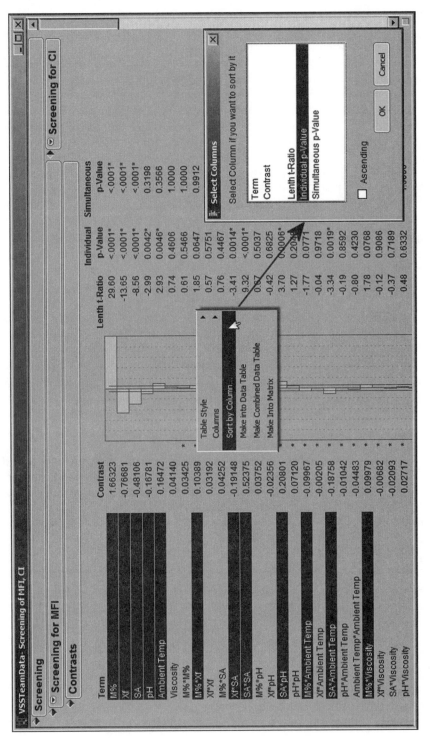

EXHIBIT 8.54   Context-Sensitive Menu with Sort by Column Option

The default sort is in descending order, which turns out to be very convenient. This is because the sorting pushes the significant effects to the bottom of the list, where there is a **Half Normal Plot** and a button to **Make Model**. Exhibit 8.55 shows the bottom part of the list of 105 terms for MFI, along with the **Make Model** (and **Run Model)** buttons.

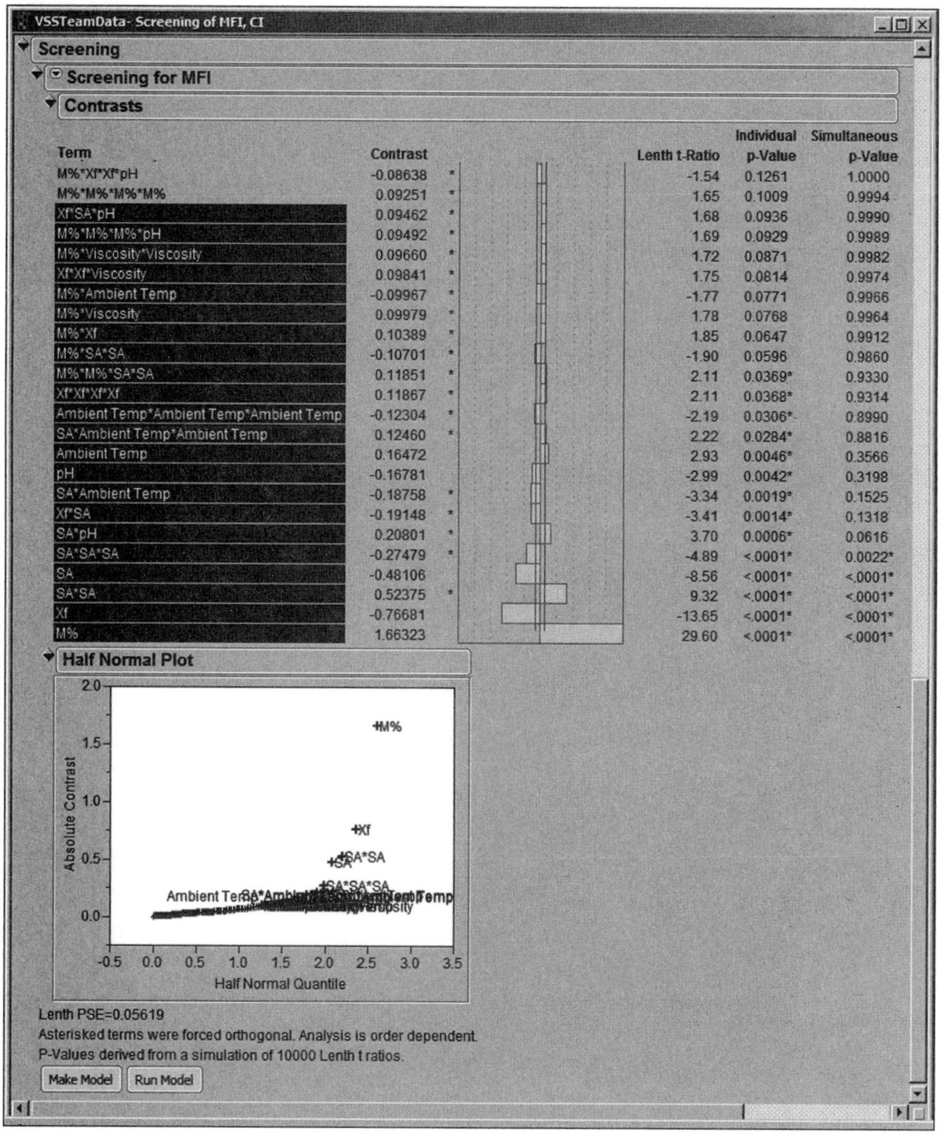
VSSTeamData- Screening of MFI, CI
Screening
Screening for MFI
Contrasts
Term | Contrast | Lenth t-Ratio | Individual p-Value | Simultaneous p-Value
M%*Xf*Xf*pH -0.08638 * -1.54 0.1261 1.0000
M%*M%*M%*M% 0.09251 * 1.65 0.1009 0.9994
Xf*SA*pH 0.09462 * 1.68 0.0936 0.9990
M%*M%*M%*pH 0.09492 * 1.69 0.0929 0.9989
M%*Viscosity*Viscosity 0.09660 * 1.72 0.0871 0.9982
Xf*Xf*Viscosity 0.09841 * 1.75 0.0814 0.9974
M%*Ambient Temp -0.09967 * -1.77 0.0771 0.9966
M%*Viscosity 0.09979 * 1.78 0.0768 0.9964
M%*Xf 0.10389 * 1.85 0.0647 0.9912
M%*SA*SA -0.10701 * -1.90 0.0596 0.9860
M%*M%*SA*SA 0.11851 * 2.11 0.0369* 0.9330
Xf*Xf*Xf*Xf 0.11867 * 2.11 0.0368* 0.9314
Ambient Temp*Ambient Temp*Ambient Temp -0.12304 * -2.19 0.0306* 0.8990
SA*Ambient Temp*Ambient Temp 0.12460 * 2.22 0.0284* 0.8816
Ambient Temp 0.16472 2.93 0.0046* 0.3566
pH -0.16781 -2.99 0.0042* 0.3198
SA*Ambient Temp -0.18758 * -3.34 0.0019* 0.1525
Xf*SA -0.19148 * -3.41 0.0014* 0.1318
SA*pH 0.20801 * 3.70 0.0006* 0.0616
SA*SA*SA -0.27479 * -4.89 <.0001* 0.0022*
SA -0.48106 -8.56 <.0001* <.0001*
SA*SA 0.52375 * 9.32 <.0001* <.0001*
Xf -0.76681 -13.65 <.0001* <.0001*
M% 1.66323 29.60 <.0001* <.0001*
Half Normal Plot
Absolute Contrast
Half Normal Quantile
M%
Xf
SA*SA
Ambient Temp
-0.5 0.0 0.5 1.0 1.5 2.0 2.5 3.0 3.5
0.0 0.5 1.0 1.5 2.0
Lenth PSE=0.05619
Asterisked terms were forced orthogonal. Analysis is order dependent.
P-Values derived from a simulation of 10000 Lenth t ratios.
Make Model
Run Model

EXHIBIT 8.55 Bottom Part of Contrasts Panel for MFI

Carl studies the information in this report. He checks the sizes of the contrasts, using the bar graph shown to the right of the contrasts. Although his data are observational, the size of the contrast does give an indication of the practical importance of the corresponding effect. Carl also studies the **Half Normal Plot**, which shows the absolute values of the contrasts plotted against quantiles for the absolute value of the normal distribution. Terms that contribute random noise will fall close to their corresponding quantiles, and hence close to the line in the plot. Significant terms will fall away from the line and toward the upper right of the plot.

Carl resizes the **Half Normal Plot** to lengthen the vertical axis. To do this, he places his cursor over the horizontal axis and positions it so that a double arrow appears. Then, he clicks and holds, dragging the plot downward (just like making an application window bigger in Windows or OS-X). The resized plot is shown in Exhibit 8.56.

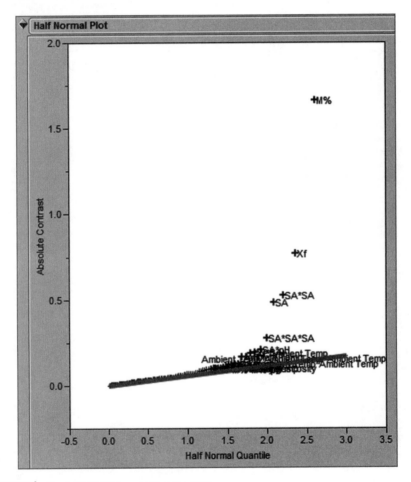

EXHIBIT 8.56   Resized Half Normal Plot for MFI

Looking at this plot, Carl decides that he will select all effects with **Absolute Contrast** values equal to or exceeding that of SA*SA*SA. He selects these in the plot by dragging a rectangle around them, as shown in Exhibit 8.57. He could also have selected them by control-clicking effect names in the report.

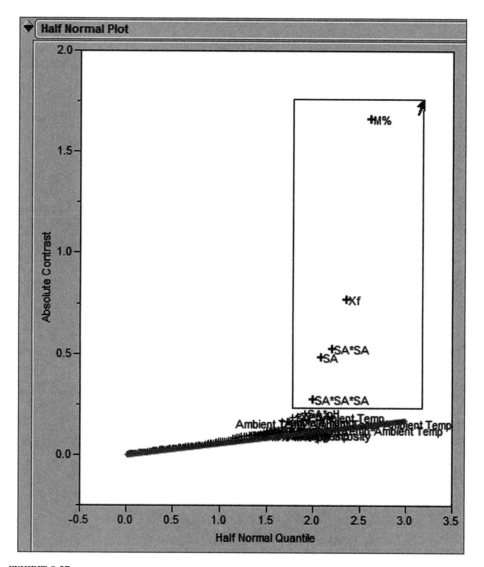

EXHIBIT 8.57   Selecting Terms with Rectangle in Half Normal Plot for MFI

The five selected effects are shown in Exhibit 8.58. Carl notes that these include all of the effects with **Simultaneous p-Values** less than 0.05. Carl could have considered more effects, but his sense from the p-values and the **Half Normal Plot** is that his selection will include the terms that are likely to have an effect on the process. With this choice, Carl thinks that he has achieved a reasonable balance between overlooking potentially active terms and including terms that do not contribute. (We encourage you to investigate models that contain more effects; these are quite interesting.)

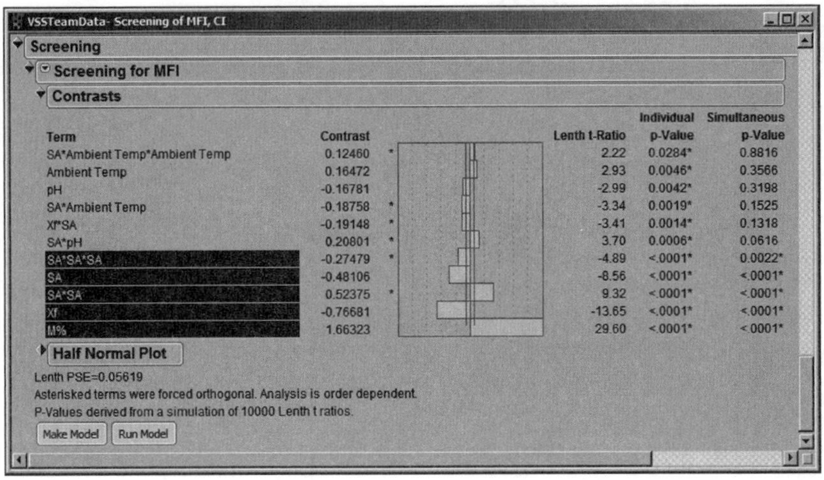

EXHIBIT 8.58   Terms Selected as Potential Predictors for MFI

Obtaining a Final Model for MFI

Carl clicks the **Make Model** button located below the **Half Normal Plot**. This opens the **Selected Model** dialog, shown in Exhibit 8.59. The effects that were selected in the screening platform are entered in the **Construct Model Effects** text box. Carl saves this dialog as **Screening Model for MFI**.

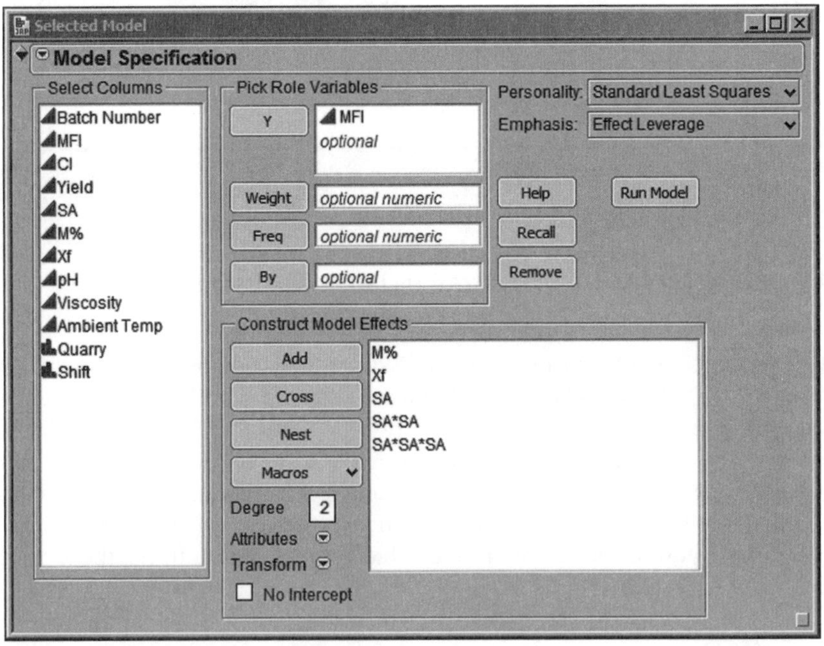

EXHIBIT 8.59   Selected Model Dialog for MFI

Carl is about to run this model when he remembers Quarry. The plan was to enter Quarry as an effect in the **Construct Model Effects** list and also to add all two-way interactions with Quarry. So, Carl clicks on Quarry in the **Select Columns** list and clicks **Add** to place it in the **Construct Model Effects** list. Then, to add all two-way interactions with Quarry, he selects Quarry in the **Select Columns** list, selects M%, Xf, and SA in the **Construct Model Effects** list, and clicks **Cross**. Carl also changes the **Emphasis** in the drop-down at the top right of the dialog to **Effect Screening** to fine tune the output in the report. The resulting **Selected Model** dialog is shown in Exhibit 8.60. Carl saves this dialog as **Model for MFI with Quarry**.

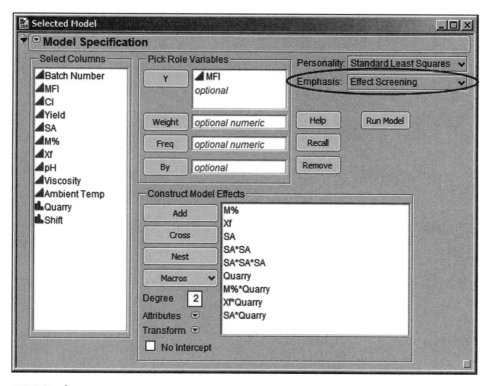

EXHIBIT 8.60 Selected Model Dialog for MFI with Quarry Terms Added

Now Carl clicks on **Run Model**. In the report, shown in Exhibit 8.61, the **Actual by Predicted** plot indicates that the model fits the data well. Carl realizes that he could also check the residuals using the traditional **Residual by Predicted Plot**, which can be obtained by selecting **Row Diagnostics > Plot Residual by Predicted** from the red triangle. But this latter plot is essentially a rotated version of the **Actual by Predicted Plot**, so Carl forgoes the pleasure.

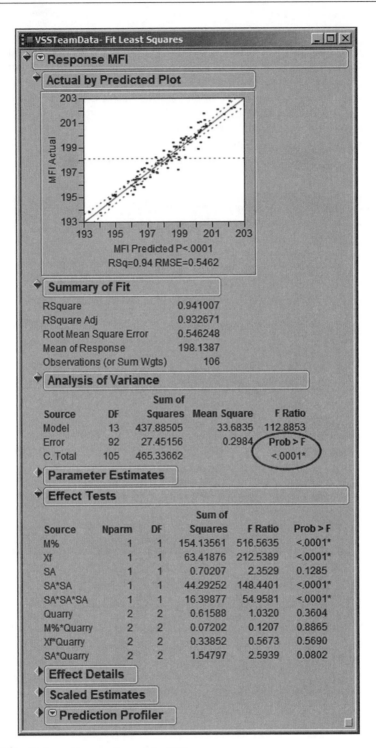

VSSTeamData- Fit Least Squares

Response MFI

Actual by Predicted Plot

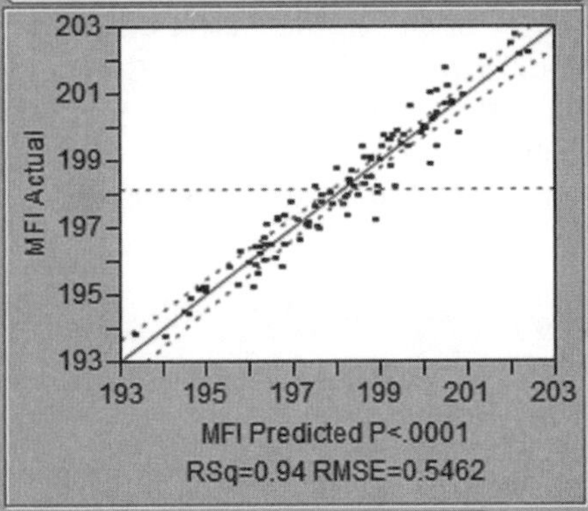

Summary of Fit

RSquare	0.941007
RSquare Adj	0.932671
Root Mean Square Error	0.546248
Mean of Response	198.1387
Observations (or Sum Wgts)	106

Analysis of Variance

Source	DF	Sum of Squares	Mean Square	F Ratio
Model	13	437.88505	33.6835	112.8853
Error	92	27.45156	0.2984	Prob > F
C. Total	105	465.33662		<.0001*

Parameter Estimates

Effect Tests

Source	Nparm	DF	Sum of Squares	F Ratio	Prob > F
M%	1	1	154.13561	516.5635	<.0001*
Xf	1	1	63.41876	212.5389	<.0001*
SA	1	1	0.70207	2.3529	0.1285
SA*SA	1	1	44.29252	148.4401	<.0001*
SA*SA*SA	1	1	16.39877	54.9581	<.0001*
Quarry	2	2	0.61588	1.0320	0.3604
M%*Quarry	2	2	0.07202	0.1207	0.8865
Xf*Quarry	2	2	0.33852	0.5673	0.5690
SA*Quarry	2	2	1.54797	2.5939	0.0802

Effect Details

Scaled Estimates

Prediction Profiler

EXHIBIT 8.61 Fit Least Squares Report for MFI

The model is significant, as indicated by the **Prob > F** value in the **Analysis of Variance** panel. The **Effect Tests** panel indicates that there are a number of effects in the model that are not statistically significant. Carl decides to reduce the model before doing further analysis.

Carl could remove effects one by one, refitting the model each time, since the **Prob > F** values will change every time the model is refit. But, in the training that he had with Tom, Tom suggested the following approach, which he prefers especially for models with many terms. Place the **Selected Model** dialog and the **Fit Least Squares** report side-by-side. Then remove all effects with **Prob > F** greater than 0.20.

This seemed a bit odd to Carl at the time, but Tom explained that as you remove terms one-by-one from a model, the **Prob > F** values as a whole tend to drop. So you may be painting an unrealistic picture of which terms are truly significant. Tom pointed out that removing terms in a block partially overcomes this issue and might actually be more appropriate when dealing with multiple tests.

Carl decides to follow Tom's advice. He places the **Selected Model** dialog and the **Fit Least Squares** report side-by-side, as shown in Exhibit 8.62. He identifies the effects that have **Prob > F** values greater than 0.20 and are not involved in higher-order terms or interactions. Only two terms qualify: M%*Quarry and Xf*Quarry. Carl removes these terms from the **Selected Model** dialog by selecting them in the **Construct Model Effects** list, then clicking the **Remove** button above the list.

He reruns the model (Exhibit 8.63). The interaction term SA*Quarry has a **Prob > F** value of 0.1011, and the main effect Quarry has a **Prob > F** value of 0.2718. Carl had been thinking about a 0.10 cut-off for **Prob > F** values, so as to minimize the risk of overlooking active effects. He is undecided as to whether to leave the borderline interaction, and hence the main effect, in the model or to remove both effects. Finally, he comes down on the side of not overlooking a potentially active factor. He can always remove it later on.

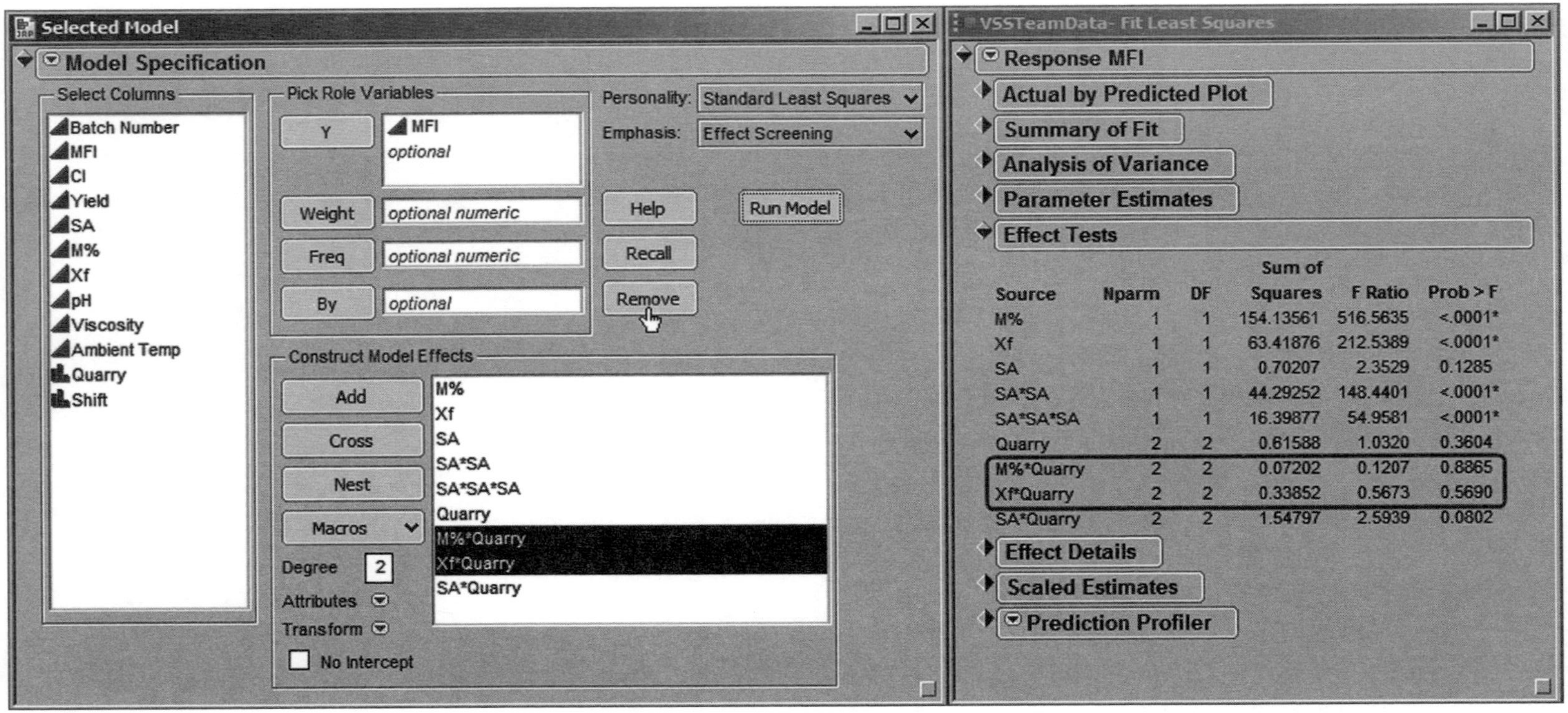

EXHIBIT 8.62   Selected Model Dialog and Least Squares Report

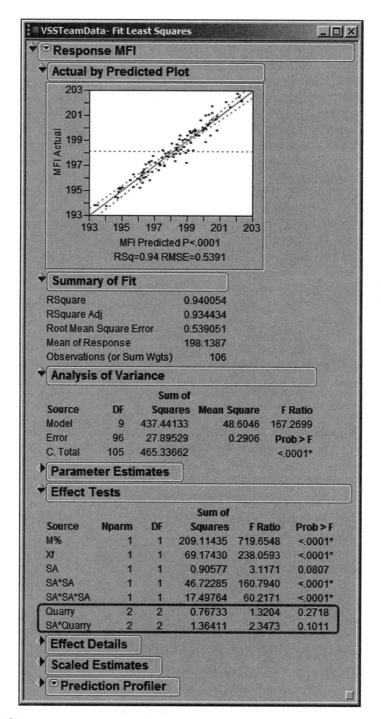

EXHIBIT 8.63   Fit Least Squares Report for MFI, Reduced Model

He saves the dialog window that created this model, shown in Exhibit 8.64, as **Reduced Model for MFI**. He notes that the Hot Xs for MFI are M%, Xf, and SA, with Quarry potentially interesting as well.

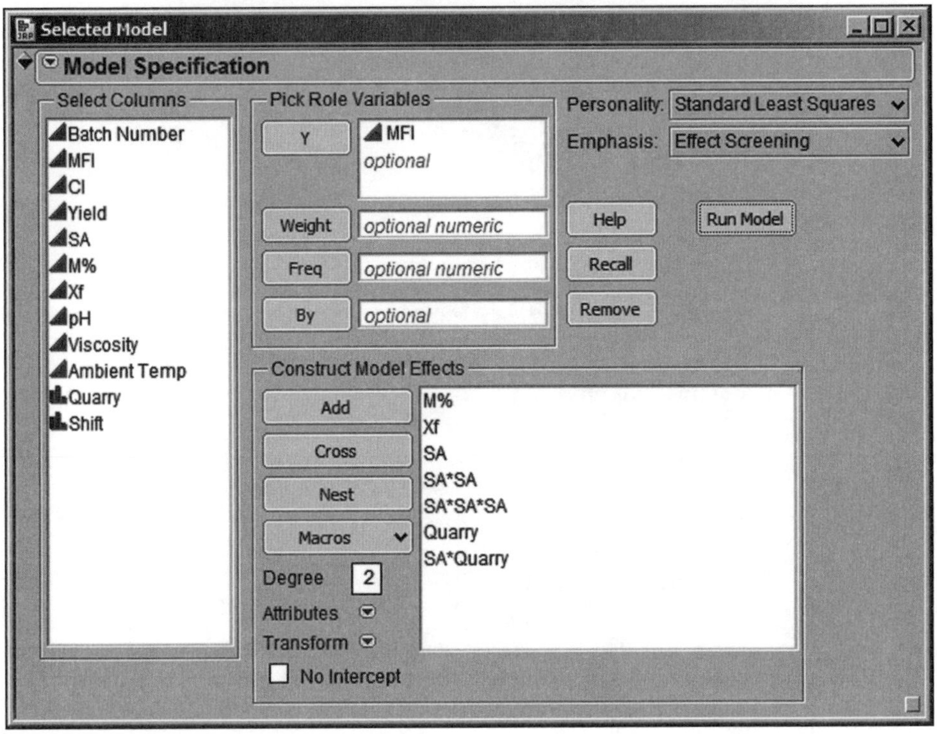

EXHIBIT 8.64   Reduced Model for MFI

Happy with this model, Carl returns to the report shown in Exhibit 8.63. He wants to save the prediction formula given by this model for **MFI** to the data table. He knows that he will want to simultaneously optimize both **MFI** and **CI**, so it will be necessary to have both prediction equations saved in his table. To add a column containing the prediction formula to the data table, Carl clicks the red triangle at the top next to **Response MFI** and selects **Save Columns > Prediction Formula**. (Alternatively, you can run the script **Prediction Formula for MFI**.)

A new column called Pred Formula MFI appears in the data table. In the columns panel next to the column's name, there is a plus sign, indicating that the Pred Formula MFI column is given by a formula. Carl clicks on the plus sign to reveal the formula, which is shown in Exhibit 8.65. After a quick look, he closes the formula box by clicking **Cancel**. He also notes the asterisk next to the plus sign. He clicks on it to learn that the **Spec Limits** property that he previously defined for MFI has been included as a **Column Property** for the prediction formula. How nifty!

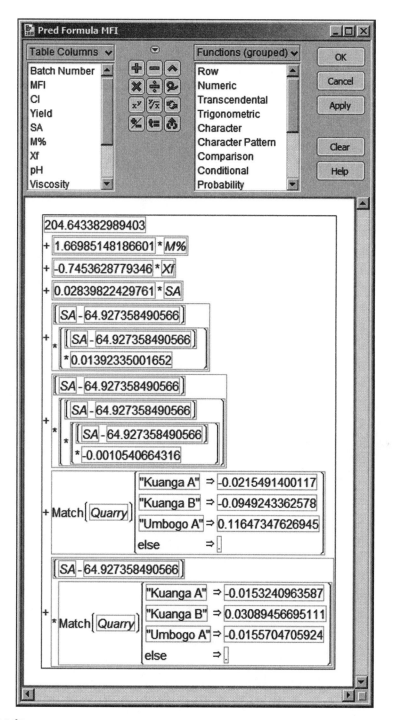

EXHIBIT 8.65   Prediction Formula for MFI

Before continuing, we note the following points:

1. There is no absolute procedure on how to decide which terms to consider for a model and no absolute procedure for how to reduce a model. You might take quite a different approach to developing a model for MFI, and it might lead to a model that is even more useful than Carl's. Remember that all models are wrong, but some of them are useful. All you can do as an analyst is aim for a useful model.
2. There are many model validation steps in which you could engage before deciding that a final model is adequate. Although we do not discuss these here, we do not want to give the impression that these should be disregarded. Checks for influential observations, multicollinearity, and so on are important.

Obtaining a Final Model for CI

Now Carl conducts a similar analysis for CI. He returns to the **Screening** report, sorts the **Terms** in the **Screening for CI** panel by **Individual p-Value**, and examines the **Half Normal Plot**. As he did for MFI, in the plot he selects the effects that appear to be significant using a rectangle, shown in Exhibit 8.66. This selects the bottom five effects in the **Terms** list: SA, Xf, a quadratic term in Xf, a cubic term in Xf, and a cubic term in SA.

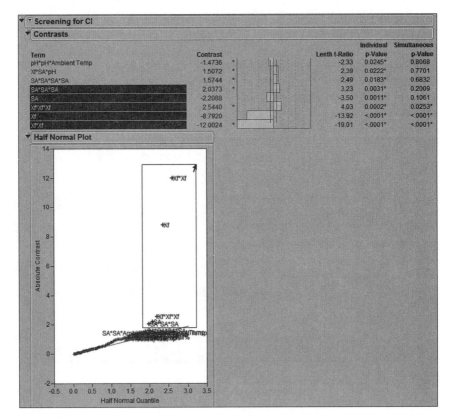

EXHIBIT 8.66   Selecting Terms with Rectangle in Half Normal Plot for CI

Carl notes that his selected effects include all of the effects with **Simultaneous p-Values** below 0.20. He checks the effects in the **Term** list immediately above the ones that he has chosen. Although some of these are two-way interactions, a number are third- and fourth-degree terms. Since fourth-degree terms are rarely important, and since they do not appear significant in the **Half Normal Plot**, he is content to proceed with the five effects that he has chosen.

He clicks **Make Model**. In the interest of maintaining model hierarchy, he adds the SA*SA term. He does this by selecting SA in the **Select Columns** list as well as in the **Construct Model Effects** list and clicking **Cross**. He saves this dialog as **Screening Model for CI**. Next, Carl adds Quarry and the two-way interactions of Quarry with Xf and SA to the model. He saves this script as **Model for CI with Quarry**.

Reducing this model by eliminating terms where **Prob > F** exceeds 0.20 results in the elimination of only SA*Quarry. When Carl reruns the model, it seems clear that SA*SA and SA*SA*SA should be removed, based on their large **Prob > F** values. When he reruns this further-reduced model, he notes that the Xf*Quarry interaction has a **Prob > F** value of 0.1423 and that the Quarry main effect has a **Prob > F** value of 0.954. He considers this to be sufficient evidence that neither the interaction nor the main effect is active. So, he removes these two terms as well. Although SA is now significant only at 0.1268, he decides to retain it in the model.

He checks the resulting model and notes that it appears to fit well. He concludes that the Hot Xs for CI are Xf and SA. Finally, he saves the resulting model dialog as **Reduced Model for CI** (see Exhibit 8.67) and saves the prediction formula to the data table. (The script **Prediction Formula for CI** will also save this formula to the data table.)

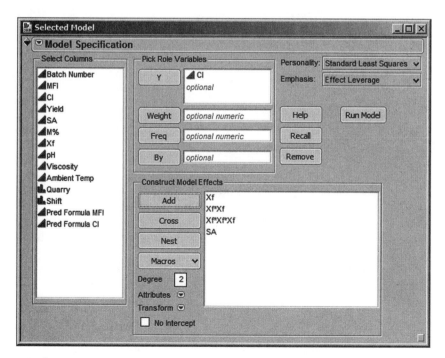

EXHIBIT 8.67   Reduced Model for CI

Revising Knowledge

Having constructed models for **MFI** and **CI** and having identified the relevant Hot Xs, Carl and his team are ready to proceed to the Revise Knowledge step of the Visual Six Sigma Data Analysis Process. They will identify optimal settings for the Hot Xs, evaluate process behavior relative to variation in the Hot Xs using simulation, and run confirmatory trials to verify improvement.

Determining Optimal Factor Level Settings

With both prediction formulas saved to the data table, Carl is ready to find settings for the Xs that will simultaneously optimize **MFI** and **CI**. To find these optimal settings, Carl selects **Graph > Profiler**. He enters both prediction formulas as **Y, Prediction Formula** (Exhibit 8.68).

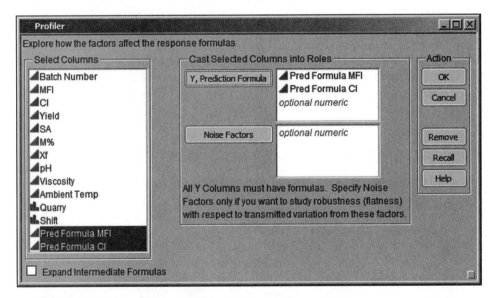

EXHIBIT 8.68   Launch Dialog for Profiler

Clicking **OK** displays the profiler report shown in Exhibit 8.69, and Carl immediately saves this script as **Profiler**. Carl thinks back to what he learned in his training. The idea is to think of each prediction formula as defining a response surface. The profiler shows cross sections, called *traces*, of both response surfaces, with the top row of panels corresponding to **MFI** and the second row corresponding to **CI**. The cross sections are given for the designated values of **M%**, **Xf**, **SA**, and **Quarry**. To explore various factor settings, the vertical red dotted lines can be moved by clicking and dragging, showing how the two predicted responses change.

Consider only the top row of plots, which relate to **MFI**. Carl has estimated a prediction model for **MFI** that is based on the factors **M%**, **Xf**, **SA**, and **Quarry**. For a given value of **Quarry**, this is a response surface in four dimensions: There are three factor values, and these result in one predicted value. Given the settings in Exhibit

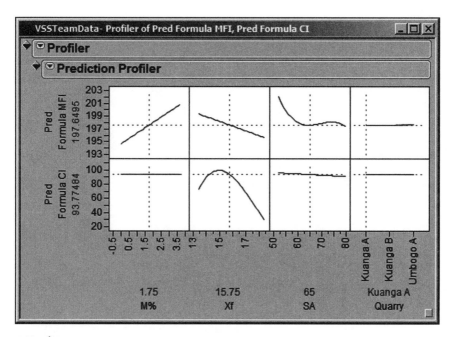

EXHIBIT 8.69   Initial Profiler Report

8.69, the profiler is telling us, for example, that when **Quarry** is Kuanga A and **M%**
= 1.75 and **Xf** = 15.75, the predicted **MFI** values, for various settings of **SA**, are
those given in the panel above **SA**. In other words, given that **Quarry** is specified,
for specific settings of any two of the continuous factors, the profiler gives the cross
section of the response surface for the third continuous factor.

Understanding the Profiler Traces

"Ha," thinks Carl. It is getting late in the day, and the idea of visualizing these traces
by plotting a response surface sounds like a wonderful diversion. Then, maybe he
can see more easily what these traces represent. So, he selects **Graph > Surface Plot**
and enters **Pred Formula MFI, SA, M%, Xf,** and **MFI** as **Columns**. When he clicks **OK**,
a surface plot appears.

Carl is interested in visualizing the interesting trace for **MFI** above **SA** in the
prediction profiler in Exhibit 8.69. To do this, in the **Independent Variables** panel,
Carl selects **SA** as **X** and **Xf** as **Y**, as shown in Exhibit 8.70. He sets **M%** to 1.75, its
value in the prediction profiler. Glancing beneath the **X** and **Y** buttons, he notes that
Quarry is set at Kuanga A, as in the profiler. The points for **MFI** are plotted, and the
surface that is being used to model these points is displayed.

Carl notes that if he puts his cursor over the plot and clicks he can rotate the
surface so as to better see various features. He rotates the plot to bring **SA** to the
front and to make the **Xf** axis increasing from front to back. Carl notes that he can
set a grid in the **Independent Variables** panel. He checks the box for **Grid** next to **Xf**
and checks to verify that the **Value** is set at 15.75 (Exhibit 8.71).

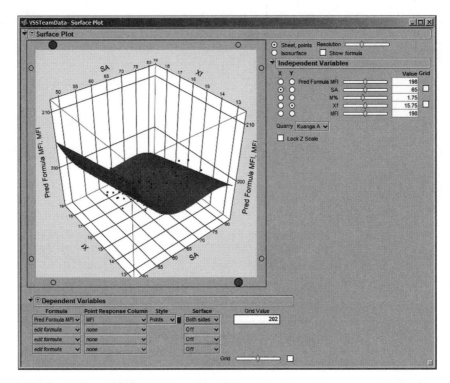

EXHIBIT 8.70   Surface Plot for Pred Formula MFI

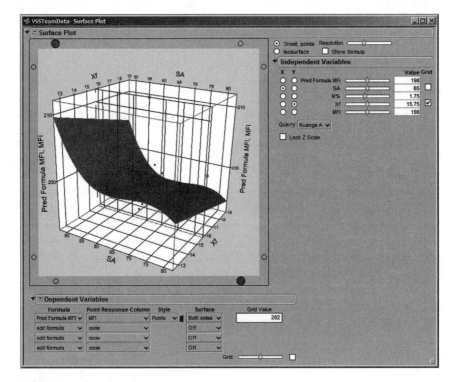

EXHIBIT 8.71   Surface Plot for Pred Formula MFI with Grid for Xf

This vertical grid cuts the surface in a curved shape. This is precisely the trace shown for SA in the profiler in Exhibit 8.69. Carl saves this script as **Surface Plot – SA and Xf**.

Now, Carl does realize that the profiler gives that cross section when Xf = 15.75 *and* M% = 1.75 *and* Quarry = Kuanga A. Carl varies the value of M% by moving the slider in the **Independent Variables** panel. He notes how the trace across the surface changes. This behavior is exhibited in the profiler when he changes settings as well.

Carl also explores the effect of **Quarry**, choosing the other quarries from the drop-down menu in the **Independent Variables** panel. The prediction surface changes slightly as he runs through the three quarries.

This exercise in three dimensions gives Carl some intuition about the profiler traces. He realizes that when he changes the settings of factors in the prediction profiler the traces correspond to cross sections of the prediction equation at the new settings.

Back to Simultaneous Optimization

"Well," Carl thinks, "That was fun! I need to show that to the team members later on. They will love it." Carl proceeds to his next task, which is to find optimal settings for the Hot Xs. To do this, he returns to the profiler. By now, he has lost that window, so he simply clicks on one of his reports, selects **Window > Close All Reports**, and then reruns the **Profiler** script.

To find optimal settings, Carl will use the JMP desirability functions. He clicks on the red triangle next to **Prediction Profiler** and chooses **Desirability Functions**, as shown in Exhibit 8.72. He saves this script as **Profiler – Desirability Functions**.

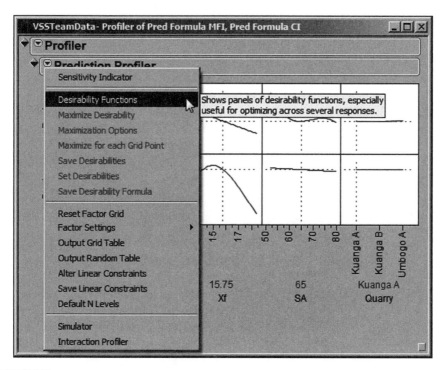

EXHIBIT 8.72   Profiler Menu Showing Desirability Functions Option

This has the effect of adding a few more panels to the profiler. Two panels are added at the right, one for each of the responses (Exhibit 8.73). These show the desirability of various values of the responses, based on the specification limits that Carl entered into **Column Info** for MFI and CI earlier, in the section "Dealing with the Preliminaries." For example, values of MFI near 195 have desirability near 1, while values above 198 and below 192 have desirabilities near 0. Similarly, large values of CI have high desirability.

VSSTeamData- Profiler of Pred Formula MFI, Pred Formula CI
Profiler
Prediction Profiler
Pred Formula MFI 197.6495
Pred Formula CI 93.77484
Desirability 0.188678
1.75
M%
15.75
Xf
65
SA
Kuanga A
Quarry
Desirability

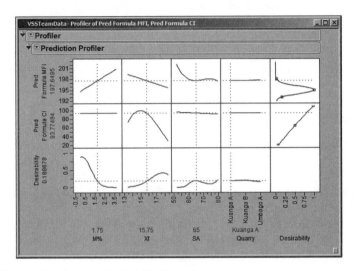

EXHIBIT 8.73 **Profiler Showing Desirability Functions**

To see the description of the desirability function for a given response, Carl double-clicks in the desirability function panel for that response. For MFI, he obtains the **Response Goal** dialog shown in Exhibit 8.74. After reviewing this, he clicks **Cancel** to exit with no changes.

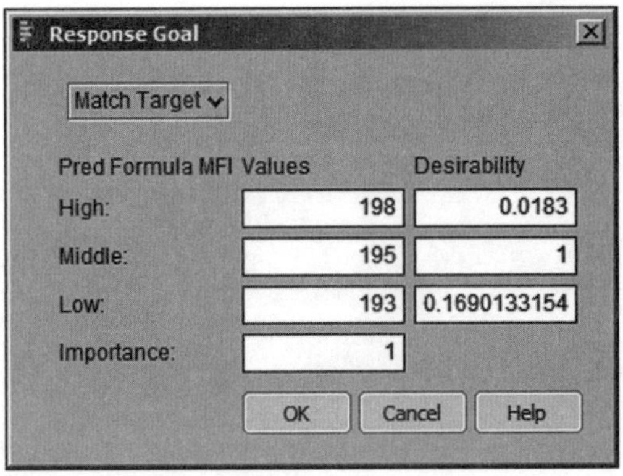

Response Goal
Match Target
Pred Formula MFI Values
Desirability
High:
198
0.0183
Middle:
195
1
Low:
193
0.1690133154
Importance:
1
OK
Cancel
Help

EXHIBIT 8.74 **Response Goal Dialog for MFI**

New panels have also appeared at the bottom of the profiler, in a row called **Desirability** (Exhibit 8.73). This row gives traces for the desirability function, which, like the predicted surface, is a function of M%, Xf, SA, and Quarry. For example, Carl sees that if M% = 1.75 and SA = 65, then low values of Xf are not very desirable. This is true for all three settings of Quarry; Carl sees this by setting the vertical red line at each of the three values of Quarry.

Of course, the goal is to find settings of the factors that maximize the desirability value. To do this, Carl returns to the red triangle next to **Prediction Profiler** and chooses **Maximize Desirability**. He obtains the settings shown in Exhibit 8.75. The plot indicates that optimal settings for the three continuous Hot Xs are M% = 0, Xf = 15.1, and SA = 62.3. The optimal Quarry is Kuanga B. At Carl's settings, the predicted value of MFI is 195.069 and of CI is 99.740, both well within their specification limit ranges. Note that you may not obtain these same settings, since, in most cases, many different settings can maximize desirability. (Carl's exact settings can be obtained by running the script **Profiler – Desirability Maximized.)**

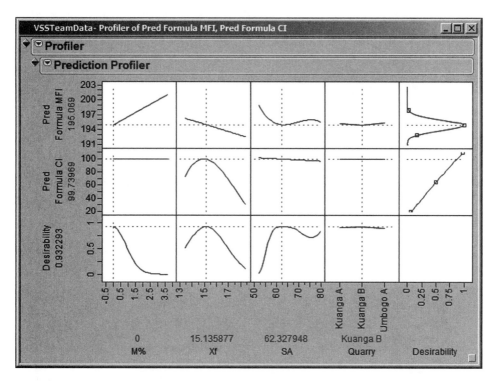

EXHIBIT 8.75 Profiler with Desirability Functions Maximized

"Now," thinks Carl, "it is not likely that we can rely on only a single supplier. What happens if we run at the optimal settings of the continuous variables, but obtain product from the other quarries?" He sees that for the optimal settings of the continuous variables all three quarries have desirability close to 1. He also reminds himself that Quarry is in the model for MFI but not for CI, so it does not affect the predicted value of CI.

Carl moves the vertical dashed line for **Quarry** to Kuanga A and notes that the predicted value for **MFI** increases by about 0.2 units to 195.26. He moves it to Umbago A and notes that the predicted value for **MFI** is about 195.40. It is clear that at the optimal settings of **M%**, **Xf**, and **SA**, **Quarry** does not have a large impact on **MFI**.

The plot also indicates that for the optimal settings of **M%** and **SA**, if **Xf** drifts to the 16- or 17-unit range, then desirability drops dramatically. By dragging the vertical dashed line for **Xf** to 16.5 and higher while looking at the **Pred Formula CI** trace for **Xf**, Carl sees that **Pred Formula CI** drops below 80 when **Xf** exceeds 16.5 or so. He concludes that **CI** is very sensitive to variation in **Xf** at the optimal settings of **M%** and **SA**.

Assessing Sensitivity to Predictor Settings

In fact, this reminds Carl that he learned about a sensitivity indicator in his training. From the **Prediction Profiler** red triangle, Carl selects **Sensitivity Indicator**. This adds little hollow triangles to the prediction traces. He saves the script as **Profiler – Optimized with Sensitivity Indicators**.

Carl leaves **M%** and **SA** at their optimal values and moves **Xf** to about 16.5 (Exhibit 8.76). He observes how the sensitivity indicator for **CI** in the **Xf** panel gets larger as he increases **Xf** to 16.5. He remembers that the sensitivity indicator points in the direction of change for the response as the factor level increases and that its size is proportional to the change. Carl concludes that maintaining tight control over **Xf** is critical.

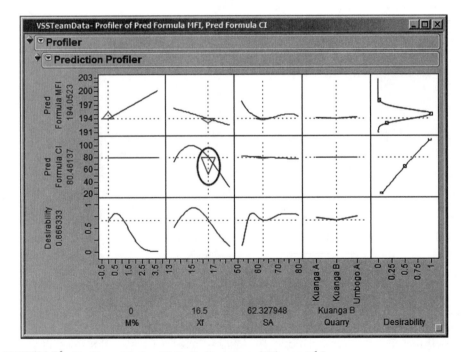

EXHIBIT 8.76   Profiler with Sensitivity Indicators and Xf near 16.5

Carl reruns the script **Profiler – Optimized with Sensitivity Indicators** since, by exploring sensitivity, he has lost his optimal settings. This time, he moves the SA setting to its left a bit. The sensitivity indicator for MFI shows that MFI is highly sensitive to SA excursions to 60 and below (see Exhibit 8.77, where SA is set at 58). Carl also observes that in the design region shown in the profiler, CI is linearly related to SA, but CI is relatively insensitive to SA (the triangle for CI above SA is so small that it is barely visible). Also, MFI is linearly related to, and somewhat sensitive to, Xf. But, Carl concludes, the big sensitivities are those of MFI to low SA and CI to high Xf.

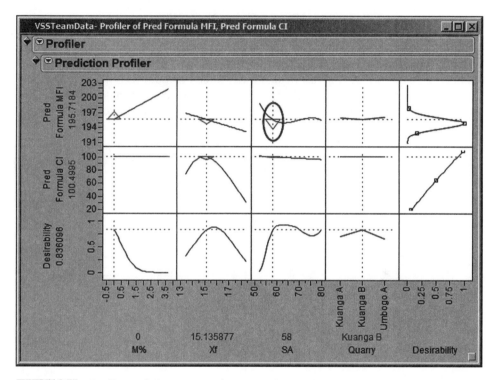

EXHIBIT 8.77   Profiler with Sensitivity Indicators and SA at 58

Carl reexamines the optimal settings, which he retrieves by rerunning the script **Profiler – Desirability Maximized**. Carl finds them very interesting: The optimal setting for M%, the viscosity modifier, is 0! So, adding the modifier actually degrades MFI (M% is not involved in the model for CI).

When Carl brings this information to the team members, they are surprised. It was always believed that the modifier helped the melt flow index. The team members talk with engineers about this, and it is decided that, perhaps, the modifier is not required—at least they are interested in testing a few batches without it.

Based on Carl's sensitivity analysis, the team concludes that both SA and Xf must be controlled tightly. The team members get started on developing an understanding of why these two factors vary, and on proposing procedures that will ensure tighter control over them. They propose a new control mechanism to monitor **SA** (amps for slurry tank stirrer) and to keep it on target at the optimal value of 62.3 and within narrow tolerances. They also develop procedures to ensure that filler and water will be added at regular intervals to ensure that **Xf** (percent of filler in the polymer) is kept at a constant level close to 15.1 percent.

Carl instructs the team members to test their new controls and to collect data from which they can estimate the variability in the **SA** and **Xf** settings in practice.

Simulating Process Outcomes

This takes the team members a few weeks. But they return with data that indicate that when they attempt to hold **Xf** and **SA** on target their effective settings do vary. They appear to have approximately normal distributions with standard deviations of 0.4 and 1.9, respectively. Carl's plan is to use these estimates of variation, together with simulation, to obtain reliable estimates of capability for both responses of interest.

With the team present, Carl reruns his profiler script, **Profiler – Desirability Maximized**. From the second-level red triangle he chooses **Simulator** (Exhibit 8.78).

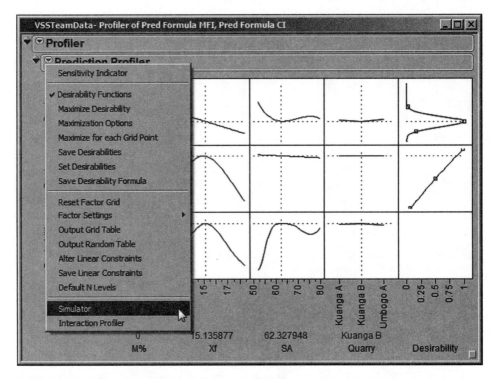

EXHIBIT 8.78   Profiler Menu Showing Simulator Option

This adds options to the report (see Exhibit 8.79). In particular, below the factor settings, the report now contains drop-down menus that allow the user to specify distributions to use in simulating factor variability.

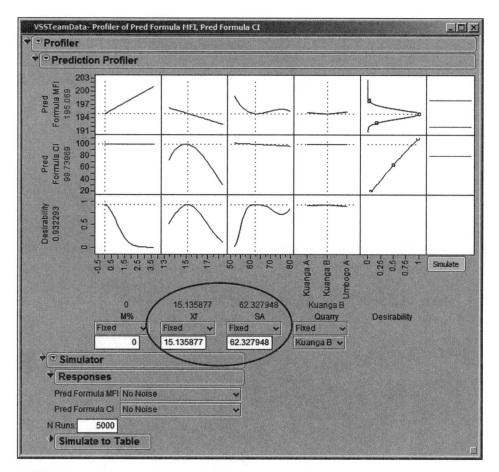

EXHIBIT 8.79 Profiler with Simulation Options

The work of the team members has shown that estimates for the standard deviations of **Xf** and **SA** are 0.4 and 1.9, respectively. Carl enters these as follows. For **Xf**, he clicks on the arrow next to **Fixed** (circled in Exhibit 8.79). From the drop-down list for **Xf**, he chooses **Random**. The default distribution is **Normal**. But Carl clicks on the arrow next to **Normal** and chooses **Normal weighted** from the list of distributions that appears (see Exhibit 8.80). This option results in sampling from a normal distribution, but in a fashion that estimates the parts per million (PPM) defective rate with more precision than would otherwise be possible. The mean is set by default at the optimal setting. Carl enters 0.4 as the **SD** for **Xf**.

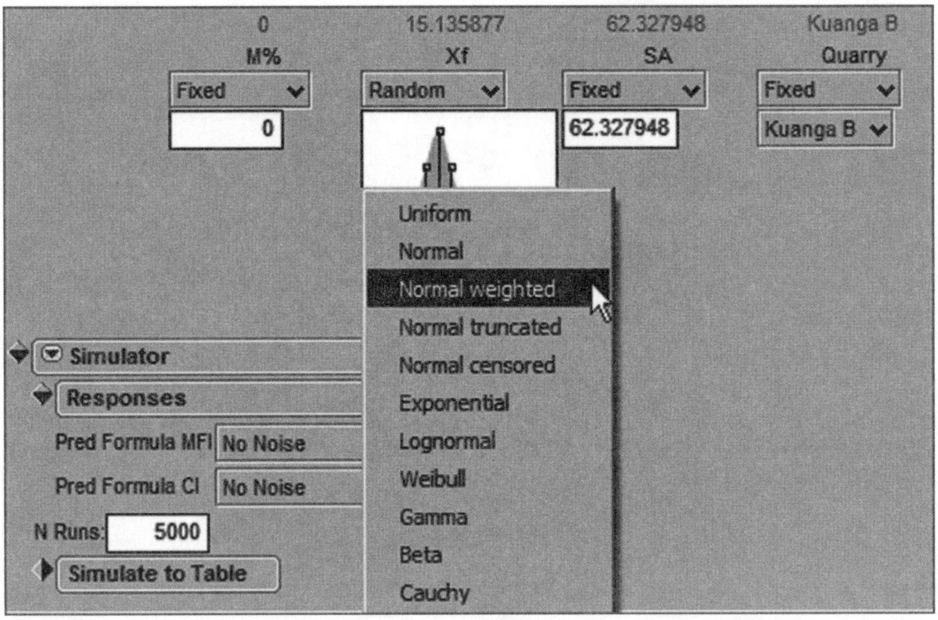

EXHIBIT 8.80   Simulator with Choices of Distributions

In a similar fashion, for **SA**, Carl chooses **Normal weighted** and adds 1.9 as the **SD** (see Exhibit 8.81). Then he saves the script as **Profiler – Simulator**.

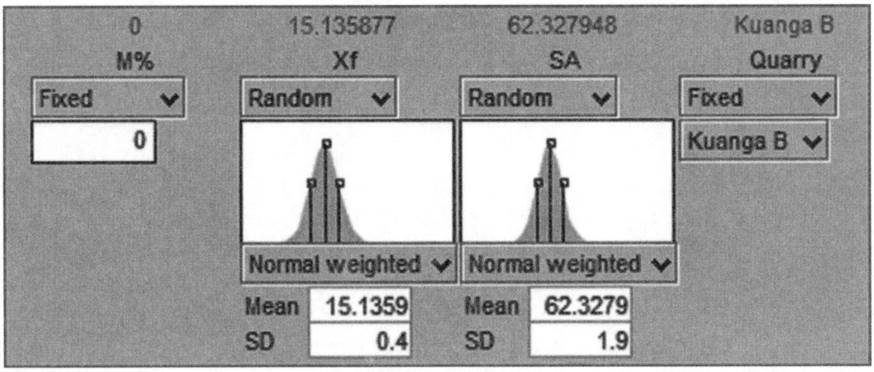

EXHIBIT 8.81   Simulator with Values Entered

Now, the moment of truth has arrived. The team waits with anticipation (a drum roll is heard) as Carl clicks the **Simulate** button. A panel appears below the **Simulate** button (Exhibit 8.82). Carl right-clicks in these results and selects **Columns > PPM**. When the team members see the **PPM** value of 360, they erupt in congratulations. Carl runs the simulation a few more times, and although there is some variation in the **PPM** values, that first value of 360 seems to be a reasonable estimate.

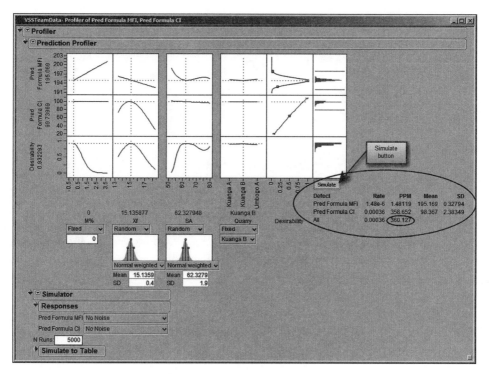

EXHIBIT 8.82   Simulation Results

In the **Defect** table below the **Simulate** button, Carl notices that the majority of defective values are coming from **CI**. He remembers that **CI** is sensitive to **Xf** values in the region of the optimal settings. If the standard deviation for **Xf** could be reduced, this might further reduce the estimated **PPM** rate. Nonetheless, the team has very good news to report. Everyone is anxious to meet with Edward, the manufacturing director, and to test these predictions in real life.

Confirming the Improvement

Edward is thrilled with the team's report and gives them the go-ahead to run formal confirmation trials, measuring yield through to the molding plant. In the limited experience they have had to date with running the process at the optimal settings, they have only monitored the polymer plant yield. Together, the team and Carl decide to perform tests on five batches using the target settings and controls for **SA** and **Xf**. The batches are followed through the molding plant, so that, in line with the original definition, **Yield** is measured using both polymer plant and molding plant waste. The measurements for these five batches are given in the data table **ConfirmationData.jmp**, shown in Exhibit 8.83.

ConfirmationData

	Batch Number	MFI	CI	Yield	SA	M%	Xf	Stage
1	4121	194.9	91.2	100	62.5	0	15.0	Confirmation
2	4122	193.6	87.5	100	62.9	0	14.9	Confirmation
3	4123	194.7	95.4	100	63.0	0	14.6	Confirmation
4	4124	193.6	98.9	100	62.2	0	14.9	Confirmation
5	4125	194.9	99.3	100	62.7	0	15.1	Confirmation

EXHIBIT 8.83 Confirmation Data from Five Batches

What a delight to see all MFI and CI values well within their specifications and to see 100 percent Yield on all five batches! Carl and his team are ecstatic.

Utilizing Knowledge

In spite of this very promising result, Carl reminds his teammates to remain cautious. Even if they had made no process changes, history shows that a crisis is only expected about once every quarter. During the single crisis that occurred over the team's baseline period, MFI values were unusually high. So there is statistical evidence that keeping MFI within the specification limits will alleviate crisis periods. But it will be important to continue to monitor Yield to ensure that the new optimal settings and controls really do address the root cause of a crisis. As they gather additional data over a longer time span, they will have more assurance that keeping MFI and CI within their specification limits really does alleviate crises.

This is an interesting situation where, although success has been confirmed in the short term, the longer time horizon of the historical problem requires a heightened sense of vigilance during the control phase. So, although the team is ready to see its project move to the Utilize Knowledge step of the Visual Six Sigma Data Analysis Process, that step will still retain some aspect of providing confirmation that the problem has been solved.

With this in mind, Carl and his team report their results to Edward. He is very impressed by the outcome of the confirmation runs and is extremely pleased by the work that Carl and his team have done. He appreciates the logic and discipline they have imposed throughout the knowledge-building process. It appears that because of their diligence the crisis periods may finally be eliminated.

Edward approves the fitting of a new control mechanism for the fill process to monitor SA and to keep it on target and within tight control. He approves of the procedures proposed by the team to maintain Xf on target with little variation. These procedures are shared with technicians and operators in a formal training session.

Once these procedures are implemented, production batches are monitored closely, to ensure that nothing goes amiss, for the first month of production. Data on MFI, CI, Yield, SA, M%, and Xf for the 79 batches produced that month are given in the data table **ControlPhaseData.jmp**.

Verifying Process Stability

The first thing that Carl checks is whether the process is stable. He opens **Control-PhaseData.jmp**. To construct control charts for MFI, CI, and Yield, Carl selects **Graph > Control Chart > IR**. In the resulting dialog, he enters MFI, CI, and Yield as **Process**, Batch Number as **Sample Label**, and unchecks the box for the **Moving Range** chart. The resulting control charts are shown in Exhibit 8.84. Carl saves the script as **Control Charts**.

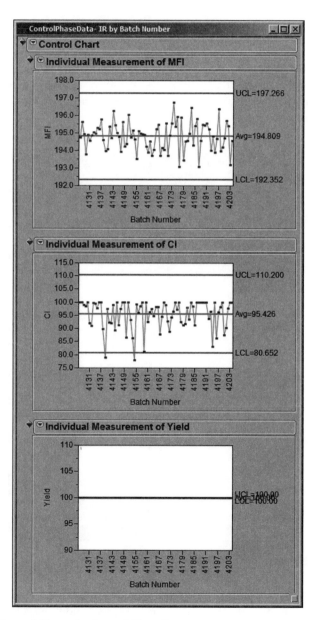

EXHIBIT 8.84   Control Charts for Control Phase Data

The MFI measurements are stable and fall well below the upper specification limit of 198. But the CI measurements appear unstable. However, note that their distribution is highly skewed, as we would expect. The individual measurement chart's control limits are valid for normally distributed data, and CI is not normally distributed. What to do?

Even in a case where the underlying data are highly non-normal, the means of samples are approximately normal, even for small samples or subgroups (this follows from the Central Limit Theorem). This means that an XBar chart can be used to assess process stability.

So, for CI, Carl decides to construct XBar and R charts, subgrouping the measurements into consecutive subgroups of size five. To do this, he selects **Graph > Control Chart > XBar** and inserts CI as **Process**. He notes that the default subgrouping is **Sample Size Constant**, set at five, so he leaves this alone. He clicks **OK** to obtain the charts in Exhibit 8.85 and saves the script as **XBar Chart**. The absence of out-of-control points and unstable patterns is evidence that the CI measurements have come from a stable process.

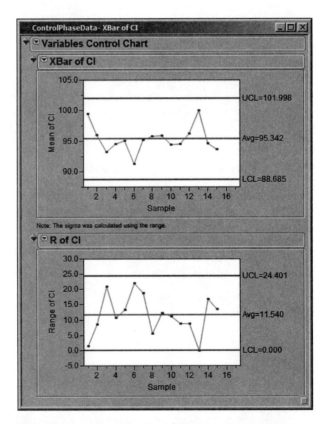

EXHIBIT 8.85   XBar and R Charts for Subgrouped CI Measurements

Finally, back to the analysis of the three charts in Exhibit 8.84—the **Yield** control chart appears a bit strange. But this is because, astoundingly, all **Yield** values are 100 percent!

Carl and the team members are very pleased with these results. Still, Carl stresses that it is important to assess capability for **MFI** and **CI** in order to know how these Ys are behaving relative to their specification limits. These are the process characteristics that will need to be controlled to ensure good yields, and so understanding their capability is important. Fortunately, both **MFI** and **CI** are stable, which allows the team to assess process capability for **MFI** and **CI**.

Estimating Process Capability

Carl first obtains histograms for **MFI** and **CI**. He selects **Analyze > Distribution** and enters MFI and CI in the **Y, Columns** box. He clicks **OK** and, when he sees vertical histograms, clicks the red triangle at the top, next to **Distributions**, and chooses **Stack**. This lays the histograms out horizontally, as shown in Exhibit 8.86 (where we have closed the **Capability Analysis** panels). Carl saves the script as **Distributions**.

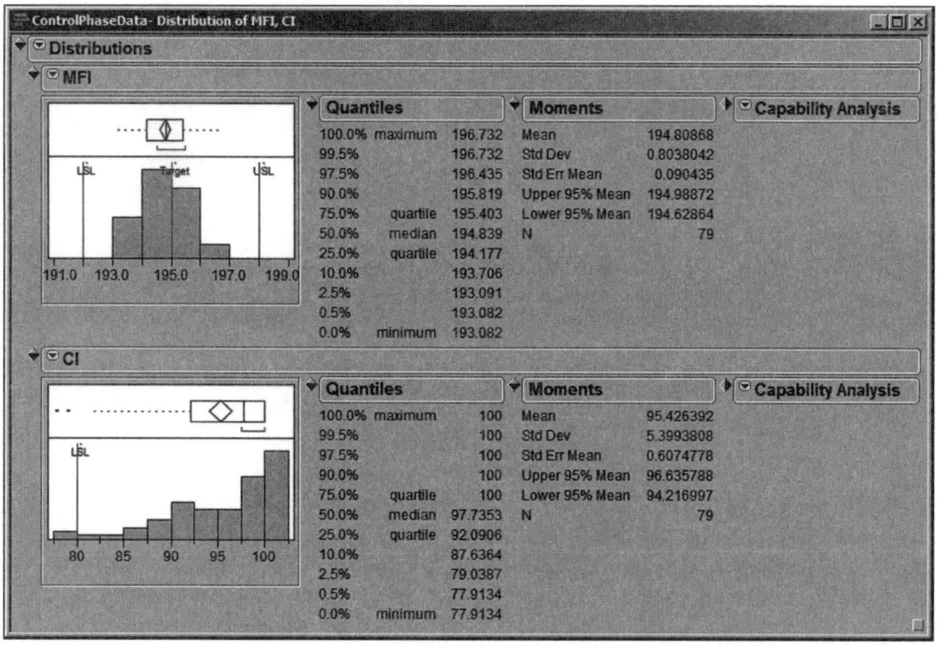

EXHIBIT 8.86 Distribution Reports for MFI and CI

The **MFI** distribution falls well within the specification limits. On the other hand, **CI** is nearly always above its LSL—only 2 batches out of 79 are below 80. Since specification limits have been entered in the columns for these two variables, JMP automatically computes normality-based capability analyses.

Both **Capability Analysis** reports are shown in Exhibit 8.87. The distribution of MFI appears to be approximately normal, indicating that the default normality-based **Cpk** is appropriate. MFI has a **Cpk** of 1.165 and an estimated defective rate (**PPM**) of 274 batches per million. This is quite amazing, given previous process behavior.

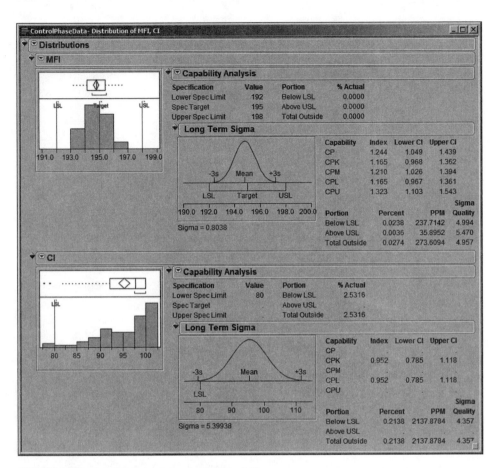

EXHIBIT 8.87   Capability Analyses for MFI and CI

Since CI is highly skewed, as shown in Exhibit 8.87, a normal distribution does not provide a good fit. It follows that basing a capability index on a normal fit is not very useful. The **Cpk** value of 0.952 for CI given in Exhibit 8.87 is based on the fit shown by the normal curve in the **Capability Analysis** panel, clearly a bad fit to the CI data. "But," a team member asks, "What do we do to assess capability?"

"Well," Carl says, "let's try another fit!" To remove the normal fit, in the report shown in Exhibit 8.87, Carl clicks on the red triangle next to CI and unchecks **Capability Analysis**.

For a left-skewed distribution, such as this one, Carl can think of only one good option and that is to fit the distribution *nonparametrically*, that is, using a method that does not specify a particular functional shape or form. To do this, Carl selects **Continuous Fit > Smooth Curve** from the red triangle next to CI. He obtains the report in Exhibit 8.88 and saves the script to the data table as **Distribution – Smooth Fit**.

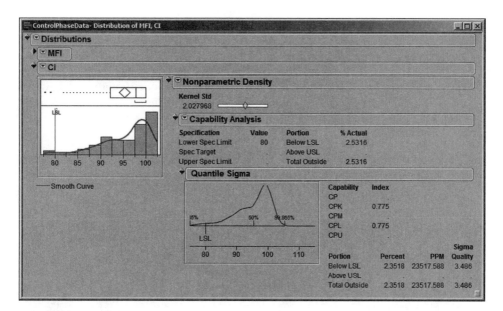

EXHIBIT 8.88   Smooth Curve Fit to CI

Well, the curve is smooth, but a bit bumpy. Yet, it describes the distribution quite well. The computed capability index is 0.775, and the **PPM** rate is 23,518, or about 2.35 percent. Based on the graph, the team feels comfortable with this estimate of capability and **PPM**, and they realize that the earlier normality-based **Cpk** value was very optimistic and incorrect.

It is also apparent to the team that their simulations underestimated the **PPM** rate. Recall that their estimate of **PPM** was 360. Their actual data, especially for **CI**, shows a much higher estimated **PPM** rate.

What to do with this knowledge? Well, a 2.35 percent out-of-specification rate is clearly not acceptable. This is an area that will need further investigation. One of the team members suggests that the lower specification limit of 80 may in fact be too tight, given that all batches had a **Yield** of 100 percent. Certainly, if it is possible to loosen the specification without incurring any loss in quality, this is a worthwhile endeavor. Carl documents the need for a resolution to this **CI** capability issue and puts it on a list of future projects.

Tracking Improvement

To visualize progress over the life of the project, Carl will concatenate the tables **VSSTeamData.jmp**, **ConfirmationData.jmp**, and **ControlPhaseData.jmp** into a single data table, which he will call **VSSTeamFinalData.jmp**. Before doing this, though, he looks at his list of open windows under **Window**, which shows a lot of windows open. At this point, he could simply **Close All**. But, by looking at the drop-down list of open data tables on the toolbar, he sees that the three data tables he wants are open. So, he clicks on a report to make it active and selects **Window > Close All Reports**. Then, one by one, he closes the data tables that are not of interest. When he is finished, only the three data tables mentioned above are left open.

Carl simply wants to concatenate the three data tables, which means that he will append rows from one data table to another. He first examines the column structure in the three data tables (Exhibit 8.89). He notes that **ConfirmationData.jmp** and **ControlPhase.jmp** have the same structure, but **VSSTeamData.jmp** contains columns that the previous two data tables do not. Although it's not required, Carl wants to assure that all three tables contain precisely the columns that are of interest to him.

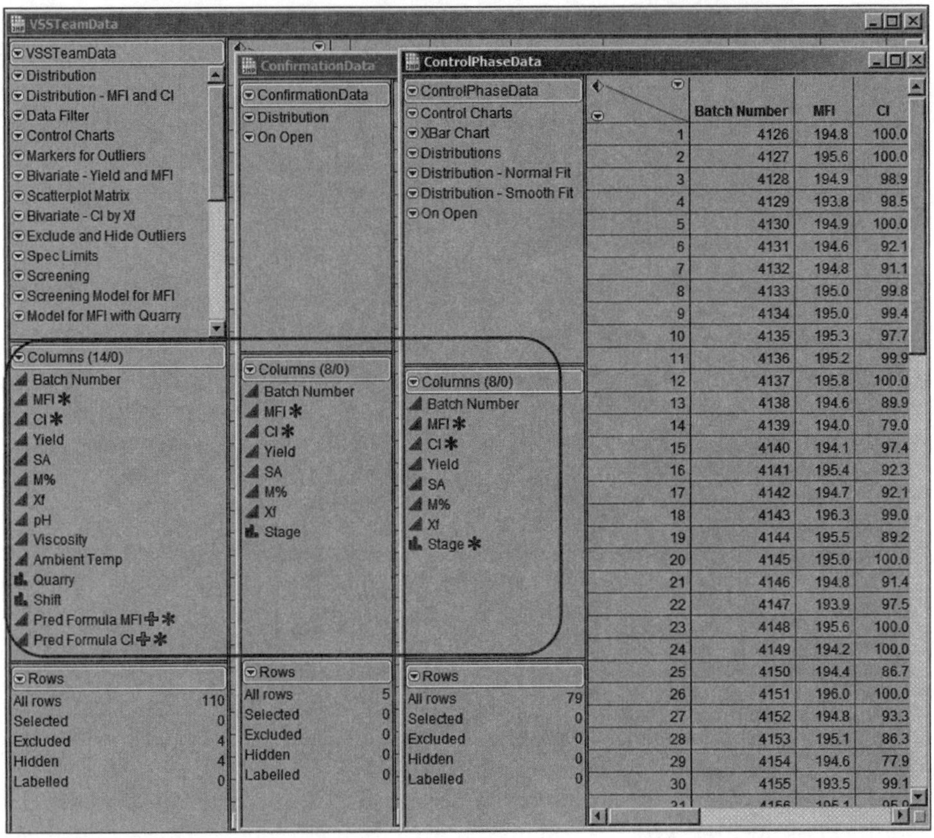

EXHIBIT 8.89   Column Panels for Three Data Tables

He clicks on **VSSTeamData.jmp** to make it active and saves it as **TempData.jmp**, indicating by the name that he can delete it later on. In the columns panel of this new data table, Carl selects the columns from **pH** to **Pred Formula CI**, inclusive, right clicks in the highlighted selection area, and chooses **Delete Columns**. Carl notes that scripts have been carried over to this temporary data table, and that some of these involve variables that he deleted, so they may not run.

Now, he needs to add a **Stage** column. In **TempData.jmp**, Carl double-clicks in the column header area to the right of the last column, **Xf**. This creates a new column. He right-clicks in the column area to open the **Column Info** window. For **Column Name**, he types in **Stage**. Then he clicks **OK**. In the first cell, he types "Old

Process" and then clicks away from this cell. He right-clicks back into it and chooses **Fill > Fill to end of table**. This copies the text "Old Process" into all of the data table rows.

Now, he is ready to concatenate the three tables. Under **Tables**, he chooses **Concatenate**. Since **TempData.jmp** is the current data table, it appears first in the list of **Data Tables to be Concatenated**. Carl adds the other two table names in the order shown in Exhibit 8.90 and enters a name for the new table, **VSSTeamFinalData.jmp**. (If you are doing this on your own, please choose a different name to avoid possibly overwriting Carl's table.)

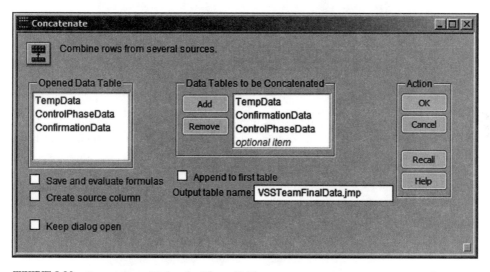

EXHIBIT 8.90   Concatenate Dialog for Three Tables

When he clicks **OK**, Carl sees the new table. He checks it to make sure it is what he had intended, and it is. He notices that all scripts have been carried over to the new table. Some may not be meaningful since they had been developed for portions of the data. But some might be meaningful. For example, he runs the **Control Charts** script, and it shows the three control charts for all of the data. He deletes **TempData.jmp** at this point.

However, Carl has something different in mind—he wants to see control charts by Stage. So, to avoid confusion, he deletes all the scripts other than **Source**. The **Source** script code tells him how the current data table was obtained, so he retains that for documentation. (If you prefer, at this point, you may close your table and open the saved table called **VSSTeamFinalData.jmp**.)

Carl will construct **IR** charts for MFI and Yield and **XBar** and **R** charts for CI, since its distribution is skewed. To construct the **IR** charts, he selects **Graph > Control Chart > IR**. He enters MFI and Yield as **Process**, Batch Number as **Sample Label**, and Stage as **Phase**, then unchecks **Moving Range** (Exhibit 8.91). Carl saves the script as **Control Charts – MFI and Yield**.

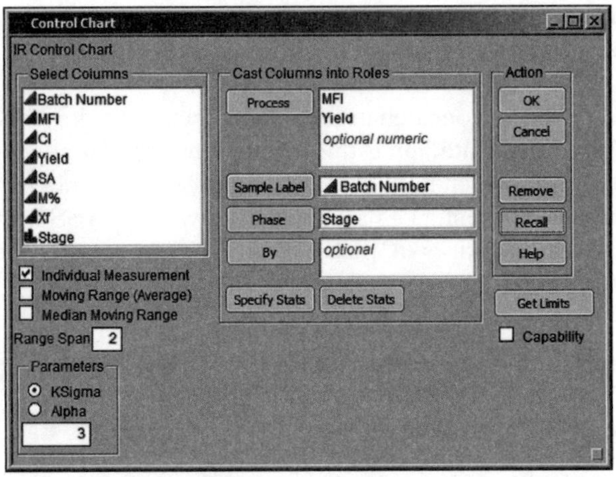

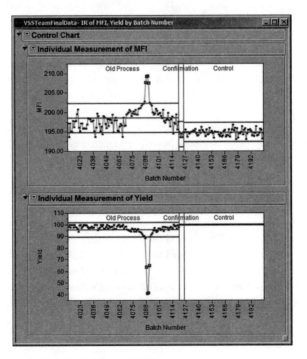

EXHIBIT 8.91   Launch Dialog for Stage Control Charts for MFI and Yield

The resulting control charts are shown in Exhibit 8.92. In these charts, the limits are calculated based on the data obtained in the specified **Stage**. Both charts indicate that the process behaves consistently in the confirmation and control stages. Carl notes that the upper control limit for **MFI** in the control phase is below the upper specification limit of 198. The chart for **Yield** shows the 100 percent yields obtained starting in the confirmation stage. The four outliers from the original process data are still marked and colored, which Carl likes.

EXHIBIT 8.92   Control Charts for MFI and Yield

Since CI has such a skewed distribution, to obtain a control chart with meaningful control limits, Carl once again chooses an **XBar** chart. He selects **Graph > Control Chart > XBar** and populates the dialog as shown in Exhibit 8.93.

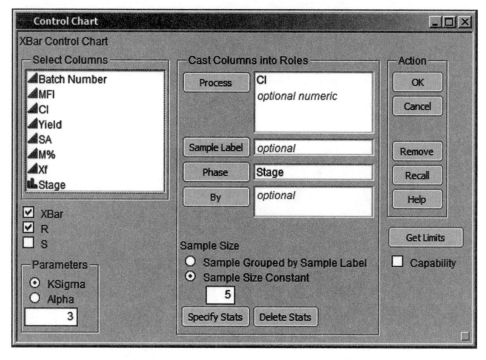

EXHIBIT 8.93   Launch Dialog for XBar and R Charts for CI

The resulting charts are shown in Exhibit 8.94. Starting with the confirmation stage, the CI process looks stable, both in terms of centering and spread. It is operating with much less variability and appears to be centered at about 95. Since this is an **XBar** chart, we cannot compare the control limits (based on averages) directly with the specification limits (based on individuals). But that has already been done in the non-normal capability analysis. Carl saves the script as **Control Chart – CI**.

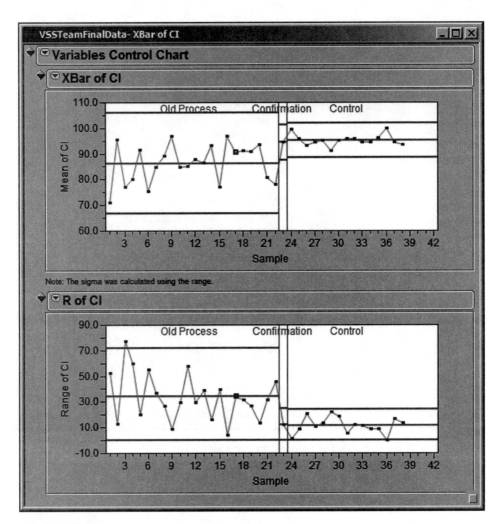

EXHIBIT 8.94   XBar and R Charts for CI

Conclusion

The original project goal was to eliminate the periods of crisis with a goal of achieving a yield rate of 95 percent. One and a half years have now passed since completing this project, and although very few batches do fall slightly below the lower limit for color index, this issue is resolved by blending low color index batches with high color index batches. To date, the molding plant has not rejected a single batch of white polymer since the changes have been implemented.

The savings from rejected batches alone are slightly over £750,000 per annum. Additionally there are now no processing restrictions on the molding plant, resulting in an additional annualized margin of £2,100,000 per annum and a very happy customer. The actual costs incurred on the project were minimal.

This was the project that convinced the skeptics, Edward included. It solved a major manufacturing problem with huge business benefits. In the final project close-out meeting, the key lessons were summarized as follows:

- Never trust a measurement system—it was only when these issues were resolved that it was possible to get meaningful results from the analysis.
- DMAIC methodology in conjunction with the Visual Six Sigma Roadmap delivers high levels of process understanding in a simple, straightforward manner.
- Visual Six Sigma techniques enable technical and business users to apply the principles of statistical thinking to solve problems rapidly and effectively.
- Visual Six Sigma greatly facilitates the communication of results to a wide audience in a simple visual form.

Note

1. C. F. Jeff Wu and Michael Hamada, *Experiments: Planning, Analysis, and Parameter Design Optimization* (Hoboken, NJ: John Wiley & Sons Inc., 2000), 112.

CHAPTER 9

Classification of Cells

Cellularplex is a small cell phone provider anxious to attract new customers. Jeremy Halls, the director of marketing, faces the challenge of running targeted and well-timed marketing campaigns. To that end, he wants to explore the value of *predictive analytics*, namely, the use of modeling techniques to predict future trends and behavior. Mi-Ling Wu is a statistical analyst with prior experience in both marketing and medical research. Jeremy enlists her help in developing strong marketing programs that will expand Cellularplex's customer base.

A test campaign aimed at identifying new customers who would take advantage of a specific offer is being launched. The data collected will allow the marketing group to explore the impact of a large number of demographic characteristics, as well as how the offer was made, on the response rate. The key response is the category into which a respondent falls, and there are four possible outcomes: an inquiry about the offer, the purchase of the promoted offer, the purchase of a different offer, or a rejection of the offer. The information from this test campaign will be used to design a large-scale drive to attract new customers.

The test campaign duration is set to three months. During this time, Mi-Ling starts learning about JMP, focusing on its powerful visualization and modeling capabilities. Because she will need to be ready to analyze the campaign data quickly when the responses arrive, Mi-Ling searches for some practice data, preferably a data set with a large number of potential predictors and where classification into two or more outcomes is required. She finds a published data set called the Wisconsin Breast Cancer Diagnostic Data. These data resulted from a study to accurately classify breast growths as malignant or benign, based on a computer characterization of a fine needle aspirate. The data include 569 records and 30 potential predictor variables.

This case study follows Mi-Ling through her self-study, as she explores features of JMP that support classification and data mining. After some basic data preparation, she makes extensive use of visualization techniques to build an understanding of the data set. After dividing the data into a training set, a validation set, and a test set, she fits four models to the training data. These include a logistic model, a partition model, and two neural net models. Comparing their performance on the validation set leads her to choose one of these as her preferred model. She then assesses its performance using the test set.

Mi-Ling is the sole investigator in this endeavor. Through her experience, you can see how Visual Six Sigma can be used by a single analyst to drive sound business or scientific decisions. She would delight in the pleasure of your company as she uncovers exciting patterns in her data and develops a good classification model. Who knows, you might be able to find a model that outperforms her final choice!

A list of the JMP platforms and options that Mi-Ling uses in this case study is shown in Exhibit 9.1. The JMP data tables that she uses are available at http://support.sas.com/visualsixsigma.

EXHIBIT 9.1   Platforms and Options Illustrated in This Case Study

Menus	Platforms and Options
Rows	Exclude/Unexclude
	Hide/Unhide
	Color or Mark by Column
	Data Filter
Cols	Column Info
	Column Properties
	Formula
	Hide/Unhide
	Exclude/Unexclude
	Group Columns
Analyze	Distribution
	Histogram
	Frequency Distribution
	Fit Y by X
	Bivariate
	Fit Line
	Contingency
	Fit Model
	Stepwise
	Nominal Logistic
	Modeling
	Neural Net
	Partition
	Multivariate Methods - Multivariate
	Correlations
	Scatterplot Matrix
Graph	Graph Builder
	Scatterplot 3D
	Surface Plot
Other Options	Add Table Variable
	Broadcast Command
	Copy from/to Row States
	Define Row State Columns
	Group By (In Bivariate)
	Preferences
	Row Legend
	Save Prediction Formula
	Save Script to Data Table
	Sort by Column (In Report Window)
	Value Ordering

Setting the Scene

Cellularplex is a small cell phone provider that is poised and anxious to expand its customer base. Jeremy Halls, the director of marketing, has been hearing about *predictive analytics* and how it can be successfully used to focus marketing strategies. He believes that statistical and data-mining models of customer characteristics and proclivities could greatly enhance his ability to run marketing campaigns that are targeted and well-timed, reaching potential customers with the right offers and using the right marketing channels.

Mi-Ling Wu has recently been hired by Cellularplex. Her previous position was with a medical research firm, where she conducted statistical analysis relating to clinical trials. Prior to that position, Mi-Ling worked with a retail firm doing predictive analytics in the marketing area.

Mi-Ling is a key member of a team that Jeremy forms to design a test campaign aimed at identifying new customers for a specific offer that Cellularplex will market in the coming year. The goal of the test campaign is to identify demographic characteristics of individuals who would likely purchase the offer and to determine the best delivery method for various combinations of demographic characteristics. The knowledge gained will be employed in designing a subsequent large-scale campaign to attract new customers.

The team members brainstorm a large number of characteristics that they think are indicative of people who might respond positively. Then they work with a data vendor to obtain a list of people with these characteristics. They also obtain the contact details for a small random sample of people who do not have the characteristics that they have identified, realizing that information from a group outside their chosen demographics could yield information on customers who might otherwise be overlooked. The team also determines different delivery methods for the offer, and with Mi-Ling's help they include these in their design. Finally they agree on how to measure customer response—for each contact, they will record whether the result was a customer inquiry, purchase of the offer, purchase of a different offer, or rejection.

The duration of the test campaign is set at three months, starting in the second quarter. Mi-Ling will support the effort, but in the meantime she wants to devote some thought to how she will analyze the kind of data it will generate. She will need to use the numerous measured characteristics and the response of each individual to classify each into one of the four possible categories, and thus determine those likely to become customers and those unlikely to become customers. Mi-Ling starts learning about JMP, which is used by the engineers at Cellularplex, and soon finds out that it has powerful visualization and modeling capabilities, which she hopes to put to good use when the real data arrive.

Knowing that she will have to undertake this analysis quickly once the data become available, Mi-Ling looks for a published data set that she can use for practice, both to learn how to use JMP and to see how it performs relative to other software that she has used. Specifically, she would like a data set with a large number of descriptive characteristics where classification of subjects into two or more categories is of primary interest.

Given her previous medical background, she easily finds and downloads an appropriate data set—the Wisconsin Breast Cancer Diagnostic Data Set. Her plan is to use various techniques in JMP to fit classification models to this data set. Realizing that some of the Cellularplex engineers are experienced JMP users, Mi-Ling connects with a few of her associates to ask if they would be willing to help her if necessary. James, an experienced JMP user, spends a couple of hours with Mi-Ling, giving her an introduction and offering to help her with further questions as they arise. What James shows Mi-Ling impresses her and gives her a good starting point for learning more on her own.

In this case study, you will join Mi-Ling as she works with some of the JMP capabilities for exploring and modeling high-dimensional data. She begins by using visualization techniques to help build an understanding of the Wisconsin Breast Cancer Diagnostic Data Set. After dividing the data into a training set, a validation set, and a test set, she applies three different modeling approaches to the training data—she fits a logistic model, a partition model, and two neural net models. Then she compares the performance of these four models on the validation set, chooses one of these as her final model, and uses the test set to assess its predictive performance.

This case study uses the principles of Visual Six Sigma to construct knowledge. This type of knowledge can eventually be used to guide sound business decisions. By its nature, this case study continues through the Model Relationships step of the Visual Six Sigma Data Analysis Process, but it does not involve the Revise Knowledge and Utilize Knowledge activities. These activities will become relevant once the classification scheme that Mi-Ling eventually develops for the marketing data is implemented as part of the formal marketing campaign.

Framing the Problem and Collecting the Data: The Wisconsin Breast Cancer Diagnostic Data Set

The Wisconsin Breast Cancer Diagnostic Data Set arises in connection with diagnosing breast tumors based on a fine needle aspirate.[1] In this study, a small-gauge needle is used to remove fluid directly from the lump or mass. The fluid is placed on a glass slide and stained so as to reveal the nuclei of the cells. An imaging system is used to determine the boundaries of the nuclei. A typical image consists of 10 to 40 nuclei. The associated software computes ten characteristics for each nucleus: radius, perimeter, area, texture, smoothness, compactness, number of concave regions, size of concavities (a *concavity* is an indentation in the cell nucleus), symmetry, and *fractal dimension* of the boundary (a measure of regularity of the contour). Values of the last seven characteristics were computed in such a way that larger values correspond to more irregular cells.[2]

A set of 569 lumps with known diagnoses (malignant or benign) was sampled, and each resulting image was processed as described above. Since a typical image can contain from 10 to 40 nuclei, the measurements were summarized. For each characteristic, the mean, max, and standard error of the mean were computed, resulting in 30 variables. The model developed by the researchers was based on separating hyperplanes.[3] A best model was chosen by applying cross-validation to estimate prediction accuracy, using all 569 records as a training set. This best model involved only three variables, mean texture, max area, and max smoothness (which, because of how smoothness was computed, indicates *least* smoothness), and achieved an estimated classification accuracy of 97.5 percent. Even more remarkably, 131 subsequent patients were diagnosed with 100 percent accuracy.

Mi-Ling downloads this data set from http://archive.ics.uci.edu/ml/datasets.html, where it is called *Breast Cancer Wisconsin (Diagnostic)*. The data file downloads as comma-delimited text, which she imports into JMP using its text filter under **File > Open**. She enters the column names and saves the file as **CellClassification_1.jmp.** A partial view of the data table is presented in Exhibit 9.2.

Image ID	Diagnosis	Mean Radius	Mean Perimeter	Mean Area
842302	M	17.99	122.80	1001.00
842517	M	20.57	132.90	1326.00
84300903	M	19.69	130.00	1203.00
84348301	M	11.42	77.58	386.10
84358402	M	20.29	135.10	1297.00
843786	M	12.45	82.57	477.10
844359	M	18.25	119.60	1040.00
84458202	M	13.71	90.20	577.90
844981	M	13.00	87.50	519.80
84501001	M	12.46	83.97	475.90
845636	M	16.02	102.70	797.80
84610002	M	15.78	103.60	781.00
846226	M	19.17	132.40	1123.00
846381	M	15.85	103.70	782.70
84667401	M	13.73	93.60	578.30
84799002	M	14.54	96.73	658.80
848406	M	14.68	94.74	684.50
84862001	M	16.13	108.10	798.80
849014	M	19.81	130.00	1260.00
8510426	B	13.54	87.46	566.30
8510653	B	13.08	85.63	520.00
8510824	B	9.50	60.34	273.90
8511133	M	15.34	102.50	704.40
851509	M	21.16	137.20	1404.00
852552	M	16.85	110.00	904.60

EXHIBIT 9.2   Partial View of CellClassification_1.jmp

There are 32 columns: an ID column, a column indicating the diagnosis into malignant (M) or benign (B), and the 30 summary variables. These are arranged as the ten *Mean* variables, followed by the ten *Max* variables, followed by the ten *standard error (SE)* variables.

Uncovering Relationships

As suggested by the Visual Six Sigma Roadmap (Exhibit 3.30), Mi-Ling begins her analysis of the Wisconsin Breast Cancer Diagnostic Data Set by visualizing the data one variable at a time, two variables at a time, and more than two at a time. This provides her with the knowledge that there are strong relationships between the 30 predictors and the diagnosis into benign or malignant masses.

One Variable at a Time

Mi-Ling opens the data table **CellClassification_1.jmp**. As a first step, she obtains distribution reports for all of the variables other than ImageID, which is simply an identifier. She notes that each variable other than **Diagnosis** has a name beginning with Mean, Max, or SE, indicating which summary statistic has been calculated—the mean, max, or standard error of the mean of the measured quantity. She selects **Analyze > Distribution** and populates the launch dialog as shown in Exhibit 9.3.

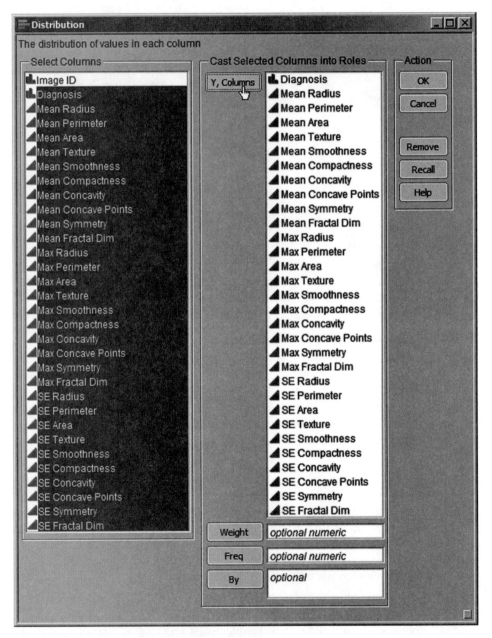

EXHIBIT 9.3   Launch Dialog for Distribution Platform

Upon clicking **OK**, she sees 31 distribution reports, the first four of which are shown in Exhibit 9.4. The vertical layout for the graphs is the JMP default. Mi-Ling knows that she can change this either interactively or more permanently in **File > Preferences**, but she is happy with this layout for now.

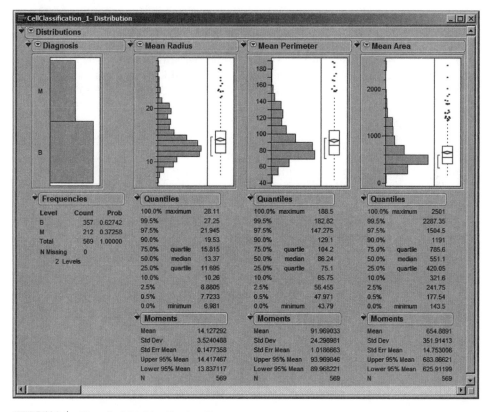

EXHIBIT 9.4   First 4 of 31 Distribution Reports

The bar graph corresponding to **Diagnosis** indicates that 212, or 37.258 percent, of the tumors in the study were assigned the value M, indicating they were malignant rather than benign. Scrolling through the plots for the 30 predictors, Mi-Ling assesses the shape of the distributions and the presence of possible outliers. She notes that most distributions are skewed toward higher values and that there may be some outliers, for example, for **SE Concavity**. She also determines, by looking at **N** under **Moments**, that there are no missing values for any of the variables. All in all, the data are well-behaved—she expects her marketing data to be much messier—but she decides that this is a good practice data set given her goal.

Mi-Ling saves a script to recreate the analysis in Exhibit 9.4 to her data table as described in Chapter 3, calling it **Distribution – 31 Variables**. When she does this, the script name is placed in the table panel at the upper left of the data table. To run this script in the future, Mi-Ling can simply click on the red triangle next to its name and choose **Run Script**.

Two Variables at a Time

DISTRIBUTION AND DYNAMIC LINKING   Next, Mi-Ling addresses the issue of bivariate relationships among the variables. Of special interest to her is whether the predictors are useful in predicting the values of **Diagnosis**, the dependent variable.

To get some initial insight on this issue, she returns to her distribution report. In the graph for **Diagnosis**, Mi-Ling clicks on the bar corresponding to M. This has the effect of selecting all rows in the data table for which **Diagnosis** has the value M. These rows are dynamically linked to all plots, and so, in the 30 histograms corresponding to predictors, areas that correspond to the rows where **Diagnosis** is M are highlighted.

For four of the histograms that correspond to Mean characteristics, Exhibit 9.5 shows the highlighting that results when Mi-Ling selects M in the **Diagnosis** bar chart. She notes that malignant masses tend to have high values for these four variables. By scrolling through the remaining plots, she sees that there are relationships with most of the other variables as well. In fact, for most, but not all, of the variables, malignant masses tend to have larger values than do benign masses.

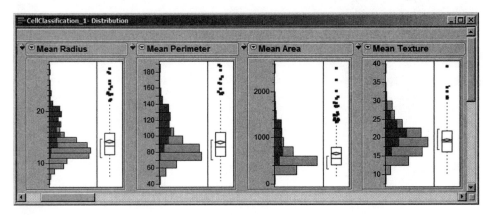

EXHIBIT 9.5   **Histograms for Four Mean Variables, with Malignant Masses Highlighted**

Mi-Ling then clicks on the bar for **Diagnosis** equal to B for additional insight. Mi-Ling concludes that there are clear relationships between **Diagnosis** and the 30 potential predictors. She is optimistic that she can build good models for classifying a mass as malignant or benign based on these predictors.

CORRELATIONS AND SCATTERPLOT MATRIX   Mi-Ling is also interested in how the 30 predictors relate to each other. To see bivariate relationships among these 30 continuous predictors, she decides to look at correlations and scatterplots. She selects **Analyze > Multivariate Methods > Multivariate**. In the launch dialog, she enters all 30 predictors, from **Mean Radius** to **SE Fractal Dimension**, as **Y, Columns** (see

Exhibit 9.6). There is a drop-down menu at the bottom of the dialog that allows the user to choose one of five estimation methods; this choice is driven by considerations such as the nature of the data and the extent of missing values. Mi-Ling trusts JMP to choose the best method for her.

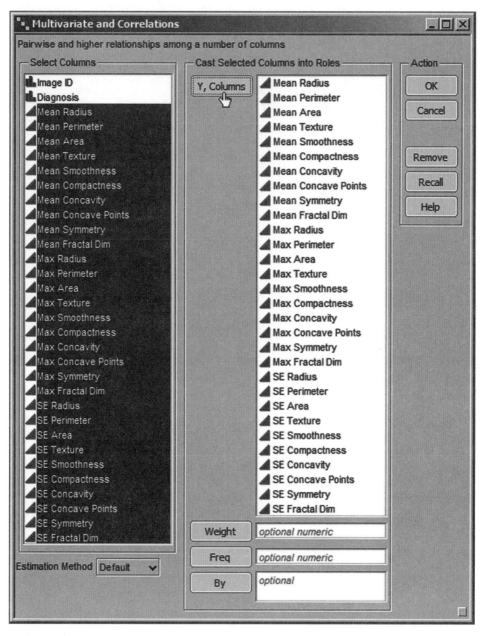

EXHIBIT 9.6   Launch Dialog for Multivariate and Correlations Report

When Mi-Ling clicks **OK**, a report containing a correlation matrix appears (a partial view is shown in Exhibit 9.7).

	Mean Radius	Mean Perimeter	Mean Area	Mean Texture	Mean Smoothness	Mean Compactness	Mean Concavity
CellClassification_1- Multivariate							
Multivariate							
Correlations							
Mean Radius	1.0000	0.9979	0.9874	0.3238	0.1706	0.5061	0.6768
Mean Perimeter	0.9979	1.0000	0.9865	0.3295	0.2073	0.5569	0.7161
Mean Area	0.9874	0.9865	1.0000	0.3211	0.1770	0.4985	0.6860
Mean Texture	0.3238	0.3295	0.3211	1.0000	-0.0234	0.2367	0.3024
Mean Smoothness	0.1706	0.2073	0.1770	-0.0234	1.0000	0.6591	0.5220
Mean Compactness	0.5061	0.5569	0.4985	0.2367	0.6591	1.0000	0.8831
Mean Concavity	0.6768	0.7161	0.6860	0.3024	0.5220	0.8831	1.0000
Mean Concave Points	0.8225	0.8510	0.8233	0.2935	0.5537	0.8311	0.9214
Mean Symmetry	0.1477	0.1830	0.1513	0.0714	0.5578	0.6026	0.5007
Mean Fractal Dim	-0.3116	-0.2615	-0.2831	-0.0764	0.5848	0.5654	0.3368
Max Radius	0.9695	0.9695	0.9627	0.3526	0.2131	0.5353	0.6882
Max Perimeter	0.9651	0.9704	0.9591	0.3580	0.2389	0.5902	0.7296
Max Area	0.9411	0.9415	0.9592	0.3435	0.2067	0.5096	0.6760
Max Texture	0.2970	0.3030	0.2875	0.9120	0.0361	0.2481	0.2999
Max Smoothness	0.1196	0.1505	0.1235	0.0775	0.8053	0.5655	0.4488
Max Compactness	0.4135	0.4558	0.3904	0.2778	0.4725	0.8658	0.7550
Max Concavity	0.5269	0.5639	0.5126	0.3010	0.4349	0.8163	0.8841
Max Concave Points	0.7442	0.7712	0.7220	0.2953	0.5031	0.8156	0.8613
Max Symmetry	0.1640	0.1891	0.1436	0.1050	0.3943	0.5102	0.4095
Max Fractal Dim	0.0071	0.0510	0.0037	0.1192	0.4993	0.6874	0.5149
SE Radius	0.6791	0.6918	0.7326	0.2759	0.3015	0.4975	0.6319
SE Perimeter	0.6742	0.6931	0.7266	0.2817	0.2961	0.5489	0.6604
SE Area	0.7359	0.7450	0.8001	0.2598	0.2466	0.4557	0.6174
SE Texture	-0.0973	-0.0868	-0.0663	0.3864	0.0684	0.0462	0.0762
SE Smoothness	-0.2226	-0.2027	-0.1668	0.0066	0.3324	0.1353	0.0986
SE Compactness	0.2060	0.2507	0.2126	0.1920	0.3189	0.7387	0.6703
SE Concavity	0.1942	0.2281	0.2077	0.1433	0.2484	0.5705	0.6913
SE Concave Points	0.3762	0.4072	0.3723	0.1639	0.3807	0.6423	0.6833
SE Symmetry	-0.1043	-0.0816	-0.0725	0.0091	0.2008	0.2300	0.1780
SE Fractal Dim	-0.0426	-0.0055	-0.0199	0.0545	0.2836	0.5073	0.4493

EXHIBIT 9.7   Partial View of Correlation Matrix for 30 Predictors

Mi-Ling prefers to see plots, so she clicks on the red triangle at the top of the report next to **Multivariate** and chooses **Scatterplot Matrix**. This gives a 30 × 30 matrix showing all bivariate scatterplots for the 30 predictors. The 6 × 6 portion of the matrix corresponding to the first six Mean variables is shown in Exhibit 9.8. She saves the script that generates this output to the data table as **Scatterplots – 30 Predictors**.

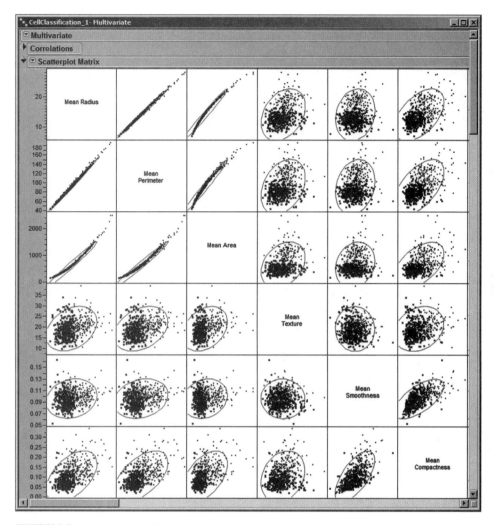

EXHIBIT 9.8 Partial View of Correlation Matrix: Six Mean Variables

"It would be nice to see how **Diagnosis** fits into the scatterplot display," thinks Mi-Ling. James had shown her that in many plots one can simply right-click to color or mark points by the values in a given column. So, she right-clicks in various locations in the scatterplot. When she right-clicks in an off-diagonal square, the menu shown in Exhibit 9.9 appears. Mi-Ling hovers over **Row Legend** with her cursor, reads the tool-tip that appears, and realizes that this is exactly what she wants—a legend that colors the rows according to the values in the **Diagnosis** column.

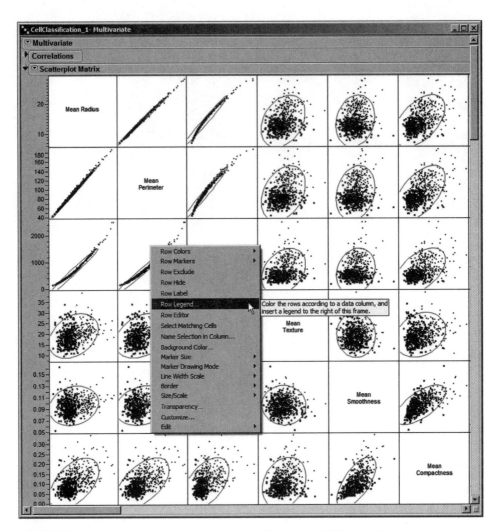

EXHIBIT 9.9   Context-Sensitive Menu from Right-Click on an Off-Diagonal Square

When Mi-Ling clicks on **Row Legend**, a **Mark by Column** dialog appears. Here, she chooses Diagnosis. The default colors don't look appropriate to her—red, a color typically associated with danger, is associated with B, which is a good outcome, and blue is associated with M, a bad outcome (Exhibit 9.10). She would like to see these colors reversed.

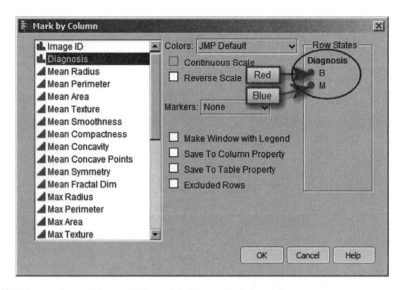

EXHIBIT 9.10   Mark by Column Dialog with Diagnosis Selected

So, she checks the box next to **Reverse Scale**—this switches the colors. Then, she explores what is available under **Markers**, viewing the updated display in the dialog's **Row States** panel. She settles on **Hollow** markers, because these will show well in grayscale printouts. After a quick telephone call to James, at his suggestion, she checks **Make Window with Legend** and **Save to Column Property**. James indicates that **Make Window with Legend** will provide her with a separate legend window that is handy, especially when viewing large or three-dimensional plots. He also suggests **Save to Column Property**, as this will save her color scheme to the Diagnosis column, which she may find useful later on. The launch window with her selections is shown in Exhibit 9.11. She clicks **OK**.

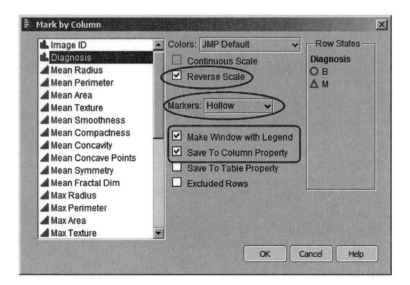

EXHIBIT 9.11   Completed Mark by Column Dialog

Mi-Ling observes that the colored markers now appear in her data table next to the row numbers. Also, an asterisk appears next to **Diagnosis** in the columns panel. She clicks on it, and it indicates **Value Colors** (Exhibit 9.12). Clicking on **Value Colors** takes her to the Diagnosis **Column Info** dialog, where she sees that the colors have been applied to B and M as she requested.

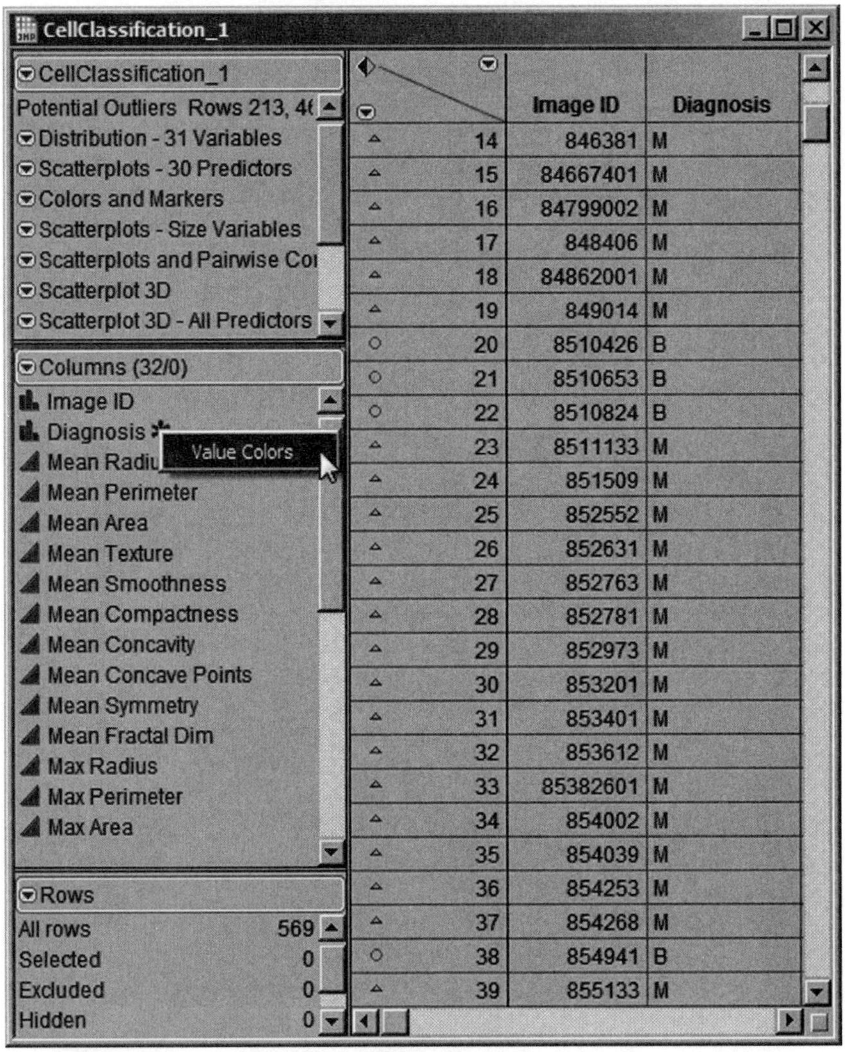

	Image ID	Diagnosis
14	846381	M
15	84667401	M
16	84799002	M
17	848406	M
18	84862001	M
19	849014	M
20	8510426	B
21	8510653	B
22	8510824	B
23	8511133	M
24	851509	M
25	852552	M
26	852631	M
27	852763	M
28	852781	M
29	852973	M
30	853201	M
31	853401	M
32	853612	M
33	85382601	M
34	854002	M
35	854039	M
36	854253	M
37	854268	M
38	854941	B
39	855133	M

CellClassification_1 panel:
- CellClassification_1
- Potential Outliers Rows 213, 4(
- Distribution - 31 Variables
- Scatterplots - 30 Predictors
- Colors and Markers
- Scatterplots - Size Variables
- Scatterplots and Pairwise Co
- Scatterplot 3D
- Scatterplot 3D - All Predictors
- Columns (32/0)
  - Image ID
  - Diagnosis
  - Mean Radiu — Value Colors
  - Mean Perimeter
  - Mean Area
  - Mean Texture
  - Mean Smoothness
  - Mean Compactness
  - Mean Concavity
  - Mean Concave Points
  - Mean Symmetry
  - Mean Fractal Dim
  - Max Radius
  - Max Perimeter
  - Max Area
- Rows
  - All rows   569
  - Selected   0
  - Excluded   0
  - Hidden   0

EXHIBIT 9.12   Markers in Data Table and Value Colors Property

The colors and markers appear in the scatterplots as well, and a legend is inserted to the right of the matrix as part of the report. Exhibit 9.13 shows the rightmost part of the scatterplot matrix along with the inserted legend.

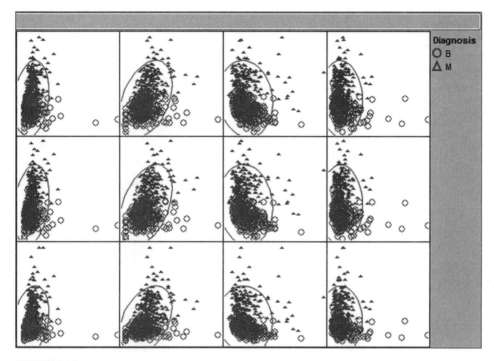

EXHIBIT 9.13   Top Right Portion of Correlation Matrix with Legend for Markers and Colors

Mi-Ling has also created the portable legend window that is shown in Exhibit 9.14. (The script **Colors and Markers** will add the colors and markers but will not produce the freestanding legend window.)

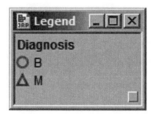

EXHIBIT 9.14   The Portable Legend Window

Mi-Ling moves the portable legend into the upper left portion of her scatterplot matrix, as shown in Exhibit 9.15. Here, she has clicked on the B level for **Diagnosis**. This selects all rows where **Diagnosis** is B and highlights these points in plots, as can be seen in the portion of the scatterplot matrix shown in Exhibit 9.15. To unselect the B rows, Mi-Ling holds the control key as she clicks on the B level in the legend. Note that the built-in legend shown in Exhibit 9.13 can also be used to select points.

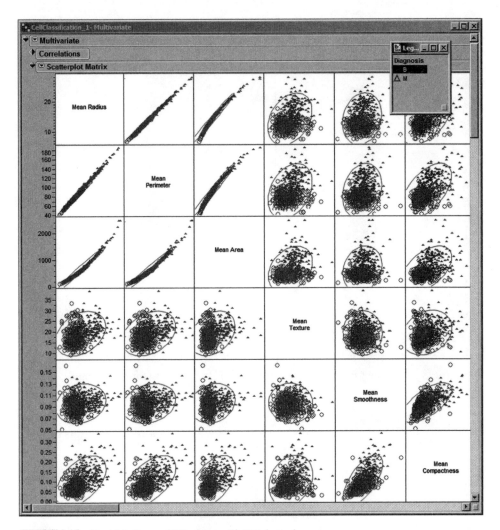

EXHIBIT 9.15   Portable Legend Window with B Selected

Mi-Ling turns her attention to the radius, perimeter, and area variables. She thinks of these as *size* variables, namely, variables that describe the size of the nuclei. **Mean Radius, Mean Perimeter**, and **Mean Area** show strong pairwise relationships, as do the Max and SE versions of the size variables. To view these relationships in greater detail, Mi-Ling obtains three **Multivariate** reports: one for the Mean size variables, one for the Max size variables, and one for the SE size variables. The reports for the Mean and SE size variables are shown in Exhibit 9.16. (The script is **Scatterplots – Size Variables**.)

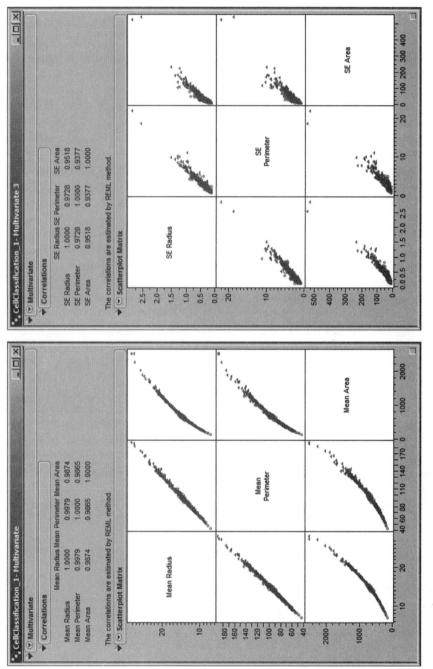

EXHIBIT 9.16   Scatterplot Matrices for Mean and SE Size Variables

For example, Mi-Ling sees from the plots that **Mean Radius** and **Mean Perimeter** are highly correlated. Also, the **Correlations** panel indicates that their correlation coefficient is 0.9979. Given what is being measured, she notes that this is not an unexpected result. She also sees that **Mean Area** is highly correlated with both **Mean Radius** and **Mean Perimeter**. These relationships show some curvature and appear to be quadratic. Giving this a little thought, Mi-Ling realizes that this is reasonable, since the area of a circle depends on the square of its radius and circumference.

Similar relationships extend to the variables **Max Radius**, **Max Perimeter**, and **Max Area**, as well as to the variables **SE Radius**, **SE Perimeter**, and **SE Area**, albeit in a weaker form.

For documentation purposes, Mi-Ling would like to save a single script that recreates all three of these **Multivariate** reports. To do this, she saves the script for one of the reports to the data table. The script is automatically saved with the name **Multivariate 2**, where the **2** is added because the table already contains a script called **Multivariate**. Then, Mi-Ling clicks on the red triangle to the left of **Multivariate 2** and selects **Edit**.

In the script text box, she enters a semicolon after the very last line; this is how JMP Scripting Language (JSL) glues statements together. Then she copies the code that is there and pastes it twice at the very end of the code in the text window. Having done this, Mi-Ling then changes the variable names in the obvious way, replacing Mean with Max in the second **Multivariate** function and Mean with SE in the third. She renames the script **Scatterplots – Size Variables**. (If you rename your script using this name, a suffix of 2 will be added as part of its name in the data table, since Mi-Ling's script with this name is already saved to the data table. In her script, for convenience, you will see that we have added a **Color by Column** command.)

PAIRWISE CORRELATIONS   At this point, Mi-Ling wonders which variables are most strongly correlated with each other, either in a positive or negative sense. The scatterplot certainly gives her some clear visual information. However, a quick numerical summary showing correlations for all pairs of variables would be nice.

She closes the three size variable reports that she has just created and returns to the **Multivariate** report for the 30 predictors (if you have closed this report, you can retrieve it by running the script **Scatterplots – 30 Predictors**). She clicks on the disclosure icons next to **Correlations** and **Scatterplot Matrix** to close these parts of the report, and then selects **Pairwise Correlations** from the red triangle next to **Multivariate**. Mi-Ling saves this new script as **Scatterplots and Pairwise Correlations**.

Mi-Ling would like to see the correlations sorted in descending order. She remembers something that James showed her. In the **Pairwise Correlations** panel, Mi-Ling right-clicks, and the menu shown in Exhibit 9.17 appears. James had mentioned that this is a standard menu that usually appears when you right-click in a report containing text or numeric results.

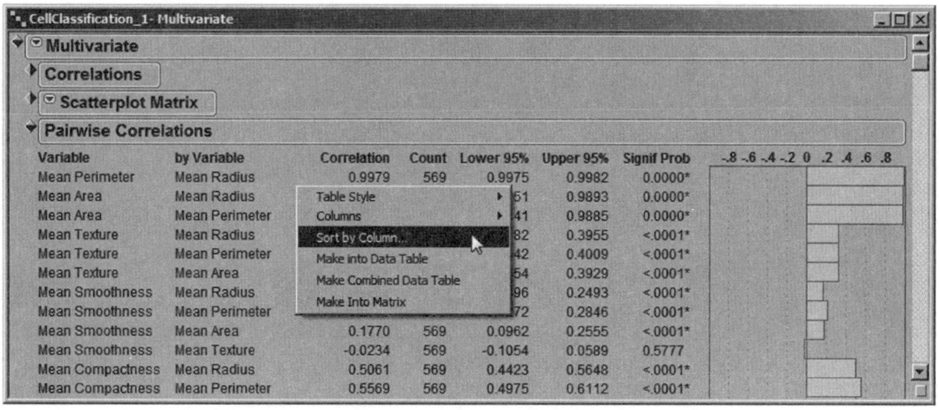

EXHIBIT 9.17   Context-Sensitive Menu from a Right-Click in Table Panel

Mi-Ling selects **Sort by Column**, and a pop-up list appears allowing her to choose the column by which to sort. She chooses Correlation (Exhibit 9.18) and clicks **OK**.

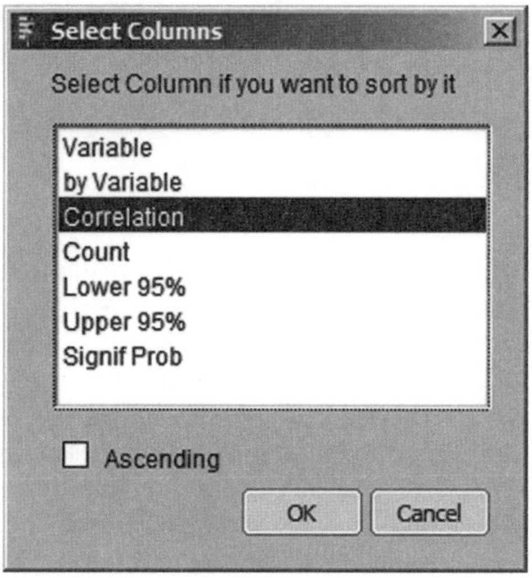

EXHIBIT 9.18   Pop-Up List for Column Selection

"How many pairwise correlations are there?" Mi-Ling wonders. She reasons: There are 30 variables, each of which can be paired with 29 other variables, giving $30 \times 29 = 870$ combinations; but these double-count the correlations, so there are $870/2 = 435$ distinct pairwise correlations. These 435 correlations are sorted in descending order. Exhibit 9.19 shows the 20 most positive and 10 most negative correlations.

CellClassification_1- Multivariate

▼ **Multivariate**
▶ **Correlations**
▶ **Scatterplot Matrix**
▼ **Pairwise Correlations**

Variable	by Variable	Correlation	Count	Lower 95%	Upper 95%	Signif Prob	-.8 -.6 -.4 -.2 0 .2 .4 .6 .8
Mean Perimeter	Mean Radius	0.9979	569	0.9975	0.9982	0.0000*	
Max Perimeter	Max Radius	0.9937	569	0.9926	0.9947	0.0000*	
Mean Area	Mean Radius	0.9874	569	0.9851	0.9893	0.0000*	
Mean Area	Mean Perimeter	0.9865	569	0.9841	0.9885	0.0000*	
Max Area	Max Radius	0.9840	569	0.9812	0.9864	0.0000*	
Max Area	Max Perimeter	0.9776	569	0.9736	0.9810	0.0000*	
SE Perimeter	SE Radius	0.9728	569	0.9680	0.9769	0.0000*	
Max Perimeter	Mean Perimeter	0.9704	569	0.9652	0.9748	0.0000*	
Max Radius	Mean Radius	0.9695	569	0.9642	0.9741	0.0000*	
Max Radius	Mean Perimeter	0.9695	569	0.9641	0.9741	0.0000*	
Max Perimeter	Mean Radius	0.9651	569	0.9590	0.9704	0.0000*	
Max Radius	Mean Area	0.9627	569	0.9562	0.9683	0.0000*	
Max Area	Mean Area	0.9592	569	0.9521	0.9653	0.0000*	
Max Perimeter	Mean Area	0.9591	569	0.9520	0.9652	0.0000*	
SE Area	SE Radius	0.9518	569	0.9434	0.9590	<.0001*	
Max Area	Mean Perimeter	0.9415	569	0.9314	0.9502	<.0001*	
Max Area	Mean Radius	0.9411	569	0.9309	0.9498	<.0001*	
SE Area	SE Perimeter	0.9377	569	0.9269	0.9469	<.0001*	
Mean Concave Points	Mean Concavity	0.9214	569	0.9080	0.9329	<.0001*	
Max Texture	Mean Texture	0.9120	569	0.8971	0.9249	<.0001*	
SE Smoothness	Mean Perimeter	-0.2027	569	-0.2802	-0.1225	<.0001*	
Max Perimeter	Mean Fractal Dim	-0.2052	569	-0.2826	-0.1251	<.0001*	
SE Smoothness	Max Perimeter	-0.2173	569	-0.2942	-0.1376	<.0001*	
SE Smoothness	Mean Radius	-0.2226	569	-0.2993	-0.1430	<.0001*	
SE Smoothness	Max Radius	-0.2307	569	-0.3071	-0.1514	<.0001*	
Max Area	Mean Fractal Dim	-0.2319	569	-0.3082	-0.1526	<.0001*	
Max Radius	Mean Fractal Dim	-0.2537	569	-0.3290	-0.1751	<.0001*	
Mean Fractal Dim	Mean Perimeter	-0.2615	569	-0.3364	-0.1832	<.0001*	
Mean Fractal Dim	Mean Area	-0.2831	569	-0.3570	-0.2057	<.0001*	
Mean Fractal Dim	Mean Radius	-0.3116	569	-0.3840	-0.2355	<.0001*	

EXHIBIT 9.19   Most Positive 20 and Most Negative 10 Correlations

In this report, Mi-Ling again notes the high correlations among the Mean size variables, the Max size variables, and the SE size variables, which appear in the top part of Exhibit 9.19. She also notes that the Max size variables are very highly correlated with the Mean size variables. Again, this is an expected result. In fact, scanning further down the report, Mi-Ling observes that the Mean and Max variables for the same characteristics tend to have fairly high correlations, as expected.

Many of the large negative correlations involve fractal dimension and the size measures. Recall that the larger the fractal dimension the more irregular the contour. Six such correlations are shown in the bottom part of Exhibit 9.19. This suggests that larger cells tend to have more regular contours than smaller cells. How interesting! Mi-Ling wonders if this apparent relationship might be an artifact of how fractal dimension was measured.

A BETTER LOOK AT MEAN FRACTAL DIMENSION   To get a better feeling for relationships between size variables and fractal dimension, Mi-Ling explores Mean Fractal Dim and Mean Radius. She selects **Analyze > Fit Y by X**, enters Mean Radius as **Y, Response**, Mean Fractal Dim as **X, Factor**, and clicks **OK**. Her bivariate report is shown in Exhibit 9.20.

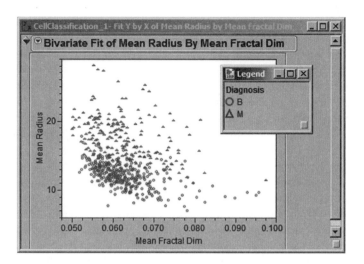

EXHIBIT 9.20   Bivariate Plot for Mean Radius and Mean Fractal Dim

As the correlation coefficient indicates, the combined collection of benign and malignant cells exhibits a decreasing relationship between **Mean Radius** and **Mean Fractal Dim**. However, given a value of **Mean Fractal Dim**, **Mean Radius** appears to be higher for malignant cells than for benign cells.

Mi-Ling would like to fit lines to each **Diagnosis** grouping in Exhibit 9.20. She clicks on the red triangle in the report and selects **Group By**. This opens a list from which Mi-Ling can select a grouping column. She selects **Diagnosis** and clicks **OK**. Then she clicks again on the red triangle and selects **Fit Line**. The report updates to show the plot in Exhibit 9.21. She saves this script as **Bivariate**.

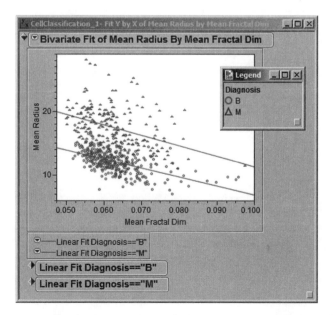

EXHIBIT 9.21   Bivariate Plot for Mean Radius and Mean Fractal Dim, with Lines Fit by Diagnosis

In fact, there is a very big difference between the two diagnosis groups, based on how **Mean Radius** and **Mean Fractal Dim** are related. Mi-Ling can see that for many pairs of values on these two variables one could make a good guess as to whether a mass is benign or malignant. She can see where she would need additional variables to help distinguish the two groups in that murky area between the fitted lines. But this is encouraging—it should be possible to devise a good classification scheme.

At this point, Mi-Ling remembers that one of the pitfalls of interpreting correlations of data containing a grouping or classification variable is that two variables may seem highly correlated, but when broken down by the levels of the classification variable, this correlation may actually be small. This was clearly not the case for **Mean Radius** and **Mean Fractal Dim**. However, she wonders if this might be the case for any of her other correlations.

From their plot in the scatterplot matrix, Mi-Ling suspects that **Mean Area** and **Mean Compactness** may provide an example of this pitfall. The correlation matrix indicates that their correlation is 0.4985, which seems somewhat substantial. To see the relationship between these two variables more clearly, she selects **Analyze > Multivariate Methods > Multivariate**, and enters only Mean Area and Mean Compactness as **Y, Columns**. Clicking **OK** gives the report in Exhibit 9.22. The points as a whole show a positive relationship, with **Mean Area** increasing with **Mean Compactness**.

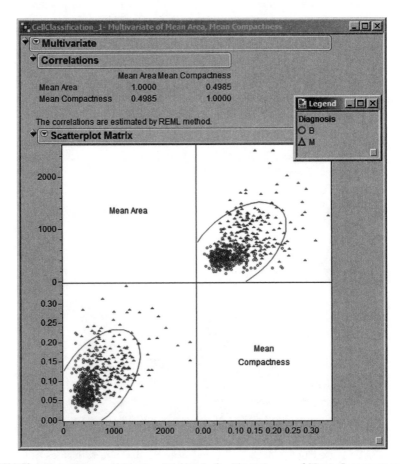

EXHIBIT 9.22   Correlation and Scatterplot Matrix for Mean Area and Mean Compactness

But what happens if the two Diagnosis groups are separated? Mi-Ling returns to **Analyze > Multivariate Methods > Multivariate**, clicks on **Recall** to repopulate the menu with the previous entries, and adds Diagnosis as a **By** variable. (The script is saved as **Multivariate**.) As she suspected, the resulting report, shown in Exhibit 9.23, shows that for each Diagnosis grouping there is very little correlation between these two variables.

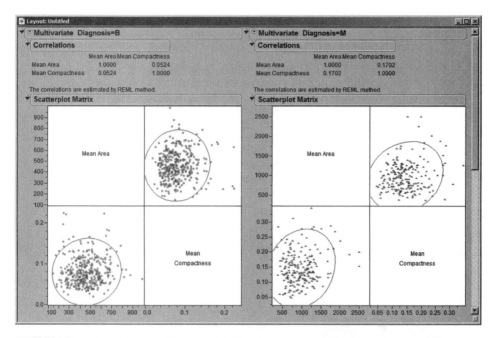

EXHIBIT 9.23   Correlations and Scatterplots for Mean Area and Mean Compactness by Diagnosis

The apparent correlation when the data are aggregated is a function of how the two Diagnosis groups differ relative to the magnitudes of the two predictors. She makes a note to keep this phenomenon in mind when she is analyzing her test campaign data. (We note in passing that the arrangement seen in Exhibit 9.23 is created using **Edit > Layout**. You can learn about this feature in **Help**.)

Part of what motivates Mi-Ling's interest in correlations is simply that they help to understand pairwise relationships. Another aspect, though, is that she is aware that strong correlations lead to multicollinearity, which can cause problems for *explanatory* models—model coefficients and their standard errors can be too large and the coefficients can have the wrong signs. However, Mi-Ling realizes that her interest is in *predictive* models. For these models, the individual coefficients themselves, and hence the impact of multicollinearity, are of less importance, so long as future observations have the same correlation structure.

In examining the scatterplot matrix further, Mi-Ling notes that there may be a few bivariate outliers. If this were her marketing data set, she would attempt to obtain more background on these records to get a better understanding of how to deal with them. For now, she chooses not to take any action relative to these points.

However, she makes a mental note that later she might want to revisit their inclusion in model-building since they have the potential to be influential. (We invite you, the reader, to explore whether the exclusion of some of these outliers might lead to better models.)

More Than Two Variables at a Time

Thinking back to her analysis of pairwise correlations, Mi-Ling realizes that the ability to color and mark points by **Diagnosis** class, a nominal variable, has in effect allowed her to do three-dimensional visualization. But what if all three variables of interest are continuous? What if there are more than three variables of interest? Mi-Ling is anxious to see how JMP can help with visualization in this setting. At this point, Mi-Ling tidies up by closing all her open reports but leaves the portable legend window open.

Under **Graph**, Mi-Ling sees something called **Scatterplot 3D**. She thinks that this might be a useful tool for three-dimensional explorations. To start, she is interested in viewing the three-dimensional relationship among the three size variables, **Mean Radius**, **Mean Perimeter**, and **Mean Area**. She selects **Graph > Scatterplot 3D** and enters the three size variables as **Y, Columns** (see Exhibit 9.24).

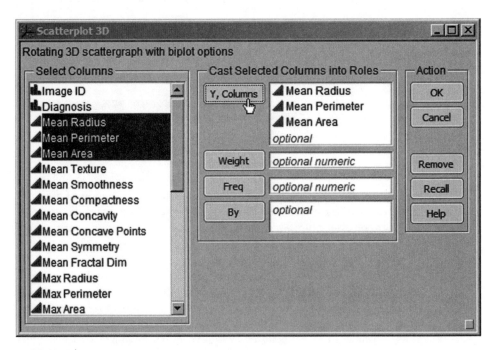

EXHIBIT 9.24   Launch Dialog for Scatterplot 3D

When she clicks **OK**, a rotatable three-dimensional plot of the data appears. She rotates this plot to better see the relationships of the three predictors with **Diagnosis**

(Exhibit 9.25). The strength of the three-dimensional relationship is striking. However, it is not clear where one would define a split into the two Diagnosis classes. Mi-Ling saves the script that generates this plot as **Scatterplot 3D**.

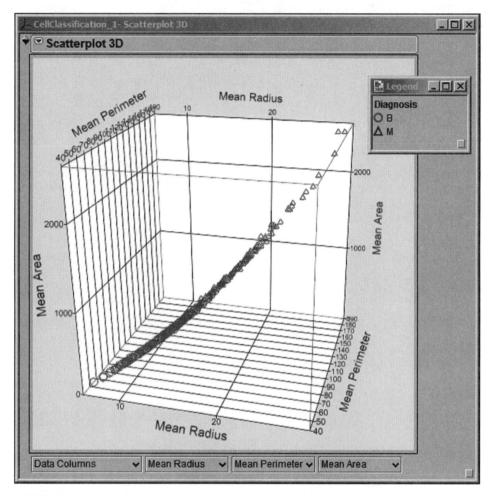

EXHIBIT 9.25   Three-Dimensional View of Mean Size Variables, by Diagnosis

Mi-Ling returns to **Graph > Scatterplot 3D** and enters all 30 predictor variables as **Y, Columns** in the **Scatterplot 3D** launch dialog. She clicks **OK** and obtains a plot showing the same three variables as in Exhibit 9.25, since they were the first listed. She sees that JMP allows the user to select any three variables for the axes from the drop-down lists at the bottom of the plot (Exhibit 9.26). In fact, Mi-Ling discovers that by clicking on the arrow at the bottom right of the plot, she can cycle through all possible combinations of three axis choices, of which there are many.

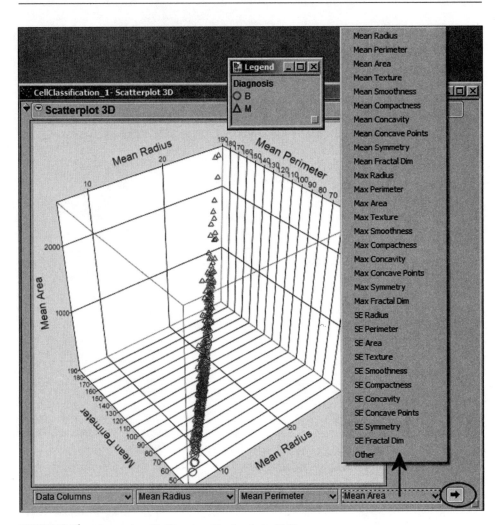

EXHIBIT 9.26   Scatterplot 3D Showing List for Axis Choice

One of the plots catches her attention. To see it again, Mi-Ling makes selections from the lists to redisplay it, choosing **Max Radius, Max Concave Points,** and **Max Texture**. She rotates this plot (Exhibit 9.27) and notes that the two diagnosis classes have a reasonable degree of separation in this three-dimensional space. This is encouraging, again suggesting that a good classification scheme is possible. She saves the script that generates this rotated plot, as well as 3D plots for all the other variables, as **Scatterplot 3D – All Predictors**.

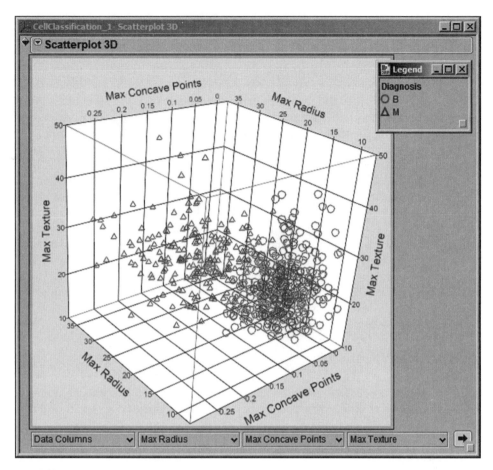

EXHIBIT 9.27 Scatterplot 3D for Max Radius, Max Concave Points, and Max Texture

Pleased that she can view the data in this fashion, Mi-Ling decides to move on to her modeling efforts. She suspects that she will want to pursue more three-dimensional visualization as she develops and assesses her models. She closes all reports, as well as the legend window.

Constructing the Training, Validation, and Test Sets

At this point, Mi-Ling has accumulated enough knowledge to realize that she should be able to build a strong classification model. She is ready to move on to the Model Relationships step of the Visual Six Sigma Data Analysis Process. However, she anticipates that the marketing study will result in a large and unruly data set, probably with many outliers, some missing values, irregular distributions, and some categorical data. It will not be nearly as small or as clean as her practice data set. So, she wants to consider modeling from a data-mining perspective.

From her previous experience, Mi-Ling knows that some data-mining techniques, such as recursive partitioning and neural nets, fit highly parameterized nonlinear models that have the potential to fit the anomalies and noise in a data set, as well as the signal. These data-mining techniques do not allow for variable selection based on hypothesis tests, which, in classical modeling, help the analyst choose models that do not overfit or underfit the data.

To balance the competing forces of overfitting and underfitting in data-mining efforts, one often divides the available data into at least two and sometimes three distinct sets. Since the tendency to overfit data may introduce bias into models fit and validated using the same data, just a portion of the data, called the *training set*, is used to construct several potential models. One then assesses the performance of these models on a hold-out portion of the data called the *validation set*. A best model is chosen based on performance on the validation data. Since choosing a model based on the validation set can also lead to overfitting, in situations where the model's predictive ability is important, a third independent set of the data is often reserved to test the model's performance. This third set is called the *test set*.[4]

With these issues in mind, Mi-Ling proceeds to construct three analysis data sets: a training set, a validation set, and a test set. She defines these in her data table and runs a quick visual check to see that there are no obvious issues arising from how she divided the data. Then she uses row state variables to facilitate selecting the rows that belong to each analysis set.

Defining the Training, Validation, and Test Sets

Admittedly, Mi-Ling's data set of 569 observations is small and well-behaved compared to most data sets where data-mining techniques are applied. But she reminds herself that she is working with this smaller, more manageable data set in order to learn how to apply techniques to the much larger marketing data set that she will soon need to analyze, as well as to any other large databases with which she may work in the future.

Mi-Ling will divide her data set of 569 rows into three portions:

- A training set consisting of about 60 percent of the data.
- A validation set consisting of about 20 percent of the data.
- A test set consisting of the remaining 20 percent of the data.

This is a typical split used in data-mining applications, where a large share of the data is used to develop models, while smaller shares are used to compare and assess models.

Mi-Ling wants to assign rows to these groups randomly. With some help from James, she sees how she can accomplish this using the formulas for random number generation provided in JMP. Mi-Ling inserts a new column in her data table. (If you prefer not to work through defining this new column, you can insert it by running the script **Random Unif**.) She does this by double-clicking in the column header area to the right of the column that is furthest to the right in the data table, **SE Fractal Dim**. The text **Column 33** appears and is selected, ready for her to type in a column name. But she is not ready to do this yet, and so she clicks away the column header, and then double-clicks back on it. This opens the **Column Info** window. From the **Column Properties** menu, Mi-Ling selects **Formula** (see Exhibit 9.28).

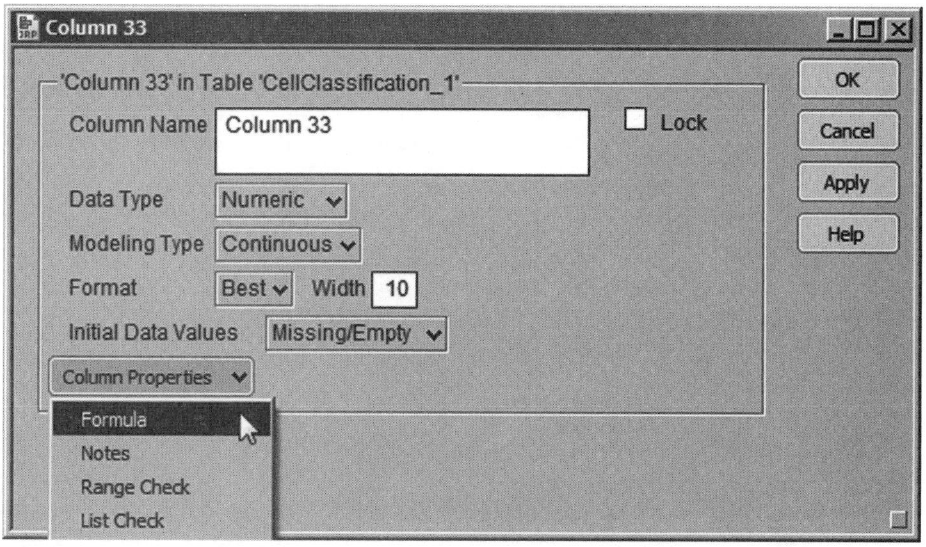

EXHIBIT 9.28   Column Info Dialog with Formula Selected from Column Properties

Once she has selected **Formula**, the **Column Info** menu updates with a panel for the **Formula** and an **Edit Formula** button (Exhibit 9.29). Had a formula already been entered, it would display in this **Formula** panel.

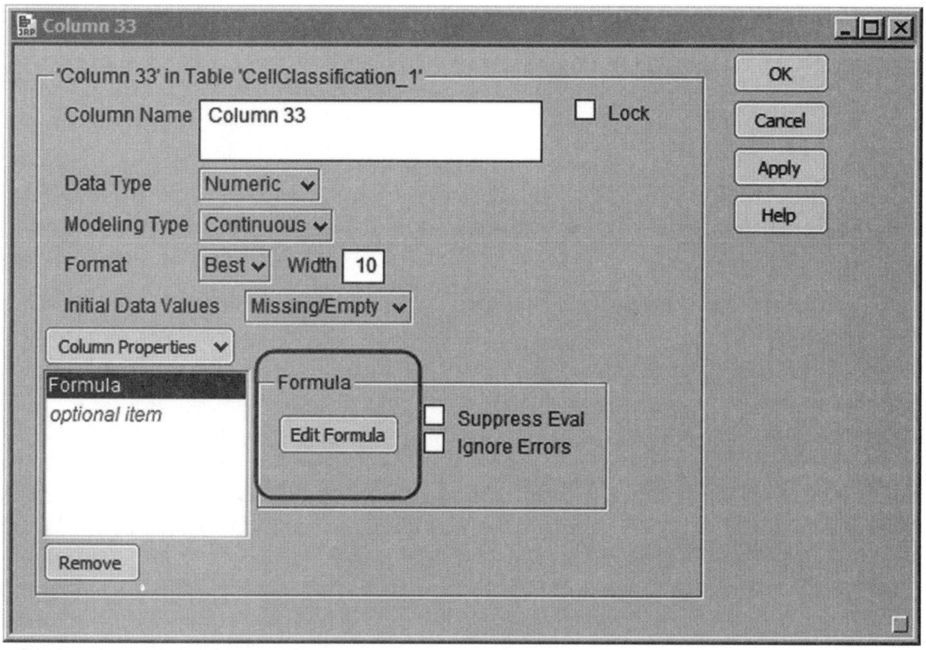

EXHIBIT 9.29   Column Info Dialog with Formula Panel

Since Mi-Ling wants to enter a formula, she clicks **Edit Formula**. This opens the formula editor. Here, Mi-Ling notices that the formula expressions are arranged into groups, in the list **Functions (grouped)**. She scrolls down until she comes to **Random** (Exhibit 9.30). Here, she is impressed with the many different types of distributions from which random values can be generated. She recalls that a uniform distribution is one that assigns equal likelihood to all values between 0 and 1 and realizes this will make it easy for her to assign rows to her 60-20-20 percent sampling scheme. She selects **Random Uniform**, as shown in Exhibit 9.30.

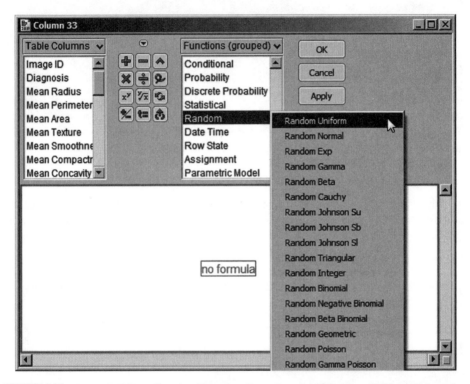

EXHIBIT 9.30   Formula Editor Showing Function Groupings with Random Uniform Selected

The formula **Random Uniform()** appears in the formula editor window. Mi-Ling clicks **Apply** in the formula editor. This enters values into her new column. She checks these values, and they appear to be random values between 0 and 1. Just to see what happens, she clicks **Apply** again. The values change—it appears that whenever she clicks **Apply,** new random values are generated. This is very nice, but Mi-Ling sees that it could lead to problems later on if she or someone else were to access the formula editor for this column and click **Apply**. So, since she no longer needs the formula, she clicks on the box outlining the formula to select it and then clicks the delete key on her keyboard.

Then Mi-Ling clicks **OK** and returns to the **Column Info** dialog, which is still open. She types in Random Unif as the **Column Name** and clicks **OK**. The new column in the data table now has the name Random Unif, and it is populated with values randomly chosen between 0 and 1.

Because the random uniform command chooses values between 0 and 1 with equal likelihood, the proportion of values in this column that fall between 0 and 0.6 will be about 60 percent, the proportion between 0.6 and 0.8 will be about 20 percent, and the proportion between 0.8 and 1.0 will be about 20 percent. Mi-Ling will use this as the basis for her assignment of rows to the training, validation, and test subsets. She will define a column called **Data Set Indicator** that will assign values in these proportions to the three analysis subsets. (If you prefer not to work through setting up this column and defining the assignments, you may run the script **Data Set Indicator**.)

Mi-Ling inserts another new column by double-clicking to the right of **Random Unif**. She replaces the highlighted **Column 34** with the name for her new column, **Data Set Indicator**. She will define values in this column using a formula, but this time she takes a shortcut to get to the formula editor. She clicks away from the column header and then right-clicks back on it. The context-sensitive menu shown in Exhibit 9.31 appears. From this menu, Mi-Ling chooses **Formula**. This opens the formula editor window.

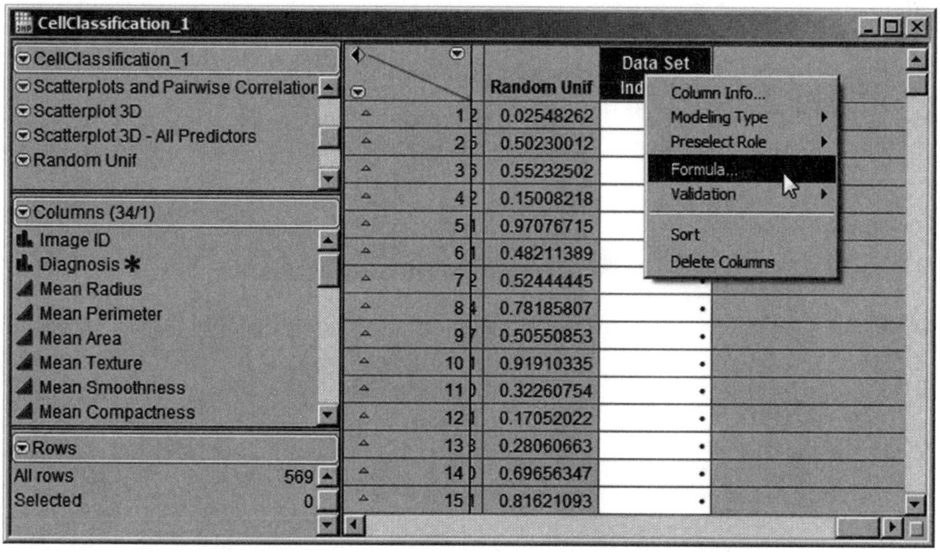

EXHIBIT 9.31 Context-Sensitive Menu Obtained from Right-Click in Column Header Area

Once in the formula editor, Mi-Ling begins the process of entering the formula (shown in its completed form in Exhibit 9.38) that assigns rows to one of the three data sets based on the value of the random uniform value assigned in the column **Random Unif**. Here are the steps that Mi-Ling follows in constructing this formula:

- From **Functions (grouped)**, Mi-Ling chooses **Conditional > If** (Exhibit 9.32). This gives the conditional function template in Exhibit 9.33.
- Since she wants four conditional clauses, Mi-Ling proceeds to insert these. She selects the last box in the template, which is a placeholder for the **else clause** (Exhibit 9.34).

- Then, she locates the insertion key in the top right corner of the keypad (Exhibit 9.35). She clicks the insertion key four times to obtain her desired configuration (Exhibit 9.36).
- Now Mi-Ling needs to populate the boxes. She selects the first **expr** box and clicks on Random Unif in the **Table Columns** listing. This inserts Random Unif into the selected box, as shown in Exhibit 9.37.
- Using her keyboard, Mi-Ling types the symbols: **< = 0.6**. This completes the first expression.
- Now, she selects the first **then clause** box. She clicks on it and types in the text **"Training Set"** with the quotes. She realizes that quotes are needed, because she is entering a character value.
- She completes the second and third clauses in a similar fashion. When she is finished, her formula appears as in Exhibit 9.38.
- She leaves the final **else** clause as is. This has the effect of assigning a missing value to any row for which Random Unif does not fall into one of the three groupings defined in the preceding clauses. Although Mi-Ling knows that she has covered all possible values of Random Unif in the first three expressions, she realizes that it is good practice to include a clause to catch errors in a conditional formula such as this one.
- Finally, she clicks **OK** to close the formula editor. The Data Set Indicator column is now populated based on the values of Random Unif. In addition, as she notes from the columns panel, the column Data Set Indicator has been assigned a nominal modeling type, consistent with its character data values.

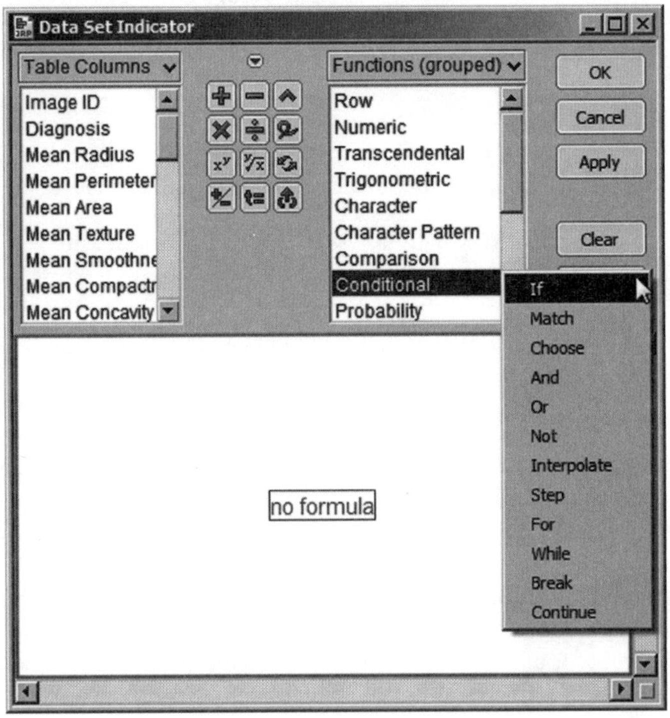

EXHIBIT 9.32   Conditional Function Choices

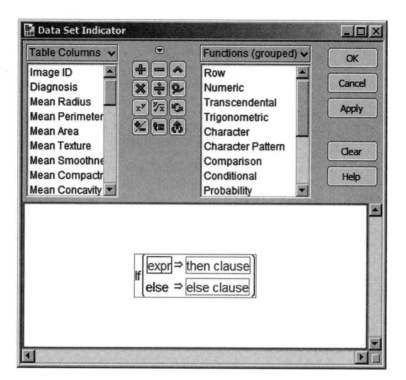

EXHIBIT 9.33   Conditional Formula Template

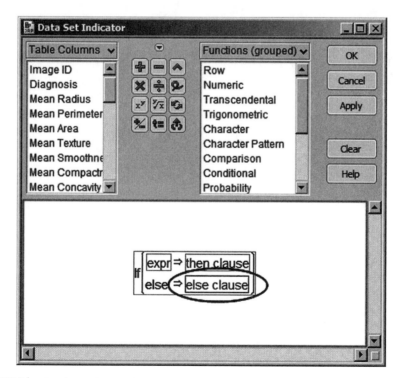

EXHIBIT 9.34   Conditional Formula Template with Else Clause Selected

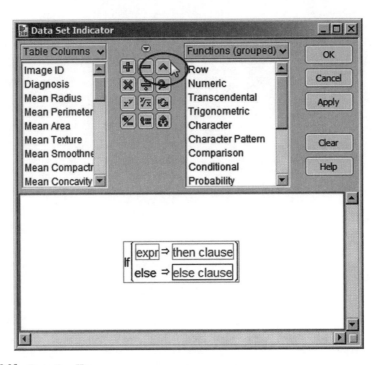

EXHIBIT 9.35   Insertion Key

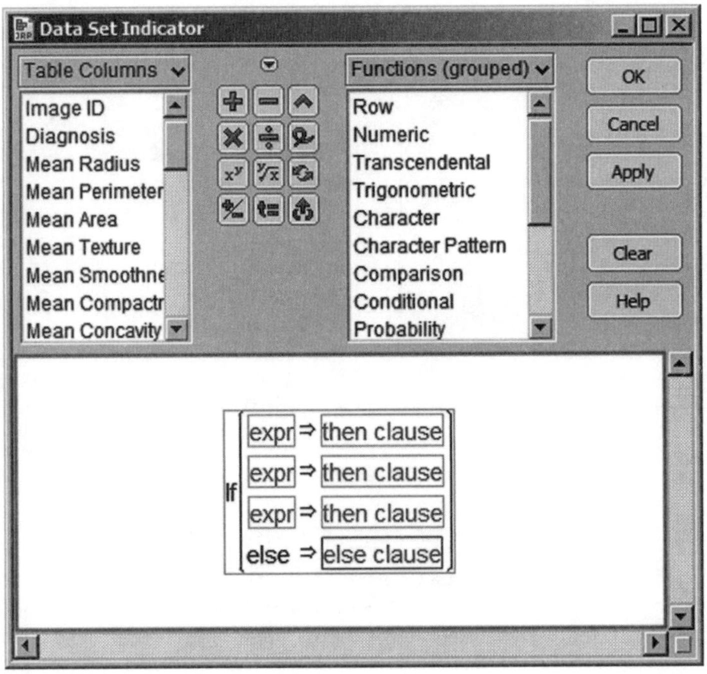

EXHIBIT 9.36   Conditional Template after Four Insertions

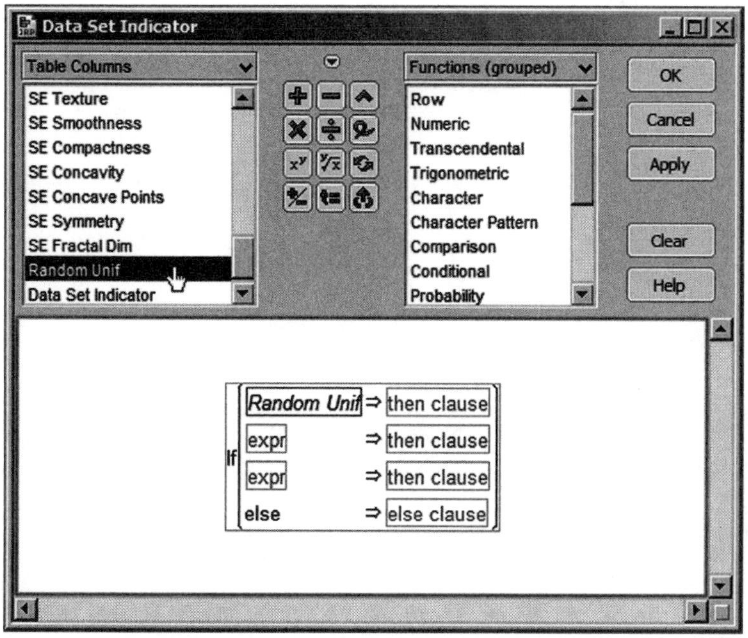

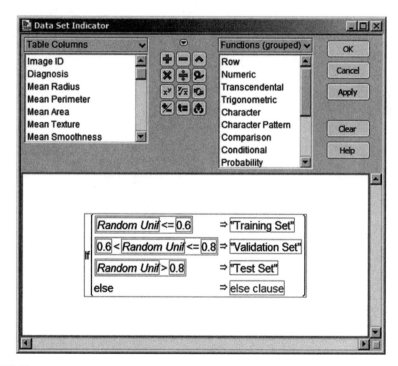

EXHIBIT 9.37   Insertion of Random Unif into Expr Box

EXHIBIT 9.38   Formula Defining Data Set Indicator Column

There is one last detail that Mi-Ling wants to address before finishing her work on the column **Data Set Indicator**. When she thinks about her three data sets, she associates a temporal order with them: First, the training set, second, the validation set, and, finally, the test set. When these data sets appear in plots or reports, she wants to see them in this order. This means that she needs to tell JMP how she wants them ordered. She can do this using the **Value Ordering** column property.

By double-clicking in the column header area for **Data Set Indicator**, Mi-Ling opens the **Column Info** dialog window. (She could also right-click in the **Data Set Indicator** column header area, then choose **Column Info** from the options list.) Under **Column Properties**, she chooses **Value Ordering** (Exhibit 9.39).

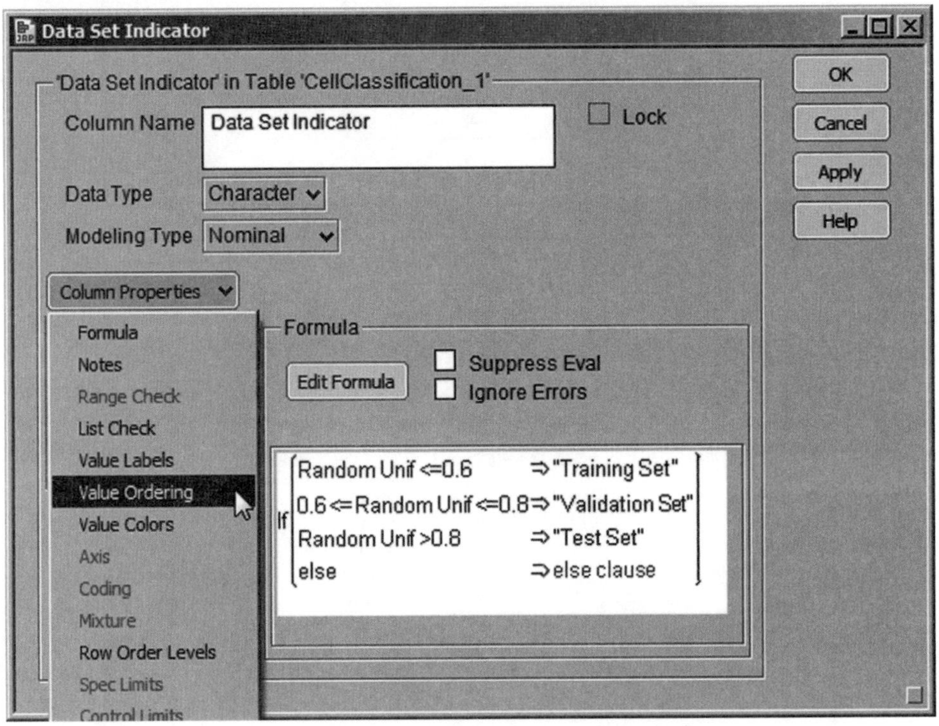

EXHIBIT 9.39   Value Ordering Choice from Column Properties Menu

Once this is selected, a new dialog opens where she can set the ordering of the three values (Exhibit 9.40). She would like these values to appear in the order: Training Set, Validation Set, and Test Set. All she needs to do is to select Test Set, and then click **Move Down** twice. (This property can be assigned by the script **Value Ordering**.)

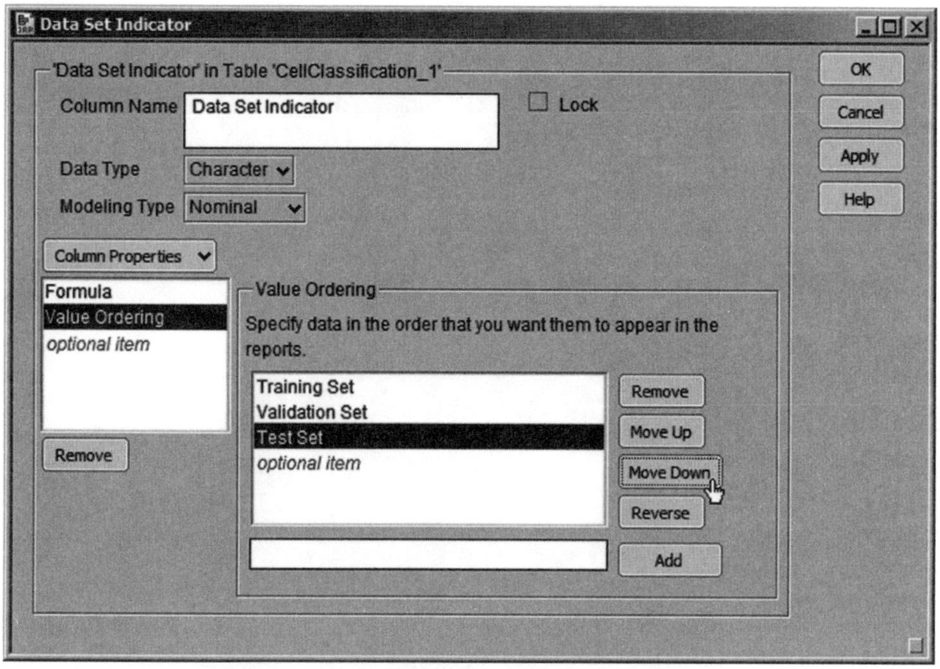

EXHIBIT 9.40   Value Ordering Dialog with Sets in Desired Order

When Mi-Ling clicks **OK**, this property is assigned to Data Set Indicator and is marked by an asterisk that appears next to the column name in the columns panel. Clicking on this asterisk opens a list showing the property **Value Ordering**. Clicking on **Value Ordering** takes Mi-Ling to that column property in **Column Info**.

Mi-Ling realizes that she will not have further need for the column Random Unif. She could delete it at this point, but decides to retain it, just in case. However, she would rather not see it in the data table or in lists of columns in launch dialogs. So, she decides to hide it and exclude it. To this end, Mi-Ling right-clicks on the column name in the columns panel and chooses both **Hide** and **Exclude** (Exhibit 9.41). Two small icons appear to the right of the column name to indicate that it is hidden and excluded (Exhibit 9.42).

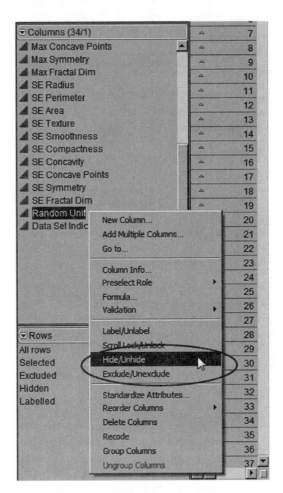

EXHIBIT 9.41   Context-Sensitive Menu Obtained in Columns Panel

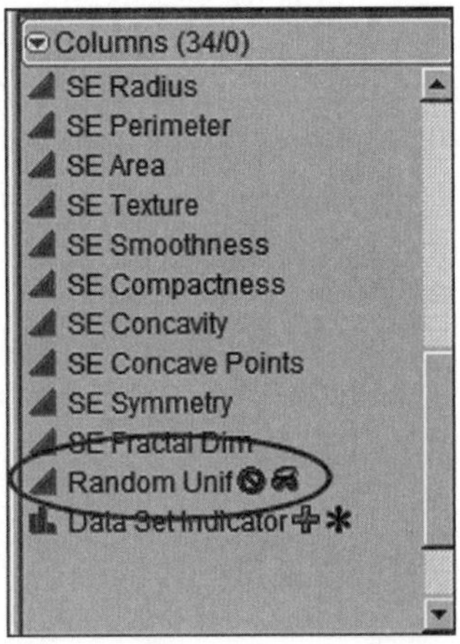

EXHIBIT 9.42   Columns Panel Showing Exclude and Hide Symbols for Random Unif Column

Checking the Analysis Data Sets Using Graph Builder

Now, if you have been working along with Mi-Ling using **CellClassification_1.jmp** and have constructed these two columns, then you realize that since Random Unif contains randomly generated values, your columns and Mi-Ling's will differ. At this point you should switch to a data table that contains Mi-Ling's training, validation, and test sets. The data table **CellClassification_2.jmp** contains her work to this point. Her analysis will continue, using this second data table.

Now Mi-Ling wants to examine her three analysis data sets, just to verify that they make sense. She begins by running **Distribution** on Data Set Indicator (Exhibit 9.43). She observes that the proportion of rows in each set is about what she wanted.

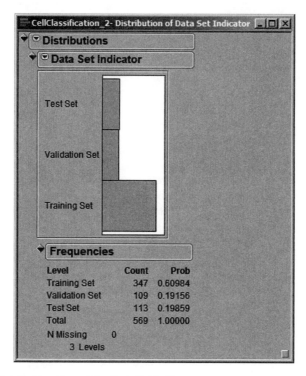

EXHIBIT 9.43   Distribution Report for Data Set Indicator

She is also interested in confirming that her training, validation, and test sets do not differ greatly in terms of the distributions of the predictors. James introduced Mi-Ling to **Graph Builder** (a new option in JMP 8), which is found under **Graph**. He demonstrated that it provides an intuitive and interactive interface for comparing the distributions of multiple variables in a variety of ways. She is anxious to try it out, thinking that it may be very useful in understanding her marketing data, which she anticipates will be messy.

Mi-Ling envisions a plot that has three vertical layers: one for the Mean variables, one for the Max variables, and one for the SE variables. She also envisions three horizontal groupings: one for each of the training, validation, and test sets. She selects **Graph > Graph Builder**. For a first try, in the window that appears, she selects all ten of the Mean variables and drags them to the Y zone in the template. She obtains the plot in Exhibit 9.44.

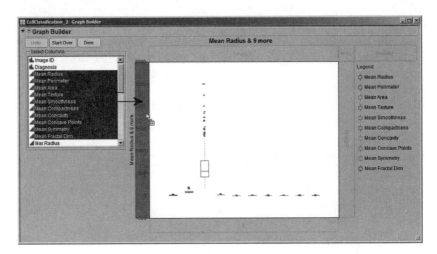

EXHIBIT 9.44   Graph Builder View of Ten Mean Variables

She notes that the scaling of the ten variables presents an issue. The third variable, **Mean Area**, covers such a large range of values that the distributions of the other nine variables are obscured. Mi-Ling clicks **Undo** in order to start over, this time using all Mean variables except for **Mean Area**. The resulting plot (Exhibit 9.45) is still unsatisfactory. It does suggest, though, that she might obtain acceptable plots if she were to construct three sets of plots:

- One for the Area variables only.
- One for the Radius, Perimeter, and Texture variables.
- One for the remaining variables.

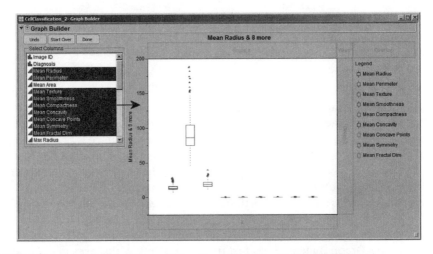

EXHIBIT 9.45   Graph Builder View of Nine Mean Variables, Excluding Mean Area

She begins with the Area variables, which cover such a range that they will be given their own plot. Mi-Ling clicks **Start Over**. She selects **Mean Area** and drags it to the **Y** zone. Then she selects **Data Set Indicator** and drags it to the **Group X** zone at the top of the template. This results in three box plots for **Mean Area**, one corresponding to each analysis set (Exhibit 9.46). Mi-Ling examines the three box plots and decides that the three data sets are quite similar relative to the distribution of **Mean Area**.

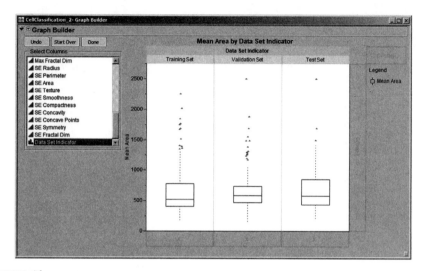

EXHIBIT 9.46   Graph Builder View of Mean Area by Data Set Indicator

What about the distributions of **Max Area** and **SE Area**? To add **Max Area** to the plot shown in Exhibit 9.46, Mi-Ling clicks and drags **Max Area** from the **Select Columns** list to the **Y** zone, dragging her cursor to that part of the **Y** zone that is just above 0, as shown in Exhibit 9.47. An *add to the bottom blue polygon* appears, creating a new layer of plots.

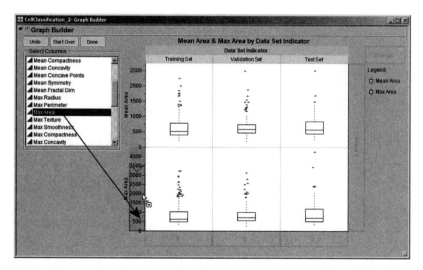

EXHIBIT 9.47   Mean Area and Max Area by Data Set Indicator

She repeats this procedure with **SE Area** to obtain the plot in Exhibit 9.48. Mi-Ling saves the script for this analysis to the data table as **Graph Builder – Area**.

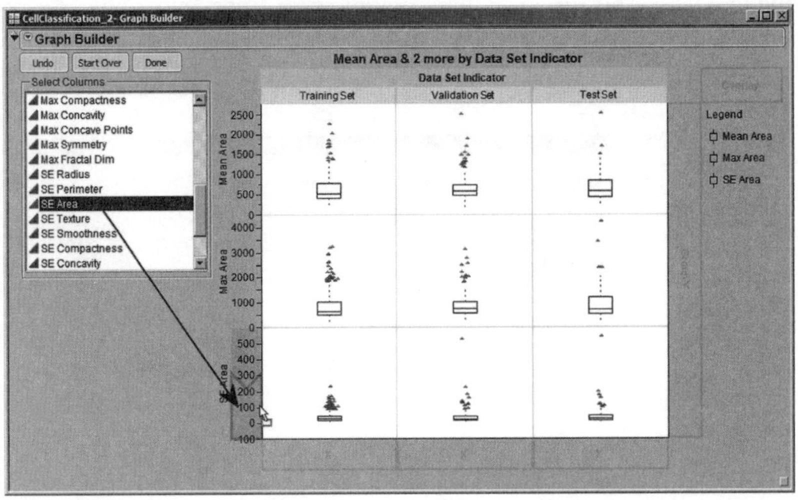

EXHIBIT 9.48   Mean Area, Max Area, and SE Area by Data Set Indicator

Mi-Ling reviews the plots in Exhibit 9.48 and notices the two large values of **SE Area**. These points fall beyond the range of **SE Area** values reflected in her training data set. Otherwise, the distributions of the area variables seem relatively similar across the three analysis data sets.

She uses her cursor to hover over each of these two outliers and identifies them as rows 213 and 462. To make sure that she does not forget about these, she adds this information to her data table as a **Table Variable**. In her data table, Mi-Ling clicks the red triangle to the left of the data table name and selects **New Table Variable**, as shown in Exhibit 9.49.

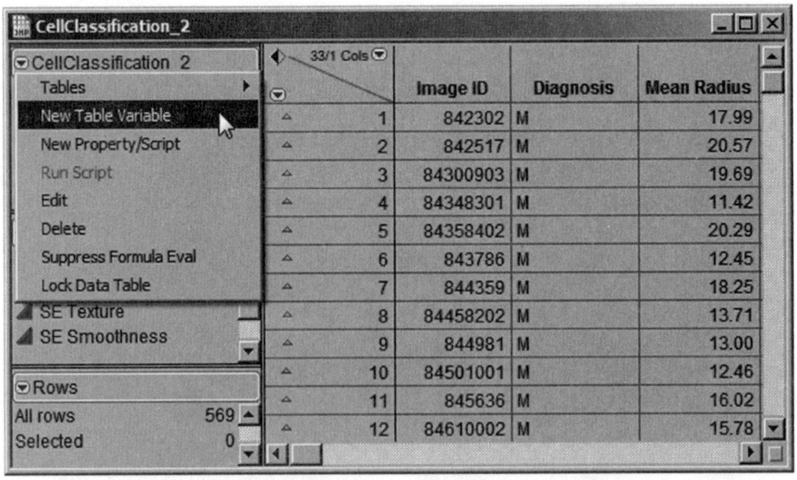

EXHIBIT 9.49   New Table Variable Selection

She fills out the text window that opens as shown in Exhibit 9.50. Then she clicks **OK**.

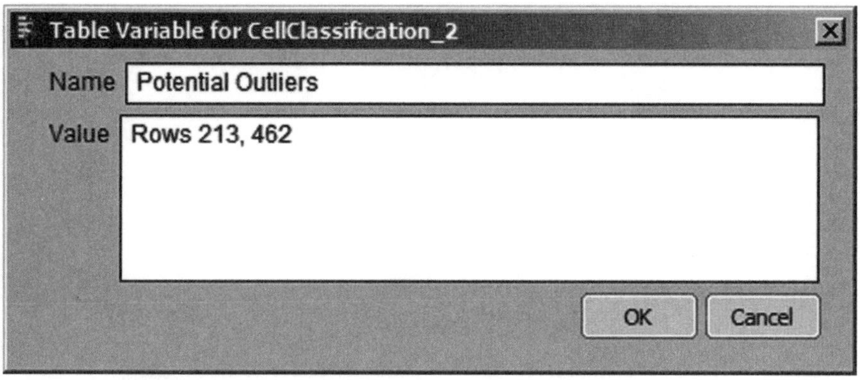

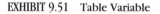

EXHIBIT 9.50 Table Variable Text Window

This information now appears in the table panel, as shown in Exhibit 9.51. Mi-Ling likes this. Defining a **Table Variable** is a convenient way to document information about the data table.

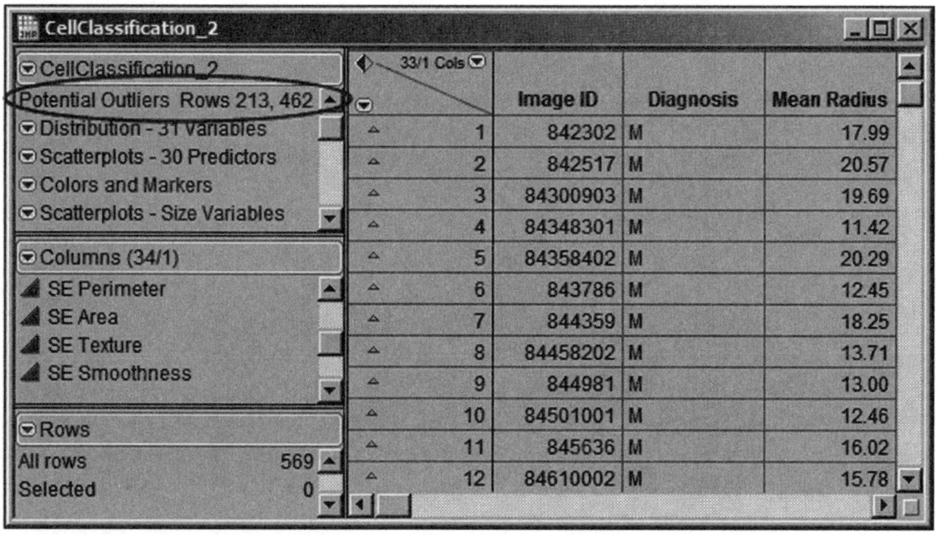

EXHIBIT 9.51 Table Variable

She now returns to her plot (Exhibit 9.48). Out of curiosity, Mi-Ling right-clicks in the top row of the plot area. A context-sensitive menu appears. She notices that she can switch to histograms or points, or add these to the plots, and that she can customize the plot in various ways. Just for fun, she chooses to change to histograms, making the choices shown in Exhibit 9.52.

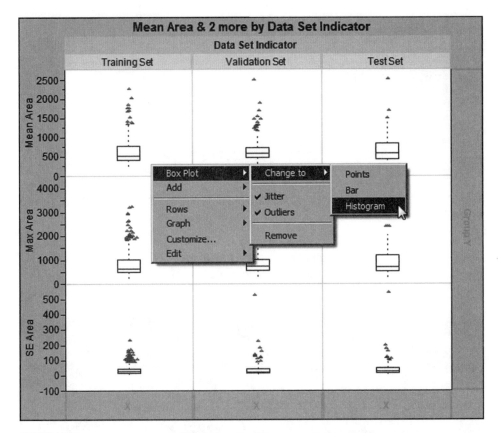

EXHIBIT 9.52   Context-Sensitive Menu Showing Histogram Option

When she clicks on **Histogram**, each plot in the first row changes from a box plot to a histogram. Since this change appears to work for one row at a time, to get the remaining two rows of box plots to appear as histograms, Mi-Ling goes to one of the other two rows, holds down the control key before right-clicking in one of these rows, and then releases it. She remembers that the control key can be used to *broadcast* commands, so it makes sense to her to try it here. Then she selects **Box Plot > Change to > Histogram**. As she had hoped, this turns all box plots in the display into histograms (Exhibit 9.53). Had she held the control key down prior to her initial click in the top row, all rows would have been changed at that point.

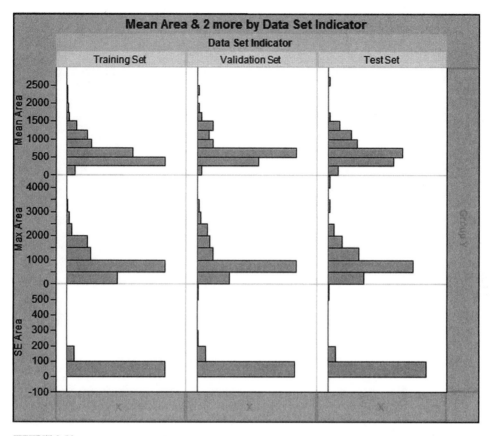

EXHIBIT 9.53   Histograms Replacing All Box Plots

Now Mi-Ling proceeds to study the other 27 variables. Her next plot involves the Mean, Max, and SE variables associated with Radius, Perimeter, and Texture. To construct this plot, she uses the same procedure that she used with the area variables. The only difference is that she selects three variables for each row of the plot; for example, for the first row, she selects **Mean Radius, Mean Perimeter**, and **Mean Texture**. The completed plot is shown in Exhibit 9.54. To the right of the plot, JMP provides color-coding to identify the groupings. Mi-Ling saves the script as **Graph Builder – Radius, Perimeter, Texture**.

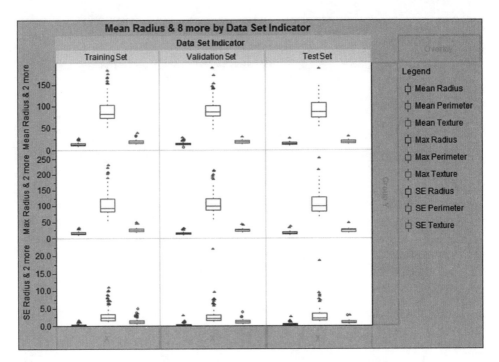

EXHIBIT 9.54   Graph Builder View of Radius, Perimeter, and Texture Variables

Mi-Ling observes that the distributions across the three analysis data sets are similar, with the exception of outlying points for **SE Perimeter** in the validation and test sets. She suspects that these outliers are associated with the outliers for **SE Area**. And they are: By hovering over these points, she notes that they correspond to rows 213 and 462.

Yet, she is curious about where these points appear in all of her plots to date. She places the plots shown in Exhibits 9.48 and 9.54 next to each other, as illustrated in Exhibit 9.55. Then she selects the two outliers in the plot for **SE Area**. When she selects them, these two points appear as large triangles in all plots. The linked view of the plots allows her to see where these points fall for all 12 variables across the **Data Set Indicator** groupings. She notes that they are somewhat outlying for **Mean Area** and **Mean Perimeter** as well, but do not appear to be an issue for the Texture variables.

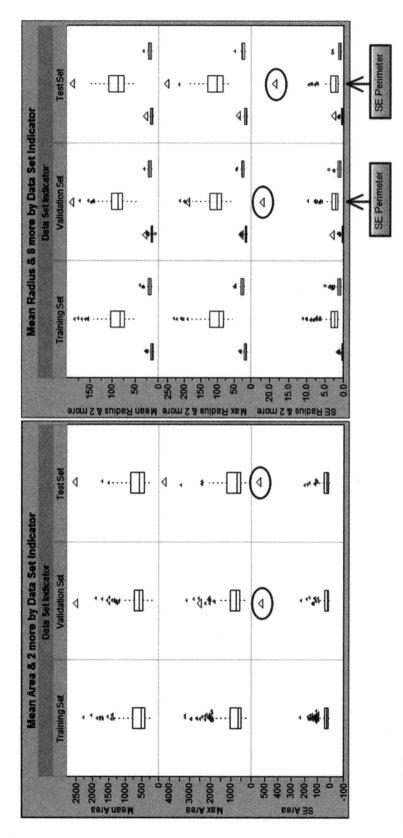

EXHIBIT 9.55   Selection of Outliers for SE Area

Since these are not in her training set, Mi-Ling is not overly concerned about them. However, she does note that they could affect her validation results (we will leave it to the reader to check that they do not). Before proceeding, she deselects these two points by clicking in the plots next to, but not on, the points. Alternatively, she could deselect them in the data table by clicking in the lower triangular area above the row numbers or by pressing the escape key while the data table is the active window.

Finally, Mi-Ling uses **Graph Builder** to construct a plot for the remaining six features: Smoothness, Compactness, Concavity, Concave Points, Symmetry, and Fractal Dim. This plot is shown in Exhibit 9.56; she saves the script as **Graph Builder – Smoothness to Fractal Dimension**.

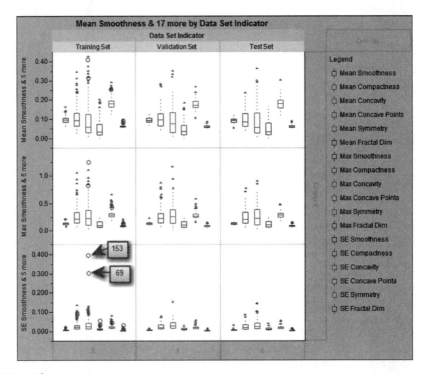

EXHIBIT 9.56   Graph Builder View for Remaining Six Variables

These distributions seem consistent across the three analysis data sets. The only exceptions are two large values for **SE Concavity** in the training set, which Mi-Ling identifies as rows 69 and 153. She selects these two points by dragging a rectangle around them in the **SE Concavity** box plot for the training set. Looking at the plots for the other 17 variables, she concludes that they do not appear anomalous for the other variables. Nonetheless, to keep track of these two rows, which could be influential for certain models, she adds them to her list of potential outliers in her **Potential Outliers** table variable.

Her graph builder analysis leaves Mi-Ling satisfied that she understands her training, validation, and test sets. She finds that they are fairly comparable in terms of predictor values and are not unreasonably affected by unruly data or outliers.

Thinking about her marketing data, she can see how **Graph Builder** will provide great flexibility for interactive exploration of multivariate relationships.

Mi-Ling is ready to start thinking about how to work with these three analysis data sets. At this point, she closes all of her open reports.

Defining Row State Variables

Mi-Ling realizes that she will want to start her work by developing models using her training data set, but that later on she will want to switch to her validation and test sets. She could segregate these three sets into three data tables, but it would be much easier to retain them in one data table. For example, as part of her modeling efforts, she will save prediction formulas to the data table. If her validation rows were in a separate table, she would have to copy her prediction formulas to that other table. That would be inconvenient. She prefers an approach that allows her to select each of the three analysis sets conveniently in a single table.

James suggested that Mi-Ling might want to use row state variables. A *row state* is an attribute that changes the way that JMP interacts with the observations that make up the data. There are six row state attributes: Selected, Excluded, Hidden, Labeled, Color, and Marker. For example, if a row is excluded, then values from that row are not used in calculations. However, values from that row will appear in plots. The hidden row state will ensure that a row is not displayed in plots. To both exclude and hide a row, both row state attributes must be applied.

James showed Mi-Ling how to define *row state variables*—these are columns that contain row state assignments, indicating if a particular row is selected, excluded, hidden, labeled, colored, or marked. Mi-Ling plans to make it easy to switch from one analysis set to another by defining row state variables.

First of all, Mi-Ling will identify her training set. She checks to make sure that she still has colors and markers assigned to the rows in her data table. (If you have cleared yours, be sure to reapply them before continuing. You may run the script **Colors and Markers**.) Then, she selects **Rows > Data Filter**. This opens the dialog window shown in Exhibit 9.57. She selects Data Set Indicator and clicks **Add**.

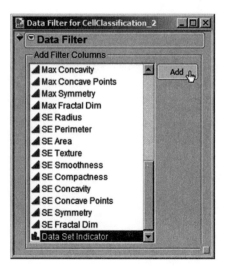

EXHIBIT 9.57   Dialog Window for Data Filter

She is interested in identifying her training set and excluding all other rows. In the **Data Filter** dialog window that appears, she clicks on Training Set, unchecks **Select**, and checks **Show** and **Include**, as shown in Exhibit 9.58.

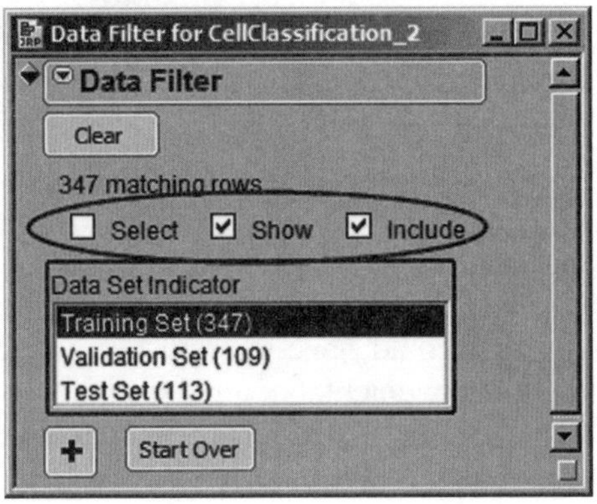

EXHIBIT 9.58   Data Filter Settings

Show has the effect of hiding all rows for which **Data Set Indicator** is not Training Set. **Include** has the effect of excluding all rows for which **Data Set Indicator** is not Training Set. So, with one easy dialog box, Mi-Ling has excluded and hidden all but the Training Set rows. Mi-Ling checks her data table to verify that the exclude and hide symbols appear to the left of rows belonging to the validation and test sets.

The row states defined by the icons next to the row numbers are the *row states in effect*. Mi-Ling is going to store these row states as a column for later use.

With a little perusal of the JMP Help files (searching on *row states* in the Index), Mi-Ling figures out how to save these row states in a **Row State** column. By double-clicking in the column header area, she creates a new column to the right of the last column, **Data Set Indicator**. She names her new column **Training Set**. She clicks off the column and then double-clicks back on the header to open **Column Info**. Under **Data Type**, she chooses **Row State**, as shown in Exhibit 9.59. She clicks **OK** to close the **Column Info** dialog.

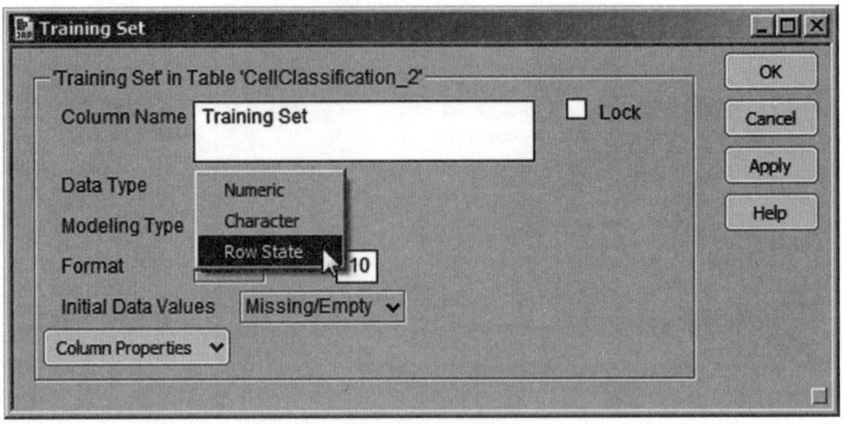

EXHIBIT 9.59   Column Info Dialog with Choice of Row State as Data Type

This has the effect of creating a column that can *store* row state assignments. To place the row states in this new column, Mi-Ling goes to the columns panel to the left of the data grid. She notices that her new column, **Training Set**, has a star-shaped icon to its left (Exhibit 9.60).

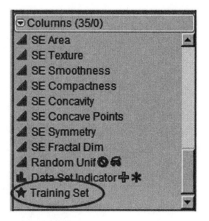

EXHIBIT 9.60   Row State Icon for Training Set Column

Mi-Ling clicks on the star and sees four options. She chooses **Copy from Row States** (Exhibit 9.61).

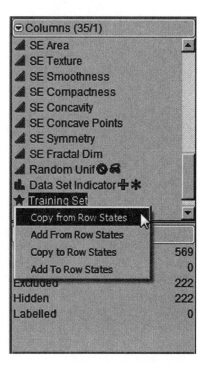

EXHIBIT 9.61   Options under Row State Icon Menu

Now Mi-Ling checks the column **Training Set** and sees that the exclude and hide row states have been copied into that column. The colors and markers, which are also row states, have been copied into that column as well (Exhibit 9.62).

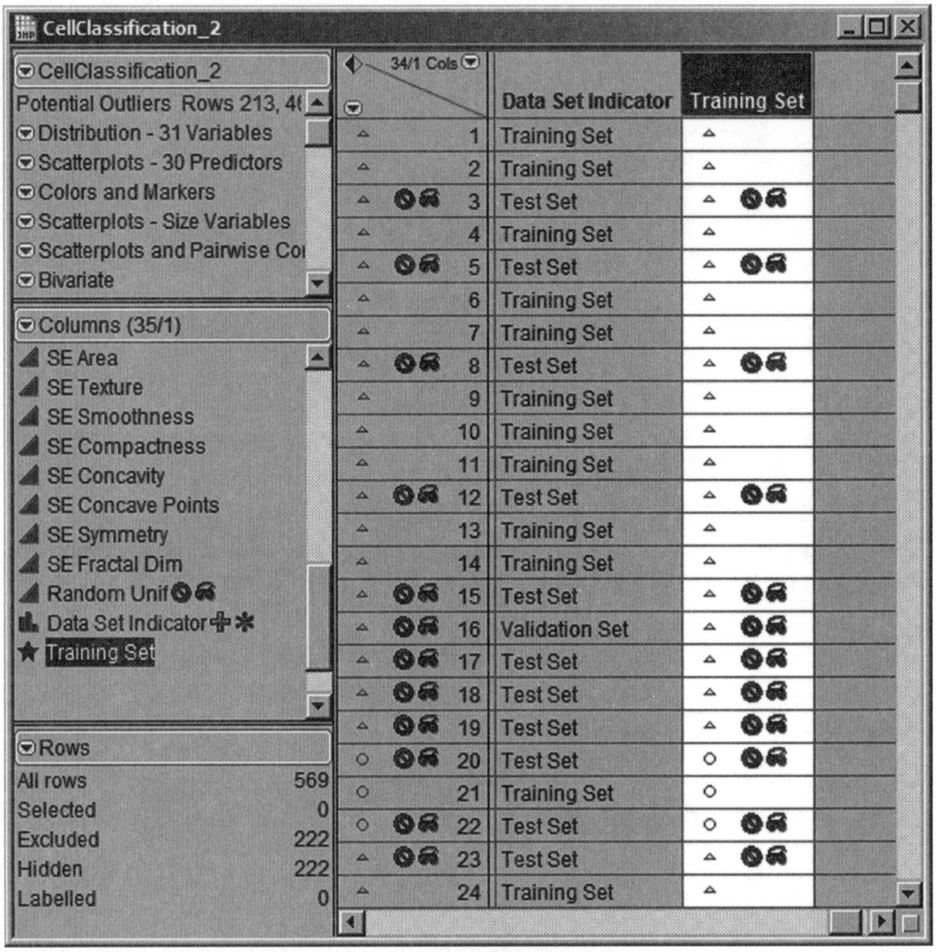

EXHIBIT 9.62   Training Set Column Containing Row States

In the **Data Filter** specification window, she clicks **Clear**. This command only affects the row states that have been imposed by **Data Filter**, removing the **Hide** and **Exclude** row symbols next to the row numbers, but leaving the colors and markers intact.

To construct the Validation Set and Test Set columns, Mi-Ling repeats the process she used in constructing the Training Set column. (We encourage the interested reader to construct these columns.) When she has finished, she again clicks **Clear** and closes the **Data Filter** window. The only remaining row states are the colors and markers. (The three row state columns can be constructed using the scripts **Training Set Column**, **Validation Set Column**, and **Test Set Column**.)

When she has finished constructing these three columns, Mi-Ling checks that she can apply these row states as she needs them. She does this by clicking on the star corresponding to the appropriate data set column in the columns panel and choosing **Copy to Row States**. With these three subsets defined, she is ready to embark on her modeling expedition.

Modeling Relationships: Logistic Model

Recall that Mi-Ling intends to explore three modeling approaches: logistic regression, recursive partitioning, and neural nets. She considers using discriminant analysis, but recalls that discriminant analysis requires assumptions about the predictor variables—for each group, the predictors must have a multivariate normal distribution, and unless one uses quadratic discriminant analysis, the groups must have a common covariance structure. Thinking ahead to her test campaign data, Mi-Ling notes that some of her predictors will be nominal. Consequently, discriminant analysis will not be appropriate, whereas logistic regression will be a legitimate approach.

Mi-Ling begins her modeling efforts with a traditional logistic model. But before launching into a serious logistic modeling effort, Mi-Ling decides that she wants to *see* how a logistic model, based on only two predictors, might look. She begins by fitting a model to only two predictors that she chooses rather haphazardly.

Once she has visualized a logistic fit, she proceeds to fit a logistic model that considers all 30 of her variables as candidate predictors. She uses a stepwise regression procedure to reduce this model.

Visualization of a Two-Predictor Model

Since she will use only the training data in constructing her models, Mi-Ling copies the values in the row state variable Training Set to the row states in the data table **CellClassification_2.jmp**. As she did earlier, she clicks on the star to the left of Training Set in the columns panel and selects **Copy to Row States**. In the rows panel, she checks that 222 rows are **Excluded** and **Hidden**.

To be able to visualize a logistic model in a simple situation, Mi-Ling begins by fitting a model to only two predictors, Mean Perimeter and Mean Smoothness, which she chooses simply because these variables have caught her attention. She selects **Analyze > Fit Model** and enters Diagnosis as **Y**. When she does this, she notices that JMP instantly inserts **Nominal Logistic** as the **Personality** for this model. In **Fit Model**, JMP provides a number of *personalities*—these are essentially different flavors of regression modeling. In this case, JMP notices that Diagnosis is nominal and that, consequently, a logistic regression model is appropriate. In the **Select Columns** list on the left, she selects Mean Perimeter and Mean Smoothness and clicks on the **Add** button to the left of the **Construct Model Effects** box (Exhibit 9.63). She saves the script for the launch dialog to the data table as **Logistic – Two Predictors**.

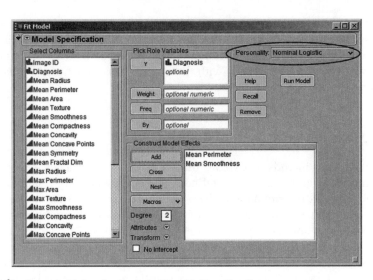

EXHIBIT 9.63 Launch Dialog for Logistic Fit with Two Predictors

When she clicks **OK**, she sees the **Nominal Logistic Fit** report shown in Exhibit 9.64. She is pleased to see that the **Whole Model Test** is significant and that the p-values in the **Effect Likelihood Ratio Tests** portion of the report, given under **Prob > ChiSq**, indicate that both predictors are significant.

CellClassification_2- Fit Nominal Logistic

Nominal Logistic Fit for Diagnosis

Iteration History

Whole Model Test

Model	-LogLikelihood	DF	ChiSquare	Prob>ChiSq
Difference	154.08666	2	308.1733	<.0001*
Full	73.26356			
Reduced	227.35022			

RSquare (U) 0.6778
Observations (or Sum Wgts) 347
Converged by Gradient

Lack Of Fit

Source	DF	-LogLikelihood	ChiSquare
Lack Of Fit	344	73.263563	146.5271
Saturated	346	0.000000	Prob>ChiSq
Fitted	2	73.263563	1.0000

Parameter Estimates

Term	Estimate	Std Error	ChiSquare	Prob>ChiSq
Intercept	-26.068551	3.241072	64.69	<.0001*
Mean Perimeter	0.18306571	0.0227746	64.61	<.0001*
Mean Smoothness	88.3379833	16.537594	28.53	<.0001*

For log odds of M/B

Effect Likelihood Ratio Tests

Source	Nparm	DF	L-R ChiSquare	Prob>ChiSq
Mean Perimeter	1	1	270.976724	<.0001*
Mean Smoothness	1	1	35.2810081	<.0001*

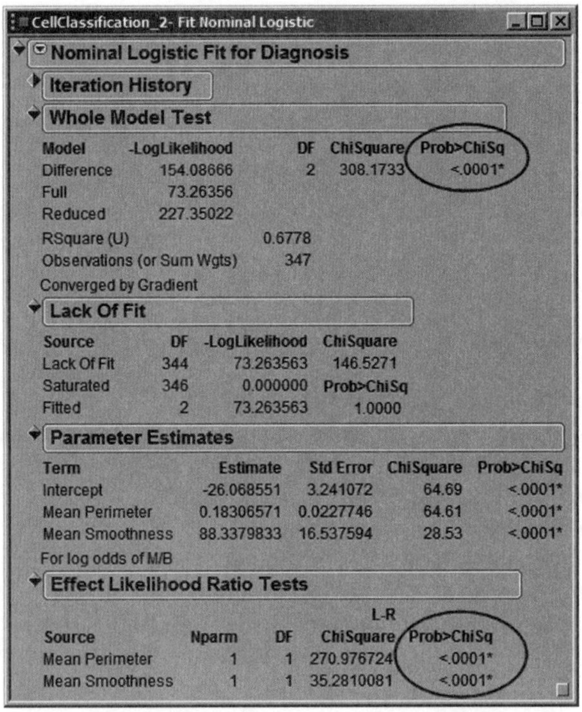

EXHIBIT 9.64 Fit Nominal Logistic Report for Two-Predictor Model

Now Mi-Ling is anxious to see a picture of the model. She remembers that for one predictor a logistic model looks like an S-shaped curve that is bounded between 0 and 1. She wonders what the surface for a model based on two predictors will look like. She clicks on the red triangle at the top of the report and chooses **Save Probability Formula** (Exhibit 9.65).

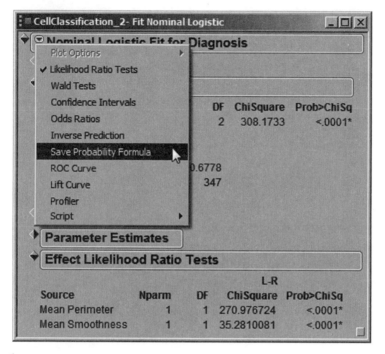

EXHIBIT 9.65   Options for Fit Nominal Logistic

This saves four formula columns to the data table. The two columns that most interest Mi-Ling are **Prob[M]** and **Most Likely Diagnosis**. The column **Prob[M]** gives the predicted probability that a mass is malignant (of course, **Prob[B]** = 1 − **Prob[M]**). Mi-Ling notes that all of these predicted values are between 0 and 1, as they should be. She clicks on the plus sign that follows **Prob[M]** in the columns panel to see the formula (Exhibit 9.66). The formula is a logistic function applied to **Lin[B]**, which in turn is a linear function of the two predictors. So **Prob[M]** is itself a nonlinear function of the two predictors.

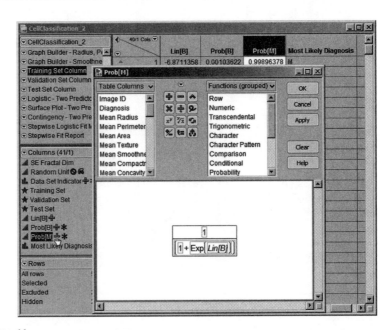

EXHIBIT 9.66   Formula for Prob[M]

Mi-Ling also checks the formula for **Most Likely Diagnosis** (Exhibit 9.67). She figures out that the formula says, "If the larger of **Prob[B]** and **Prob[M]** is **Prob[B]**, then predict B. If the larger of **Prob[B]** and **Prob[M]** is **Prob[M]**, then predict M." So the formula is predicting the outcome class that has the largest predicted probability. That means that B is assigned if and only if **Prob[B]** exceeds 0.50, and similarly for M.

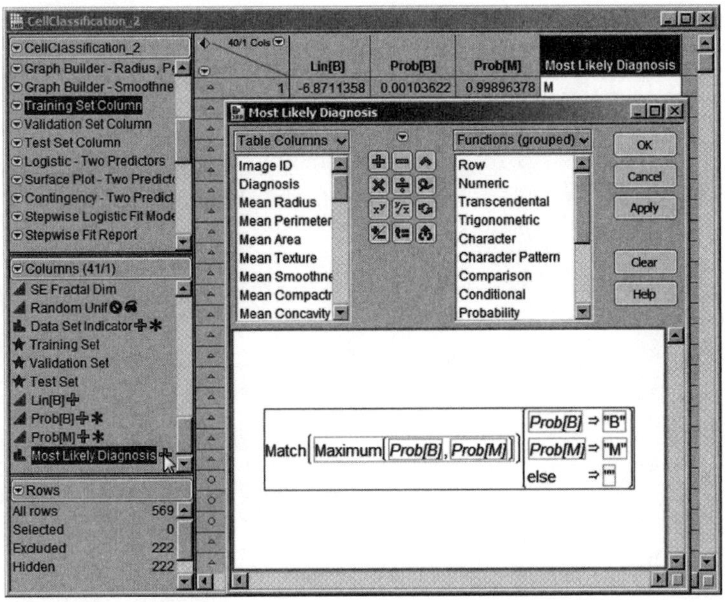

EXHIBIT 9.67   Formula for Most Likely Diagnosis

To construct a picture of the prediction surface, Mi-Ling selects **Graph > Surface Plot**. Since she wants to see how Prob[M] varies based on the values of Mean Perimeter and Mean Smoothness, she populates the launch dialog as shown in Exhibit 9.68.

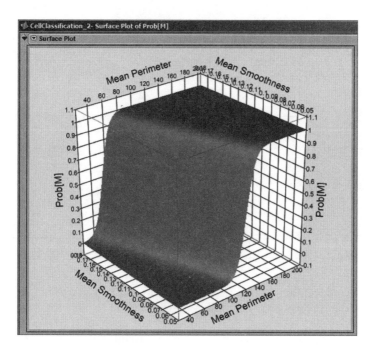

EXHIBIT 9.68 Launch Dialog for Surface Plot

When she clicks **OK**, she sees the surface plot shown in Exhibit 9.69. She takes her cursor over to the plot, which she then rotates by holding down the left mouse button. This allows her to see the surface from various angles. She sees that the surface has an S shape, with all **Prob[M]** values between 0 and 1, as they should be.

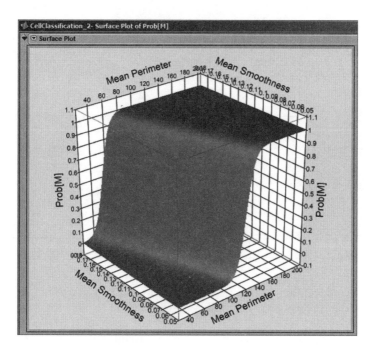

EXHIBIT 9.69 Surface Plot of Prob[M]

But what about the individual points? She would like to display their predicted values, along with their Diagnosis markers and colors, on the plot. To plot the points, she goes to the **Dependent Variables** panel beneath the plot. She sees that Prob[M] is the only formula entered, as it should be. To the right of Prob[M], in the second column, called **Point Response Column**, she chooses Prob[M] (see Exhibit 9.70, where the markers have been made solid and enlarged for visibility). This has the effect of plotting Prob[M] values for the points on the three-dimensional grid. Since the surface that is plotted is the prediction surface, all the predicted values fall on that surface.

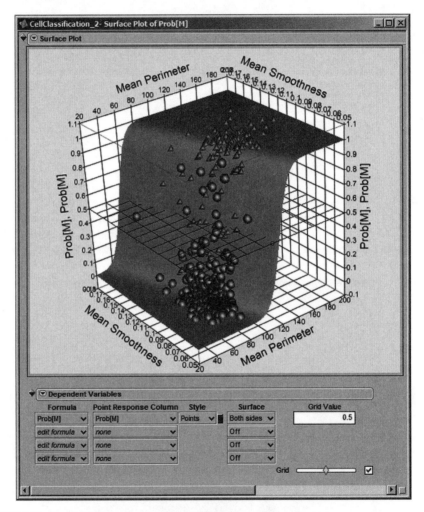

EXHIBIT 9.70   Surface Plot of Prob[M] with Points and Grid

However, since the points are colored and marked according to the actual outcome, Mi-Ling easily sees the points corresponding to malignant masses—they are depicted by red triangles. She wonders, "Are most of these predicted to be malignant?" Well, a mass is predicted to be malignant if Prob[M] exceeds 0.50. On the far right in the **Dependent Variables** panel, Mi-Ling notices a text box labeled **Grid Value** and, below it, a **Grid** slider. The **Grid Value** is already set to 0.5. Mi-Ling checks the box to the right of the **Grid** slider, which inserts a grid in the plot at Prob[M] = 0.5 (Exhibit 9.70).

She sees that most points that correspond to malignant masses (identified by triangles) are above the grid at 0.5. However, a number fall below; these correspond to the malignant masses that would be classified as benign, which is a type of misclassification error. Similarly, most benign points (plotted as circles) are below the grid, but again, a few are above it; these correspond to benign masses that would be classified as malignant, another type of misclassification error. Mi-Ling saves the script for the plot as **Surface Plot – Two Predictors**.

Mi-Ling concludes that the model is not bad, but the two types of misclassification errors appear consequential. She realizes that an easy way to quantify the misclassification errors is to compare Most Likely Diagnosis with the actual values found in Diagnosis using **Fit Y by X**. She selects **Analyze > Fit Y by X**, where she inserts Most Likely Diagnosis as **Y, Response** and Diagnosis as **X, Factor**. She clicks **OK** and obtains the report shown in Exhibit 9.71.

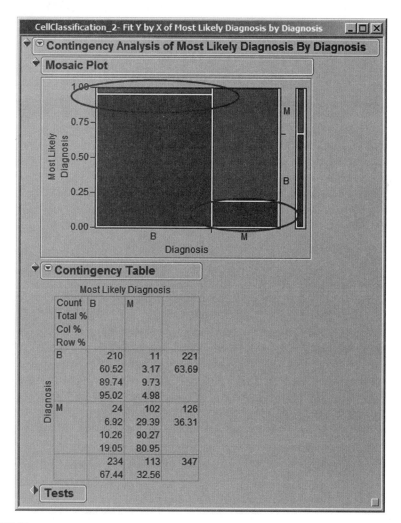

EXHIBIT 9.71 Contingency Report for Two Predictor Model

In the mosaic plot, the two circled areas indicate misclassifications. The circled (blue) area above B indicates masses that were benign but that were classified as malignant, while the circled (red) area above M indicates masses that were malignant but that were classified as benign.

Mi-Ling finds the contingency table informative. From the **Total %** value, she sees that malignant masses are classified as benign 6.92 percent of the time and benign masses are classified as malignant 3.17 percent of the time.

To better focus on **Count** and **Total %**, Mi-Ling sees that she can remove **Row %** and **Column %** from the contingency table by deselecting these options from the red triangle menu provided next to **Contingency Table**. But she realizes that in her analyses she will be constructing several contingency tables, and would prefer not to have to deselect these options every time. In short, she would like to set a *preference* relative to what she sees when she runs a contingency analysis.

She closes the **Contingency** report. Then, she selects **File > Preferences**, selects **Platforms**, and then selects the **Contingency** platform. In the list of options, she deselects **Row %** and **Col %**. She clicks **OK**. Then she reruns her **Fit Y by X** analysis by selecting **Analyze > Fit Y by X** and clicking the **Recall** button in the **Action** column, followed by **OK**. She obtains the output in Exhibit 9.72. Mi-Ling saves the script for this analysis as **Contingency – Two Predictors**.

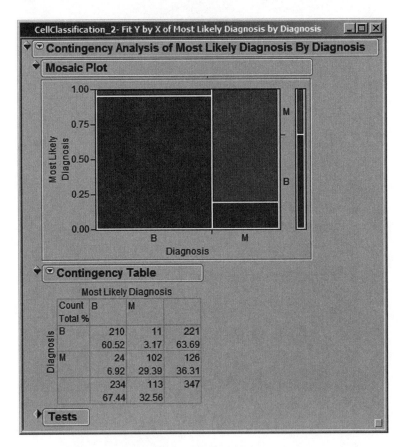

EXHIBIT 9.72   Contingency Report Showing Modified Table

In the revised **Contingency Table**, Mi-Ling easily sees that masses that are actually malignant are classified as benign in 24 instances, while masses that are benign are classified as malignant in 11 instances. In other words, there are 24 false negatives and 11 false positives. The overall misclassification error is 35 (24 + 11) divided by 347, or 10.1 percent. This is not very good, but Mi-Ling realizes that she did not choose her two predictors in any methodical way. Yet, this exercise with two predictors has been very useful in giving Mi-Ling insight on logistic modeling.

At this point, Mi-Ling is ready to get serious about model construction. She sees no further need for the four columns that she has saved to the data table, given that she can reproduce them easily enough by running the script **Logistic – Two Predictors**, running the model, and saving the probability formula columns. So, she deletes them. To do this, she selects all four columns, either in the data grid, as shown in Exhibit 9.73, or in the columns panel. She right-clicks in the highlighted area and selects **Delete Columns**. (If you are working along with Mi-Ling, please delete these columns in order to avoid complications later on.)

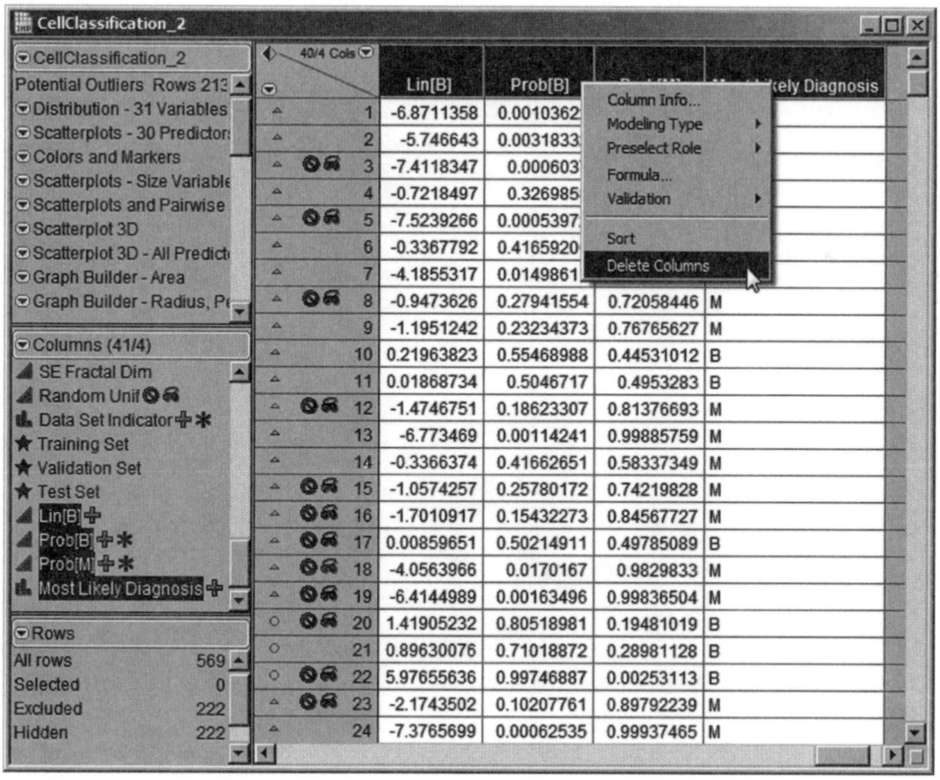

EXHIBIT 9.73   Deleting the Four Save Probability Formula Columns

Fitting a Comprehensive Logistic Model

GROUPING PREDICTORS   In fitting her models, Mi-Ling realizes that she will often want to treat all 30 of her predictors as a group. James showed her that JMP can group variables. When a large number of columns will be treated as a unit, say, as potential predictors, this can make analyzing data more convenient. She decides to group her 30 predictors.

To do this, Mi-Ling selects all 30 of her predictors, from **Mean Radius** to **SE Fractal Dim**, in the columns panel. Then she right-clicks in the highlighted area and selects **Group Columns**, as shown in Exhibit 9.74.

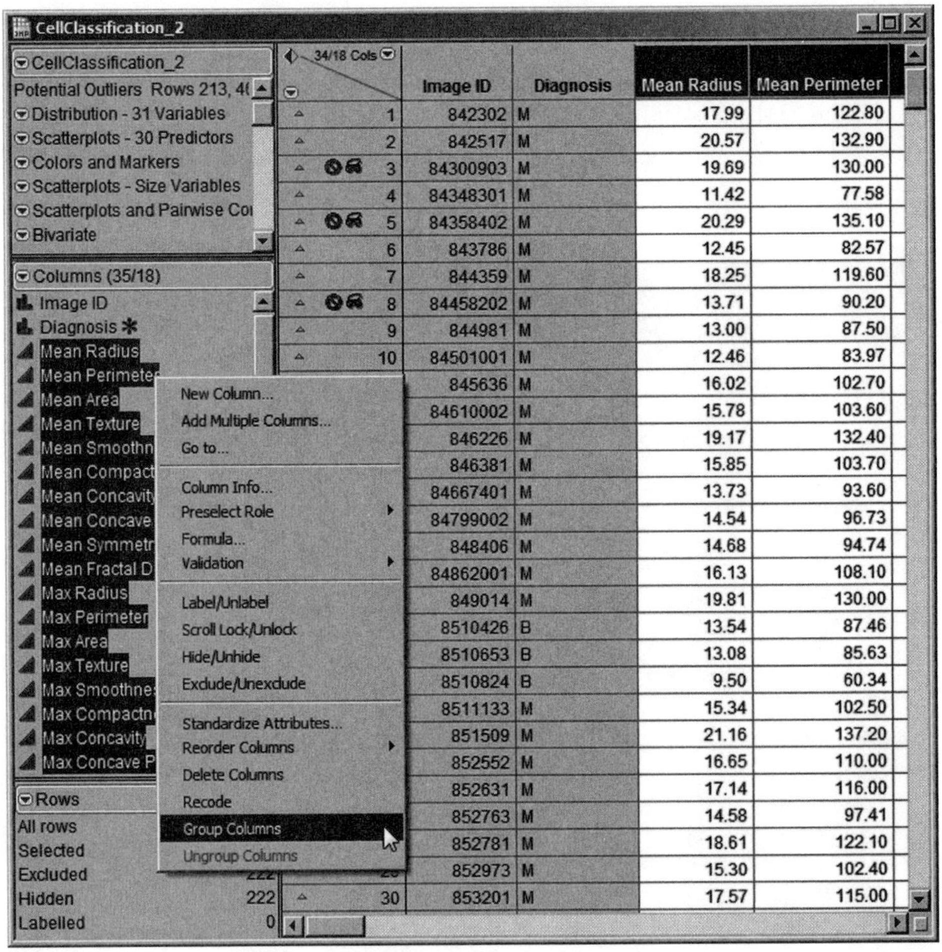

EXHIBIT 9.74   Selection of Group Columns

This has the effect of placing all 30 variables in a group designated by the name of the first variable. Mi-Ling double-clicks on the name that JMP has assigned—**Mean Radius etc.**—and changes it to **Thirty Predictors** (Exhibit 9.75). To view the columns in the group, Mi-Ling need only click the disclosure icon to the left of Thirty Predictors. (The script **Group 30 Columns** creates the group Thirty Predictors.)

CellClassification_2					
		Image ID	**Diagnosis**	**Mean Radius**	**Mean Perimeter**
CellClassification_2					
Potential Outliers Rows 213, 4(	1	842302	M	17.99	122.80
Distribution - 31 Variables	2	842517	M	20.57	132.90
Scatterplots - 30 Predictors	3	84300903	M	19.69	130.00
Colors and Markers	4	84348301	M	11.42	77.58
Scatterplots - Size Variables	5	84358402	M	20.29	135.10
Scatterplots and Pairwise Co	6	843786	M	12.45	82.57
Bivariate	7	844359	M	18.25	119.60
Multivariate	8	84458202	M	13.71	90.20
Scatterplot 3D	9	844981	M	13.00	87.50
Columns (37/0)	10	84501001	M	12.46	83.97
Image ID	11	845636	M	16.02	102.70
Diagnosis *	12	84610002	M	15.78	103.60
Thirty Predictors (30/0)	13	846226	M	19.17	132.40
Random Unif	14	846381	M	15.85	103.70
Data Set Indicator	15	84667401	M	13.73	93.60
Training Set	16	84799002	M	14.54	96.73
Validation Set	17	848406	M	14.68	94.74
Test Set	18	84862001	M	16.13	108.10
	19	849014	M	19.81	130.00
Rows	20	8510426	B	13.54	87.46
All rows 569					
Selected 0					
Excluded 222					

EXHIBIT 9.75   Grouped Columns with Name Thirty Predictors

FITTING A STEPWISE LOGISTIC MODEL   Mi-Ling begins her thinking about fitting a logistic model by pondering the issue of variable selection. She has 30 potential predictors, and she knows that she could expand the set of terms if she wished. She could include two-way interactions (for example, the interaction of Mean Perimeter and Mean Smoothness), quadratic terms, and even higher-order terms. Even with only 30 predictors, there are well over one billion different possible logistic models.

To reduce the number of potential predictors that she might include in her logistic model, Mi-Ling decides to use stepwise regression. But which potential predictors should she include in her initial model? Certainly all 30 of the variables in her data set are potential predictors. However, what about interactions? She calculates the number of two-way interactions: $(30 \times 29)/2 = 435$ (the same as the number of correlations). So including main effects and all two-way interactions would require estimating $30 + 435 + 1 = 466$ parameters. Mi-Ling realizes that she has a total of 347 records in her training set, which is not nearly enough to estimate 466 parameters.

With that sobering thought, she decides to proceed with main effects only. She also plans to explore partition and neural net models; if there are important interactions or higher-order effects, they may be addressed using these modeling approaches.

She checks to make sure that the row states for her training set have been applied. Once more Mi-Ling selects **Analyze > Fit Model**, where she enters Diagnosis as **Y** and all 30 of her predictors, which now have been grouped under the single name Thirty Predictors, in the **Construct Model Effects** box. Under **Personality**, she chooses **Stepwise**. This **Fit Model** dialog is shown in Exhibit 9.76. So that she does not need to reconstruct this launch dialog in the future, she saves its script as **Stepwise Logistic Fit Model**.

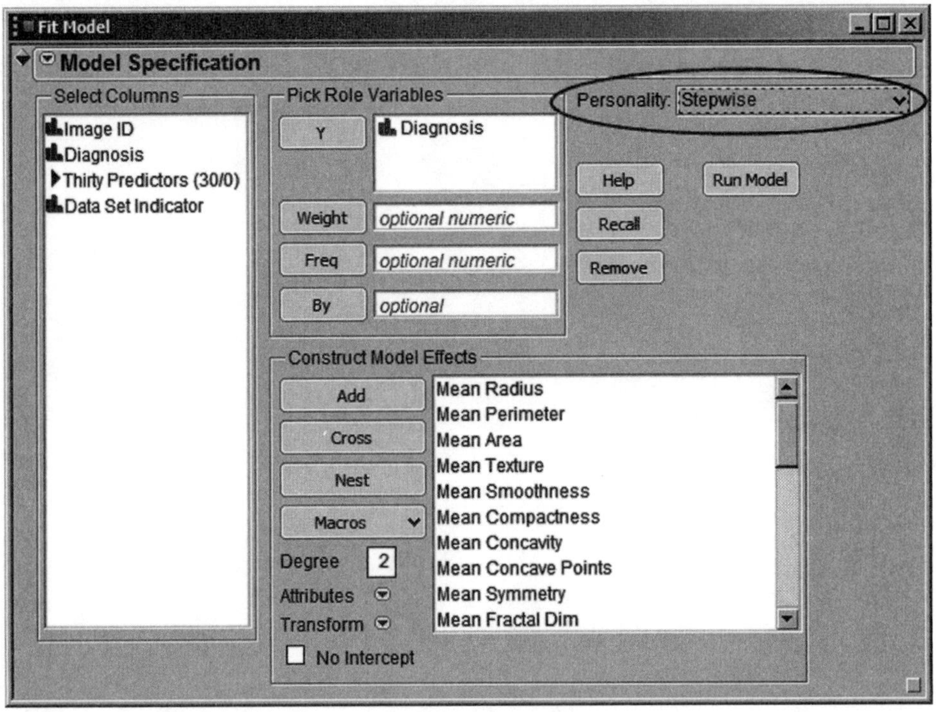

EXHIBIT 9.76   Fit Model Dialog for Stepwise Logistic Regression

Clicking **Run Model** creates the **Fit Stepwise** report (Exhibit 9.77). In the **Stepwise Regression Control** panel, Mi-Ling can make stepwise selection choices similar to those available in linear regression analysis. Mi-Ling reminds herself that a *forward* selection procedure consists of sequentially entering the most desirable term into the model, while a *backward* selection procedure consists of sequentially removing the least desirable term from the model. The **Current Estimates** panel shows estimates of parameters and significance probabilities for the model under consideration at a given time.

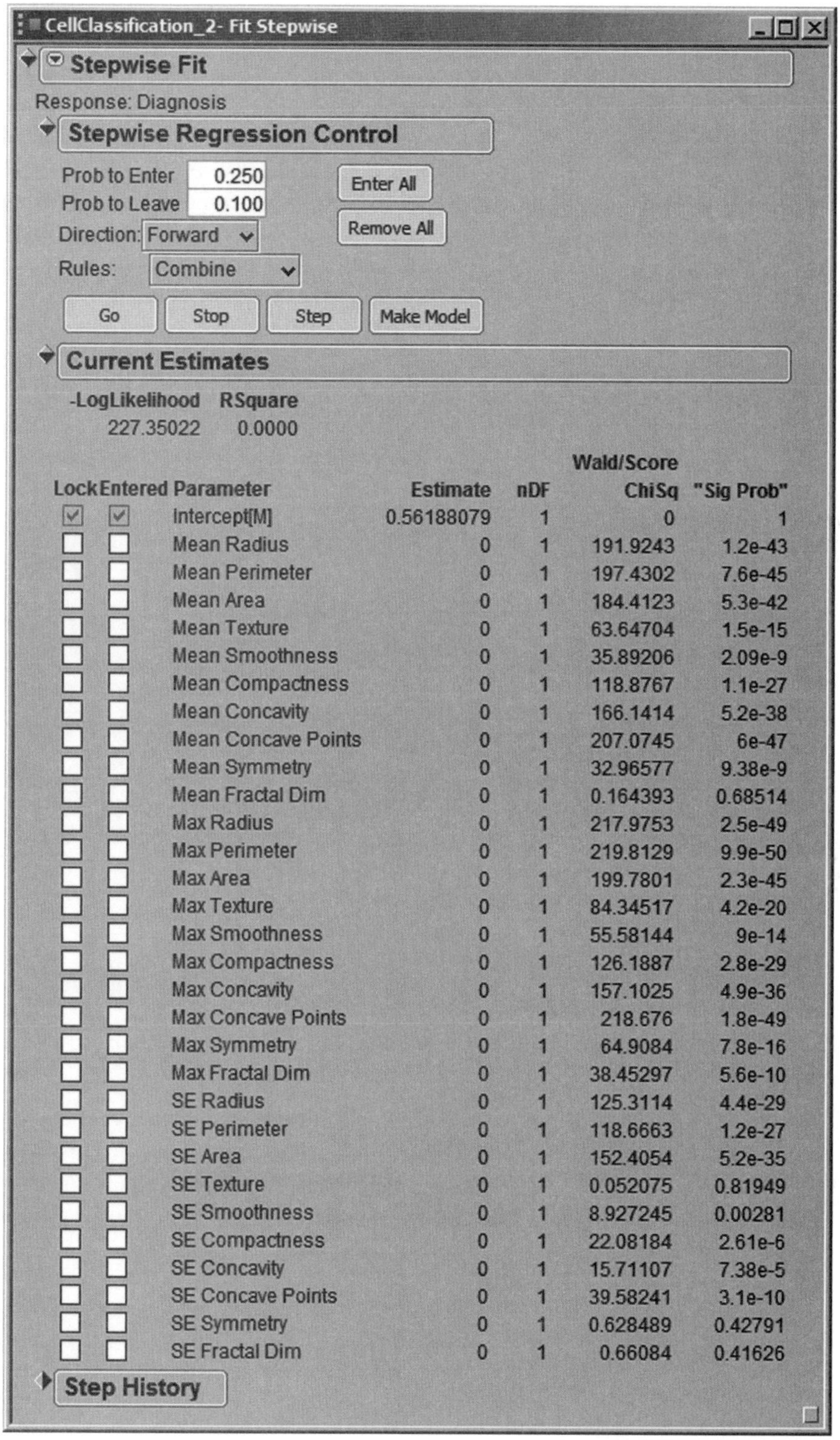

CellClassification_2- Fit Stepwise					

Stepwise Fit

Response: Diagnosis

Stepwise Regression Control

Prob to Enter 0.250   Enter All
Prob to Leave 0.100
Direction: Forward ⌄   Remove All
Rules: Combine ⌄

Go   Stop   Step   Make Model

Current Estimates

-LogLikelihood   RSquare
227.35022   0.0000

Lock	Entered	Parameter	Estimate	nDF	Wald/Score ChiSq	"Sig Prob"
☑	☑	Intercept[M]	0.56188079	1	0	1
☐	☐	Mean Radius	0	1	191.9243	1.2e-43
☐	☐	Mean Perimeter	0	1	197.4302	7.6e-45
☐	☐	Mean Area	0	1	184.4123	5.3e-42
☐	☐	Mean Texture	0	1	63.64704	1.5e-15
☐	☐	Mean Smoothness	0	1	35.89206	2.09e-9
☐	☐	Mean Compactness	0	1	118.8767	1.1e-27
☐	☐	Mean Concavity	0	1	166.1414	5.2e-38
☐	☐	Mean Concave Points	0	1	207.0745	6e-47
☐	☐	Mean Symmetry	0	1	32.96577	9.38e-9
☐	☐	Mean Fractal Dim	0	1	0.164393	0.68514
☐	☐	Max Radius	0	1	217.9753	2.5e-49
☐	☐	Max Perimeter	0	1	219.8129	9.9e-50
☐	☐	Max Area	0	1	199.7801	2.3e-45
☐	☐	Max Texture	0	1	84.34517	4.2e-20
☐	☐	Max Smoothness	0	1	55.58144	9e-14
☐	☐	Max Compactness	0	1	126.1887	2.8e-29
☐	☐	Max Concavity	0	1	157.1025	4.9e-36
☐	☐	Max Concave Points	0	1	218.676	1.8e-49
☐	☐	Max Symmetry	0	1	64.9084	7.8e-16
☐	☐	Max Fractal Dim	0	1	38.45297	5.6e-10
☐	☐	SE Radius	0	1	125.3114	4.4e-29
☐	☐	SE Perimeter	0	1	118.6663	1.2e-27
☐	☐	SE Area	0	1	152.4054	5.2e-35
☐	☐	SE Texture	0	1	0.052075	0.81949
☐	☐	SE Smoothness	0	1	8.927245	0.00281
☐	☐	SE Compactness	0	1	22.08184	2.61e-6
☐	☐	SE Concavity	0	1	15.71107	7.38e-5
☐	☐	SE Concave Points	0	1	39.58241	3.1e-10
☐	☐	SE Symmetry	0	1	0.628489	0.42791
☐	☐	SE Fractal Dim	0	1	0.66084	0.41626

Step History

EXHIBIT 9.77   Fit Stepwise Report

Because it tends to consider a large group of models, Mi-Ling decides to use a *mixed* procedure, meaning that each forward selection step will be followed by a backward selection step. To communicate this to JMP she sets **Direction** to **Mixed** in the **Stepwise Regression Control** panel. She also sets both the **Prob to Enter** and **Prob to Leave** values at 0.15. This has the effect that at a given step, only variables with significance levels below 0.15 are available to enter the model, while variables that have entered at a previous step but which now have significance levels exceeding 0.15 are available to be removed. The **Stepwise Regression Control** panel, as completed by Mi-Ling, is shown in Exhibit 9.78. She saves this in the script **Stepwise Fit Report**.

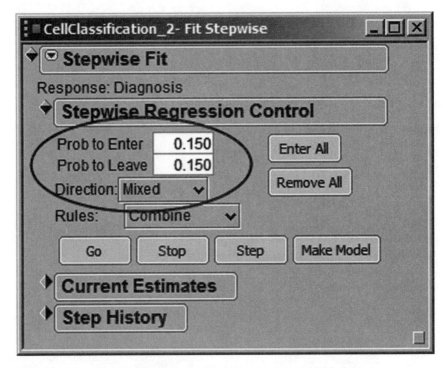

EXHIBIT 9.78   Stepwise Regression Control Panel for Logistic Variable Selection

When Mi-Ling clicks **Go**, she watches the **Current Estimates** panel as seven variables are selected (Exhibit 9.79). Alternatively, she could have clicked **Step** to see exactly how variables enter and leave, one step at a time.

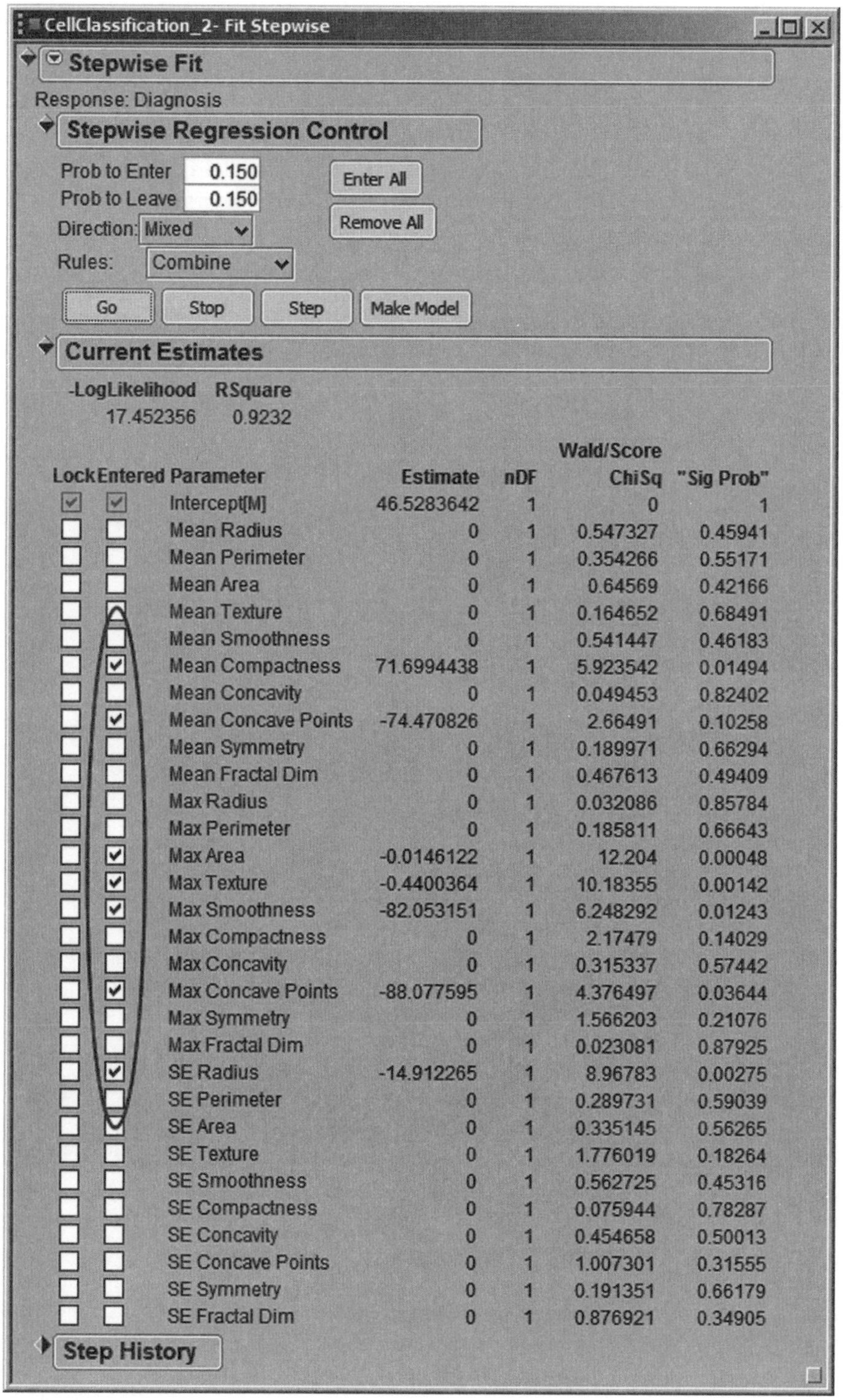

Lock	Entered	Parameter	Estimate	nDF	Wald/Score ChiSq	"Sig Prob"
☑	☑	Intercept[M]	46.5283642	1	0	1
☐	☐	Mean Radius	0	1	0.547327	0.45941
☐	☐	Mean Perimeter	0	1	0.354266	0.55171
☐	☐	Mean Area	0	1	0.64569	0.42166
☐	☐	Mean Texture	0	1	0.164652	0.68491
☐	☐	Mean Smoothness	0	1	0.541447	0.46183
☐	☑	Mean Compactness	71.6994438	1	5.923542	0.01494
☐	☐	Mean Concavity	0	1	0.049453	0.82402
☐	☑	Mean Concave Points	-74.470826	1	2.66491	0.10258
☐	☐	Mean Symmetry	0	1	0.189971	0.66294
☐	☐	Mean Fractal Dim	0	1	0.467613	0.49409
☐	☐	Max Radius	0	1	0.032086	0.85784
☐	☐	Max Perimeter	0	1	0.185811	0.66643
☐	☑	Max Area	-0.0146122	1	12.204	0.00048
☐	☑	Max Texture	-0.4400364	1	10.18355	0.00142
☐	☑	Max Smoothness	-82.053151	1	6.248292	0.01243
☐	☐	Max Compactness	0	1	2.17479	0.14029
☐	☐	Max Concavity	0	1	0.315337	0.57442
☐	☑	Max Concave Points	-88.077595	1	4.376497	0.03644
☐	☐	Max Symmetry	0	1	1.566203	0.21076
☐	☐	Max Fractal Dim	0	1	0.023081	0.87925
☐	☑	SE Radius	-14.912265	1	8.96783	0.00275
☐	☐	SE Perimeter	0	1	0.289731	0.59039
☐	☐	SE Area	0	1	0.335145	0.56265
☐	☐	SE Texture	0	1	1.776019	0.18264
☐	☐	SE Smoothness	0	1	0.562725	0.45316
☐	☐	SE Compactness	0	1	0.075944	0.78287
☐	☐	SE Concavity	0	1	0.454658	0.50013
☐	☐	SE Concave Points	0	1	1.007301	0.31555
☐	☐	SE Symmetry	0	1	0.191351	0.66179
☐	☐	SE Fractal Dim	0	1	0.876921	0.34905

EXHIBIT 9.79 Current Estimates Panel in Fit Stepwise

The **Step History** panel (Exhibit 9.80) gives a log of the sequence in which variables were entered and removed. Also provided are various statistics of interest. Mi-Ling thinks back to the fact that her training set contained two rows with unusually large values of SE Concavity. She sees that SE Concavity did not appear in the **Step History** and that it does not appear in the final model. In a way, this is comforting. On the other hand, it is possible that these rows were influential and caused SE Concavity or other predictors not to appear significant. At a future time, Mi-Ling may consider fitting a logistic model with these two rows excluded. For now, she continues with her current model.

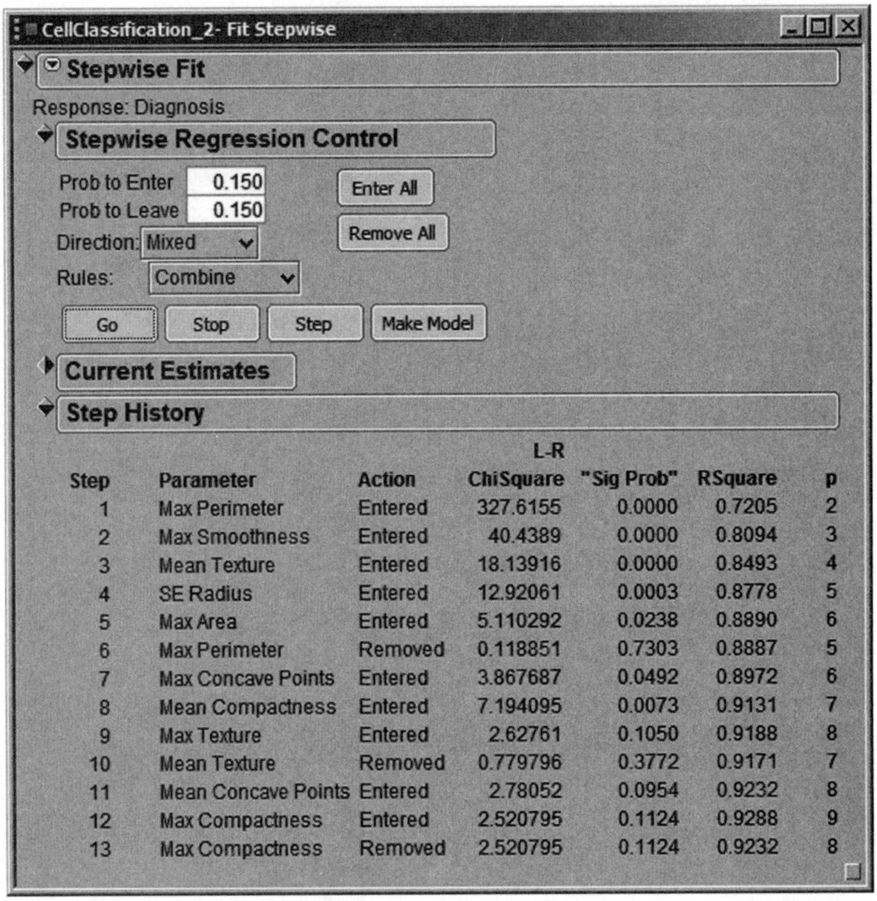

Step	Parameter	Action	L-R ChiSquare	"Sig Prob"	RSquare	p
1	Max Perimeter	Entered	327.6155	0.0000	0.7205	2
2	Max Smoothness	Entered	40.4389	0.0000	0.8094	3
3	Mean Texture	Entered	18.13916	0.0000	0.8493	4
4	SE Radius	Entered	12.92061	0.0003	0.8778	5
5	Max Area	Entered	5.110292	0.0238	0.8890	6
6	Max Perimeter	Removed	0.118851	0.7303	0.8887	5
7	Max Concave Points	Entered	3.867687	0.0492	0.8972	6
8	Mean Compactness	Entered	7.194095	0.0073	0.9131	7
9	Max Texture	Entered	2.62761	0.1050	0.9188	8
10	Mean Texture	Removed	0.779796	0.3772	0.9171	7
11	Mean Concave Points	Entered	2.78052	0.0954	0.9232	8
12	Max Compactness	Entered	2.520795	0.1124	0.9288	9
13	Max Compactness	Removed	2.520795	0.1124	0.9232	8

EXHIBIT 9.80   Step History Panel in Fit Stepwise

To fit the seven-predictor model obtained using her training set, Mi-Ling clicks on **Make Model** in the **Stepwise Regression Control** panel. This creates a **Stepped Model** launch dialog containing the specification for Mi-Ling's seven-predictor model (the saved script is **Stepwise Logistic Model**).

Finally, Mi-Ling clicks **Run Model.** The report (Exhibit 9.81) shows details about the model fit. The overall model fit is significant. The **Effect Likelihood Ratio Tests** show that all except one predictor is significant at the 0.01 level.

```
CellClassification_2- Fit Nominal Logistic            _ □ ×
```

▼ Nominal Logistic Fit for Diagnosis

  ▶ **Iteration History**

  ▼ **Whole Model Test**

Model	-LogLikelihood	DF	ChiSquare	Prob>ChiSq
Difference	209.89787	7	419.7957	<.0001*
Full	17.45236			
Reduced	227.35022			

RSquare (U)	0.9232
Observations (or Sum Wgts)	347

Converged by Gradient

  ▶ **Lack Of Fit**

  ▶ **Parameter Estimates**

  ▼ **Effect Likelihood Ratio Tests**

Source	Nparm	DF	L-R ChiSquare	Prob>ChiSq
Mean Compactness	1	1	9.63654184	0.0019*
Mean Concave Points	1	1	2.78052009	0.0954
Max Area	1	1	29.7063969	<.0001*
Max Texture	1	1	26.3022599	<.0001*
Max Smoothness	1	1	8.63654934	0.0033*
Max Concave Points	1	1	7.17330457	0.0074*
SE Radius	1	1	18.0721689	<.0001*

EXHIBIT 9.81   Fit Nominal Logistic Report for Stepwise Model

Mi-Ling clicks the red triangle in the report and chooses **Save Probability Formula**. Recall that this saves a number of formulas to the data table, including Prob[B] and Prob[M], namely, the probability that the tumor is benign or malignant, respectively, as well as a column called Most Likely Diagnosis, which gives the diagnosis class with the highest probability, conditional on the values of the predictors.

To see how well the classification performs on the training data, Mi-Ling selects **Analyze > Fit Y by X**. As before, she enters Most Likely Diagnosis as **Y, Response** and Diagnosis as **X, Factor**. The resulting mosaic plot and contingency table are shown in Exhibit 9.82. Of the 347 rows, only five are misclassified. She saves the script as **Contingency – Logistic Model**.

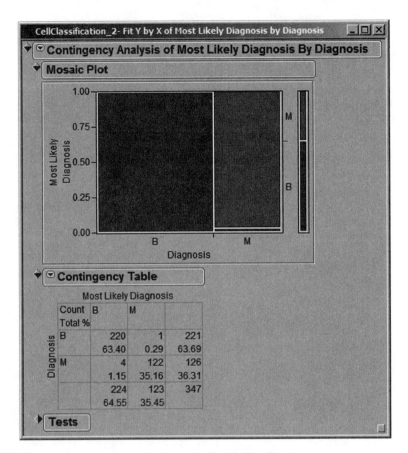

EXHIBIT 9.82   Contingency Report for Logistic Model Classification

Mi-Ling thinks this is great. But reality quickly sets in when she reminds herself that there is an inherent bias in evaluating a classification rule on the data used in fitting the model. Once she has fit her other models, she will compare them all using the validation data set. At this point, she closes the reports that deal with the logistic fit. She is anxious to construct and explore a model using recursive partitioning.

Modeling Relationships: Recursive Partitioning

Mi-Ling turns her attention to the JMP partition platform, which implements a version of classification and regression tree analysis.[5] The partition platform allows both the response and predictors to be either continuous or categorical. Continuous predictors are split into two partitions according to cutting values, while predictors that are nominal or ordinal are split into two groups of levels. Intuitively, the split is chosen so as to maximize the difference in response between the two branches, or *nodes*, resulting from the split.

If the response is continuous, the sum of squares due to the difference between means is a measure of the difference in the two groups. Both the variable to be split and the cutting value for the split are determined by maximizing a quantity, called the **LogWorth**, which is related to the p-value associated with the sum of squares due to the difference between means. In the case of a continuous response, the fitted values are the means within the two groups.

If the response is categorical, as in Mi-Ling's case, the splits are determined by maximizing a **LogWorth** statistic that is related to the p-value of the likelihood ratio chi-square statistic, which is referred to as **G^2**. In this case, the fitted values are the estimated proportions, or response rates, within the resulting two groups.

Mi-Ling remembers hearing that the partition platform is useful both for exploring relationships and for modeling: It is very flexible, allowing a user to find not only splits that are optimal in a global sense, but also node-specific splits that satisfy various criteria. The platform provides a simple *stopping rule*—that is, a criterion to end splitting—based on a user-defined minimum node size. This is advantageous in that it allows flexibility at the discretion of the user.

To fit her partition model, Mi-Ling selects **Analyze > Modeling > Partition**. She enters Diagnosis as **Y, Response** and the Thirty Predictors grouping consisting of all 30 predictor variables as **X, Factor**. When she clicks **OK**, she sees the initial report shown in Exhibit 9.83. The initial node is shown, indicating under **Count** that there are 347 rows of data. The bar graph in the node and the plot above the node use the color red to indicate malignant values (red triangles) and blue to indicate benign values (blue circles).

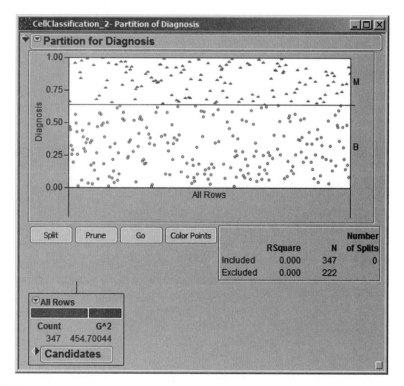

EXHIBIT 9.83   Initial Partition Report

Mi-Ling would like JMP to display the proportions of malignant and benign records in each node, so she selects **Display Options > Show Split Prob** from the red triangle at the top of the report. When she clicks on this, the diagram updates to show the split proportions in the initial node, and will show these in all subsequent nodes as well.

Now the report appears as shown in Exhibit 9.84. Mi-Ling sees that the benign proportion is 0.6369 and the malignant proportion is 0.3631. She infers that the horizontal line separating the benign points from the malignant points in the plot at the top of the report is at about 0.64. Mi-Ling saves the script for this analysis as **Initial Partition Report Window.**

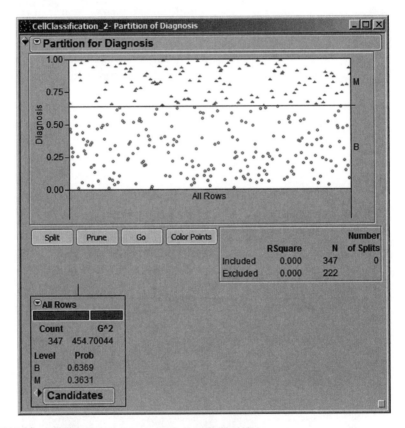

EXHIBIT 9.84   Initial Partition Report with Split Probabilities

Now, Mi-Ling begins to split by clicking once on the **Split** button. JMP determines the best variable on which to split and the best cutting value for that variable.

The tree, after the first split, is shown in Exhibit 9.85. The first split is on the variable **Max Concave Points,** and the observations are split at the value where **Max Concave Points** = 0.14. Of the 111 observations where **Max Concave Points** ≥ 0.14 (the leftmost node), 96.40 percent are malignant. Of the 236 for which **Max Concave Points** < 0.14, 91.95 percent are benign. Mi-Ling notices that the graph at the top updates to incorporate the information about the first split, suggesting that the first split has done very well in discriminating between benign and malignant tumors.

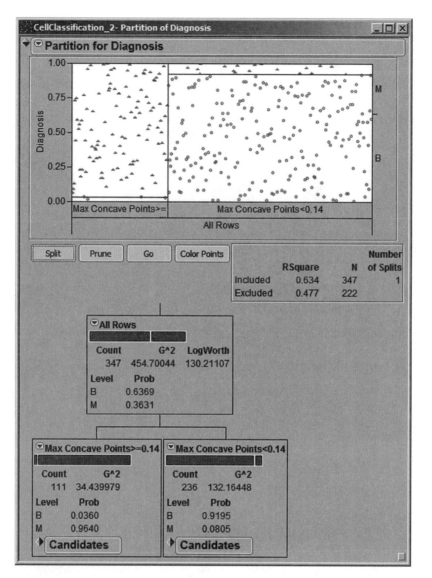

EXHIBIT 9.85 Partition Report after First Split

Mi-Ling continues to split for a total of eight splits (Exhibit 9.86). At this point, she notices that no further splits occur. After a little thinking and a call to James, she realizes that splitting stops because JMP has set a minimum split size. In the drop-down menu obtained by clicking on the red triangle at the top of the report, Mi-Ling finds **Minimum Size Split**. By selecting this, she discovers that the minimum split size is set at five by default. She realizes that she could have set a larger **Minimum Size Split** value, which would have stopped the splitting earlier. In fact, she may have overfit the data, given that some of the final nodes contain very few observations. All the same, she decides that she will consider the eight-split model. (You might like to explore models obtained using larger values of **Minimum Size Split**.)

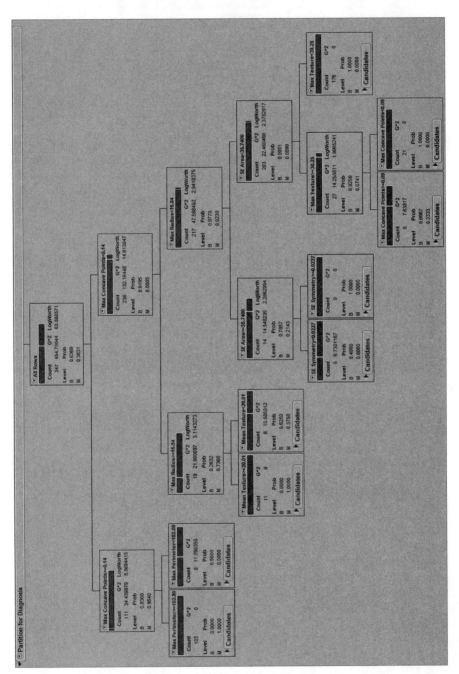

EXHIBIT 9.86 Partition Tree after Eight Splits

Mi-Ling notices that there are many options available from the red triangle menu at the top of the report, including **Leaf Report**, **Column Contributions**, **K-Fold Cross Validation**, **ROC Curve**, **Lift Curve**, and so on. She has used ROC and lift curves before. They are used to assess model fit. For this model, Mi-Ling plans to assess model fit by computing the misclassification rate, as she did with her logistic fits. For reasons of space, we will not discuss these additional options. We do encourage you to explore these using the documentation in **Help**.

A **Small Tree View** that condenses the information in the large tree is provided as shown in Exhibit 9.87. This small schematic shows the split variables and the split values in the tree. Mi-Ling notices that the eight splits resulted in nine *terminal nodes*, that is, nodes where no further splitting occurs. The splits occurred on **Max Concave Points**, **Max Perimeter**, **Max Radius**, **Mean Texture**, **SE Area**, **SE Symmetry**, and **Max Texture**. So, concavity, area, texture, and symmetry variables are involved.

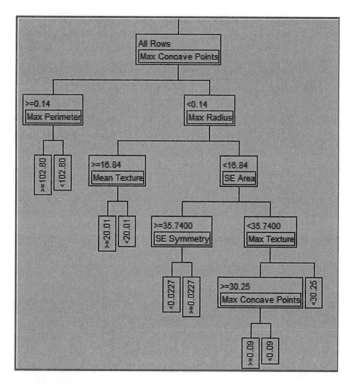

EXHIBIT 9.87 Small Tree View for Partition Model

Mi-Ling saves her report as the script **Partition Model**. She is now ready to save the prediction equation to the data table. From the red triangle at the top of the report, she chooses **Save Columns > Save Prediction Formula**. She sees that this saves two new columns to the data table, Prob(Diagnosis==B) and Prob(Diagnosis==M).

By clicking on the plus sign to the right of Prob(Diagnosis==M) in the columns panel, Mi-Ling is able to view its formula, shown in Exhibit 9.88. She sees that this formula has the effect of placing a new observation into a terminal node based on its values on the split variables, and then assigning to that new observation a probability of malignancy equal to the proportion of malignant outcomes observed for training data records in that node. It follows that the classification rule consists of determining the terminal node into which a new observation falls and classifying it into the class with the higher sample proportion in that node.

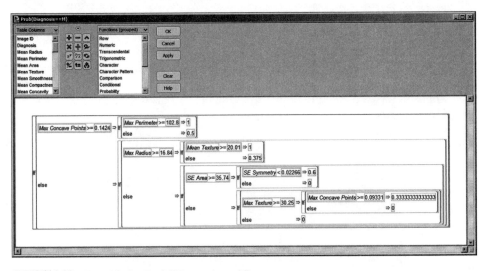

EXHIBIT 9.88   Formula for Prob(Diagnosis==M)

To define the classification rule, Mi-Ling creates a new column called **Partition Prediction**. She constructs a formula to define this column; this formula classifies an observation as M if **Prob(Diagnosis==M) >= 0.5**, B if **Prob(Diagnosis==M) < 0.5**, and missing otherwise. Mi-Ling's formula is shown in Exhibit 9.89. (Alternatively, you may run the script **Partition Prediction** to create this column from the saved probability columns.)

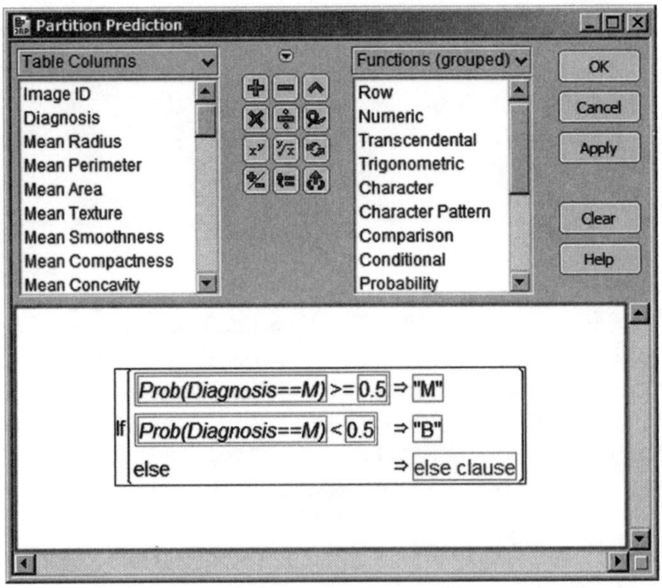

EXHIBIT 9.89   Formula for Partition Prediction

She then returns to **Analyze > Fit Y by X**, and enters Partition Prediction as **Y, Response**, and Diagnosis as **X, Factor**. The resulting mosaic plot and contingency table are shown in Exhibit 9.90. Of the 347 rows, 11 are misclassified. At first blush, this model does not seem to be performing as well as the logistic model, which had only five misclassifications in the training set. In a later section, Mi-Ling will compare this model to the logistic model by evaluating it on the validation data set. She saves the script as **Contingency – Partition Model**.

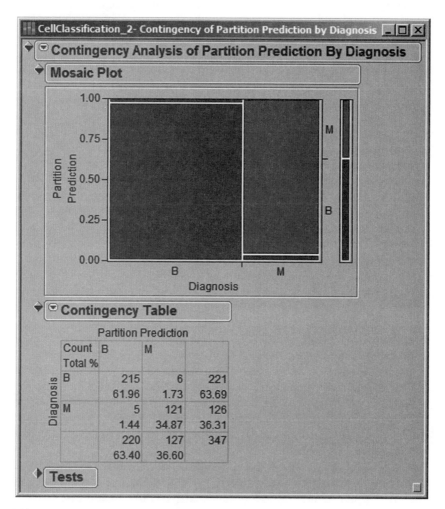

EXHIBIT 9.90   Contingency Report for Partition Model Classification

Modeling Relationships: Neural Net Models

In her study of data-mining techniques, Mi-Ling has read about how *neural nets* can be used for classification and prediction. She is interested in exploring neural net classification models for her data. Mi-Ling has read that cross-validation can be used to mitigate the effects of overfitting the data. With this in mind, she decides to fit one neural net model in a naive way, without considering cross-validation, and to select a second neural net model based on the value of a cross-validation statistic for her training data.

Background

Neural net algorithms were originally inspired by how biological neurons are believed to function. Starting in the 1940s, scientists in the area of artificial intelligence pursued the idea of designing algorithms that can *learn* in a way that emulates neuron function in the human brain.

In fact, the science of biologically informed computation has its origins in a seminal paper called "A Logical Calculus of Ideas Immanent in Nervous Activity."[6] Implicit in this paper's use of logic and computation to describe the nervous system was the concept that *ideas* are carried by the collection of neurons as a whole, rather than being tied to a specific neuron. Research since these early days has leveraged this idea of distributed processing, and neural nets typically have an input layer of neurons, an output layer, and a hidden layer where processing occurs.[7]

Mi-Ling realizes that in a mathematical sense a neural net is nothing more than a nonlinear regression model. She learns that in its implementation of neural nets, JMP uses standard nonlinear least squares regression methods. Although a general neural net can have many hidden layers, one layer is considered sufficient for most modeling situations; for this reason, JMP uses a single hidden layer. Each hidden neuron or node is modeled using a logistic function applied to a linear function of the predictors. In a classification situation such as Mi-Ling's, the output value results from a logistic function applied to a linear function of the outputs from the hidden nodes. For example, this means that for 30 input variables, one response, and k hidden nodes, the number of parameters to be estimated is $(31 \times k) + (k + 1)$.

With so many parameters, it is easy to see that a major advantage of a neural net is its ability to model a variety of patterns of response. But fitting this many parameters comes at a cost. Because the criterion that is optimized usually has many local optima, convergence to an optimum can be difficult. Also, with so many parameters, Mi-Ling can see why overfitting is problematic. She reminds herself that this is why validation sets are critical to neural net modeling strategies. Another disadvantage of neural net models is that they are not interpretable beyond the relationship between inputs and output, due to the hidden layer.

The implementation used by JMP provides a user-specified overfitting penalty to help minimize overfitting issues. Because of its similarity to a ridge-regression penalty function, the neural net overfitting penalty not only addresses overfitting, but also helps mitigate the effects of multicollinearity. The user is also able to set the number of nodes in the hidden layer. Note that a small number of hidden nodes can lead to underfitting and a large number can lead to overfitting, but *small* and *large* are relative to the specific problem under study. For a given number of hidden nodes, each application of the fitting algorithm has a random start, and JMP refers to these individual fits as tours. About 16 to 20 tours are recommended in order to find a useful optimum.

JMP also provides two methods to help a user select a neural net model that will extend well to new data. One of these methods is called **Random Holdback**. In this method, a sample of the observations is withheld (the *holdback* sample) while the remaining observations are used to train a neural net. JMP computes an R^2 value for the training sample, then applies the neural net to the holdback sample and calculates an R^2 for that sample, which is called the *cross-validation R^2*, denoted **CV RSquare** in the JMP report. The user can vary the number of hidden nodes and the overfit penalty in an attempt to find a model that generalizes well to the holdback sample. This method works well for large numbers of observations, where one can easily fit a model to 75 percent or fewer of the observations. JMP uses two-thirds of the complete data set by default.

The second method is called **K-Fold Cross-validation**. Here, a neural net model is fit to all of the data to provide starting values. Then, the observations are divided randomly into K groups (or *folds*). In turn, each of these groups is treated as a holdback sample. For each of the K groups, a model is fit to the data in the other (K − 1) folds, using estimates from the full fit as starting values. The model is then extended to the holdback group. An R^2 is calculated for each holdback sample, and these are averaged to give a **CV RSquare** that represents how the model might perform on new observations. The estimates from the full fit are used as starting values because the function being optimized is multimodal, and this practice attempts to bias the estimates for the submodels to the mode of the overall fit.

A First Model: Neural Net 1

Mi-Ling decides to begin by fitting a model to the breast cancer data without any use of cross-validation. To fit a neural net model, she selects **Analyze > Modeling > Neural Net**. Consistent with the other modeling platforms, she enters Diagnosis as **Y, Response** and her grouping, Thirty Predictors, as **X, Factors**. She leaves the **Crossvalidation** option in the launch dialog set at **No Crossvalidation**. When she clicks **OK**, she sees the **Control Panel** (see Exhibit 9.91).

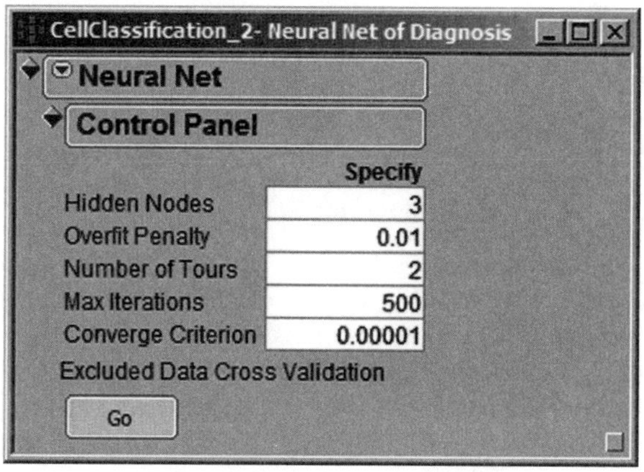

EXHIBIT 9.91 Neural Net Control Panel

In the **Control Panel**, Mi-Ling sees that the default fit is a model with three hidden nodes. To get a picture of this model, she clicks on the red triangle and chooses

Diagram. The diagram shown in Exhibit 9.92 illustrates the 30 input variables, the three hidden nodes (H1, H2, and H3), and their combination in the prediction of the probability of Diagnosis classes. The final model will be a logistic function of a linear combination of three models, each of which relates one of the hidden nodes, H1, H2, and H3, to the 30 predictors.

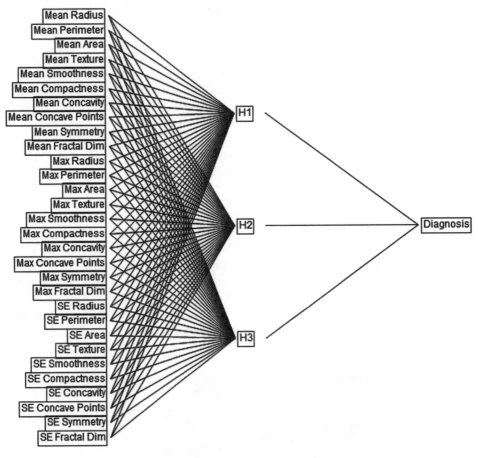

EXHIBIT 9.92   Diagram of Neural Net Model for 30 Predictors with Three Hidden Nodes

Reexamining the default **Control Panel** settings, Mi-Ling notes that the **Overfit Penalty** is set at 0.01, a value that she accepts for this model. She realizes that smaller values of the overfit penalty may lead to overfitting, while larger values may result in underfitting. She plans to explore this in a second neural net model. She does change the **Number of Tours** to 20, though, in order to increase the likelihood of finding an optimum (see Exhibit 9.93). Then, she clicks **Go** to fit a model. The model fitting does not take long, but she does realize that depending on the data set size and the settings in the **Control Panel**, the fitting procedure could take a noticeable amount of time.

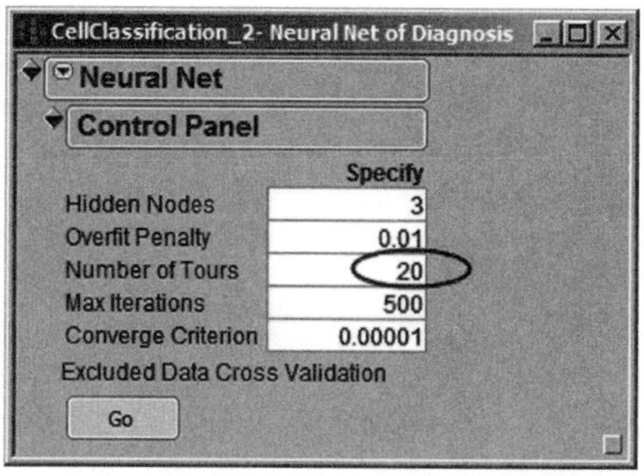

EXHIBIT 9.93   Neural Net Control Panel Settings

The **Current Fit Results** panel (Exhibit 9.94) shows Mi-Ling's results for the current fit. In her sequence of 20 tours—recall that each has a random start—only 1 of the 20 tours **Converged at Best**, meaning that it satisfied the convergence criterion. This is the fit that JMP uses. In total, 97 parameters (**Nparm**) have been estimated. These are listed in the **Parameter Estimates** panel, but they are not of intrinsic interest. (Note that because of the random starts, when you run this report your results will differ slightly from Mi-Ling's.)

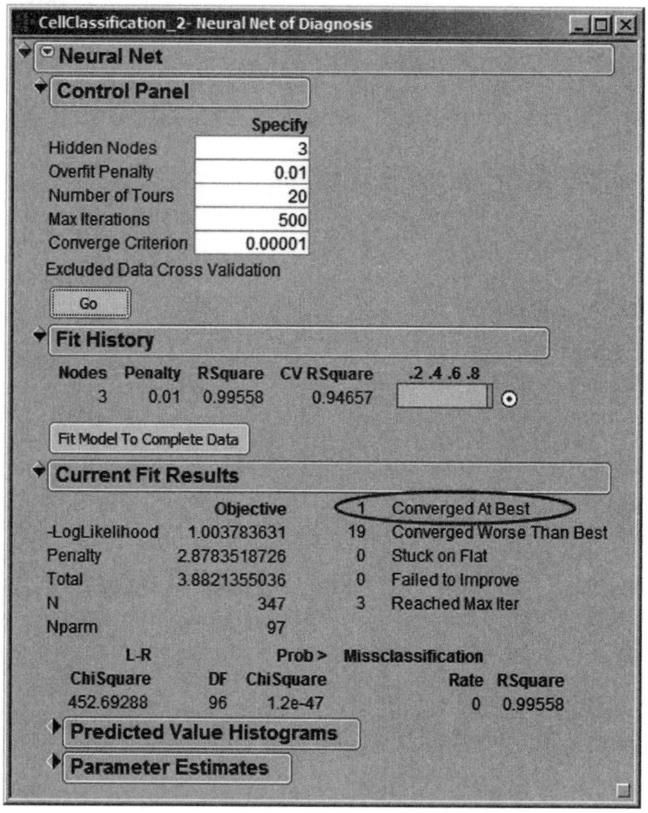

EXHIBIT 9.94   Results of Neural Net Fit to Diagnosis with 30 Predictors

In order to be able to refer to the same model and the same results in her future work, Mi-Ling saves a script to the data table that reproduces the model that is chosen by the 20-tour analysis in Exhibit 9.94. She does this by including the random seed, shown under **Parameter Estimates** (Exhibit 9.95) in her script. She calls her script **Neural Net 1**. If you are following using JMP and want to obtain Mi-Ling's exact results, at this point you should run the script **Neural Net 1**.

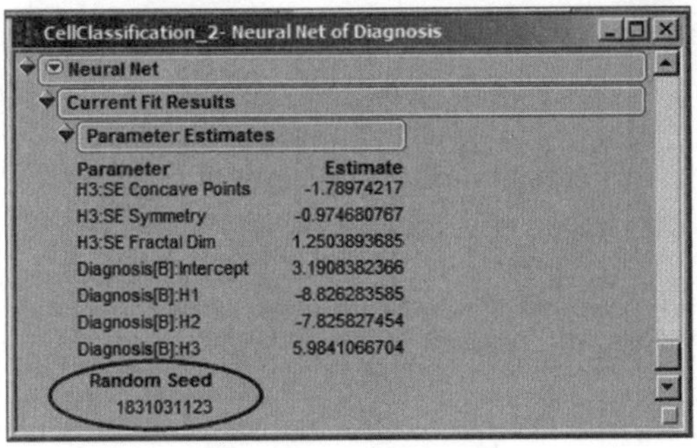

EXHIBIT 9.95   Random Seed for Neural Net 1

Mi-Ling notices that histograms for the probabilities predicted by the model, conditioned on whether the actual **Diagnosis** is malignant or benign, are provided in the **Neural Net** report, as shown in Exhibit 9.96. She notes that for the training data, the probabilities predicted by the model appear to classify masses into the two classes quite successfully. She also notes that the **RSquare** for the model, fit to the training data, is 0.99558. This sounds wonderful, but Mi-Ling realizes that this is likely a consequence of overfitting the data.

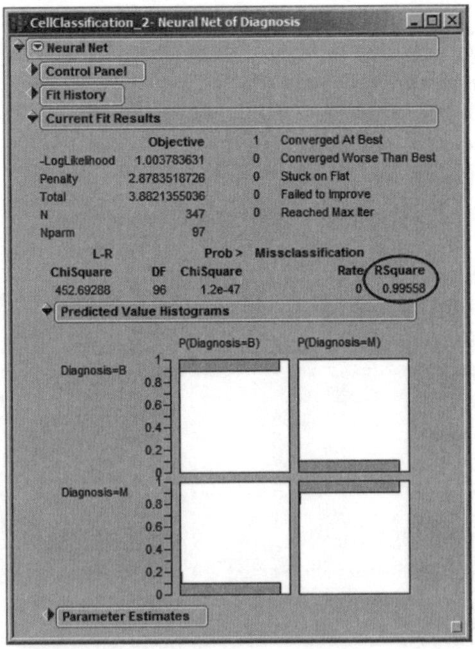

EXHIBIT 9.96   Histograms for Neural Net Probabilities

To get a sense of what her 30-predictor model looks like, Mi-Ling looks at a few other options provided by the **Neural Net** report. From the red triangle at the top of the **Neural Net** report she chooses **Categorical Profiler**. This opens a **Prediction Profiler**, a portion of which is shown in Exhibit 9.97.

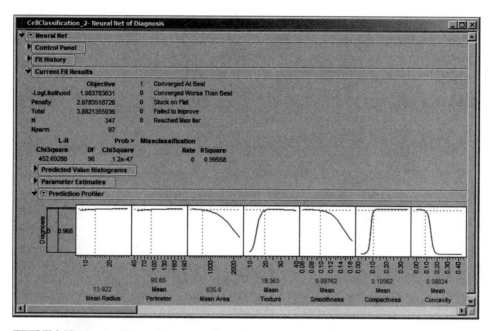

EXHIBIT 9.97 Partial View of Categorical Profiler for Neural Net Model 1

The dotted vertical red lines represent settings for each of the predictors. The trace shown in the profiler cell above a given predictor represents the cross section of the fitted model for **Prob(Diagnosis=B)** for that variable, at the given settings of the other variables. When she changes one variable's value, Mi-Ling can see the impact of this change on the surface for all other variables. For example, Mi-Ling moves the dotted vertical red line for **Mean Fractal Dimension** through its range of values. As she does this, she observes its impact on the traces for the other variables. As she changes values for other predictors and scrolls through the plots, she observes that the surface appears fairly smooth, with some steep peaks, but no very jagged areas.

Mi-Ling then chooses another way to visualize the surface, selecting **Surface Profiler** from the top red triangle menu. This gives a three-dimensional view of the effect of predictor variables, taken two at a time, on **Prob(Diagnosis=B)** and **Prob(Diagnosis=M)**. Exhibit 9.98 shows the relationship between the predictors **Max Area** and **SE Compactness** and the predicted response **Prob(Diagnosis=M)**. The plot shows that as **Max Area** increases and **SE Compactness** decreases, the probability of malignancy increases essentially to one. But, Mi-Ling realizes that this is just one of the many (435) possible surface plots for **Prob(Diagnosis=M)**. She explores a number of these.

Now Mi-Ling would like to assess the performance of her model relative to misclassification. In the report, from the top red triangle, Mi-Ling chooses the option

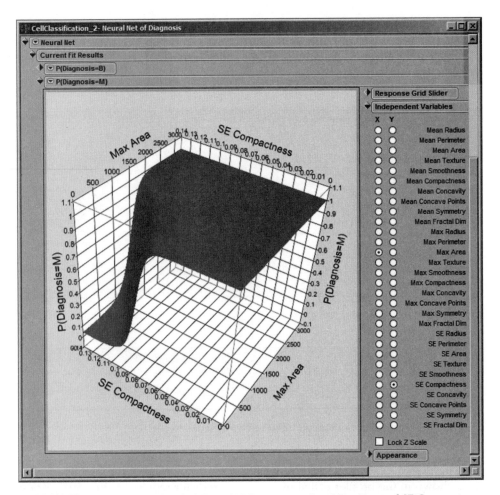

EXHIBIT 9.98   Surface Plot of Probability of Malignancy against Max Area and SE Compactness in Neural Net Model 1

Save Predicted. This adds three new columns to the data table: **Pred Diagnosis[B]**, which gives the predicted probability that a mass is benign; **Pred Diagnosis[M]**, which gives the predicted probability that a mass is malignant; and **Pred Diagnosis**, which gives a prediction of benign or malignant, based on which predicted probability is larger.

Had Mi-Ling chosen to **Save Formulas**, she would have obtained five formulas: the formulas for the three hidden nodes, called **H1 Formula**, **H2 Formula**, and **H3 Formula**; a formula called **SoftSum**, which calculates an intermediate result; and the final estimated probability called **Diagnosis[B] Formula**, which applies a logistic function to the estimated linear function of the hidden nodes. If you would like some insight on what a neural net fit is like, explore these formulas.

To see how well the model classifies training set observations, Mi-Ling runs a **Fit Y by X** analysis using Pred Diagnosis as **Y, Response** and Diagnosis as **X, Factor**. She saves the script as **Contingency – NN1**. The report for the training set is shown in Exhibit 9.99. Mi-Ling is surprised to see that there are no misclassifications, but she keeps in mind that neural nets have a tendency to overfit the training set. A little belatedly, she notices that the overall **Misclassification Rate** is also given in the **Current Fit Results** panel in Exhibit 9.94.

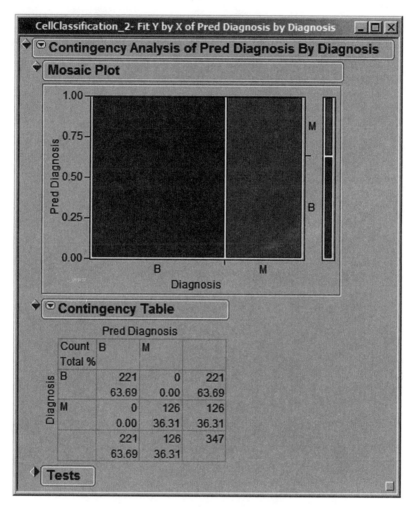

EXHIBIT 9.99   Contingency Report for Neural Net Model 1 Classification

A Second Model: Neural Net 2

At this point, Mi-Ling proceeds to explore various neural net model architectures using K-fold cross-validation. She closes all reports. She selects **Analyze > Modeling > Neural Net** and fills in the launch dialog as before, with Diagnosis as **Y, Response** and 30 Predictors as **X, Factor**. However, in this dialog, she selects **K-Fold Crossvalidation** from the drop-down menu at the bottom of the launch dialog, as shown in Exhibit 9.100.

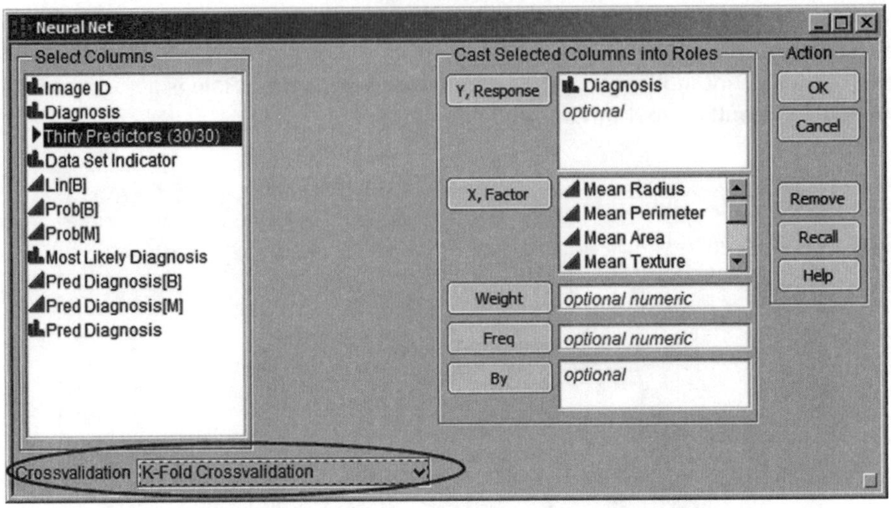

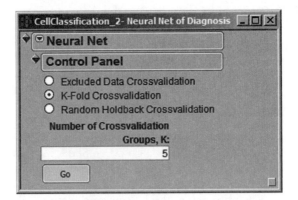

EXHIBIT 9.100   Launch Dialog for Neural Net with K-Fold Crossvalidation

Mi-Ling realizes that since her validation and test sets are excluded, she will be doing cross-validation within the context of her 347-observation training set. In another context, she might well include all of her training and validation data in this cross-validation-based modeling, because the nature of the algorithm attempts to minimize overfitting. However, in order to be consistent with her other three models and to retain the complete independence of her validation (and test) sets, she proceeds to apply this technique to her training set only.

Clicking **OK** opens the **Control Panel** (Exhibit 9.101). The default number of **Groups, K** is five, which Mi-Ling considers reasonable given the size of her data set. She has 347 observations, and so each of the five training samples will contain at least 276 rows (there are 347 / 5 or about 69 observations in each fold, and four folds in the training sample, so about 69 × 4 = 276 observations in each training sample).

EXHIBIT 9.101   Initial Control Panel Dialog for K-Fold Crossvalidation

When she clicks **Go**, the **Control Panel** updates to give her the choices that she saw earlier. However, this time Mi-Ling will explore the effect of different numbers of hidden nodes and various values of the overfit penalty on the fit. To do this, she selects **Sequence of Fits** from the red triangle in the **Neural Net** report.

She populates the dialog box that opens as shown in Exhibit 9.102. The default specification under **Hidden Nodes** allows her to explore models with two, three, and four **Hidden Nodes**. The values for **Overfit Penalty** are scaled multiplicatively, and JMP presents a default scaling factor of two, which Mi-Ling accepts. She starts her range for **Overfit Penalty** at 0.01 and ends at 1.28, exploring a total of eight values: 0.01, 0.02, 0.04, 0.08, 0.16, 0.32, 0.64, and 1.28. This gives a total of 24 models. She clicks **OK**.

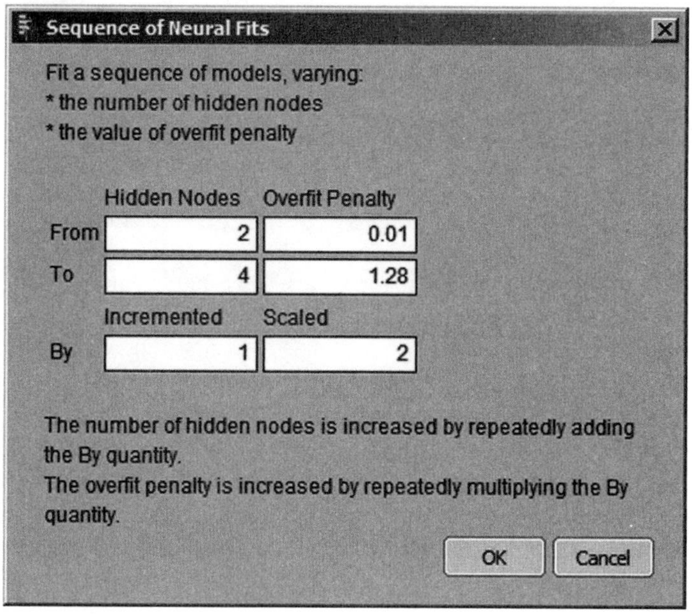

EXHIBIT 9.102   Sequence of Neural Fits Dialog

The models that JMP calculates in the sequence of fits are summarized in the **Fit History** panel. Again, keep in mind that because of random starts, your results will not exactly match Mi-Ling's. Her results are shown in the **Fit History** panel in Exhibit 9.103. She obtains three models with a **CV RSquare** of 0.85 or better. Two of these have four nodes (and so 129 parameters), and one has three nodes (97 parameters). Since simpler models are usually more desirable, Mi-Ling chooses the three-parameter model with an overfit penalty of 0.64 as her current model. She clicks the radio button to the right of this model, and the **Current Fit Results** panel updates to show a report for this model.

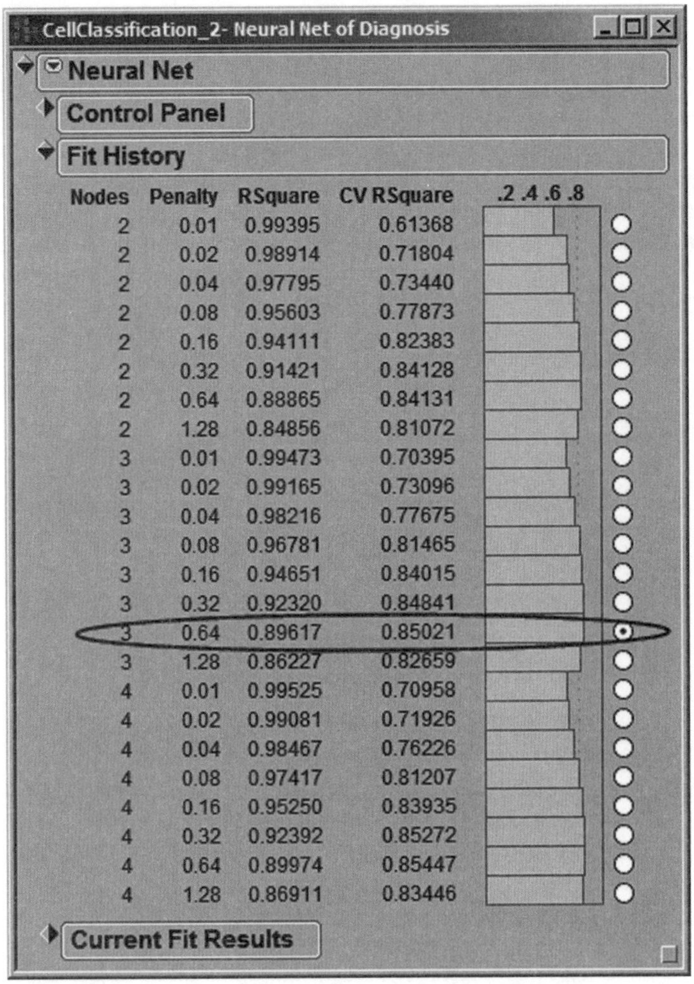

Nodes	Penalty	RSquare	CV RSquare
2	0.01	0.99395	0.61368
2	0.02	0.98914	0.71804
2	0.04	0.97795	0.73440
2	0.08	0.95603	0.77873
2	0.16	0.94111	0.82383
2	0.32	0.91421	0.84128
2	0.64	0.88865	0.84131
2	1.28	0.84856	0.81072
3	0.01	0.99473	0.70395
3	0.02	0.99165	0.73096
3	0.04	0.98216	0.77675
3	0.08	0.96781	0.81465
3	0.16	0.94651	0.84015
3	0.32	0.92320	0.84841
3	0.64	0.89617	0.85021
3	1.28	0.86227	0.82659
4	0.01	0.99525	0.70958
4	0.02	0.99081	0.71926
4	0.04	0.98467	0.76226
4	0.08	0.97417	0.81207
4	0.16	0.95250	0.83935
4	0.32	0.92392	0.85272
4	0.64	0.89974	0.85447
4	1.28	0.86911	0.83446

EXHIBIT 9.103 **Fit History Panel for 24 Exploratory Model Fits**

To ensure that she can recapture the specific model that she has chosen, Mi-Ling saves a script that contains the random seed for her chosen model, which she finds, as before, in the **Parameter Estimates** panel under **Current Fit**. She calls this script **Neural Net 2** and verifies that it reproduces the final model that she chose. (If you are following along, please run **Neural Net 2** at this point.)

From the report's red triangle menu, Mi-Ling clicks on **Categorical Profiler** and **Surface Profiler** to get a sense of what this second model looks like. When she does this, she sees that this model seems considerably smoother than her Neural Net 1 model. For comparison, we show some of the profiler traces for both models in Exhibit 9.104.

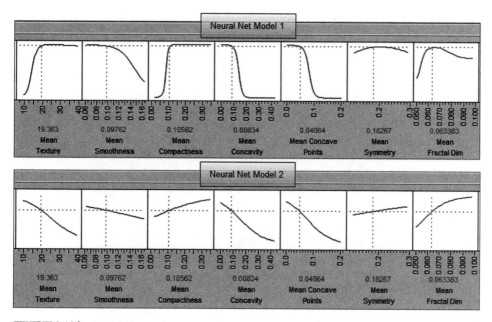

EXHIBIT 9.104 Partial View of Prediction Profilers for Neural Net Models 1 and 2

As before, Mi-Ling saves this model's formulas to the data table by choosing **Save Predicted** from the red triangle next to **Neural Net**. This inserts three new columns into the data table: Pred Diagnosis[B] 2, Pred Diagnosis[M] 2, and Pred Diagnosis 2.

Now the wiser, Mi-Ling observes that the **Misclassification Rate** given in the **Current Fit Results** panel is 0.012. Yet, she is interested in how this breaks down, so she obtains the **Contingency** report shown in Exhibit 9.105 (the script is called **Contingency – NN2**). This shows four misclassifications: three false negatives and one false positive. Mi-Ling recalls that there were no misclassifications for Neural Net 1 on the training data (Exhibit 9.99). Perhaps Neural Net 1 did indeed overfit the data. The profiler traces suggest that this might be the case. She will keep this in mind during the model validation step, which she is anxious to begin.

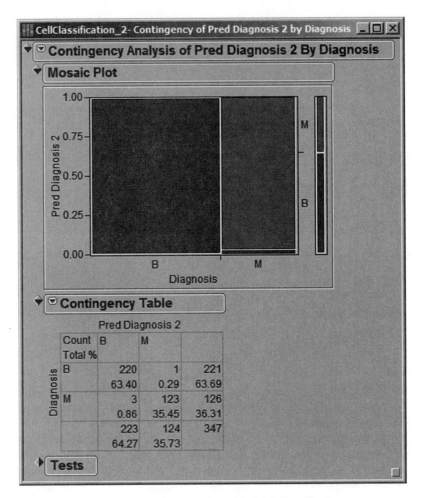

EXHIBIT 9.105   Contingency Report for Neural Net Model 2 Classification

Comparison of Classification Models

At this point, Mi-Ling is excited. She will select a single model by comparing the performance of all four models on her validation set. For now, she is content to use a single performance criterion, namely, the overall misclassification rate. Of course she realizes that in certain settings, a criterion that weights the two types of misclassification errors differently might be more appropriate. For example, since overlooking a malignant tumor is more serious than incorrectly classifying a benign tumor, one might penalize that first error more severely than the second. For the moment, Mi-Ling puts that issue aside. (We note that one can fit models with general loss functions in the JMP nonlinear platform.)

Mi-Ling switches to her validation set by locating the row state variable **Validation Set** in the columns panel of the data table, clicking on the red star to its left, and selecting **Copy to Row States**. All but the 109 observations in her validation set are now excluded and hidden. Next she selects **Analyze > Fit Y by X**, and enters, as **Y, Response**, the variables Most Likely Diagnosis (the logistic classification), Partition Prediction, Pred Diagnosis, and Pred Diagnosis 2 (these last two being the neural net classifications). As **X, Factor**, she enters Diagnosis (the actual diagnosis). She clicks **OK**.

When the report appears, she decides to remove the **Mosaic Plot** and **Tests** reports. To do this, while holding down the control key, she clicks on any one of the red triangles in the report and unchecks **Mosaic Plot**. In a similar fashion, she removes the **Tests**. Recall that holding down the control key broadcasts the command to other similar open reports. (The script is saved as **Model Comparison – Validation Data**.)

The report is shown in Exhibit 9.106, and this information is summarized in Exhibit 9.107. The logistic and neural net models outperform the partition model. Neural Net 2 slightly outperforms Neural Net 1 and the logistic model.

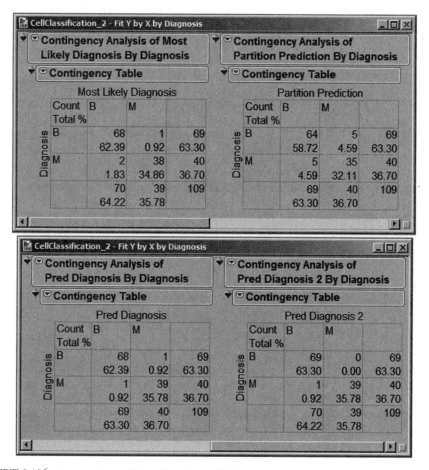

EXHIBIT 9.106   Comparison of Four Models on Validation Data

	Model	M Misclassified	B Misclssified	Total Misclassified
1	Logistic	2	1	3
2	Partition	5	5	10
3	Neural Net 1	1	1	2
4	Neural Net 2	1	0	1

EXHIBIT 9.107   Model Validation Summary

In thinking about the two neural net models, Mi-Ling refers back to the sequence of fits report shown in Exhibit 9.103. She notes that Neural Net 1, which has three nodes and an overfit penalty of 0.01, is represented, in the sequence of fits, by a neural net model that has a **CV RSquare** of 0.70395. Neural Net 2, with an overfit penalty of 0.64, had a **CV RSquare** of 0.85021. For this data, larger overfit penalties seem to result in better cross-validation results. She concludes that this is partially why Neural Net 2 performed slightly better on the validation data than did Neural Net 1. Since Neural Net 2 appears to be the best performer on the validation data, Mi-Ling chooses Neural Net 2 as her model for classification.

Now, to obtain a sense of how this model will perform on new, independent data, she applies it to her test set. She applies the row states from the row state variable **Test Set** to the data table in order to exclude all but the test set observations. She selects **Analyze > Fit Y by X**, then clicks **Recall** and **OK** to run the same analysis as before, but now on her test set (this script is saved as **Model Comparison – Test Data**).

Although the report (Exhibit 9.108) shows results for all four models, Neural Net 2 is of primary interest to Mi-Ling at this point, as this is her chosen model. This model gives a misclassification rate of 3 out of 113, or 0.027 on the test data; stated differently, it has a classification accuracy of 97.3 percent. Mi-Ling takes this as an indication of how this model will perform when classifying new observations. Interestingly, this is almost exactly the classification accuracy obtained by the Wisconsin study researchers, which you may recall was 97.5 percent. Certainly Mi-Ling's approach and theirs differ in significant ways, but all the same, this similarity is worthy of note.

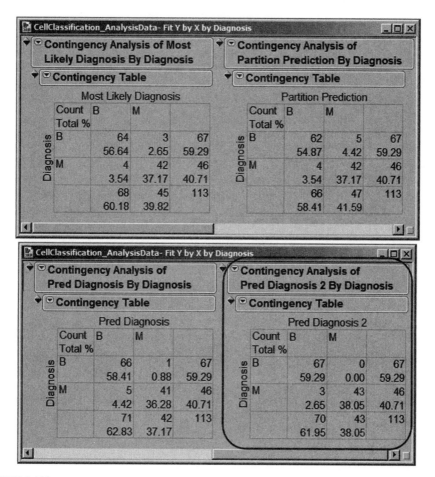

EXHIBIT 9.108   Performance of Four Models on Test Data

Conclusion

Mi-Ling's goal in this analysis was to explore some of the features that JMP provides to support classification and data mining. She began by using various visualization techniques to develop an understanding of the data and relationships among the variables. Then, she used formulas and row states to partition her data into a training set, a validation set, and a test set.

Mi-Ling was interested in investigating logistic, partition, and neural net fits. Given that her goal was to learn about these platforms, she constructed models in a fairly straightforward way. She fit four models using the training data: a logistic model, a partition model, and two neural net models. The best classification, based on performance on her validation set, was obtained with a neural net model whose structure was chosen using K-fold cross-validation. We note that Mi-Ling could have taken a number of more sophisticated approaches to her modeling endeavor, had she so desired.

Among Mi-Ling's four models, the partition model had the worst performance. In our experience, single partition models tend not to perform as well as nonlinear (or linear) regression techniques when the predictors are continuous. They can be very useful when there are categorical predictors, and especially when these have many levels. Moreover, unlike neural net models and even logistic models, partition models are very intuitive and interpretable, which makes them all the more valuable for data exploration. In Mi-Ling's situation, where classification was the primary goal, the interpretability of the model was less important than its ability to classify accurately.

We also wish to underscore the importance of guarding against overfitting, which, in the case of neural net models, often results in claims of exaggerated model performance. The application of K-fold cross-validation helped Mi-Ling arrive at a neural net model that was simple but also generalized well to her test set. In the case of neural nets, where overfitting is so easy, we strongly recommended that model performance be assessed on a genuinely independent data set. Without such an approach, claims about the model's predictive performance are likely to be overly optimistic.

Notes

1. Olvi L. Mangasarian, W. Nick Street, and William H. Wolberg, "Breast Cancer Diagnosis and Prognosis via Linear Programming," *Mathematical Programming Technical Report* 94–10 (December 19, 1994): 1–9.
2. For more detail on these characteristics, see W. Nick Street, William H. Wolberg, and Olvi L. Mangasarian, "Nuclear Feature Extraction for Breast Tumor Diagnosis," *International Symposium on Electronic Imaging: Science and Technology* 1905 (1993): 861–870.
3. Mangasarian, Street, and Wolberg, "Breast Cancer Diagnosis and Prognosis via Linear Programming"; and Trevor Hastie, Robert Tibshirani, and Jerome Friedman, *The Elements of Statistical Learning: Data Mining, Inference, and Prediction* (New York, NY: Springer, 2001), 108–111, 371–389.
4. The validation and test sets are sometimes used in roles different from the ones we have described. We follow the convention proposed in: Christopher M. Bishop, *Neural Networks for Pattern Recognition* (New York, NY: Oxford University Press, 1995), 372; Trevor Hastie, Robert Tibshirani, and Jerome Friedman, *The Elements of Statistical Learning: Data Mining, Inference, and Prediction* (New York, NY: Springer, 2001), 196; and B. D. Ripley, *Pattern Recognition and Neural Networks* (New York, NY: Cambridge University Press, 1996), 3–8.
5. John P. Sall and Cathy Maahs-Fladung, "Trees, Neural Nets, PLS, I-Optimal Designs and Other New JMP® Version 5 Novelties," *SUGI 27*, http://www2.sas.com/proceedings/sugi27/p268-27.pdf (accessed July 31, 2009).
6. Warren S. McCulloch and Walter Pitts, "A Logical Calculus of the Ideas Immanent in Nervous Activity," *Bulletin of Mathematical Biophysics* 5 (1943): 115–133.
7. Michael J. A. Berry and Gordon Linoff, *Data Mining Techniques: For Marketing, Sales, and Customer Relationship Management* (New York, NY: John Wiley and Sons, Inc., 1997), 286–334; Trevor Hastie, Robert Tibshirani, and Jerome Friedman, *The Elements of Statistical Learning*, 347–369; Simon Haykin, *Neural Networks: A Comprehensive Foundation*, Second Edition (New York, NY: Prentice Hall, 1998); and Ripley, *Pattern Recognition and Neural Networks*, 143–180.

Index